EXODUS!

GIULIA BONACCI

EXODUS!

HEIRS AND PIONEERS, RASTAFARI RETURN TO ETHIOPIA

Translated by Antoinette Tidjani Alou

Foreword by Elikia M'Bokolo

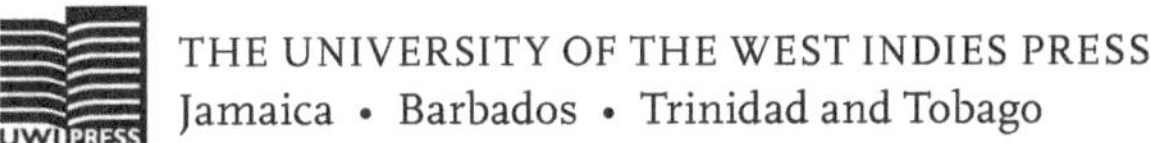

THE UNIVERSITY OF THE WEST INDIES PRESS
Jamaica • Barbados • Trinidad and Tobago

The University of the West Indies Press
7A Gibraltar Hall Road, Mona
Kingston 7, Jamaica
www.uwipress.com

5–7 rue de l'Ecole Polytechnique, 75005 Paris, France
First published in 2010 as *Exodus! L'histoire du retour des Rastarfariens en Ethiopie*.
This edition has been translated and published under licence from Editions L'Harmattan.

A catalogue record of this book is available from the National Library of Jamaica.

ISBN: 978-976-640-503-8 (print)
978-976-640-514-4 (Kindle)
978-976-640-525-0 (ePub)

Cover photograph: Bob Marley holding Yosef in his arms, one of the first Rastafari children born in Shashemene, Ethiopia, 1978. Photograph by Yohannes Bisrat. Private archives, Mebrat Bekele © DR.

Cover and book design by Robert Harris

Set in Minion Pro 10.5/14.2 x 27

Printed in the United States of America

In memoriam

Yenenesh – Kuky

Kenny Lockheart

Ras Freedom

Yosef – Baba

Bongo Solomon

Ayele Olana

Abere Jembere

ልቤ፡አዝኗል

One bright morning when my work is over,
I will fly away home, fly away home to Zion, fly away home . . .

– Bob Marley, "Rastaman Chant" (1973)

From the universities must come men, ideas, knowledge, experience, technical skills, and the deep humane understanding vital to fruitful relations among nations. Without these, world order, for which We have so long strived, cannot be established. From the universities, too, must come that ability which is the most valuable attribute of civilised men everywhere: the ability to transcend narrow passions and to engage in honest conversations; for civilisation is by nature the victory of persuasion over force. Unity is strength. No nation can divide itself and remain powerful.

– Haile Selassie I, 19 December 1961

CONTENTS

APPENDICES

ILLUSTRATIONS

FOREWORD

The Return!

IT WAS, TO TELL THE TRUTH, QUITE UNTHINKABLE. But not only did they nourish the thought, they also brought it to fruition. *They* refers to the sons and daughters of Africa who were taken into slavery against their will, through unimaginable violence, and who, despite all they endured in the Americas, continued to nurture the dream of a return to mother Africa. "Return to Guinea" was the expression used by those of St Domingue. For many, "going back to Guinea" spelled death, death chosen over a life in slavery: death awaited as a liberation. For the more determined, it meant death assumed, wilfully precipitated by an act of suicide. But how were we to imagine that return would really occur, and that it would be followed by life, there, in Africa?

In the history of migrations, force has almost always been the cause of departure. Even those who apparently freely chose to leave almost always did so because life on the spot was no longer possible or had become unbearable: structural poverty, or impoverishment attributed to those in power, expropriations and pogroms, victimizations and repressions on the part of the state, ethnic and religious stigmatization, the cultural oppression of minorities, dictatorship and despotism are the forms of violence which preside over such individual and collective departures. These are clearly voyages with no return, embarked on with multiple practices diabolizing the country of departure and hopes of a new life or even rebirth in the host country. Africa, too, in the context of the slave trade, had its "doors of no return", like today's Ouidah. But, regardless of the reasons and conditions of their transformation into slave-goods, the lives lived by Africans overseas as enslaved producers could in no manner make them forget their "native land". Hence the importance of this problematic of "return" on which Giulia Bonacci's book sheds an entirely new light.

For there are all sorts of returns. While the imagination of enslaved Africans was peopled by hopes and dreams of escape, the slave-holding and slave-trading powers, obsessed with "the black question", began to plot massive "dismissal" of black people back to Africa. Such was the case of the United Kingdom, embarrassed by what the powers in place regarded as an "invasion" of blacks: increasing numbers of slaves during the eighteenth century who fled the New World to set foot on British soil, which they knew would make them automatically free; former soldiers, engaged on the British side in the American War of Independence. This teeming, vindicatory multitude, cherishing freedom, prompt to bring before the courts any issue liable to endanger this freedom, linked by strong bonds of solidarity, quickly appeared to be a force which sooner or later would become impossible to contain and control. From this hysterical fear, largely polluted by racism, arose the project to establish in Africa a colony to receive these "returning" slaves. Beginning in 1787, this led to the creation of Sierra Leone.

Confronted with the same influx of "Negroes", perceived as synonymous with "slaves", France under Louis XVI chose an even more radical policy of "return": the blacks who came to France in the vain hope of enjoying there the freedom recognized since the fourteenth century for any person who set foot on the soil of the kingdom were "returned" to the colonies and to the condition of slaves.

These men and women in revolt and in search of redemption worried the slave colonies too, especially following the victorious insurrection of Saint-Domingue. It is not by chance that, at the beginning of the nineteenth century, there emerged in the United States all manner of philanthropists cleverly providing black people wanting to "go back" to Africa the wherewithal for the foundation of Liberia.

It is a known fact that returns of this nature, swollen by the flood of slaves released from the ships of slave traders after 1815, generated painful forms of colonization on the African continent, which were all the more incomprehensible and unbearable for the natives as the new masters were themselves natives.

The story that Giulia Bonacci tells is quite different. She begins by taking us into the history of the slave trade, of slavery, and of the "return" to a land like no other – to Ethiopia, exalted in the minds of Africans as a symbol with multiple resonances: a symbol of the primacy of Africa in the construction of thousand-year-old empires; a symbol of resistance and African independence; a symbol of the wellspring of the African Renaissance. Along the way, she tackles the history of pan-Africanism. Prior to this work, this was primarily the fragmented history of an ideology with multiple orientations, the history of the successful emancipation of the old European colonial territories in Africa, of other old slave colonies and, finally, the history of a wide-reaching movement of global dimensions broken into a few great iconic moments and figures.

Giulia Bonacci disrupts this schema, which has become the norm, at least at three levels. First, she presents pan-Africanism, starting with the "returns" to Ethiopia, as a social history reaching beyond "great figures", strongly illuminating the decisive role played by ordinary people. She goes on to propose a cultural history which, before or beyond ideological constructions, is particularly attentive to religion, to art – musical developments in particular – and to the symbolic dimension of a process whose complexity is thereby restored. She offers, finally, a long history of pan-Africanism, covering at least two centuries, during which many themes, claims, postures and projects surface distinctively through repetition.

The great gap disturbing this long interval, and which ultimately forms the central object of *Exodus!*, reposes on the fact of a voluntary return, as oppposed to the new forms of deportation which produced Sierra Leone and Liberia. Far from claiming the foundation *ex nihilo* of a state of black "returnees", what this book presents is the extraordinary odyssey of those black people who organized a "return" to an existing state, one upon which the pan-African imagination had seized more than half a century before, one whose hard realities on the ground the "returnees" were about to discover. The waves of return to Ethiopia, starting at the end of the nineteenth century, also corresponded with the sudden emergence of dynamics that would deeply affect the foundation of the oldest state of the African continent: imperialist encirclement; the aggression of Fascist Italy; British then American leanings towards an encroaching neocolonialism; the false starts of African unity; the meanderings of a revolution which claimed to be communist; the fratricidal war with Eritrea; finally, the slow reconstruction of state and society.

By ordering these apparently disparate facts and by giving them more than convincing coherence, this book renews not only the history of diasporas and returns but also that of Africa and Ethiopia. The author takes apparent pleasure in combining several levels. The result is a plurality reflecting the complexity of the phenomena examined. The connections thus highlighted reveal the coherence of the processes involved. These principal levels also comprise the three sections of the book.

The first part is, as it were, on the outside of this division since it provides the historical background of the "ideological and social roots of the return to Ethiopia". This is primarily an intellectual, cultural and spiritual history, rather than an ideological one, revealing the maturation of the problematics of return within the pan-African movement.

The second part unfolds at the "macro" level of the world and, more particularly, of the pan-African networks, highlighting the connections and pinpointing the actors to show how this ample intellectual movement of a global character was ultimately embodied, so to speak, in the concrete and almost commonplace project of the return to and settlement in a remote corner of Africa enjoying the privilege of belonging to the great kingdom of the *negusä nägäst*.

The third part leads us to Shashemene, the destination of a long journey from diaspora to "return", in which the first stirrings of pan-African drive would integrate the realities of a state obliged to make room for these new comers while observing its own dynamics and fatally unpredictable convulsions – the fall of the prestigious Haile Selassie and of a legendary imperial regime, the introduction of communism and Red Terror, the civil war, the advent of a federal and democratic regime. Giulia Bonacci shows that these three levels are connected to one another. Thanks to meticulous research based on archival sources (enlightening "macro" elements) and fieldwork (related to the presence of individual narratives), Bonacci demonstrates that the main lead connecting all three levels which ground her problematics is made up of, paradoxically, the individual itineraries which crop up in all the adventures and all the great moments of the pan-African movement and the problematics of return.

This, then, is the gist of an innovative book, no doubt the fruit of painstaking effort. The historical discourse is conceived on the basis of first-hand materials, the "sources" so dear to specialists. None of these are missing: sources derived from public and private records unearthed in Ethiopia, Europe, the Caribbean and the United States; oral enquiry of an unprecedented breadth in this field. To accomplish the last, Giulia Bonacci was obliged to rise to the challenge of difficult fieldwork conditions (because of her status as a woman and of the insecurity of many of her research sites) not only in Jamaica, particularly Kingston, but also in the United Kingdom, especially the poor suburbs of London and other towns; in American cities, in particular certain districts of New York where the pan-Africanism of Marcus Garvey blossomed at the beginning of the twentieth century; and Ethiopia, of course, in Shashemene and Addis Ababa; and finally, in the Ghanaian capital, Accra, which Bonacci is, moreover, the first to reveal as one of the most important links of pan-Africanism and of Rastafari in Africa, in the past as in the present.

This book is therefore the product of a beautiful adventure of discovery, intelligence, solidarity and fraternity. It unveils Africa, Africans and the black world as they are, in their struggles, achievements, desire for unity, and their fierce and enduring will to foster the emergence of a better world.

Elikia M'Bokolo
Director of Research
Ecole des Hautes Etudes en Sciences Sociales, France/Université de Kinshasa, Democratic Republic of Congo

PREFACE TO THE ENGLISH EDITION

TO COME TO LIFE, THIS TRANSLATION REQUIRED THE indefectible support of a number of persons and institutions. They understood the significance of making this book available in English, endorsed the importance of the story it told, and thus deserve many thanks. Special thanks are due to Sir Hilary Beckles, vice chancellor of the University of the West Indies, whom I met in 2010 at a workshop on the Back-to-Africa movement, organized in Johannesburg by the Centre for Advanced Studies of African Society; he was instrumental in providing the necessary funds for the translation. I am very grateful for the chance he gave this story to reach its English readership. The translator, Antoinette Tidjani Alou (Université Abdou Mamouni, Niger), has worked wonders; with passionate dedication, she has crafted a text that sounds even better than the original. Our discussions, through unstable Internet connections between Niamey and Addis Ababa, over the use of a term or over variations in meaning between two languages, reflect what I regard as exemplary collaboration. Many thanks to Hillina Seife, a doctoral candidate at the University of Michigan, Ann Arbor, and a fervent researcher of this historic "Ethiopian nation" abroad, who generously helped in finding missing references in English. Erin MacLeod (Vanier College, Montreal), who read the French version as early as 2007, always believed in the need to get it across in English. Her unfaltering confidence was expressed through an early translation of the introduction, used to draft a proposal for the English market and to make contacts in the Caribbean and American publishing worlds. I wish to thank Derek Bishton for the permission to reproduce the wonderful photographs he took in Shashemene in 1981, originally published in *Black Heart Man: A Journey into Rastafari* (London: Chatto and Windus, 1986). The editors of the University of the West Indies Press never wavered when faced with the length of the book and showed their support at every step of this translation. L'Harmattan publishing house, the publisher of the second edition of the French text, kindly facilitated the birth of this translation. The Institute of Research for Development, thanks to which I have been posted for four years in Addis Ababa, provided me with a great working environment.

Since the first publication of this book in French, change has come to the "Jamaican neighbourhood" of the town of Shashemene. Roads have replaced houses, asphalt now covers pebbles and new constructions mount to the sky. The development of Shashemene has gradually become a reality, and the landscape is deeply affected by this change. Construction sites are on the rise, barriers are constructed, while space shrinks and trade diversifies. The horse-drawn *gari* carriages have been dethroned by the *bajaj*, small enhanced motorbikes imported from India, which decrease the length of trips. Jamaicans still form the majority of the eight hundred or so Rastafari residing on the periphery of Shashemene, but other groups are rapidly increasing. There are almost a hundred Trinidadians, and the nearest Trinidad and Tobago ambassador, posted in Uganda, came to pay them a visit a couple of years ago. French-speaking Rastafari from Guadeloupe, Martinique and metropolitan France are also forging ties with Ethiopia and Shashemene. The Rastafari community in Shashemene has developed its own social institutions, and it vividly contributes to the Ethiopian social and cultural landscape. Life in Shashemene, on the "land grant", continues to reflect the social and economic transformations traversing Ethiopia and the larger world and nurtures the very special alliance between the Rastafari and Ethiopia.

Exodus! offers keys to decipher the historical progression of the idea and practices of return to Africa and clarifies the concurrent ideological and social challenges. This work retraces the history of African Americans and Caribbeans in Ethiopia and, in particular, the history of the Rastafari community in Shashemene. It allows us to understand the complex relations that this community maintains with its Ethiopian environment and underscores their historic significance.

To you, dear readers, I say: Enjoy the journey to Shashemene. *Bon voyage*!

Ethiopia
March 2014

ACKNOWLEDGEMENTS

IT IS WITH PLEASURE AND GRATITUDE THAT I extend thanks to those who assisted me in the successful completion of this work.

Elikia M'Bokolo trusted me from day one. He guided me in my journeys and discoveries, and his unfailing support proved invaluable. The doctoral programme in history and civilizations at the Centre d'Etudes Africaines (Centre for African Studies) of the Ecole des Hautes Etudes en Sciences Sociales (School for Advanced Studies in Social Sciences) provided space for thought and initiative as well as the moral and financial support which made this research possible.

Barry Chevannes warmly welcomed me at the University of the West Indies at Mona, Jamaica, and facilitated my use of its libraries and resources. Gérard Prunier and Berhanou Abebe, through the Centre Français des Etudes Ethiopennes (French Centre for Ethiopian Studies) in Addis Ababa, generously supported my extended periods of enquiry in the field. These were also facilitated by the Institute of Ethiopian Studies and its former director, Baye Yimam, and by the Department of History of the University of Addis Ababa and its former director, Tekle Haymanot Gebre Sellassie. Girma Balcha, then responsible for immigration and nationality affairs, played a crucial role by sharing his analyses. The civil servants of the National Urban Planning Institute, particularly Belachew Kalechristos, and of the Ethiopian Mapping Auhority and those in charge of the archives of the Ministry of Foreign Affairs and the Ministry of the Interior responded patiently and attentively to my many requests.

The mayor of Shashemene, Shimelis Haylu Dinagee, and the employees and the experts of the municipality showed great generosity. Wahib Adamu and Ayele Olana assisted me in my field enquiries in Shashemene and facilitated numerous encounters.

The staff of the National Library and the National Archives in Jamaica; the Charles E. Young Research Library at the University of California, Los Angeles; the Biscayne Bay Campus Library in Florida; the International University in Miami; and the Schomburg Center for Research in Black Culture, in Harlem, New York, were all exceedingly kind and helpful.

Discussions, exchanges and reflections with many colleagues contributed greatly to my learning. I extend my sincere thanks to them, in particular to Edward Alpers, Henriette Asséo, Shimelis Bonsa, Louis Brenner, Christine Chivallon, Myriam Cottias, Marie-Laure Derat, Vincent Duclert, Teshome H. Gabriel, Nancy Green, Pauline Guedj, C.R.D. Halisi, Randal Hepner, Robert A. Hill, Bertrand Hirsch, Jakes Homiak, Marie-José Jolivet, Jean-François Mayer, Louis Moyston, Pap Ndiaye, Jalani Niaah, Richard Pankhurst, Jean-Claude Penrad, Christophe Prochasson, Vanina Profizi, Jean M. Rahier, William Scott, Hillina Seife, Ida Tafari, Jean-François Tribillon, Waibinte Wariboko, Anaïs Wion, Michael Witter and Bahru Zewde. The generosity of Andrea Gandini, Dimitri Béchacq, Katia Girma, Paolo Israel, Boris Lutanie, Thomas Osmond and Estelle Sohier was never lacking. Formatting of cartography is due to the talents of Marie-Therese Manchotte and Nicolas Buchet de Neuilly. Bruno Blum nourished this research over the years, thanks to many discussions and a remarkable discography. He followed this edition of the book step by step and his rigour, patience and generosity must be saluted.

Roy Morrison and Wayne Modest (Kingston), Timothy Green (Los Angeles), Joseph Selbonne (Paris), Sophie Heckett (Addis Ababa), Ras Kawintseb Mehert Sellassie, Patrick Campbell and Sharon Joseph (Shashemene) guided my steps over tricky ground and always encouraged me. Their patience and their affection often taught me much more than years of study – how could I ever give you back your part?

Thanks are also due to I and I, to the Rastafari from around the world too numerous to mention by name, to those in Ethiopia and beyond, whose hospitality, confidence, reasoning and sharing gave life to this great adventure. Thank you to all the officers who opened the doors of their organizations. Heroes of what is no longer Utopia, this history is yours, but the shortcomings are mine alone. *Nuff love and guidance!*

And to my nomadic family, the beloved, the first to inspire in me the taste for Africa and who launched me on the search for "a home", words are not enough – thank you.

INTRODUCTION

> "You take this, my testimony, and you get another person testimony, when you get back home you will have all that to pick out the sense from the nonsense."
>
> – *Mama Wellete, Shashemene*

> "You hear about the land that was promised, And now it is not the promised land anymore, it is for those who are not here, it is promised to them, but for me it is a given land, I dwell upon it, not promised anymore, that was a vision, now it is my heaven, my Utopia, my heaven."
>
> – *Bongo Solomon, Shashemene*

SHASHEMENE IS A CITY SITUATED 250 KILOMETRES TO the south of Addis Ababa, the capital of Ethiopia. Located at the hollow of the Rift valley, at 1,900 metres above sea level, Shashemene is a town of passage that has been traversed throughout time by commercial roads, colonial and revolutionary armies, migrants, peasants, and administrators. It is a unique part of the Ethiopian landscape because since the 1950s, several hundreds of Caribbean men, women and children have come, primarily from Jamaica, but also from Trinidad and Tobago, St Kitts, Montserrat, Dominica, Barbados, the United States, and Great Britain to live in Shashemene. They are Rastafari. They define themselves as the "true Ethiopians" and claim to have "repatriated" to Ethiopia, to "have returned home". It is not by chance that they settled close to Shashemene. This is the site of the land that Emperor Haile Selassie I of Ethiopia offered to the black people of the world to thank them for their support during the Italo-Ethiopian war (1935–41). They were invited to come and settle there to contribute to the rebuilding and the development of the country. Initially they arrived in small numbers, and it is only at the end of the 1960s that the arrivals became more regular, when Jamaican Rastafari seized this opportunity to accomplish the return to Africa that they had been demanding for years from the Jamaican government. They were followed by Rastafari from all over the Caribbean and the English-speaking metropolises, and currently form one of the largest diaspora settlements on the African continent.

The social history of this land and the return to Africa staged there are at the heart of the present work. The focus is not simply on the Caribbean, Ethiopia or Rastafari but rather on the return of those who identified with Ethiopia, namely the Rastafari and their predecessors. While taking into consideration the challenges specific to each context, I will focus on giving form to the "return to Ethiopia" and clarifying the processes by which a territory and identities are connected. To this end, I will examine the place of Ethiopia in the black imagination, and the impact of the pan-African policies of Haile Selassie I and their evolution in the course of the regimes that succeeded the empire. Beginning with the diaspora, I will present the practices of the return and the reasons that brought the Rastafari to Shashemene. A particular point of interest is the part played by two organizations, the Ethiopian World Federation (EWF), to which the administration of this land was entrusted, and the Twelve Tribes of Israel, which mobilized around the objective of the return to Shashemene. Finally, I will evoke the vicissitudes of this settlement, marked by the contradiction that characterizes the relations between Africa and its diasporas. The study of the return to Ethiopia, to Shashemene, provides an approach to the entanglement of racial, political and religious ideologies at the core of the black experience and offers the analysis of an unfamiliar mobility, one which remains nonetheless, in the words of William Shack, a "historical reality" (1974, 143).

"Black", "white", "race", "racial" are nouns and adjectives distasteful to the French and are used here in keeping with the Anglo-Saxon intellectual tradition. "Race" is not a biological reality; on the contrary, biologically, genetically, it does not exist. Indeed, "race" is constructed by individuals and societies on the basis of attributes of phenotype and plays a social and political role. It represents herein a matrix of meanings anchored in the slave trade and slavery. It is generated by specific historical conditions, by discriminatory social relations, represented in a variety of ways in and out of Africa. Although the actors of this return are black people – peasants, singers, intellectuals, activists, politicians, religious leaders or prophets – theirs is in no way a community-oriented version of history; it is not a history of black people for black people. The history of the return to Ethiopia has universal value because it is also the history of the violence of political relations, of the injustice of social conditions, of the powers of mobilization of the poorest of the poor and of the force of their imagination.

Back to Africa

To go home, to return, to stay, to leave, to set off again, to go back home, to repatriate, these are all verbs signifying movement, mobility and circulation between places – simple words covering a great variety of experiences. The return to Africa in which we are interested is identified by the expression "Back to Africa". This term designates a social movement deployed over several centuries, whose objective was "to repair" the delocalizations due to slavery and to escape the socio-economic conditions and the colonial status thus engendered. This return also subsumes the notion of the before and the elsewhere representing a golden age, a kind of backward movement in time and space supposedly endowed with the power to erase the degradations endured. It is in this sense an ideological approach, reconstructing an origin, a trajectory, and following the traces showing the way back "home". The designation of one's "home", of a land of origin (fatherland, motherland, homeland), enabled by feelings of belonging, by emotional ties and identity constructions linking various symbolic spaces, systems or realities is a characteristic of diasporas. The concept of diaspora has aroused complex and exciting debates. In French, several works have been published in recent years presenting its uses, limitations and challenges (Dufoix 2003, 2011; Chivallon 2004; Anteby-Yemini et al. 2005; Berthomière and Chivallon 2006).

Whereas these works sometimes approach the question of return of diasporas, the question of the return to Africa lacks methodical investigations, in the African context in particular. Indeed, the return to Africa is generally studied in its symbolic or cultural dimensions, ignoring the issue of physical mobilities. These shortcomings compromise attempts to define the African diasporas. As underlined by George Shepperson (1993, 44), "the study of the back-to-Africa movement is an essential part of the concept of the African diaspora, which loses much of its force if it is limited to dispersal in an outward direction only". If return is indeed an essential part of the diaspora, the aim of this study is to show how the diaspora takes shape in the accomplishment of return. Observed from the standpoint of Ethiopia, the arrivals of returnees reveal the contours of an "Ethiopian" diaspora originating in the transatlantic slave trade.

Ethiopia

Ethiopia was not spared from internal, Indian Ocean, Eastern and trans-Saharan slave trades, but because of its geographical location, far from the Atlantic coast, it never appeared as a source or a go-between in the human traffic that occurred over several centuries. However, the "returnees" to this East African country insist on the reality of a trajectory of enslavement originating in Ethiopia. In Shashemene, a Jamaican asked me one day: "So, your work is to show that we came from here?" He was probably hoping to hear I was gathering proof that his Ethiopian forebears had also been carried away to the plantations of the Americas. Instead, my aim was to understand how one could *imagine* coming from here. How could someone be born in Kingston, Jamaica, and "return" to

Shashemene? Grow up in London and "return" to Addis Ababa? Leave Port of Spain, Trinidad, to live in Brooklyn, New York, and "repatriate" to Ethiopia? Speak English with the transformed syntax of former provinces of the British Empire and "be Ethiopian"? A clue was offered by Kamari Clarke, who had worked on Yoruba networks stretching between West Africa and the United States. She stressed that returns to Africa, like other "contemporary movements[,] may not be linked to empirically derived dispersals, but instead to social memories and imaginaries" (Clarke 2004, xiii). It thus becomes a matter of finding the forms and contours of the memories and social imaginaries specifically related to Ethiopia within the African diaspora. To revert to a distinction often made by Elikia M'Bokolo, the focus here is not on a history of origins but rather on a history of the processes through which an Ethiopian origin, Ethiopian filiations, and an Ethiopian nationality were imagined, transformed into practices and realized, sometimes via the return to Ethiopia. The transatlantic space, which is too often restricted to its coasts, will be widened to include the symbolic and political relations between Ethiopia and other black worlds. The study of return will therefore contribute to the development of research on "the imaginary of destinations" (Green 2002, 3).

The Caribbean

Among the returnees to Ethiopia, the predominance of Caribbeans over Americans, Brazilians and Central Americans is more than obvious. I will attempt to state the reasons and conditions behind this phenomenon. The term *Caribbeans* is used here to refer to people from the Caribbean space as defined by Christine Chivallon (2004, 36–39), especially those who share a common "transatlantic heritage", that is, the descendants of Africans. My use of the term also includes persons originating in the second wave of Caribbean diaspora, namely, Caribbean migrants to Central America and the English-speaking urban centres of Great Britain and the United States.

The complexities of Caribbean identity constructs regarding Africa have occupied many anthropologists and generated a great deal of literature. However, Caribbean migrations in the direction of West Africa have largely gone unnoticed, as demonstrated by a remark made by Robin Cohen (1992), who states not without caution that Caribbeans had never migrated to the continent. I will demonstrate the opposite through a particular focus on Jamaica, the largest English-speaking island of the Caribbean, without disregarding other islands or migratory spaces. Tangible and intangible circulations between these various spaces will constitute points of special interest. Distinguishing between Caribbeans and African Americans enables us to highlight the commitment of the former to the black and pan-African nationalist projects and to the mobility targeting a return to the continent.

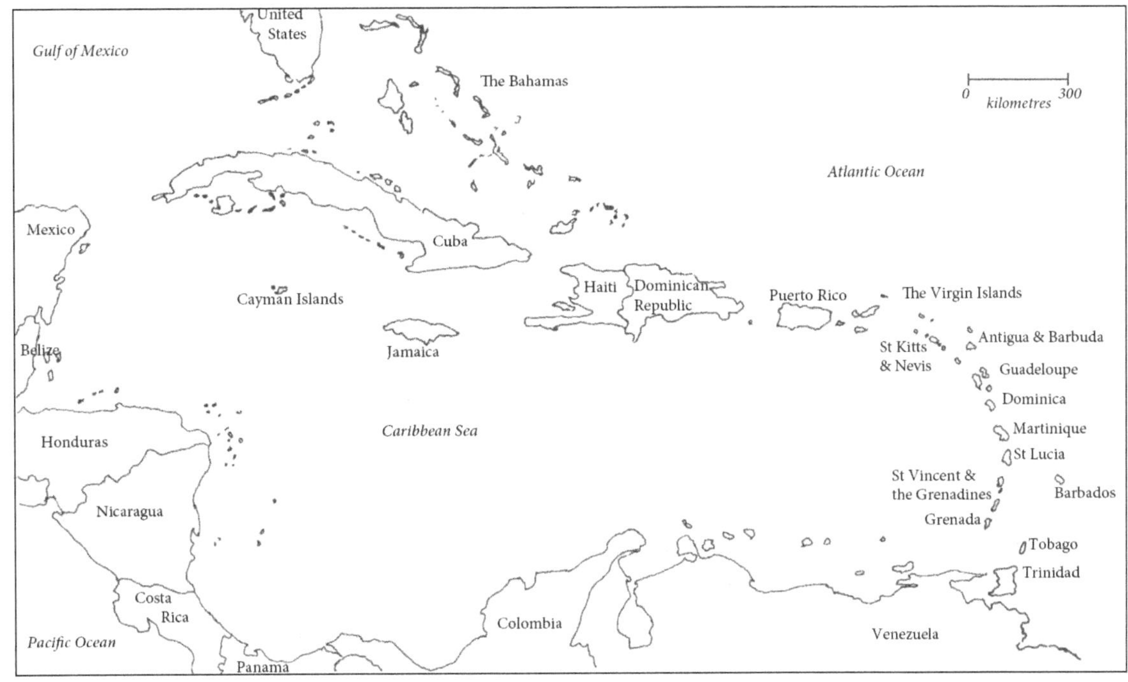

Figure I.1. Map of the Caribbean

Rastafari

Jamaicans occupy a unique place in the history of the return to Ethiopia and, among them, the Rastafari[1] can lay claim to further distinction in this regard. The Rastafari still suffer the brunt of prejudices associating them with illegal practices, a marginal religion or an exotic folklore. They are generally studied through the lens of their musical expressions – namely, reggae. In French, since the work of Denis-Constant on the sources of reggae (1982) and the collection of articles published by *Les Cahiers du CERI* (Angles et al. 1994), only one dissertation has appeared in this field, bearing on the bonds between reggae and Rastafari (Daynes 2001). In addition, journalists who specialize in Jamaican music have written on the subject (Lee 1999; Lutanie 2000; Blum 2004). These exceedingly rare references in French testify to an existing and unacceptable cleavage between French-speaking and English-speaking spaces, leading to the ignorance of a movement that marked Jamaica, the Caribbean and, beyond the islands, the production of cultural identities in the modern and postmodern world. The scope of the present book does not allow for an exhaustive analysis of the Jamaican history of the Rastafari movement, which began in 1930 and has produced several hundreds of reference works in English. It is possible, however, to offer a few remarks.

Most treatises on the Rastafari movement begin with a note of caution: the movement is extremely difficult to circumscribe, it eludes definition and resists categorization. It has at times been regarded as "a political cultism" (Simpson 1955), "an escapist cult of the outcast" (Patterson 1964), "a messianic movement unique to Jamaica" (Barrett 1997), "a millenarian movement" (Albuquerque 1977), "a form of cultural resistance" (Campbell 1994), "a social movement" (Lewis 1993) or "a cultural movement" (Chevannes 1998b). Rastafari was initially studied as a marginal cult specific to the poorest strata of the black classes of Jamaica. But the use of the term "movement", though incapable of encompassing the variety of participants in the Rastafari movement, has become increasingly prevalent since the 1970s. The name *Rastafari* derives from the title and the first name of Emperor Haile Selassie I prior to his coronation in 1930: *ras*, translating literally as head, is a title of nobility and *Täfäri* is a passive form of the verb *fära*, to fear, and means "he who is feared".

The various categories of analysis used to define the movement depend on the disciplines to which scholars belong and the ideological positions from which they approach Rastafari. They also reflect the complexity of the movement and the variety of interpretations the actors themselves have offered. Certain typical statements by the Rastafari, like "each one must find out the truth for himself", are used to explain why Rastafari is considered "an innate conception" (Yawney and Homiak 2001, 263). Each person being free to identify with Rastafari, to live like a Rastafari and to explain what Rastafari is, there are probably as many interpretations as practitioners. Consequently, Rastafari has often been understood as an allegory for extreme, individual freedom, as a constant insubordination to homogenizing and dominating dogma of any type (see Chevannes 1998b, 31–33; Chivallon 2004, 212–14). It is therefore difficult to make generalizations based on discourses on the Rastafari movement without distorting the object itself.

Some common features are nevertheless characteristic of Rastafari. First, there is the attribution of a divine nature to the emperor of Ethiopia, Haile Selassie I, and its corollary, the inversion of the symbolic values assigned to black identity and white identity. Then, there is identification with the Hebrews carried away into slavery and a dichotomous vision of the world flagged by the terms *Zion* and *Babylon*. Zion represents Africa, which is at once the land of origin and the promised land, while Babylon symbolizes the Western world and its administrations. Lastly, there is the claiming of Ethiopian or African nationality as a right and, consequently, the right to return to Ethiopia or any other part of Africa.

Rastafari *livity*, or lifestyle, is marked by the wearing of dreadlocks (natural and "dreadful" knots of hair), the eating of *ital*, that is, "vital" and vegan food, and by the ritualized use of weed or *ganja* (*Cannabis sativa*). Rastafari livity, ritual (*nyabinghi*) and linguistic (*Italk*) innovations are transmitted within spaces of sociability like the *reasoning*. Age hierarchy is important and a dialectical movement characterizes the staging of the Rastafari word. All these practices follow a continuum going from the strictest to the most liberal forms, and differences in livity are part of the diversity inherent in the movement.

The cultural system developed by the Rastafari, initially nourished by the Jamaican context, has aroused the interest of numerous anthropologists, who have, for the most part, underscored the idea that a symbolic "return to Africa" was achieved through the development of this cultural system. However, the question of actual returns to Ethiopia, of physical settlements in Shashemene, is always overlooked. Thus, *The Rastafari Reader*, the best reflection of the state of research on the movement, fails to devote a single chapter to the question of the return (Murrell et al. 1998). How can we explain this silence surrounding the practices of the key actors of the return to Ethiopia? Does this reflect the disproportion between the masses of Rastafari who demanded to return and the small number of those who actually made the journey? Or is this related to the discomfort of Jamaican intellectuals regarding a population bent on leaving the island even after its independence in 1962? Or is it a question of chasm yawning between Caribbean and African historiography?

Rastafari and Return

Some specialists of the Rastafari movement eventually made the voyage to Shashemene during the 1980s. Horace Campbell, in a work of reference (1994), devotes seven pages to the settlement in Shashemene. His analysis, which is political and nationalistic, approaches the Rastafari movement as the legacy of popular practices of resistance. Although he considers the return of African descendants to Africa as their right, his judgement, in the light of the transformations induced by the Ethiopian Revolution of 1974, is that the return to Ethiopia is a conservative and even a colonial expedient contrary to the interests of African peoples. To his mind, the accomplishment of the return would imply a material and social process in contradiction with the emancipatory nature and free spirit of the Rastafari movement. British writer Derek Bishton (1986) narrated his visit to Shashemene and brought back wonderful photographs of the Caribbeans who had settled there. William F. Lewis (1993), an anthropologist and Catholic priest who spent only a few days in Shashemene, presented his first impressions and provided two individual life stories. Robert Hill, a historian specializing in Marcus Garvey and black ideologies, visited Shashemene but published nothing on the subject. Carole D. Yawney (2001) and John (Jake) P. Homiak (2001), American anthropologists, wrote two articles, respectively, with a specific focus on the question of Rastafari return. Starting from Jamaica and the United States and their immersion in specific groups within the movement, they offer interesting information, devoid of data derived from Ethiopia, which they finally visited in 2002.

Barry Chevannes, a Jamaican anthropologist who did remarkable work on

Rastafari, adopted a clear-cut position on the question of return. He too sees Rastafari as the legacy of popular practices of resistance but defines it as a movement whose impact and form are essentially cultural ones, in which the return to Africa occupies a merely theological, millenarian function. This purportedly explains why return is regularly emphasized by the Rastafari with no actual realization. In "New Approach to Rastafari", Chevannes stresses that in a sixty-year period there have been few initiatives of return: "The Repatriation picture then roughly looks like this: the first twenty years [1930–1950], one episode at the beginning; the next ten years [1950s] three episodes within a three-year span; *thereafter none*" (1998b, 30; emphasis mine). This *none* is quite disconcerting since, as we shall see, there are records of settlement in Shashemene as of the 1950s; in fact, Jamaican Rastafari were on the spot at the end of the 1960s.

The reality of the effective returns to Ethiopia is thus swept aside, alongside the structuring role of the processes of popular and collective organization that made them possible, and which this work will highlight. To this end, beyond the dichotomy – between culture and religion on the one hand and nationalism and politics on the other – which traverses and determines the historiography on Rastafari, I will favour an approach taking into account the political *and* the religious factors, whose interactions or, to quote Max Weber, whose "elective affinities" occupy a central place in the construction of social reality (1967, 103–4).

Itineraries

From the Caribbean to Ethiopia, there are no accessible sources on the history of return seen as a distinct and predefined corpus. Consequently, such data had to be sought after with perseverance. In fact, a paper providing an in-depth discussion of the research conditions leading to the present book might be useful. The enquiry had to begin in Shashemene and, as is often the case in the history of the migrations, so as to work from "the point of arrival to the point of departure, then advance, alongside the migrant, from the country of origin to the adopted country" (Green 2002, 3). Thus, between 2000 and 2003, I made several long visits to Ethiopia, where I consulted various archives – national, ministerial, municipal, and cartographic – providing a "ground-level" approach. Above all, I conducted over fifty interviews, life histories for the most part, in Shashemene and Addis Ababa, as well as in Kingston, Jamaica, and at times in the United States. This oral research allowed me to check and supplement the data in the census of the repatriated population of Shashemene carried out in 2003 by the Offices of Immigration and Nationality Affairs in Addis Ababa.[2] The fusion of these sources provides a corpus of 169 persons arriving in Shashemene in three waves between 1950 and 2003.

Before 1965, a few Caribbeans who had migrated to the United States as well as a few Americans of various religious affiliations arrived in Shashemene. After

1966, some Jamaican Rastafari landed directly from Kingston, helped by two organizations, the EWF and the Twelve Tribes of Israel. After 1991, Rastafari still arrived, from all over the Caribbean as well as the United States and Great Britain. I will focus minutely on these three waves and their interconnections with the political and social history of Ethiopia. This social chronology of the arrivals in Shashemene pinpoints various places of departure and, concomitantly, the trajectories, organizations and circulations which form the history of return.

In order to document a territorialized history paradoxically characterized by multiple locations, I made several research trips to London, Kingston, Accra, Los Angeles and New York. There I found printed sources, most of them quite rare, comprising pan-African newspapers and magazines and public records. These sources indicated a very interesting pathway: the return to Ethiopia could not be studied as the initiative of Rastafari alone. On the contrary, the Rastafari emerged as the heirs of older discourses and practices, some of them dating from the eighteenth century. These sources bound the small community repatriated to Shashemene with others dotted along the West African coast and inscribed it in circulations between the black worlds, through migrations but also via symbols, songs and imaginaries. The musical sources, for their part, have served as the "backbone" of this history, given their remarkable capacity to convey, around the Atlantic and beyond, these imaginaries of Ethiopia and of return. They include the hymns of the 1920s which are still sung today, Rastafari ritual music, the *nyabinghi*, and, of course, reggae. Confrontations between these various sources – oral, printed, archival, press, cartographic, musical, audio-visual – with their complementarities and contradictions give life to this history.

Heirs and Pioneers

At the heart of this history of return lies a fundamental contradiction. It could be illustrated by the words of these Jamaicans living in Shashemene since the 1960s and reported in a documentary:[3]

> I really came as a pioneer. A pioneer is one who prepare the way for those coming behind. (Inez Baugh)

> Pioneer? No, I don't see myself as a pioneer, I am an heir. A pioneer is who leave their home behind him to go to another country and seek life there and bring their people there. I am not like that, I was sold from here and taken there, so I am repatriated, I came back, this is my heritage. (Noel Dyer)

Heirs and *pioneers*, these two identificatory terms used by Jamaicans living in Shashemene are simultaneous and concurrent. They reflect the tensions and contradictions of black identity and the diaspora experience. In this sense, they echo the "double consciousness" evoked by W.E.B. Du Bois: "A peculiar sensation", "Two souls, two thoughts, two unreconciled strivings; two warring ideals in one dark body, whose dogged strength alone keeps it from being torn asunder" (1996, 5). Paul Gilroy's work on "the black Atlantic" is organized around this ambivalence. He identified thus the conditions of its emergence: "the double consciousness emerges from the unhappy symbiosis of three ways of thinking, being and seeing. The first is racially particularistic; the second nationalist . . . the third diasporic" (1993, 127). Here, race, nation and belonging form the triptych embodying the tensions of the duality generated by the mobility of return. While studying precisely their modes of dissemination and transmission, this work will put forward the hypothesis that the filiations and the legacies claimed by the returnees to Ethiopia and, more generally, the "Ethiopians of the world" are signs of this double consciousness which still produces contradictions in the spaces which once existed only in the imagination.

Inevitably, choices had to be made in the weaving of this work. In order to develop, historical writing constructs "with a coherent set of grand units a *structure* similar to the architecture of places and characters in a tragedy. But the system of this staging is the space where the *movement* of documentation, that is, of small units, introduces disorder into this order, eludes established divisions and activates a slow erosion of the organizing concepts" (de Certeau 1975, 136). The staging adopted herein is based on three grand units, forming the three parts of this book: the ideological and social roots of the return to Ethiopia (part 1), the Rastafari movement and the return to Ethiopia (part 2), and the fortunes of "the true Ethiopians" in Shashemene (part 3). The disorder will take the form of the regular documentary exchanges between the Americas, the Caribbean and Ethiopia, of the variety of scales at which the writing had to be done, and also of the many voices which recall, narrate and reveal the itineraries of return and make sense of the encounter between Africa and its diasporas.

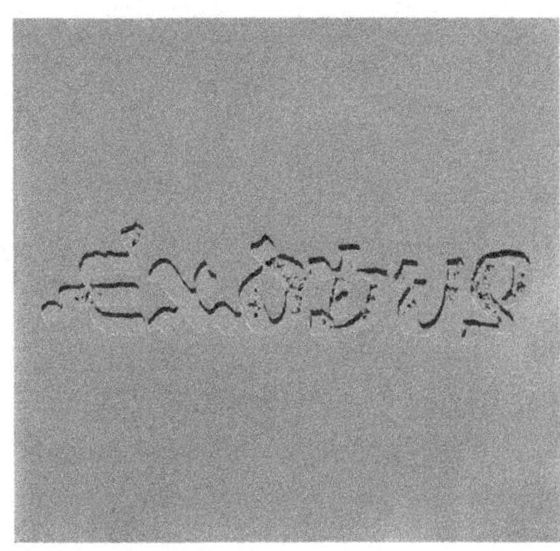

Figures I.2a–b. Designed by Neville Garrick in 1977, the font on the recto of Bob Marley and the Wailers' album *Exodus* evokes the Ethiopian syllabary, the *fidäl*.

Part 1

THE IDEOLOGICAL AND SOCIAL ROOTS OF THE RETURN TO ETHIOPIA

"We are not racist, we are race conscious."
– *Ras Dawit, Shashemene*

"We are the real Ethiopians!"
– *Bro Darka, Shashemene*

We know where we're going
We know from where we're from
We're leaving Babylon
We're going to our Father's land
Exodus!
– *Bob Marley, "Exodus" (1977)*

TODAY, ETHIOPIANS AND VISITORS TO ETHIOPIA RAPIDLY ASSOCIATE Shashemene with the repatriated population living on its periphery. Rastafari are part of the social and tourist landscape of Ethiopia, and for most of them, the history of this settlement starts with their gradual arrival since the end of 1960s. It is possible to approach the history of the return to Ethiopia by focusing only on the commitment of the Rastafari and analysing the consequences of this settlement on the Rastafari movement. The consequence of such an approach would be the erasure of the memory of those who arrived there before them: Americans,

Caribbeans, black Jews, Baptists and black Muslims. We would also lose sight of the enduring symbolic and concrete relations between the Ethiopian state and the black people of the world. Hence the will to inscribe the history of the return to Shashemene within a broader and more profound framework. This is the challenge: to deconstruct the "roots", the "origins" of a movement itself in search of roots and origins.

Part 1 sets out to identify the factors which prompted the desire for departure and finally departure itself, and to distinguish the specific traits of the return to Ethiopia compared to the other historical returns to the West African coast. The preponderant involvement of Caribbeans in nationalist and pan-African projects will then be underlined. Thereafter, it will be a matter of defining the place of Ethiopia in the racial imaginary and of following its religious and political variations. I will offer a comprehensive view of the ideology called Ethiopianism, regularly redynamized by the consideration of Ethiopian sovereigns for the black people of the world and their pan-African policy. Particular pains will be taken to recall the context in which the land in Shashemene was gifted and the role of the Ethiopian World Federation, an organization founded in New York in 1937 at the order of Haile Selassie I. The response of the black communities to this gift announces the convergence of two ideologies and their practices, the return to Africa and Ethiopianism. This framework will enable an outline of some of the material and immaterial legacies which circulated around the Atlantic, and a reminder of the ways in which the genealogies of return to Africa as well as the symbolic geographies of Ethiopia were transmitted in time and space, transforming Rastafari into the heirs of a longer history in which racial, political and religious paradigms were closely intertwined.

CHAPTER 1

SAILING AGAINST THE TIDE

Going Back to Africa

AT THE THRESHOLD OF THIS BOOK, IT IS imperative to take a new look at the history of the returns to Africa. The desire for return circulated in the Americas as a social and political alternative to the coercive conditions under which African descendants existed. The emergence of racial belonging, of a black identity characteristic of most of the societies of the Americas – variations notwithstanding – are the matrix in which the projects of return and their political, nationalist and pan-African practices developed. The imaginaries, spaces and conditions of return will be discussed, as will governmental and individual initiatives. Special attention will be given to the Caribbean actors of return, and their predominant role will be underlined.

Imaginaries of Return

The desire "to go back to Africa" is closely related to the history of transatlantic slavery; it was born in the belly of the slave ships which moved towards the large slave markets of the Americas. The individual memories of Africa were forged in the boats which furrowed the Atlantic. They initially took the shapes of a family, a house, a village or a landscape. Facing the horror of experience, these individual memories formed the idealized image of another place, of a past, of a place beyond the sea, a place which was lost, left behind, gone. For each first generation of Africans taken away into slavery, the desire to return was strong, as St Clair Drake underlines, and there was always, somewhere, a first generation since 1518 throughout the next three hundred and forty years (Drake 1993, 471). But after each first generation, the effect of time and the reconstruction of memories pushed the lands of origin into the fog of forgetting. The impulse of return, as Edouard Glissant insisted, "thus yielded, as the memory

Figure 1.1.
Repatriation now! Billboard in an exhibition, downtown Kingston, 2002. Photograph: G. Bonacci © DR.

of the ancestral land became blurred. Everywhere (in the Americas) where the technical rhythm was maintained or renewed for a transshipped population, whether oppressed or dominant, the impulse of Return declined little by little, absorbed by the taking into account of the new land" (1997, 46–47).

The taking into account of the new land ousted the memories of the land of origin, which subsided into obscure and mythicized forms. This "impulse" seems to emerge from the subconscious, to conceptualize that which is not directly controllable and which returns, resurfaces, in sometimes unexpected forms. The resurgence of the impulse was often triggered by the "legitimacy" of control, the perpetuation of technologies of coercion and the violence exercised via the institutions of slavery. In this sense, the impulse to return was the indicator par excellence of symbolic and real violence visited on and experienced by the black populations. Once the individual memories of a family, a village or a landscape had disappeared, other collective, social memories were deployed, associating return with new and henceforth imagined lands.

The scope for action at the disposal of the enslaved was quite limited. To break away from slavery, to change one's status meant becoming a "maroon",[1] buying freedom or gaining liberty under certain conditions. The last solution was suicide or the common abortive practices which were sometimes linked, in popular belief, to the hope of a post-mortem return. Joseph Ki-Zerbo evokes in this regard a "pathetic nostalgia":

> The cult of the ancestors, which is so characteristic of the religion of Africans, for whom the dead are not alive, but enjoy an existence more powerful than they did here below, assumed in this context a sublimely touching significance: the dead, released now from the rule of a tyrannical Master, were thought to retrace in the opposite direction the infernal crossing of the Ocean. Sailing without obstacles towards the

beloved continent, they were on their way to joining the assembly of the ancestors, over there, beyond the "great waters", over there in the country of Guinea. (1972, 224)

This popular tradition of the "flying slave" was transmitted from generation to generation and sometimes cropped up in Caribbean funeral practices where the deceased were placed facing the east in order to facilitate their return, as reported by St Clair Drake (1993, 471–72). A broad comparative work remains to be done since the flight over water knew multiple variants in the Americas. Thus in Saint-Domingue, the myth of the transmigration of souls to Guinea, evoked by Ki-Zerbo, took shape at an early date. "Guinea" indicated the paradise to which the dead returned after their life in exile. For every first generation of *arrivants* it probably identified their region of origin, the Gulf of Guinea, but the term quickly came to symbolize an idealized land whose men were virtuous, bold and brave in battle. Guinea lost its historicity and its territoriality and became the mythicized origin as well as a collective site of identification and of resistance to slavery (Montilus 1993).

In Jamaica, Monica Schuler unearthed the oral traces of stories saying that those who hoped to go back to Africa after death should not eat salt (1980, 93–96). Schuler recognized that the cosmological meaning of salt consumption remained obscure. She nevertheless linked it to the ritual of baptism introduced by the Portuguese into the kingdom of Kongo at the end of the fifteenth century. More than the sprinkling with water, the Portuguese used salt, placed on the tongue of the baptized. In Jamaica, refusal to eat salt might have become a metaphor of resistance to "foreign practices", including conversion to Christianity. The deprivation of salt offered a certain purity, a faithfulness to the African practices which would allow flight back home since "spirits do not eat salt" (96). The potency of such symbolism, linking food and post-mortem return, is illustrated by the practices of the Rastafari whose ital – literally vital – food is natural, vegan and generally without salt (Homiak 1985, 249–51). A popular verse, used by Bob Marley in his song "Rastaman Chant" (1973) evokes this: "One bright morning when my work is over / I will fly away home / fly away home to Zion, fly away home."

In connecting return by flying over the sea to the biblical trope of Zion, Bob Marley expressed an association often made between the transshipped African populations and biblical people. Very early on, the slaves or ex-slaves seized upon biblical narrative to put words to their experiences and the book of Exodus served them as a political and moral template (Glaude 2000; Callahan 2006). In response to the "curse of Ham" – the third son of Noah, who, after having seen the nudity of his father, was supposedly condemned by his father to be his brothers' servant (Genesis 9:18–29) – erected as a primordial truth and used to justify the subordinate social position of blacks in the Americas, what better language to use than that of Exodus to express the desire to leave existing conditions, to go elsewhere? The metaphor of the Hebrews, a holy people subjected to bondage, was continuously pressed into service to illustrate the degraded situation of the black populations and their critique of the racist societies in which they lived. The second book of the Bible tells the story of Moses and his mission to release the Hebrews from the oppression of the Egyptians. The words that the God of Israel is said to have pronounced permeate the imagination of numerous congregations: "I have surely seen the affliction of my people which are in Egypt and have heard their cry by reason of their taskmasters; for I know their sorrows. And I am come down to deliver them out of the hand of the Egyptians, and to bring them up out of that land, unto a good land and a large, unto a land flowing with milk and honey" (Exodus 3:7–9).

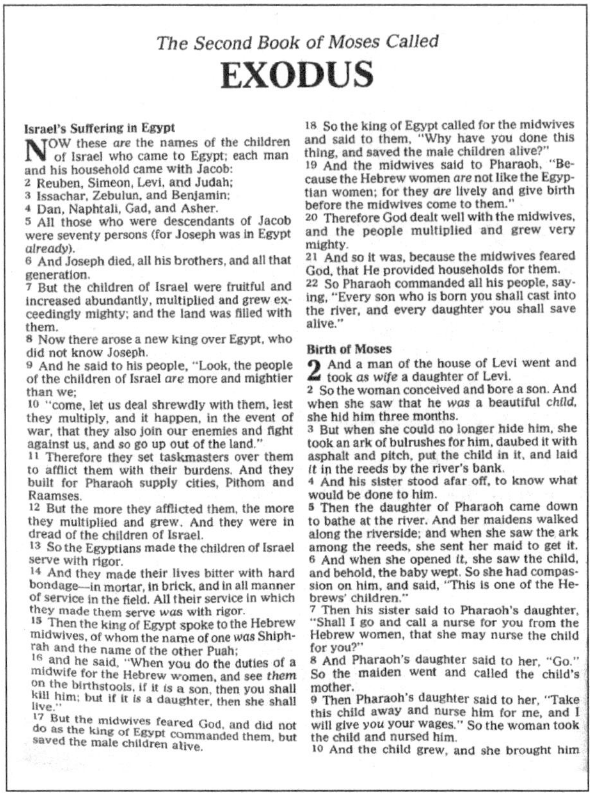

Moses embodied par excellence the figure of the leader with which many activists and "potential Messiahs" were compared – when they did not attribute his qualities to themselves. Exodus represented escape, but also the promise of a land elsewhere. Miracles led to it, as did laws, the terms of the covenant between men and God, the condition based on which the divine cloud could guide them out of the land of bondage into the land of abundance. Depending on the period and the place, various spaces were identified as this elsewhere, a point to which we will return. The uses of Exodus underline the power of the imagination, the capacity to identify the present with the past, to create filiations, to chart other future worlds, to think freedom as a possibility and as a struggle. As Robin D.G. Kelley (2002, 16) reminds us, the back-to-Africa idea was almost universally labelled as escapist or was associated with essentialist or romantic conceptions of black cultural unity. Critics underlined the utopian character of these projects as well as their impracticability and chanted the litany of failures. They were not wrong. However, to deny the tenacity of the desire to leave one place for another, an elsewhere which becomes a "home" of "one's own", is to deny what these movements have to tell us about the way in which black people imagined real freedom (Kelley 2002, 16). To deny the extent of the debates, discussions, efforts and mobilizations to accomplish return is to deny the social criticism made by the return to Africa, which produced territorialized symbols of origins as well as political practices. Bearing testimony to this is its inscription in black political ideologies, especially nationalism and pan-Africanism.

The Second Book of Moses Called

EXODUS

Israel's Suffering in Egypt

NOW these *are* the names of the children of Israel who came to Egypt; each man and his household came with Jacob:
2 Reuben, Simeon, Levi, and Judah;
3 Issachar, Zebulun, and Benjamin;
4 Dan, Naphtali, Gad, and Asher.
5 All those who were descendants of Jacob were seventy persons (for Joseph was in Egypt *already*).
6 And Joseph died, all his brothers, and all that generation.
7 But the children of Israel were fruitful and increased abundantly, multiplied and grew exceedingly mighty; and the land was filled with them.
8 Now there arose a new king over Egypt, who did not know Joseph.
9 And he said to his people, "Look, the people of the children of Israel *are* more and mightier than we;
10 "come, let us deal shrewdly with them, lest they multiply, and it happen, in the event of war, that they also join our enemies and fight against us, and *so* go up out of the land."
11 Therefore they set taskmasters over them to afflict them with their burdens. And they built for Pharaoh supply cities, Pithom and Raamses.
12 But the more they afflicted them, the more they multiplied and grew. And they were in dread of the children of Israel.
13 So the Egyptians made the children of Israel serve with rigor.
14 And they made their lives bitter with hard bondage—in mortar, in brick, and in all manner of service in the field. All their service in which they made them serve *was* with rigor.
15 Then the king of Egypt spoke to the Hebrew midwives, of whom the name of one *was* Shiphrah and the name of the other Puah;
16 and he said, "When you do the duties of a midwife for the Hebrew women, and see *them* on the birthstools, if it *is* a son, then you shall kill him; but if it *is* a daughter, then she shall live."
17 But the midwives feared God, and did not do as the king of Egypt commanded them, but saved the male children alive.
18 So the king of Egypt called for the midwives and said to them, "Why have you done this thing, and saved the male children alive?"
19 And the midwives said to Pharaoh, "Because the Hebrew women *are* not like the Egyptian women; for they *are* lively and give birth before the midwives come to them."
20 Therefore God dealt well with the midwives, and the people multiplied and grew very mighty.
21 And so it was, because the midwives feared God, that He provided households for them.
22 So Pharaoh commanded all his people, saying, "Every son who is born you shall cast into the river, and every daughter you shall save alive."

Birth of Moses

2 And a man of the house of Levi went and took *as wife* a daughter of Levi.
2 So the woman conceived and bore a son. And when she saw that he *was* a beautiful *child*, she hid him three months.
3 But when she could no longer hide him, she took an ark of bulrushes for him, daubed it with asphalt and pitch, put the child in it, and laid *it* in the reeds by the river's bank.
4 And his sister stood afar off, to know what would be done to him.
5 Then the daughter of Pharaoh came down to bathe at the river. And her maidens walked along the riverside; and when she saw the ark among the reeds, she sent her maid to get it.
6 And when she opened *it*, she saw the child, and behold, the baby wept. So she had compassion on him, and said, "This is one of the Hebrews' children."
7 Then his sister said to Pharaoh's daughter, "Shall I go and call a nurse for you from the Hebrew women, that she may nurse the child for you?"
8 And Pharaoh's daughter said to her, "Go." So the maiden went and called the child's mother.
9 Then Pharaoh's daughter said to her, "Take this child away and nurse him for me, and I will give *you* your wages." So the woman took the child and nursed him.
10 And the child grew, and she brought him

Figure 1.2. The book of Exodus in the New King James Version of the Bible.

Back to Africa: A Nationalist and Pan-African Theme

The return to Africa is a theme traversing questions regarding the formation of black nationalism and its corollary, the development of a pan-African ideology. The theme of return appears in every work on these questions and often short-circuits preliminary definitions of the nation, nationalism and pan-Africanism. In order to reduce the profusion of definitions and so better distinguish and establish the place of return in two of the most important black political ideologies, nationalism and pan-Africanism, let us reconsider for a moment these discourses which, as Chivallon stresses, could not "do without one another: the desire for sovereignty on a territory (nationalism) generally through reference to Africa whose unity is thought through solidarity among its people (Pan-Africanism)" (2004, 165).

Black Nationalism

In an address to the Sorbonne on 11 March 1882, Ernest Renan exposed his definition of the nation, stripping away elements formerly associated with it, in particular by the Germans J.G. Herder and J.G. Fichte, who had a more organic approach to the phenomenon. For Renan, it was not race, language, religion, community of interests or geography that determined the definition of the nation. The nation was above all a "soul, a spiritual principle", "a moral conscience", comprising two elements: "joint possession of a rich legacy of memories" and "the current assent, the desire to live together, the will to continue to advance the heritage received undivided". This heritage was defined more precisely: "a heroic past, great men, glory (I mean the true one), this is the social capital on which a national idea is grounded" (Renan 1996, 240). This text by Renan, which founded the interpretation of the nation as a contract, in fact advocated against the search for purity and an essentialist vision of men and nations. Renan requested acceptance of the mixity at the origin of the nations, in order to transcend the differences among men and allow them to pursue a joint project born of the desire to live together. The glorious heritage would be at the base of nation-building, and its definition implied a reinterpretation of the past and a rewriting of history. The historical processes resulting in nations were slow and painful, and all required a dose of amnesia and compromise. Compromise "led to the anchorage of the loss of the memory of slavery in the national narrative" (Cottias 2007, 89–90), whereas slavery was a resource allowing the imagination of another nation – a black one. Thus, Renan presented a perspective which was naturally very European, one plunging into ancient history and making detours through Italy, Germany, England and France. Using another approach, Benedict Anderson proposed to define nations as the fruit of the human imagination, offering a better inroad into the black political universe: "[The nation] is *imagined* because the members of even the smallest nation will never know most of their fellow-members, meet them, or even hear of them, yet in the minds of each lives the image of their communion" (2002, 19).

The nation was imagined as a community because, in spite of the inequalities it encompassed, it was perceived as a profound, horizontal camaraderie, it was limited because it could not be coextensive with all of humanity; it was sovereign because the sovereign state was a guarantee of this community. The power of this symbolism grounded in shared cultural heritages lent, in political life, a universal legitimacy to the nation. The tight bonds between nation and nationalism are often questioned through the pre-existence of the one or the other. For Ernest Gellner, nationalism created the nation, and not the other way around. Nationalism was then defined as "primarily a political principle, affirming the inevitable congruence of political unity and national unity" (1989, 11). The nationalist sentiment was "the sentiment of anger" caused by the absence of congruence between these political national unities, comprising the hallmarks of oppressive and dysfunctional regimes. As Anderson also underlined, using Renan's terms, nationalism invents nations where there were none before, for multiple reasons (2002, 19). The nation, whose subjective antiquity was defined by nationalists, remains in the eyes of the historians an objectively modern phenomenon. Anderson insisted: "nationalism has to be understood by aligning it, not with self-consciously held political ideologies, but with the large cultural systems that preceded it, out of which – as well as against which – it came into being" (1991, 12).

In this sense, it is in the theoretical and practical framework of European nationalisms and European national practices that one can understand how black nationalism was formed, developed, and came to a head. It was at once a part of this phenomenon, given the importance of print capitalism (of which the black press is a good example) and opposed to it – that is, it was also a nationalism of reaction to white domination, born in a context of bondage and resistance. Wilson Moses defines black nationalism thus: "[It] differs from most other nationalisms in that its adherents are united neither by a common geography nor by a common language but, by the nebulous concept of racial unity" (1978, 17).

Black nationalism sought to go beyond the differences between black people in order to unify them politically, whether they were Africans living in Africa or Afro-descendants. It was nationalism to the extent that it imagined the unity of all the members of a black racial family and often, but not always, had the objective of creating an independent black nation state with precise geographical borders – be it on the African continent, or elsewhere. As Gellner pinpointed, "for these kinds of nationalism [of diaspora], the acquisition of territory was the first and perhaps the main problem" (1983, 106).

The desire to create a national haven expressed not only dissatisfaction with the living conditions in the black Americas,[2] but also a desire for independence and a determination to demonstrate the ability of black people to establish a government, a national administration and to manage themselves. Moses proposed a temporal agenda in which black "protonationalism" supposedly originated at the end of the eighteenth century, like most of the other nationalisms covered by Anderson (1996, 6). In the United States, after a relative deceleration in the 1830s, nationalist expressions swelled again around 1850, due notably to the Fugitive Slave Law which obliged the police in all states to help with the capture of runaway slaves, thus transforming the protection of slavery into a national policy. A few years later, in 1857, the Dred Scott ruling, validated by the United States Supreme Court, stated that no black person was a citizen and had no rights that white people were obliged to respect.

The first half of the nineteenth century was marked by a national debate on slavery and two ideologies took shape. On the one hand were the integrationists, who hoped for a society where colour would be unimportant and where individual work and successes would largely determine the life of blacks. On the other were the nationalists, who sought to establish their own economic interstices and geopolitical spaces – a territory, a state, or settlements *elsewhere*. The influence of the "emigrationists", for whom emigration out of the United States was a precondition to any kind of freedom, was particularly significant. Eclipsed by the years of the American Civil War (1861–65) and following the emancipation of the slaves as sanctioned by the adoption of the thirteenth amendment of the constitution in 1865, black nationalism resurfaced in the guise of a "technocratic black nationalism" (Moses 1978, 28). Booker T. Washington (1856–1915) and W.E.B. Du Bois (1868–1963) were its public representatives, though in contrasted and sometimes opposing ways. At the beginning of the twentieth century, Marcus Garvey and his Back-to-Africa movement were milestones of black nationalism. In addition to integration or nationalism, a third strategic vision emerged during the twentieth century, notably propelled by black working-class consciousness: the possibility of changing, of radically transforming the United States through the redistribution of resources. These three visions – integration, nationalism/emigrationism, and transformation – were not mutually exclusive and were sometimes quite interconnected (Marable and Mullings 2000, xxi). Depending on the period, various possibilities of action became available to the black populations, be they slaves or free. The complexity of these black ideologies resided in the tensions, attractions, and repulsions between these social visions. This study will focus on the aspect of nationalism related to the foundation of a black nation and on the emigrationism according to which this black nation could not be created on American soil but only outside it, on the African continent in particular.

Pan-Africanism

Black nationalism, seeking to politically unite all black people be they Africans or Afro-descendants, was intrinsically linked to the development of pan-Africanism. The actors of both were often the same and appear in works on both fields. Moses detected the object of pan-Africanism in the prefix "pan" which, as in pan-Germanism and pan-Slavism, sought to unify independent ethnic groups under a collective nationalist banner on the basis of histories and cultures presumed to be similar (1978, 17). Imanuel Geiss, in a reference book on pan-Africanism, immediately recognizes the difficulty in offering a simple and precise definition of pan-Africanism, but he proposes a preliminary one:

> 1. Intellectual and political movements among Africans and African Americans who regard or have regarded Africans and people of African descent as homogenous. This outlook leads to a feeling of racial solidarity and a new self-awareness and causes African Americans to look upon Africa as their real 'homeland', without necessarily thinking of a physical return to Africa.
> 2. All ideas that have stressed or sought the cultural unity and political independence of Africa, including the desire to modernize Africa on a basis of equality of rights. The key concepts here have been respectively the "redemption of Africa" and "Africa for the Africans".
> 3. Ideas or political movements that have advocated, or advocate, the political unity of Africa or at least close political collaboration in one form or another. (Geiss 1974, 3)

This first definition echoes the preceding discussions of nationalism: racial solidarity, Africa as land of origin and sometimes land of the future, and the cultural and political unity of Africans and Afro-descendants. Geiss inscribed this definition in what was still an imperfect temporal framework: proto-pan-Africanism before 1900, the formation of pan-Africanism proper between 1900 and 1945, and pan-Africanism as a political movement for the unity of the African continent after 1958. This chronology, following the tempo of the pan-African congresses,[3] seems to have been determined by the time at which Geiss did his research (1964–66) and by the space in which he situated the birth and development of pan-Africanism. His work supposed an almost total geographical equivalence between the pan-African movement and the British Empire. Indeed, he defended the idea that it was first and almost exclusively in the British Empire – due to its scale and its colonial policies – that pan-Africanism developed.

Elikia M'Bokolo disputed this approach by pointing out the pre-existence of at least two other spaces of triangular relations namely – the French-speaking and Portuguese-speaking spaces (1995b, 2006a). The French-speaking space, stretching from Haiti to Guadeloupe and Martinique, had relationships with Paris and West Africa and produced by the 1860s pan-Africanist intellectuals and activists like Anténor Firmin and Benito Sylvain.[4] The Portuguese-speaking space, which is still little known, extended from Brazil to Portugal and the coastal regions of Africa which were formerly Portuguese. Luanda, the Angolan capital, probably played in the 1870–90 period the same role in the development of pan-Africanism as Paris and London did at the end of the nineteenth and at the beginning of the twentieth century. M'Bokolo also insists on the reappropriation of pan-Africanism by the political and intellectual African elites, beginning in the 1900s and completed by 1950. They contributed to renovate and transform the pan-African ideology, which "remains the most ambitious and inclusive ideology Africa ever produced for itself since the nineteenth century" (M'Bokolo 2006a, 1). This was an ideology, in the sense of being "a system of ideas, representations, and social conceptions, which expresses the interests of categories and social groups, provides a total interpretation of the world such as it is organized and implies points of view, standards of behaviours and directives for action" (1).

Pan-Africanism was constantly presented in a variety of modes by historians and was often studied through a double prism: its links to the birth of nationalisms and its expressions in specific spaces (American, Caribbean, West African, East African and so on). Moreover, reference was sometimes made to ideological pan-Africanism, considered to be represented by the work of the Trinidadians C.L.R. James and George Padmore, and to political pan-Africanism, whose watersheds were thought to be the various pan-African conventions, to which W.E.B. Du Bois was deeply committed. These aspects were supposed to form what George Shepperson (1962) defines as "Pan-Africanism", with a capital *P*. With a small *p*, "pan-Africanism" purportedly designated all the various, sometimes transitory, movements claiming a bond between Africans and the descendants of Africans, in which the cultural element was seen as predominant. This, supposedly, was the case of cultural pan-Africanism, through which intellectuals rewrote the history of the continent: literary pan-Africanism, of which negritude is an example and musical pan-Africanism, in which artists consciously mix themes of diverse origins and universal resonance. Evangelical pan-Africanism, which retraced the itinerary and relations between the black churches around the Atlantic, would probably be half-way between Pan-Africanism and pan-Africanism. Shepperson himself recognized that this dichotomy between Pan-Africanism and pan-Africanism was not absolute and that many elements interacted between these two poles. As Winston James pointed out, these categories had institutional connections, and the implicit hierarchy between them was really neither desirable nor justifiable. Indeed, pan-African (small *p*) organizations like, for example, that of Marcus Garvey, sometimes had far greater impact than the five Pan-African (capital *P*) conventions on the mobilization of Afro-descendants and on the processes of decolonization in Africa and in the Caribbean (James 2004, 126). Following this remark by James, I have chosen to use *pan-Africanism* herein as a generic term englobing these various policies or cultural efforts, pending, in another framework, a fuller contribution to more precise definitions.

This wealth of complexity in definitions augurs well for the future of research on pan-Africanism, to which the study of the returns to Africa remains a bonafide contribution. Indeed, the Back-to-Africa movement occupied a crucial place in the history of pan-Africanism: the actors of return contributed to the formation and diffusion of the pan-African ideology, and vice versa – the great pan-Africanists activists of the Americas often visited or lived on the continent. The relations formed between Africans and the descendants of Africans through the movements of return contributed to create pan-Africanism, thus pulling what was often a very intellectualized ideology in the direction of its less-known social practices, which nonetheless participated in making it "real" and lived.

Spaces and Itineraries of Return

The "triangle" of the Atlantic slave trade had its apexes in Europe, in Africa and in the Americas, and it is no surprise that the itineraries of return inscribed themselves in this geography. The starting points were generally associated with the United States and England or, at times, Brazil (Verger 1968). West Africa or, to be more precise, the coast of West Africa, from the Gulf of Benin to the Gulf of Guinea, formed one apex of the itineraries of return. Placed in the long-term context, these returns constituted a stage in the construction of an "Atlantic community", consisting not of one-way relations of Africa towards the Americas or of the Americas towards Africa, but, on the contrary, of reciprocal relations and constant interactions (Law and Mann 1999). The role of this "Atlantic community" was discernible in the historical development of a community of persons sharing family and commercial relations, identities and cultural practices as defined all around the ocean. The Atlantic community revisited and scrambled the triangular spaces, and, depending on the local situations, it was anglophone, lusophone or francophone. At all events, the returns to the continent contributed to the acceleration, complication and development of these multidirectional relations. Moreover, as St Clair Drake emphasized, unknown sources on return, whether failures or successes, are constantly being exhumed from archives (1993, 471). Joseph Harris (1987) showed this in his work on returnees and refugees in colonial Kenya. Since the 1870s, in Freretown on the coast of the Indian Ocean, the settlement of "returnees" from India, in particular from Bombay, and the British Caribbean, as well as of migrants arriving from Sierra Leone and recaptured slaves who were freed at sea, formed, with the local population, a cosmopolitan society. Harris suggested that in spite of their connections with Europeans and notwithstanding the missionary consciousness which often animated them, they enabled the development of the

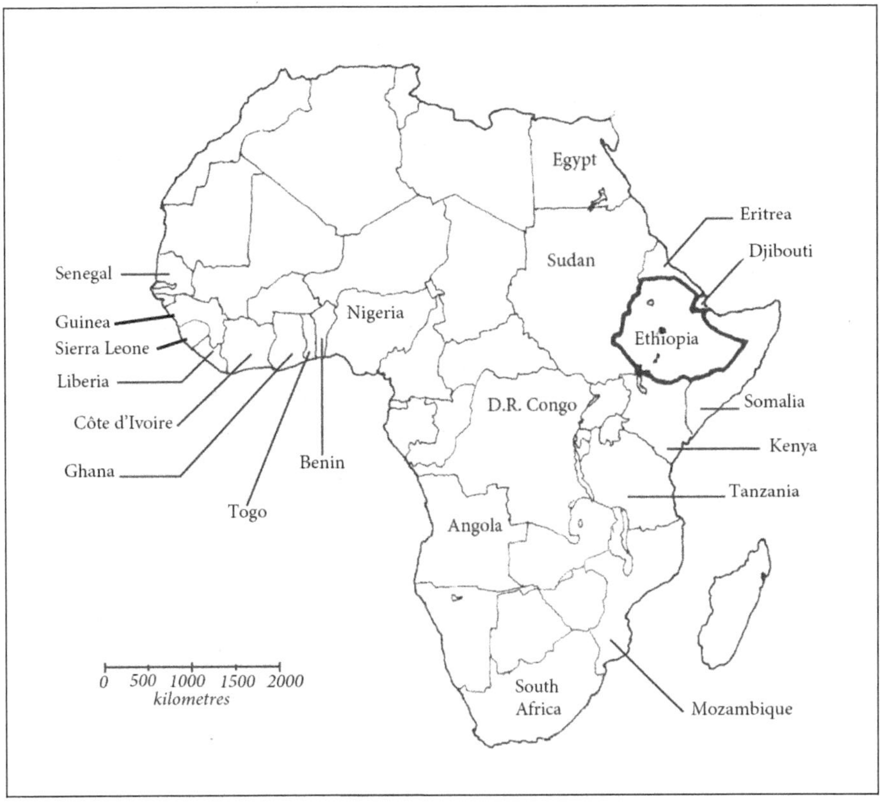

Figure 1.3.
Map of Africa.

cause of Kenyan nationalism. This is another aspect of return that has come to light, one which throws wide open the threshold of the slave trade, of another space, which is not our focus here. Our incursion into East Africa will transit via Ethiopia, without taking into account the entire coast stretching from the Horn to the Cape. It will suffice for the moment to pinpoint the "classic" spaces and itineraries of return, namely, to the coast of West Africa.

The return to Sierra Leone is the first classic example of return to Africa, although such was not the main concern of its instigators. As early as 1783, an Englishman, Henry Smeathman, conceived the idea of a settlement in Sierra Leone, and three years later he made contact with the "Committee for the Relief of the Black Poor" founded by gentlemen concerned about the miserable living conditions of coloured persons in England. Joined by high-society abolitionists, Thomas Clarkson, Granville Sharp and William Wilberforce, their campaign could only be carried out by combining humanitarian intentions and practical, notably commercial, advantages. Thus, in February 1790, the Sierra Leone Society was founded, putting an end to the autonomy of the "Free province" and directing from London the establishment of Freetown, which was growing. The involvement of the English philanthropists in the establishment of Sierra Leone marked its economic and political development and impacted the entire West African region, in particular through the missionaries who originated there.

The first and best-known repatriated population came from these "Black Poor". Far from passive, these blacks participated in the development of the project of return (Braidwood 1982). They wanted "to go back home", being mostly from the United States, from the Thirteen Colonies or from the British Caribbean, but the practices of the slave trade there presented a danger. When alternative places of settlement were discussed by the committee gentlemen, who also considered Nova Scotia (Canada), the Black Poor joined ranks with Smeathman and agreed to go to Sierra Leone, provided they were protected from the risks of the slave trade, still rampant in the region. In April 1787, 459 persons left for Sierra Leone, but few survived the climate and living conditions. Those who did were not alone for long; through other routes arrived the populations which contributed to the formation of the Krio social group (Wyse 1993). The first to arrive were the "Black Loyalists" who had fought on the side of the English during the American War of Independence, who were taken to Nova Scotia after the defeat of the English. They were ready to leave a hostile environment to go to Africa, and in January 1792 a contingent of 1,196 blacks arrived on the coast of West Africa, quickly followed by a second contingent in March of the same year. They founded Freetown, close to the first settlement of repatriates called Granville Town. Then the Jamaican maroons arrived. After the Second Maroon War in the British island (1795–96), they were exiled to Nova Scotia. In 1800, the Jamaican maroons arrived with their history of resistance and their culture, after a long journey which had led them from the mountains of the Cockpit Country in Jamaica to wintry Canada (Campbell 1993). Despite the condescension with which they were treated by the other returnees, with time the group became more homogeneous. To alleviate administrative difficulties, Sierra Leone was made the first British Crown Colony in Africa on 1 January 1808, whereas from 1807 British citizens were forbidden to engage in activities related to the slave trade. This partial abolition of the slave trade introduced the fourth and largest group of immigrants, comprising manumitted Africans, originating in the region and from all over West Africa. They introduced themselves little by little into the social stratification in progress and submitted to British infrastructures. Krios were in the making, born of the encounter between the itineraries of return which had crossed the Atlantic and of the intermingling of these extremely different cultures: loyalists, resisters and manumitted. Initially forming a polyglot, international society seeking among Western norms and community practices the means to develop themselves and to develop relations from the coast towards the interior, they later migrated all over West Africa (Geiss 1974, 41–57).

The arrival of the Brazilians is another major example of return of Africans or Creoles to the West African coast, this time from Rio de Janeiro and from Bahia, in Brazil. From 1807, slave uprisings took place in Bahia, culminating in the Malé Revolt of 1835. These revolts were a form of resistance to the inhuman treatments handed out by slave owners, but were also supposedly due to the concentration of Africans of a "warlike nature" brought from only one region of Africa, and who were followers of Islam (Verger 1968, 325–50). Subsequent to police measures, they were massively expelled from Bahia, and a movement of return to the Gulf of Benin ensued, often guided by "fidelity to the land from which they had been unwillingly severed" (599). They were quickly followed by other Brazilians who had been freed or who had bought their liberty. Many of them were aided by members of their families, relations, religious congregations or abolitionist associations. The return movement gained importance after 1835 and, in spite of the difficulty in obtaining statistics, it is believed that between 1820 and 1899 nearly eight thousand people made the journey from Bahia (Lindsay 1994, 25). These Brazilians settled around the four ports of the Coast of Mina – Grand Popo, Ouidah, Jaquin and Apa – and in Porto Novo, Lagos and Accra. Largely influenced by the cultures and practices developed in Brazil, they returned with customs, habits, practices and lifestyles to which they remained attached. Instead of finding roots, they created new, interstitial spaces between the European and African populations already on the spot. They also encountered many immigrants from the Sierra Leone, with whom they had few affinities. The latter formed a kind of middle class who spoke English, were Protestant and British subjects, and were consequently closer to the English civil servants and merchants from the metropolis than to the Brazilian immigrants. These Brazilians had little wealth on their arrival, spoke another language, were Catholic or Muslim, and were foreigners. Some were peasants, but many more were businessmen or merchants, often engaged in the slave trade. These Brazilians had a considerable impact on the African economy and on the culture of the West African coast. Francisco Felix de Souza (d. 1849) became the iconic figure of the Brazilians engaged in the slave trade out of Ouidah. Following his support of the coup d'état which brought the brother of the king of Dahomey to the throne, he became the only intermediary of the new king in the slave trade market, with the title of "chacha". As a testimony to the aura of this character, the writer Bruce Chatwin (1980) dedicated a novel to him, and several documentary films have been made on the descendants of the de Souza family in Benin.

The case of Liberia is another inevitable example of the practices of return to Africa. In December 1816, the American Colonization Society was founded in the United States, with the objective to finance the return of Afro-descendants to Africa. The society arose from a coalition of idealistic philanthropists, some of whom intended to serve the interests of African Americans, considering that equality was unattainable in the United States, while others, who were openly racist, hoped to consolidate the slave system in the south of the country by deporting the free and manumitted population. Sierra Leone was to some extent a model, but the negotiations between the Americans and the British concerning the possibility of deporting blacks to Sierra Leone having failed, the officers of the American Colonization Society bought land in Cape Mesurado in 1822 by coercing the indigenes (Geiss 1974, 81). This settlement was called Liberia. In 1820, a boat bearing about eighty persons arrived in the region but, disembarked on an island not far from Freetown, they were decimated by fevers, and the survivors took refuge in Fourah Bay, on dry land. In the course of the nineteenth century, nearly eighteen thousand former slaves came from the United States, men and women in equal proportions, and disembarked in Liberia. Some were freed on the condition that they emigrate, whereas others were forcefully deported. Some five thousand persons freed along the coast also settled there, in addition to a small group from Barbados in the Caribbean (Ham 1993). Together, they formed a group of so-called Libero-Americans who, though they contributed to the development of the region, especially through trade and education, nevertheless became a small parasitic elite, exploiting the local African populations by introducing practices akin to the slavery from which they had only just escaped. Liberia, which became independent in 1847, played an important role in the formation of the black nationalist discourse in the United States, in spite of its racist foundations. We will return later to some of the characters, like Paul Cuffe or Edward W. Blyden, who devoted their life and efforts to this cause.

It is important to make mention of the popular efforts whose objective was to counter the forced emigration to Liberia: the projects of emigration to Haiti. Since the revolts which devastated Saint-Domingue starting in 1791, and which led to the independence of the first black republic in 1804, Haiti exerted a profound fascination on the black American populations (Drake 1991, 36). Icon of a successful slave revolt, symbol of the ability of blacks to overthrow Western powers and to establish an independent nation, Haiti was, far from the African coasts, another possible point of relocation for emigrationists. James Theodore Holly (1829–1911), a freeborn black man from the United States, was one of the defenders of emigration to Haiti. The arguments developed were identical to those advocating the return to Africa: emigration to Haiti would prove that blacks were capable of managing a government and developing a national identity, and it was the complete opposite of the policies of forced return that Liberia represented. Richard Allen (1760–1831) founded the African Methodist Episcopal Church, in Philadelphia, in 1816; it was the first independent African American denomination, and he became its bishop. A pioneer among American black intellectuals, the author of treatises against the inequality of the races, he contributed significantly to the development of an African American political consciousness and protested against the forced returns to Liberia. But when in 1824 Jean-Pierre Boyer, president of the unified Haitian Republic (1822–44), invited free blacks to emigrate to his country, Allen supported the project and directed the Society for Promoting the Emigration of Free Persons to Hayti, founded that same year (Geiss 1974, 34, 86). American emigration to Haiti between 1824 and 1825 was, at the time of Geiss's writing, estimated at approximately two thousand people, many of whom were members of the African Methodist Episcopal Church (86). Recent research escalates these figures and indicates that, during the 1820s, between eight and thirteen thousand people probably emigrated to Haiti.[5] The project quickly lost momentum; President Boyer was overwhelmed by the mass of newcomers, and tensions rapidly developed between Haitians and immigrants. The project of emigration to Haiti was nonetheless reclaimed by President Lincoln in 1861. He supported the idea of a deportation of the black populations either to Africa or to Haiti – or even to Panama. Supported by a few black American leaders like Henry Highland Garnet (1815–82), this project was violently disputed by others, especially Frederick Douglass (1817–95). Of the last newcomers, very few succeeded in settling in the country. It was a fiasco, but one largely unknown to historians. It would appear that the integration of the African Americans who remained into Haitian society has never been precisely documented.

The "classic" examples of return to Africa share a localization on the coast of West Africa and have in common the involvement of whites: Americans and Englishmen. The experiences of Sierra Leone and Liberia were initially conceptualized by westerners who, for humanitarian or racist reasons, saw them as a good means of "saving" or discarding black populations who had become a burden. These first colonies on African soil laid the foundations of an economic and social development on which large Western enterprises grafted themselves in order to exploit the natural resources, develop maritime trade or propagate Christian missions. The settlement of the Brazilians was, to a certain extent, encouraged by the British authorities who saw them as extremely useful intermediaries and serious workers. The increase of returns to the West African coast by of the end of the eighteenth century served as a launching pad for generations of black nationalists who engaged themselves body and soul in debates on the legitimacy of Liberia and on the development of the region. The project of emigration to Haiti, an unexpected form of "return" and a legitimate alternative to "white" projects, introduces a crucial dimension: that of black initiatives with respect to departure from the United States, around which black nationalism constructed itsel by the beginning of the nineteenth century.

A Few Trajectories and Initiatives

Several works recall the numerous initiatives by individuals who sought, by one means or another, to go back to Africa or to organize the return of black populations. Among these figure the works of Edwin S. Redkey (1974) and of Robert G. Weisbord (1974), which are quite comprehensive, even though the first is limited to the period 1890 to 1910, while the second covers the nineteenth and twentieth centuries. Furthermore, classic works on black nationalism offer access to various sources, letters, calls and manifestos for return, sometimes dating from the eighteenth century (Moses 1996). To plunge into the back-to-Africa discourses is to open complex fields concerning the formation of black nationalism and pan-Africanism. Since it is not the objective of the present work to evaluate all accessible resources on the subject, I will limit myself to underlining the involvement of a few personalities in order to evaluate the importance of the question of emigration and return in the development of a black and pan-African political consciousness and to underline the ideological framework in which the movements of return developed. In a happy – though sometimes reductive – critique of the engagement of black nationalists in Africa, a book has underscored the similarities of their ideology of "redemption" with that of the "civilizing mission" developed by European empires. Tunde Adeleke thus emphasizes the idea that Europeans defined their intrusion in Africa as a humanitarian effort, inspired by a philanthropic commitment to the universalization of the benefits allotted to a "higher" European civilization (Adeleke 1998). By shedding light on the ideological and cultural bonds between black nationalism and the European "civilizing mission", Adeleke defines the engagement of these nationalists through an "imperialist" gaze, one shared to a certain extent with Europeans, hence their profound duality. It is within this "civilizing" framework that the concepts of the regeneration and redemption of Africa took shape and allowed African Americans to define their crucial role in this enterprise, which they themselves often described as "colonial".

The first concrete project of return from the United States was developed by Paul Cuffe (1759–1817), of African and American Indian descent, born in Massachusetts, who became a Quaker in his adulthood. He was a ship captain when the news of Sierra Leone reached him in early 1810. He travelled there with an African American crew. He was later invited to London to discuss the possibilities of settlement with the abolitionists who had founded an "African Institution" with the view of maintaining their relations with the continent, since Sierra Leone had become a British colony. Cuffe's project presented a good mix of settlement and commerce and, as some of his letters indicate, he had hopes of making huge profits through the development of maritime trade between the United States and Africa.[6] After delay due to the war of 1812 between the British and the Americans, he set out again in February 1816 for Sierra Leone, carrying on board thirty-eight African Americans who had for the most part financed their own journeys (Geiss 1974, 84–85; Weisbord 1974, 14–15). Two hundred people were on the waiting list for return, but Cuffe's death in 1817 prevented them from making the journey. The spirit of economic independence which guided him was to become one of the outstanding features of emigrationism, one which was sometimes paradoxical as it was also used to justify the exploitation of the local African populations. Contained in the term "colony" or "colonization", which often designated the nature of the black settlements on the continent, this association between emigration and the development of commerce was representative of one of the core characteristics of the black "civilizing mission": the aim was to build an economic power which could either overwhelm or rival that of Europeans.

Another project, among the most important, was developed by Martin R. Delany (1812–85). Born free in the south of the United States, he engaged himself at an early age in abolitionist activities and, between 1843 and 1846, published out of Pittsburgh a newspaper called *Mystery*. He studied medicine at Harvard and published two works during this time. The first, *The Condition, Elevation, Emigration and Destiny of the Colored People of the United States*, published in 1852, deployed an emigrationist propaganda. Delany stressed the general poverty of African Americans, defines them as "a nation within a nation" and, by virtue of the oppression to which they were subjected, as "really a *broken people*" (1852, 209). He defines Liberia as "not an Independent Republic: in fact, *it is not* an independent nation at all; but a poor *miserable mockery* – a *burlesque* on a government – a pitiful dependency on the American Colonizationists" (169). His acerbic criticism of Liberia did not prevent him from thinking about emigration – quite the contrary – and there is a question that resurfaces throughout the book: "Where shall we go?" According to him, the hand of Providence pointed to the American continent as a refuge for the nations of the world, and he gave serious thought to projects of settlement in Canada, in Central and South America or in the Caribbean. However, in an appendix, "A project for an adventure to the Eastern coast of Africa" was proposed, in view of its implementation by a "Confidential Council" whose objective would be to identify the most appropriate place for a settlement. Delany's conquering spirit was particularly explicit at the end of the project: "The land is ours – there it lies with inexhaustible resources; let us go and possess it" (214). In spite of his outspoken opposition to Liberia, it was, of course, aboard a Liberian boat that he set off in 1859 for a voyage to Liberia. With Robert Campbell (1829–84), a Jamaican printer, he travelled to Lagos, where they signed a treaty with King Docemo, who seemed to accept the idea of an African American settlement.

Delany's second book, quite a short one, was published in 1861 with the title *Official Report of the Niger Valley Exploring Party*. East Africa was put aside and Delany confirmed that large businesses, especially in cotton production, could be established around the river Niger. He underlined the crucial role which African Americans could play, as "legitimate descendants of Africa", in the introduction of civilization, in regeneration and in the foundation of a "grand nationality" (Delany, 1861, 76–77). Regardless of his words of respect for the local institutions, chieftaincies and royal families, there was no doubt in Delany's mind that the blacks of America had a (pre)dominant role to play. He coined an expression whose first half at least was to become famous, to the point of being reappropriated as *the* pan-African slogan by the leaders of African independence in the 1960s: "Africa for the African race, and black men to rule them". The second half of the expression, for its part, was clarified by the phrase which followed: "By black men I mean, men of African descent who claim an identity with the race" (82). There was therefore a clear indication of the role African Americans were to play in the development of African "civilization". In their hands, the exercise of power and control on the continent, its resources and numerous populations became legitimate. Interrupting Delany's great projects of conquest of Africa, the American Civil War, which began the same year (1861), forced him to remain in the United States.

Upon his arrival in Liberia, he had been welcomed by Edward W. Blyden (1832–1912) and Alexander Crummell (1819–98), who had settled there since 1851 and 1853, respectively. Born in St Thomas in the Danish Virgin Islands, Blyden, in the face of the refusal of several American tertiary institutions to accept him because he was black, embarked in 1851 for Liberia under the auspices of the American Colonization Society. There he brilliantly completed classic studies and became a professor in Liberia College, the first secular tertiary English-speaking institution in sub-Saharan Africa. As soon as he arrived, he became a correspondent for the *Liberia Herald*, which had just lost a famous editor, the Jamaican John B. Russwurm.

Blyden was a prolific and brilliant writer, one who was highly critical of American slavery, against which he wrote statements of advocacy defending the history and the destiny of the "black race". In *A Voice from Bleeding Africa* (1856), Blyden exposed what has been called the "redemptionist" aspect of black nationalism. The mission of Liberians and that of black Americans was to be "the redemption of Africa, and the disenthralment and elevation of the African race" (E. Blyden 1856, cited in Lynch 1971, 10). Blyden believed, as did many Liberians, that the emergence of a powerful African civilization would help to overthrow the slave-owning and slave-trading powers. In another publication, "The Call of Providence to the Descendants of Africa in America" (1862) he went even further with his redemptionist vision while maintaining that God had allowed slavery so that African Americans could accomplish fully their predestined role. Providence would allow the suffering of the slave trade to lead to a good, materialized by the manifest destiny of African Americans who, by returning to their ancestral homes, would bring with them Christianity and civilization and thus contribute "to regenerate" a "degraded" Africa (30). Despite his public criticisms of the deficiencies of the new state, he remained the champion of the independence of Liberia, whose legitimacy and symbolic character he always defended (*The Significance of Liberia* [1906], quoted by M'Bokolo 2006a, 14). He travelled widely in West Africa and in 1866 visited Egypt, Palestine and Syria. An accomplished linguist, Blyden was acclaimed as the "First African personality" to have succeeded in developing a complete philosophy of Africanness capable of winning over his contemporaries and influencing several generations of Africans (Pawliková-Vilhanová 1998, 175).

In 1853, two years after his arrival, Blyden was joined by Alexander Crummell. Born free in New York, of a father who was brought as a slave from Africa but who quickly succeeded in freeing himself, he developed an elitist ideology in which the popular cultures of the slave South had no part. Once in Liberia, though he considered that "as far as West Africa is concerned there is no history",[7] he was impressed by the local cultures, while realizing that they procured neither wealth nor power to the populations. Crummell, convinced that Christianity was the source of the military and economic power of the British, became its defender – thus taking the opposite view of Blyden, who, though permeated by Christianity, thought that Islam would be less disastrous for Africa. Crummell also endeavoured to promote the use of English in Liberia which, with the rise of Christianity, would allow the advance of "civilization" in West Africa. He explained thus the reasons behind the importance of Liberia: fifteen thousand civilized black Americans controlled a half-million "bold and warlike heathens"; in spite of its small size Liberia was the only producer of sugar, wood and bricks for export in the region (Crummell 1861, 181). Shocked by the coup d'état of 1871 which overthrew the fifth democratically elected president of Liberia, Edward James Royce, Crummell returned to the United States (Moses 2004, 103–20).

After the end of the American Civil War in 1865, two characters served as a bridge between the centuries and prepared the ground for the most massive campaign of return to Africa, that of Marcus Garvey. These were Bishop McNeal Turner (1834–1915) and Chief Alfred Sam (ca. 1879/80–1930s?). A free black from the US South, Turner was very soon to confront racism and the fragility of his situation and, as a young man, became an itinerant preacher. A member of the African Methodist Episcopal Church, he was also influenced by the sermons of Alexander Crummell, who defended the idea that Africa was the "true home of the American negro and indicated a way of escaping the frustrations of segregation" by returning to Africa (Redkey 1969, 229). Known for having developed the doctrine that "God is a Negro", Turner tried to revive the black nationalism of the period preceding the American Civil War. His programme, which depicted Africa as "a promised land" and defended a massive migration to the continent, did not however gain the support of the intellectual middle-class, contrary to the nationalism of the mid-nineteenth century. Turner, in developing his "African dream", became a sharp critic of the racial policies of the United States and, in his opinion, any radical change of the situation of the blacks necessarily transited through emigration to Africa. In relation with the American Colonization Society, he was also engaged in other emigration projects like the "Liberian Exodus Association", based in South Carolina, which sent a ship full of emigrants to Liberia in 1878. In 1891, authorized by the African Methodist Episcopal Church to visit the continent, he left for Sierra

Leone and Liberia. Turner cried tears of emotion upon his arrival and sent dithyrambic reports on the living conditions, despite the difficulties of the climate and the fevers in these coastal countries. On his return to the United States, he published a newspaper, *Voice of Missions*, a tribune which allowed free range to the expression of his militancy. In 1893 and 1895 he returned to Liberia and to Sierra Leone to supervise ecclesiastical conferences. Anxious about the increasing presence of Europeans, he accelerated his campaign of emigration and colonization of Africa. In 1898, he consolidated a branch of the African Methodist Episcopal Church in South Africa and thus contributed indirectly to the development of the African Independent Churches, to which we will return in the following chapter. In the United States, he employed all possible means of opposition to the passing of coercive laws against blacks in the states of the American South. He remained an activist until his death in 1915. His emigration campaign bore few fruits, as many blacks still regarded Africa as a wild continent. His commitment contributed, however, to often sharpen the criticism of discrimination affecting the black population and to develop a mutual interest, of a missionary character, between Africans of the continent and those of the diaspora (Redkey 1969, 242).

Chief Alfred Sam remains a somewhat mysterious character whose dates are uncertain. Born in the Gold Coast, he was representative of those West Africans who were both traders and nationalists and who crossed the ocean to develop commercial prospects with African Americans. As in the case of others, this was a means of escaping commercial stifling from the quasi-monopoly of the English in the region (Hill 1987, 58). He arrived in the United States in 1910 and founded the Akim Trading Society, in New York. Its objectives being purely commercial, his plan was to buy a boat and develop maritime trade. He also bought lands with mineral resources a hundred kilometres from Cape Coast. Having heard of his activities, black leaders asked him for information about the possibility of obtaining land in the Gold Coast for the settlement of African Americans. Once an agreement was reached with the chiefs of Akyem region, from where he originated, his commercial society widened its services to include the support Afro-American immigration to the Gold Coast. He returned to Boston in 1913 to announce the news there and bought a boat. It would appear that this maritime company was called the Ethiopian Steamship Line, a precursor, to some extent, of Marcus Garvey's Black Star Line (Langley 1973, 43). Consequently, an "African movement" developed, producing many volunteers for emigration. After several arrests by American authorities alarmed about his success, he went on a journey rendered perilous by the state of the boat with forty-six people on board. They experienced difficulties in disembarking on the West African coast, were obliged to stop in Sierra Leone and Liberia, and finally landed at Axim, on the Gold Coast, in January 1915. After several weeks of prospection inland, Sam abandoned the group of African Americans and

Figure 1.4. The steamer *Booker T. Washington*, part of the Black Star Line founded by Marcus Garvey. © DR.

disappeared. Some of the African Americans who remained settled in Cape Coast, Winneba, Accra and in Nigeria. Chief Sam, it seems, left via the Ivory Coast to Liberia, but precious little is known about the end of his life. Yet he was heralded by contemporaries as a forerunner who had made an important step towards the "regeneration of Africa", and he was long regarded by certain Ghanaians as a pioneer of the economic and political nationalism of the Gold Coast (Hill 1987, 72).

Many other persons were engaged in plans of emigration and colonization, and hot debates occupied the black leaders who defended or criticized the possibilities of return. This study has chosen to limit itself to the itineraries of a few personalities who made a significant contribution to the pro-emigration propaganda and to the return to Africa of the black populations. Their trajectories pinpoint one of the crucial factors which fuelled, if not actual departure, at least the dream of another place: the terrible conditions of slavery and segregation to which they were all opposed. Many attempts at return failed, for a variety of reasons. The prejudices concerning Africa, interiorized by the blacks, were rampant, and the frequent bad news from emigrants, either victims of disease or bloated with their sense of superiority, dampened enthusiasm. Notwithstanding the development of the black press, communication at the national level was not easy; the poverty of the majority of blacks limited their investment in transatlantic firms. Last, the constant claim, even by emigrationists, to American nationality and the attached privileges inserted the projects of return in a contradictory framework. The campaigns for return, though often fruitless, were conducted by brilliant intellectuals and entrepreneurs who contributed to the development of a critical consciousness regarding the living conditions in the United States. Indeed, involvement in a migration movement constituted a form of resistance (Barnes 2004, 181). Central to it was the belief in the historical responsibility of African Americans in the development of the African continent and people. Regeneration, redemption, providence, and evangelization were themes which traversed the writings of most of these nationalists. The position of the majority of these black migrants was in fact paradoxical; they depicted Africa as their "home", but at the same time were convinced that the development of European-style capitalism, coupled with missionary Christianity, offered every chance for the development of a great civilization. We must at this point shift our focus somewhat, away from the back-to-Africa discourses in United States. The United States obviously formed a vital platform in the development of black nationalism, yet from the very outset activists from the Caribbean engaged themselves in projects of return, to which we will now direct our attention.

Caribbeans in Africa

The involvement of Caribbeans in projects of return, and more generally in nationalist and pan-African discourses and practices, is difficult to discern to the extent that they are often included in the generic term of African Americans. In his effort to define "pan-Africanism", George Shepperson underlined in passing the existence of a "West Indian Factor" whose persistence in all pan-African projects he qualified as "remarkable" (Shepperson 1962, 356). Recognizing the low visibility of Caribbeans, Winston James sought to explain their disproportionate involvement in pan-African projects and in return migrations (James 2004). His conclusions may be summed up as follows:

1. Caribbeans had always travelled since abolition, in particular Jamaicans and Barbadians;
2. Economic prospects were extremely limited in the British Caribbean at the end of the nineteenth and the beginning of the twentieth century;
3. Because of the "colour line" in the Caribbean, many sought opportunities in Africa, where the resistance to racial and colonial structures seemed completely legitimate;
4. Caribbeans probably had greater affinities with Africans since new migrants, born in Africa, continued to arrive in the islands even after abolition, whereas the black population in the United States had reproduced itself since the end of the eighteenth century;
5. While the French colonial authorities sometimes co-opted African or Caribbean elites, this was not the case with the English, whose reticence to absorb the same elites also explained the dissatisfaction of black intelligentsia. (James 2004, 151–53)

Migrations were clearly structurally inscribed in the formation of Caribbean societies. They were closely related to economic development which either demanded slave labour, cheap labour, or forced migrant workers after the economic structures inherited from the plantation system were transformed by abolition. Though it seems certain, moreover, that the continuous deportation of Africans to the Caribbean, over a longer period and more consistently than to the United States, played a crucial role in the cultural formation of creole societies, it remains difficult to affirm that it was due to "affinities" with Africans that Caribbeans specifically migrated to Africa. In analysing the dynamics which moved them to migrate, it is important not to overlook the ideologies and imaginaries thanks to which individuals constructed common narratives and destinies between Africans and Afro-descendants. Similarly, the role of the black elites, a determining factor in the diffusion of nationalism and pan-Africanism, should not be allowed to obscure the role of others, namely the workers and "lower classes" who comprised the majority of returnees to the continent and who, probably because of incomplete sources or their lesser significance for the public sphere, were unable to attract the attention of historians. While there are no total figures quantifying Caribbean presence in Africa from the end of the eighteenth century, several "profiles" of the Caribbeans in Africa have, however, come in for discussion. In her book on West Indians in Sierra Leone between 1808 and 1880, Nemata Blyden distinguishes between two types: Caribbean missionaries and Caribbean foreigners (Blyden 2000, 231–44).

Many Caribbeans were missionaries attached to European missions which hoped to facilitate the diffusion of the Christian message thanks to intermediaries who "resembled" the local population. W. Wariboko underlined the paradoxes in the situation of the Jamaican clergy within the mission in Niger of the Church Missionary Society. Though black, the Jamaican clergy made a point of being regarded as "foreigners", on par with the white missionaries, in order to claim the same economic advantages, which were not offered. Most of them resigned, until the Church Missionary Society stopped recruiting Caribbeans in 1925. While some found more lucrative employment in the region, the majority returned, as they had no intention of settling durably in West Africa (Wariboko 2004).

The group of Caribbeans studied by Nemata Blyden was mainly composed of officials employed in the British colonial administration. They arrived voluntarily in Sierra Leone as part of a privileged group, and the majority did not intend to reside permanently on the continent. N. Blyden used three criteria to discuss the identity problems raised by these Caribbeans in Africa: race or colour; class; and nationality or place of origin. She used these criteria to define the changing forms of identification among Caribbeans in Sierra Leone. Their African ancestry, while never questioned, did not prevent distinctions being made between Caribbeans and the local populations. Similarly, the self-perceptions of Caribbeans also differed at times from that of the group formed by the forementioned blacks of other origins living in Sierra Leone: black poor, black loyalists, maroons and Africans. Without presenting a homogenizing view of the Caribbean community of Freetown, N. Blyden underlines more generally the history of identity politics in Sierra Leone and their continuous reconfiguration. She analyses, finally, the position of Caribbeans in Africa in the nineteenth century by extending the discussions of William Shack and Elliott Skinner concerning strangers in Africa. Shack and Skinner adapted to African societies the idea of the "stranger" by the German sociologist George Simmel (1971 [1908]) and discussed the challenges of the continuous presence of strangers, blacks or whites, in Africa (Shack and Skinner 1979). They underlined the ways in which the social role and the status of foreigners affected the social and legal distinctions between hosts and foreigners in specific societies. They showed how the relations between hosts and foreigners, as well as the structural position of foreigners, helped to define the dynamics of accommodation and identification.

Using the paradigm of the stranger, N. Blyden highlights the processes of creation of a distinct Caribbean identity. With a constant back-and-forth between the various levels and components of these migrant groups, and their distinctions of colour and class, she ultimately underlines the attachment that they all had for their place of origin, Jamaica, the Bahamas, Trinidad and so on, and their fidelity to the British colonial administration, in whose service several occupied the position of governor of Sierra Leone, in particular John B. Russwurm, William Fergusson, John Carr and Robert Dougan (Blyden 2000, 57–85). However, by restricting her study to the relations between Caribbeans and the immigrant black community in Sierra Leone, Blyden has overlooked a crucial aspect of this figure of the foreigner: the relations with the indigenous African population. An important contribution to the sociology of Caribbean migrants to West Africa in the nineteenth century, the work of N. Blyden and its limitations illustrate the complexity of the study of black migrant groups in Africa. More so than the figure of the missionary, the figure of the foreigner is flexible and adaptable to various social groups in various spaces. As we will see later in the case of Ethiopia, the paradigm of the foreigner can be used to question the ways in which emigrationists, pan-Africanists and other champions of a homogenizing ideology linking the continent and the diaspora constructed or experienced their relation to host countries and populations.

Many of the Caribbeans who repatriated voluntarily to Africa have been forgotten, leaving only traces of those who occupied the public sphere or who exercised activities of a collective nature. This was the case of several Caribbean settlers in West Africa who contributed, for example, to the development of printing in the region. For example, John Brown Russwurm (1799–1851), a Jamaican of mixed blood, became one of the first three blacks to graduate from an American institution (James 2004, 127–33; James 2010). While still in the United States in 1827, he founded *Freedom's Journal*, the first black newspaper in the country. An abolitionist with a critical view of the American Colonization Society, Russwurm had thought of emigrating to Haiti before leaving, in 1829, for Liberia. There he founded, the following year, the *Liberia Herald*, the first black newspaper in West Africa. He also participated in the colonial administration: he became, in 1836, the first black governor of Liberia. Russwurm occupied this position until his death in 1851, when E.W. Blyden, also of Caribbean origin, arrived in Liberia and took over as editor of the *Liberia Herald*. There was another Caribbean man who played a crucial role in the development of the press: Robert Campbell (1829–84), a Jamaican printer, who had already travelled to Central America and who, in spite of his light complexion, was unable to secure employment in the United States. He accompanied Martin Delany in the "mission of exploration" of the Niger valley but, unlike him, was determined to live on the continent and he settled in Lagos in 1861 with wife and children. Despite a marked mistrust on the part of the British governors there, he published the *Anglo-African* which, by 1863 became more than a newspaper, a training site for the first generation of printers of the city. Winston James (James 2004, 145) stresses that Campbell "simply sought to contribute to the advancement of Africa while making a living for his family" and was not a nationalist or a talented orator such as Delany or J. Albert Thorne.

A little-known character, J. Albert Thorne was born in 1860 in Barbados and lived in Jamaica. It appears that, between 1890 and 1920, he tried to organize a journey and the settlement of Caribbeans in Central Africa, in Nyasaland, but this project seems to have been a failure. Thorne maintained close relations with Marcus Garvey and the Universal Negro Improvement Association (UNIA). Certain historians even insinuate that he saw himself as a competitor with the UNIA and accused Garvey of having plagiarized his Back-to-Africa programme (Weisbord 1974, 41–44), while others indicate that he supported Garvey from the very beginnings of the UNIA in Kingston in 1914 (Martin 1986, 112). Regardless of the inaccuracies which remain concerning Thorne, he is a pivotal character linking us to another Caribbean man, a printer and a nationalist in search of a territory: Marcus Garvey. Their involvement in creating, editing and distributing the press reminds us of the importance of the impact of print capitalism on formulating the imagination of nations. These Caribbean men, involved in the production of an independent black press, contributed to the birth of West African nationalisms but also to the production of a transatlantic "black nation". News from diverse spaces, colonial conflicts, the fate of blacks on the continent and in the Americas was transmitted in the pages of many newspapers and thus participated in creating among their readers "ties", references and a shared symbolic universe.

Marcus Garvey: The Return of Moses

A Caribbean man played a decisive role in the development of nationalism, pan-Africanism and returns to Africa. Marcus Garvey (1887–1940) was a fascinating character in more ways than one. He was one of the first to abandon an intellectualized discourse in order to reach the masses. He pulled the arguments of black nationalism to the extreme and the mark he left on black communities is still felt today. Many historians studied his itinerary and have bequeathed an exceptionally rich literature (Cronon 1969; Langley 1973; Martin 1986; Stein 1986; Lewis 1988; Grant 2009). Moreover, in an exhaustive enterprise of bringing together the archives and documents concerning Garvey and his organization, numerous volumes were published under the title *The Marcus Garvey and UNIA Papers*, offering unprecedented access to the history of black nationalism at the beginning of the twentieth century.[8]

Marcus Mosiah Garvey was born on 17 August 1887 in St Ann's Bay, on the northern coast of Jamaica, of peasant parents thought to descend from the maroons. He left school at an early age and, like many other Jamaicans, migrated to Kingston, the capital. At eighteen, he was already a professional printer and was noticed for his political engagement during the workers' strikes in the National Club which fought the privileges of British colonialism in the island. In 1910 and in the two subsequent years, he travelled to Central America as a seasonal worker, publishing his first newspapers and relentlessly advocating better protection of workers. In this way, he visited Ecuador, Costa Rica, Panama and British Honduras, where he familiarized himself with the fate of the numerous Caribbean migrants who had left in search of work in banana plantations or on the building sites of the Panama Canal. In autumn 1912, he arrived in England, where he worked for *Africa Times and Orient Review*, the pan-Africanist newspaper of the time, founded by Duse Mohammed Ali (1867–1944), an Egyptian, author of a book on the history of Egypt, *In the Land of the Pharaohs*, published in London in 1911. Garvey's stay in England was extremely influential as he got acquainted with the actors of pan-Africanism and with the colonial conflicts in the Middle East. Moreover, at the time of his stay in Europe, he visited Scotland, Ireland, France, Italy, Spain, Austria, Hungary and Germany before returning to Jamaica in July 1914. He then founded with Amy Ashwood, who became his first wife, the Universal Negro Improvement and Conservation Association and African Communities (Imperial) League, a society whose name reflected the international vision fostered by his voyages and the fear of extinction of the black race under the conditions of the time. He expressed himself publicly on the occasion of several meetings in Kingston and St Ann's Bay, but in 1915 he had only a hundred members at his side. Garvey then decided to leave for the United States and arrived in New York in March 1916. He planned a fund-raising tour of the country intended to last five months but which in fact took him nearly a year. He settled thereafter in Harlem, held discussions with many African American representatives and regular meetings which attracted greater and greater numbers.

In fact, Harlem was in the process of becoming a black capital, where

Caribbean migrants met with migrants arriving from the south of the United States. The great migration (1915–30) was transforming a southern, rural African American peasant population into a national, urban and industrial population, thus creating new spaces of civil and political activism (Hahn 2003, 465). Moreover, this migration was integrated into a religious imaginary in which the north became the equivalent of "Canaan", a paradise, a land of freedom to be reached at all costs (Raboteau 2001). These double flows of arrivals had a decisive social impact: the face of neighbourhoods like Harlem were transformed; the interethnic relations between people of different Caribbean origins and between them and African Americans were renewed; cultural effervescence produced the black Renaissance; and Marcus Garvey's UNIA was about to find its social base and its international springboard. We would do well to recall that the impact of Caribbeans in the United States was out of all proportion with their actual numbers: Caribbeans founded nationalist organizations like the UNIA but were also at the origin of the political trends of revolutionary socialism; they provided brilliant radical intellectuals, including Hubert Harrison, Cyril Briggs, Claude McKay as well as Arturo Schomburg and Jesús Colón (James 1998, 184). Steven Hahn, unveiling the geographies of Garveyism, emphasized that the UNIA was able to take root where emigrationism enjoyed popular support, especially in the rural south. He shows that the adaptability of "traditions of popular organization" had a genealogy anchored in slavery and that emancipation, which pushed the blacks to defy the nation, enabled African Americans and Caribbeans to rally around a charismatic character like Marcus Garvey (Hahn 2003, 467–76).

Figure 1.5. Marcus Garvey, president of the Universal Negro Improvement Association, ca. 1920 © DR.

With a social base of this nature, the UNIA logically relocated its Kingston headquarters to New York. Although several branches were already functioning there, the UNIA was officially registered in New York in July 1918. Garvey began to be recognized as one of the most important radical figures in Harlem. His newspaper, *Negro World,* was circulated to black communities in the Americas, and in 1919 the Black Star Line Steamship Corporation was established. Garvey survived a murder attempt, and in 1920 he organized the First Convention of the Negro Peoples of the World in which thirty-five thousand persons participated.

Figure 1.6. Marcus Garvey in official regalia, during the procession of First Convention of the Negro Peoples of the World, Harlem, 1920. © DR.

The same year, he founded the UNIA's Negro Factories Corporation to manage a printery and firms. By 1921, Garvey had become the leader of the largest black organization in history. He was at that time extremely criticized by European and American governments and by black integrationist intellectuals like W.E.B. Du Bois and his National Association for the Advancement of Colored People, founded in 1910.

After marrying Amy Jacques, his second wife, Garvey established the Black Cross Navigation and Trading Company in 1924. But the previous year he had been judged guilty of fraud in the administration of the Black Star Line, and in February 1925 he was sent to jail in Atlanta. Released earlier than expected, he was forced to leave the United States and set off for Jamaica, where he arrived after a stopover in Panama, in 1927. He continued to travel, especially to England and Canada, but he also launched out in the Jamaican political arena by founding the People's Political Party in 1929. At the end of 1933, he began to publish another newspaper, the *Blackman*, and the following year he moved the centre of his activities to England, from whence he continued to promote the activities of the UNIA. He fell ill and died in London in June 1940.

Race, Nation and Belonging

Without making claims to an exhaustive presentation of the characteristics, strengths and limitations of Marcus Garvey's movement, I would like to highlight a number of factors capable of informing the history of return to Africa. To understand the international character of the UNIA, we must consider for a moment the coverage of its local branches. Garvey often declared that he was at the head of "four hundred million blacks", an exaggeration characteristic of his immoderate personality. However, in 1921, the UNIA counted a total of 859 branches, and in 1926 six million persons were apparently registered members. Tony Martin, based on lists discovered in 1970 and drawn up between 1925 and 1928, indicates that 725 branches were established in the United States, and 271 outside the United States, for a total of 996 (Martin 1986, 15–17, cited by Tété-Adjalogo 1995, 248–56). In the United States, the Southern states were the paramount region in the world regarding the penetration of the UNIA among the popular masses, with seventy-four branches in Louisiana alone. Outside the United States, the greater Caribbean, which includes Central America and the northern part of South America, was the most important bastion of Garveyism. For example, Cuba had fifty-two branches, Panama forty-seven, Trinidad thirty, Costa Rica twenty-three and Jamaica eleven. South Africa had eight active branches, but Martin points out that the branches in Dahomey and the Belgian Congo were omitted from these lists. He also stated that the UNIA was represented in all parts of the world with an important black population, notably Canada, Europe and Australia. The statistics are not extremely reliable: certain branches did not always forward information on the number of their members, others had a troubled and sporadic existence, but the geographic and demographic scope of the UNIA was unprecedented. The *Negro World*, by publishing reports and inserts on the conditions and activities of black populations in several countries and in several languages, reflected the UNIA's internationalism. The distribution of this newspaper was frequently prohibited in several countries, for example British Honduras and Trinidad, whose authorities feared the influence of the black organization, as well as in the European colonies of Africa.

Indeed, since the beginnings of the UNIA in Jamaica in 1914, the question of the primacy of race was central, and all of the organization's activities sought to develop self-esteem and to inculcate colour pride in black women and men. The black race, its beauty, its purity and its redemption formed the ideological core generating an entire range of practices and positions. Garvey's focus on the destiny of black people inevitably led him in the direction of racial separatism, expressed through cultural activities (poetry, plays, relations with the actors of the Harlem Renaissance), through commercial activities that would make the race economically independent (often expressed at the local level by a social system of mutual aid within UNIA branches), as well as efforts to set up schools and other training structures. To inspire in the race the power he deemed necessary, Garvey made use of biblical metaphors, religious phraseology, and practices akin to those of church congregations, strategies aimed at channelling the religious enthusiasm of his members. Analysing the fact that most churches taught that God created man in his own image, he deduced that black people should also be able to represent God in *their* image, that is, as black. In a speech at the beginning of the 1920s, Garvey defended his approach:

> If the white man has the idea of a white God, let him worship his God as he desires. If the yellow man's God is of his race let him worship his God as he sees fit. We, as Negroes, have found a new ideal. Whilst our God has no colour, yet it is human to see everything through one's own spectacles, and since the white people have seen their God through white spectacles, we have only now started out (late though it be) to see our God through our own spectacles. . . . We Negroes believe in the God of Ethiopia, the everlasting God – God the Father, God the Son and God the Holy Ghost, the

> One God of all ages. That is the God in whom we believe, but we shall worship Him through the spectacles of Ethiopia.[9]

In conformity with the attention given to racial primacy, the idea of God could be adjusted to accommodate identities and phenotypes. Garvey, to a certain extent, reappropriated God and inserted this reappropriation into the broader perspective of the social and economic rehabilitation of black people by black people. But not only was God black, he had a territory and a nationality ascribed to him, namely, Ethiopia. The image of these spectacles was very sharp; it showed that a share of choice and willpower determined the way in which men saw God. By recovering a symbolism of the previous century in which the "God of the Ethiopians" was already declared, in particular by David Walker, Garvey championed Ethiopianism, a corpus of references to Ethiopia which formed part of the militant Afro-American heritage and had contributed to the shaping of black nationalism and pan-Africanism.[10] The UNIA had many religious avatars, but was usually associated with the African Orthodox Church of Alexander McGuire from St Croix (1866–1934). Founded in 1921, the church played a significant role in disseminating Garveyism and in spreading information regarding its objectives. Bishop McGuire wrote the "Negro Catechism" used by Garveyites. It was a document in which garveyist ideas on the religion as well as the basic principles of the UNIA were reproduced.[11]

The separatism that Garvey preached led him to excesses for which he was widely criticized. Not only did he entertain good relations with white radicals engaged in the anti-colonial and anti-imperialist struggle, he also conferred on several occasions with the proponents of white supremacy, with whom he initially shared "the race first" doctrine and that of the separation of the races. His correspondence with Earnest Cox, the founder of the White America Society, who supported the return of blacks to Africa in view of separating the races, was a great shock to many UNIA members as well as to the general public.[12] This ambiguous relationship to white power was also reformulated in the comparisons Garvey made between his organization, the nation which it was supposed to represent and governments of Adolf Hitler and Benito Mussolini. The indoctrination of the youth, the conversion of multitudes to discipline, the exceptional eloquence of the leaders and the atmosphere surrounding these movements were similarities which did not elude Garvey's contemporaries. The latter announced in 1937: "UNIA was before Mussolini and Hitler were heard of. Mussolini and Hitler copied the program of UNIA – aggressive nationalism for the black man in Africa" (cited in Martin 1986, 60).

Marcus Garvey's "aggressive nationalism" was related to the racial primacy which he defended, and the idea that the UNIA represented a government of the "black nation" was at the heart of his ideology. George Padmore, the famous Trinidadian pan-Africanist, thus pertinently defined the UNIA's nationalism: "Marcus Garvey founded his Negro Empire in New York in the year 1920.

Territory, it had none; but its subjects were counted by the millions and scattered throughout the world" (Padmore 1971, 70). Padmore's reference was to the First Convention of the Negro Peoples of the World, held in New York that year. On this occasion, the UNIA sought to deploy all the attributes of a nation. It established a constitution and announced a "Declaration of Rights of the Negro People of the World" (cited in Hill 1983, 575–76) defining the position of the organization on various subjects. An anthem with military and Ethiopianist imagery was adopted, the "Universal Ethiopian Anthem", to be discussed later. A flag was chosen, with red, black and green as the official colours of the black race. The various bodies of the UNIA – the Universal African Legions, the Universal Motor Corps, the Universal African Black Cross Nurses, the Juveniles and the like had specific uniforms, ranks and statutes, with which they paraded in the streets of Harlem.[13] Garvey himself was designated on this occasion as the "provisional president of Africa".

Though often derided by his critics, both black and white, Garvey nevertheless defended the right to represent a black nation with all the attributes of modern nations. He maintained correspondence with the League of Nations and named several "ambassadors" to represent the UNIA before other nations (Martin 1986, 45–50). With Garvey, black nationalism was taken to unexpected heights in terms of popular support, international diffusion and effective communication. Western governments were all quite reserved facing the disemmination of Garvey's imagery propaganda; they were fully aware of the social and political potential of this movement. Garvey's nation was huge, his subjects were in the millions, but a vital ingredient was missing: territory. Garvey's nation had no territory, and it is on Africa that he set his sights, spent his efforts and based his slogans.

Back to Africa

One of Garvey's most famous slogans, partly recovered from a phrase popularized in 1860 by Martin R. Delany, was: "Africa for the Africans, at home and abroad." Faithful to the legacy of the nineteenth-century nationalists like Bishop Turner, Chief Alfred Sam and J. Albert Thorne, whose emigrationist efforts had influenced the collective consciousness, Garvey defined a crucial stake: the return to Africa of the black populations. An argument which was often shared by the champions of the separation of the races, the Back-to-Africa project promoted by the UNIA was an important factor behind the attraction which the UNIA held for the masses. At the time of the first convention in August 1920, Marcus Garvey explained his programme of return in these terms:

> The doctrines of going "Back to Africa" must be clearly understood. We are not preaching any doctrines to ask all the Negroes of Harlem and of the United States to pack up

LET US GUIDE OUR OWN DESTINY

BY FINANCING OUR OWN COMMERCIAL VENTURES.
HELP US TO HELP YOU HELP YOURSELF AND THE NEGRO RACE IN GENERAL
YOU CAN DO THIS BY PLAYING A MAN OR WOMAN'S PART IN THE WORLD OF COMMERCE;
DO YOUR FULL SHARE IN HELPING TO PROVIDE
A DIRECT LINE OF STEAMSHIPS OWNED, CONTROLLED AND MANNED BY NEGROES TO
REACH THE NEGRO PEOPLES OF THE WORLD
AMERICA, CANADA, SOUTH AND CENTRAL AMERICA, AFRICA AND THE WEST INDIES

There should be no trouble about making up your mind to help your race to rise to a position in the maritime world that will challenge the attention and command the admiration of the world. "Men like nations fail in nothing they boldly attempt when sustained by virtuous purpose and firm resolution."
Money awaiting an advantageous investment should go to purchasing shares in the Black Star Line and reap the reward that is bound to follow.

DO A MAN'S PART RIGHT NOW

Send In and Buy Your Shares Today

"THE BLACK STAR LINE," Inc.

Capitalized at $10,000,000 Under the Laws of the State of Delaware

2,000,000 shares of common stock now on sale at par value of $5.00 each for a limited time only at the office of the corporation, 56 West 135th Street, New York City. Phone Harlem 2877.

The Black Star Line, Inc., is the result of a Herculean effort on the part of Hon. Marcus Garvey, world-famed Negro orator, who in July, 1914, founded a society known as the Universal Negro Improvement Association and African Communities League, of which he is now President-General.

The Association now has a membership of over three million persons, with branches all over the United States, Canada, South and Central America, the West Indies and Africa

THE BLACK STAR LINE, Inc.

Is backed today in its operations by the full strength of its organization to say the least, of millions of other Negro men and women in all parts of the world.

BUY SHARES TODAY AND NOT TOMORROW

CUT THIS OUT AND MAIL IT

SUBSCRIPTION BLANK

"THE BLACK STAR LINE, Inc."
56 West 135th Street, New York City

Date ....

Gentlemen:
I hereby subscribe for .... shares of stock at $5.00 per share and forward herewith as full payment $...........

Name ....
Street ....
City ....
State ....

Figure 1.7. An application form for shares in the maritime enterprise the Black Star Line. © DR.

> their trunks and to leave for Africa. We are not crazy, because we have to wait until we get a Lenox Avenue and a Seventh Avenue before we could get the Negroes of Harlem to leave for Africa. . . . But we are asking you to get this Organization to do the pioneering work. The majority of us may remain here, but we must send our scientists, our mechanics, and our artisans and let them build railroads, let them build the great Educational and other institutions necessary and when they are constructed, the time will come for the command to be given, "Come home" to Lenox Avenue, to Seventh Avenue. Not until then. . . . We are going to live for a higher purpose, the purpose of a free and redeemed Africa, because no security, no success can come to the Black man, so long as he is outnumbered in the particular community where his race may become industrially and commercially strong. (Hill 1983, 2:559)

The project of return was no longer considered a "project of adventure" on unknown African coasts or as a humanitarian enterprise to evangelize the African populations, but rather the construction of a replica of Harlem, hence the evocation of well-known landmarks, Lennox and Seventh Avenues, which cross Harlem from north to south. Garvey identified the first stage of the project, the sending of technicians and engineers "to build" Africa. Once this work was completed, the second phase would be to "order" the people to depart, to leave the soil of the United States. He was convinced that this order would be respected. The freedom and the safety of Africa were still presented as crucial issues, but these were attributed to the majority status the black people of the diaspora would attain on the continent. The danger associated with being a minority was underlined, tacitly pinpointing the example of the south of the United States, which had experienced a disastrous lynching campaign the previous summer. A majority status supposedly permitted the sovereignty that would lead the black populations to industrialization and business successes, economic independence and political autonomy – the necessary qualities of nationhood.

However, the relations between Garvey and Liberia, "our Liberia" as he would sometimes say, appeared uncomfortable at times. A first emissary was sent in 1920 and, given his success, a delegation of six UNIA officials and technicians left for Liberia the following year. Land on the periphery of Monrovia was allocated to them by the government and was speedily exploited and cultivated. However, the lack of funds and the growing suspicion of the authorities accelerated the departure of the delegation a few months later. In December 1923, another delegation sent by Garvey was to finalize the preparations for the reception of twenty to thirty thousand families who would arrive shortly. Following their warm welcome, another team of technicians arrived in Monrovia in May 1924 to study the site on which dwellings were to be constructed. But they were unexpectedly deported by the Liberian government in July 1924 and the UNIA was prohibited in the country. M.B. Akpan (1973) stressed that President King justified this break by citing his relations with the neighbouring colonial powers, to whom he did not want to give the impression of supporting an anti-colonial movement based on race, in order to protect, if necessary, the borders of the country. But Akpan also underlined that behind Garvey's failure lurked the determination of the oligarchy in power "to defend their privileged position against any 'intruders' and their role as parasites who lived by exploiting the indigenous African population" (108). Indeed, the position of the oligarchy was fragile in the face of a local population whose numbers greatly exceeded theirs and who might have reacted to Garvey's anti-colonialist discourses by confronting them directly. The warm welcome extended to the representatives of the UNIA was therefore more the mark of political duplicity than that of real commitment. Garvey represented a danger to this elite, and with his title of "provisional president of Africa", his boats and his millions of members, he might have short-circuited the power structures in Liberia. Moreover, the establishment of the UNIA in Liberia ran the risk of disrupting the relations of the country with the United States, a major economic partner, especially since the 1923 investment of Harvey S. Firestone for rubber cultivation for export had boosted the national economy (122). By banishing the UNIA from the territory, the Liberian government put an end to the project of return advocated by Garvey, to the delight of his opponents.

One of Garvey's famous detractors, W.E.B. Du Bois, was, moreover, sent to Liberia as the representative of the United States at the investiture of President King in 1924. This visit allowed the United States to reaffirm their interest in Liberian business while contributing to weakening the ties between Liberia and the UNIA. On the questions of emigrationism and return to Africa, Du Bois changed his mind several times in the course of his long and brilliant career. An editorial published in 1919 in his newspaper, *Crisis* (17, no. 4 [February 1919]: 166), when Garvey was already a hero of black nationalism and return to Africa, is sufficiently illustrative of his ambivalent position:

> Once and for all, let us realize that we are Americans, that we were brought here with the earliest settlers, and that the very sort of civilization from which we came made the complete adoption of western modes and customs imperative if we were to survive at all. In brief, there is nothing so indigenous, so completely "made in America" as we. It is as absurd to talk of a return to Africa, merely because that was our home

300 years ago, as it would be to expect the members of the Caucasian race to return to the fastnesses of the Caucasus mountains from which, it is reputed, they sprang.

But it is true that we as a people are not given to colonization and that thereby a number of essential occupations and interests have been closed to us which the redemption of Africa would open up. The African movement means to us what the Zionist must mean to the Jews, the centralization of race effort and the recognition of a racial fount to help bear the burden of Africa does not mean any lessening of effort in our own problem at home. Rather it means increased interest. For any ebullition of action and feeling that results in an amelioration of the lot of Africa tends to ameliorate the condition of coloured peoples throughout the world. And no man liveth to himself.

All of the paradoxes of black nationalism and emigrationism seem to be contained in this passage. On the one hand, Du Bois affirmed that black people were indeed Americans, that they were the acme of what it meant to be American, and he underlined what nonsense it was to try "to return to Africa". But on the other hand, he maintained that the colonization of Africa by blacks was crucial as it would open numerous opportunities to them, commercial ones in particular. Hence, racial solidarity was deemed both capable of "saving" Africa and of improving the condition of blacks in the United States. Despite a thinly veiled criticism of Garvey, Du Bois, by obviously binding the fate of Africa to that of the blacks of the world, was in line with the classic legacies of nationalism and pan-Africanism. He made a comparison with Zionism that was interesting in more ways than one. The Zionist struggle of the Jews was often referenced by black nationalists, and in particular by Garvey, who held in high regard their capacity to organize themselves in the objective of founding a Jewish nation. Garvey's Back-to-Africa programme was, moreover, labelled as "black Zionism" by George Padmore (1960, 97–113). While this amalgamation is somewhat hasty, Zionism in fact served as a nationalist paradigmatic model for the UNIA and, more generally, for black nationalists (Washington 1984; Weisbord and Kazarian 1985, 15–18).

It is therefore not surprising that Marcus Garvey was so often compared to Moses, the man chosen by God to guide the Israelites out of the land of bondage into a land of abundance. In addition to his second name, Mosiah, the fact that Garvey himself never set foot in Africa, in the same way that Moses never got to the promised land, strengthened the biblical symbolism of the book of Exodus, which the thousands of black militants, whether members of the UNIA or not, reappropriated to illustrate their destiny and the role of a leader, Marcus Garvey, who was both venerated and despised. It is important to stress that at the beginning of the twentieth century Marcus Garvey represented the most radical manifestation of black nationalism. A man whose charisma and popularity superseded that of all his predecessors, he is now regarded as the ancestor of all later manifestations of black nationalism. Constantly evoked, repeated and used, the reference to Marcus Garvey has progressed far beyond political circles, permeating popular discourse and, in doing so, inspiring many other organizations. The UNIA became a metaphor evoking the black nation and its symbols were often reappropriated. Branches of the UNIA are still active today, and the colours of the red, black and green flag are still brandished and carried as visible signs of the attachment to black nationalism and as a globalized cultural reference.

THE DESIRE TO RETURN TO AFRICA EXISTED IN the imaginary and in the actions of Africans since the inception of the slave society which brought Africans to the coasts of the Americas. Return was instrumental to the production of the black ideologies of nationalism and pan-Africanism as it staged the hope of a territory wherein racial solidarity between Africans and Afro-descendants could prosper. Whether defended or decried, actual returns to the West African coast and sometimes to Haiti as well were effectuated by dint of government policies and individual initiatives. The paramount role of Caribbeans in the projects of return and, more largely, in nationalist and pan-African discourses has been highlighted. Marcus Garvey was the most charismatic and most famous Caribbean figure among them, and his projection of an Ethiopian God for black people underlines the power of a black imaginary linked to Ethiopia. The sources and contours of this imaginary are the subject of the following chapter.

CHAPTER 2

SOURCES AND CONTOURS OF ETHIOPIANISM

A BEAUTIFUL SCHOLARLY COMPARISON COULD BE MADE BETWEEN the different imaginaries arising from conceptions of Ethiopia. Such a comparison would examine, in Ethiopia itself, the scholarly and popular constructions of the dynasty of King Solomon and the traditions and practices related to the sacred royalty. It would also visit Western representations of the Kingdom of Prester John, which was for centuries the object of the quests of missionaries, adventurers and diplomats seeking to discover, understand and – sometimes – corrupt it. Around the Atlantic, it would consider the identity constructs in which Ethiopia served as a metaphor of black peoples and of Africa. I will restrict myself for the moment to the last: the imaginaries produced by the representations of Ethiopia. As used herein, the term *Ethiopianism* designates the ideological matrix created from the fount of Ethiopia and disseminated throughout the black worlds. This chapter will attempt to reveal their textual origins and changing symbolic valence. It will recall the existing scholarly knowledge on Ethiopianism and propose an innovative reading of the spaces in which it circulated. By introducing the concept of modern Ethiopianism, it will show how this ideology changed, shifting from an identification of the African continent with Ethiopia to an association of the symbolic Ethiopia with the Ethiopian state, thanks, in particular, to the pan-African policies of the sovereigns of Ethiopia. Ethiopianism is a central paradigm in the history of return to Ethiopia, concretized by the relations between African Americans and the Ethiopian state since the end of the nineteenth century.

The Black Imagination of Ethiopia

The pan-African library invariably mentions, in one place or another, in a few lines or entire chapters, the power of Ethiopianism in the formation of social and religious black nationalist thought. In fact, Ethiopianism is indissociable from a racial reading of the world: Ethiopia and Ethiopians, through the analogy of phenotypes, served to designate black people. This associative process found its origins in the reading and literal interpretation of the Bible, wherein Ethiopians were identified as black. In the King James Version or authorized English version of the Bible, published in 1611, translators used the term *Ethiopian*, which was quite popular at the time, to render the Hebrew *Kush* or the Greek *Aἰθιοπία*, designating black people. This term covered a rather vague expanse, an origin extending beyond modern Ethiopia to all of sub-Saharan Africa (Shepperson 1968, 5). This choice of translation had an unexpected impact over the centuries: the slave populations of the Americas and the evangelized populations of Africa learned to read into or to deduce from these evocations of Ethiopia or Ethiopians references to their lost origin and to their glorious biblical heritage, also lost. Most historians associate the birth of Ethiopianism with the use of a biblical verse, Psalm 68:31, "Princes shall come out of Egypt; Ethiopia shall soon stretch out her hands unto God". Interpreted as a prophecy, as the sign that black people were predestined to have a special and privileged connection to the divine plan, this verse was incessantly used in numerous contexts, sometimes to different ends. This interpretation might seem arbitrary and decontextualized, but it is explicable, and not only in the light of the historical situation of blacks in the Americas. According to Imanuel Geiss, the same interpretation was present in modern Protestant theology. This psalm was a triumphal song of King David, referring to the political situation of Israel, caught between the powers of Assyria and Egypt. It was an eschatological hymn with an interpretation deemed to be valid for all times (Geiss 1974, 134). The biblical references to Ethiopia were used as a foil for the degraded situation of black people and contributed to reflecting an admirable past and the promise of imminent freedom, as contained in the "soon" of verse 31. As highlighted by George Shepperson, an author prolific on the subject of Ethiopianism, in the last quarter of the eighteenth century, this verse became a contemporary slogan marking the aspirations of black people wherever the Bible – in its 1611 version – was understood (Shepperson 1968, 250). Indeed, this verse was frequently cited in the written productions of black writers and in the work of historians, but the foundation of Ethiopianism was not limited to this alone. However, Psalm 68:31 served to epitomize all other mentions of Ethiopia and Ethiopians in the biblical text.

The prophetic function was not the only one to be activated by the use of these references; Ethiopianism was also formed by the usage of a broader biblical and Ethiopianist nomenclature. Various references were called upon to offer to black people an image of themselves other than the one relayed by their environment. Let us take a few significant examples. In the second chapter of Genesis, Ethiopia is mentioned in the geographies of paradise. The second river flowing out of Eden, to the east, "is Gihon: the same it is that compasseth the whole land of Ethiopia" (Genesis 2:13). Ethiopia, thus named, was associated with the creation of the world, pre-existing the fall of man and woman into the sin of knowledge. It thus became a place, a symbol of the golden age and of the abundance of heavenly lands. When God showed Moses the extent of his powers, after the transformation of the prophet's staff into a snake, Moses "put his hand into his bosom, then he took it out, behold his hand was leprous like snow" (Exodus 6:6–8). This passage was used "to show" that Moses's skin was not white, a colour synonymous with disease. Implicitly then, Moses was associated with a darker colour, similar to that of Africans. Moreover, Moses, fleeing Egypt after the murder of an Egyptian whom he allegedly saw striking a Hebrew, was accommodated by Jethro, "a priest of Madian" who gave him his daughter, Zipporah, with whom he had two sons. Zipporah was a "Kushite", an "Ethiopian". The fact that Moses, a criminal chosen for a saving mission, had an "Ethiopian" wife indicated in the prelude to the Exodus the presence of black people and, what is more, their confidence in the mission of Moses, illustrated by Zipporah, who did not hesitate to circumcise her son with a sharp stone in the night of the desert (Exodus 4:24–26).

The fifth verse of the Song of Solomon also made a direct reference to the phenotype of its protagonists: "I am black but comely" (Song of Solomon 1:5). Although the translations hesitate over the conjunction: black but beautiful, black and beautiful, black and yet beautiful, black people were nevertheless centre stage in this great love poem. The books of the prophets mentioned Ethiopians; thus Jeremiah in his oracles enquired: "Can the Ethiopian change his skin, or a leopard his spots?" (Jeremiah 13:23). He associated the specific black skin tone of the Ethiopian with the impossibility of alteration. And the prophet Amos continued: "Are ye not as the children of the Ethiopians unto me, O children of Israel?" (Amos 9:7). The latter constantly contravened the divine plan, but this comparison indicates that they had a special place, just like the Ethiopians who, for their part, had remained irreproachable.

At the other end of the Bible, in the Acts of the Apostles, an Ethiopian eunuch, who was a "man of great authority under Candace, queen of Ethiopia, who had charge of all her treasure", returning from a pilgrimage to Jerusalem, met the apostle Philip on the road (Acts of Apostles 8:26–40). Poring together over a prophecy of Isaiah, the Ethiopian accepted the "good news" and was baptized, thus becoming, according to the text, one of the first propagators of Christianity in Ethiopia. The eunuch represented the divine instrument that allowed the introduction of the benefits of Christianity to Ethiopians and, by extension, to the black people who identified with them. These references, in Genesis, Exodus, the Song of Solomon, the Prophets and the Acts of the Apostles are but a few among the many references to Ethiopia and Ethiopians circulating in the biblical text and crystallized in Psalm 68:31. The biblical references to Ethiopia, once appropriated by means of identification, served a psychosocial function. St Clair Drake explained it in these terms: "They [the people of the black diaspora] knew they were Africans and 'of African descent', but white men invested the name of Africa with attributes that brought on feelings of shame. Compensatory beliefs backed up by convincing authority – great *myths*, the source of every people's deepest strengths – were needed to bolster their self-esteem" (Drake 1991, 10–11; author's italics).

The Bible, practised literally, provided "proof" that, countering the tarnished image of Africa circulating in the slave worlds, there existed *another* Africa, with a different significance, namely, Ethiopia. In the search for memories and origins, in a bid to reconstruct what existed before and elsewhere, the nationalist imaginary was magnetized by Ethiopia, which simultaneously represented a place, a colour and a black lineage. Consequently, Ethiopia was able to operate as "living" myth, "providing models for human behaviour and consequently conferring significance and value on existence" (Eliade 1963, 12). "To live" a myth is really a "religious" experience, as Mircea Eliade underscores, but there is also contained in this experience potential forces of political and social change (33). Accordingly, Drake insisted that " 'Ethiopianism' became an energizing myth in both the New World and Africa itself for those pre-political movements that arose while the powerless were gathering their strength for realistic and rewarding political activity" (Drake 1991, 11).

Ethiopianism, nourished in the churches, temples and congregations, was at the core of the formation of black religious, social and nationalist thought. The black imagination of Ethiopia was expressed in multiple forms – in biblical references, certainly, but also in pamphlets, the rewriting of history, anti-colonial manifestos and the creation of separate institutions. The trope of Ethiopia circulated widely in the black continental or insular worlds, far removed from contemporary life in the Horn of Africa. Before revisiting these spaces traversed by Ethiopianism, I will attempt to elucidate the conditions of production and the limitations of the knowledge historians have provided on this phenomenon.

Knowledge of Ethiopianism

The knowledge produced on Ethiopianism is characterized by a certain fragmentation, which limits the dialogue between its African and its American expressions. In a collective work on Christianity in Africa, George Shepperson proposes in one chapter a chronology of Ethiopianism, qualified as the best example of an "eccentric ecclesiastical etymology" produced by Christian churches in Africa (Shepperson 1968, 249). He indicates four periods corresponding to the different phases of Ethiopianism. The first and longest, 1611–1871, entails the biblical references to the term Ethiopia and their uses, mentioned above. While "Ethiopianism" was not yet in use, for Shepperson these references nevertheless correspond to a period marked by the first experiences of "Negro liberation".

The second period, 1872–1928, is referred to as the classic period since

Ethiopianism is thought to have exerted at this time its strongest political influence, noted in the international, American, European and African press. Shepperson insists on the fear Europeans had of Ethiopianism, on the threat felt vis-à-vis what was considered to be "a pan-African conspiracy" seeking to counter European supremacy in Africa (Shepperson 1968, 252). The formation of the African Independent Churches, especially in southern Africa, was at the centre of this classic period. The complex process of the formation of these churches was due to several factors: the stimulation provided by secessionist European churches; reaction to the high-handed discipline exercised by European missionaries; the desire of the African clergy to increase its power and control over church structures; the creation of tribal churches which integrated non-Christian local practices; the rejection of the colour line observed in the European churches. After a cursory treatment of English West Africa, Shepperson stresses that few "Ethiopian" churches were established there, but that a new ideological dimension was attributed to Ethiopianism, represented by the nationalist J.E. Casely Hayford (1866–1930). His book, published in 1911, was entitled *Ethiopia Unbound*. It emphasized that what Africa needed was not so much African Americans but "Africans or Ethiopians". For Hayford, Africa, "cradle of humanity", was in a position to free itself from the bonds woven by foreigners and colonizers (cited by Shepperson 1968, 260). The third period of Ethiopianism, 1929–63, is characterized, Shepperson maintains, by a growing confusion between the terms Ethiopianism and "Watch Tower", designating "the independent African religio-political 'conspiracy'" feared by Europeans (261). "Watch Tower" was an American movement with an apocalyptic creed introduced into South Africa in 1907 by an Englishman, Joseph Booth. Booth played a role in the development of Ethiopianism by popularizing the slogan "Africa for the Africans" that interested the black Americans and the Africans he had trained.[1] Two of his disciples, Elliott Kenan Kamwana and John Chilembwe, fomented local disorder, including the great 1915 revolt against the English in Nyasaland, led by Chilembwe (Shepperson and Price 1963).

The last period identified by Shepperson began in 1963 and was by far the shortest, his work being written in 1968. He had time only to indicate "trends" of the future of Ethiopianism and its study: first, a separation of the Independent Churches from the development of nationalism; then, an accent on the non-separatist African churches; finally, renewed interest for the theology of the Independent Churches and their use of Ethiopianism.

The main remark to be made on this periodization of the phenomenon of Ethiopianism concerns the approach of Shepperson, a specialist in the religious and social history of southern Africa. Indeed, for him, the expressions of Ethiopianism were defined first and foremost in Africa, especially in the formation of the African Independent Churches. This specialist glance, though rich and interesting, prevented a more global and comprehensive approach to the dynamics of Ethiopianism. The difficulty in arriving at a global understanding of Ethiopianism is conceivable, since this requires submitting several centuries and continents to rigorous local examination and to comparison over a spatially vast expanse. Imanuel Geiss adopts a standpoint that is similar to that of Shepperson. Although he mentions on several occasions the affection of Africans in the Americas for Ethiopian symbolism, his chapter on Ethiopianism is also limited to the formation of the African Independent Churches. He recognized the influence of African American missionaries on the development of Ethiopianism in Africa but underlined precisely that, as of the 1870s, the religious communities referred to as "Ethiopian" were formed in South Africa. In a slight widening of this problematic typically linked to the regions of South Africa, he includes the Gold Coast, Sierra Leone and Nigeria, where variants of Ethiopianism played a pivotal though sometimes limited role in the emergence of nationalisms (Geiss 1974, 132–59).

On the other side of the Atlantic, historians specializing in black American thought also developed their studies and definitions of Ethiopianism. William Scott opens a brilliant work on the relations between black Americans and Ethiopians during the Italo-Ethiopian war (1935–41) with a chapter on the "Ethiopian tradition" (Scott 1993, 12–22). In a more recent article, he reconsiders the difficulties involved in the knowledge and definition of Ethiopianism (Scott 2004). He begins by underlining the limitations of the American historiography of Ethiopianism: little research has been devoted to this field, resulting in gaps that prevent the detailed narration of the long history of this ideology. He goes on to attempt a definition of Ethiopianism:

> It may be defined as a religious-political concept of race revival. It is a distinctively black nationalist idea that was active among black Protestants in much of Anglophone Africa and the Diaspora throughout and after slavery and colonialism. A biblically derived myth of black nationality and destiny, it identifies all people of African descent with Ethiopia of the Bible, a respected black land in antiquity, and ordains global black redemption from the sovereignty of all other races. (Scott 2004, 44)

This proposal clearly pinpoints a number of factors. Ethiopianism is indissociably linked to a racialized vision: Ethiopians *are* black and blacks *are* Ethiopians. The theme of the redemption of the race, of the revival of the black world, traverses, as mentioned previously, the discourses of most of the instigators of return to Africa. It is reformulated in this instance from a sovereignist point of view: the subjugation of the black subject by nations who are neither black nor Ethiopian is refused by the producers of Ethiopianism. The corollary of nations, nationality, is also mentioned in this text. The belief in an Ethiopian destiny was thought to be materialized by the claim to an Ethiopian nationality. This issue is of prime importance for our study of Rastạfari and of the consequences of return to Ethiopia. It allows us, moreover, to highlight one of the principal drawbacks of this definition. Without denying the importance of the Bible in the genesis of Ethiopianism, or of the mimetic rhetoric through which it was expressed, it is probably reductive to restrict the *identification* of black people with the biblical Ethiopia, an ancient land which disputed with Egypt the status of the foundation of human civilization. The historical appropriation of themes related to biblical Ethiopia is undeniably at the base of Ethiopianism but, as will be demonstrated later, the *identification* with modern Ethiopia is a crucial component of Ethiopianism, one that allowed this idea to pass undiminished beyond the end of the nineteenth century.

Scott later defines three trends of Ethiopianism: millenarian, cultural and messianic (2004, 48–49). The first, millenarian Ethiopianism, supposedly arose at the end of the nineteenth century in the Southern United States, at the heights of segregation. This trend is said to affirm that at a divinely ordained time, whites and blacks will be judged, thus positing a kind of "pan-African millennium". Pamphlets of an apocalyptic nature, like Robert Alexander Young's *Ethiopian Manifesto* (1829) or David Walker's *Appeal in Four Articles* (1829), are allegedly its antecedents. They are, besides, well known by historians of the formation of black nationalism. The second trend, cultural Ethiopianism, bridging the nineteenth and the twentieth centuries, produced in the United States a corpus of literary, theatrical and poetic texts permeated with references to Ethiopia, to which is attributed the emergence of an "Ethiopian expressionism". The third and last trend is purportedly a messianic Ethiopianism. Provoked by the Adwa victory (1896) in which the armies of Emperor Menelik defeated the Italians, this trend can be found, according to the author, in Marcus Garvey's UNIA. In fact, the members of the UNIA, were, to his mind, not only captivated by Garvey's redemptionist theories, but also by the dream of the restoration of a black government whose dominion over the world was thought to have existed in ancient times. Scott's effort to work out distinctions between these various trends of Ethiopianism is creditable and remains a fundamental contribution to the elucidation of this nebulous concept. We are nevertheless left to question the utility or relevance of a distinction between the millenarian, cultural, and messianic categories. Restricting ourselves to Scott's references limits analysis. Let us take two examples.

First, what he rightly described as cultural Ethiopianism was in fact closely connected to the political events taking place in Ethiopia. Admittedly, the famous poem "Ode to Ethiopia" by Paul Laurence Dunbar, quoted by Scott, dates back to 1893, three years before the repercussions of Adwa, but most of the other literary works on the Ethiopian theme are subsequent to this event. This applies to George Schuyler's *Ethiopian Stories*, a collection of short stories written in the effervescence surrounding the Italo-Ethiopian war.[2] In the same way, Ethiopianism permeated the Harlem Renaissance, and the visual, theatrical and artistic productions of the 1920s relayed, with different canons, the inescapable image of a primordial Ethiopia, nourished by its ancient localization close to Egypt but also by new policies coming out of East Africa (Schmeisser 2004, 263–86). It is interesting to note that militant poetic practices were very popular in Marcus Garvey's *Negro World*, which published, in each issue, songs and poems on the Ethiopian, nationalist or redemptionist theme.

Further, Scott regards the texts of Walker and Young as the forerunners of millenarian Ethiopianism. In this, he is partially right. But where do we draw the line between millenarian and messianic Ethiopianism? An attentive reading of Young's text confirms its messianic references. The *Ethiopian Manifesto* was addressed to "Ethiopians" and constantly associated blacks, Ethiopians and Africans. Young (1829, 65) announces the arrival of a prophet or a Messiah to save the black race: "As came John the Baptist, of old, to spread abroad the forthcoming of his master, so alike are intended these our words, to denote to the black African or Ethiopian people, that God has prepared for them a leader, who awaits but for his season to proclaim to them his birthright."

Young defined himself as an "oracle" and announced that the arrival of the Messiah would free the slaves from the bonds of slavery. As is characteristic in messianic processes, the redeemer whose arrival he announces bears a strange resemblance to Young himself. Indeed, at the beginning of the text (1829, 62), after an announcement of the universal and imminent liberation of the black people, the redeemer is described as a "mixture" of white and black, which does not prevent him from swearing allegiance to the black race. Here is Young's description of this messianic "chief": "Know ye, then, if a white man ever appeared on earth, bearing in himself the semblance of his former race, the man we proclaim ordained of God, to call together the black people as a nation in themselves. We say, in him will be seen, in appearance, a white man, although having been born of a black woman, his mother" (62). Behind this antiquated turn of phrase, it is in fact a mulatto saver in his own image whom Young announces. He thus echoes the interstitial position, between black and white, occupied by those of "mixed blood", a question which constantly agitated black nationalists and, more specifically, black leaders, who were also measured and judged according to their phenotype. Why, then, should this text by Young, which is both millenarian and messianic, be included only in one category, that of millenarianism? These two examples emphasize the arduous nature of the task of categorizing Ethiopianism. The three trends suggested by Scott intersect with one another and are sometimes juxtaposed, proof of their insufficient differentiation.

St Clair Drake makes an interesting remark in his work devoted to the religious and social forms of Ethiopianism. He considers Ethiopianism to be "an enduring legacy to the people who fight for Black Power in the twentieth century" (Drake 1991, 11). Further, he offers his own definition of Black Power: "Two goals began to take shape as to what *Black Power* should be used for: to return 'home', to

Africa; and to wrest the land where they toiled from the men who kept them in subjection – an extension of the Maroon pattern into *black nationalism*" (18).

Other definitions of Black Power have been evoked by its partisans, actors of American social revolutions in the 1960s (Carmichael and Hamilton 1967), but Drake's approach is particularly interesting for several reasons. He identified Ethiopianism as a legacy – that is, a transmitted intangible and symbolic baggage – which permeates black actors, consciously or unconsciously, one that they evoke directly or indirectly through a biblical rhetoric. Then there are the objectives for which this heritage is activated: to return to Africa, to go "home", or to ensure domination on the land by the bonded men and women toiling there. These objectives might seem contradictory: flee the Americas, on the one hand, and regain there a form of territorial sovereignty on the other. Herein resides, in fact, the tension entailed in black nationalism, reflected in this sentence. Beyond an apparent contradiction, the link between Africa and territory is underlined, a land for black people, a land of black people, a land holding where black people were no longer subjugated but free, as evoked by the reference to the maroon communities.

The knowledge on Ethiopianism produced by researchers is marked by the difficulty of categorization and by a notable geographical dichotomy: on the one hand, Ethiopianism in southern Africa and, on the other, Ethiopianism in the United States, with, at times, a recognized bridge between these two spaces through the intervention of black or white missionaries (Martin 1985, 31–46; Mutero Chirenje 1987). This dichotomy, which overlooks the Caribbean, is the inevitable mark distinguishing different research fields, despite a common objective. While keeping in mind the racial bias of Ethiopianism as well as the characteristics underlined by Drake, the notions of heritage, return and territory, I will now propose another reading of Ethiopianism.

Spaces of Ethiopianism

In accordance with the term "black belt" used to describe spaces of the US South, where the black populations were the most numerous, I propose to use of the term *Ethiopian belt* to designate, globally, the spaces in which Ethiopianism appeared. This particular geography is characteristic of the places where colonial and racial policies converged, provoking in their wake practices of sociocultural resistance and innovation. The United States, the Caribbean and southern Africa form three inevitable poles among which a material and intangible "Ethiopian heritage" circulates, transported by biblical references, written and oral textualities and individuals. These are the contours of the Ethiopian belt, understood as a fundamental layer in the better-known geographies of black nationalism, pan-Africanism and Garveyism. I will now focus on three complementary expressions of Ethiopianism in order to illustrate with greater precision the expanse of this Ethiopian belt: the writing of the history of Africa, a church with an international vocation, and the foundation of "Zion Cities", terrestrial counterparts of the heavenly Zion. By illustrating the notions of heritage, return and land, these examples open new perspectives on the symbolic place of Ethiopia in black practices and discourses.

Ethiopianism and the Writing of History

Numerous works by Caribbean or American intellectuals could be called upon to demonstrate the influence of Ethiopianism on the writing or rewriting of the history of Africa. Without any pretence at exhaustiveness, two texts will be referenced here in this respect. The first is a lecture produced by E.W. Blyden for the American Colonization Society in 1880, entitled "Ethiopia Stretching Out Her Hands unto God; or Africa's Service to the World". The second is a work by W.E.B. Du Bois entitled *The World and Africa: An Enquiry into the Part Which Africa Has Played in World History,* published in 1946, with a chapter exclusively devoted to ancient Ethiopia. Despite their different nature and the fact that they were written almost seventy years apart, these texts remain comparable due to their similar objectives: to reinsert Africa into the history of the world by insisting on their continuous contacts; to pinpoint the slave trade as the cause of the obscuring and transformation of the history of Africa. These two prolific authors marked their time, influenced their contemporaries and left behind a currently valid intellectual heritage. It is Blyden and not Du Bois who was described as an "intellectual Ethiopianist" (Drake 1991, 54–70), but the remarkable continuity between their treatment of Ethiopia is more a shared feature than a dividing factor. Blyden was steeped in biological determinism, which earned him many a criticism from Du Bois, who, though writing after the Second World War, made recourse to the classification of the races – Caucasoid, Mongoloid and Negroid – while signalling its limitations (Du Bois 1946, 116). Blyden introduced in his text a formula characteristic of Ethiopianism: "It is pretty well established now, however, that by *Ethiopia*, is meant the continent of Africa, and by *Ethiopians*, the great race who inhabit that continent" (Blyden 1880, 113).[4]

Based on this homogenizing definition, which identified the entire continent as Ethiopia and all blacks as Ethiopians, Blyden drew upon Herodotus, the "father of the history", to define two types of Ethiopians. They had the same appearance, but those from the East supposedly had straight hair while those from the West, "the Libyans", had kinky hair (Blyden 1880, 113). Du Bois used Greek etymology to define Ethiopia as the "land of the burnt faces" and also quoted Herodotus, specifying that he distinguished four types of Ethiopians: two endogenous and two exogenous. The two endogenous types are those referenced by Blyden, and the exogenous ones are said to be the Phoenicians and the Greeks (Du Bois 1946, 122). Blyden, like Du Bois, endeavoured to find references to Ethiopia in the work of Greek authors. Both quoted Homer, who in the *Iliad* evoked "blameless Ethiopians" among whom the gods of Olympus regularly feasted and who offered them warm hospitality (Blyden 1880, 116; Du Bois 1946, 119). Du Bois went even further in the study of Greek mythological figures, stressing that a number of them were black or of mixed blood and were known to the Ethiopians. He gave the examples of the son of Zeus and Io, Epaphus, whom Aeschylus described as black, and of Andromeda, the black daughter of Cepheus, king of Ethiopia and of Cassiopeia (Du Bois 1946, 119, 121, 226). He also cited other mythical or historical Greek figures who were black, like Aesop and Sappho (120). These examples enabled him to defend the idea that there was no colour line in the cultures of the ancient Mediterranean but rather a struggle between barbarity and civilization in which black people did not have the prerogative of barbarity (227). The use of Greek authors to evoke the place of Africa in history thus served two objectives: to lend legitimacy to their writing of history and to underline the absence of prejudices against black people in the ancient worlds.

To contradict the theories of the eternal inferiority of black people, both authors insisted on the bonds between Ethiopia and Egypt, though in a different way. In Blyden's text, Egypt was a pretext to highlight the technological accomplishments attributed to Ethiopians, which remained mysterious to the scientists of the nineteenth century: "Science, in its latest wonders, has nothing to show equal to some of the wonderful things even now to be seen in Africa. In Africa stands that marvellous architectural pile – the great Pyramid – which has been the admiration and despair of the world for a hundred generations" (Blyden 1880, 116–17).

Probably influenced by the impulsion given to Egyptology by Jean-François Champollion (1790–1832) and by his own voyage to Egypt in 1866, Blyden evoked a tangible achievement among the most outstanding, the great pyramid, attributed to black genius, thus making way for the formulation of a continuity between ancient "Ethiopian" civilizations and the "Ethiopian" people of his time. He also evoked the Sphinx as a metaphor of Africa, sitting "on the highway of the world", of the intertwining of continents and cultures, connected to the most famous names and events in the "annals of time" (Blyden 1880, 117). Without going into the details of Egyptian history, he settled for the place of Egypt in the Bible, where Abraham sheltered in times of famine (Genesis 12:10), Moses received his education, and the Holy Family took refuge in their flight from King Herod and his plans of massacre. In fact, Blyden used the Bible as a historical source, to the point of qualifying it, elsewhere, as an ethnographic document, while continuously legitimating his approach through references to numerous exegeses in support of his interpretations.[3]

Du Bois, for his part, entered into greater detail regarding the vicissitudes of the reigning dynasties of Egypt, but framed his remarks by explaining in a few points what the history of the northeast of Africa must have been like:

> In Ethiopia the sunrise of human culture took place, spreading down into the Nile valley. Ethiopia, land of the blacks, was thus the cradle of Egyptian civilization. Beyond Ethiopia, in Central and South Africa, lay the gold of Ophir and the rich trade of Punt on which the prosperity of Egypt largely depended. Egypt brought slaves from black Africa as she did from Europe and Asia. But she also brought citizens and leaders from black Africa. When Egypt conquered Asia, she used black soldiers to a wide extent. When Asia overwhelmed Egypt, Egypt sought refuge in Ethiopia as a child returns to its mother, and Ethiopia then for centuries dominated and successfully invaded Asia. (Du Bois 1946, 117)

In a few sentences, the central and fundamental role of Ethiopia in the genesis of humanity and in the survival and prosperity of Egyptian society is underlined. Ethiopia was identified as a maternal figure, one that is, moreover, still current in the term "motherland", used to designate the African continent. It was therefore impossible to write the ancient history of Africa without pointing out the organic link between Egyptian civilization and black Africa. The long discussion on this organic link led Du Bois to evoke, in turn, the emergence of the "nation of the Hebrews" (Du Bois 1946, 124–31). In the text quoted above, he had already included biblical motifs, such as the reference to the incense of Punt and the gold of Ophir (Psalm 45). Regarding the Hebrews, he evoked the "classic" biblical references to Ethiopia: Jeremiah saved from prison by a black functionary, Ebed-Melech (Jeremiah 38:7, 10, 12), Moses and his leprous hand, the Song of Solomon, the prophet Isaiah (Isaiah 20:3–5) and, of course, Psalm 68:31. In fact, Du Bois was only partially distanced from a historical practice that regarded the Bible as an objective source.

The important intracontinental migrations originating in Ethiopia and the nurturing bond between Ethiopia and Egypt were particularly underlined by both authors, especially Du Bois, who developed this question further. He wrote seventy years after Blyden, and his text demonstrates the stability of the attention paid to the role of Ethiopia in the birth of African civilizations. Du Bois's insistence on Egypt might reveal the slow but certain shift *towards* Egypt in the interest of black American intellectuals studying Ethiopia, as if to show that the move from Ethiopianism to Egyptocentrism was only a small step away, one for which Du Bois was preparing the ground. Indeed, in 1955, less than ten years after the publication of this work by Du Bois, Cheik Anta Diop published his seminal work, *Nations nègres et cultures* (*Black Nations and Cultures*), on the anteriority of Negro civilizations and the role of ancient Egypt in the formation of a continental cultural unity. Cited by American intellectuals, this work was to give rise to a process of rewriting of the history of Africa, called Afrocentrism, in which Egypt became an inevitable reference.[4]

The Ethiopianism which emerged in these texts, especially that of Blyden, was closely linked to biblical references – like an Ethiopia that encompassed the entire continent – and to a movement of redemption and return to Africa. Consequently, Ethiopianism influenced Blyden in his writing of the history of Africa. This influence is visible also in Du Bois's writing of history, despite its inscription within a broader pan-African framework, with which the work opens and closes. History enabled him to explicate his political engagement during a period which was quite different from that of Blyden, some fifteen years before his departure to live in Ghana. The increasingly accentuated shift towards Egypt was, however, to become a distinctive mark of many American intellectuals as of the 1960s, and thus indicates how, in almost one hundred years, Ethiopianism took, little by little, second place in black intellectual work, whereas the grand hours of Egyptocentrism were barely beginning. This also shows that if Ethiopianism gradually disappeared from the intellectual productions related to the writing of the history of Africa, it is elsewhere, and not among scholars, that the richest references to Ethiopianism could be found. As Du Bois suggested in reference to the pan-African movement of the 1920s: "Then, too, there came simultaneously another movement, stemming from the West Indies. This was a people's movement rather than a movement of the intellectuals. It was led by Marcus Garvey and it represented a poorly conceived but intensely earnest determination to unite the Negroes of the world" (Du Bois 1946, 236). Du Bois thus distinguished a popular movement *as opposed to* an intellectual movement and stated precisely that it came from the British Caribbean, the West Indies. The popular aspect is of particular interest to the present work, since it is therein that Ethiopianism found a home and means of sustenance. Whereas the intellectuals set off for Egypt, the others continuously imagined Ethiopia and the identifications that bonded them with that land.

An International Ethiopian Church

We already mentioned the movement of Christian revival which, as of the 1890s, drove the development of the African Independent Churches all over Africa, and in South Africa especially. George Shepperson, as mentioned, associated the second period of Ethiopianism (1872–1928) with the first great wave of formation of these churches (Shepperson 1968, 250–60). They were quite numerous, often had fragile administrations, and assembled congregations of various sizes, from less than a hundred to several thousands. In the main, they arose from a break with established, often missionary churches or due to the emergence of a leader of charismatic or prophetic character. In his 1902 thesis, Maurice Leenhardt (1976) studied these churches, which he brought together under the term "Ethiopian movement". Later, Bengt Sundkler (1961 and 1976) identified two types of Independent Churches, the Ethiopian churches and the Zionist churches, which will be addressed later. The Ethiopian churches had only an indirect link with today's Ethiopia, reposed on the biblical corpus characteristic of Ethiopianism and appropriated the nationalist slogan "Africa to the Africans", while largely rehabilitating their organization based on the model of the Protestant missionary churches (Sundkler 1961, 54). The first among them was the Ethiopian Church founded by Mangena M. Mokone in 1892 in Witwatersrand. A pastor of the Wesleyan mission, James M. Dwane (1848–1915), following separation from his church, joined Mokone and founded in 1900 the Order of Ethiopia under an Anglican denomination (Sundkler 1961, 41). Mokone and Dwane were in contact with the African Methodist Episcopal Church founded by Richard Allen in 1816 in Philadelphia and with its bishop, Henry McNeal Turner, partisan of the "return to Africa", who travelled to South Africa for the first time in 1898 (Sundkler 1961, 40–42; Geiss 1974, 141–45). One of these Ethiopian churches, the Afro-Athlican Constructive Church (AACC), is intriguing for the reason that it is particularly unfamiliar. It was mentioned by Sundkler, who stated that it was based in Kimberley, South Africa, and he underlined the fact that Marcus Garvey left a special imprint there (Sundkler 1961, 58). He offered very little information on the formation and the congregation of this church but insisted that the colour line was clearly asserted in it: it was strictly reserved for the "children of Ethiopia" or the "children of Kush" (59). Future research in South Africa will probably unearth more information on the AACC, but it is remarkable that information on this church, available in the national archives in Jamaica, in a file gathering original documents and police reports dating from February 1926 to September 1927, has not been analysed.[5]

The doctrine and organization of the AACC are explained in a small book of about forty pages, signed by Robert Athlyi Rogers, founder of the AACC. This book, entitled *The Holy Piby*, sometimes called *The Blackman's Bible*, provides some biographical information on Robert Athlyi Rogers.[6] Born in Anguilla, a small island in the eastern Caribbean, at an unknown date, Rogers migrated to the United States and settled in Newark, New Jersey.[7] There he preached the "redemption of Ethiopia" in the streets, and later in the buildings of the African Methodist Episcopal Church. In 1919, branches of the AACC opened in Springfield, Massachusetts, and Woodbridge, New Jersey, while a parade was organized in Newark. In 1921, for an entire year, Rogers travelled by boat to Central and South America, proselytizing the black populations. In 1922, Marcus Garvey addressed a division of the UNIA in Newark, in a great meeting in which Rogers was invited to speak. This encounter with Garvey had a significant impact on the development of the doctrines of the AACC. In them, Garvey was portrayed as an "apostle of the Lord God for the redemption of Ethiopia and her suffering posterities" (Rogers 2000, 55). This allowed the AACC to position itself as a movement equivalent to the UNIA, but working strictly on a spiritual level.[8] Nevertheless, the similarities of or perhaps the adaptation of the Garvey programme to the doctrines of the AACC was particularly remarkable in the emphasis placed on the necessary development of work, trade and industry.

A document entitled "The Living and Trading Scheme" presents a plan to improve the standard of living of its members, to protect them from poverty and ignorance, to propel them towards sobriety and prosperity.[9] The equivalent of a tithe was required, intended to constitute the first capital through which an internal trade network of the church would develop: "A trading branch which will enable our people – unitedly working together to throw in their pennies which will in due time amount to pounds, which amount will be used in buying and selling such class of goods that the people demand daily." An industrial branch was also suggested, with the aim of allowing the members to provide for their needs and for the community to take charge of burials. Indeed, to "live industriously", "to be fruitful", to establish black-owned trade, to generate money were themes close to those of Garvey, for whom redemption was also a matter of the economic independence of black communities. In 1924 Rogers published *The Holy Piby*, a "holy book" composed of several parts. The first part, "Athlyi", quickly recounts the story of the Creation and underlines the persecutions to which the "Ministers of the Gospel" were subjected (Rogers 2000, 23). The second part and the longest, "Aggregation", narrates in a symbolic and very cryptic language various visions of paradise as well as the anointing of Ethiopia and pronounces a prophecy on the imminent arrival of the saviour: "prepare ye the way for a redeemer" (28). The hierarchy of the church was set forth in this document: first, God (*Elijah*); second, Pastor Rogers; next, the various apostles who administrated "the children of Ethiopia" (30–31). The twelve commandments of the "Holy Law" formed a doctrinal framework and chiefly addressed the daily life and sociability of the members, by mentioning values such as love, work, unity, cleanliness, punctuality, honesty and so on. The creed of the AACC was expressed as follows:

> O God of Ethiopia, thy divine majesty; thy spirit come in our hearts to dwell in the path of righteousness lead us, help us to forgive that we may be forgiven, teach us love and loyalty on earth as to heaven, endow us with wisdom and understanding to do thy will, thy blessing to use that the hungry be fed, the naked clothed, the sick nourished, the aged cared for. Deliver us from the hands of our enemies that we prove fruitful, then in the last day when life is o'er, our bodies in the clay, or in the depths of the sea, or in the belly of a beast, O give our souls a place in thy kingdom forever and forever. Amen. (Rogers 2000, 39)

Using terms that sometimes recall the Lord's Prayer (Luke 6:2–4), this AACC creed found a posterity that Rogers was probably far from imagining. Indeed, recited during the assemblies of the AACC in Jamaica in the 1920s,[10] this creed is known even today as the "Ethiopian prayer" and is recited by most Rastafari, alone or in a community setting, in all of their organizations. It represents a formidable element of continuity, with a text that has undergone only minute changes and which indicates the extent to which Ethiopianism, despite significant changes during the twentieth century, continues to permeate the Rastafari movement.[11]

The third part of *The Holy Piby* is entitled "The Facts of the Apostles". It relates the various revelations addressed to the "apostles of the twentieth century" of the church, and God is portrayed addressing himself directly to Marcus Garvey: "Prepare ye a bill of arrangement, saith the Lord, and give it in the hands of thy colleague [Rogers] that he go to the land of Ethiopia (Africa) and to the nations at the entrance of the land and request them to open the door for the return of thy children" (Rogers 2000, 83–84). The return to Africa is mentioned several times in the text and the object of Rogers's visions and messianic prophecies is somewhat more clearly defined therein: "I saw the natural man standing in the east and the star of his crown gave light to the pathway of the children of Ethiopia" (86–87). The fourth and last part, "Precautions", begins with an allegory of the voyages of Athlyi Rogers and the taboos related to purity: filiation without racial intermingling, the submission of women, social relations avoiding the impure. The objectives of the church contained in *The Holy Piby* were thus read at several levels: at the general level, the "safety of the posterities of Ethiopia" (86–87); at the social level, to "set up a real religious and material brotherhood among the children of Ethiopia" (101); at the nationalist level, "then shall the children of Ethiopia return to their own land and there establish a light with which no nation shall compare, nor will there be any power sufficient to douse it" (84); at the utopian level, to "establish Heaven on earth" (19); and, finally, at the messianic level, "I am Messiah unto Ethiopia, therefore my word reign forever and ever. I shall be cast into prison for your sake, but my spirit shall go out of jail and fight for Ethiopia" (98). The centrality of Ethiopia, its personification and the identification of its genealogies highlight the AACC as a unique example of a congregation whose doctrines are largely based on the corpus of Ethiopianism.

In Jamaica, the doctrinal contents of the AACC have permeated popular Ethiopianism, but the institution itself did not seem to have enjoyed great success. Its establishment by Rogers in South Africa in 1924 might have contributed to its local prestige in Jamaica.[12] Mrs Grace J. Garrison, recently returned from Panama and called "the Comet", was in charge of the institution, whose first stone was laid on 20 November 1925 in Kingston. But a building never materialized.[13] Moreover, branches are thought to have been opened in Morant Bay and Bath, in the east of the island; in St Andrew, not far from Kingston; in Spanish Town, the second city of the country; and in Montego Bay, on the north coast.[14] The first pastor, Malcolm McCormack, was a professional broom-maker, and the AACC counted some forty members at the time. The following year, certain gatherings attracted nearly three hundred visitors.[15] By then Charles F. Goodridge, from Barbados, was in charge. He was supposed to live on the contributions of the members of his church. Police reports indicate that several disturbances arose within the congregation – first because the UNIA distanced itself from this denomination, calling its members "impostors"; second, due to financial issues: former members accused Goodridge of misappropriating the funds of the church.[16] These disagreements, fuelled by persons who were simultaneously members of the UNIA and members of the AACC and by others who had paid their tithe without dividends, obliged Goodridge to request police protection on leaving services.[17] The local life of the church, which was tense, unstable, financially limited, remains rather obscure, despite the fact that, as it turned out, the sermons, discourses and especially the songs exercised a certain fascination on the working classes of Kingston. The hymn book, printed in Kingston in 1925, provides a corpus of twenty-two very interesting texts.[18] Associating the psalms and biblical symbolism with recurrent images of Ethiopia and the children of Ethiopia, the hymns of the AACC may be seen as heralding *nyabinghi*, the ritual music of the Rastafari. As for Rogers, it appears that he committed suicide on 24 August 1931.[19] He had, in the *Piby*, formulated a wish: "My God, My God, what shall happen to the apostles of the Twentieth Century? Father if it's me, even I that shall pass from the presence of men grant that the Piby live forever that the children of Ethiopia, through the teaching of the Afro-Athlican Constructive Church, may obtain salvation forever" (Rogers 2000, 88).

Whereas the fragility of the organization, its marginality and the predatory attitudes of its pastors did not augur well for a fruitful posterity of the AACC, Rogers might have been surprised to discover that his doctrines and the hymns of his Ethiopian church marked the twentieth century and were integrated into the legacy of Ethiopianism diffused by Rastafari. As eccentric as it may appear, the AACC was a denomination which, from the United States to Jamaica and South Africa, helped to draw the contours of an "Ethiopian belt", wherein was formulated the quest for an identity, a nationality and a land – and a holy one, if possible.

Zion Cities in Africa

In South Africa, the second type of independent churches identified by Bengt Sundkler is the Zionist churches – with no relationship to the contemporary Jewish movement (Sundkler 1961, 48). These were charismatic groups, often motivated by the desire to establish Zion cities, thought to be the earthly counterparts of the heavenly Zion.[20] The Zionist churches shared, in the main, the Ethiopianism of the Ethiopian churches but remained much closer to local ritual practices; hence they had a more pronounced "African" character (Sundkler 1961, 55). Adrian Hastings stated, in addition, that the Ethiopian churches attracted the African elite of the clergy as well as learned laity irritated by European control, whereas the other – apostolic or Zionist – churches often assembled the poorest, who valued the power conferred by the Christian faith and were less interested in education and elitist personal development (Hastings 1994, 533). This is not the place to recall the complex history of the growth and the multiple schisms of these churches, but what is necessary here, however, is to underline an element characteristic of a great many of them – that is, the foundation of Zion Cities, which offered the illusion of a territorialized sovereignty of divine nature.[21]

The city is a recurrent theme in the Bible, from the accursed cities (Enoch, Babel, Sodom, Gomorrah) to the Holy City, embodied by Jerusalem. The ancient name of the acropolis of Jerusalem was Zion – a city conquered by King David, in which King Solomon built the temple according to divine instructions (1 Kings 6–7, 2 Chronicles 3–4). The symbol of the alliance between God and men, the Ark of the Covenant, holding the Tables of the Law, was placed in this city. The term Zion, first introduced in the book of Genesis (14:17–18), appears many times in the books of the prophets and in the psalms as the "Holy Mountain" chosen and favoured by God. In the New Testament, Zion is opposed to Babylon, representing the forces of evil (Revelation 14:7–12). Eschatological battles were staged in Jerusalem, and the last book of the Bible closes on the vision of the heavenly Jerusalem, the New City: "And I saw the Holy City, new Jerusalem, coming down from God, . . . it had twelve gates, and at the gates twelve angels" (Revelation 21:2, 12). Announcing eschatological times, the new Jerusalem entailed the promise of the redemption of the just.

In the South African context, to establish a Zion City was both an identity act and a political gesture. It was a way of appropriating a space, a territory in which the population could feel protected and independent. The earthly Zions, mirroring the heavenly Zion, were generally established on mountaintops and inevitably attracted populations with no access to land. To emphasize the importance of this question of land, Sundkler reminds us that the Israelites of Enoch Mgijima had settled in Bulhoek, near Queenstown, sure that Jehovah had guided them there, out of the situation of subjection imposed on them. Because they occupied crown land and had no titles of property for the land on which the three hundred huts of their "City" stood, the Israelites were finally massacred by police forces in 1921 (Sundkler 1961, 72–73, and 1976, 315). Zion cities did not all meet such a tragic end. They represented an aspiration to freedom, community life as well as faith in the purifying function of the city. The symbolism of the Zion Cities put an end to the need of the people to project themselves into a dubious eschatological future, where hopes were reserved for another life; they could, "here and now", work out their salvation and their redemption (Sundkler 1976, 194). This accomplished eschatology also countered the unfulfilled apocalyptic message of the European or American missionaries. The disillusions caused by missionary teaching could thus be finally reversed by the concrete reality of an African Zion (Daneel 1987, 264). The Zion Cities were often built on mountains; to go up to Zion represented both a physical and a spiritual effort. Mountains were regarded as places predisposed to the practice of divine communication by reason of their elevation; they acted as a link between earth and heaven, offered a sense of closeness to God and invited asceticism (Sundkler 1976, 315).

Isaiah Shembe (ca. 1867–1935), one of the best-known "Zulu prophets", established his Church of the Nazarites in 1910 in Ekuphakameni, not far from Durban. The mountain was, first, the place where Shembe is said to have had his first vision, like Moses, who went to the mountain to communicate with God (Exodus 31:18, 32–34). There he ordained his first pastors, and the place became a site of annual pilgrimage (Sundkler 1976, 314). Ekuphakameni, meaning "the Elated place", was called by various names: Zion, Nazareth, Jerusalem, "new Eden", "the heavenly place" and so on. Isaiah Shembe's successor edited and published 218 hymns in 1940, most of which were already in circulation among the members of the congregation (Vilakazi et al. 1986, 139; Sundkler 1976, 186–205). Many of the hymns were devoted to Ekuphakameni. Accordingly, hymn 160 evokes an "elevated place which enlightens all the nations", and a "city built on a mountain". Like the heavenly Jerusalem, twelve doors were supposed to allow entry to it. It would seem only one door gave access to Ekuphakameni, but it was nonetheless a symbolic passageway, at whose threshold shoes had to be removed and through which not everyone could pass (Becken 1978, 165). Hence, hymn 63 repeated: "Let me hurry, let me hasten / to enter Ekuphakameni / before the gates are shut" (Sundkler 1976, 200).[22] A constant interweaving of biblical meaning and local reality transformed Ekuphakameni into the glorious Zion Church of the Nazarites.

Dialungana K. Solomon, the second son of Simon Kimbangu, who directed the business of the Church of Jesus Christ on the Earth by the Prophet Simon Kimbangu, also set to work on the convergence between reality and biblical meaning, after the death of his father in 1951. In 1961, he finished the third version of a text entitled *The Beloved City*, which sought to legitimate the presence of the new Jerusalem in Nkamba – a village at the top of a mountain, surrounded by water and protected by guarded doors – and to counter the claims of other religious movements. This relatively short text, translated by Wyatt MacGaffey (1969, 132–41), started with numerous biblical references to the four names of the Holy City: Salem, Jerusalem, City of David, City of God. In short, he explained the vision of the new Jerusalem, Nkamba, seen as capable of relieving the suffering of the people. The identification of the members of the congregation with the children of Israel was illustrated by the torments of the slave trade and of forced labour to which they were subjected. Lastly, the revelation incarnated by Prophet Simon Kimbangu as well as his miracles was narrated as the means allowing him to guide men and women to repentance and faith. The "hills of Satan", represented by sorcerers, fetishists, missionaries and the Belgian government – none of whom accepted that the new Jerusalem had "descended" unto Africa – came under constant attack. The text ended with the listing of ten reasons why the congregation should love the new Jerusalem like the Hebrews loved the one of old. MacGaffey underlined the "cyclical time" of the existence of the church: the contemporary events were said to be identical to those of the past, as demonstrated by the analogy between the seventy years of biblical exile and the duration of the colonial past in Central Africa (141–45). Despite some chronological confusion, faith and confidence in Nkamba were reiterated; the present time and space were sacralized, thanks in particular to the presence of the mausoleum, or temple, in which Simon Kimbangu rested; the "beloved City" was at the centre of the emotions and practices of the congregation.

These are but a few examples reminding us of the degree to which the foundation of Zion Cities by many prophets represented a central element of the southern African Zionist churches, which capitalized on local practices and ritual traditions. It is sometimes touching to note the extent to which the aspirations of the people were related not only to economic independence but also to spiritual independence. The foundation and control of a terrestrial Zion thus laid the ground for an independent and territorialized social organization. For the congregations involved in these Cities, to live in Zion was to take on a new life and a new identity (Sundkler 1976, 305). Representing the need to have "a place of one's own", a "home" protected by its sacred status, the Zion Cities seemed to offer, for Africans living in Africa, the illusion of a certain freedom and protection with respect to the powerful social changes surrounding them. More than through direct political action, it is in the form of biblical reappropriation and symbolic fulfilment of the prophecies contained in the Bible that social change was imagined, as a means of projection into the future and, more importantly, of living.

The three expressions of Ethiopianism chosen here – the writing of the history, an international Ethiopian Church and the foundation of Zion Cities – were deployed in a vast space representing the Ethiopian belt, as defined above. They underline the similarity between local situations in which racial and colonial policies converged, creating in their wake social resistance, cultural innovation and a desire for change. At the confluence of the nineteenth and the twentieth centuries, white power was symbolically defied in similar ways in the United States, in Jamaica and in South Africa – three poles of this Ethiopian belt. Ethiopianism, the ideological matrix associating black people and their salvation with Ethiopia, was clearly, at times, a limited but useful instrument. Whether in the case of intellectuals who made use of it in rewriting the history of Africa or in the case of the "ordinary people" who founded churches meant to ensure both their material and spiritual salvation or, in the case of the prophets who founded Zion Cities, Ethiopianism was an amazing and inexhaustible symbolic reservoir. These three expressions of Ethiopianism gave, in their own way, historical depth to the popular identification which motivated certain individuals to repatriate to Ethiopia. By identifying heritages, defending symbolic return to the continent and identifying Holy Cities, lands and mountains, these expressions of Ethiopianism indicate that physical settlements in Ethiopia were not the result of "caprice" but were, to the contrary, the fruit of a long, symbolic narrative which assumed multiple forms in various places. There is still, however, another factor crucial to a fuller understanding of Ethiopianism – namely, the role played by modern Ethiopia, the "real" Ethiopian state, without which Ethiopianism would have remained one of the ideologies that nourished black nationalism and pan-Africanism without becoming the cornerstone of the return to Ethiopia.

Modern Ethiopianism

Most writings on the subject of Ethiopianism disregard an extremely important element: the place of the Ethiopian state in the formation of Ethiopianism, its role, its capacity as agent and its interactions with the promoters of the Ethiopianist corpus. While the living conditions of black people in the diaspora as well as the black imagination of Ethiopia played a fundamental role in the formation of Ethiopianism, it would be mistaken to think that Ethiopia itself had nothing to do with this phenomenon. Admittedly, since the seventeenth century, Ethiopia was almost entirely a trope of the black imaginary. But at the end of the nineteenth century, when Ethiopia positioned itself more precisely in the geography of colonial and racial policies, its image changed.

At the beginning of the nineteenth century, European interest in Ethiopia was renewed through the interrelated commercial, missionary and scientific enterprises which began to arrive in the region. Kasa Hailu, who became Tewodros II, King of Kings of Ethiopiam, in 1855, following internecine wars, was sometimes regarded as the first Ethiopian sovereign with a modernizing project (Crummey 1969). He had begged for military and technical aid from Europeans, but with little success. After alienating himself from the Catholics and the French, he alienated the English by imprisoning the British consul, Captain Cameron; the rare Protestant missionaries whom he had obliged to work in the arms factory; as well as the official envoy in charge of negotiating the release of the prisoners, whose ranks he eventually joined. The main object of the expedition led by Sir Robert Napier was to release these persons and to punish Tewodros. Added to this was the fact that England had few commercial interests in the region. Twenty years prior to the partition of the African continent by Europeans, the sacking of the citadel of Meqdala in 1868, the final refuge of Tewodros, and his suicide put an end to the efforts of the modernizer. The English rapidly withdrew, but the Italians were not far off, and by 1885 they occupied the port of Messawa, where they succeeded the Egyptians. While attempting an invasion from the south, the Italian troops were decimated at Dogali in January 1887 by the troops of *Ras* Alula, the general of the King of Kings, Yohannes IV, crowned in 1872 in Axum. The latter died in Matamma in 1889 during a battle with the mahdist armies, and his successor, Menelik, in charge of Choa, was crowned that same year. While leading his troops out to the south of Ethiopia, in view of the expansion of the empire, as will be seen later, Menelik II had strategically established his capital in Entotto, on the hills north of Addis Ababa, in 1881. The capital was moved to Addis Ababa in 1892, the same year that the "great famine" was to strike all regions of the empire. The Treaty of Wechale (Ucciali), signed in 1889 by Count Pietro Antonelli, who arrived in the region in 1882, and by Menelik, had divergent translations of article 17, whose Amharic version indicated that Menelik "*reserved the faculty* to make use of Italian government officials for his relationships with the European powers", whereas the Italian version had it that "that *he must*" (Berhanou Abebe 1998, 128). Menelik denounced the Italian version, which effectively transformed Ethiopia into an Italian protectorate, whereas the Italians continued, in the north, to exercise a policy of subversion, occupying the land and joining ranks with the princes and other notables of Tigray. Rebellions broke out in the north as early as 1894 and the military option remained the only way forward for Menelik.

Figure 2.1. Menelik II in court dress, ca. 1903 © DR.

The Adwa campaign took place in three stages: a great battle at Amba Alague; the siege of Meqele, the headquarters where the Italians had built a fort; and finally, the defeat of the Italians in Adwa. At the side of Menelik, a heroic figure distinguished himself: *Ras* Makonnen, the father of Tafari Makonnen, the future emperor (Petridès 1966). On 1 March 1896, the battle of Adwa became a victory, Italian colonial ambitions crumbled, and an independent Ethiopia survived. Having escaped by a hair from European colonial influence, Ethiopia alone preserved its independence when Africa and its resources "were divided up" during the Berlin conference (15 November 1884–26 February 1885). The national and international political and military processes presiding over the formation of the modern Ethiopian state culminated in Adwa. They paved the way for the visibility and knowledge of the Ethiopian state and its sovereigns, who no longer restricted themselves to European diplomatic relations. Ethiopia was then on the verge of becoming the symbol of resistance, independence and freedom from colonization and oppression of the black populations of the world. The victory of Adwa in 1896 thus marked the advent of what I will call modern Ethiopianism.

Figure 2.2. The child Tafari at the side of his father, Makonnen, ca. 1900 © DR.

The term *modern Ethiopianism*, as used here, refers to the transformation of the Ethiopianist corpus due to the relations between Ethiopia and the black worlds within and beyond Africa. With the growing presence of Ethiopia on the international scene, as of 1896, the myth of Ethiopia, announced in the corpus of Ethiopianism, was gradually *incarnated* via representations of the Ethiopian state and of the personalities who gave flesh to the Ethiopian state, especially its emperors, Menelik II and Haile Selassie I. To "incarnate" is understood here in the etymological sense of *carno*, *carnis*, "flesh", meaning "to cover" (a spiritual body) with a fleshly body; to represent in oneself. (*Dictionnaire Robert* 1996). That which previously belonged to the realm of symbolism and cultural innovation – the biblical Ethiopia, the blackness of Ethiopians, filiation between Ethiopians and black people, Ethiopia as the place of origin of humanity, Ethiopia as coterminous with the entire African continent – gradually shifted towards an often incomplete (ac)knowledge(ment) of the modern Ethiopian state. Activated by a double identification with the only independent country in Africa and with the Ethiopian royalty, seen as an incarnation of black power and freedom, nourished by initially infrequent contacts, modern Ethiopianism designates the special relations between Ethiopia and the black people of the world since the end of the nineteenth century. As will be seen, the pan-African policies of the Ethiopian sovereigns contributed to transform Ethiopianism, changing the symbolic relations between Ethiopia and black people of the world into tangible ones. These Ethio-Atlantic relations form the central theme of the work of Fikru Negash Gebrekidan (2005), an Ethiopian researcher working in the United States. Providing rich information, this book, resulting from his dissertation, occasionally sins through overgeneralization. Naturally, Ethiopianism occupies place of pride in it. His analysis revolves around the Italo-Ethiopian war of 1935–41, and Ethiopianism is defined therein as a predecessor of black nationalism (Fikru Negash Gebrekidan 2005, 37–47). The definition of modern Ethiopianism proposed by Fikru resonates with my own when he affirms: "Modern Ethiopianism is, however, much more than a quest for an idyllic past. Given the state-of-the-art means of communication, Ethiopia is no longer a far-off abstraction, even if Ethiopian realities often coexist with Ethiopia's mythic image as a racial homeland. Contemporary Ethio-Atlantic ties are articulated by tangible historical events" (Fikru Negash Gebrekidan 2005, 1).

Modern Ethiopianism allows us to discern the convergence or even the juxtaposition of myth and reality in the dynamic histories that structure the relations between Ethiopia and the black people of the world. In order to clarify the events which allowed the transformation of Ethiopianism at the end of the nineteenth century, it is helpful to revisit a particular moment in this process of the gradual incarnation of the black imagination of Ethiopia through the beginning and development of Ethio-Atlantic relations.

Relations with the Ethiopian State

The gradual incarnation of classic Ethiopianism in the representations of the Ethiopian state and sovereigns is due to at least two interrelated factors: the impact of the victory of Adwa and the arrival of the first Caribbeans in Ethiopia. Articles and editorials in the black American press immediately relayed the narrative of the Italian debacle at Adwa. While the sources of the black press were not fundamentally different from those that fed the white press, their interpretations were quite different. William Scott stressed that Adwa as well was a major awakening of the consciousness of African Americans and produced a deep reverence for modern Ethiopia, thereby reinforcing the older tradition of Ethiopianism (Scott 1993, 21). The Ethiopian victory, the sign of a strong African nation, instilled in African Americans a feeling of personal pride. This victory, as Sylvia Jacobs (1981, 194) affirms, "became a kind of folk story that was well known to all blacks and passed among individuals within the black community in beauty parlours and barber shops, at church congregations, at various meetings and gatherings, and in family circles". Yet, in the Caribbean, the news of Adwa seemed to pass relatively unnoticed. Based on the example of Trinidad and Tobago, Rita Pemberton (1998, 605) explained that this relatively low impact "was due to the lack of knowledge in the country of Ethiopia and its activities. This lack of information was assisted by the established media which primarily focused on issues that were important to the interests of the ruling class it represented. But, preoccupation with domestic problems also assisted this situation to develop. Thus, Adwa seemed to pass unnoticed in Trinidad and Tobago in 1896."

The disparity in the impact of the news of Adwa on the United States and on the Caribbean might therefore be due to the presence of the independent black press, which was more developed in the United States than in the English-speaking Caribbean. To a certain degree, Trinidad caught up later on, at the time of the Italo-Ethiopian war (1935–41). Adwa was mentioned there in the popular music, calypso, as the first Ethiopian victory over the Italians.[23] The news of the victory of Adwa was also perceived differently depending on social distinctions: with a weak impact in popular milieux compared to a strong repercussion in intellectual circles, the best example being probably that of Benito Sylvain (1868–1915).

A Haitian and a musician, having finished his initial studies in Port-au-Prince, Benito Sylvain went to further them in France, in the navy, before starting to study philosophy. He was only twenty years old when his articles defending the black race created a sensation in Paris. After serving for a time as a journalist in Haiti, he was engaged in the diplomatic service of his country and was posted to London in 1889. In 1890, he launched his first newspaper, *La Fraternité* (*Fraternity*), "to defend in Europe the interests of the black race" (Sylvain 1901, 508). In the following years, he assumed numerous responsibilities: president of the Oriental and African committee of the Society of Ethnography in Paris, coordinator of a special delegation sent to the French Caribbean by the steering committee of the Alliance Française, Haitian representative to the first anti-slavery conventions which took place in Paris in 1890 and in Brussels in 1891. Upon the announcement of the victory of Adwa, Sylvain prepared to leave for Ethiopia with a letter of friendship for Menelik II from General Nord Alexis (Lara 2000, 285). He travelled to Marseille in 1897 via Port Said and Djibouti, then onward by road. He made a first stop in Harar, where he met *Ras* Makonnen, and later obtained an audience with Emperor Menelik II: "I alone among all the many travellers who have visited Abyssinia since the memorable victory of Adwa, went there with the sole concern of seeing the emperor, Menelik, to help him, in a completely altruistic manner, maintain the national independence of his empire and to ensure, in the plenitude of his sovereign rights, a normal course of progress" (Sylvain 1906, p. Ethiopia/Liberia).

Not without a certain pretentiousness, Sylvain distinguished himself from all the European visitors to Ethiopia through emphasis on his altruism. On several occasions, Sylvain and the emperor discussed international issues, racial solidarity, and slavery in Ethiopia. He is said to have received the title of "aide-de-camp" (Lara 2000, 190–97). On his return to Europe, Sylvain met Henry Sylvester Williams (1869–1911), a lawyer from Trinidad who had founded the African Association in 1898 with the view of organizing a conference "to start influencing public opinion on the facts and conditions affecting the wellbeing of people originating in the various regions of the British Empire" (Mathurin 1976, 48). With Sylvain's help, this conference was to reach beyond the borders of the British Empire to become the first pan-African conference. Held in 1900 in London, it brought together the black leaders of the time, with Sylvain representing both Haiti and Ethiopia. In the wake of these events, Sylvain defended his doctorate in 1899 and published it in 1901. Entitled *Du sort des indigènes dans les colonies d'exploitation* (*On the Fate of the Natives in the Colonies of Exploitation*), it launched a severe attack on slavery, racism and colonialism. Its final chapter explained the objectives of the Pan-African Association, founded at the time of the 1900 conference.

Sylvain's numerous activities cannot all be cited here; it is, however, possible to underline two elements. First, as the representative of a group of eighteen thousand black persons from the Congo established in Cuba subsequent to their deportation to the island as slaves some thirty years earlier, he tried to negotiate their repatriation to the Congo, disputing the prerogatives exercised there by Leopold II. Although this mission was a failure, it nevertheless offered Sylvain the opportunity to define the objectives of an undertaking of that kind: "But, in the absence of a mass emigration, which is neither necessary nor practical, we must encourage the very creditable motivation which leads an increasing number of groups of civilized blacks from the United States or other countries of America to contribute to the education and moral liberation of their fellows in Africa" (1901, 520). Sylvain approach's was pragmatic: he did not choose to advocate massive return to the continent, at a time when emigrationists like Henry McNeal Turner were defending their "African dream" of a promised land. But he contributed to linking the first fruits of the pan-African movement to the defence of the *right* of Africans to return to the continent (518).[24]

Second, it is remarkable to note that Sylvain travelled four times to Ethiopia. Although the dates of these voyages remain uncertain, it would seem that in addition to the voyage of 1897, he returned there the following year, then in 1903 with William H. Ellis, an African American entrepreneur, to whom we will return, and again in 1906 (Sylvain 1906, 108). He hoped to consolidate the diplomatic and friendly relations between Haiti and Ethiopia and to develop the scope of the activities of the Pan-African Association. On the whole, little information has been preserved concerning Sylvain's activities in Ethiopia, though a few references survive in Ethiopian historiography (Prouty 1986, 192, 202, 270, 277n; Pankhurst 1967, 65–67). By 1904, a manuscript of his travel impressions was ready but, for reasons Sylvain deliberately left unelucidated, he was not keen on publishing at that time, and probably died before being able to do so.

An intellectual and a pan-Africanist militant, Sylvain was close to other Haitian intellectuals like Anténor Firmin and engaged on several occasions in Haitian politics, although his commitment had an internationalist dimension. His last newspaper, *L'étoile africaine* (*African Star*), announced the creation of L'Oeuvre du relèvement social des Noirs (the Association for the Social Improvement of Blacks), founded in Rome in 1905 with the blessings of Pope Pius X. Sylvain was probably unwise in putting complete trust in the papacy, but the objectives, aimed at coordinating pan-African efforts and preserving the rights of the African race "too often despoiled, oppressed and vilified", confer on him the status of a key pioneer of the modern fight against racism (Sylvain 1906, 108).

In the wake of the battle of Adwa, the first great anti-colonial victory, the trajectory of Benito Sylvain reveals the extent to which the visibility of the modern Ethiopian state participated in the emergence of modern Ethiopianism and the construction of pan-Africanism. After Adwa, other factors also contributed to the gradual incarnation of Ethiopianism in representations of the state and of Ethiopian sovereigns, in particular the rise to power of *Ras* Tafari, the son of *Ras* Makonnen, whom Sylvain met (Bonacci 2013). In fact, after his victory, Menelik left the Italians established on the coast, and Franco-Ethiopian relations blossomed thanks to the "scientific" mission of Commander Marchand (1863–1934). However, the economic and social situation of the country was fragile, notwithstanding the stability preserved through several agreements establishing the borders with Eritrea, British Somalia, Anglo-Egyptian Sudan and Kenya (Berhanou Abebe 1998, 140–41). Menelik, who had been ill since 1906 and inactive since 1908, died in 1913, resulting in internecine conflicts over his succession. In his will, Menelik had designated *Lejj* Iyassu as his successor, but the intention of Taytu, the empress, was to leave the matter ambiguous, in an attempt to bring to the throne Zawditu, the daughter of Menelik. She was finally obliged to retreat to the palace, and *Bitwäddäd* Tessemma became regent. He was to prepare *Lejj* Iyassu for his future charge, but he died prematurely in 1911. As Iyassu had not come of age, he could not be crowned, but he travelled constantly throughout the empire. His numerous marriages, his sympathy for the Ottoman Empire and his leaning towards Islam made him a very controversial figure.

The First World War had begun, remapping European alliances, when France (which had recently signed the agreement for construction of the railway line between Awash and Addis Ababa), Great Britain and Italy approached the Ethiopian Council of Ministers to draw their attention to the internal and external dangers to which the young prince Iyassu was exposing his country. This was enough to provoke the coup d'état of 27 September 1916, in which the notables obtained from the *Abuna*, the head of the church, the agreement that they were released from the oath of fidelity to Menelik's testament. The *Abuna* publicly agreed. Zawditu, the daughter of Menelik, was named empress, and *Ras* Tafari, the son of *Ras* Makonnen, became heir to the throne. Iyassu tried to oppose this new policy by returning to Wollo to foment a rebellion, with his father *Negus* Mikael, but they were defeated and imprisoned. The reign of Zawditu and the regency of Tafari inaugurated a domestic policy centred around education and the consolidation of power, with the creation of the first modern college and the first printing press, *Berhanenna Selam* (light and peace), in 1925. The vicissitudes of Ethiopian domestic policy and these first efforts at modernization probably went unnoticed by the black communities of the world. To the contrary, Ethiopian foreign policy, in the charge of foreign legations opened by Menelik in Addis Ababa and Ethiopian legations in Paris, London and Rome, enabled Tafari to take control of foreign relations and to acquire international visibility (Berhanou Abebe 1998, 156–57).

Two interrelated political processes marked the regency of Tafari: the abolition of slavery in Ethiopia and membership in the League of Nations. Alain Rouaud's (1998) apt analysis of these processes may be summarized as follows: notwithstanding previous but unsuccessful measures against slavery taken by Tewodros, Yohannes IV and Menelik II, Europeans seized upon this issue, comparing slavery in Ethiopia to slavery in the Americas, in order to blackmail the Ethiopian government and suggest the division of Ethiopia as the way of ending these practices. For Tafari, who was aware of the implication of Europeans in this human traffic, the solution was to take measures against slavery in a bid to legitimize his power in the country and, ultimately, to gain entrance for Ethiopia to the League of Nations, the only way, in his opinion, of protecting the country from the colonial appetites of European powers. In 1922, a large press campaign was launched in Great Britain against the Ethiopian government, accused of weakness in facing the recrudescence of the slave trade, and Tafari promptly took severe steps to punish anyone involved in it. After prolonged hesitation regarding the potentials and the internal and external risks, the regent finally submitted the country's candidature to the League of Nations, with the support of France. In 1923, the fourth assembly of the admissions commission of the League of Nations, after heated debates, finally rendered a positive judgement. To prove the good faith of his government, Tafari published, in September 1923, a decree against slavery that was even more severe than the previous ones, and two weeks later, Ethiopia entered the League of Nations. Other decrees followed: a more complete one in 1924, and still another in 1931, setting new objectives. While the actual applications of these decrees progressed slowly, and though they were incapable of swiftly eradicating a practice that was widespread in the empire, these approaches nevertheless invested Ethiopia with an exceptional aura in the black world.

The abolition of slavery had a special resonance for the black people of the Americas, and Tafari's great voyage to Europe in 1924, following the Ethiopian accession to league membership, allowed the regent to emerge in images on the international scene and contributed to his prestige. Still, the duplicity of the Europeans on issues regarding slavery insinuated two elements which provoked debates in the black communities: the "slave-trading" stigma of the regent, but especially, the question of the identity of Ethiopians who, if they were slave owners, could, consequently, not be regarded as black. The question of colour and that of the identity of Ethiopians filled the contemporary literature produced in the Americas and seemed crucial for black intellectuals. The embodiment of Ethiopianism in the Ethiopian state and its representatives that started with Adwa became increasingly concrete with Tafari. The relations between Ethiopia and the black people of the world quickly developed, despite concerns with respect to the phenotype of Ethiopians.

Can the Ethiopian Change the Colour of His Skin?

The following interrogation expressed in 1946 by W.E.B. Du Bois (1946, 118) is a good introduction to the debates regarding the phenotype of Ethiopians:

> So here in Ethiopia, "Land of the Blacks", country of the "Burnt faces", we are continually faced with the silly paradox that these black folk were not Negroes. What then are Negroes? Who are Africans? Why has the whole history of Ethiopia been neglected or ascribed to white "Hamites"? And why does every historian and encyclopaedist, whenever he writes of the civilization of the upper Nile, feel compelled to reiterate that these black people were "not Negroes"?

By his reference to the "Hamites", Du Bois was echoing a hypothesis traversing African studies about the colour of the Hamites. This question was in fact symptomatic of the nature of the interracial relations which, changing over time, provoked various interpretations of the nature of this biblical people (Sanders 1969). At the heart of these discussions are the biblical references to Ham, the youngest son of Noah, cursed by his father (Genesis 9:18–29). Condemned to serve his brothers, Ham was ostensibly used as a divine legitimation of the subjection of black people to transatlantic slavery. The new hamitic conception elaborated at the beginning of the nineteenth century reversed this paradigm, especially with regard to explaining the origins of the great Egyptian civilization, with which Europeans had become more familiar in the wake of Napoleon's campaigns. Largely driven by the clergy, this reinterpretation indicated that only Canaan, son of Ham, was cursed, and not Ham himself. Consequently, the Egyptians were Caucasoid Hamites, had never been cursed and were capable of civilization.

Supported by American anthropology and philology, the new hamitic theory developed and was firmly established at the beginning of the twentieth century. Supplanting theology, science affirmed that the Hamites were a branch of the Caucasian race that had gone to Africa, were not endogenous to the continent and spoke a specific family of hamitic languages. By extension, the Hamites, often described through their activity, pastoralism, thus gained a cultural identity, and all the traces of civilization found in Africa were attributed to these "foreigners" who had come from elsewhere. It is only the era of independence that historians, freed from colonial bonds, finally began to express doubts about the viability of these interpretations, which nevertheless had made a great impact (Sanders 1969).

Regarding Ethiopia, it might be an erroneous shortcut to evoke the application by European historiography of this new hamite theory dating from the beginning of the nineteenth century. However, certain aspects of historiography, dominant until the 1970s, are relatively close to this tendency in certain respects, notably in the effort to attribute ancient Ethiopian civilization to external factors alone. The "Semites", who supposedly came to Ethiopia from the south of

Arabia, were thus credited with the origins of the Ethiopian civilization of the highlands. Given the weight of the theories of philologists and orientalists in historiography, ancient Ethiopia, limited to the Kingdom of Axum, became the cornerstone of Ethiopian history and identity, thereby obscuring the memory of the cultural contributions of the kushite, omotic and nilotic linguistic groups (Teshale Tibebu 1995, xvi–xvii, xxiii–xiv).

The question of the "race" of the Ethiopians was in fact as important for blacks as it was for whites. The best way of approaching these debates is to draw a parallel between the lavish invitations of the Ethiopian government to the black people of the world and the way in which Europeans reacted to the resulting thin but steady migratory flow. As early as the reign of Menelik, several black persons had taken the road to Ethiopia. Benito Sylvain mentioned "the incredible hostility on the part of Europeans" (1906, 108), and the Caribbeans and African Americans who followed him learned this at their expense.

Little is known about Joseph Vitalien, a Martinican (Scott 1993, 201) or Guadeloupian (Pankhurst 1967, 65–66; Prouty 1986, 283; Lara 2000, 184–85) doctor, who was born in 1868, arrived in Djibouti in 1899 and became, in 1904, the personal doctor of Emperor Menelik (Pankhurst 1967, 65). In 1909, Dr Vitalien told a journalist of the *Journal de Paris* newspaper:

> It has been ten years since my appointment by the Emperor: I was living in a village in Burgundy, friends pressed me to go there; I went to the country of the Abyssinians, among the Gallas, my black brothers; I was going to organize a medical camp in Djibouti. One day, Ras Makonnen summoned me; it was a twelve days walk from the coast, through the Somali deserts. I did a few cures, I became the doctor and councillor of Ras Mahonnen [*sic*]; then Menelik said: "I am the king, the good doctor is mine." Makonnen accompanied me to the court of the Negus. And I became his doctor. (Quoted in Lara 2000, 184–85)

The reasons that spurred Vitalien to undertake the long voyage to Ethiopia remain unclear, but his competence did not go unnoticed at the court. In addition to his medical responsibilities, the education of the young Tafari was entrusted to him, before his replacement by Monseigneur Jarousseau (Berhanou Abebe 1998, 163). Dr Mérab, a naturalized Frenchman originally of Georgian nationality, who arrived in Ethiopia in 1908, reports his contempt for Vitalien: "a negro from Guadeloupe, originally from the Slave Coast, mounted from the Lower Niger to the Upper Nile; under the pretext of curing people, he got into politics . . . but one soon discovered the kind of wolf that had entered the devastated sheepfold disguised as a shepherd" (Mérab 1912, 212).

While Vitalien was highly respected at the court (Prouty 1986, 283–84, 292), Mérab wrongly stressed that Emperor Menelik was as "horrified" by the Negro doctor as he was by another, an Indochinese, who arrived a few years later. Dr Mérab hated Vitalien and used many terms, like "Black Skin", "*mano negra*", "black tongue", "termites of French influence", to refer to him without ever using his name. He indicated that "the skin of the negro, regardless of its hue, washed off on all those who approached it" and that "the negro, whose soul was darker than his skin, had returned from Europe" and was "incapable by heredity of appreciating the honour" of a promise (Mérab 1912, 213–14). Despite this congenital biological specificity attributed to his colleague, Dr Mérab was, however, unable to prevent Dr Vitalien from becoming, in 1909, the director of the country's first hospital, the Menelik II Hospital, opened in Harar (Robbins 1933, 69). Besides, it would seem that Menelik offered to Dr Vitalien the post of minister of public health, although foreigners, in spite of their influence in the creation of the first cabinet of the emperor in 1907, were excluded from membership. Facing the opposition of the European powers of the day, the French Ministry of Foreign Affairs apparently asked Vitalien to decline the offer (Pankhurst 1967, 66–67). In one of his multiple reports sent to the French government, Vitalien expressed the matter as follows: "I can also assure you . . . that Menelik urgently pressed me to take the ministry of Public Health which he had created for me, but I knew that by accepting, I would provoke the susceptibilities of Rome and London, so I refused to become a Minister for the Negus and devoted myself entirely to my more modest but useful role as a missionary doctor" (quoted by Lara 2000, 185).

Whether in Rome, London or Paris, the foreign legations shared Dr Mérab's colour prejudice and disapproved of public responsibilities being held by blacks, even those of French nationality. This was the same type of disapproval that William H. Ellis (Guillaume Enriques Ellesio) experienced. Born in Texas near 1865, Ellis was a mixed-blood polyglot with Cuban and Mexican parents. He was an entrepreneur with several lines of business speculation in cotton and wool, brokerage on Wall Street, and management of industrial fortunes. He met with *Ras* Makonnen and *Käntiba* Gebru Desta, mayor of Gondar, in London, during the coronation of King Edward VII in 1902, and was invited to visit Ethiopia. He made the journey in 1903, accompanied by the Haitian Benito Sylvain, who was on his third voyage, thus becoming perhaps the first African American to visit Ethiopia, with the responsibility of presenting Menelik with the first trade treaty signed between Ethiopia and the United States. The unique source on this event is a long article by Richard Pankhurst assembling information on Ellis's trajectory, a few elements of which will be recalled below (Pankhurst 1972).

William Ellis was primarily interested in trade and paid great attention to the opportunities offered by Ethiopia, where he hoped to develop the banking sector as well as wide-scale cotton production, on concessions offered by the emperor. Following the arrival of Robert P. Skinner, the American consul in France, in Ethiopia at the end of 1903, the American authorities proved reticent to entrust to a coloured person the continuation of negotiations for the establishment of a trade relation between the two countries. Skinner insistently defined Ethiopia as "Caucasian Kushite" and Ethiopians as "Caucasian Semites". Seeking to establish a difference – or even racial antagonism – between Ethiopians and African Americans, he claimed to be sure of the fact that Menelik himself identified as Caucasian (Negusse Ayele 2003, 48). Notwithstanding the prejudices of the American consul, Ellis was a member of the subsequent mission, owing to his closeness to the emperor and his knowledge of the country. He thus returned to Ethiopia in 1904 to ratify the document. Although he was a figure often discussed in the American press, it remains regrettable that, "for most of his life, we are able to see him only through the eyes of an essentially hostile white press, interested in sensational news, written by journalists whose traditions forced them to ridicule or disparage their black compatriots" (Pankhurst 1972, 110).

Ellis, who claimed to have "African blood" and to be "racially related to Menelik" (Pankhurst 1972, 105, 103), helped to connect the emperor with the American philanthropist Andrew Carnegie, who supported the education of blacks. In a letter dated November 1903, Menelik thanked Carnegie for his "gift to the African Americans of the United States, to assist and help" their educational development (Pankhurst 1972, 93). Ellis's will to link the situation of blacks to bilateral commercial projects in the making was realized in 1911 in a contract between Germany and the United States – a document founding a trading company in Ethiopia, entirely reproduced by Pankhurst. Extremely comprehensive, studying the commercial possibilities in minerals, cattle, agricultural products as well as target markets and proposing a financial plan, this contract seems to be the first document to propose the sending of African Americans to Ethiopia. From the beginning, at the time of the presentation of the parties, it was specified that Ellis was "connected by blood to the Hamitic races" and that, added to his great experience as an entrepreneur, he was an inevitable actor in the installation of this company. Under the heading "labour", the idea was formulated "to import several hundreds of African Americans from the United States of America to Abyssinia" as teachers or foremen, in view of transmitting specific skills like the cultivation of wheat or cotton (Pankhurst 1972, 113–14). This commercial project never received the financial support of the American authorities that Ellis had expected. The announcement of Menelik's death in 1913 suspended all commercial prerogatives and left hanging the issue of the land concessions the emperor had given to Ellis and, through him, to the Americans.

Daniel Alexander was, for his part, spared the prejudices of the westerners. This was surely due to the fact that although he was also Menelik's protégé, he occupied no official or governmental position and did not seek to become a relay between Ethiopia and foreign governments. Originating in Missouri, it appears that Daniel R. Alexander was a missionary as well as a blacksmith, who arrived in Ethiopia in 1908 (Scott 1993, 86). He established a farm not far from Addis Ababa and had "many servants and cattle on his property" (Robbins 1933, 69). He is often regarded as the first African American who settled in Ethiopia. Very little information has been preserved concerning him, but he remained in the country at least until 1935. It is, moreover, probable that the group of black Americans who settled in the 1920s and formed a "community on the Amhara highlands" mentioned by historian Angelo Del Boca (1969, 38) in fact refers to Alexander's estate, which hosted several visitors at the time. However, the assertion that, in a letter dictated on his deathbed by Menelik in 1909, six million acres of land were reserved for black people desirous of "returning home", while not improbable, could not be verified (Ellison 1977, 76).

Once Tafari took over the regency, and especially the foreign affairs of the empire, new dynamics came into play. Without ceasing to take advantage of the passage and competence of African Americans or Caribbeans visiting Ethiopia, Tafari, through a policy of overture and invitation, offered, on several occasions, the opportunity to the black people of the world to come and settle in Ethiopia in order to contribute to the country's development. The first opportunity arose in 1919 when the Ethiopian government sent a delegation to the United States to congratulate Belgium, Great Britain, France and the United States for their successful conclusion of the First World War. *Däjazmač* Nadew, a nephew of Empress Zawditu, in command of the imperial army, as well as *Blatténguéta* Heruy Wolde Selassie, the mayor of Addis Ababa; *Käntiba* Gebru, the mayor of Gondar; and *Ato* Sinkas, the secretary of Nadew, made up this delegation. The American vice-consul in Aden, Addison E. Southard, was also posted to Ethiopia and had warned the American authorities of the risks this delegation might incur regarding the colour line in place in America and the repercussions on the budding relations between the two countries.

The black American press gave wide coverage to this visit, which African Americans saw as an important occasion "to identify with the official representatives of an independent African country, one that figured prominently in their heritage" (Harris 1994, 4). Given a warm welcome by the US government, the Ethiopians nevertheless experienced American-style racial discrimination when the entry to a New York club was refused them on the pretext of colour. The very next business day, the affair made the headlines of newspapers, and this unpleasant experience contributed to erasing in the United States the notion of a racial difference between African Americans and Ethiopians (5). Of even greater importance, *Käntiba* Gebru launched a call for emigration to Ethiopia. Educated in Switzerland, he had already met Benito Sylvain and William Ellis. His invitation to black Americans encouraged them to get involved in the development of Ethiopia, and many of them later declared that they were inspired by this message (6). Marcus Garvey's UNIA had obtained permission from *Däjazmač* Nadew to address the Ethiopian public, but the authorities obstructed the opening of the space that was to accommodate them (Hill 1983, 1:459–60). But the address was merely delayed, since in August 1922 Mr Topakyan, the consul general of Persia, who was then the representative of the Ethiopian government in the United States, gave Marcus Garvey a letter read *in absentia* during the third UNIA convention. This message from the "King and Queen of the cradle of civilization, Abyssinia", extending an invitation to settle in Ethiopia, was welcomed with sustained applause: "Assure them [members of the UNIA] of the cordiality with which I invite them back to the home land, particularly those qualified to help solve our big problems, and to develop our vast resources, teachers, artisans, mechanics, writers, musicians, professional men, women, all who are able to lend a hand in the constructive work which our country so deeply feels and greatly needs" (Hill 1985, 4:1006–7).

Thereafter, the invitation was reiterated through the intermediary of *Azaž* Workneh Esheté (Dr Charles Martin), a doctor then ambassador in London. Passing through the United States in 1927 for diplomatic discussions concerning the construction of a large dam on Lake Tanna, he met a delegation of African Americans and encouraged "farmers, engineers, mechanics, physicians, dentists" and the like to come to Ethiopia (Harris 1994, 6; Garretson 2012, 159–60). He assured them that they would receive land and good wages, but no one left with him for Ethiopia. In July 1930, Southard, who had become the representative of the United States to Ethiopia, addressed a lengthy report to the department, in which he stressed that "new developments in Ethiopian attitudes toward foreigners appear to tend toward a distinct favouring of those with dark skins" (Harris 1994, 8). Southard recognized that the modernization of Ethiopia required foreign professionals and technicians, but he worried about the attitude of Tafari, who had pointed out the arrogance of certain of these white foreigners. He suggested solving the problem by engaging more black professionals, to prevent Ethiopians from bearing the brunt of these feelings of superiority.

These various initiatives promoted by Tafari might appear marginal when compared to other international political developments but are nonetheless extremely important. For the first time, a policy of requesting help from the black communities of the United States was directly put into practice by the Ethiopian authorities. The classic identification with Ethiopia was thus renewed by the appearance on the international scene of the official representatives of the Ethiopian state, guided by the hand of Tafari. A growing consciousness of common interests and a common destiny was one of the results of these invitations. Though the invitations were not immediately honoured, African American nationalists were nevertheless inspired by these events and various popular organizations were formed following these contacts, including the Star Order of Ethiopia and the Ethiopian Missionaries to Abyssinia, founded by Cleveland Redding (Harris 1994, 7). The invariable reservations of the Europeans in Addis

Ababa regarding both these invitations and the slow but steady migratory flow revealed their thoroughly racist mentalities, which was nowhere near depletion. For the European powers, it was dangerous to allow this identification and cooperation between Ethiopia and the black people of the world to develop beyond their control. On several occasions, Ethiopians on official visits had denied that they were "Negroes", a reaction which was not at all surprising. Why would they want to identify with a second-class American population which was socially and economically marginalized, segregated, and lynched? Besides, Ethiopian officials never used term *Negroes* but rather the term *African* to refer to black people.[25] The regent's pan-African policy, activated by these contacts, messages, invitations, meetings, has to date been ignored by Ethiopian historiography, gave the lie to the then current allegations that Ethiopians were not, or did not regard themselves as, black people.

Ethiopia, whose representation had been nourished by biblical textuality and the first anti-colonial victory at Adwa, became, thanks to Tafari, more and more "real". The apogee of this incarnation was the consecration of Tafari as *negusä nägäst*, King of Kings, on 2 November 1930, following his coronation on 7 October 1928 when he had become *negus*, king. The base of his power was consolidated and he took the name and the symbolically loaded titles of Haile Selassie I (Power of the Trinity), Conquering Lion of the Tribe of Judah, King of Kings, Lord of the Lords, Elect of God, Emperor of Ethiopia. The emperor in ceremonial apparel made the front page of many newspapers and magazines, and in addition to the official guests at the coronation, many journalists, curiosity seekers and visitors took the opportunity to travel to Ethiopia. The relations between Ethiopia and the black people of the world were strengthened. The fortune of modern Ethiopianism was established and Rastafari was born in its wake. More and more black migrants tried to settle in what had been the ancient kingdom of the Queen of Sheba, and had now become the modern incarnation of black power.

EHIOPIANISM WAS AN IDEOLOGICAL MATRIX CREATED AROUND THE name and symbolism of Ethiopia circulating in the black worlds. Based on a biblical substrate, the name Ethiopia became synonymous with Africa and the black race, operating a symbolic inversion for the black people of the Americas living in societies that had barely moved beyond slavery. In the face of a historiography opening little or no dialogue between Ethiopianism in Africa and Ethiopianism in the United States, I have used "Ethiopian belt" to designate the spaces in which Ethiopianism was alive and in circulation. In defining the notion of modern Ethiopianism, I have highlighted the moments and the reasons which moved this imaginary of Ethiopia towards its incarnation in the structures and representatives of the Ethiopian state. Progressing beyond symbolism, the tangible relations between Ethiopia and the black people of the world took shape thanks to the first – frequently Caribbean – migrants to Ethiopia. They were supported by the Ethiopians, who on several occasions deployed a pan-African policy by inviting black professionals to emigrate, despite the racism of the majority of Europeans residing in Ethiopia. The events of the 1930s and the beginning of the settlement in Shashemene form the object of the following chapter.

CHAPTER 3

FIRST STEPS OF THE RETURN TO SHASHEMENE

IN ORDER TO ELUCIDATE THE FIRST STEPS OF the return to Shashemene, it is crucial to consider a number of interrelated dynamics. The objective of the present chapter is to identify and explicate them. Following the 1930 coronation of Haile Selassie I, the Italo-Ethiopian war (1935–41) contributed to the dissemination of a sentiment of racial and international solidarity with Ethiopia that included religious and political variations. The arrival in Ethiopia of Caribbean migrants who identified with the country highlights how the "Ethiopian nation" took shape outside Ethiopia. This chapter will focus in particular on the ways in which the creation, in 1937, of the Ethiopian World Federation (EWF), a pro-Ethiopian organization in New York, contributed to the nurturing of this sentiment. Retracing the process which brought Haile Selassie I to offer to this organization land on the periphery of Shashemene will allow us to clarify the convergence of two ideologies and their practices: Ethiopianism and the return to Africa. The first arrivants in Shashemene illustrate a turning point at which the prestige of Ethiopia was losing ground in the face of the African independences. At this stage, the expressions of Ethiopianism swung from the United States to Jamaica.

The Universal Ethiopian Anthem and Arnold J. Ford

The Universal Ethiopian Anthem was declared the "hymn of the black race" during the First Convention of the Negro Peoples of the World organized by Marcus Garvey in New York in 1920 (Hill 1983, 2:575). This equivalent of a national anthem for a black nation without a territory comprises three verses and a refrain:[1]

I
Ethiopia thou land of our fathers
Thou land where the gods loved to be,

As storm cloud at night suddenly gathers
Our armies come rushing to thee.
We must in fight be victorious
When swords are thrust outward to gleam;
For us will the vict'ry be glorious
When led by the red, black and green

Chorus
Advance, advance to victory,
Let Africa be free
Advance to meet the foe
With the might
Of the red, the black and the green

II
Ethiopia, the tyrant's falling
Who smote thee upon thy knees,
And thy children are lustily calling
From over the distant seas;
Jehovah the great one, has heard us,
Has noted our sighs and our tears,
With His spirit of Love He has stirred us
To be the One through the coming years

III
Oh Jehovah the God of the ages,
Grant unto our sons that lead
The wisdom Thou gave to Thy sages,
When Israel was sore in need.
Thy voice thro' the dim past has spoken,
Ethiopia shall stretch forth her hand,
By Thee shall all fetters be broken,
And Heav'n bless our dear fatherland

Like most national anthems, the Universal Ethiopian Anthem was a song of war, struggle and, finally, victory, identifying the elements that constitute a nation, and operating through a series of analogies. The nation was embodied by Ethiopia, "the land of our fathers", to which was attributed a prophetic destiny marked by the allusion to Psalm 68, "Ethiopia shall stretch forth her hands [unto God]", characteristic of the corpus of Ethiopianism. The terms Ethiopia and Africa figure in this hymn as a single national entity whose "sons" are compared to Israel's "children" scattered across the seas, sending their cries up to the "God of all the ages". An "Ethiopian nation" was created, one in which thousands of UNIA members took part. The posterity of this hymn went far beyond Garvey's organization. It was the result of various reappropriations by religious congregations and popular or secular organizations, which gave form to an imagined multi-sited "Ethiopian nation" located within the spaces of the African diaspora. Subsequent to the practice of UNIA members in the 1920s, it was sung by "Ethiopian" activists in the United States up until the 1950s.[2] In Jamaica, starting with the first generation of Rastafari, who were Garveyites, the hymn has been sung continuously and is currently known and sung by Rastafari within and beyond Jamaica. The Universal Ethiopian Anthem is like a thread running through the century, which, once unravelled and followed, might prove capable of revealing the forms of this "Ethiopian nation" getting ready to "go home" (Bonacci 2014).

The first member of this "Ethiopian nation" to make the return to Ethiopia was Arnold Josiah Ford (1877–1935), a co-author of the anthem. The other co-author was Benjamin Ebenezer Burrell (1892–1959), a Jamaican who arrived in the United States in 1917 and worked for a time in the military industry before resuming his initial profession as a journalist. He did not remain a UNIA member for long, and in July 1920, he began co-editing, with his brother, Theophilus, the *Crusader*, the official organ of the African Blood Brotherhood, founded in 1919 by Cyril Briggs. From the Caribbean island of St Kitts, Briggs arrived in the United States in 1905. African Blood Brotherhood was opposed to Garvey, and Burrell became its director of historical research. He was later involved in various trade union organizations (Hill 1983, 1:227; James 1998, 155–84). Arnold Josiah Ford followed quite another trajectory. Born in Barbados, he was a composer, musician, linguist and theologian. He had been a member of the musical corps of the British Royal Navy during the First World War (Hill 1983, 2:398). Arriving in Harlem after the First World War, he joined a congregation of black Jews (Ottley 1943, 144). The members of the congregations of black Jews, then in full development, identified with both the Hebrews and the Ethiopians – a matter to which we will return in a moment. Thanks to his exhaustive study of the Torah, the Talmud and Hebrew, Ford rose to the position of rabbi. Like many Caribbeans and black Jews in Harlem, he joined Marcus Garvey's organization, the UNIA, and became its musical director.

Besides the Universal Ethiopian Anthem, he composed many songs, twenty-one of which are collected in a booklet entitled the Universal Ethiopian Hymnal.[3] Filled with biblical references, these songs of a religious nature are representative of the variety of cultural influences present in Harlem at the time. Some of these songs popularized expressions such as "Awake!" or "Perfect Love", while others used the name of Africa in their title; one song quotes the UNIA slogan: "One God, One Aim, One Destiny", and others still, like "God Bless Our President" and the Potentate's Hymn, are devoted to the glorification of Garvey. While the song "Ethiopia's Children" popularized, ten years before the coronation of Haile Selassie I, the title King of Kings and Lord of Lords, others are in praise of Allah and allude to mosques. Four songs indicate that they are "derived from the Hebrews". Ford inevitably became a figure in the small New York community of black Jews. After the decline of the UNIA in 1925, he founded the House of the Sons of Abraham, *Beth B'nai Abraham*. Despite schisms and divisions, Ford established his congregation and choir, continued to teach Hebrew and to preach the Ethiopian identity of the "true Jews" (Landes 1967, 180–83).

In his brilliant depiction of the Harlem of the first half of the twentieth century, Jervis Anderson showed that "Black Jew" was an epithet frequently used to designate Caribbeans in Harlem. It referred to their professional over-representation and their business reputation (Anderson 1982, 301–4). This usage is also referenced by Christine Chivallon, who mentions the "myth of the black Jew" labelling West Indians, and Jamaicans in particular, laying the foundation of the reputation of a dynamic ethnic minority within US society (Chivallon 2004, 100). "Black Jew" referred to the migrant communities originating in the Caribbean. It alludes to their commercial vitality but also to the many preachers and congregations of the same name. Such communities, in which these same Caribbeans were highly involved, mushroomed in the nineteenth century in the large North American cities where they lived. The numerical weight of the black Jewish congregations is hard to determine. It varies between a minimalist approximation, in the 1920s, indicating at least eight congregations in Harlem (Brotz 1964, 10), and a maximalist one, in the 1930s, counting ten thousand black Jews in New York and a few hundred thousand in the United States (Ottley 1943, 142). But we do well to recall that these congregations were mobile and characterized by their variability (Moors 1967, 175). The conditions of creation of the forms of worship and temples of the black Jews has been addressed by James Landing (2002) and Jacob Dorman (2004), whose work updates the links between the black Jews, the world of rural Pentecostalism in the US South and that of the practioners of "science", of freemasonry and of the occult. Beginning with the eighteenth- and nineteenth-century identification with the biblical Hebrews in bondage, continuing with association of the black Jews with the twelve tribes of Israel, numerous reappropriations have emerged, based on readings of the Old Testament.

Yvonne Chireau (2000, 16) pinpoints two recurrent themes of these encounters between the Jewish people and the black people. First, there are the analogies between the experiences of the Jewish people and those of the black people, notably their common history of dispersion, slavery, persecution and emancipation. These analogies facilitated various appropriations of Judaism by black congregations through the adoption of the languages and written symbolism, and via the creation of specific rituals. Then, there is the self-identification of the black people as Jews through a double symbolic association. The black Jews identified with the people of Israel and recognized in the mythical encounter between King Solomon and the Queen of Sheba the foundation of a line of Ethiopian and Hebrew kings, coming down to the Emperor of Ethiopia, Haile

Selassie I[4] (Brotz 1964, 18, 51). Paintings and portraits of the emperor were prominently displayed in certain synagogues (Trevisan Semi 2002, 95). The Jewish idea of a chosen people was reappropriated to affirm that the descendants of Africans, called Ethiopians, were chosen by God for a specific mission in his plan of redemption (Chireau 2000, 20). The black Jews therefore reconnected with Ethiopianism, to which they gave a new interpretation, contemporaneous with those that permeated black religious and nationalist movements. The presence in the Harlem of 1920s and 1930s of Jacques Faitlovitch, a Polish Jew born in 1881, engaged alongside the Ethiopian Jews (*Falashas* or *Béta Israel*) in missions of education and information, helped to maintain this cultural matrix ready to find its roots in Ethiopia (Trevisan Semi 2002, 92–93). The news of Faitlovitch's "discovery" of Jews in Ethiopia enabled the Harlem congregations to identify "scientifically" with this social group, which was both Jewish and Ethiopian (Brotz 1964, 49).

In 1930, Arnold J. Ford decided to leave for Ethiopia with some members of his synagogue. He thus contributed "to materialize" the relation between the black Jews of Harlem and those of Ethiopia and to feed the imaginary of Ethiopian identity and of "return" to Ethiopia. With the support of donations from almost six hundred members of his congregation, Ford set off for Ethiopia in 1930. Countering the claim that he was a co-founder of the Nation of Islam (Brotz 1964, 11), the historian William Scott (1993, 181–84) has offered one the best accounts of Ford's settlement in Ethiopia. Accompanied by Eudora Paris, a singer who was well known in the circles of Harlem nationalists, and by Mr Jackman and Mr Helliger, he later attended the coronation of Emperor Haile Selassie I, in November 1930. Despite the death of Helliger at sea, the small party met with Daniel Alexander, who had settled in 1908, with Herbert Julian, a Harlem aviator in residence there since the spring of 1930, with Mrs Hattie Kofi, a Garveyite from New York, and a few others. In a handwritten letter dated 5 June 1931 and addressed to Rabbi Matthew, another important figure among the black Jews in Harlem, Ford mentioned his cordial relations with the emperor and the Ethiopian nobility, pressed the rabbi to gather money for the purpose of "building and development", and insisted: "Do wake up."[5] In rather authoritative terms, he asked Matthew to write letters, to mobilize congregations and to encourage their speedy migration and settlement. This anxiety was due to the opportunities which, he said, had been opened up by the Ethiopian authorities: "I have told them, we want homes for ourselves and our generations for ever, we want religious freedom, we want farms, horses, mules, cattle poultry and opportunity for work on the great dam, we want land in that vicinity. All of these things they have granted us. Yes, with love and goodwill, they have answered Yes. Go ahead. Come. Build. Occupy. "[6]

There are two interpretations of Ford's stay in Ethiopia. Jacob Dorman (2004, 292–93) stressed that Ford's project was "to occupy" and "to civilize" the country, like the Italians, who were already in the process of preparing their invasion of Ethiopia. Yet Ford's correspondence shows greater concern with the responsibility of establishing a viable settlement than with the pretension of civilizing the country. Dorman also underlined that the Ethiopians treated Ford and his disciples badly because of their colour. While underlining, rightly, that the Ethiopians had cultural prejudices regarding the darker populations living in the south of the country, the historian drew on the work of C.S. Coon to show that Caribbeans experienced racial prejudice (1935, 293–94). A specialist in the biology-oriented field of physical anthropology, Coon travelled at the same period to Ethiopia to carry out cranial measurements, but his mission came up against all kinds of obstacles and could not be concluded. Coon was in fact a racist American who supported Italy's "noble idea" of "civiliz[ing] a people with an ancient culture", and his condescension regarding the settlement of African Americans is therefore not surprising (145, 139).[7] For William Scott, who did several interviews with members of this small community, the relations between the Ethiopian elite and the members of Rabbi Ford's group were characterized by "a large dose of good will and harmony" (1971, 2). Consequently, Eudora Paris, who arrived at the same time as Ford, performed at several receptions at the palace, and she and her mother became dressmakers in great demand by the ladies of the Ethiopian nobility. The connections with several important families gave them access to certain privileges and Scott interprets these relations as the mark "of a partial absorption into the Ethiopian elite" (15). Scott underlines how the prejudices of the diplomatic missions, French and American especially, often capitalized on the traditional prejudices of the Amharas and the Tigreans, thus contributing to the circulation of the image of tense relations between African Americans and Ethiopians (24).

Little information is available on the reactions of the Ethiopian government to the Jewish identity of these Caribbean migrants who came from the United States, but Ethiopian Jews (*Falashas* or *Béta Israel*) were generally ostracized. The black Jews of Harlem were perhaps primarily regarded as foreigners rather than assimilated with Ethiopian Jews. Notwithstanding the contrasted interpretations of Scott and Dorman, the position of Rabbi Ford in Ethiopia was not completely in phase with that of the residents of Harlem. The repeated invitations extended to black Americans, the cordiality of the Ethiopian elites and the support offered on the spot contrasted with the concrete means of action of the congregations of Harlem who lacked capital, had limited competence and no diplomatic or commercial support. Ford's greatest problem was his inability to respond to the Ethiopian opportunities and expectations, thus impairing the efforts of the black congregations he represented.

Two years after Rabbi Ford, another group arrived, encouraged by the good news received from Ethiopia. The arrivants included the parents of Eudora Paris, Nancy and Thomas Paris; Albertha Thomas; Jane Foster; Ada and Augustine

Bastian; and Mignon Innes from Barbados, who later married Rabbi Ford. They were all from the Caribbean, mainly the Virgin Islands, and had all been involved in Marcus Garvey's movement and/or Ford's congregation, *Beth B'nai Abraham* (Scott 1971, 14). By 1930, almost a hundred African Americans and Caribbeans were present in Ethiopia. The majority originated in the most modest social classes, but some possessed technical skills that were extremely useful in Ethiopia. There was William Weeks, who was already advanced in years, a clock- and watchmaker from Harlem; John Sandiford, a cabinetmaker; Oswald Nanton, a carpenter; James Alexander Hart, a mechanic from British Guiana; George A. Smith, who taught first in Addis Ababa, then in Dire Dawa, where he organized the Ethiopian Boy Scouts Association; and Mr Helweig, to whom *Käntiba* Gebru gave land (18–20). In 1934, several African Americans were attached to the ministries of education and of public health, like John B. West from Washington, a graduate of Howard University who came with his wife, and Dr Reuben S. Young from New York, who served as a medical officer in the municipality of Dire Dawa. The factotum of the American major L.B. Roberts, who had designed the road to Lake Tana in 1930, was a black man from Georgia named John Henry Ware.

In the terms of a white American visitor, most of the African Americans in Ethiopia were there "to build roads, kill monkeys for their skin, open hairdressing salons, offer dental care, teach the jazz and *spirituals*, . . . open cabarets and cinemas" (Robbins 1933, 69). One such business in Addis Ababa, called Tambourine, was opened by a Corsican. African Americans artists performed there, the singer Eudora Paris played the piano and records received from the United States. She was accompanied by Ford, who played the banjo for a foreign audience comprising Frenchmen, Belgians, Italians and Germans (Coon 1935, 130–34). This small community participated in the social life of Addis Ababa thanks to its skills in the craft industry or entertainment, but thanks also to positions of responsibility in the sectors of education and health. This tendency would have progressed in all likelihood in spite of the death of Thomas Paris and Arnold J. Ford in 1935, but the approach of the Italian invasion put an end to its development. Most African Americans were obliged to leave Ethiopia in 1936, except Albertha Tomas and Mignon Ford, who was by then a widow (Harris 1994, 151). Difficult years arrived, during which the social and political landscape of Ethiopia was greatly disrupted, while Ethiopia emerged forcefully on the international scene.

"The Rape of Abyssinia"

Since his march on Rome in October 1922, Mussolini had come to power and had submitted the country, the administrative organs of the state and the people to a Fascist dictatorship. When his claims on Austria failed in 1934, Mussolini went elsewhere in search of glory and power, and Africa was envisaged as a possible space for these accomplishments. He had, for a few years, been harbouring the project of resuming his campaign against Ethiopia. All he needed was a pretext, provided by the Walwal incident of December 1934. Walwal, a frontier post between Italian Somaliland and Ethiopia, was invaluable for its many wells situated on the Ethiopian side but was occupied by the Italians. A conflict arose between Italian and Ethiopian forces, following which the Italians demanded reparations unacceptable in the eyes of the Ethiopians. Ethiopia brought the conflict before the League of Nations, while both sides began preparing for war. At the beginning of 1935, with the volte-face of France and the support of England, which feared the alliance between Mussolini and Nazi Germany, Italy had free rein in this situation. In October 1935, directly before the League of Nations judgement condemning the Italian aggression at Walwal, the Fascist armies crossed the Marab river and invaded Ethiopia. They took Adwa and rapidly established themselves in Meqele. The war escalated with Marshal Badoglio at the head of the Italian corps and with the use of chemical gases, prohibited by the Geneva Convention of 1925. The Ethiopians finally riposted in January 1936 but were crushed by the Italian air force. The battle of Maychaw, on 31 March, sealed the Italian military victory in the north, while Marshal Graziani was arriving from the south. Numerical superiority, more advanced military technology and more effective logistics transformed the Italians into formidable combatants who entered Addis Ababa on 5 May 1936, satisfied with their revenge for the humiliation at Adwa in 1896. Haile Selassie I was the first Ethiopian emperor to face the choice of exile. Shortly before the fall of the capital, he took the train to Djibouti, passed through Jerusalem, then Geneva; he was hosted in Bath, England, while Ethiopia was organizing popular resistance (Bahru Zewde 2000, 166–76). The aggression against Ethiopia had a vast international impact and was particularly upsetting for the black populations for whom the Ethiopian nation was the compelling symbol of freedom in an Africa divided up among European powers. The sentiment of indignation and the spontaneous popular opposition to the war have been studied in their African (Asante 1977), American (Venturini 1990; Scott 1993; Watkins-Owens 1996) and Caribbean (Yelvington 1999) dimensions and traverse most of the works on twentieth-century pan-Africanism (Esedebe 1994; Meriwether 2002; Edwards 2003; Fikru Negash Gebrekidan 2005).

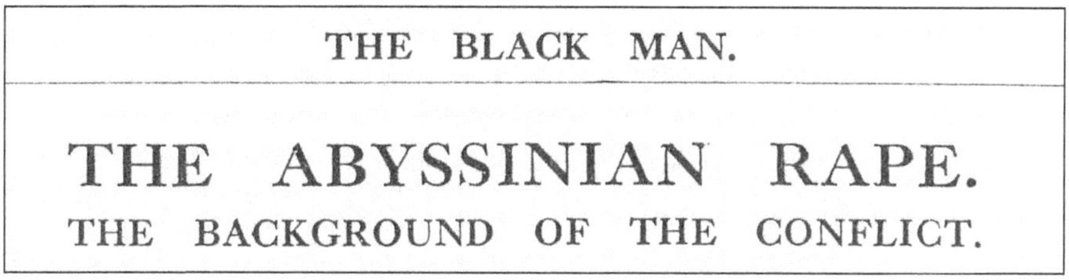

THE BLACK MAN.

THE ABYSSINIAN RAPE.

THE BACKGROUND OF THE CONFLICT.

Figure 3.1. *Black Man* 1, no. 19 (August–September 1935): 16. © DR.

The Black American Mobilization

The Italo-Ethiopian war contributed to the crystallization of the feelings of racial solidarity and to the redefinition of the relations between Africans and Afro-descendants. In the United States, the popular mobilization was unprecedented and, as noted by the historian John Hope Franklin, with the Italian invasion of Ethiopia, "almost overnight even the most provincial among Negro Americans became international-minded" (Franklin and Moss 1988, 385). Very quickly, riots broke out, in Harlem especially, between black and Italian communities at odds over the fate of Ethiopia (Venturini 1990). The black press capitalized on the news of the war and its consequences and continuously relayed information, points of view and analyses of the events and their symbolic meaning. The Trinidadian pan-Africanist George Padmore, who was then in London, expressed in these terms the feeling that traversed the black communities:

> The brutal rape of Ethiopia combined with the cynical attitude of the Great Powers convinced Africans and peoples of African descent everywhere that black men had no rights which white men felt bound to respect if they stood in the way of their imperial interests. . . . With the realization of their utter defenselessness against the new aggression from Europeans in Africa, the blacks felt it necessary to look to themselves. (1971, 123–24)

Seeking "to take care of themselves", black intellectuals and activists created many associations whose objective was to support the Ethiopian cause and to defend the black race. To take a few American examples: by 1934, the Ethiopian Research Council was founded by the anthropologist W. Leo Hansberry (Harris 1994, 20–28), and in February 1935 delegates of twenty Harlem organizations, including the UNIA and Masonic lodges, created the Provisional Committee for the Defense of Ethiopia. Journalist Robert F.S. Harris organized the Committee for Ethiopia, and Dr Willis N. Huggins, after meeting with Ethiopian ministers in France and England, founded in Harlem the Friends of Ethiopia in the United States. Other associations were also created: the Medical Committee for the Defense of Ethiopia, the Pan-African Reconstruction Association, the Menelik Club and United Aid for Ethiopia, which already federated the activities of several groups. The activities of these pro-Ethiopian groups took various forms: petitions and appeals to the Italian government, the League of Nations, the English government and American officials, popular demonstrations, anti-Italian boycotts, and campaigns calling for financial contributions and volunteers (Ross 1972). "Ethiopian volunteers" sought to enlist in the defence of Ethiopia. Some were successful. Their fortunes were nevertheless diverse.

Two aviators, Hubert Julian and John Robinson, enrolled in the Ethiopian armed forces, and whereas Julian was accused of treason, Robinson went on to become a legendary figure in Harlem. Born in Trinidad, Julian migrated to

Canada, where he learned to fly aeroplanes. Then, in 1921 in Harlem, he became an officer in the African Legion, Marcus Garvey's paramilitary UNIA unit. Renowned for his aerobatics and reputed to be a big spender, he was recruited in 1930 by Melaku Beyen, an Ethiopian medical student at Howard University, to perform during the coronation of the emperor in Addis Ababa. "The black eagle", as he was called, performed a parachute jump for which he was honoured. But two days before the coronation, without authorization, he flew one of Tafari's new planes and had an accident from which he escaped miraculously. Banished from the empire, he returned in 1935 to train infantry recruits. Very soon, he was regarded badly due to his pretentious speeches concerning his role at court, his street brawls and his attempts at seducing the emperor's daughters. He resigned in November 1935. On his return to the United States, he launched a campaign of denigration and denunciation of the emperor and definitively alienated himself from the African American community when, after the fall of Addis Ababa in 1936, he departed for Italy, where he accepted Italian nationality (Scott 1993, 81–95; Harris 1994, 54–57). Odd and despised, he was highly criticized by most African Americans, who found a hero in the other aviator, John Robinson, called the "brown condor".

Born in 1903 in Florida, Robinson pursued his technical studies at the Tuskegee Institute, founded in 1881 by Booker T. Washington. Unsuccessful in finding work in the south, he left for Detroit, where he worked as a mechanic. By dint of patience and tenacity, he managed to enter an aeronautical school, which had earlier refused him because of his colour, and he became the first African American pilot. On hearing news of the war, he sought to engage in Ethiopia and, in 1935, met Melaku Beyen. The latter, regardless of his inconclusive experience with Hubert Julian, transmitted Robinson's request to the emperor, who accepted it. In April 1935, Robinson arrived in Ethiopia, where he was promoted to the rank of officer in the imperial army. He survived the bombardments on the northern front, and made frequent liaison flights between the military fronts and the headquarters. He left the country shortly before the Italian victory and received a triumphant welcome in Harlem. Robinson made lecture tours, spoke at receptions and used his visibility to defend the Ethiopian cause (Scott 1993, 69–80; Harris 1994, 56–57; Tucker 2012). Consequently, these were two aviators were contrasting figures, who each marked the black American imagination. Though unable to make a real difference in the war on the side of Ethiopia, they nevertheless contributed – especially Robinson – to the reinforcement of the pan-African bonds between Ethiopia and the black communities of the Americas.

The War Viewed from the Caribbean

Though less well documented than in the United States, the reactions to the Italo-Ethiopian war nevertheless ignited the English-speaking Caribbean.

Fortunately, rarely discussed Jamaican archives and an attentive reading of the international black press are enlightening in this regard. Many volunteers attempted to engage in the Ethiopian army, but the embassies and offices of British foreign affairs were obviously not in support of an undertaking of this kind. In Jamaica, brief references to reactions to the Italo-Ethiopian war show that the conflict was perceived as a prelude to the social unrest leading to the workers' uprisings of 1938. The effect of the war was seen as a simple "awakening" or "agitation" of the black consciousness. Hence Ken Post's affirmation that

> In 1935 Jamaican Ethiopianism broadened and deepened. A white Italy, led by the dictator Benito Mussolini, attacked Ethiopia, and immediately a great wave of sympathy for the black state and its ruler swept Jamaica – as it did black people everywhere. . . . Nevertheless, what is significant is that this sympathy took no real organisational form before 1938; there were no 'Committees for the Defence of Ethiopia', such as emerged in the U.S.A. (Post 1970, 195)

However, as brilliantly demonstrated by Kevin Yelvington (1999) concerning Trinidad, the war played a central role in local constructions of ethnicity, culture and class. The war and the identification with Ethiopia permeated the sermons preached in many churches and were relayed by the local and the pan-African press, such as *New Times and Ethiopia News*, published in England. The Italo-Ethiopian crisis sent people to the streets in huge demonstrations and numerous organizations were created with a view to raising funds and volunteers for Ethiopia. They traversed social sectors, schools, churches, trade unions and so on. The cultural and religious dimensions of the "war in Trinidad", in the words of Yelvington, were not negligible: the coronation of the emperor, commemorated on 2 November 1935, brought together almost two thousand five hundred persons; calypso groups called the Ethiopians or Heroes of the Dark Continent sang of the fall of Mussolini (1999, 218–19). These events finally led Trinidadians to question the colonial authority on the island and provoked the great strikes of 1937.

In the case of Jamaica, the reactions to the war have not come in for the type of attention Yelvington gives to Trinidad. A few preliminary remarks can, however, be made. As of August 1935, following a public meeting, the Kingston branch of the UNIA addressed a telegram to the Italian consul in London expressing concern about the preparations for war: "Jamaican negroes' convention strongly protest Italy's interferance [*sic*] Ethiopia's sovereignty."[8] A mere two days after the Italian crossing of the Marab River, a large assembly was held in Kingston, at which a resolution was adopted under the patronage of the Ethiopian Alliance of the World. Article 16 of the charter of the League of Nations, recommending the protection of member countries, was evoked.[9] Another great public meeting was held at the Ward Theatre on 13 October, and about a fortnight later, at least four petitions were addressed to the colonial government protesting against the developments in Ethiopia. In the main, these petitions underlined the loyalty of the petitioners to the British crown and recalled that Jamaicans had fought for the British Empire during the First World War, "in order to maintain the integrity of the great British Empire [we] offered our services and we contributed with our lives and finances to that end. That in the same way we helped to safe guard the integrity of other races, we are asking that our race be protected at this crucial moment."[10]

The racial identification with Ethiopia was the cornerstone of these protests. These correspondences contained several references to the awareness, notwithstanding their loyalty to the British Empire, that Jamaicans had been forcefully removed from Africa and that it was their duty to defend Ethiopia at all costs. Accordingly, a handwritten letter from the Spanish Town branch of the UNIA insisted: "Be it further resolved that we are willing to fight on behalf of the one and only Negro Empire . . . [it is] quite reasonable that we be allowed to defend the integrity of the Ethiopian Empire from the continual attack of the enemy."[11] The "Ethiopian volunteers" were thus ready to leave for combat, but, unsurprisingly, the British government stated that it was not possible for British subjects to engage at the side of foreign states in war against other states at peace with the British crown. In other words, because England was not then at war with Italy, British subjects could not engage in combat in support of Ethiopia. The letter of the colonial secretary indicated, moreover, that no exemption from these rules could be made for "particular categories of British subjects", that is, for the descendants of slaves, who were now colonial citizens.[12]

Ken Post's argument that the war did not provoke the emergence of specific organizations in Jamaica seems incomplete. Admittedly, there is little information in the archives on the popular organizations specifically founded during the mobilization surrounding the Italo-Ethiopian crisis, but the social transversality of this mobilization is quite obvious. In addition to the UNIA, various types of organizations featured among the numerous signatories of diverse petitions: the Citizen's Association, the Jamaican National League, the Jamaica Poetry League, the Debating Association, the Ex-Service Men's Association, the Jamaica Development Association, the Trade Men's Association, the Association of Lodges and Benevolent Societies, the Parochial Boards Association, as well as the mayor of Kingston and the Council of Kingston and St Andrew Corporation. There was a priori no reason for a lesser degree of popular emotion in Jamaica than in Trinidad. Given the extent of mobilization of Jamaican associations, from the social and municipal services to trade unions, lodges, ex-volunteers of the British West Indies Regiment, and cultural organizations, the lack of information concerning other spontaneous organizations is due primarily to the gap in historical research – which needs to include the ways in which popular mobilization took shape. As will be seen in the next part of this study, this period is also marked by the resurgence of requests to return to Africa. Highlighting social and anti-colonial criticism, this popular mobilization prefigured the great workers' uprising of 1938. That year, the uprisings, largely organized and supported by black nationalism and racial consciousness, challenged the colonial state and gave rise to the two main political parties in Jamaica, the People's National Party and the Jamaica Labour Party (Campbell 1994, 81–85).

Marcus Garvey and Haile Selassie I

On the threshold of the Italo-Ethiopian war, Marcus Garvey's movement had already experienced a rapid decline. He was sentenced in 1923 and later banished from American soil. Upon his return to Jamaica in 1927, Garvey attempted unsuccessfully to make room for himself in the Jamaican political arena. He was then in a weak position, despite which many branches of the UNIA continued to function. UNIA branches complained to American and British authorities concerning the threats to Ethiopia. Six issues of Marcus Garvey's last newspaper, the *Blackman*, were published in Jamaica before the newspaper's transfer to London in 1935. The first issue dates back to December 1933, but the publication was somewhat irregular – at times, issues appeared on a monthly basis, and at others, the publication was bimonthly. In England, the title was modified to the *Black Man*, with a final issue in June 1939. In the columns of this newspaper, Marcus Garvey was able to comment on the development of the Italo-Ethiopian crisis. As early as June 1935, he vehemently criticized Mussolini and hoped that the League of Nations would keep its commitments with respect to Ethiopia.[13] In the following issue, he underlined the "universal sympathy" expressed with regard to Ethiopia.[14] On several occasions, the *Black Man* reprinted articles published by other newspapers, recalling the long-standing independence of Ethiopia, the history of the conflict since Adwa as well as the various treaties signed between Italy and Ethiopia until Ethiopia's entry in the League of Nations.[15] Previously noted for his use of Ethiopianism, his identification with the God of Ethiopia in the image of the black man, Garvey stated in December 1935 his boundless admiration for the besieged emperor:

> The Emperor of Abyssinia will fight not only by himself but by the guidance of that Divine Power and Force that never fails. Already he has triumphed in his diplomacy. . . . This is only the first triumph, but it is an indication of the final victory. Scattered and dispersed Africa has sent not only her sympathy but her allegiance to the Emperor of Abyssinia. . . . Let Abyssinia, therefore, go forward with the sword in hand, and as Gideon's Band became triumphant against the presumptive superior forces of the enemy, so shall Haile Selassie lead Ethiopia back to her ancient glory, and inspire the black man to the hope of once more worshipping under his own vine and fig tree.[16]

These few lines offered an eschatological vision of Ethiopia: guided by a divine hand, it could only overcome, backed by the multitude of black communities,

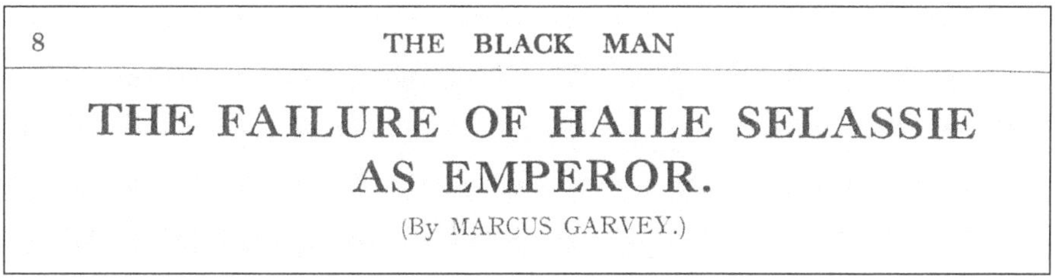

8 THE BLACK MAN

THE FAILURE OF HAILE SELASSIE AS EMPEROR.

(By MARCUS GARVEY.)

Figure 3.2. *Black Man* 2, no. 6 (March–April 1937): 8. © DR.

seen as having sworn loyalty to the emperor. The biblical references to the sword, to ancient glory, to the vine and the fig tree conjured up the image of a battle between the forces of good and evil and recalled the potent symbolism which was still attributed to Ethiopia. However, by March 1936, a degree of criticism of the emperor began to appear in the articles signed by Garvey, and in the July–August 1936 issue, he published an incendiary article on the emperor who had left the country to take refuge in England.

For Garvey, this departure was an abdication, considered to be the consequence of several factors. Garvey expressed his resentment of the emperor, perceived as having chosen to surround himself with white advisers, to rely on white institutions like the League of Nations, and to give attention only to white delegations and representatives. Garvey was indignant at the lack of will or the incapacity of the emperor to organize the support of the black people outside Ethiopia: "If Haile Selassie had negotiated the proper relationship with the hundreds of millions of Negroes outside Abyssinia – in Africa, in South and Central America, in Canada, the West Indies and Australia, he could have had an organization of men and women ready to do service, not only in the development of Abyssinia, as a great Negro nation, but on the spur of moment to protect it from any foe."[17]

Garvey was indignant that the emperor had established no consulate, diplomatic representation or minister of foreign affairs to represent the country before the black peoples of the world. He was still of the opinion that the UNIA represented a great black nation – regardless of the absence of territory and international legitimacy – and thus deserved the full attention of the Ethiopian state. With the bitterness of a settling of scores, Garvey stressed that, in 1920, the Ethiopian government had not responded to his invitation to attend the first UNIA conference; that, upon its arrival in London, the Ethiopian government in exile had neglected to receive black delegations, contrary to its treatment of white ones; that the letters addressed to Haile Selassie I were extremely difficult to deliver; and that no black institution was invited to the first receptions that the latter had held in London. Garvey pointed out that his intention was not to condemn the emperor, but the defeat of Ethiopia was, in his opinion, due to the fact that he refused to identify with Negroes and had "separated himself from the Negro people of the world".[18] This line of argument was developed in subsequent articles.[19] This reduction of the emperor's position to a racial

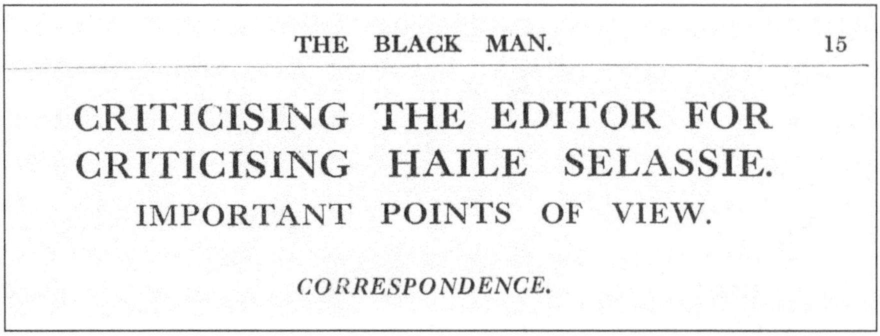

THE BLACK MAN. 15

CRITICISING THE EDITOR FOR CRITICISING HAILE SELASSIE.

IMPORTANT POINTS OF VIEW.

CORRESPONDENCE.

Figure 3.3.
Black Man 2, no. 3 (September–October 1936): 15. © DR.

policy of identification with whites reignited an old debate about the colour of Ethiopians. Was Garvey's grievance due to the fact that the emperor had declined to receive him (Scott 1993, 174)? There is no source to corroborate this anecdote, and the emperor did not refuse contact with black organizations as he received, that same year, a delegation from the United States, which will be addressed in a moment.

Haile Selassie I kept Garvey at a distance, owing not to racial discrimination but to the fact that Garvey had, at the time, lost his former aura: he had been accused of embezzlements, had been imprisoned and expelled from the United States; over the last ten years, his prestige had declined. On the other hand, though exiled, Haile Selassie I still represented the Ethiopian crown and was treated as such by the English. And there was no love lost between them and Garvey. They considered him to be a radical and would probably not have encouraged an interview liable to place him in the limelight. For such reasons, the emperor thought it best not to meet with Garvey, who consequently produced in the columns of the *Black Man* a relentless campaign of criticism against him. Many persons reacted to Garvey's allegations and criticism.

A letter from Una Brown, published by Garvey, expressed the conflict which members or sympathizers of the UNIA experienced when facing the gross error of judgement their "great leader" had made regarding the Ethiopian emperor, whose double symbolic value – both religious and national – were still intact despite his exile: "We hated Du Bois for antagonizing you; and you who have done so much for the race, surprise the entire race for saying the Emperor has outlived his usefulness and should seek asylum in a monastery."[20]

Garvey's position apparently created a great rift among the troops of the UNIA, and even Joel Rogers (1880–1966), a Jamaican historian and journalist who had been living in the United States since 1911, sought to destroy Garvey's statements point by point. The only war correspondent for the black press who covered Ethiopia in 1935–36, Rogers was well known for his sometimes exaggerated reports on Ethiopian victories. He published in 1936 an assessment of his stay in Ethiopia, in which he commented on the question of the race of Ethiopians, presented photographs of the Ethiopian population, revisited the question of slavery and resumed the debate on the attitude of Ethiopians regarding African Americans. On each point, he assumed the most positive stance possible about Ethiopia, thus presenting to his African American readership an engaging portrayal of Ethiopia. An Ethiopian official reportedly told him: "We think of ourselves as a nation, not as a race. This does not mean that we do not recognise our kinship with peoples of African descent in the New World. We wish you would urge as many as possible of your skilled farmers, mechanics, and scientists to come to Ethiopia. We need them here and would give them land free" (Rogers 1936, 30).

Was Rogers's writing a piece of rhetoric aimed simply at opposing Garvey? Or was it merely pan-African propaganda, reporting previous invitations and drawing on the powerful symbolism of land? In any case, his reports were widely read in the Americas, and following his interview with the emperor during his stay in Ethiopia, Rogers returned to Harlem covered in glory (Scott 1993, 198–201). Rogers's task was to make a "faithful" portrayal of the emperor, and after describing his political and moral aptitudes and his gracious and Christian behaviour, he described his racial appearance in these terms:

> In features he is Oriental, a fact accentuated by his beard. In colour he is a lightish black-brown, and considerably darker than one would infer from the published pictures of him. In reality he is what one would call in the United States a dark mulatto, judged by his colour and his hair. In his general expression he has been aptly described by one writer as a "black edition of the pictured Christ". (Rogers 1936, 29)

Garvey's representations were at variance with Rogers'. For one, the emperor had betrayed the race by seeking "to be white"; for the other, he was a light-skinned African who might be seen as a black version of Christ – or at any rate, as having a phenotype that was familiar in the United States. Garvey and Rogers did not exhaust the debates on this question, which continued to traverse black American communities. The local and international constructions of the black race, the identification with Ethiopia as well as pan-African solidarity were impacted by the Italo-Ethiopian war. Outside the intellectual circles, the disagreement between Marcus Garvey and Emperor Haile Selassie I seems to occupy little or no place among the social legacies ascribed to both men. For example, while certain Garveyites or historians of Garveyism refused to admit a filiation between Garvey and the Rastafari movement because of this quarrel (Stein 1986, 275–76; Tété-Adjalogo 1995, 171–72), most Rastafari have no problem constructing a fundamental complementarity, or even continuity, between Garvey and the emperor and integrating both in a specific cosmology, albeit with different functions. These legacies will be discussed later. In the meantime, an important question must be posed.

The emperor's exile to Bath and the room for manoeuvre then available to him are rather poorly documented. We are left with this question: did Garvey's often unjustified remarks influence Haile Selassie I's decision to make a concrete gesture in the direction of the black communities who supported the Ethiopian cause? Did the reproach of inability to organize the black people who identified with the fate of his country push him to approve the requests regularly received from blacks in the United States (Haile Selassie 1994, 27–31)? The 1937 foundation of the EWF in New York might provide a good illustration.

The Foundation of the Ethiopian World Federation

The EWF is an important organization in more ways than one: it was the first institution to emanate from a political decision made by the emperor with respect to black communities. Notwithstanding its fragility, it remains active today. It is totally overlooked, despite the fact that the fate of the settlement in Shashemene was indissociably related to its existence and function. Insofar as it was the result of a popular initiative, it illustrated the need "to take care of themselves" which traversed the black communities. In 1936, a mission was established representing several American black associations, United Aid for Ethiopia, the Ethiopian Research Council, and the Medical Committee for the Defense of Ethiopia. It was led by Dr Phillip Savory, accompanied by Reverend William Imes and Cyril Philips, who made a very discreet departure from the United States so as not to be obstructed by the American authorities. They went to Bath, England, where the emperor was in exile. The delegates met with Haile Selassie I, Melaku Beyen and Dr Charles Martin, to whom several documents were delivered, including strong criticisms of John H. Shaw, the consul – a white man – who represented Ethiopia in the United States. One pressing request of the mission was to receive a representative of the emperor on American soil, in order to lend legitimacy to the actions undertaken by various pro-Ethiopian associations and to channel the funds yet to be received by the emperor (Harris 1994, 104–19). Their request was approved, and in September of the same year, Melaku Beyen arrived with his family in New York to found the EWF. They were welcomed by the delegates and other black personalities. As stated by Joseph Harris (1994, 120), it was a historic moment, the first fruit of a mission entirely designed and led by African Americans in view of opposing the aggression launched by a European nation on African soil.

Melaku Beyen (1900–1940) had done his preparatory studies in Bombay, India; along with Beshawered Habte-Wold and Werqu Gobene, he was one of the first Ethiopians to have studied in the United States. All three were registered at Muskingum College in Ohio. Werqu never finished his studies, whereas Melaku graduated in 1928, majoring in chemistry, and Beshawered in 1929, specializing in economics in 1929. Melaku's stay in the United States was marked by his closeness to African Americans. He recruited the aviators Hubert Julian and John Robinson for the emperor and married an African American woman

(Bahru Zewde 2002, 89–91). Melaku was eminently qualified to succeed in the mission of federating the pro-Ethiopian organizations. On his return to New York in 1936, he re-encountered the racialized spaces, which had changed little during his absence, and set quickly to work. He travelled throughout the United States, organized public meetings, made many speeches and set up the Haile Selassie Fund Drive, aimed at the financial mobilization of the black lower middle class and tradesmen in Harlem. The newspaper *Voice of Ethiopia,* whose first issue was published in January 1937, served as a forum to publicize Melaku's actions, to report on antifascism, to teach the history of Ethiopia, as a directory of the businesses in Harlem and as a means of advertising community activities. To provide an institutional framework for these pro-Ethiopian activities, Melaku founded, on 25 August 1937 the EWF, whose Local 1, as the head office was called, was situated in New York.[21] The primary goal of the federation was set forth thus in its constitution:

> To promote the love and good will among Ethiopians at home or abroad in order to maintain the integrity and the sovereignty of Ethiopia, to disseminate the ancient Ethiopian culture among our members, to correct wrongs, to end oppression and to cut out for ourselves and our posterity a destiny worthy of our ideal of perfect humanity and the aim for which God created us; not only to save ourselves from annihilation but find our place in the sun; in this effort we are determined to seek peace and to pursue it, for this is God's will for man.[22]

Figure 3.4. Melaku Beyen, founder of Ethiopian World Federation, n.d. Archives G. Robinson, Shashemene © DR.

Making an indirect allusion to the call, popularized by Marcus Garvey, to Africans at home and abroad, the EWF clearly formulated an ambition of reaching the dispersed "Ethiopians" and thus contributed to nurturing the political identification and racial policy linking the Ethiopians from Ethiopia and the black Americans who were supposed to be "the Ethiopians abroad". Racial solidarity, considered a result of this identification, had long been advocated by Melaku, and it assumed a concrete and material form with the EWF. "[Since 1921], these two thoughts, the solidarity of the Black race, and the undying determination of our people at home to be free, have become realities and offer the greatest assurance of the perpetuation of Ethiopia's independence" (Beyen 1939, 8).

Local 1 in New York continued its fundraising drives, organized balls and evening events in honour of Ethiopia and the emperor and invited many personalities passing through Harlem to perform.[23] The EWF was structured precisely around "international officers" residing in New York: a president, a first and second vice-president, an executive secretary, a treasurer, an organizer and a chaplain. With a few additional members, they formed the executive council. Groups of at least twenty-five persons desirous of forming a local affiliated to the federation had to apply to the executive council to obtain a charter enabling them to elect their own officers.[24] By 1938, nearly ten locals were opened in the United States; in 1939, they rose to nineteen, with twenty-two pending applications for the creation of new locals (Scott 1972, 136; Harris 1994, 127). These branches opened quickly in the United States, especially Chicago, whose local was very active thanks to its president, Harry Broome. Like Melaku, he had spent years travelling throughout the south of the country to rally forces to the Ethiopian cause (Harris 1994, 128). The first international congress of the federation was held in July 1939 in New York and allowed many delegates to meet and prestigious guests to speak. The birthday of Haile Selassie I was celebrated with a great ball, and the congress ended in a parade of the Ethiopian colours organized by Colonel Robinson.[25] In 1940, there were twenty-two active EWF branches, including one in Latin America and another in the Caribbean. The first Jamaican local opened in June 1939, followed in November by branches in Honduras and Havana, Cuba. Moreover, thanks to the impact of its press organ, the *Voice of Ethiopia*, letters and funds were received by the headquarters of the federation from places as distant as the islands of the Caribbean, Panama, Colombia, Venezuela, Jerusalem, Sudan, Nigeria and Brazil. Whereas the real extent of the financial support of the EWF to the Ethiopian cause is hard to estimate, its moral support may be appreciated from the speedy creation of these national and international branches.

The various branches of the EWF reposed on the historical geographies of Ethiopianism and Garveyism and drew the contours of a pan-African space in which the identification of black people with the Ethiopian people and a global popular uprising supporting the war effort converged. Melaku recognized the EWF's symbolic debt to the UNIA, but he did so tardily, in 1940 (Harris 1994, 130). On 4 May of that same year, one year before the liberation of Ethiopia, Melaku passed away due to fragile health. This was a great loss for the federation, for he had become its symbol and source of inspiration. In addition to his family, he was survived by another Ethiopian, *Lejj* Araya Abebe, who had joined him in New York at the command of the emperor. Araya had served as the treasurer of the federation and was in charge of Amharic lessons in *Voice of Ethiopia*. After Melaku's death, and until his return to Ethiopia in 1943, Araya Abebe remained the sole link between the federation and the Ethiopian government (Fikru Negash Gebrekidan 2005, 108).

Added to this renewed identification between Ethiopians and the black people of the West, two other elements characterized the EWF: first, its pan-African perspective, sustained in *Voice of Ethiopia*. This was done through articles on Ethiopia, on Haiti, and on the black presence in the United States, in the

Caribbean and in Africa. Melaku Beyen wrote: "We are out to create the United States of Africa", a political slogan that was to remain at the heart of the pan-African issues that arose at the time of independence of the the African nations. Certain branches of the EWF offered classes in Amharic and Ethiopian history and published numerous inserts on black "heroes" as well as reviews of books by W.E.B. Du Bois, George Padmore and Joel Rogers. Padmore and Nnamdi Azikiwe themselves contributed to *Voice of Ethiopia* (Harris 1994, 131–32).

The second element characteristic of the EWF was its ecumenical perspective that may be illustrated by a meeting held at the beginning of 1955 in the small theatre of the Young Men's Christian Organization in Harlem. There, the EWF presented, to "an audience composed of Christians, Ethiopian Falasha Jews, Moslem Copts, all in their colourful costumes and headdress", a forty-minute recording of the Ethiopian Orthodox liturgy.[26] The evening continued with short addresses by Ethiopian students and EWF officers, including Mayme Richardson, who sang *Ethiopia*, a hymn of her own composition. A film, *Focus on Ethiopia*, was also shown. The cohabitation between these unusual religious persuasions and the sharing of an Ethiopian liturgical recording amply illustrate the extent to which the identification with Ethiopia traversed the black congregations. Inscribed in its constitution and in the practices of its members, the religious aspect of the EWF did not preclude political prerogatives but contributed to making it into an inclusive space where members of various congregations, independent and established churches alike, could come together around a common concern for the symbolic and political vocation of Ethiopia.

The Reconstruction of Ethiopia

Five years to the day after the Italian arrival in Addis Ababa, Emperor Haile Selassie I made a triumphal entrance into the capital. He arrived there via Sudan, supported by Ethiopian freedom fighters and the British armed forces, which had entered through Eritrea and Kenya to re-secure Ethiopia's independence. Italy's unconditional surrender took place only in September, by when the British military administration had already replaced the fascist colonial order. Extricating himself from the tripartite treaty of 1906, which had divided Ethiopia into European zones of influence, the emperor signed the treaty of January 1942, which laid down the principle of Anglo-Ethiopian cooperation – a cooperation that was unequal, since the English maintained control of the military and of foreign affairs. Causing many frictions, this treaty was finally replaced by another in 1944, without damage to Ethiopia's independence. In this last treaty, English replaced French as the empire's language for international relations. It inserted Ethiopia even more deeply into the complex relations between England and the United States (Marcus 1983). A new era – *Addis zemen* – began, during which time the reorganization of the empire (somewhat impeded by the problems of Ogaden and Eritrea) and its development emerged as priorities and led to a visible improvement of social, economic and financial conditions (Berhanou Abebe 1998, 193–207).

On the other side of the Atlantic, with the end of the Second World War and the return of the African American soldiers, the activism scene was gradually transformed. It is difficult to appreciate the place of the EWF in the post-war United States, as sources are fragmentary and no historian has yet addressed the work of reconstructing the American dynamics of this organization, whose various branches formed a complex international network. However, the identification with Ethiopia and the large wave of solidarity which took hold of the black worlds seemed to continue after the war; it remained imbued with religious references drawn from the gospels or from interpretations related to the lineage of King Solomon.[27] Most EWF meetings and encounters began with lessons from the Bible and hymns such as the *Universal Ethiopian Anthem*, co-authored for the UNIA by Arnold J. Ford.[28] Illustrative of the contradictions of their "double consciousness", the officers of the EWF claimed to be "loyal Americans of Ethiopian blood and descent",[29] and the EWF, while continuing to nurture this Ethiopian identification, durably contributed to attributing to Ethiopia a "mythical", biblical, spiritual as well as a "real", political and territorial form.

Up until the 1950s at least, EWF officers paid great attention to the political evolution of Ethiopia. The newspaper *New Times and Ethiopia News,* founded in 1936 by Sylvia Pankhurst and published in London, provided them with an important platform.[30] In its pages, they were able to read news of Ethiopia and to publish their official correspondence, articles and opinions. Regularly, they took stands on questions related to the English protectorate established in Ethiopia, petitioned the US government to adopt anti-imperialist positions and defended the idea of a "great Ethiopia" joined together with Eritrea and Somaliland.[31] The *New Times and Ethiopia News* offers an interesting pathway to which we will return later: in the early 1950s, even if most of the EWF's official mail was sent from the United States, there was an increase in the reception of mail and correspondence from the English-speaking Caribbean – Jamaica, British Guiana, and Trinidad and Tobago. Because it regarded Ethiopians from Ethiopia and Ethiopians from abroad as one people and institutionalized that idea, the EWF was quickly associated with the possibility of return to the continent. The possibility was fuelled by the news of persons who had already made the trip to Ethiopia. This news was then circulating in pan-African newspapers like *African Opinion*. For W. Shack, one of the objectives of the federation was to finance a group of immigrants to Ethiopia (Shack 1974, 149). The EWF was based on a strict and precise constitution with no reference whatsoever to the terms "return", "repatriation" or "Back to Africa". Nevertheless, even if it was rarely ever translated into action, the emigrationist will of its members helped to change the objectives and priorities of the organization.

With or without the EWF, in Ethiopia itself, an entire pan-African generation set to work on the reconstruction of the country. Teachers, professionals, technicians, journalists, photographers and administrators got going, and many made the trip to this war-ravaged land. They made a crucial contribution to the development of Ethiopia in the 1940s–1950s. But many of their trajectories remain fragmentary. We are still left with unanswered questions, and rare are the evaluations of the social impact of their contributions and of their skills deployed in Ethiopia (Shack 1974; Harris 1994). Joseph Harris has revisited the role of Yilma Deressa, the Ethiopian vice-minister of finance, who was to submit requests for financial and military cooperation to the American State Department. Hosted at Howard University during his stay, he took advantage of his situation to meet and recruit African American teachers and technicians.

A first group arrived in Ethiopia in December 1943: Edgar D. Draper of Baltimore, along with Hiley A. Hill and Edgar F. Love, left for the Ras Makonnen School in Harar; Obdulio Vazquez-Delgado from Puerto Rico taught electricity at the Addis Ababa School of Art; and William M. Steen became director of the English section of the department of press and propaganda of the Ministry of the Pen. He replaced a Briton, Ian H. Simpson, as editor of the weekly magazine *Ethiopian Herald*, published the monthly magazine *Ethiopian Review* and supervised the government's radio programmes in English (Harris 1994, 142–52).

The second group arrived in January 1944. It was headed by Colonel Robinson, who had returned to train the first Ethiopian pilots of Ethiopian Air Lines, and comprised James William Cheeks of Ohio, Edward Eugene Jones of Chicago and Joseph Muldrow of South Carolina. These mechanics and specialists in aeronautics were accompanied by Hester, a pilot with administrative skills, and Thurlow Evans Tibbs, a schoolmaster from Washington, DC. As for David Abner Talbot, of British Guiana, he was a journalist and succeeded Steen as an editor-in-chief of the *Ethiopian Herald*. Like his cousin T.R. Makonnen[32] (King 1978, 54n2), David Talbot was one of the great – albeit disregarded – figures of pan-Africanism. A graduate of New York University, he had edited a monthly magazine, the *African*, had frequented African students in the United States and had engaged in the civil rights struggle. He wrote several books on Ethiopia, broadcast radio programmes received as far as South Africa, and continuously informed the interconnected destinies of Ethiopian independence and black resistance in the United States. Married to an Egyptian woman, Talbot was moreover the president of the EWF local in Addis Ababa, which was probably opened at the end of the 1940s.[33] One of his books, *The Musical Bride* (1962), retraced the difficulties encountered by a young female Ethiopian musician who, educated in Europe, returned to Ankober in the hope of modernizing her society of origin and making it more amenable to women.[34] The narrator of this story was the host of a group of African Americans who arrived in Ethiopia overland to take up positions in the Ethiopian government. This was the second group, arrived in 1944. Their experience is narrated in an opening chapter filled with anecdotes evoking the discovery of an Ethiopia for which the African Americans had prepared themselves through reading. Many misunderstandings accompanied their voyage, and the question of their identity was frequently raised. Indeed, their host did not understand the origins of this delegation:

> "You are all *franji,*" he [their host] said, meaning foreigners; how then, are you similar in looks to us Ethiopians?'. Mr Gibbs, one of the members of our party, started to explain the slave origin of these strangers with non-white skins. Since Mr Gibbs was an octoroon and of light complexion, the *Chika Sum* said that the question was not meant for him.
>
> "You are Italian, aren't you?" he questioned Mr Gibbs. Mr Webster then took the floor and explained that, in the United States from which we hailed, if a man had one drop of African blood, he was considered coloured, as coloured as the Ethiopians.
>
> "No no no, I don't need glasses to see; this man is *natch* (meaning white) isn't he? We have seen plenty of them. Emperor Menelik had to capture thousands of them at Aduwa to teach them the lesson that Ethiopians are an unconquerable people." (Talbot 1962, 10, his transcriptions from Amharic)

In the eyes of the Ethiopian hosts, these visitors were first *franji*, foreigners, but their dark skin colour was disturbing. The light skin tone of one of their party was without a doubt the same as that of the Italians, defeated by his countrymen. For an African American who was, moreover, a pro-Ethiopian activist, to be compared to an Italian because of his light complexion might have been perceived as an insult and was certainly shocking. The Ethiopian host continued by adding that he did not understand how these black people had lost their mother tongue and preferred to speak the language of the *franjis*, thus putting them, at times, in an embarrassing situation. This encounter illustrated how the borders of belonging and race could be blurred and transformed by the meeting between Ethiopians and African Americans. The remainder of the journey plunged the visitors into an experience of strangeness and novelty, and the narrative was filled with many amusing anecdotes.

On their arrival in the capital, they found the immigrant community as well as the Caribbeans who had been living there since the 1930s. Mignon Ford, the widow of Rabbi Ford, was still present and, with the aid of Albertha Thomas, had opened a school in 1941. It was named the Princess Zennebe Worq School in 1943. In 1945, it was moved to an urban lot provided by Empress Menen (Harris 1994, 151). There were also other persons present, about whom little is known to date. Their traces have been left in the black press of the time, and future research should bring to light more precise information about their lives. Among them are Dr T. Thomas Fortune Fletcher from New York, who directed the Medhane Alem School in Addis Ababa; Clarence Perry, who taught at the same school; Homer Smith, a journalist from Minnesota, who had lived fourteen years in Moscow; Cecil Herbert DuValle from Philadelphia, who was a driving instructor, and so on.[35] Having been recruited without appeal to the opinion of the British, who were used to functioning based on the colour line, the African Americans occasionally found themselves at the centre of international tensions between the Ethiopians, British and Americans. They were, for the most part, technicians and professionals, who stayed until the termination of their contracts, then returned home, with the exception of Mignon Ford and David Talbot, who spent the rest of their lives in Ethiopia. They settled in urban areas, in Addis Ababa or Harar, except for one couple, Helen and James Piper, who appear in an *Ebony* article about this pan-African generation engaged in Ethiopia. It has been reported that James Piper taught carpentry in the Grundrandt School in Addis Ababa. Although James and Helen Piper are mentioned only in passing by specialists on this period (Scott 1993, 218), they are of great interest to this study, owing primarily to the fact that they were the first to leave the capital, after a few years, to settle in a rural environment, on the periphery of Shashemene.

Helen and James Piper

Helen and James Piper were born at the beginning of the century, probably a little before 1910, on the small island of Montserrat in the eastern Caribbean (Bishton 1986, 34; Campbell 1994, 222). Montserrat covers about sixty square kilometres, nearly a third of which is mountainous, non-arable land. In 1911, almost eighty years after the abolition of slavery, the population of African descent was a hundred times more numerous than the colonists, comprising Irishmen for the most part (Philpott 1973, 19, 23). The inhabitants of Montserrat migrated massively to the huge construction sites of the Panama Canal as of 1904. After the completion of the canal, large-scale emigration continued, notably in the direction of the United States, where the Pipers too went, in all probability between 1930 and 1940. During the 1950s and 1960s, the flow of the migrants from Montserrat shifted to England and formed, in absolute figures, the greatest outmigration in the history of the island and, proportionally, the most important in the Caribbean (Philpott 1973, 29).

During their stay in the United States, the Pipers acquired American nationality, and while their place of residence in the United States remains unclear – was it Harlem,[36] Chicago[37] or perhaps both? – they circulated within urban spaces which were then in the throes of transformation. They were too young to have been members of the UNIA at the beginning of the 1920s when the movement was at its zenith. Following Garvey's sentence in 1923 and the fast decline of his movement in subsequent years, the UNIA encountered by the Pipers no longer possessed its former institutional forms, but its claims lived on and were relayed by a militant black population. The Pipers were Caribbean migrants whose racial identity proved problematic in the contrasting rhythms of socio-economic mobility in a segregated America (Watkins-Owens 1996, 53); they had heard of Garvey's history, seen photographs and collected testimonies with which they identified. A letter the Pipers wrote to the pan-African magazine *African Opinion* resonates with this Garveyite tradition:

> We turn our thoughts to the Immortal, the late Hon. Marcus Garvey whose life-dreams were "Africa for the Africans at home and abroad". He would have been happy to see this day but was called to the great beyond. He is gone but his "motto" remains in the hearts of those who loved him. It would have pleased the great spirit of Mr Garvey to see the march of Black people from the West to their native land, "Africa".[38]

The Pipers placed Garvey on a pedestal as a model, as an "immortal" hero; it was the vision he preached that they sought to bring to pass by settling in Shashemene. This bond is a clear illustration of the mark left by Garvey on the imaginary of those who formed the "black nation" in search of a territory. This influence is all the more important to underline for its visibility over time and its presence, under different guises, among the transatlantic migrants who later arrived in Shashemene. The Pipers' identification with the "native" land, subsumed by the generic "Africa", was quite common, but there is an interesting element that reveals that their attachment to Ethiopia surpassed the importance they gave to Liberia, which was also present in Garvey's Back-to-Africa projects. It concerns the religious connection that made the call of Ethiopia so attractive: in a milieu and during a period marked by extremely remarkable religious vitality and diversity, the Pipers could have chosen among a number of black congregations, but they were black Jews who identified simultaneously with the Hebrews and with the Ethiopians, as did Rabbi Ford, who had arrived almost twenty years earlier.

Helen and James Piper celebrated every Saturday morning, and in their home in Ethiopia they did not have an image of Christ but a *tabot*.[39] *Tabot* is an Amharic word that has retained the Ge'ez plural and designates replicas of the Tables of the Law kept in the Ark of the Covenant that God entrusted to Moses and to the Israelites (Exodus 20:34). All Ethiopian churches are consecrated by the presence of the *tabot*, which takes part in the rituals, feast days and celebrations of Ethiopian Christianity (Chaillot 2000, 102–3). Gladstone Robinson, who arrived from the United States in 1964, and who will come in for further mention, presents the Pipers as follows:

> James Piper was a black Jew, a Hebrew, went to all ceremonies like Friday they lock down everything, no work, they cook and they stay in the house. [Once in Ethiopia] they tried to get me into that because I sat in a [Sabbath] session with them, and he do all the rituals and things and the sad part is when His Imperial Majesty came down and ask for Mr Piper he said he can't come out "cause he is praying to his God". He wasn't a Rasta, 'cause Rasta can't say that! God come to you and [*sucks his teeth*]. . . . The Emperor turned around and left right back to Addis. I didn't get involved with the black Jews cause they don't believe in Haile Selassie, they would connect the line

> of Judah and all of that, Solomon, but they don't say the Emperor is God like we do, but we worked with them and get along with them cause they helped [previously in the United States]. We had black Jews working right with us.[40]

For Robinson, the recognition of the divine character of the emperor was what made the difference between him, a Rastafari, and the black Jews. It would have been unthinkable for a Rastafari to refuse to meet the emperor, whereas, for the Pipers, the observance of the Sabbath from Friday evening and all day Saturday was a ritual practice which allowed no exception, even in the presence of Haile Selassie I. Robinson nevertheless emphasized the activities that linked Rastafari and black Jews from similar sociocultural backgrounds. The trajectory of Leonard P. Howell, one of the founders of the Rastafari movement, illustrates this proximity: a cosmopolitan Jamaican, he became familiar with the congregations of black Jews in Harlem before returning to Jamaica in 1932 to preach the divinity of *Ras* Tafari, who had become the emperor. Howell's trajectory and his role, which are now recognized in the genesis of the Rastafari movement (Lee 1999; Hill 2001), illustrate the circulations then at work in the "Ethiopian belt". These congregations gave mutual support to one another and were constructed on similar social and interpretative bases, despite marked distinctions in their understanding of the human or divine nature of the emperor.

When the Italo-Ethiopian war broke out in October 1935, Helen and James Piper were young adults; they read the press, attended many meetings, took part in the protests, marched in parades and contributed to the funds raised for Ethiopia. Prior to the war, were they imbued with the ideological and religious filiations mentioned earlier? Or was it the Italian aggression that motivated their decisive involvement in the popular "traditions of organization" represented by Garveyism and the congregations of black Jews (Hahn 2003, 473–76)? The concrete forms of their commitment are not clear, but an Ethiopian who knew them in Shashemene recalled that what "[he had] heard, is that when the Italians arrived in Ethiopia, Mrs Piper organized demonstrations".[41] The Pipers were predisposed to being affected by this war and to reacting to it: they were black, migrants, Caribbeans, Garveyites and black Jews. From 1935, they were perhaps affiliated with some of these pro-Ethiopian organizations and went on to become members of the EWF.

In 1947, Harry Broome, the president of Local 10 of the federation in Chicago, announced to the Ethiopian ministry of information that sixty-eight members of the EWF were ready to leave for Ethiopia with funding, material and tools. This underlined the vitality of the members of this local as well as their capacity to organize and to raise funds (Shack 1974, 151). It is possible that this enthusiasm was caused – or encouraged – by the reception, that same year, of a handwritten letter of thanks from the emperor addressed to the members of the EWF, emphasizing that "the help and assistance given to Us by you will never be erased from Our thoughts. We hope and wish the communication between you and Our nationals will be of lasting significance."[42]

W. Shack has noted that, for unknown reasons, this migration did not occur, but when he indicated that it is only at the end of the 1950s that about six families from the federation arrived in Ethiopia, he had forgotten the Pipers (Shack 1974, 151). In fact, Helen and James Piper arrived in Ethiopia in 1948; they were, besides, members of the EWF and were probably part of the militant contingent trained in Chicago. On his arrival, James Piper accepted a job as a teacher at the Gundrandt Technical School in Addis Ababa, and Helen Piper occupied an administrative position on the site of the airport. They were part of a movement that went beyond the members of the EWF and that led many African Americans to settle in Ethiopia in order to participate in the reconstruction of the country.[43] The Pipers shared many things with the other representatives of this generation: a pan-African commitment, a militant trajectory, skills and, in the case of some, an Afro-Jewish affiliation. There was, however, one thing which certainly set them apart: whereas most African Americans resided in urban areas, especially in Addis Ababa, the Pipers chose to settle in a rural environment, which was, moreover, isolated from the African American community.

In 1952, James and Helen Piper set out again for the United States, where they gave an enthusiastic description of Ethiopia to the members of the EWF. They returned to Ethiopia in 1953 (*Majority Report* 1961, 5).[44] They settled near Shashemene, a town then counting a few thousands of inhabitants and situated two hundred and fifty kilometres to the south of Addis Ababa.[45] A donation of land there had been made by the emperor to the members of the EWF to thank them for their support during the Italo-Ethiopian war and to enable them to settle and contribute directly to the development of the country. This land was destined to become a continuous and still current pole of attraction for members of the "Ethiopian diaspora" living on the other side of the Atlantic.

The Land Grant in Shashemene

To attempt to reconstruct the process of the granting of land in Shashemene constitutes a major historical challenge. This was, in fact, the first initiative of the kind on the part of an African head of state with respect to the black people of the world. A political gesture sealing the pan-African policies of Ethiopian emperors since Menelik II and reinforcing the image of Haile Selassie I, this land grant was a crucial moment in these transatlantic relations. About ten years after the end of the Italo-Ethiopian war, which had had important international repercussions, Ethiopia was redefining its economic development, and the power of the emperor was sliding in the direction of absolutism. Nonetheless, he received a request reiterating the determination of African Americans to continue developing relations with the country and to secure the means of settling there. In May 1950, the New York offices of the EWF wrote a letter of petition to the emperor. It was delivered to him by Reginald Birch, a member of the advisory council of the federation, sent specifically to Ethiopia for this mission. Two requests were formulated in this letter: "concessions of land for settlement of a large number of the members of the Federation desiring to travel to Ethiopia for permanent settlement" and an "easing of visa restrictions to facilitate the voluntary entry of such members wishing from time to time to travel to Ethiopia to settle, visit and otherwise pursue ways for strengthening their relations with the Motherland".[46] Various types of mobility were therefore considered: migration in view of permanent settlement in Ethiopia, for which a land concession was required, and circulations requiring customs and governmental waivers.

The need for a relationship with the "motherland", Ethiopia, is obvious in this letter. This is indeed the particularity of modern Ethiopianism: it is constructed in relation to an "imagined" but also to a very real Ethiopia, materialized and nurtured thanks to the country's encounter with black mobility. The emperor's official response is not documented, and mystery still surrounds the steps that were taken, the administrative process of attribution and the exact date of the donation. The date most frequently retained and cited is 1955, as the news of the donation was publicly announced in Kingston, Jamaica, that year. Naturally, it marked minds as well as historiography. This point will be discussed later. However, several elements encourage us to think that the donation was prior to 1955. Even EWF officers in Ethiopia, questioned on several occasions, were hesitant in quoting an exact date. During a collective interview conducted in Shashemene, the question was posed to them directly:

> "Do you know when was the land granted?" [*Silence*]
> Officer 1: "1955"
> Officer 2: "Two dates are known: 1955 and 1952."
> Officer 3: "One understands it is 1948, 1950 or 1956. "[47]

Gladstone Robinson, who arrived in 1964 in Shashemene from the United States and who was a long-standing member of the EWF, mentioned 1951. Another EWF officer, who left England to settle in Addis Ababa in 1988, has indicated 1948 as the date of the gift. This is his explanation of the uncertainty surrounding it: "There is no actual date that we can define that's the date [of the grant], from Rasta tings [things] coming down from elders, a lot of it is not written, or recorded except in these last ten, fifteen years, but they are the ones that told us from the year 1948, come home."[48]

The oral tradition around which the Rastafari movement was formed provided the transmission belt relaying the news of the grant, in the absence of public documentation. Several groups, including EWF's Research and Repatriation Committee, founded in London in 1980 by Rastafari, undertook the search for an official document indicating the dates, statutes and procedures of the gift, but without success. Whereas the intention to return had been transmitted to the younger generation, the date, for its part, was forgotten. In the same way, even today, the Ethiopian authorities are unable to provide precise details, and neither the Ministry of Foreign Affairs nor the Offices of Immigration seem to be in possession of this information. In the land archives of the former regime, recently transferred to the Welde Meskel Memorial Archives Research Center in Addis Ababa, an inevitably selective research – considering the volume of the archives – was conducted. Given the bonds between Princess Tenagne Worq, daughter of the emperor, and the transatlantic migrants, her archives were selected. Among these archives, comprising a multitude of extremely interesting documents on the life and activities of the princess as well as many others documents concerning the royal domains (concessions, exploitation, jurisprudence and regulations of conflicts), we diligently examined some three hundred and fifty files – but to no avail. The archives of the Ministry of the Pen, attached to the emperor, and which might have survived the political upheavals of the last thirty years, were inaccessible, being situated within the palace, currently occupied by the presidential offices of the Federal Democratic Republic of Ethiopia. Moreover, in post-war Ethiopia, many agreements on land concession and construction were concluded verbally, and it is also possible that the granting of the land in Shashemene was never sealed by a specific document (Bahru Zewde 2000, 192).

Nevertheless, two persons who might have contributed to concretizing the promise of land have been identified. First, there was *Lejj* Araya Abebe, who had worked with Melaku Beyen and the EWF in New York at the order of the emperor and who returned home in 1943. He is thought to have taken up a semi-official charge as an intermediary between the government and the African American community in Ethiopia and might have played an active role in the granting of land on the periphery of Shashemene (Fikru Negash Gebrekidan 2005, 108). Even more important was David A. Talbot, who arrived in Ethiopia in 1943 during the great influx of African American professionals. He was particularly well integrated into the Ethiopian society and had participated in the creation of a local of the EWF in Addis Ababa, where he assumed the function of president, while James and Helen Piper served, respectively, as secretary and treasurer. Together, alongside Julia Green, a Jamaican from Annotto Bay, they "explored the countryside until they came to Shashemani [*sic*]".[49] Extremely occupied with his professional tasks in town and already in charge of land in Ambo (Fikru Negash Gebrekidan 2005, 166), it was not Talbot's priority to settle in Shashemene, but it would appear that he "is really the one that negotiated the land grant but he said I am not the one who will live there, so he got Piper and Madame to go down".[50]

What is more, a house in Addis Ababa had been put at the disposal of potential migrants to Shashemene: the EWF called for a financial contribution from its members to carry out refurbishing and encouraged "carpenters, painters, plumbers, electricians, upholsterers, farmers and cabinet makers" to get ready to emigrate. Especially stressed was the request that "only those who have proven or shall have proven their worth as true Ethiopians" should come to settle in Ethiopia.[51] While the expression "true Ethiopians" called upon the familiar Ethiopianist racial and biblical symbolism, its use as criterion for measuring individual commitment was surely problematic. This was a direct call for emigration addressing militants of the federation; it was, however, scarcely relayed by the press. The *New Times and Ethiopia News* announced this grant in 1956, and *African Opinion* mentioned it only in 1964, whereas news on repatriation to Africa had been diffused in each of its issues over the previous fifteen years.[52]

Was it that the EWF, proud of having been granted land in its own name, retained the information to preserve its privilege? Was it the fragility of the organization and its officers, who, maybe relatively demobilized at the beginning of the 1950s, when Ethiopia was no longer under Italian fire, obstructed the dissemination of the news to its own members? Was it that the EWF was no longer attracting the membership of black activists and had started to decline? A few answers probably reside in the person of Mayme Richardson. Born in 1912 in Michigan, she was black, Catholic, a soprano singer and an officer in the EWF in charge of international organization. After giving a number of prestigious concerts in the United States, she left in 1948 to give a series of twenty-two concerts in Palestine, followed by performances in Cyprus and Egypt (Fleming and Burckel 1950, 438). She was invited to Ethiopia and discovered Addis Ababa:

Figure 3.5. Mayme Richardson dressed as an Ethiopian woman, *African Opinion* 1, no. 4 (January 1950): 11. © DR.

> There's something strange, strange like magic about putting your foot on the soil of Africa that gives you a sensation you've never had before in your life. I felt it and experienced it but cannot explain it. Yes, I was completely overcome by the spirit of freedom, untrammelled freedom! I was at home once more with my people. I felt happy, secured and moved. It was indeed the land of my heritage.[53]

The emotion she expressed is hardly astonishing: this was Richardson's first encounter with Ethiopia, a land to which her imagination was deeply attached; she found herself in a place where the majority of the population was black, where what differentiated her from others was no longer colour, but language, attitude or attire. She performed before the emperor and was completely fascinated by the Ethiopian court, by "the royalty of these great Blacks", by the gold ornaments and the pageantry. She reported these words of the emperor in response to the spirituals she had sung: "No one could hear you sing and interpret the songs of such a great race without being deeply moved and touched. They are indeed soul stirring and borne out of hearts praying and fighting for freedom. I recognize the kinship between American blacks and our own people."[54]

The idea of kinship between Ethiopians and black Americans must have touched Richardson deeply. The testimony of her visit to Ethiopia was widely diffused in the press, and her account was quoted by *African Opinion* until 1969.[55] Before returning to the United States in 1949, the singer performed before George Merrill, the American ambassador to Ethiopia, toured the country and also stopped over in Greece, Italy and France. Motivated by this experience, she resumed her activities in the federation as soon as she returned. She was present at most of the great congresses of the EWF, founded Local 34 in Chicago, to which she gave the name of Princess Tsehay, one of the daughters of the emperor, and above all, ceaselessly diffused the news about this gift of land and the possibility of settlement – a prospect which seemed increasingly feasible.[56]

The EWF was then at a crucial turning point, one at which its existence was at stake: most its officers had been present since its foundation in 1937 and were well advanced in age. They had militated during the Italo-Ethiopian war and, since the death of Melaku Beyen in 1940, had been directly involved in the collection of funds, the dissemination of information on Ethiopia, the survival of the organization, and some had even travelled to Ethiopia. The thirteenth annual convention of the EWF, held in New York in July 1952, celebrated with "honor and devotion" the sixtieth birthday of the emperor and initiated discussions on the state of the federation. A brilliant speaker, Brother Johnson, president of Local 12 in Kansas City, asked that black people intensify their efforts to make the federation grow throughout the world. Mayme Richardson, who was more pragmatic, asked for the launching of a vast membership campaign, "especially to attract young people".[57] It was not in the United States that Mayme Richardson managed to find younger and more dynamic members. As will be seen later, she went, at the beginning of the 1950s, to the place where real popular support of the federation was to be found: in the Caribbean, and especially in Jamaica. Other members left the United States for Ethiopia and Shashemene. These arrivals were rare, separate, intermittent, and occurred only in the mid-1960s, almost fifteen years after that of Helen and James Piper, bearing witness to the decline of the activities of the federation.

Gladstone Robinson

Very little information is available on the handful of Americans who migrated to Ethiopia at the beginning of the 1960s and sought to settle in Shashemene.

Their trajectories and personalities seem to have been erased from memory. There were at least eight such persons, but they arrived separately and at different times. They were members of the EWF, but the diversity of their religious affiliations is amazing: William Hillman, who arrived with his wife and daughter, was a Baptist pastor born in Georgia. He is said to have heard about Shashemene for the first time at a public meeting with Malcolm X in Pennsylvania at the beginning of the 1960s (Bishton 1986, 29); Delval and his wife, Doughty, were black Jews, like the Pipers; Tuwills was a black Muslim, who came with his two wives and two daughters; Gladstone Robinson was a Rastafari. Of Lynch and Dawson, two other African Americans, no memory has remained. This diversity confirms one of the characteristics of the EWF: its concerns were not fundamentally of a religious order. Its officers and members were nonetheless believers, and all were imbued with Ethiopianist biblical and symbolic values.

To return for a moment to the trajectory of Gladstone Robinson: he was the only Rastafari arriving from the United States. To a certain extent, he was a bridge between two waves of arrivals in Shashemene: the first, American, and the second, Jamaican. Robinson was born in August 1929 in Brooklyn, in the midst of the great depression, of a sailor father from Barbados and a Cherokee Indian mother from North Carolina. This double heritage accounts for two strong sentiments: "Two claims against Babylon, one for the Indian tragedy where two millions was slaughtered and also for repatriation, four hundred years of slavery."[58]

His mother had founded a Pentecostal church and had nourished the hope that her son would become a pastor: "She say it's a means of income and also to stay out of trouble."[59] Gladstone grew up in a religious atmosphere but was a brilliant schoolboy who wanted to study medicine. Owing to a lack of means, he fell back on pharmacy, which he studied at the Brooklyn College of Pharmacy. He was also a sportsman and took part in inter-university competitions. He continued his studies at the University of Long Island. But something crucial occurred: "I got the African bug and I quit school after three years, because I become involved in the Back-to-Africa movement then, I went to lectures that captivated me, and I lived with an Ethiopian who taught me a lot about African History. These things made me reject the system I was in. I became radically inclined in that sense, it was an awakening to me, and that cause family problems."[60] This "radical inclination" also pushed him to become a member of the EWF, but his wife, of Afro-Mexican and European origin, had no patience with the "African bug" and left him, with their two children, to settle in California. Gladstone then decided to quit his job in a pharmacy in New York. He left for Los Angeles, where he distributed newspapers for four years and got involved in Local 35 of the federation, which was named after Dr Melaku Beyen. He settled later in Houston, where he completed his master's degree in pharmacy, and, having become the Western organizer of the federation, he founded a local there. This Southern city, which was still segregated, was a new environment for him. He connected with students from Africa and the Middle East and was engaged in religious and militant organizations. On his return to New York, with his diploma in hand, Gladstone Robinson found work in a pharmacy on Sugar Hill in Harlem and continued his activities within the federation, where he established close connections with many black Jews. It was at this point in time that he made a crucial encounter.

During the first four months of 1964, he hosted in his home Douglas Mack, Filmore Alvaranga and Samuel Clayton, three Rastafari from Jamaica on their way to Nigeria, Kenya and Ethiopia. They were travelling with complaints: a petition with three thousand signatures addressed to the United Nations and the newly created Organization of African Unity. They formed what was known at the time as "the second mission to Africa". Their self-financed tour was independent and organized in the name of the Rastafari community of Kingston, whom they represented. Two of them, Mack and Alvaranga, had participated in the first mission. Approved by the Jamaican state, this first "semi-governmental" mission left in 1961. It visited Ethiopia, Nigeria, Ghana, Liberia and Sierra Leone in order to examine the possibilities of "repatriation" and settlement of Jamaican citizens. The origins and forms of these mobilizations will be discussed later. For Robinson, this meeting was extremely significant. No doubt, he was already aware of these missions. The popular mobilization for repatriation in Jamaica had been largely relayed by the pan-African press. Robinson was introduced into the Jamaican and Rastafari community of New

Figure 3.6. Douglas Mack, Gladstone Robinson, Filmore Alvaranga, *Lejj* Ayelework Abebe (Ethiopia representative to the United Nations), Samuel Clayton, New York, 1964. Archives G. Robinson, Shashemene © DR.

York, and he introduced his hosts to a group of black Jews called the House of Judah (Mack 1999, 122; Landing 2002, 250). Together, they undertook several official initiatives in New York and Washington – in particular, in the direction of the new African embassies which had opened there and whose prestige was still intact.

Weekly meetings were organized at Robinson's home, where the African Repatriation Committee was founded. Thanks to this New York mobilization, the three Rastafari found the funds needed to continue their journey, and in April 1964, they left for a one-year stay on the African continent. Robinson, who remained in New York, decided to go to Jamaica as the representative of the African Repatriation Committee, counter to the advice of the three Jamaicans, and left in the company of a Jamaican, Noel Scott, and his son.

Gladstone Robinson kept a diary in which he made daily entries on the details of this trip as well as his encounters in Jamaica. This small, twenty-three page manuscript has not been published, but provides rich information.[61] The objective of this mission to Jamaica was to visit all the EWF locals in Kingston as well as the various Rastafari groups, in view of bringing them together under the aegis of the African Repatriation Committee. The idea was to establish a strong militant base capable of demanding repatriation to Africa. Following a large meeting presided over by Ras Mortimo Planno, about whom more will be said, various Rastafari organizations agreed to federate under the name of the African Repatriation Committee, which was regarded as an offshoot of the EWF in New York, despite Robinson's frequent insistence on the need "to

Figure 3.7. Berthal J. Moody, Mortimo Planno, Gladstone Robinson, Solomon Wolfe, Kingston, 1964. Archives G. Robinson, Shashemene © DR.

Figure 3.8. Gladstone Robinson, Mortimo Planno, Noel Scott, Solomon Wolfe, ?, Kingston, 1964. Archives G. Robinson, Shashemene © DR.

put order" in the affairs of the New York headquarters of the EWF.[62] Robinson remained curiously discreet about an experience which was surely an enormous culture shock. This young, mixed-blood American, with close-cut hair, who always wore a suit and a tie, carried an attaché case, wore glasses and was very well-bred, betrayed little of his personal impressions on meeting with the Rastafari of Kingston, who, in contrast, often came from the poorest milieu and had experienced several years of violent repression at the hands of colonial and postcolonial authorities. Gladstone Robinson nevertheless participated in several celebrations with the Rastafari, thus acquainting himself with their specific cultural practices.

Subsequent to this double experience of hosting Rastafari in New York and meeting with Rastafari in Jamaica, Robinson defined himself as a "Rasta" by defending the divine nature of the emperor and by progressively adopting Rastafari cultural practices. His authority over the African Repatriation Committee was however shaken on his return to New York. His legitimacy and that of the committee were questioned by the EWF, and it would appear that, at the EWF annual convention held in July, Robinson's initiative was repudiated. Similarly, when the three Rastafari returned from their mission on the African continent in May 1965, they strongly reacted to Robinson's visit to Jamaica and accused him of having sown confusion and discord within the movement (Mack 1999, 143–44). In Jamaica, this initiative by the African Repatriation Committee

Figure 3.9. Helen Piper, Gladstone Robinson and James Piper in Shashemene, 1964. Archives G. Robinson, Shashemene © DR.

was inscribed in a history of continuous efforts and of frequent organizational failures and thus bore no fruit. But just a few days after his return to New York, Robinson left the internal EWF conflicts and power struggle between New York and Kingston behind him and went to Ethiopia, where he met Helen and James Piper. He was one of the last Americans to arrive in Shashemene before the organization of the return to Ethiopia was irreversibly taken over by the Jamaicans.

New Pan-African Causes

The Italo-Ethiopian war of 1935–41 revealed the influence of Ethiopianism in the world and caused one of the greatest pan-African mobilizations in history. This mobilization led many Afro-American technicians and professionals to get involved in the reconstruction of Ethiopia. In 1954, Haile Selassie I travelled to the United States, where he devoted time to the organization of meetings with representatives of black organizations and visited several churches including the Abyssinian Baptist Church, founded in 1808. On his first visit to Harlem, almost thirty thousand people came out to welcome and acclaim him, attesting to his continued prestige.[63] In contrast with this international influence, due in part to the presence of Ethiopia at the Conference of the Non-Aligned Nations in Bandung in 1955 and to its intervention in the crisis in the Congo, the Ethiopian domestic political situation was less visible, and the regime had hardened out of all proportion. The emperor had crushed a coup d'état fomented by his own imperial guard in 1960 while he was on a trip to Brazil; in 1963, the peasants of Bale, a region east of Shashemene, rose up in protest against the social inequality between Christians and Muslims; and the federal compromise negotiated with Eritrea, for its part, was falling to pieces. The autocratic Ethiopia of the ageing monarch seemed to be lagging behind the rest of an African continent that was wide awake and was fast becoming a kind of laboratory for progressive politics and ideology.

The fifth Pan-African Congress, held in Manchester in 1945, had established itself as an actor in the anti-colonial struggles conducted by a generation of dynamic young leaders who placed Africa again at the centre of pan-African concerns. Strategies of action were put in place: the organization of the masses through trade unions and political parties, the fight for political power through non-violence and, if necessary, through armed combat (Geiss 1974, 408). Kwame Nkrumah (1979, 53–54) emphasized in his autobiography the watershed that this meeting represented: "Like Garveyism, the first four conferences were not born of indigenous African consciousness. Garvey's ideology was concerned with *black* nationalism as opposed to *African* nationalism. And it was this fifth Pan-African Congress that provided the outlet for African nationalism and brought about the awakening of African political consciousness. It became, in fact, a mass movement of Africa for the Africans."

By placing the first four pan-African congresses on the same plane with Garveyism, Nkrumah insisted on the complementarity of the two movements, and even on their interdependence. He announced that Africans had taken over the pan-African struggle for liberation and that African nationalisms were ready to emerge massively on the scene. In this way, Nkrumah dissociated himself from Garvey and especially from the primacy of race, which he embodied. By recognizing the shift from black nationalism to African nationalism, he announced the maturity of his own nationalist thought. While he was still a teacher in Accra, he was initiated into nationalism in 1926 by Kwegyir Aggrey (1875–1927). A year before his death, Aggrey was the first African teacher of the Prince of Wales College in Achimota, Ghana, inaugurated with great pomp by the British governor: "[Kwegyir Aggrey] was extremely proud of his colour and hostile to any racial segregation, and although he could understand the principle which Marcus Garvey recommended, namely "Africa for the Africans" he never hesitated to fight against this principle" (Nkrumah 1960, 28).

The position of interracial cooperation recommended by Aggrey – represented by the white and black keys of the piano necessary to create harmony – was not easily acceptable to the young Nkrumah. However, with time, his position evolved insofar as he came to the awareness that the use of racial primacy as a base for political action would not suffice to unite the populations of a vast continent, who were certainly black but with multiple internal demarcations of class, caste, language, region, ethnicity and so on. And yet, it was to the slogan "Africa for the Africans", popularized and even globalized by Garvey, that Nkrumah resorted. The road had been long since Delany (1861, 82) defended the idea of "Africa for the Africans, and black men to lead them"; that is, power to the descendants of Africans who "identified with the race". Their principal role was still contained in Garvey's slogan: "Africa for the Africans, at home and abroad." Nkrumah thus confirmed a double movement: recognition of the Garveyite and the pan-African heritages and, at the same time, recognition of the need to be freed from these genealogies through their transformation. Contrary to Aggrey, he chose not to oppose this racial principle but to work to transform it into a continental principle (M'Bokolo 2006b). When, in 1957, Ghana proclaimed its independence, Kwame Nkrumah represented – to cite another symbol popularized by Garvey and, before that, by Benito Sylvain – a rising black star for the liberation of the African peoples and for continental pan-Africanism. The celebrations surrounding the independence of Ghana marked a turning point in the relations between black Africa and the Americas and in their respective identities: "Africa, tossing off white rule and taking independence, no longer remained a place easily stereotyped as 'backward' and needing to be 'redeemed' or 'uplifted'. Africa's drive for freedom had moved further, faster, than that of black America. Africans, while transforming their continent, pushed African Americans to dismiss old notions and articulate new ideas" (Meriwether 2002, 159).

Many personalities attended the celebration of Ghanaian independence, including Martin Luther King, Charles Diggs (who had lived in Ethiopia), George Padmore, intellectuals and delegates from newspapers, black organizations and churches (Meriwether 2002, 159–60).[64] A new era was dawning, one in which contemporary Africa became an inspiration for black Americans. In 1954, the judgment *Brown v. Board of Education* had initiated the desegregation of schools in the United States; civil resistance embroiled the country; and the fight for equality nourished the hopes of each and everyone. The references to Africa were still present, but Africa had changed. It was no longer stuck with the degraded and negative image which had circulated for such a long time. It was no longer a continent that needed to be "civilized" but one engaged in nationalist successes with a deep impact on the black imaginary: "Beyond inspiring black Americans to continue the struggle, the sweep of African independence boosted the pride and confidence that African Americans felt in their heritage and themselves" (Meriwether 2002, 201).

The process of decolonization of the continent contributed to the revalorization of African Americans. Finally, promising nations were emerging, nations with which they could identify. The political and cultural practices of African Americans drew on continental current affairs, whereas their objectives were

Figure 3.10. Haile Selassie I and African heads of state at the first summit of the Organization of African Unity, Addis Ababa, 1963.

increasingly related to the transformation of their country, the fight for equality and change in their social conditions. In 1963, the foundation of the Organization of African Unity in Addis Ababa assembled the new nations and bore witness to the geopolitical changes. On this occasion, Haile Selassie I consolidated his image of "father of Africa", but the dynamism of the "sons" – the heads of the newly independent countries – promptly supplanted him. At a time when independence was drawing, for the first time, the contours of other black nations in addition to historic Liberia and modern Ethiopia – familiar icons of freedom and black power – the return to the continent might have become an outdated option. George Padmore was, moreover, singularly opposed to it. Projects of repatriation like Garvey's were, for him, "the repetition of colonialist projects which he rejected with the same severity" (M' Bokolo 2006b, 9).

Yet, with the increase in exchanges between the continent and the diaspora, returns and settlements were incessant and more frequently in the direction of independent Africa. The possibilities of access to land for the diaspora were unequalled, and though the flow seemed to have dried up, this is more the effect of historiographic distortion than that of documented analysis. In 1951, Nkrumah, who received an honorary doctorate from the University of Lincoln, had already recalled the role that black Americans had to play in Africa (Nkrumah 1960, 171), and following independence, many of them went to settle in Tanzania, Ghana or Liberia.

Though unable to provide details here on a history deserving more comprehensive research, a few examples may be mentioned. A group of 175 African Americans went to Liberia in 1967 and experimented with rural life, but their settlement was a failure. They were "Hebrew Israelites", a religious movement originating in the black Jewish congregations of the beginning of the twentieth century, mentioned above (Weisbord and Kazarian 1985, 61–91; Markowitz 2006). In 1969, an article published in the black American magazine *Ebony* indicated that Joseph Mobutu had invited the black people of the diaspora to come and work in the Congo. President Hastings Banda was, for his part, less sure that African Americans would enjoy Malawi, where there was not even a single movie theatre. In Tanzania, between 1964 and 1969, at least two hundred African Americans are reported to have acquired Tanzanian nationality and to have found refuge from the racial violence exercised in the United States. Certain heads of state, like Léopold Sédar Senghor of Senegal, Emile Zinsou of Dahomey and Milton Obote of Uganda, were, for their part, more cautious and seemed to encourage black Americans to continue *at home* their fight against the racist policies of the US government.[65] Others had more ambiguous positions, like Tom Mboya (1930–69), a great Kenyan figure, treasurer of the party of Jomo Kenyatta, and founder, in 1957, of the People's Convention Party. In 1959, he affirmed: "Black Americans have been told they are not wanted in Africa. This is a deliberate erroneous propaganda. You may come home whenever you want, Africa is your heritage. You are awaited and needed."[66] Ten years later, shortly before his assassination, he expressed his disagreement with the projects of return to Africa and denounced the feeling of racial solidarity: "The idea of American Negroes coming here to live, to make Kenya their home just because they are black, is wrong."[67] He was booed by an assembly in Harlem for these words. He explained his opinions in an article which gave due importance to the relations between Africans and African Americans, but stressed that the concerns of the new nations were of a different nature and could not be limited to racial identification, as they were engaged in the construction of viable states. On this occasion, Mboya made the distinction between a call for massive return, which he discouraged for practical reasons, and individual returns, even in the thousands, which could surely contribute to the development of African institutions.[68]

This differentiation between the propaganda of massive return, like Garvey's, and individual returns is interesting and recalls, to a certain extent, the fears of the Liberian government, in the mid-1920s, regarding the risks related to the massive arrival of members of Garvey's UNIA. But in 1960, Garvey was no longer there, and his emigrationist movement counting millions of members was no longer at the forefront. On the other hand, many African Americans repatriated individually. Whereas some, like Richard Wright, travelled to the Gold Coast in 1954, others like George Padmore (1957), W.E.B. Du Bois (1961) or Maya Angelou (1962) went to live there after independence. Some engaged in the pan-African movement from the continent, like Bill Sutherland – first in Ghana, then, after the coup d'état which overthrew Nkrumah in 1966, in Tanzania, where he contributed to the sixth Pan-African Congress in 1974 (Sutherland

and Meyer 2000). A small book by Ernest Dunbar touchingly recalls the biography of a few American expatriates, with no dissimulation of their hopes or failings (Dunbar 1970). Their reasons for leaving were numerous but remained closely related to the American sociopolitical situation. All these initiatives, it must be repeated, stand in need of further research, but what surfaces is the fact that independent Africa attracted most of these migrants, who visited and sometimes settled on the continent. This movement was representative of an era when the prestige of Ethiopia was rapidly declining: it remained one of the iconic lands of black and African liberation movements, but seemed to have become outdated and impracticable.

Consequently, several specialists perceived the post-1945 period as announcing the demise of Ethiopianism. William Scott mentioned, at the time, its "eclipse and virtual evaporation" (Scott 2004, 43). St Clair Drake affirmed in 1970: "the force [of Ethiopianism] is now almost spent" (Drake 1991, 11). William Shack, who did not comment directly on the survival of Ethiopianism, underlined the influence that African Americans "heroes" had had, and tried his hand at futurology: "But I would hazard a guess that many of the currently popular slogans which African Americans have fashioned out of their struggles, such as 'seize the time', 'power to the people', and the like, will be reinterpreted within the framework of the changing political scene in Ethiopia" (Shack 1974, 155).

To a certain extent, he was not wrong, and it could be argued that the American slogans did not cause but, we could say, were echoed in others, heard in Ethiopia at the dawn of the 1974 revolution: "*Itiopia teqdem*" ("Ethiopia first"), "*märét larashu*" ("the land to the labourer", that is, to the people). The location of these three researchers in the US space in which Ethiopianism circulated blinkered their gaze. They gave a royal burial to an ideology which had contributed greatly to the formation of black nationalism and pan-Africanism, for the reason that, before their very eyes, African Americans were regarding the independent African countries with increased attention. However, as I will show in the next section, there was a large wave that they did not foresee. Or rather, one which had been unfurling for several years at the time of their writing, but which they were unable to decipher: the incoming wave of Jamaicans. Eternal migrants, frequently transiting through the American hub, it is from Jamaica that they took hold of the torch of Ethiopianism. Although there was no reason to expect this, the arrivals in Shashemene slowed down in keeping with the changing concerns of the black American communities; the new African nations attracted all eyes, and returnees and activists settled there, while, slowly but surely, Rastafari from Jamaica started to arrive in Ethiopia. They had vocally claimed their right to return and had organized themselves to finance their voyages. Moving completely against the tide, they began to appropriate Shashemene and to demonstrate at the same time the continuity of Ethiopianism and the permanence of the desire for return.

THE REAPPROPRIATIONS OF THE UNIVERSAL ETHIOPIAN ANTHEM, WHICH became in 1920 "the anthem of the black race", outlined the contours of the "Ethiopian nation" outside Ethiopia. In 1930, one of its authors, Arnold J. Ford, a black Jew from the Caribbean and a migrant in the United States, left for Ethiopia. The end of the Italo-Ethiopian war pushed a generation of pan-Africanists to go to Ethiopia and to contribute to the rebuilding of the country. However, the EWF, the pan-Ethiopian organization which institutionalized the identification of the black people with Ethiopia, mobilized with difficulty in response to Haile Selassie's invitation to its members to come and settle on the land in Shashemene. Launching the dynamics of the return to Shashemene, the first newcomers, who were previously little known, James and Helen Piper, were Caribbean migrants in the United States and they were followed by a few Americans including Gladstone Robinson. Few in number, they were, in fact, the first comers, the pioneers of this rural settlement. The prestige of Ethiopia weakened facing the independence of other African nations, but the relations specific to modern Ethiopianism were about to shift from the United States to Jamaica, from whence the dynamics of the return to Shashemene would rebound.

CONCLUSION TO PART 1

THE DESIRE TO RETURN TO AFRICA IS GENERATED by the reconstruction of origins, the violence in the societies originating in slavery, and the power of the imagination. It may be interpreted alternatively as a metaphor of escape or as a metaphor of freedom. An enterprise with a utopian character, the return to the continent, whether defended or disparaged, was closely related to the formation of black nationalism and of pan-Africanism and was used to claim unity in the nature and destiny of the black populations around the Atlantic. Whereas governmental, English and American initiatives led many African descendants to form cosmopolitan societies in Sierra Leone and Liberia as of the end of the eighteenth century, other paths were also taken, in the direction of Nigeria, Benin, or Haiti. The black intellectuals engaged in the defence of return projects sometimes participated in these initiatives but also developed their own projects of return. Conflating return plans, evangelization and trade, their discourses were contradictory, and their human and financial efforts of mobilization, depending on their local situation in the Americas, often failed. The disproportionate role of Caribbeans in these pan-African projects has been underlined; many came to settle on the continent during the nineteenth century. Marcus Garvey's movement, which climaxed at the turn of the 1920s, was the most powerful example. Garvey himself never managed to visit the continent, but the legacy of his movement was remarkable, despite obvious contradictions and ambiguities.

In his programme, which gave pride of place to racial nationalism, Garvey recalled the spiritual corollary of the social and economic independence of black people: identification with the God of Ethiopia. Continuously excluded from the process of reflection on the phenomenon of return to Africa, Ethiopia nevertheless occupied a distinct place in the workings of the black nationalist and socioreligious imaginary defined as Ethiopianism. Nourished by a biblical substrate, Ethiopianism was activated by a double identification with the Ethiopian people as the ultimate representation of the black people and with the Ethiopian royalty as an incarnation of power and of the black nation.

Ethiopianism, an overlooked and complex ideology, invariably surfaced in the spaces where colonial and racial conflicts converged – in the United States, in the Caribbean and in southern Africa at the beginning of the nineteenth century. Following the Ethiopian victory against the Italians in Adwa (1896), the coronation of Emperor Haile Selassie I (1930), and the Italo-Ethiopian war (1935–41), Ethiopianism moved beyond the symbolic sphere proper and developed *in relation to* the modern Ethiopian state. The evolution of these relations is particularly visible through the study of the African descendants present in Ethiopia as of the end of the nineteenth century. These pan-Africanists were doctors, entrepreneurs and craftsmen from various horizons and often collided with the racism of the Western diplomatic services. They were invited on several occasions, by Emperors Menelik II and Haile Selassie I, to settle in the country and to contribute to its development.

As of the 1930s, the dynamics that would lead to a rural settlement close to Shashemene were put in place. The Italo-Ethiopian war having provoked an unprecedented pan-African mobilization, the "Ethiopian volunteers" sought to enrol in the Ethiopian armed forces. Few managed to do so, owing to obstruction by the English and the American governments, but many went to Ethiopia in the 1940s to take part in the rebuilding of the country. Despite or because of Marcus Garvey's criticism of the emperor's choice of exile, the latter decided to create a pan-Ethiopian device to gather the moral and financial support manifested in the Americas. Consequently, the EWF was created. To thank the members of this organization for their mobilization, Haile Selassie I invited them to come and settle on a land concession situated on the periphery of Shashemene. The first donation of land to the diaspora by an African head of state, the settlement of Shashemene was a crucial step in the development of the relations between Ethiopia and the black people of the world. A few American and Caribbean migrants arrived in a slow trickle and settled there until the middle of the 1960s. When the gaining of independence by other African nations recharted the transatlantic landscape, visitors and returnees moved to these new countries symbolizing independence and freedom. Contrary to appearances, the reterritorialization of pan-African concerns and the deceleration of Ethiopianism did not mark the end of migrations to Shashemene. Quite unexpectedly, a wave of Jamaicans relayed this movement of return and appropriated the land in Shashemene, erasing the memory of those who had gone before them.

By expanding the transatlantic space to include Ethiopia, this part of the book has endeavoured to identify and unravel the ideological and social roots of the return to Ethiopia. The tangible and intangible heritages entailed in black nationalism, pan-Africanism and Ethiopianism circulated widely in these changing spaces and nourished the imaginary of return. The "Ethiopians from abroad" were less visible during the African independences, but the symbolic appeal of the land of Ethiopia – seen as black, free and, sometimes, as holy

– remained. Perpetuating while transforming the genealogies of return, the activists invited to Shashemene, black Jews and other members of the EWF, laid the groundwork of return. They were pioneers, the first to establish a rural settlement, certain that their skills could change the social landscape; they were also heirs to nationalist contradictions, which strove to invest them with a leading role in the domination and control of the continent. They were pioneers in view of their fundamental disparity with pan-African concerns of the 1960s; they were also symbolic heirs to the land in Ethiopia offered by an emperor who was to become the representative of earthly and divine powers. Simultaneously a head of state and a Messiah, he incarnated, despite himself, liberty, the nation and the status of a chosen people, all of which had helped to form the religious, social and political mindscape of African descendants.

Part 2

THE RASTAFARI MOVEMENT AND THE RETURN TO ETHIOPIA

"They took us by boat and we're coming back by plane."
– *Bro Trika, Shashemene*

"I man remember even in the seventeenth century from Jamaica, went to Canada and to Sierra Leone. Repatriation is a fulfilment. Father was building I and I spiritually before we come on the land, we have a commandment since the times of Israel. Moses build we again within deh concept deh. When man reach certain perfection, man could a go through repatriation programme same way."
– *Priest Paul, Shashemene*

Hear what Israel say
Send us home to Shashemene land
The Land that was given by our Father
Emperor Haile Selassie I Jah Rastafari
Send us home to Shashemene land.
– *Peter and Paul Lewis, "Ethiopian Land" (1976)*

THIS SECOND PART PROPOSES A REREADING OF THE relations between the Rastafari movement and Ethiopia. More precisely, what it proposes is another history of the Rastafari movement, made possible by the analysis of the arrivals in

Ethiopia. Analyses of the practices of return being absent from most major works on the Rastafari movement, the first challenge is to demonstrate their "historical reality" (Shack 1974, 143). The return to Africa was defined through the millenarian theological function that it had for the Rastafari, with the result that it was continually staged without ever being fulfilled (Chevannes 1998b, 30). Consequently, the second challenge is to show that return also entails a nationalist function, closely related to its religious function.

Paying attention to the interactions or, to use Max Weber's term, to the "elective affinities" (1967, 103–4) between nationalism and religion, is a significant component of the approach of this work. There exists an interesting historiographic tension regarding the organizations which make up the Rastafari movement. Constructed as an allegory of extreme individual freedom because of the insubordination of its practitioners to all types of homogenization and dominant dogmas, the movement was almost always described as acephalous (Barrett 1997, 172; Chevannes 1998b, 31). Rastafari social organizations have nevertheless been studied, and their fluid, destructured and often ephemeral aspects have been underlined (Homiak 1985, Homiak and Yawney 2001). Nearly seventy Rastafari organizations with various fortunes have been inventoried (van Dijk 1993, 360–69). The activities of a number of them have been the object of detailed typologies (Rogers 1970), but there is no information concerning the history of their formation.

The third challenge is therefore to show that shifting the angle of approach to the study of Rastafari – that is, by moving away from Jamaica in order to revisit the history of the movement from the vantage point of Ethiopia, provides another image. Seen from Ethiopia – the structuring role of Rastafari organizations in the practices of return becomes obvious. It is not a question of denying the extreme fluidity of the movement – in fact, "free spirits", with no organizational affiliations, went to Ethiopia. The concern here is to clearly highlight the manner in which the return to Ethiopia was initially carried out by Rastafari organizations. What is at stake, in fact, is to demonstrate that return structured the Rastafari organizations which placed the question of settling in Shashemene at the centre of their propaganda and development. Restituting the processes of popular and collective organization, starting with the arrivals in Ethiopia, thus makes room for the writing of another history of the Rastafari movement.

This part will show that the return to Africa was not merely a claim made by the Rastafari, since several sectors of the Jamaican population had stepped into the breach at the same time or even before the Rastafari became the torchbearers. The divinity attributed to Haile Selassie I, in whom converged religious and nationalistic symbolism converged, transformed the invitation to Shashemene into a gesture appropriated by the Rastafari. This section will show how Jamaican Rastafari accomplished the project of return by integrating the historical pan-Ethiopian organization, the EWF, and by creating another organization, the Twelve Tribes of Israel. This section will also draw attention to the manner in which these organizations, which remain more or less unknown, structured the return to Ethiopia and the Rastafari movement. Finally, I will analyse how, following the internationalization of the movement, starting in the 1970s, Rastafari of the entire world, and particularly those of the English-speaking metropolises, also left for Shashemene. This should allow us to fill in the blank spaces on the map of the "Ethiopian nation" outside Ethiopia – a cartography which we can only construct once these "Ethiopian nationals" are back "home". The "return" of this Ethiopian nation transforms Rastafari into the heirs of Ethiopianism and of black nationalism of the postcolonial era. Their pioneering commitment is revealed by their choice of linking their destiny to that of the land of Ethiopia.

CHAPTER 4

JAMAICA

The Political and Religious Stakes of the Return to Ethiopia

IN JAMAICA, THE ABOLITION OF SLAVERY IN 1834 led to the emergence of "two Jamaicas", to borrow Philip Curtin's term (cited by Patterson 1975, 287): one characterized by an Afro-Jamaican cultural system extending the popular practices formed during slavery and the other oriented towards a European cultural system, understood as the renewal of British civilization maltreated during slavery. This bipolarization continues to characterize the country. In this strongly polarized context, the representations of Africa and the values associated with the continent underwent various changes – from reappropriation to rejection – on the part of a largely black population.[1] The historical complexity of the representations of Africa seen from Jamaica could produce an entire volume of in-depth study. This present chapter will limit itself to a particular mode of representation which saw Africa not only as the land of origin but also as a land of migration and repatriation.

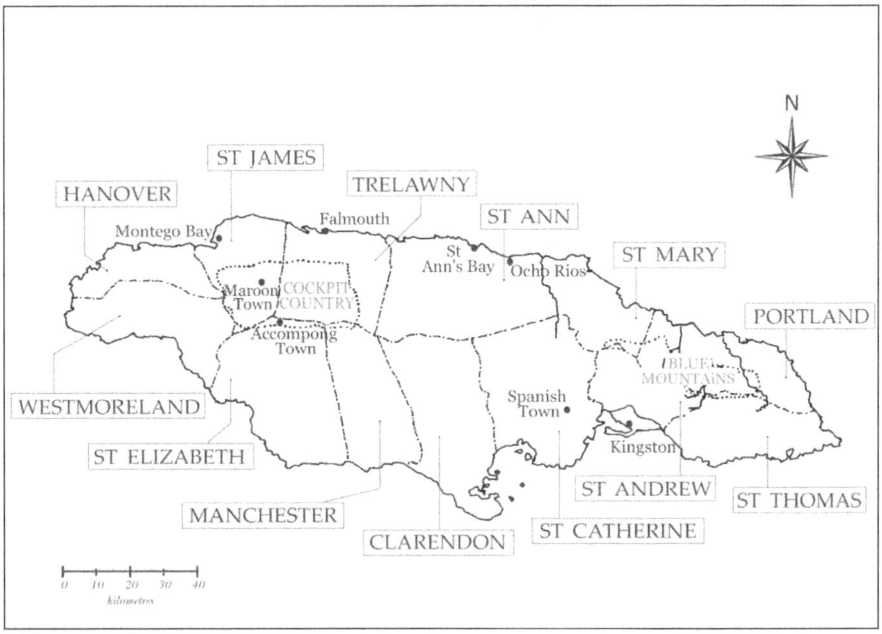

Figure 4.1.
Map of Jamaica

The result of a meticulous study of the Jamaican archives gathered under the title "Repatriation to Africa", this chapter reveals the challenges raised by the question of the return to Africa for colonial and postcolonial Jamaican society. It will become clear that the desire for return resurfaced regularly in Jamaica, bearing witness to the violence of the social conditions, largely inherited from slavery, which structured the social struggles of the popular masses and their relations to the colonial government. I will go on to show how Rastafari reappropriated this claim to the right to return, making it into an alternative to the

Figure 4.2.
The Blue Mountains in Jamaica. Photograph: G. Bonacci © DR.

migratory movements characteristic of this insular society. The images of the Ethiopian nation, the references to an Ethiopian nationality, the incarnation of God in the body of Haile Selassie I were for Rastafari the expression of a radical social criticism. Following the announcement of a land grant in Ethiopia, and despite the reluctance of the EWF concerning the integration of Rastafari, the desire for return became a mass movement, marked by several spectacular failures. I will discuss the consequences of the independence of Jamaica in 1962 with respect to the desire for return and underline, finally, the impact of Haile Selassie's 1966 visit on the practices of return.

"Back to Africa" and the Jamaican Society

The historical scope of the desire for return from Jamaica to Africa extends beyond the Rastafari movement itself. The Sierra Leoneans engaged as workers by the British government in the nineteenth century, the Caribbean veterans of the colonial armies in the 1930s and the Garveyite activists, after Garvey's death in 1940, had already asserted the right to return to Africa: it was a right to work, for the first; a racial right, for the second; and a need in view of preserving the integrity of the races, for the last. The financing of this return was regarded as a responsibility of the British and was requested from them. These various groups illustrate the social diversity of those who demanded the right to return. Nevertheless, their internationalist identity brought them together; they had migrated to Jamaica or had lived abroad and had been activists in international organizations. Seen from Jamaica, the Back-to-Africa claim was therefore a part of the familiarization with the international language of black unity – an important and rarely underlined antecedent of the claim of Rastafari.

The Sierra Leoneans

Following the emancipation of the slaves, proclaimed in 1834 and made effective in 1838 after the years of "apprenticeship" which made little or no change in the conditions of the workers, the British launched a campaign of recruitment of Sierra Leoneans to work in Jamaica. Thousands of Sierra Leoneans were engaged, many of whom wanted to return to their country of origin at the end of the period of indenture, which generally lasted five years. As a result of decreasing wages and the fall in their standard of living in Jamaica, very few managed to return (Schuler 1980, 88–93). Between 1843 and 1845, less than three hundred persons made the return journey by boat. A number of Africans freed in Cuba, some veterans of the colonial armies and immigrant children born in Jamaica slipped in among these returnees. A new period of indenture began, and the Jamaican authorities disregarded the questions related to the repatriation of the indentured workers. Between 1849 and 1857, at least two hundred and thirty persons asked to be repatriated, but only a few were successful. Many petitions were addressed from Sierra Leone to the Queen of England requesting the return of relatives exiled in Jamaica. In 1861, seventy-four Africans embarked for Sierra Leone by personally defraying the cost of the crossing, while the colonial government denied any future responsibility regarding repatriation to Sierra Leone. Thousands of immigrants were forced to remain in Jamaica, nurturing a collective imaginary of Africa and of return, largely sustained by the increasing internationalization of the Jamaican migratory landscape. In fact, as of the 1880s, massive migrations of Jamaicans to Central America and North America disrupted the social landscape of the country and contributed to the internationalization of the practices and experiences of Jamaican peasants.

With the constant decline of the sugar industry since emancipation and with the emergence of banana cultivation, which gradually developed into a mass production, the fate of the peasants was sealed. The unemployment of sugar workers, the starvation wages of the workers in the banana industry, an unjust system of land taxation and a rise in prices of land due to the development of banana plantations forced the Jamaican peasants to migrate massively to the urban areas, where they lived in extremely unsanitary conditions. Between 1871 and 1911, the percentage of the population employed in agriculture continued to fall while that of employees in the urban "domestic sector" rose constantly. Indentured workers from China, and especially from India, added to the economic pressure of the poorest members of the working class (James 1998, 22–23). Whereas Jamaicans of black and mulatto extraction who became teachers, secretaries, clergymen and lawyers began to form a literate and active middle class aspiring to assimilation and cooperation with white culture and authority, as of the 1880s, the peasants, rural and urban residents and other poor people made up the contingents of outmigrants to Central America and the United States (Campbell 1994, 39). Migratory flows were initially unequal. For example, in 1906, 3,018 persons originating from all over the Caribbean entered the United States, and 10,533 Jamaicans left for Panama. At the beginning of the 1920s, New York became the primary destination of Jamaican migrants (James 1998, 49). This migratory movement was particularly important as it allowed Jamaican migrants to familiarize themselves with the international language of racial unity. As noted by Winston James (1998, 71): "Many of these travelled Caribbeans developed an internationalist, pan-Africanist perspective through interacting with black people from different countries and through observing the common oppressed condition of black humanity around the world. . . . It was easier for those who have travelled than for those who have not, to develop a pan-Africanist consciousness."

This pan-African consciousness increased considerably in Jamaica, and Marcus Garvey's trajectory was exemplary in this respect: previously engaged in trade union activities in Jamaica, he travelled to Central America and resided in London before founding the UNIA in New York in July 1918. His slogans, "Back to Africa" and "Africa for the Africans at home and abroad", had raised high the hopes of a Jamaican population undergoing important social changes at the beginning of the twentieth century, and the claim to return to Africa persisted after the decline of the UNIA in the 1920s. The first spontaneous petitions of Jamaicans claiming the assistance of the government to return to Africa date back to the 1930s. At the time, Jamaica was experiencing the impact of the stock market crash of 1929 and the subsequent economic depression. The majority of workers were not yet unionized; the wages of the sugar workers had not increased since 1838; and unskilled activities, like transporting banana, were carried out in violent and degrading conditions (Campbell 1994, 78–79). The workers of the urban areas were particularly affected by the Great Depression, and their standard of living declined. Malnutrition, diseases, lack of education and of social services added to urban overpopulation, and the development of slums transformed the decade of 1930s into a period of harsh living conditions.

The Veterans of the British West Indies Regiment

The Caribbean veterans who had participated in the First World War under British command wrote to the government, as early as 1933, to request repatriation to Africa. They were not the only ones to nourish this desire, but taking the step of writing to the governor of Jamaica was probably facilitated by their prior experiences and contact with the British administration. The British West Indies Regiment was founded in 1915 in spite of the initial refusal of the British War Office and Colonial Office, which did not want black combatants on European soil (James 1998, 55). Being good colonial subjects, numerous Caribbeans were eager to enrol, and approximately fifteen thousand men were finally recruited – two thirds of whom were Jamaicans – to form eleven battalions, with four hundred officers, mostly white and mulatto Caribbeans – but they were excluded from the European front and confined to Egypt, Mesopotamia, Palestine, Cameroon and Tanganyika. It is only after the success of the Bermuda Voluntary Artillery in France in the winter of 1915–16 that the Caribbean regiments began to arrive in Europe to take part in the combat (56, 61). The experience of segregation and humiliation suffered by these black soldiers in the British army contributed to their political awakening. With inferior wages, housing and food, a second-class status in the hospitals and camps, strict segregation in all activities – except cricket – the constant inequalities of treatment and the humiliation were strongly resented by the soldiers and by the island populations (56–60). Hence, an entire Caribbean generation was radicalized. The war experiences gave rise to increased nationalist and racialized ideologies, with C.L.R. James as a famous example.

The pan-African awakening due to the internationalization of the Jamaican experience and the radicalization that it clearly produced was witnessed in the reiterated requests to the British government to facilitate the return to Africa. Return was the object of an initial series of six letters written in 1933 by Gilbert McKenzie, a native of Barbados, addressed to the governor of Jamaica, and all were signed, except the first, by several veterans. McKenzie stressed that his ancestors had been taken away as slaves from Lagos to Jamaica in 1806, just one year before the abolition of the slave trade by the English.[2] He also declared to be in the company of Sierra Leonean descendants who had been recruited as workers in 1826. They were all reported to have served in the British West Indies Regiment. On his return to Jamaica, McKenzie continue to serve in the armed forces for some time, but after the dissolution of the regiment in 1927 and the financial crash of 1929, he fell on hard times and sought work: "I applied at the various institutions and departments within the Corporate area of Kingston and Saint Andrew, viz.– Hospitals, Asylum, Poor House, Railways, Custom, Public work and other well-known places, and no employment to be had."[3] As a last resort, he approached the regiment's benevolent fund, but failed to obtain social aid. Indignation and anger surfaced in his letters, which all followed the same narrative scheme: McKenzie revisited the history of Jamaica, the extermination of the Indians by the Spanish, the conquest by the English, and the importation of "tens of thousands of West Africans of West Africa [who] were robbed, and exploited, and brought to this colony to work as slaves in the various plantations by the English race".[4] He often insisted with pride on the fact that he was African, born in the West Indies but colonized and losing his language and his name to find himself stranded with the English language and an English or Scottish name. McKenzie relayed Garvey's nationalism: "The Universe knows that we are scattered Africans in the West Indies and Africa is for the Africans at Home and Abroad."[5] Winston James has underlined the extent to which the veterans reinforced the UNIA (James 1998, 66–68), whose specific terminology is to be found in these letters. The veteran asserted the right to return to Africa, framing it as a "racial right". He also used several terms to evoke the subject of return, first "a free deportation to Africa, the land of my sires, where I can earn a living to better my poverty stricken condition and regain what is lost".[6] In the following letter, he used the term "repatriation": "We know there are millions of square miles of land in Africa not yet developed and we should be there to assist in developing those lands and gather from it the wealth of the resources. We are now asking to be repatriate [*sic*] to Africa, the home of our fore-parents."[7]

Africa was directly associated with land, perceived as a source of economic independence, a powerful factor underlying the desire for return. Two weeks later, he used the term "emigration": "We positively know, in full conscience of spirit and with racial feelings that our request to emigrate in Africa is based on the racial rights of a right cause."[8] Be it deportation, repatriation, or emigration, at all events, McKenzie called on the responsibility of the colonial government. He frequently mentioned the right of the "black race" to return to Africa and the duty of the English to contribute to this return. Whereas an officer of the colonial government, recalling that return was one of the elements of Garvey's programme, exclaimed: "these men cannot be so ignorant as might be supposed to the conditions in Africa", probably without considering the living conditions of unemployed Jamaicans.[9] The governor, Sir Alexander R. Slater, who seemed more understanding, added that "theoretically the argument of the petitioners is not without force and it commands my sympathy".[10] But the question of return encountered a major obstacle: "if Government recognized it [the right to return] we should logically have to repatriate all the descendants of African slaves who claimed that right – a number which <u>might</u> easily run to hundreds of thousands."[11]

In fact, the repatriation of thousands of African descendants was not a priority of the British government. This governor, Sir A.R. Slater, had previously served in the Gold Coast and recalled an initiative taken by African Americans who had chartered a boat to repatriate African descendants. The migrants were not welcome, a "tragedy"; added to which, many died of fever. As for the survivors, they were once again "repatriated", this time probably to the United States, at the expense of the government of the Gold Coast.[12] On 26 April 1933, McKenzie received a definitive answer: repatriation of the population was impracticable; there were no funds at hand, and this solution was not in the interest of the petitioners. McKenzie refuted these arguments, announced that two hundred and thirteen people were ready to leave for Africa and that the conditions there were of no importance – it was the responsibility of the British to respond to the request of the veterans.[13] Two years later, when the Italian threats to Ethiopia brought greater strength to racial consciousness, McKenzie returned to the attack and reiterated his request for assistance to return to Africa.[14] In the last petition, addressed directly to the king in London, he recalled the "accidental birth" of Africans in the Caribbean, emphasized the commitment of the Caribbean soldiers to the empire during the First World War and, in a prose sprinkled with Garveyite slogans, the urgency of the war in Ethiopia and racial justice, he continued to claim the right to return.[15]

In 1938, driven by Garveyite nationalism exacerbated by the Italo-Ethiopian war, great revolts shook Jamaica: peasants, port and sugar workers, domestic servants and the poor of all walks of life took up arms to demand better working conditions and increased wages. Sometimes regarded as a "social and political revolution", this great revolt was a historic moment (Nettleford 2001, 122). The popular involvement in political action was the fruit of the development of racial consciousness and showed that great sections of the proletariat had organized (Nettleford 2001, 122; Campbell 1994, 81–85). Important political figures took off on this occasion, in particular Norman Manley and Alexander Bustamante, two cousins who, based on the trade union organizations of 1938, founded the two Jamaican political parties, which are still rivals today: the People's National

Party and the Jamaica Labour Party. The response of the colonial authorities to the great revolts of 1938 was a terrible repression, and since the social conditions remained unchanged, the requests for repatriation aid continued to flow into the offices of the colonial government. On 1 August 1938, a march was organized to protest against the repression following the revolts and to propose as a solution that the government "send us back to Africa". Addressed to "Ethiopians", the circular announcing the march bore the slogans of the UNIA, "One God, One Aim, One Destiny" and "Africa for Africans at Home and Abroad". Africa was celebrated as land where all was possible: "Africa the Land of oppertunity [*sic*]! Africa the Land of untold and undiscovered Treasures! Africa the glourious [*sic*] of all Lands."[16] In 1938, McKenzie continued, unsuccessfully, to send petitions, and other veterans took over. J.A. Atkinson, who had already signed the letters written by McKenzie, wrote, in his turn, a petition in June 1939. He declared his desire to return to Africa "in the same manner that Jews are being returned to Jerusalem" and pointed out that lands were free in Nigeria and that they wanted to go and develop them.[17]

Copeland Robinson was particularly disgruntled and began his letter by saying: "we the Black Nation form the Black Race". He reminded the government that it was no longer possible for black people to continue to be maltreated, killed and wrongfully repressed. Robinson requested to return "home" and he concluded his letter by reiterating his seriousness.[18] Nilton Gordon, for his part, had been deported from the United States two years earlier. His small church did not allow him to make a living and attain a respectable position because "there is none for a poor black man in this country. The system, Sir, is against him." Refusing to be the subject of any race or nation, Gordon asked to be sent back to Africa.[19] Following in the wake of the veterans, persons of all types relayed the back-to-Africa claim. The letters sent to the colonial government form the visible part of a social distress that imagined no solution save departure to the continent. To these letters, the government systematically replied that it had no intention of supporting such claims, that they were neither fundable nor desirable, and no job offer or alternative was ever proposed to the petitioners.

The Universal Negro Improvement Association in the 1940s

After the death of Marcus Garvey in London in 1940, the UNIA experienced an unquestionable decline in terms of international activities and visibility. However, in 1937 in Jamaica, a branch of the UNIA, the Whitfield Division, located in Trench Town, a popular neighbourhood in Kingston, was reorganized by Clifford Gayle upon his return from British Honduras (Belize), where he had spent a year and a half.[20] By September 1941, the secretary of this local, Florence Pitters, wrote to the governor of Jamaica, Sir Arthur Richards, to inform him that the UNIA was going to conduct a "missionary work" in the country in order to collect signatures supporting a bill on return called the Repatriation Bill.[21] Three weeks later, Mrs Pitters took up her pen once again to confirm that, despite the numerous petitions the government had already received on this subject, their request remained legitimate, especially in view of the social conditions in which the majority of Jamaicans lived. By recalling the fact that the British supported the liberation of Ethiopia in 1941, she amalgamated the country with a race, that of the Ethiopians and, by extension, with the black people of the world:

> For how can a great and powerful nation recognize as an ally a Race while some of the said race are kept as partial slaves under the hand of its powerful ally? . . . if the British government should make the grave mistake of not keeping to her word of giving justice to Ethiopia, which must include justice to all her children those at home and those abroad, [it] will cause the entire race to lose the confidence they had in the words of the British Government.[22]

Florence Pitters borrowed the discourses associating black nationalism and modern Ethiopianism by identifying the descendants of Africans with Ethiopians and by requesting their relocation to the continent. But it is unlikely that this letter threatening the British with the loss of confidence of their colonial subjects made a great impression on them. In January 1942, the Repatriation Bill of Jamaica and the West Indies, written by Mrs Pitters at the order of the general president of the UNIA, James R. Stewart, arrived on the desk of the governor of Jamaica.[23] The Garveyites had previously supported the Bill for Voluntary Resettlement of American Negroes in West Africa, also known as the Greater Liberia Act, submitted to the American Senate on 24 April 1939 by Theodore G. Bilbo (1877–47). A Democrat senator of the Mississippi, Bilbo was a racist convinced that, in order to safeguard the integrity of the races and to solve the "racial problem" in the United States, the return to Africa of the descendants of slaves was an absolute priority. Supported by the most extremist among the black nationalists, he stated that three million blacks had signed this petition (Bilbo 1947, 213). The Repatriation Bill promoted by Whitfield Division of the UNIA in Trench Town reused large sections of Bilbo's text[24] and, using the threat of intermingling, asked for a complete separation of the races. This essentialist vision designated the mulattos as a danger and incriminated, in the same breath, birth control purportedly aimed at reducing the demography of the black race. Her discourse having been re-tailored to fit the Jamaican context, Pitters mentioned the subsidies Queen Victoria had granted to slave owners during abolition. These compensations amounted to twenty million pounds: had the money been granted to the ex-slaves, they would not have lived in such conditions. In conclusion, Pitters underlined the similarity in the destiny of Afro-descendants and the children of Israel, whose Exodus liberated them from Egyptian slavery: "So we, the oppressed children of African decent [*sic*], have taken up the cry.

– Send us back to Africa. Remember 10 plagues was the chastisement on the House of Pharoah [*sic*] for hardness of heart; and I venture to say – every Race, Group or Nation that turns a deaf ear to the call of Justice, shall be paid likewise."[25]

The Exodus archetype was still functioning: Afro-descendants were assimilated with the Hebrews, and the British government, associated with the Pharaoh, was implicitly threatened with future disasters. Furthermore, in October 1942, Florence Pitters forwarded a copy of this document directly to the secretary of state for the colonies, in London, probably for fear that the governor of Jamaica might refrain from informing his superiors of the claims of the UNIA. She affirmed, moreover, that the UNIA had 25,000 registered members who had signed this petition and that they were representative of the 760,000 black Jamaicans.[26] Reiterated in another letter welcoming the new governor of Jamaica, Sir John Huggins, in 1943, her social criticism remained unchanged. She accused the middle class, associated with mulattos, of refusing to support the progress of the black population, while at the same time distancing herself from the "communist threat" embodied by the People's National Party and from the capitalist class which left "the poor masses gapping on a meagre existence".[27] The last, dislodged by the bauxite industry progressively established in the countryside, inflated the contingents of migrants who moved first in the direction of the cities, then towards the Americas and England. The land was bought from small farmers, leading to their displacement, and between 1943 and 1970, nearly half a million Jamaicans were consequently forced to leave the countryside, while Jamaica became one of the largest bauxite producers in the world, exploited by Canadian and American multinationals (Campbell 1994, 86).

In 1944, while the impoverishment of the population increased as bauxite replaced sugar at the centre of the economy, the transfer of the constitutional power from Great Britain to Jamaica began. Universal suffrage, a bicameral legislature comprising an elected assembly, and the rudiments of a ministerial administration placed Jamaican politics on the road to independence (Nettleford 2001, 116). Nevertheless, these gains appeared quite limited in the eyes of nationalist and pan-Africanist Jamaicans, who were then in the process of discussing the clauses of the Atlantic Charter signed by the president of the United States, Franklin D. Roosevelt, and the British prime minister, Winston Churchill, in 1941. In the middle of the Second World War, the Atlantic Charter expressed Anglo-American solidarity and laid the groundwork of the future Charter of the United Nations Organization. Its third clause indicated "the right of all people to choose the form of government under which they will live" and the right to self-determination of the peoples who had been deprived of it by force (Padmore 1960, 162). Winston Churchill had stressed that this charter did not apply to the populations of colour of the colonial empire, a position that was unacceptable for African and Caribbean nationalists. On the initiative of Nnamdi Azikiwe, who was then the director of the National Council of Nigeria and Cameroon, a memorandum was published in 1943, entitled the *Charter of the Atlantic and British West Africa*, in which the principle of self-determination was approved and the immediate abrogation of the colonial administration was demanded (162). In Jamaica, Amy Jacques Garvey, Garvey's second wife, published, in 1944, a *Memorandum Correlative of Africa, the West Africa, and the Americas* for submission to the leaders of the post-bellum world: Winston Churchill, Chiang Kai-shek, Joseph Stalin and Franklin D. Roosevelt (Goldthree 2005).

The pan-African mobilization around the Charter of the Atlantic and the slow administrative changes in Jamaica fuelled the nationalist and political dynamism of Jamaican militants, and in 1948 the Whitfield Division recommenced its demands concerning the voluntary return of the population to Liberia, this time along with a targeted call for funds and a united petition signed by various activist groups. The UNIA, with "all allied societies in the island working towards Back-to-Africa", but in actual fact with the Afro–West Indian Welfare League, founded in 1938 under the name of Negro Welfare League, presented a petition signed by 57,860 "Afro-Jamaicans" asking the British government for financial support to allow them to go to Liberia, where, according to the document, they would be welcome.[28] The militancy of 1948 generated the enthusiasm of numerous persons, and individual initiatives rallied to these claims, like that of Samuel Hall, who also wanted to go to Liberia with six members of his family.[29] Two years later, the petitioners received a dry, short and inevitably negative reply from the colonial secretary.[30] This mobilization at the end of the 1940s resulted in a collective failure. It has remained particularly disregarded and deserves in-depth research. Indeed, while the People's National Party became the party of the masses in 1949, defending "democratic socialism", a number of Jamaicans, financing their own voyage, nevertheless managed to leave the island for Liberia and for West Africa in general. The history of their settlement has not been documented yet (Campbell 1994, 85).[31]

The letters and petitions mentioned above all stated that their writers had gathered tens of thousands of signatures, but such affirmations were probably inflated in the hope of drawing the attention of the government. However, exaggerated or not, these figures attested to the liveliness of the imaginary of return. It is not difficult to imagine the veterans of the British West Indies Regiment and the officers of the UNIA going from door to door to present their requests to the population. As return was presented as a responsibility of the British administration, the Jamaican workers were probably quite willing to sign petitions. The return to "Africa" remained geographically vague, and Africa remained an unknown continent. On rare occasion, the petitioners showed a remote knowledge of Africa and mentioned Nigeria, for example. Liberia remained central to the imaginary of the Garveyites, whereas their use of the name Ethiopia generally alluded to racial belonging.

It was thanks to the Rastafari that Ethiopia became the centre of the imaginary of return. For the sufferers, return was presented as the only real alternative for economic and social improvement. McKenzie, the earlier mentioned veteran of the British West Indies Regiment, used the term "sufferers" for the first time in 1933.[32] It was reutilized by the Rastafari to represent the majority of the population, which remained, in the unequal development of the country, black, poor and economically marginalized. Rastafari and Back-to-Africa activists developed complex bonds and reciprocal influence in the 1930s and 1940s. The dynamism and radicalism of the Rastafari inspired the black militants, whose constant agitation for return marked the beginning of the Rastafari movement. Whereas the militant elite, like Marcus Garvey, partially disavowed the cultural practices of the Rastafari (Lewis 1998b), many individuals circulated between the two tendencies. This was the case of Clifford Gayle, who, on his return from British Honduras, reorganized the Whitfield division of the UNIA in Trench Town in 1937. A portrayal of Gayle, written by the secretary of that branch of the UNIA, indicated:

> It was a customary sight around the Corporate Area of Kingston and St Andrew, to see [Clifford Gayle] with two drums, a flag rolled up, a lamp post all tied to the drums, and saddled to his back, with the lamp in his hand. Struggling under his load to some favoured corner or square, where he put down his load and hoisted the flag. While thumming [*sic*] on the Bass Drum, he would raise this old familiar song: "Oh Africa awaken the morning is at hand, no more arth thou forsaken! Oh bountious [*sic*] Motherland."[33]

The street, in Jamaica, was an eminently important site of communication (Elkins 1977). Preachers, politicians, activists and passers-by gathered there. That is where Alexander Bedward, a revivalist preacher who attracted great crowds, made his debut in the nineteenth century, and the same applies to Marcus Garvey and the first Rastafari: Leonard Howell, Robert Hinds, Joseph Nathaniel Hibbert and Archibald Dunkley. Clifford Gayle was no exception to this existing practice, and accompanied by a drum, he struck up an "old familiar song", published by Arnold J. Ford, the rabbi from Barbados, the former musical director of the UNIA, who had left for Ethiopia in 1930.[34] This song also appeared in the booklet of the hymns of the Ethiopian Church, the AACC, founded by Robert Athlyi Rogers, which was popular in Jamaica.[35] Certain Rastafari also sang this song in which "Africa" was sometimes replaced by "Ethiopia" (Simpson 1955, 136). This composition, which was as popular in the United States as it was in Jamaica since the 1920s and at least until the end of the 1950s, bears witness to the cultural exchanges between black Jews, Garveyites and Rastafari. These exchanges illustrate the continuity between the legacies of Ethiopianism, nationalism and popular pan-Africanism as well as their transformations. However, the close ties between the leaders of the UNIA and the first Rastafari do not obscure their differences. What distinguished Rastafari was the symbolic and tangible centrality of the Ethiopian nation and of its emperor, Haile Selassie I.

The Rastafari and Ethiopia

The Rastafari, drawing on popular Jamaican religions like Revivalism and influenced by the black internationalism originating in the most disinherited classes of Jamaica, constructed themselves based on a central postulate which could be summarized like this: "we are the true Ethiopians". This saying, repeated in various forms, was not fundamentally different from the identification with the "Ethiopian race" of the black activists who had preceded them. But taking Ethiopianism even further, they conflated religious and nationalist languages. Haile Selassie I, the Ethiopian sovereign, became the centre of their cosmology and the symbol of their cultural and political resistance. The interactions between the literal interpretation of this Ethiopian identity and Haile Selassie I's invitation to Shashemene influenced their centralization of their claims to right of return on Ethiopia.

Ethiopianism in Jamaica

We have already studied, in the preceding part of this work, the importance of Ethiopianism in the formation of black social and religious nationalist thought. Fed by a biblical substrate, Ethiopianism was activated by a double identification with, on the one hand, the Ethiopian people, perceived as the ultimate representation of black peoples, and, on the other, with the Ethiopian royalty, seen as the embodiment of black power and of the black nation. Ethiopianism constantly emerged in the spaces of the United States, the Caribbean and South Africa, in which colonial and racial conflicts converged. It characterized popular practices of resistance and various sociocultural innovations. Ethiopianism was circulated, transmitted and inherited around the Atlantic through the intermediary of black missionaries, migrants and workers. Consequently, Robert Hill stressed that "there had been in existence in Jamaica, prior to the coronation event in Ethiopia in 1930, a considerable tradition of 'Ethiopianism' that was traceable back over a lengthy period" (Hill 2001, 17).

Despite countless references to Ethiopianism in the historiography of the Rastafari movement, the reality of this phenomenon in nineteenth-century Jamaica remains largely unfamiliar. This is surprising since "the most central institution of resistance in Jamaica has been religion " (Chevannes 1988a, 1). The Church of England began its teachings only in 1815; before this date, the Baptist, Methodist and Moravian churches had spread quickly in a context marked by practices derived from African religions (Myal, Obeah, Kumina, Convince, Revival). The Baptists, introduced at the end of the eighteenth century by George

Lisle, a former black American slave, contributed to familiarize enslaved and free Jamaicans with the biblical corpus of Ethiopianism.[36] The Baptists were, moreover, the pioneers of emancipation and education, and they defended access to land and social justice, as demonstrated by the great Morant Bay Revolt in 1865. Paul Bogle, a Baptist preacher, took the lead and forced the white oligarchy, intent on preserving its privileges, to take into account a new social force, constituted by a peasant community, galvanized by the cry "Cleave to the Black!" (Campbell 1994, 35–38; Sibley 1965). Historical gaps persist regarding the formation and the role of Ethiopianism in Jamaica in the nineteenth century, but it resurfaced forcefully at the beginning of the twentieth century. Marcus Garvey's propaganda helped to popularize the identification with Ethiopia and between 1904 and 1906 and again in 1924, certain individuals went as far as demanding official recognition of an Ethiopian lineage conferring on them the status of "black princes" (Elkins 1977, 33–41; Hill 2008). In 1927, the *Daily Gleaner* announced the birth of a "new Ethiopian religion", followed by the publication of two works which formed the interpretative base of the Rastafari movement. *The Holy Piby* and *The Royal Parchment Scroll of Black Supremacy* were published in Jamaica between 1924 and 1926, illustrating the development of Ethiopianism on the island.

The Royal Parchment Scroll of Black Supremacy

The preceding part of this book addressed *The Holy Piby* in view of illustrating the complexity and the international breadth of the "Ethiopian belt" and its incessant search for an identity, a nationality and a – preferably holy – land. Also known as *The Blackman's Bible*, *The Holy Piby*, published in 1924, contained the doctrines of the Afro-Athlican Constructive Church, founded by Robert Athlyi Rogers, from Anguilla. It will suffice to recall that the creed of the AACC, the "Ethiopian prayer", is familiar to most Rastafari.

The second text, entitled *Royal Parchment Scroll of Black Supremacy*, was published in June 1926 by Reverend Fitz Balintine Pettersburgh, who had come to Jamaica two years earlier, from the United States.[37] Little is known about the reverend, but his text did not go unnoticed. The *Daily Gleaner*, reflecting the public position on the subject, published the following in its regard: "The grammar is like the sense, which seems to us to be indistinguishable from nonsense, and the whole concoction is so putrid that we wonder what class of people could ever take such rubbish seriously."[38]

Admittedly, the language of the *Royal Parchment* is difficult to apprehend in many respects; it diverges into metaphysical, and sometimes complex cryptic, considerations which are hard to decipher. However, the "class" mentioned by the *Daily Gleaner* capable of taking such a work "seriously" was very much present. The peasants, workers, national or international migrants, economically strangled and socially marginalized masses valued the *Royal Parchment*. In it they found a religious, racial and nationalist discourse echoing that of Marcus Garvey. The *Royal Parchment* opened with a short introduction signed by "Rev. Fitz Balintine Pettersburgh, King of Kings, Creator of Theocracy, and Biblical Sovereign, the Crown Head of Holy Times". This was followed by a foreword in which the text was described as a rule book. It was described, further on, as "Ethiopia's Bible-text and Rule Book" and as the "Black supremacy, by His Majesty the King of Kings". The body of the book was made up of fifty relatively short chapters. On each page, the biblical Ethiopia was mentioned and used as a metaphor alluding to black people. The continuous juxtaposition of biblical allusions, references to Ethiopia and to black supremacy constituted a spiritual, nationalist and racial discourse. It made mention of common practices of the popular Jamaican religions subsumed by the term Revivalism: healing, baptism and fasting. However, the book sought to distance itself from Obeah, or practices of magic, and deplored the fact that the revivalists had not received the light of "the Resurrection of the Kingdom of Ethiopia". The *Royal Parchment* proposed a form of government that was simultaneously that of a black government – endowed with the prerogatives of the state, such as education, communication, and nationality – and that of a theocracy – represented by the Order of Melchisedec, a priest and king (Genesis 14:18–19). The constant association, on almost every page, of black supremacy, the "King of Kings", "King Alpha and Queen Omega" and other biblical and eschatological titles flagged the messianism underlining the text. Indeed, Reverend Pettersburgh, on several occasions, identified himself with King Alpha, while defending the institution of marriage and the presence of Queen Omega, who probably represented his wife. The throne, crown and sceptre were his royal attributes. Opposing the "Anglo-Saxon Baptist Church" (referred to as the "Anglo Saxon Slave Dynasty called White Supremacy"), the "offense of slavery" and the "Klu-Kluk-Klan" [*sic*], Pettersburgh proposed another organization, that of the "Black Supremacy The Church triumphant" with its officers, both men and women, divided into groups or "circles" of twenty-five members with, at their head, the priests of the "Royal Order of Melchisedec The King of Salem". Because "the Bible owner is the black man", this text was addressed to all black men and women who, together, were seen as representing black supremacy.

Black supremacy represented a symbolic or figurative political takeover by black people which implied a process of inversion of the racial and social hierarchy typical of the Caribbean, where black people, who were in the majority, were always "below" or "behind" (Nettleford 2001, 25). The result of an essentialist vision imagining the economic and cultural domination of blacks over whites, the invocation of black supremacy was in the first place a form of opposition to the influence of the British colonial government. The *Royal Parchment*, with its references to Robert Athlyi Rogers and Marcus Garvey, constituted a framework of intertextual references which was used and perpetuated by the first leaders of the Rastafari movement regardless of police surveillance. The secretary of Robert Hinds, one of the first preachers of the divinity of Haile Selassie I, in an encounter with Barry Chevannes, confirmed that "there was a book entitled *The Black Supremacy*. We used to read those books in public, but we were warned [by the constables] not to keep it up" (Chevannes 1994, 136). The public reading of this work and its oral diffusion through numerous urban preachers contributed to the dissemination of its contents. But another work, published eight years later, was also influential and participated in popularizing the ongoing juxtaposition between religious and nationalist languages.

The Promised Key

Leonard Howell, commonly called the "first Rasta" (Lee 1999), signed *The Promised Key* while in prison for sedition. *The Promised Key* illustrated the circulations characteristic of Ethiopianism, for it was apparently published in 1935, simultaneously in Kingston and Accra by Nnamdi Azikiwe, who was at the time the editor of the *African Morning Post*.[39] Robert Hill has claimed that *The Promised Key* "largely plagiarized" *The Holy Piby* (Hill 2001, 18), but it was, in fact, on the symbols and even, at times, the terminology of the two precursory texts, *The Holy Piby* and *The Royal Parchment Scroll of Black Supremacy*, that it drew, over approximately fifteen pages. Compared to its predecessors, *The Promised Key* was articulated around two innovations: the defence of a new world vision and the proclamation of the divinity of the emperor. Catholicism, and the Pope in particular, were identified as the enemy of Israel and the promoter of a "false religion" of a satanic nature symbolized by the number "666", whereas "civilization" was associated with "black supremacy". Howell was an essentialist who also insisted on the necessary separation of the races and the impossibility of intermarriage between blacks and whites. Regarding the "Ethiopian question", he reused the imagery developed in the *Royal Parchment*, portraying Africa as a female figure and recalled that the slave traders "went into her and robbed her lands, money and took her seeds to be slaves" (Pettersburgh 1926, 74). But Howell replaced the word Africa with that of Ethiopia. Ethiopia was obviously present in the two precursory texts, but this time Howell addressed himself directly to the Ethiopians, to the black people. It is to them that he proclaimed his profession of faith: "My dear Ethiopians, Ethiopia is the crown head of this earth field since heaven has been built by His Majesty Ras Tafari the living God. Thanks and praise the ever living God as long as eternal ages roll" (Howell, 1935, 10).

The main distinction in Howell's text was that the title of "King Alpha" that he used, as Rogers and Pettersburgh had done before, became a synonym of "King Ras Tafari" and of "His Majesty Ras Tafari". The almost systematic use of "Ras Tafari" helped to popularize the first name and the first title of the emperor. Howell described him as a "God Almighty" (Howell 1935, 14), and his titles were repeated in a direct reference to the book of Revelation (19:16): "Upon His Majesty Ras Tafari's head are many diadems and on His garment a name written King of Kings and Lord of Lords, oh come let us adore him for he is King of Kings and Lord of Lords. The Conquering Lion of Judah, The Elect of God and the Light of the World" (Howell 1935, 3).

The Promised Key starts with a lengthy description of the protocol of the coronation of the emperor and insists on the attributes of royalty, the throne, the sceptre, the crowns, the robes and the priests. The Duke of Gloucester, who went to represent the British crown at the coronation, was described as falling to his knees before the "King Ras Tafari". This was a very potent image for the British colonial subjects, symbolizing a submission of white power to black power, which Howell supported with several biblical references (Psalm 72:9–11; Genesis 49:10). Hence, Howell explicitly affirmed that the recently crowned emperor was God and that his kingdom embodied a domination of black supremacy over others. *The Promised Key* was a doctrinary digest which firmly planted the beginning of the Rastafari movement in the continuum of Ethiopianism in Jamaica: "the determinant of Rastafari origins is the underlying identification which blacks have consistently made with Ethiopia by virtue of Biblical symbolism " (Hill 2001, 16). So, not only was there a lively albeit disregarded Ethiopianism in

Figure 4.3. Card distributed by the first Rastafari in Jamaica, in particular Leonard Percival Howell. On the front, the young Emperor Haile Selassie I, on the back an official stamp marked "K.O.K. Mission" (King of Kings Mission), founded by Robert Hinds. © DR.

Jamaica as of the nineteenth century, but it underwent, in the 1930s, what could be termed a great revival, thanks to the circulation of several texts and to their reappropriation by the Jamaican popular imaginary. This probably explains why the name popularized by Howell in 1935, and which came to designate the Rastafari, is Rastafari (*Ras* Tafari), the title and first name of the emperor *before* his coronation in 1930, when he became Haile Selassie I. This phenomenon, which Clinton Chisholm, in an article on the Rastafari movement and Ethiopianism, evaluates as "a minor detail" (Chisholm 1998, 171), nevertheless pinpoints the period 1916–30 as the crucial time "of the incubation" of the Rastafari movement (Bonacci 2013). The Rastafari, by personalizing the God of the Ethiopians, by embodying the myth, elevated Ethiopianism to an acme unattained by the other well-known groups or familiar congregations of the Ethiopianist corpus. Whereas in Harlem in 1931 the members of the UNIA had paraded alongside the congregations of black Jews, carrying in the front line life-size photographs of Marcus Garvey and Haile Selassie I (Hill 2001, 16), the Rastafari transformed the young emperor into a man filled with a divine character.

The Body of the Myth

Marcus Garvey had insisted: the liberation of the black man was also spiritual, hence the need to see God through the "spectacles of Ethiopia". Several prophecies on the crowning of a black king were regularly attributed to him by researchers, with no reference whatsoever (Hill 2001, 14). The staging of his play, *The King and Queen of Africa*, in Kingston in 1930, a few months before the coronation of the emperor, was probably more impactful. The coronation on 2 November 1930, when Tafari became Haile Selassie I, literally meaning the "power of the Trinity", and when he took the titles of King of Kings, Lord of Lords, Conquering Lion of the Tribe of Judah, Elect of God, Light of the World, generally serves to date the birth of the Rastafari movement. The Jamaican and the international press circulated information on the event. The special issue of *National Geographic* devoted to the ceremony appeared in June 1931. Its coloured images and narratives reached Jamaicans and nourished the interpretations generated by the first Rastafari in their midst. Twenty-five years later, the Rastafari continued to use them (Simpson 1955, 137). Thanks to the eighty-three illustrations and two long articles covering almost seventy pages, details of the 1930 coronation and of daily life in Ethiopia became available, visible and tangible for the first time. The fascination that Ethiopia exerted on Addison E. Southard, then the ambassador of the United States in Addis Ababa, is visible in his article on "Haile Selassie the First, formerly Ras Tafari [who] succeeds to the world's oldest continuously sovereign throne " (*National Geographic* 1931, 679). Although illiteracy was widespread, the public reading of these texts wove a close relation between the spoken and the written word. Barry Chevannes explains it in these

Figure 4.4. The coronation of Haile Selassie I, Addis Ababa, 2 November 1930. © DR.

words: "What was written could only reach people by being read to them, and what was heard was surer to be true if it could be proved that it was written" (Chevannes 1994, 120). Once the reality of the event was "proven" by the text, it was soon reinterpreted by sensitized groups as the realization of biblical prophecies concerning the return of the Messiah and as the materialization of the nationalist sentiment which associated Ethiopia with the black nation. The attribution of a divine nature to the Emperor of Ethiopia and the construction of him as a prophetic figure allowed him to play, unwittingly, a crucial social role. Indeed, the fundamental identifier of a Rastafari was above all the belief in the divinity of the emperor: "in Rastafarian philosophy, the reincarnation of Haile Selassie as God transformed in the flesh is the foundation/pillar in the tenets of Rastafarian doctrine and belief systems" (I. Tafari *in* Hill 2001, 5).

The recognition that Haile Selassie I became God in his flesh was the common belief of all Rastafari. However, the individual and collective identification of the Rastafari with the emperor was based on the two facets – political and religious – represented by Haile Selassie through his coronation in 1930, followed by his defence of Ethiopia against Italian aggression. These two aspects were important because, as underscored by Horace Campbell (1994, 102): "The body of ideas and beliefs which guided Rastafari at that time was deeper than simply a deification and glorification of Haile Selassie. His Imperial Majesty (H.I.M.) stood for African independence in an uncompromising manner."

Haile Selassie I incarnated the simultaneous convergence of the political and religious imaginaries. The interpretation of this convergence in the *body* of a black man put the Emperor of Ethiopia at the heart of the Rastafari movement. The titles of the emperor were, for the Rastafari, a significant element "proving" the divine nature of Haile Selassie I. The importance they attached to the imperial titles is interesting to the extent that it reposed on the symbolic capital it entailed, and which belonged to the neo-Solomonic ideology created in the nineteenth century by the Ethiopian emperors in a bid to legitimate their power. This capital was represented by "a stock of symbols and concepts which allowed political rulers to communicate with mass following, and which allowed that following to identify with, and in some sense participate in, the polity" (Crummey 1988, 14). This "stock of symbols and concepts" originated in the Zionist ideology of the Ethiopian sovereigns, and is contained in a book entitled *Kebrä Nägäst*, the "Glory of the Kings".[40] *Kebrä Nägäst* was composed in the fourteenth century on the basis of older texts used to legitimate the power of the Ethiopian sovereigns by constructing their descent from the union of King Solomon of Jerusalem and the Queen of Sheba, and demonstrating that the country and the people of Ethiopia were the successors of Israel and of the Hebrews. The concepts related to the sacred royalty of the Ethiopian crown were, in the main, derived from this text (Ullendorff 1997, 132). Constructed like a Bible and beginning with the creation narrative, *Kebrä Nägäst* details the encounter between King Solomon and Queen Saba, briefly alluded to in the Bible.[41] The fruit of their union, Bayna-Lekem or Menelik I, returned to his father upon his majority, to retrieve – on divine command, obviously – the Ark of the Covenant, around which the temple of Jerusalem had been constructed. The Ark containing the laws given by God to Moses on Mount Sinai, and its transfer to Axum – where tradition affirms that it is still to be found today – conferred on Ethiopians and Ethiopia the status of a people and of a land elected by God. By territorializing Mount Zion, where "God resides", in Ethiopia, the foundation myth of the Ethiopian nation took shape and was elaborated on by the contributions of successive sovereigns, especially as far as titles are concerned. Tewodros (1855–68) used the daring title *s'eyumä egziabehér*, "Elect of God",

Figure 4.5. Haile Selassie, Empress Menen and two of their children, November 2, 1930, St George's Church, Addis Ababa © DR.

to refer to himself; Yohannes IV (1871–89) introduced the appellation *negusä s'eyon*, "King of Zion"; and Menelik II (1889–1913) was the first to use the title *Mo'a anbäsa zäemnägädä yehuda*, "The Lion of the tribe of Judah has prevailed", associating the Messiah with the lion, the symbol of a royal and divine dynasty represented by Israel and the house of David (Crummey 1988; Rubenson 1965, 77). The fundamental justification of nineteenth-century Ethiopian imperial power could be summed up in these words: the "power of God" (Crummey 1988, 35). These successive contributions formed the symbolic and conceptual legacy with which Tafari ascended to the Ethiopian throne. He did not abstain from referring to this neo-Solomonic ideology – quite the contrary, as illustrated, for example, in article 3 of the Ethiopian constitution promulgated in 1931: "Imperial dignity shall remain perpetually attached to the line of His Majesty Haile Selassie I, descendant of King Sahle Selassie, whose line descends without interruption from the dynasty of Menelik I, son of King Solomon of Jerusalem and of the Queen of Ethiopia, known as Sheba" (Pétridès 1964, 275).

The "direct descent" of the sovereigns since Menelik I was part of the construction of the myth, and it is clear to historians that the royal genealogies were much more complex. This reinvented lineage did not alter the symbolic force of the references contained in the imperial titles, converging in 1930 in the person of Haile Selassie I, to form, in the term of Sven Rubenson, "the Ethiopian heritage" (Rubenson 1965, 85). This heritage concerned the people of Ethiopia but also the Rastafari of Jamaica. Indeed, "Rastafari, who proclaimed that Haile

Selassie was the King of Kings and Lord of Lords, was taking the Ethiopian Movement one step further by centralising the person of Haile Selassie as the vehicle of liberation" (Campbell 1994, 3).

The genesis and the development of Rastafari was inscribed in a liberation movement because the Rastafari themselves *incarnated* the myths they generated: they gave body to the myth through their social practices. The symbolic inversion provided by the ideology of the divinity of the emperor influenced the formation of social practices by the Rastafari. They expressed their rejection of the dominant social norm in colonial Jamaica by creating another system of values. Joseph Owens expressed it as follows: "The Rastaman is a myth, a substantial, concrete, objective myth, yet you cannot kill it with guns and batons and starvation and contempt. Rasta has endured and survived because Rasta has attached itself to the people, and has developed and elaborated that myth. The Rastaman has become myth himself" (Owens 1995, 2).

In a social structure derived from the plantation system, in which everything African was devaluated and where the dominant values were European (Nettleford 2001, 36), claiming pride in the black phenotype was, strictly speaking, a social threat. Reversing the image of Africans associated with the infamous chains of slavery, the black body was asserted as the site of divinity and thus was consecrated. This inversion of the colour line associating negritude with royalty, not to mention divinity, was an explicit criticism of the social condition of black people in the British colonies. It was expressed in all Rastafari practices, which have, as a whole, been well studied by researchers (for example, Yawney 1978; Homiak 1985; Lewis 1993; Chevannes 1994; Barrett 1997). Hence the wearing of the beard and of dreadlocks, literally "terrifying locks", which transformed their appearance; the ritual use of ganja; the creation of an "egalitarian" language, Italk; the formation of ritual and social structures known as reasoning, groundation and nyabinghi are all expressions of a culture of resistance targeting mental and physical liberation and showing how ideology may be incarnated in everyday reality. Some of these practices were initiated at the Pinnacle, the ideal community founded by Leonard Howell in 1940, perched in the mountains of St Andrews, not far from Kingston, and assembling, in certain periods, more than six hundred members.[42] The development of a community-based, self-sufficient economy, beyond governmental control, was too threatening; the camp was razed twice by the police, in 1941 and in 1954 (Hill 2001; van Dijk 1993, 85–105). The Rastafari of Pinnacle, forced to descend to Kingston, added to the population of the poor neighbourhoods, and to the expansion of the movement. The social practices of Rastafari were transformed and became increasingly radical. These practices were seen as subversive by Jamaican society, and a constant dynamics of resistance and repression was set in place. It reached its apogee with the claim, by Rastafari, of the right to return to Africa. In fact, "Underlying the belief in the Emperor's divinity is the conclusion that

Black people were destined to return to their native Africa, after centuries of injustice at the hands of the Whites" (Chevannes 1998b, 26).

The logical consequence of the construction of the divinity of the emperor, added to individuals' Ethiopian filiation, attained an unprecedented level with the Rastafari. The return to Africa that Rastafari demanded was expressed in a manner conflating the political and religious registers and announced their opposition to the colonial government by ascribing to it the prerogative of illegitimacy. For Weber, the contemporary state is "a human community which, within the limits of a given territory . . . successfully asserts for its own account the *monopoly of legitimate physical violence*" (1963, 125; italics in the original).

The contemporary Jamaican state was heir to the British slave administration, and the physical violence induced by the technologies of slavery was in fact legal until 1834, the official date of emancipation. This legality made the Jamaican state fundamentally illegitimate, from the standpoint of Rastafari. By contrast, the physical violence exercised by the Ethiopian state was viewed as totally legitimate, as its objective was to preserve the independence of the country. Fuelled by Rastafari cultural innovations, the Back-to-Africa claims targeted Ethiopia in particular.

Back to Ethiopia

In Rastafari perspective, repatriation to Africa fulfilled a double function, nationalist and religious: it was simultaneously a means of territorializing the black nation and a means of concretizing its redemption. In addition to the claiming of a right due to them as the descendants of African slaves, they connected with biblical prophecies announcing the return to Zion. The "fulfilment of the prophecy" became, moreover, a central objective, one that was sometimes more rhetorical than practised. The biblical passage that was perhaps the most frequently quoted to justify repatriation as a divine plan was taken from the book of Isaiah (43:5–7):

> Fear not, for *I am* with thee: I will bring thy seed from the east and gather thee from the west: I will say to the north, Give up; and to the south, Keep not back, bring my sons from afar, and my daughters from the ends of the earth; Even every one that is called by my name, for I have created him for my glory, I have formed him; yea, I have made him.

"The fulfilment of the prophecy" was thus therefore a sign of the reappropriation of the biblical and nationalist symbolism derived from the people of Israel. The language of Exodus, the identification with the children of Israel and their return to Zion were recontextualized by the Jamaican Rastafari in response to their socio-economic conditions and their experiences of discrimination. What the Rastafari proposed was in fact an alternative national allegiance, not with the British Empire but with the Ethiopian empire. While Leonard Howell was in prison for sedition in 1934, it was reported in the press that the Rastafari were preparing to return to Ethiopia by walking over the waters, an event which, obviously, did not take place (van Dijk 1993, 92). The Rastafari were obliged to wait until the 1940s for their claims to reach the government in a more official manner. Between 1943 and 1949, at least thirty-five letters, most of them handwritten, pleading the cause of return, were received by the colonial secretariat. The fact that their authors were Rastafari was highlighted by the countless references to "our Glorious God, King Rastafari",[43] "the Negro people God and King is here and he is the King of Glory",[44] "our Black government, King and Emperor of Ethiopia",[45] or by the signatures in the name of "Haile Selassie I, Power of the Trinity".[46] The superposition of the religious and nationalist languages to which the Rastafari were heirs found expression in every one of these letters – and their receipt was not always acknowledged by the offices of the colonial secretariat.

C. Jones had worked as a driver for the Jamaica Labour Party in 1940 but had later been unemployed for three years. He begged the government to find him a job pending his return to Africa.[47] He had sent handwritten letters – the first of which is quoted in extenso below, in view of demonstrating the wealth of biblical references he used to formulate his distress and claims:

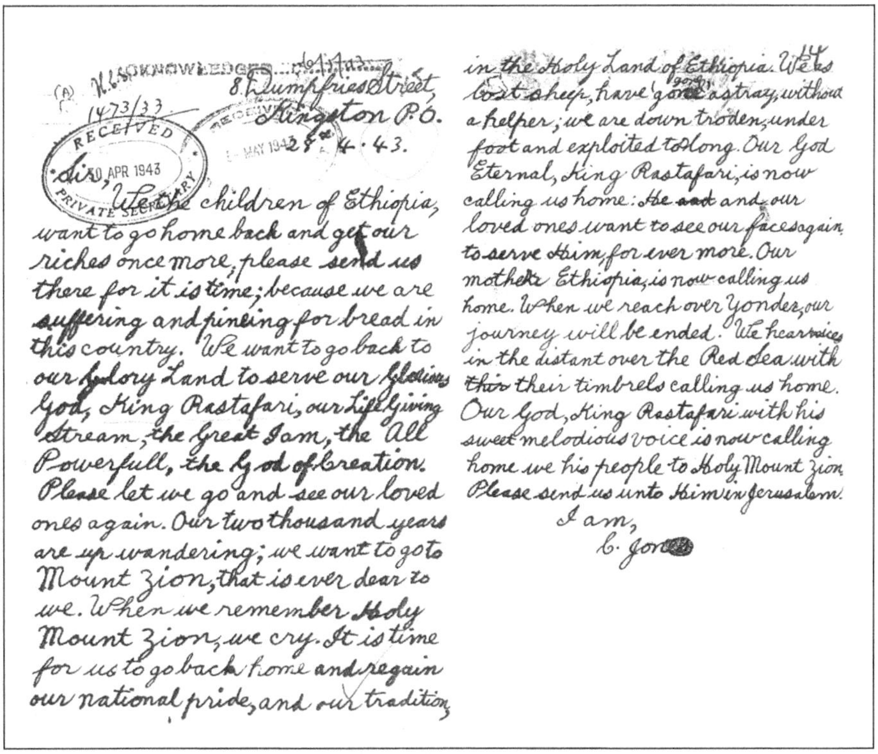

Figure 4.6. C. Jones to the colonial secretary, 4/28/1943 in 1B/5/77/390 [1933] Repatriation to Africa II, National Archives, Spanish Town, Jamaica. © DR

> We the Children of Ethiopia, want to go home to get our riches once more, please send us there for it is time; because we are suffering and pincing [*sic*] for bread in this country. We want to go back to our Glory Land to serve our Glorious God, King Rastafari, our Life Giving Stream, the Great I am, the All Powerfull [*sic*], the God of Creation. Please let we go and see our loved ones again. Our two thousand years are up wandering; we want to go to Mount Zion, that is ever dear to we. When we remember Holy Mount Zion, we cry. It is time for us to go back home and regain our national pride, and our tradition, in the Holy Land of Ethiopia. We as lost sheep have gone astray, without a helper; we are down trodden, under foot and exploited too long. Our God Eternal, King Rastafari, is now calling us home. He and our loved ones want to see our faces again to serve Him for ever more. Our mother Ethiopia is now calling us home. When we reach over yonder, our journey will be ended. We hear voices in the distant over the Red Sea with their timbrels [*sic*] calling us home. Our God, King Rastafari with his sweet melodious voice is now calling home we his people to Holy Mount Zion. Please send us unto Him in Jerusalem.
>
> I am, C. Jones[48]

The biblical turn of phrase was particularly patent in this text, containing almost unchanged quotations of passages like the following from Psalm 137, "By the rivers of Babylon, we sat down and wept, when we remembered Zion", which the Rastafari sang to the accompanimentof nyabinghi drums. This psalm was also set to music in 1969 by the Melodians and became a reggae classic, "Rivers of Babylon", and was again interpreted in 1978 by the Jamaican disco group Boney M, who transformed it into an international hit. The biblical geography – the Red Sea, the Holy Land, Mount Zion – was re-actualized with Ethiopia at its centre, functioning as a synonym of the promised land. The complaint of the exiled Israelites was completely reappropriated and served to transform the departure to Ethiopia into a return ordained by God, in the guise of "King Rastafari". The identification with the Israelites, combined with a filiation with Ethiopia, was a well-known expression of Ethiopianism that had lost nothing of its topicality for the Rastafari. It was also on the basis of this identification that Annie Harvey wrote to the colonial authorities to demand the "return of the children of Israel of Jamaica and other islands of West Indies" to the African continent, the "land of their fathers". She underlined the wealth of the African soil, which would allow the poor to live in dignity, and stated that the prophecy of the second coming of Christ had been fulfilled. One of the first consequences of this fulfilment was the necessary return of the children of Israel, that is, of the "dark people".[49]

Born in 1882, Annie Harvey had met her husband David in Port Limón in Costa Rica, and together they had circulated between Panama, Jamaica, Havana and the United States before returning to Jamaica for a few months in 1924. According to the information gathered by the police, Annie M. Harvey had declared that she "was called by a vision to go to Abyssinia to do missionary work. She and her husband therefore left for Abyssinia where they remained for five and a half years before they returned to Jamaica where she continued her missionary work."[50] Little information remains on the details of their stay in Ethiopia, but they must have been present during the coronation of the emperor, since they brought back photographs of the event. In Jamaica, they founded a congregation called "the Israelites" and identified themselves as having "African or Ethiopian" ancestors. The police superintendent discovered no bond between Harvey and the Rastafari movement, and, in fact, Anne Harvey made no mention of "King Rastafari". Nevertheless, perhaps encouraged by the place that the Rastafari were taking, little by little, in the Jamaican society, she was able, ten years after her return from Ethiopia, to put in an official and fervently religious application for the right to return to the continent.

The nationalist dimension of these claims, in which Israel was an inevitable metaphor, traversed every last one of these letters. Thus, C. Jones, in the letter referred to above, spoke about "national pride", and Egbert Smith, the author of four letters, mentioned "national laws and respect" that the black people wanted to gain. He insisted: "We want Ethiopia to know that we are ready to come home."[51] He wrote from a neighbourhood of Kingston transparently called "Dunghill" or, sometimes, "Dungle", a contraction of *dung* and *jungle*; it was a huge area of open garbage disposal inhabited by poor people and had become one of the first strongholds of the Rastafari movement.

The nationalist claim of Rastafari was articulated on the basis of their racial identification with Haile Selassie I. This was effectively demonstrated in a letter by R.E. Bennett and M.L. Henderson, signed by "over 383 others [who] agree with the plan".[52] They began by underlining "a well-known fact throughout the earth, that Emperor Haile Selassie, the King of Kings represent Black peoples all over the world". Based on this identification with the emperor, they insisted on the indisputable reality of the "sovereignty of Ethiopia" and on their need to restore their contact with "their black government". The petitioners made frequent references to the history of slavery to illustrate their right and to prove the legitimacy of their claims, for "history proves that our unsisters [ancestors] were taking [*sic*] from our Motherland Ethiopia as slaves".[53] This certainty of having really had ancestors taken away from Ethiopia was a constant argument of the Rastafari and was used "to concretize" the imagined filiation between Ethiopia and the black peoples and, consequently, to legitimate the return to Ethiopia in particular.

Four letters sent by B.L. Wilson between 1944 and 1945 directly repeated the themes put in circulation by the *Royal Parchment Scroll of Black Supremacy* and *The Promised Key*, signalled by this doubly underlined heading: "black supremacy emerges, Ras-ta-fari, the Lion of Judah reigns". Black supremacy was seen as referring to the original status of the black people prior to slavery and their fall into the hands of Europeans, their "former slaves". But it was also

Figure 4.7a–b. Photograph of Haile Selassie, recto and verso, Jamaica, ca. 1944 in 1B/5/77/390 [1933] Repatriation to Africa II, National Archives, Spanish Town, Jamaica © DR.

perceived as the rebirth of black nationalism, "the consciousness of national pride".[54] This national consciousness was witnessed by the affection for "a King, a Country, and a Flag".[55] Wilson's letters exuded barely disguised threats. One letter bore the words "the last warning" across the first page. The author pointed out that the great revolts of 1938 were not forgotten, implying that they could be renewed.[56] Claiming the name "Rastafarian", Wilson sent to the government two photographs – his own and that of Haile Selassie I – but only the latter is available in the archives.

Other letters followed, revealing the level of analysis and understanding of the early Rastafari, whose consciousness was awakened regarding the problematics of local politics and the stakes of nationalism and pan-Africanism. These requests related to the return to Africa were grounded in material and social distress. According to the petitioners, radical and complete personal or collective change could be made possible only through physical relocation to Africa. These arguments were couched in a doubly political and religious language. The UNIA petitions, added to the letters of the Rastafari, who signalled their attachment to Ethiopia via the divinity of the emperor and the attributes of the "Ethiopian nation" (hymn, flag and uniforms), challenged the Jamaican colonial government. An integral part of their cosmology, the desire for return gave rise to incessant claims as well as a great debate in a society in the throes of political transformation. At the beginning of the 1950s, great news pushed the Rastafari movement to another level of public unrest: land had been made available in Ethiopia, in Shashemene, by Haile Selassie I. By becoming "real", the possibility of a territory made way for the public visibility of the Rastafari but also led to the escalation of social tensions.

The Ethiopian World Federation and the Land Grant in Ethiopia

The EWF was founded in New York in 1937 by Melaku E. Beyen, at the order of the emperor, with the aim of centralizing the moral and financial support of the black communities at the time of the Italo-Ethiopian war. In 1939, the first Jamaican Local of the EWF opened in Kingston at the instigation of Paul Earlington. Born in 1912 in the ghetto, he was a UNIA "scout" in 1925 and found Garvey extremely fascinating. He had heard of *Ras* Tafari before the 1930 coronation and had, a few years later, a "vision of the king" in which Haile Selassie reportedly told him: "I have a work for you to do" (Hepner 1998, 69). Well acquainted with all the first preachers of Rastafari and the militants against the Italo-Ethiopian war, he wrote to the EWF in New York to express his intention to open a local of the federation in Jamaica. Thanks to a positive response, in June 1939, a year after the great popular rising of 1938, eight hundred persons attended the opening ceremony of Local 17 of the EWF in Kingston with L.F.C. Mantle as president and Paul Earlington as vice-president (68–72). The Jamaican branch of the EWF acted "to maintain the integrity of Ethiopia" and declared its loyalty "to the cause of universal freedom for the Blacks", but nevertheless requested the protection and assistance of the Jamaican government.[57] However, such a protection could not protect the militants from themselves, and the first years of the local were marked by a constant change of officers. C.P. Jackson, a mechanic, was president in January 1940, and Catherine M. Green succeeded him in February 1940, by when the local had already registered seventy members.[58] The meetings were attended in evening dress, in a room rented for six pounds a month, and concerts were occasionally organized to raise funds. But Paul Earlington left for the United States, and Local 17 soon collapsed.

Another local, Local 31, was opened with William Powell as president and a few Rastafari as officers. This new group prevented bearded Rastafari from becoming members, whereas most Rastafari wore a beard (van Dijk 1993, 113). This discrimination against bearded Rastafari might appear secondary, but it underlines, on the contrary, the importance of appearance. Throughout the history of the movement, the treatment of hair was an element of distinction and debate among the three categories of Rastafari: the combsome, who combed their hair; the bearded; and the wearers of dreadlocks, who were opposed to all baldheads, hence non-Rastafari (Chevannes 1998c). When Cecil G. Gordon, a more secular activist, took over the presidency of Local 31 in 1942, this refusal to integrate the bearded Rastafari into the EWF led to the creation of other groups, informal and non-recognized, thus fragmenting the base of legitimacy of the pan-Ethiopian organization. Due to such controversies, the EWF initially had little effect on the movement in Jamaica. Its incapacity to channel Rastafari's passion for Ethiopia and to integrate the Rastafari into its official structures had serious consequences regarding the circulation of an important piece of news: land was available in Ethiopia for the members of the organization.

It is by mail that the EWF in Jamaica learned of the existence of land available in Ethiopia for its members. On 8 July 1950, George A. Bryan, secretary of the organization in New York, informed Miss Iris Davis, the secretary of Local 31 in Kingston, that the EWF "has been granted land concession in Ethiopia", in recognition of the organization's support during the years of war, and that a house had been provided in Addis Ababa.[59] This letter insisted on the fact that all EWF members were concerned, since a petition had been sent to the emperor on their behalf. Bryan pressed the Jamaican local to assemble its members in order to relay this information and insisted on the qualities required of the candidates for departure: "only those who have proven or shall have proven their worth as true Ethiopians". Two months later, Richard A. Brown, then in charge of the administration of Local 31, wrote to the governor of Jamaica to inform him, in the obsequious language reserved for official correspondence, that the EWF in Jamaica was indeed concerned in this donation of lands and to ask him for support from the government with respect to expenditure required for the journey of the 350 members of the local, since "according to present economic conditions now existing in the Island we are financially embarrassed and cannot find the necessary finance for transportation".[60] Probably taken by surprise, a week later the colonial secretary requested precise details: how many people intended to go to Ethiopia, what was the cost of the voyage and, almost ingenuously, whether they were all of Ethiopian descent.[61] In response, the officers of Local 31 confirmed that all the members of the federation "[were] descendants of Ethiopians".[62] On this occasion, 360 persons were counted – ten more than in the letter of 6 September – and still others were announced, probably attracted to the local by this news. Certain that they would receive permanent residence in Ethiopia, Brown nonetheless asked for time to obtain details from the EWF in New York.

On 27 September 1950, the *Daily Gleaner* published the decision taken by the executive council of the colonial secretariat to study the possibilities of immigration to Liberia and Ethiopia, thus fuelling the rumours on the possibility of government support. In a hasty exchange of letters and telephone calls, the governor was informed of the visit to Kingston of a person in charge of the EWF in New York, and an appointment was fixed between Governor John Huggins and Bishop Lawson. Bishop Lawson, of the Church of Our Lord Jesus Christ, was then the international president of the EWF and had already travelled to Ethiopia.[63] He was to become, on 26 January 1951, the president of a new American branch of the EWF, Local 26.[64] Having arrived in Kingston on 8 November 1950, Bishop Lawson had time to meet the officers and members of Local 31 prior to the official meeting, which was held on 13 November. The minutes of this meeting, as reflected in the report of John Huggins, reveal the gap that existed between the EWF in New York and the EWF in Kingston. Lawson, who arrived business card in hand, began by stating that the term "Ethiopian" was generic and nonspecific, and thus applied to all of Africa, and not only to the country of Ethiopia. He conceded that the federation was closely related to Ethiopia and that one of its objectives was to encourage the emigration of people who could become useful citizens. Lawson was unable to say how many members had already made the trip to Ethiopia but insisted on the nonsectarian, ecumenical character of the federation. In particular, he distanced himself very clearly from the popular religious forms he had been able to observe during his short stay in Jamaica. As reported by the governor: "He told me that he had met some members of the Ras Tafari cult and was shocked at their belief in the Emperor as divine. The Federation had no connection at all with the Ras Tafaris."[65]

This position was devastating: the EWF in New York refused to maintain connections with the Rastafari. Lawson also took the occasion to report that the Jamaican members of the federation had the impression that the government was going to take care of the travelling expenses of the persons accepted by the Ethiopian government. Governor Huggins immediately challenged this idea, stating that the investigations in progress were "entirely exploratory and must not be regarded as indicating that assistance will be given by Government to emigration to Africa".[66] Bishop Lawson departed extremely disturbed by two concerns: the poverty of the Jamaican members and their cultural proximity to Rastafari. The position of the New York EWF was then clear: no finances would be forthcoming from the Jamaican members, and the organization dissociated itself from the popular practices which had a tendency to amalgamate their objectives with devotion to the Emperor of Ethiopia. Eleven years after the establishment of the first EWF branch in Kingston, the refusal to take into account and to integrate Rastafari into the organization persisted regardless of their numerical strength and their passion for Ethiopia, thus signalling the tenacious prejudice of this pan-African elite with respect to the sufferers.

Notwithstanding the failure of this international contact of the EWF during the 1950s, the Rastafari movement and many secular activists were operating full swing. The formal and informal groups multiplied, influenced by the news of land being available in Ethiopia. Letters flooded the government, like those of Joseph Myers, who stated that 600 members of the Ethiopian United Body were ready to leave for Ethiopia.[67] Claudius Barnes, an officer of the Afro-West Indian Welfare League who had participated in the united 1948 UNIA petition, declared that 1,540 members were ready to leave for Liberia and 1,500 for

Ethiopia.[68] On the destruction of the Pinnacle, founded by Leonard Howell, the dreadlocks flowed into Kingston, residing in the poorest neighbourhoods, squatting on garbage disposal sites and empty lots. During the year of the celebration of the Silver Jubilee, the twenty-five years of reign of the emperor, a certain visit had the effect of a bomb in the small Jamaican society.

Mrs Mayme Richardson, the soprano who was the international organizer of the EWF in New York and who had toured Ethiopia in 1948, arrived in September 1955 in Jamaica, where she remained until the end of October, before visiting other Caribbean islands.[69] For several years, she had pressed the federation to develop its base and to attract new, younger members in order to renew their ranks.[70] A large gathering in her honour was organized at Coke Hall, where the room was packed and many organizations present, including the EWF, the UNIA and the Afro–West Indian Welfare League. In 1954, she had met the emperor when he visited the United States, and she carried a message to the audience, reported by the Jamaican press: "Haile Selassie wanted the people 'to know and learn more of their ancient history; to learn their native language; to know and learn more about their own religion; and the true fidelity of Christ'. . . . There was a land grant now in Ethiopia and black people could go there and claim a bit. But they had to go in groups."[71]

Mayme Richardson also stated that the emperor was building a fleet which would sail from Addis Ababa to the United States and "there was a possibility too, that the ships would one day call here". The potent symbolism of the boat, which resonated with the character of an insular society, cannot be underestimated; it acted as an echo of the programme of Marcus Garvey and his fleet, the Black Star Line. No more was needed to raise the enthusiasm of the assembly, later relayed by the rumour that spread throughout the city. Contrary to the announcement made in 1950, the federation recognized in 1955 that its real base of support was in Jamaica and accepted to address the Jamaican activists.[72] Furthermore, coinciding with the visit of Mayme Richardson, an official letter from the executive committee of the New York EWF, addressed to Local 31 in Kingston, shared the same information: (1) land had been given through the EWF to the "black people of the West" who had helped Ethiopia in its time of distress; (2) this land was the personal property of the emperor; (3) as the Ethiopian government was not prepared for a mass migration, the migrants had to be of "pioneer calibre"; (4) people were to leave in groups and to promote a spirit of collective cooperation; (5) professionals (carpenters, plumbers, masons, electricians and so on) could help the Ethiopians and learn from them; (6) as the EWF in New York was unable to contribute financially to the journeys, the EWF locals were to raise funds in view of supporting their members.[73]

This news resulted in a considerable growth of the EWF and of the Rastafari movement; many informal groups became locals of the federation, with the support of Mayme Richardson. Cecil G. Gordon left Local 31 to found Local

19. These became the two only branches that were officially registered with the government. The officers of the Afro–West Indian Brotherhood, who had visited London in May 1955 in the costumes of Ethiopian pageantry,[74] announced that their organization was to merge with the EWF, to become Local 7.[75] The Brotherhood Solidarity of United Ethiopians and the African Cultural League merged to form Local 37. Joseph Nathaniel Hibbert merged his organization, the Ethiopian Coptic Faith, with Local 27, and Archibald Dunkley's King of Kings Mission became Local 77. Other branches in Kingston included Locals 19, 33, 40 and 41, the last being exclusively female. Members of the Ethiopian Youth Cosmic Faith affiliated themselves with Locals 7 and 33. In the country, Local 11 was opened in Rock Hall, St Andrew; Local 32 in Montego Bay; and Local 25 in Spanish Town, the country's second city. The success of the EWF, resulting from the news of the land grant in Ethiopia, did not however guarantee the establishment of locals with institutionally solid and effective administrations. Most locals were short-lived and unstable, and some, like that of Mortimo Planno, functioned only occasionally (Yawney 1978, 339). Other organizations remained distant from the EWF, like the Ethiopian Body, which was later divided into several branches. Certain members of the EWF developed their own organizations, while continuing their affiliation with the federation (Smith et al. 1960, 12). Lastly, many Rastafari remained non-affiliated and independent of any collective body. The legitimacy assumed by the EWF thanks to the announcement of the land grant was important, but did not suffice to transform the EWF into a major organization in the Rastafari milieu where the claim of the right to return to Africa was increasingly diffuse and pressing. The Rastafari were incapable of coordination based on a single institution for reasons related to appearance, organizational methods, and the predominance of charismatic, sometimes authoritarian, personalities, but also because of lack of previous administrative skills and by reason of their living conditions. These economic and social conditions curtailed the constant and regular commitment to multiple meetings. These fragmented collective practices, added to the fragility of the organizations, form one of the enduring structural characteristics of the Rastafari movement. While in the 1950s a massive outmigration to England began, the Rastafari movement entered for good into the Jamaican public sphere, at a time when the first Jamaican was arriving in Shashemene. He had no support whatsoever from the EWF, of which he was not a member. Due to his extraordinary trajectory, he became an "icon" of the return to Africa.

Noel Dyer's Incredible Adventure

A decisive social evolution was sparked in Jamaica at the beginning of the 1950s: mass migration to the United Kingdom. Migratory flows still brought migrants to the United States, but the United Kingdom became, in a few years, the primary destination. All that was needed was a passport, without the visa, health certificate or work permit generally required for other destinations (Roberts and Mill 1958, 10–11). The contacts with England, which had become closer since the Second World War, the means of transportation facilitating the voyage, and the absence of legal restrictions led to a great increase in this migratory movement between 1953 and 1955 – sevenfold for skilled workers and fourteen times for those without qualification, reaching a total of more than seventeen thousand migrants, men and women, in 1955 (Roberts and Mill 1958, 44–49). Against the backdrop of this constant outmigration and that of the news of a land grant in Ethiopia, the Rastafari movement, studied for the first time in 1953 by George Simpson, emerged as "a full-blown belief in mass migration" to Africa (Smith et al. 1960, 12). While thousands of persons were leaving for England, the desire to return to Africa surfaced powerfully and was captured in slogans such as these, to be heard in the streets of Kingston: "Africa Yes, England No" or "Repatriation Yes, Migration No" (Campbell 1994, 87).

Noel Dyer was born in St Thomas, Jamaica, probably around the 1930s. He migrated initially to Kingston and, although illiterate, seemed to show potential for an international career as a cricketer.[76] In the 1950s, he encountered Rastafari, then in full growth and effervescence, but very little information has remained concerning his affiliations with collectives. He was not a member of the EWF but had surely heard of the gift of land in Ethiopia, opening a concrete prospect of settlement on the continent. Dyer was engulfed by this "new Jamaican migration" draining an increasing number of persons with a variety of skills into England. He arrived in London in 1960 where he worked for more than three years. But, as he explained: "I was tired of hanging around. . . . The English is the ones who took us away from the motherland, and they're the ones who understand our ways. We can only understand their ways by being amongst them, and understanding the whole thing about the slave trade and captivity. London was the most appropriate place to find out about myself" (quoted by Bishton 1986, 28).

The arrival in England forced Dyer to reformat his historical consciousness and identity, owing to the fact that the integration of Jamaicans into English social and economic life was far from simple. The encounter with the metropolis, with daily racial discrimination, and the minority status of immigrants informed a process in which "black" and "Rastafari" identity became at the same time a social marker and a personal and collective identity stance. This is why, convinced that Haile Selassie I had called him in a dream, Dyer decided to leave England on 17 September 1964. With less than six pounds sterling in his pocket, he went to Victoria Station without really knowing where to go, as he could not find the train for the coastal town of Dover. A young Dutch woman reportedly asked him what he was doing and he is said to have answered: "I'm lookin' for Ethiopia. I'm the son of slave and I was taken from Africa in the seventeenth century and carried beyond the sea. Now, I'm goin' home" (quoted by Bishton 1986, 28). She helped him to find the right train, and Noel Dyer's incredible adventure began. He arrived in Paris, but his funds were quickly depleted, forcing him to work for three months in a garage to gather the money needed to take a train to Spain and a boat to Morocco. After that, Noel Dyer began to walk towards the east, towards Ethiopia, sometimes by hitchhiking, which enabled him to move faster. In this way, he crossed Morocco, Algeria, Tunisia and Libya and arrived in Egypt. It took him three weeks to get from Cairo to the Aswan dam, where he had difficulties crossing. Finally, assisted by the Egyptian authorities, he crossed the desert on foot to Sudan, where he was stopped by the Sudanese authorities as he did not have a visa. He spent several weeks in prison, until the Ethiopian embassy in Khartoum heard of this Rastaman who wanted to reach Zion on foot and allowed him, finally, to enter Ethiopia. It took Dyer more than a year to make this "return" journey from England to Ethiopia.

Owing to this journey, he became one of the best known and most respected of the Rastafari who arrived in Ethiopia. This may be gathered from audio-visual materials,[77] from Rastafari elders paying him homage[78] and from Rastafari publications.[79] The books on the Rastafari movement which make mention of Shashemene all devote a number of lines to him and are generally fascinated by this character (Bishton 1986, 28–29; Campbell 1994, 223–24). The realization of a dream by means of such willpower was indeed extraordinary, but, for Campbell, what Dyer's story represented above all is "an example of what the racism of Jamaican society has forced some black people to resort to in order to escape discrimination and exploitation" (Campbell 1994, 224). In fact, this racism was not the prerogative of Jamaica and was just as palpable in England, where black people formed a socially and economically marginalized minority. This reality pushed many persons towards Rastafari and encouraged them to envision migration to Africa, where the absence of racial hostility could be imagined.

Of Some Failures and Agitators

Noel Dyer was still in Jamaica when, in March 1958, a Rastafari by the name of Prince Emmanuel Charles Edwards called for the organization of a great Rastafari "convention" or "groundation". He had already come to the attention of the colonial authorities some ten years earlier, when he wrote to ask for help to go back to Africa.[80] He described the conditions of overpopulation, malnutrition and poverty of the sufferers and evoked a "gigantic movement" towards the motherland: "Exploited Africa is our rightful home and heritage and we are laying claim thereto. If Africa is good enough to be enjoyed by other races and Nations, it should be good enough for the people who God bestowed it upon."[81]

Whereas the terms Africa and Ethiopia were often interchangeable for Prince

Emmanuel, it is only in his last letter that Ethiopia was explicitly designated as "former home" of the descendants of slaves.[82] In this letter, the UNIA is mentioned twice. The address of the sender, which changed with each letter, testified to Prince Emmanuel's urban mobility. The great ritual convention or groundation for which he had called was held in downtown Kingston. For twenty-one days, thousands of people gathered to the sound of nyabinghi drums and lit great fires for the occasion.[83] The Jamaican press directed a horrified gaze on this gathering of Rastafari coming from all over the island. On the last day, a group attempting "to capture" Victoria Park was violently arrested by the police. The question of repatriation was on the agenda for discussion, and many Rastafari had sold their belongings in the certainty that they would be able to embark for Africa at the end of the convention (Chevannes 1994, 173). Despite this missed departure, the event was a success insofar as it brought together Rastafari from all over the island and from various groups, thus conferring a certain prestige on Prince Emmanuel. This assembly also marked "the decisive point in the deterioration of relations between the Government and the public on the one hand, and the Ras Tafari movement on the other" (Smith et al. 1960, 15). Following the convention, police pressure increased; and in May, Prince Emmanuel's camp was burned by the police. He was arrested, imprisoned, judged and finally released (van Dijk 1993, 118, and 146–49). In 1958, several similar raids were reported, during which families watched the bulldozing of their shacks and Rastafari were shot and killed by the police. In 1959, an altercation between Rastafari and the police in Coronation Market, the large market in downtown Kingston, resulted in several months' imprisonment of about ninety persons. Most were Rastafari, and many of their dwellings in the ghettos of Ackee Walk and Back-o-Wall were destroyed (118–23). The neighbouring success of the Castro brothers against Batista and the advent of the Cuban Revolution were saluted by Rastafari, who saw this event as another stage in the liberation of the people and in the fall of colonial regimes. This was enough for the Rastafari to be associated, in Jamaica, with dangerous Marxist revolutionaries (121).

Whereas in December 1958 the government counted 1,640 "cultists" on the island, with about half of them in Kingston, the official figures, two years later, for Kingston alone had increased to between ten thousand and fifteen thousand "declared" Rastafari and as many "undeclared" (Smith et al. 1960, 17). While these last figures are probably exaggerated, the 1958 census gave no idea of the impact Rastafari were going to have on Jamaican society. The report ended by insisting that "the Rastafarites have no real influence on the communities in which they live".[84] This was a great mistake, as demonstrated by the enthusiasm raised in 1959 by Reverend Claudius Henry. A Jamaican who had recently returned home from a thirteen-year stay in the United States, he had attempted, unsuccessfully, to join the EWF. He founded thereafter his own church, The

Seventh Emmanuel Brethren, soon renamed the African Reform Church. At his instigation, he was called the "repairer of the breach", in reference to chapter 58 of the book of Isaiah. That summer, he began the circulation of thousands of small blue cards on which was printed the following lines, written in a cryptic style and permeated with biblical symbolism:

> Pioneering Israel's scattered Children of African Origin back home to Africa, this year 1959, deadline Oct. 5th, this new government is God's Righteous Kingdom of Everlasting Peace on Earth, "Creation's Second Birth". Holder of this Certificate is requested to visit the Headquarters at 78 Rosalie Ave. off Waltham Park Road, August 1st 1959, for Our Emancipation Jubilee commencing at 9 a.m. sharp. Please preserve this Certificate for removal. No passport will be necessary for those returning home to Africa. Bring this Certificate with you on August 1st, for "Identification". We are sincerely, "The Seventh Emmanuel's Brethren" gathering Israel's Scattered Children for removal, with our Leader, God's Appointed and Anointed Prophet, Rev. C. V. Henry, RB. [Repairer of the Breach]
>
> Given this 2nd day of March 1959, in the year of the reign of His Imperial Majesty, 1st Emperor of Ethiopia, "God's Elect", Haile Sellassie, King of Kings and Lord of Lords. 'Israel's Returned Messiah' ".[85]

Once more, thousands of people gathered on that date in the port of Kingston, having sold their belongings and given up their homes in the hope of a "miraculous repatriation". The next day, the *Daily Gleaner* ran the following headline, "No passports, no bookings; but 'going back to Africa' ", underlining the absence of any serious preparation and the fraudulent character of this initiative.[86] After the deadline, the potential migrants left the port, bitterly disappointed; in fact, a few hundreds of them even refused to leave, as they had no means of transportation or were ashamed to confront their failure. Henry was sent to prison and obliged to pay a fine. At the end of the year, weapons were discovered in the possession of his son and of some of his disciples (see Chevannes 1976). Accused of treason and of preparing a coup d'état, Henry and some fifteen other persons were judged in a great lawsuit that made the headlines of newspapers for several weeks. Rastafari had made a significant impact on their community of faith or neighbourhood and on the public sphere. Everyone had heard of them, and the "return to Africa" was widely discussed. A Rastafari who arrived in Ethiopia at the beginning of the 1970s recalled the Claudius Henry affair:

> Henry wanted to repatriate people back to Africa. Henry me know him. . . . Me see him works, government fight against him because he want repatriate people. And if him do so, who a gonna work fe Jamaica government? If we repatriate people to Africa, who gonna work fe government? That what the government said. So better we get rid of you. Not to say Henry was the best man, but him was like Marcus Garvey, every people sell what dem have to come back to Africa.[87]

Figure 4.8. Reverend Claudius Henry in the midst of his congregation of Clarendon and St Thomas, which decided to remain at his side after the failure of the departure to Africa, *Daily Gleaner*, 10 October 1959 © DR.

Reverend Henry was compared to Garvey in terms of his objective to return to Africa and his charisma, capable of influencing the poor masses of Jamaica who hoped to leave the country. The above-quoted recollection of this Rastafari expresses his understanding of Henry's failure: the obstacle to return was the Jamaican government, which ran the risk of losing an important part of the country's workforce. The subjection of the masses through labour constituted, to his mind, one of the priorities of the government. In 1959, the Cuban Revolution was already victorious; the federation of the West Indies, under discussion; Ghana had been independent for two years; and in the United States, the black communities experienced a gradual increase in the respect given to their rights. In Jamaica, by contrast, a large part of the population, both rural and urban, was still ready to leave, to "go back to Africa". Material consideration restrained an entire layer of the population on the island, since the poorest often lacked the means to migrate to England (Maunder 1955, 50–53). These were easy meat for charismatic characters such as Henry who promised boats and other means of transportation.

Rastafari belonged, at the time, to the lowest rung of the disinherited strata of the Jamaican population, but certain leaders, ready to rebound following these failures, started to send their grievances to the pan-African press. By addressing a larger audience unfamiliar with Rastafari, they also inserted the requests for return within a broader framework. The prophecy of Isaiah was juxtaposed with the Universal Declaration of Human Rights, voted on 10 December 1948 by the United Nations. Mortimo Planno, also known as Ras Kumi, emerged at this period, alongside Prince Emmanuel, as a Rastafari of great charisma. Planno was born in Cuba in 1929 but came to Jamaica with his parents in 1932.

Several of his letters were published in *African Opinion*, where he launched a strong attack against the violence of the Jamaican government. He accused them of refusing to acknowledge the Universal Declaration, using its articles 3, 5, 6, and 7 to show that Rastafari were subjected to a persecution at variance with international law. Speaking in the name of a federation of cults called the United African Movement, he also stated: "We decided to mark that day [10 December] by claiming our nationality – Ethiopian or African – in accordance with the UN Charter . . . we have all Rights to claim our own nationality – Ethiopian where our King is our Almighty."[88] Indeed, article 15 announced: "Everyone has the right to a nationality. No one shall be arbitrarily deprived of his nationality, nor denied the right to change his nationality." If the Rastafari decided to have Ethiopian nationality, nothing, in their opinion, could prevent this; besides, there was a legal framework authorizing such a right. In another letter, Planno proposed only one alternative: repatriation or armed rebellion, an "all-out war".[89] In Planno's letter, the Rastafari were designated by various appellations: "twelve tribes of Israel", "Nazarenes, Levites, Statesmen and Sons of Kings", "Africans in Jamaica" and "Rasses", the (Jamaican) plural of *Ras*. While publicly relinking with the very characteristic religious and nationalistic language, he announced that this ultimatum concerned "forty-five thousand African Nationalists and thousands of Brothers and Sisters". This militancy, regardless of the exaggeration of the figures, earned him the goodwill of the editors of the *African Opinion*, who were unlikely, a priori, to identify with the fortune of a minority group living in the "pit of hell", as he called Jamaica.[90] This was only the beginning of the public career of Mortimo Planno, who was to play a significant role in the evolution of the manner in which Jamaican society regarded the Rastafari.

Engagements and Disengagements of the Jamaican Government

Three scholars, M.G. Smith, Roy Augier and Rex Nettleford, conducted a rapid enquiry into the history of the movement, its doctrinal particularities and its organizations, whose "complex composition and heterogeneity of elements" sometimes left them speechless (Smith et al. 1960, 29). The result of their research, known as the "1960 Report", made such an impact on historiography that it is invariably quoted as a fundamental reference, one that was long regarded by researchers such as Albuquerque (1977, 27) as the definitive history of the movement before 1960. It is now a well-known fact that the report, perhaps because of its profusion of details, contributed, on the contrary, to the feeding of a "historical myopia" which might have limited research on the history and the formation of the movement (Hill 2001, 13–14). Indeed, Robert Hill (2013) demonstrated recently that this report was an initiative of the Ministry of Interior, which had the objective to "pacify" the Rastafari movement and prevent its radicalization, as represented by Reverend Claudius Henry. This report affirmed that Rastafari were neither criminals nor madmen, contrary to what was generally circulated in the press, but underlined the threat of having Marxist ideas clothed in Rastafari ideology. The scholars pinpointed the deplorable socio-economic conditions in which the majority of Rastafari lived and publicized the claims to return to Africa. They explained the reasons for their position:

1. Every citizen has a right to emigrate if he so desires, and to change his nationality if he so desires.
2. While many Ras Tafari brethren would stay in Jamaica if they found work and good social conditions, a large number have strong religious ties with Africa, which cannot be destroyed.
3. Jamaica is over-populated, and cannot provide work for all citizens. Every effort should be made to facilitate emigration.
4. Jamaica now facilitates the settlement of emigrants in England; from a racial point of view emigration to Africa seems more appropriate.
5. Substantial emigration to Africa will not be possible unless the Jamaica government takes certain initiatives. (Smith et al. 1960, 34)

Grounded on article 15 of the Universal Declaration of Human Rights, the report also made important remarks on the freedom of individuals to emigrate and to change their nationality, on the importance of the racial, symbolic and cultural connection of Jamaicans with Africa and on the responsibility of the government to offer a job market or to support emigration, especially to Africa. It closed with recommendations to the government, which could be summarized as follows: the government should send a mission to Africa to study the possibilities of immigration, and arrangements should be discussed with the Rastafari; the majority of Rastafari were peaceful citizens, and the police should end its persecutions; low-rent dwellings should be built by the government, which should also ensure the availability of water, electricity, garbage collection and the like in the ghettos; the Ethiopian Orthodox Church should be invited to establish itself; the Rastafari should be supported in their economic projects, and their access to the press and the radio should be facilitated (Smith et al. 1960, 38). The notion of rehabilitation developed in the report implied that the social problems experienced by Rastafari were common to all persons living in the most disinherited neighbourhoods. There was also the fact that, for the first time, members of the intellectual elite were echoing the claims to return laid down by Rastafari and were directly challenging the government. The impact of the 1960 Report, published over several successive weeks in the daily press, was considerable, and if no social policy seemed to accrue directly to Rastafari as a result, a mission was in fact organized to study the possibilities of accommodation of Jamaicans in Africa. This particular recommendation, negotiated with the Jamaican government prior to the release of the report, presented the movement to Africa as "migration", not as "return", and was aimed at "coopting" Rastafari, "the only way to bring these people down to earth", in the words of Prime Minister Norman Manley (Hill 2013).

The First Mission

At the end of 1960, the leader of the People's National Party government, Norman Manley, opened discussions for the organization of a semi-official, semi-governmental mission to Africa in order to study the concrete possibilities of emigration and accommodation of Jamaicans, specifically in Ethiopia, Nigeria, Ghana, Liberia and Sierra Leone. While this mission has already been studied in detail (van Dijk 1993, 149–53), I would like to make a few remarks: the Rastafari were opposed to the fact that non-Rastafari were included in the mission, and they were bitterly divided over the choice of their representatives. The first opportunity had finally arisen for them to show a unified front and to choose a delegation representative of the movement, but the Rastafari, due to their lack of organization – or more accurately, because of the extreme mobility and fluidity of their groups and organizations – diverged on questions of leadership, representativeness and doctrinal differences. The selection of the other, non-Rastafari delegates was also problematic, and, in the end, seven delegates made the journey. Mortimo Planno (the dreadlocks), Douglas Mack and Filmore Alvaranga (who were bearded) representing the Rastafari movement, Westmore Blackwood from the UNIA, Dr B. Douglas from the Afro-Caribbean League, Cecil Gordon from the EWF, and Munroe Scarlett from the Afro–West Indian Welfare League. They were accompanied by a journalist, Victor Reid, and by Dr Leslie, a physician.[91] The presence of these organizations in the mission is a clear indication that activism regarding the return to Africa was not restricted to Rastafari but was shared by well-known nationalist militants like Scarlett, whose organization was an "offshoot of UNIA and was founded as a 'back to Africa' organization".[92] The surgeon, Douglas, represented a less radical position, since the primary goal of his organization was "not migration to Africa but development of the West Indies",[93] but he was nevertheless willing to cooperate in the event that this migration was decided on. The representatives of the EWF had excluded Rastafari from the preliminary negotiations with the government and, claiming a particular relation to Ethiopia thanks to the land grant in Shashemene, demanded a privileged role in the direction of the mission. While identifying the black people who were eager to go to Ethiopia with the Ethiopians, the EWF reiterated their loyalty to the British crown and to the Jamaican government, thereby distinguishing themselves from the majority of Rastafari, for whom the colonial government was fundamentally illegitimate.[94] These varying organizational positions did not portend perfect agreement among the representatives, and cleavages between Rastafari and non-Rastafari surfaced even in the reports produced after the mission: there was a "minority" report, signed by the Rastafari, and a "majority" report, signed by the others.

The mission arrived in Ethiopia in April 1961 after a short stopover in New York and London and a journey through Rome, Khartoum and Asmara. Received with honour in Addis Ababa, the mission remained seven days in the country and paid many visits to officials of the church and of the government in the capital and in the interior, including Shashemene, where they met Helen and James Piper, who were already established there.[95] During their meeting with Abuna Basileos, the patriarch of the Orthodox Church, a discussion arose on the question of the divinity of the emperor, which the Rastafari reported as follows: "We discussed H.I.M. [His Imperial Majesty] Emperor Haile Selassie, being the returned Messiah. His Holiness the Abuna told us at the conclusion of the discussion that the Bible can be interpreted that way. We had tea and honey wine with him" (*Minority Report* 1961, 16). The interpretation of the nature and of the eschatological role of the emperor that the Rastafari made was thus indirectly legitimated by the highest-ranking authorities of the church. These encounters were, for the Rastafari present and, by extension, for the Rastafari movement, a historic moment, whose apogee occurred on 21 April when they met with the emperor. The Rastafari had come with photographs, sculptures and craft items as gifts for the monarch. The report underlined the positive attitude expressed by the emperor: "H.I.M. told us that he knew the black people of the West and particularly Jamaica were blood brothers to the Ethiopians and he knew that slaves were sent from Ethiopia to Jamaica. He said we should send the right people. The Emperor said Ethiopia was large enough to hold all the people of African descent living outside Africa" (*Minority Report* 1961, 16–17). These words had an interesting fortune, as they were often quoted, reused and reinterpreted by Rastafari in various situations. That the emperor recognized a blood relation was a very strong sign, a "confirmation" for all Jamaicans who saw themselves as Ethiopians. The expression "the right people" also was largely repeated and discussed, with multiple argumentations on the hidden meaning: were the Rastafari "the right people"? Or did this term refer to workers? To professionals? To the Ethiopians of the world? Currently, Rastafari still refer to these words. Overall, the outcome of the mission to Ethiopia was positive, with the emperor and government officials confirming that Afro-descendants were welcome in the country.

The mission continued on its journey to Nigeria, where it was warmly received by several persons, including Nnamdi Azikiwe, then the governor general. He spoke to them about his debt to Caribbeans: "He observed that he himself had been taught by West Indian teachers and stated that the philosophies of the late Marcus Garvey were responsible in large measure for his work towards the independence of Nigeria" (*Majority Report* 1961, 6). Ministers of government and customary chiefs assured them that settlement was possible, that the return

Figure 4.9. At the foot of Haile Selassie's palace, delegates of the first mission to Africa in 1961 with tame lion. The emperor's aide-de-camp stands on the steps (top right), a representative of the Imperial Guard stands at the extreme left, and an attaché from the Ministry of Foreign Affairs is on the left of the first row. Mission members are, rear from left, Dr M.B. Douglas, Vic Reid, W.M.M. Blackwood, Douglas Mack; front row, from left, Cecil Gordon, E.H. Lake, L.C. Leslie, Z. Munroe Scarlett, Mortimo Planno, Filmore Alvaranga. *Daily Gleaner,* 6 June 1961 © DR.

to Africa was necessary for both Caribbeans and Africans. After an eleven-day stay and several visits in the interior, the mission set off once again, for Ghana. It was speedily received by President Kwame Nkrumah, who declared: "How shall I put it? Our meeting is historic. It has historic significance not only because we're blood relations but also because so many attempts were previously made and failed. Marcus Garvey tried but was prevented" (*Majority Report* 1961, 9). Nkrumah also gave his consent to this Jamaican initiative, promising that land could be provided and stressing that a joint, realistic approach should be elaborated.

The same warm welcome was extended to the mission on its arrival in Liberia, where it was received by President Tubman, who pointed out clearly that Liberia had laws facilitating immigration. Tubman was particularly interested in the Rastafari and asked them questions about their faith, after having asked them to bless the meal they were sharing. After thirteen days in Liberia, the mission went on to Sierra Leone. The prime minister, Dr Sir Milton Margai, confirmed that, in principle, Sierra Leone was open to projects of return, but he nevertheless stated that, the independence of the country having been obtained less than one month earlier (on 27 April 1961), the government was presently tied up with more urgent concerns. After some ten days, the mission left by air, via Dakar, Lisbon and Puerto Rico, arriving in Jamaica at the beginning of June. A crowd of five thousand persons rushed to the airport to welcome them enthusiastically with banners, flags, songs and drums.

Having submitted their reports to the government, the delegates communicated their findings to their partisans. Van Dijk has reported a very interesting public speech made by Mortimo Planno and heard by Roy Augier, who had co-signed the 1960 Report on the Rastafari movement:

> Mortimo Planno was making a public speech in the Coronation Market area. Not only do I remember the speech, for a long time will I remember it, because it was the most masterly political speech that I have heard. He wanted to convey to that crowd – and it was a very large crowd – that Africa was not what it had been trumped up to be. But those words never left his mouth, he just circled it, approached it, retreated, but gradually hinting. . . . I think they got the message, but he never said, let's abandon repatriation and let's stay here, we are better off over here: Jamaican society is better organized. He never said anything like that.[96]

In van Dijk's analysis, this testimony was a sign that the mission to Africa was one of the first events contributing to a gradual weakening of the doctrines of return within the Rastafari movement (van Dijk 1993, 157). He pointed to the case of the Orthodox Rastafari, especially those who had withdrawn their support for the mission and who believed their return would be accomplished through divine intervention. A more moderate and realistic segment of the movement apparently "got the message" that Africa was perhaps not really the land of milk and honey they had expected and that a mass return meant heavy negotiations between the governments concerned. However, while the organization of the mission had been complex, repatriation was not impossible. Moreover, the recognition of this claim by the government, which had taken the initiative to organize the mission, contributed to relieve the tension between the Rastafari movement and Jamaican society. Rastafari could no longer claim to be completely ignored and marginalized in the society, since they were in relation with the government, which had contributed to the study of the real possibilities of return.

Following the 1961 mission, between January and April 1962, the government sent another mission of a technical nature to Nigeria, Ghana and Ethiopia. Composed of only four persons, with no Rastafari, its task was to study "the technical problems involved in any plan for the movement of persons from Jamaica to any of the nations of Africa" (Nettleford 2001, 70). Rex Nettleford, who had co-signed the 1960 Report on the Rastafari movement, was part of this mission alongside Aston Foreman, who was to become, in 1970, the first Jamaican ambassador to an African nation – namely, Ethiopia. The technical mission reported that most West African nations preferred to receive qualified and professional Jamaicans, whereas the Ethiopian government seemed ready to provide land for Jamaican farmers. The cost of settling families was presented to the government (*Technical Mission to Africa*, 1962, 89–90). The report of this mission went unnoticed in the press, and, due to a change of government a week after its return, its results were definitively buried (Nettleford 2001, 71).

Jamaica had been engaged for several years on the road leading to independence. Following the failure, in 1961, of the West Indies federation defended by Norman Manley and the People's National Party, elections were organized in April 1962, and a date of independence was fixed within the framework of the Commonwealth, in dialogue with the British.[97] The Jamaica Labour Party, the main opposition party, led by Alexander Bustamante, won the elections and opened the independence celebrations on 6 August 1962. In the enthusiasm and popular nationalism ignited by the gaining of independence, there was little place for alter-nationalist forces like the Rastafari movement.[98] Their claim to Ethiopian nationality went hand in hand with their rejection of Jamaican nationality and was proportional to the intensity of their feeling of alienation in the insular society (Smith et al. 1960, 21). It surfaced especially regarding the motto of the new nation: "Out of many, one people", intended to be the reflection of a multicultural and supposedly non-racialist Jamaica. This idealization of the Jamaican nation, touted by the middle class, was disputed by the Rastafari and was shown to disregard the contributions of the large substrate of the black population of the island, for whom the Rastafari were the self-designated voice (Nettleford 2001, 19–37). What is more, the following year was a dark one for them, marked by what was called the "massacre of Coral Gardens" or the "Holy Thursday massacre". On 11 April 1963, six bearded Rastafari set fire to a gas station and killed a man in Coral Gardens, not far from Montego Bay, the tourist capital. Following pursuit by the police, three of them were killed, as well as a police officer and three civilians. Without entering into the details, presented elsewhere (van Dijk 1993, 164–69), the repression led by the government deserves to be underlined. Prince Elijah, a Rastafari, thus remembers the "massacre of the Holy Thursday":

> At the time of the Coral Gardens insolence, I-man was 20 years old. I never know where they call Coral Gardens. . . . The government of Jamaica, the Alexander Bustamante government, first he says, "Kill every goddamn blasted one a them," meaning the Rastafarians. The Commissioner of Police said, "Mr Prime Minister, it's impossible to kill every man because of what three men committed themselves." His answer: Harass, beat and charge for vagrancy. (Williams 2005, 7, 9)

Prince Elijah also spent time in prison. His wife and children were molested, and, as seen in his recently published book, 1963 remained a crucial date in Jamaican popular memory. All the Rastafari of the island became the targets of police raids; their locks were forcibly shorn; their houses were burned; hundreds of them were imprisoned for several long weeks; and there were many casualties and several deaths. Whereas Rastafari were perceived as a threat to the national identity in the process of formation under the postcolonial government, 1963 was by far the most spectacular instance of police violence perpetrated in Jamaica against the movement.

The Second Mission

Once the Coral Gardens massacre was over and emotions had somewhat abated, three Rastafari decided to launch a second mission to Africa. This time, without expecting financial support from the government, they carried out a fundraising campaign and managed to leave for New York in December 1963. Filmore Alvaranga and Douglas Mack had participated in the first mission; Samuel Clayton was a talented nyabinghi musician; and all three were bearded. Carrying a petition listing the professions and skills of Rastafari who wished to migrate, they were received in New York by Gladstone Robinson, the American member of the EWF and Back-to-Africa activist mentioned earlier. Together they formed the African Repatriation Committee and gathered the funds needed to continue the journey. On their arrival in Nigeria, they were housed by the government, which, after two weeks, was ready to send them back to Jamaica without granting them an audience. Facing the categorical refusal of the Rastafari, plane tickets for Kenya were offered. They remained in Kenya for four months and were housed following the instructions of President Jomo Kenyatta. They took the opportunity to travel within the country, to become acquainted with Kikuyu culture and to meet with politicians, students and congregations. The Kenyan government then financed their plane ticket to Ethiopia, where they arrived in November 1964. They were received by the Orthodox clergy, whom they visited

Figure 4.10. Delegates of the second mission to Ethiopia, Samuel Clayton, Filmore Alvaranga, the Patriarch of the Ethiopian Orthodox Church *Abuna* Theophilus, and Douglas Mack, Addis Ababa, 1964. Archives G. Robinson, Shashemene © DR.

frequently, and were acclimatized little by little with the life in Addis Ababa, where they remained, their movements restricted by lack of funds.

Nevertheless, they visited the farm of David Talbot, the Guianese pan-Africanist and journalist, in Ambo, not far from the capital. It was only in April 1965 that they were officially received by the emperor, who told them that Ethiopia was able to accommodate the Rastafari desirous of settling there. Moreover, Mack reported that "His Majesty said that the Sheshamane [*sic*] land grant was one of the areas, granted for resettlement of people of African descent residing in the Western hemisphere, who desired to return. He also said Ethiopia needed the skills of our brothers in the west to assist in her development; and his government would continue talks with the government of Jamaica" (1999, 141–42). The prospects were therefore bright in the eyes of the three men, who were then able to return to Jamaica, travelling through London and New York, as arranged by the emperor. Only two hundred people welcomed them on their return to Kingston. It is possible that the three "ambassadors" had expected another kind of welcome, but their long mission at the expense of African governments and the visit of Gladstone Robinson in their absence, followed by a series of unfortunate events, had already diminished their prestige. They insisted that they "could have remained in Ethiopia as naturalized citizens if we wished . . . but we came back to centralize and control the movement".[99] Probably because of this obvious objective to become the leaders of the Rastafari movement, they received little support in Jamaica. Besides, they were bearded and thus could not represent the dreadlocks factions. No tangible result came of their long mission, but they nevertheless founded the Rastafarian Brethren Repatriation Association in May 1965, adding to the long list of more or less effective organizations composing the Rastafari movement.

The Visit of Haile Selassie I to Jamaica

The announcement of an official visit by Haile Selassie I to Jamaica, scheduled to take place in April 1966, generated hope and excitement among the Rastafari. As was the case at the time of the announcement of the land grant in Ethiopia in 1955, during Prince Emmanuel's 1958 convention, prior to the resounding failure of Reverend Henry in 1959 and before the 1961 mission, the expectation of immediate repatriation peaked. The emperor's Caribbean tour took him to Haiti, followed by a visit to Barbados, to Jamaica and finally to Trinidad.[100] His arrival in Kingston on 21 April generated the greatest popular mobilization. The day before, nearly ten thousand persons gathered on the runway to await the "Lion of Judah". The authorities, with the stake of impending elections in mind, decided to use tact with potential voters and thus refrained from forceful evacuation.[101] A heavy rain fell on the crowd just before the arrival of the plane,[102] and as soon the emperor was sighted, "the crowd jumped down from

Figure 4.11. Arrival of the emperor's plane, Kingston, 21 April 1966, *Janhoy bäcaribiyan dässétoč* (Haile Selassie in the islands of Caribbean). 1966 [1958 *a.m.*]. Ministry of Information and Tourism, Addis Ababa © DR.

the roofs of the airport building, burst the barriers and surged towards the aircraft, overwhelming the welcoming VIPs, the police, the Guard of Honour and the band".[103] Many photographs and audiovisual documents testify to the popular passion of the crowd holding up posters, flags and banners amid clouds of ganja and the accompaniment of drums beating out nyabinghi rhythms which overpowered the unsuccessful attempts of the official reception.[104] The emperor seemed taken aback by this reception and had quite a bit of difficulty leaving the plane. Thanks to the authority he commanded, Mortimo Planno was able

Figure 4.12. Crowd overwhelming the security services and storming the runway, Kingston, 21 April 1966, *Janhoy bäcaribiyan dässétoč* (Haile Selassie in the islands of Caribbean). 1966 [1958 *a.m.*]. Ministry of Information and Tourism, Addis Ababa © DR.

Figure 4.13. Mortimo Planno helps the emperor to get down from his plane, Kingston, 21 April 1966. © DR

to persuade the crowd to allow the emperor to pass. It was a historic moment for Jamaicans, who had come together en masse, and especially for Rastafari, who were invited to take part in several receptions organized in honour of Haile Selassie I and found themselves, for the first time, mingling with distinguished guests and the notables of the island at King's House in Kingston. In addition, the emperor gave an audience the following day to Rastafari, those who had participated in the 1961 and 1963 missions, and met with the representatives of Rastafari groups and with other activist organizations that held him in high esteem.

The Jamaican government had secretly hoped that, during this visit, Haile Selassie I would repudiate the faith placed in him by Rastafari, but though he said a few words on the need to turn to the true God, they went largely unnoticed, and the government's wish remained unfulfilled (van Dijk 1993, 175). The words pronounced by Haile Selassie I which left an imprint on the Jamaican imaginary were quite different. At the national stadium, taking the floor after Donald Sangster, who was then prime minister, the emperor said:

> I know of the love which the Jamaican people entertain for the people of Ethiopia and the welcome which you have given me this day is evidence of it. I know the Jamaican people were very sympathetic when Ethiopia was occupied during the fascist regime. During that time Jamaicans as well as others who had African blood supported the Ethiopian Liberation Movement.... I know you share the African people's sentiments. The Jamaican and Ethiopian people are blood brothers and have had relationship going back a very long time. (Haile Selassie 1966)

By referring to the great pan-African movement of 1935–41 and by mentioning not only the African blood of Jamaicans but also the common blood shared by Ethiopians and Jamaicans, the emperor was sure to elicit boundless admiration on part of his Jamaican supporters. These words were taken as added proof of the legitimacy of the claims of the Rastafari, who had been requesting Ethiopian nationality for a long time by arguing that they were the true Ethiopians. That the Jamaican government was weakened by this visit was the comment made by the British, who regarded the omnipresence and power of the crowd as a sign of the weakness of national security. They also underlined the fear provoked in the ranks of middle-class Jamaicans, who saw these demonstrations as "a portent of what they have always most feared – an unruly upsurge of the black mass from below ".[105] But, for this "black mass", to meet an African king, descendant of a revered lineage, was a great experience; for the Rastafari, this moment was almost a Parousia, it was the manifestation of the Living God; with their own eyes they could finally *see* the person whom they revered. Some *saw* Christ himself in the person of Haile Selassie I, as illustrated by this testimony by Rita Marley:

> and I *looked* into his hand and there was the nail-print. It was a mark, and I could only identify that work with the Scriptures of history, saying "when you see him, you will know him by the nail-print in his hand". So when I *saw* this, I said to myself that this could be true, this could be the man of whom it was said: before the year 2000 Christ will be a man walking on this earth. (Quoted by Salewicz 2000, 132–33; italics mine)

The visit of the emperor stirred up many discussions of a theological nature among the Rastafari, some of whom had trouble seeing in the small man with light skin the black God about whom so much had been said. There were diverse interpretations of the objectives reportedly set by the emperor. Watchwords supposedly pronounced by the emperor were spread in Rastafari circles: "Organize and centralize" became a vital injunction for some, as we will see later; but "Liberation before Repatriation" contributed to a lessening of the urgency of repatriation as opposed to working for social change in Jamaica itself.[106] The second watchword resonated durably with some commentators. For the British: "any likelihood of their [the Rastafari] being 'repatriated' to Ethiopia has now faded for ever";[107] which was also the opinion of Jamaican intellectuals. Rex Nettleford, who had co-signed the 1960 Report on the movement, stated in 1970 that "the coming of Haile Selassie contributed to the waning ardour of the desire for physical Return" (Nettleford 2001, 73). The same opinion was held by Barry Chevannes, who had seen no attempt at return during the 1960s (1998b, 30). Their remarks were founded in reality only in part, as the choice of acting in Jamaica first instead of seeking to return to Africa did not concern all Rastafari. Especially in the light of the fact that, two months after the visit of Haile Selassie I, the large ghetto of Back-o-Wall was bulldozed, throwing hundreds of now homeless persons into the streets. Among them were many Rastafari who sang "Since we are squatters in Jamaica / Send us back to Ethiopia / We will be citizens there" (Barrett 1997, 157). All of the arrivals in Shashemene coming directly from Jamaica occurred after the visit of the emperor in 1966. Seen from Ethiopia, this visit – and the social repression that followed it – constituted the shock which finally pushed some Jamaicans to organize and leave the island and settle in Ethiopia. Once assured of the reality of the emperor because *they had seen him*, some Rastafari, counting on their own resources, started to organize their departure.

THE RETURN TO AFRICA REPRESENTED A THREAT FOR colonial and postcolonial Jamaican society. The establishment of a black nation, imagined through the prism of the return to Africa, loomed as an alternative to British domination and to the Jamaican nation in the process of construction. Sierra Leoneans at the end of the nineteenth century, veterans of the First World War, and Garveyites after the fall of Garvey claimed the right to return to Africa due to their status as descendants of African slaves. Rastafari helped to centre these claims on Ethiopia thanks to their interpretation of the divine nature of Haile Selassie, in whom the nationalist and religious imaginaries converged. The EWF, to which the land in Shashemene was entrusted, was reluctant to include Rastafari as members in view of their beliefs and practices. However, in a society deeply structured by internal and international migrations, Africa still appeared, during the 1950s, to be a possible alternative destination. Return was then a matter of public debate in Jamaica, maintained by a few spectacular failed mass departures by boat; by the 1960 Report, which transformed the way in which Rastafari were perceived;and by the 1961 Back-to-Africa Mission – the first government initiative to study the possibilities of return. With independence in 1962 and the new legitimacy of the government, the question of return was laid to rest, driven by the feeling that it was more important to work to change the Jamaican society. This did not prevent Noel Dyer from making the return on foot from England, but it is only after the visit of the emperor in 1966 that the Rastafari started to organize themselves – the subject of the following chapter.

CHAPTER 5

ORGANIZING AND CENTRALIZING THE ETHIOPIAN NATION

FOLLOWING THE REFUSAL OF THE GOVERNMENT OF JAMAICA to assume any responsibility in the process of return to Africa, many Rastafari took refuge in passive or mystical expectation. Some were persuaded that return would happen only through divine intervention – in this case, that of Haile Selassie I. In spite of the great popular mobilizations, which the hope of the return had provoked in the 1950s and 1960s, few Jamaicans left for the African continent. Yet urban violence was a factor that motivated their departure. Mainly financed by the political parties, it was to bleed the Jamaican popular classes for decades (van Dijk 1993, 179–80; Gunst 1995). The Rastafari who went to Ethiopia were not very different from those who remained in Jamaica. They defined themselves as the "true Ethiopians" but preferred action to waiting. They were determined to concretize their symbolic membership in the "Ethiopian nation of the world". Between 1966 and 1974, twenty-five of them entered Ethiopia, followed by another twenty-three between 1975 and 1991, signalling a deceleration of arrivals under the Ethiopian military regime called the *derg*. Based on interviews carried out in Kingston and Shashemene and on the intersection of these enquiries with other sources (the pan-African press and the archives of the Ethiopian Orthodox Church in Jamaica), this chapter highlights the fact that their efforts at organization and centralization were crucial to their departure. Rastafari finally integrated with the EWF, but its fragility encouraged the formation of another organization, the Twelve Tribes of Israel. The institutional history of this organization illustrates the efforts and the difficulties attending the gathering of people, passports and funds. This chapter also focuses on the structuring role of these organizations in the practices of return, regardless of the presence of a small group of "free spirits": the first arrivants of 1968.

Inez and Clifton Baugh

Illustrative of the determination of these "free spirits" – the countless Rastafari who were not involved in a specific organization – a small group of four adults and four children left Jamaica in February 1968. Inez and Clifton Baugh, Clifton's brother Landford Baugh and one of their friends, Vivian Thompson, left for Ethiopia, taking with them Patricia Thompson, the daughter of Vivian; Jasmine Baugh, who was barely four months old; and another baby, Anne Marie Boyd, the niece of Inez; and the young Clifton Douglas. Clifton Baugh was born in 1925 in Swift River, Portland, where he grew up before migrating to town. Inez Williams was born in 1935 in St Ann's Bay, and lived for a long time in the country before moving to the city. They met in Spanish Town, where Clifton was working in construction, while Inez held an administrative job. She had been brought up in the church, either Methodist or Catholic, whereas Clifton was, from his twenties, familiar with the Rastafari movement. One of their sons, born in Ethiopia, remembers the way in which his father told him about the origins of his interest for Africa:

> My dad . . . start reading and hearing the history of Ethiopia, start getting inspired from Marcus Garvey and the Back-to-Africa movement, those are the stuff that start them thinking of move. . . . That's where they get the inspiration. . . . From my dad it was like they used to meet with his other friends, they used to meet after work and they call it reasoning, when you sit down and talk about stuff, know what I mean? So one of the evenings, after work they meet and start talk about Africa, that's where his feelings of coming home start building, they said, they talked about coming home, but at that time nobody was financially stable to pay your fare and come home. They were these different groups and organizations, Black Star Liner, shipping people, it wasn't much a reality.[1]

The "reasoning" was the most current and widespread form of sociability among the Rastafari. It took place in a yard, the common space of the urban dwelling. There, the divinity of the emperor was constructed in a discursive mode. This was also the space in which the cultural practices specific to Rastafari were transmitted and shared (Homiak 1985). It is likely that this paternal narrative was not limited to "one of the evenings"; it is highly probable that the evocations of "home", of Africa, of Ethiopia and of the "land of their fathers" was a daily production of these social interactions. They were sustained by personal readings and reflection regarding the previous failures at return: Marcus Garvey, the congress of 1958 and Reverend Henry in 1959. The visit of Haile Selassie I in 1966 moved the Baughs from discourses of return to practices of return. Inez remembers with emotion the arrival of the emperor in Kingston. She was there on the runway, she said, with the biggest flag of all in that enthusiastic assembly.[2] Their son has confirmed the impact of this visit on the dynamics of their departure: "I remember my dad saying when His Majesty came to

Figure 5.1. The group of "pioneers", from left to right: Vivian Thompson, holding Patricia Thompson, Inez Williams holding Anne Marie Boyd, Clifton Baugh holding Jasmine Baugh, and in front, Clifton Douglas. *African Opinion* 8, nos. 7–8 (May–June 1968): 11. © DR.

Jamaica, that's when they got motivated, well, we're not going to wait anymore since our Father came already, and we saw Him, it is time for us to really move . . . as far as I see things, if we don't make our own move, we will never be able to move from here."[3]

Haile Selassie I's 1966 visit served as a catalyst. The Baughs had heard of the donation of land in Shashemene but were not members of the EWF, and the existing organizations "weren't really functioning". So, defining themselves as "pioneers", they formed a group. Most of the Rastafari with whom they reasoned "wasn't strongly motivated even if they talk about Africa, they weren't".[4] So, Clifton turned to his brother. Along with a few others, they decided to put together what they had, to sell their house and belongings to finance their trip. They went against their families and close relations, who strongly disapproved of this initiative and who reproduced the common images circulating in Jamaica identifying Africa with negative and primitive values. They told them that they were "crazy persons to leave a land and go to a no man's land cause is just starvation and war".[5] But they had made up their minds. Inez's sister, saddened by this departure and probably harbouring the hope that she would reunite with them soon, gave them her daughter. On a picture taken right before their departure, the "pioneers" appear calm and serene: the men are bearded and dressed in suits and ties with scarves in the colours of Ethiopia and Inez is also dressed in a suit with a bandana in her hair.[6] Published in the *Daily Gleaner*, the picture was reprinted in *African Opinion* in New York, accompanying a letter to the editor signed by Mortimo Planno, who noted that "these brethren have gone HOME to help in rebuilding the CONTINENT. Many more intend to go but cannot yet find the passage money."[7] Funding was the main obstacle to the mobility of poor Jamaicans, yet, in spite of the lack of capital, the idea that they could contribute to the construction of the continent was quite vivid, serving to perpetuate the nineteenth-century representations of African emigration. After a long voyage, with several changes of plane and stopovers for refuelling, they finally arrived in Ethiopia, met the handful of persons who had already settled in Shashemene, and kicked off the wave of future Jamaican arrivals, due, in particular, to their activism within the EWF.

The Ethiopian World Federation Changes "from Bottom Up"

When Mayme Richardson had announced in 1955 that land was available in Ethiopia for the members of the EWF, a dozen branches were quickly created, originating either in recently created groups or in existing congregations that became EWF locals. Some of these locals had, subsequent to the departure of Mayme Richardson and on her recommendation, been created in various parishes, but most were located in Kingston and were marked by irregular activity. Rows linked to the land grant in Shashemene had flared and subsided, but the EWF headquarters in New York was yet to facilitate the journey of a Jamaican member. The distinction between Rastafari and non-Rastafari members was significant, since the dreadlocks had been prevented from joining certain EWF locals. An EWF Rastafari residing in Ethiopia explains the ambient tensions of the times in these terms:

> At dem times Rasta wasn't invited as members [by the EWF], we were seen as escapist, drop out of society, ganja smokers and even denied employment. When we try to attend a meeting of the EWF . . . we could only stay outside by the window and we hear dem a deliberate whatever it is. But still dem don't like our presence, because what we show dem is Him is the Messiah and yet you have different religion among them, Catholic, Presbyterian, Church of England, Baptists . . . that's why dem can't have a steady progressive EWF.[8]

While the EWF, at its debut in the United States, was an ecumenical organization, tensions crystallized in Jamaica around the claiming of a Rastafari identity. Rastafari failed to find their niche within the EWF as they were not ready to put aside their faith, but also owing to the fact that the officers of the federation, who had international responsibilities and dominated the EWF administrative relations between Jamaica and New York, were non-Rastafari who rejected Rastafari. From 1956, Cecil Gordon, who was the president of Local 19 in Kingston, was the "second international vice-president for the Caribbean". Brooks chaired Local 13 and, like McLean, was also an officer of the New York Local and "the deputy international organizer" (Smith et al. 1960, 12). They thus had a control that they were unwilling to share and the Rastafari locals "became insubordinate to the baldhead initial charters".[9] The conflict between Rastafari and non-Rastafari resurfaced in the hierarchy of power and control within the EWF. Yet the distinction between formal and informal, recognized or unrecognized locals was never very clear due to constant breaks and fusions among the groups, and Rastafari were sometimes members of the most important locals. Added to this were the conflicts among locals, including tension between locals with a membership of bearded Rastafari and locals whose members were Rastafari with dreadlocks: "You have rivalry at the local level, because we're not following the constitution and procedures, we were still Rastas. We become enemy of our own thing, 'cause we're not behaving to how we should and it's a businesslike corporation. You have conventions, and settlements of officers, and duties, but at that level, InI Rastas wasn't prepared, I tell you."[10]

The EWF, because of the constitution that regulated its internal operations, was an extremely structured organization, while these locals would constantly "proselyte [*sic*] one another". Their administrations were weak, fragile and undisciplined, resulting in inevitable delay in the execution of a collective programme. Could this have been otherwise in the context of a population shunned by the handful of influential locals, and given the fact that this population was partly illiterate, lacked administrative practice and was animated by a mystical expectation sometimes at variance with concrete action?

Whereas numerous Rastafari disputed the direction of the EWF, which they considered counterproductive, a few seized the opportunities the EWF represented by sending the required documents directly to New York, whence they received in 1958 the charter allowing the creation of a new local.[11] Thus Local 43, located in Unity Lane, was created in the neigbourhood of Waterhouse. Solomon Wolfe was in charge of Local 43, and he was "strictly a EWF bredren. [He] was a business man, very cool and possesses a great sense of sympathy to people in need. He is a very charitable I-drin and a Rasta of long standing" (Jah Bones 1985, 29).[12] Following the departure of the three Rastafari who went on the second mission to Africa and subsequent to the visit in June 1964 of Gladstone Robinson, who had come from New York to promote the African Repatriation Committee, a committee of seven delegares from Local 43 went to the EWF annual convention in New York in July 1964. At this congress, Robinson's initiative, the African Repatriation Committee, was rejected, and the seven Jamaicans realized that the "EWF, as a Back-to-Africa organization, international in scope [did not] have a repatriation committee".[13] For the Rastafari, there was initially no doubt that the EWF, to which land in Ethiopia had been entrusted, was an organization dealing with repatriation to Africa. They came to understand by going to New York that organizing back-to-Africa returns was not the main objective of the EWF. No aspect of its constitution alluded to such a role, and the American members, who were few and aged, were in no hurry to go to Ethiopia. An important distinction may be used to clarify the objectives of the Rastafari as opposed to those of American and non-Rastafari Jamaican members of the EWF: "The Rastafarians have always claimed that Ethiopia is their rightful heritage and their ultimate goal is to sit under their own 'vine and fig tree'. The land grant therefore was considered by the Rastafarians to be a direct fulfilment of prophecy. They were convinced that the time had come for the sons of Africa to return. In short, to the EWF, the Back-to-Africa movement meant migration; to the Rastafarians, repatriation" (Barrett 1968, 79–80, quoted by van Dijk 1993, 115).

The Rastafari saw repatriation as a type of mobility distinct from migration, especially owing to their spiritual interpretation. Because the land had been given by the emperor in person, and in view of the special relation they saw themselves as having with him, the Rastafari defended the idea that this gift was specifically made to them. Thus, the land in Shashemene became a powerful argument in favour of repatriation and was interpreted through the literal lenses of biblical prophecies on the return to Israel. As a result, the Rastafari regarded repatriation as an operation of divine origin, one that only Jah,[14] rather than the Jamaican government, could bring to pass. Such was the theological function of return, often resulting in a certain passivity and a culture of expectation (Chevannes 1998b, 30–31). However, not all Rastafari were satisfied with mystical or passive expectation, and some acted in view of actually accomplishing a return. By extension, they made the prophecy come true. For the land was there, in Ethiopia, at the disposal of EWF members. Left to their own devices, the members of Local 43 joined ranks with Local 31, which was then the most important in terms of membership. They launched a fundraising drive, with the support of EWF international president Chester Garden, and the authorization of the Jamaican prime minister, Dr Donald Sangster. The aim was to "transport pioneers and help them settle and develop lands at Shashamene [*sic*]".[15] Zeptha Malcolm, a Rastafari, contributed more than half of these funds, and Local 31 contributed almost a third. The other subscribers were five private individuals and four companies. But once the funds had been gathered for financing the voyage, a fundamental question arose: Who was ready to leave?

Carmen Clarke

One woman was ready: Carmen Clarke. Born in 1934 in St Mary, she was an only child; she grew up in Jones Town, a neighbourhood in Kingston where her mother had settled after leaving her babyfather in St Mary. Looking back on her youth, what Carmen Clarke remembered especially was that she had had to count on herself at an early age. She dropped out of school and worked to provide for her own needs. One thing she was sure of – she did not want a child before marriage. When she was about twenty years old, she went to live in Trench Town.

Her entry into the Rastafari faith occurred gradually, through three visions received at different times. The first, which she had while she attended a "Babylon Church" disturbed her deeply: "I go to bed one night [and got a] vision of two men coming to me. One tall with the Orthodox wrap, one small, face indiscernible, they were coming from the east, spoke to me, 'What are you waiting for to accept the Lord?' "[16] Unable to decipher the meaning of this dream, she spoke about it to an EWF brother. Thanks to him, she encountered the pan-Ethiopian organization. She visited the locals on several occasions, took part in the meetings, listened attentively and, one month later, she became a member. At this time, she had a second vision:

Figure 5.2. Carmen Clarke, Kingston, ca. 1955. Archives C. Clarke, Shashemene © DR.

> [I got] another vision of two men in the same manner, they were coming from the east, many clouds. The tall man looked at corners [around] he had a pig in his hands "this was the devil that was in you". My blessing is to always negotiate with His Imperial Majesty within me. After I get the real meaning. The house they were in was me, the temple, and they leave me clean to accept the Lord.[17]

By reinterpreting the theme of spiritual rebirth, of the purification leading to a new life, Carmen Clarke was able to begin her life as a Rastafari. The collective mode in which these visions were interpreted illustrates the importance of the social interactions accompanying the construction of a Rastafari identity, in which "to be in the faith" entailed participation in a social environment. She moved again, this time to Almond Town, in the company of a man to whom her third vision was linked:

> He was not in the faith but I did my activities the same way. But he had to choose. One morning he visioned a short man that turned him back and said you're dead three times. So I ended with him. I can't stay with a dead man. I visioned again the two men. They were bright clouds, red, gold and green coming towards me. I gradually discern the short man, the face of His Imperial Majesty. Before I get the full blessing the man woke me up. Not another night you stay here I told him. It is the last time between you and me. I lost that blessing that was supposed to come to me.[18]

Dreams and visions are a constitutive element of the religious life of Jamaicans of all walks of life. Barry Chevannes has underlined their importance in the process of conversion to Rastafari. Most of the Rastafari, belonging to the generation before that of Carmen Clarke, whom Chevannes interviewed, spoke to him of dreams related to their conversion (Chevannes 1994, 110–14). For Carmen Clarke, these three visions were the stages through which the identity of Haile Selassie I – and her own by the same token – were revealed to her. After a symbolic purification, the indiscernible figure becomes a specific face, that of the emperor, surrounded by the colours of the Ethiopian flag. The progressive

Figure 5.3. On the left, Carmen Clarke. Ethiopian World Federation presents its objectives in rural Jamaica, 1950s. Archives C. Clarke, Shashemene © DR.

clarification in these visions confirmed, little by little, the assurance of her own faith and her identification with Haile Selassie I.

Carmen Clarke had been involved for several years in volunteer social and activist activities. As she was literate, she was sometimes charged to write letters on behalf of the EWF. Thus, in 1954, she sent information on Local 31 to the newspaper *New Times and Ethiopia News*, published in London by Sylvia Pankhurst.[19] Two months later, she sent another letter to the London secretariat, prefaced with greetings praising the emperor: "Long live our hero Emperor Haile Sellassie I who came to break every chain. Although the road be rough and steep, I go to the desert to find my sheep." By quoting the words of a well-known hymn, "The Lion of Judah Shall Break Every Chain", she cordially thanked the newspaper, which had informed them of the official visits of the emperor to the United States, Canada and Mexico City.[20]

Local 31, in which she participated, had 250 registered members, but only about fifty were active. Most members originated in the urban proletariat and were employed as construction workers, mechanics, post-office employees, night watchmen or waiters (Rogers 1970, 10). This local, which was democratic in principle, seemed to function, in fact, in an autocratic mode. It was involved, starting at the beginning of the 1960s, in Back-to-Africa campaigns. Following the fundraising drive launched jointly with Local 43 in Waterhouse, the question asked was, who then was ready to leave? Carmen Clarke gives us her version of the story:

> The local I was living with before, number 31, has a lot of members, whole heap of members, I think people dem they ready to accept the doctrine and the preaching of Ethiopia through the federation down there but their mind, their mind wasn't ready for Ethiopia. Because when I ready to come to Ethiopia, there was people who

in that local, years upon years who died, you know, even some before I left, they were in the local going night and day, going all round and they didn't ready, they never even have a passport when the calling come, the local is going to send people to Ethiopia, some of them no have a passport. Being in the local for years, singing "send me back to Ethiopia land" but they didn't ready, their mind didn't ready, [just] their mouth talking.[21]

The important role Local 31 played in her life is clearly underlined. This is the local in which she lived, around which most of her activities converged and where her social connections existed. Carmen Clarke criticized most of the members of the local: those who spent a lot of time there, always talking about Ethiopia, but never taking seriously the real possibilities of departure available to them. She made a distinction between lip service and true dedication. Although they were constantly speaking about return, singing about it, hoping for it, very few considered the inherent material constraints, starting with the question of passports. This general unpreparedness of the majority of the members of Local 31 illustrates the difficulty involved in moving from the rhetoric of return to the practice of return. For most individuals, whether Rastafari or not, "Back to Africa" was a slogan, a claim closely related to their condition as poor, marginalized black Jamaicans. Carmen Clarke, for her part, had a literal take on the familiar calls to return. She was thirty-five years old and she was ready: "Once I started and get the doctrine, I'm ready, I'm ready to take the trip, all my friends, outside [of] federation [say] 'you crazy, where are you going to Africa, people are starving to death' and they talk. I say OK, it's alright, let me go and see for myself."[22]

She was determined. Looking back now on all those who remained behind, Carmen Clarke still wonders what all these sermons over the years, what all these words without concrete effect in the face of a real opportunity actually meant. She represents an "older generation" of Rastafari who were pious, militant, without dreadlocks, like the majority of those with whom she made the journey. Indeed, a group of five adults and a child was formed. They came from Locals 31 and 43. Certain group members delayed their departure due to passport problems, but they left finally on 5 September 1969 via New York. The *Daily Gleaner* ran the title:

Figure 5.4. Letter of Carmen Clarke, secretary of Local 31 of the Ethiopian World Federation, addressed to the newspaper published by Sylvia Pankhurst in London. *New Times and Ethiopia News*, 11 September 1954, 3. © DR.

Correspondence

ETHIOPIAN WORLD FEDERATION
Local 31

Kingston,
Jamaica,
B.W.I.

Dear Editor,—Greetings to you and thanks for your answer to my introduction to you on behalf of dear Motherland Ethiopia, kindly publish for me in your next issue these words:

"Long live our hero Emperor Haile Sellassie I, who came to break every chain. Although the road be rough and steep, I go to the desert to find my sheep." Thanks to "New Times and Ethiopian News" for the assistance we have received on behalf of our awakened spirits. When our prayers were answered through your news: Emperor Haile Sellassie in Washington, we thank you for the publication of the journey of our distinguished monarch, the King of Kings who is proven all over the world.

We of the Federation thank you for the information you have given us from time to time.

We long for the foundation of a government for the black nations who have been downtrodden for centuries. We have long been looking towards a reunion to our family on the other side of the world behind the iron curtain of success towards the franchise of human rights. We have long been working to get some concrete agreement on such subjects, even though we are not spoken of among the famous ones of the earth.

We thank those who are for the truth—Liberty, International Justice, and the Democracy.

Thanks again for the information concerning His Imperial Majesty's tour of the United State, Canada and Mexico.

Thank you for the help your newspaper brings to us in this time of our humanitarian revolt against material success and our struggle for human rights.

SISTER M. CLARKE.

Figure 5.5. Zeptha J. Malcolm, who left for Shashemene in 1969, *African Opinion* 9, nos. 5–6 (March–April 1970): 9. © DR.

"Mission off to develop 700 acres in Ethiopia."[23] There was Carmen Clarke, the only woman who was unmarried, and Zeptha Malcolm, a dreadlocked Rastafari born in Cuba in 1927 of a Jamaican mother and a Cuban father, who had moved to Jamaica at age seventeen. He was a construction worker. He had had seven children with two women, but only one of his daughters accompanied him to Ethiopia (Gibson 1996, 211).

Frederick Pryce changed his mind in New York and returned to Jamaica. Gerald Brissett was a skilled worker, and Solomon Wolfe made the trip as the president of Local 43. They all had to invest financially to be able to pay for their trip, as the funds collected turned out to be insufficient. They stayed eleven days in New York, where they got baptized in the Ethiopian Orthodox Church. Passing through Athens and Nairobi, they arrived in Addis Ababa, and despite a few difficulties related to their vaccinations, they were able to disembark. They were followed a few weeks later by the head of the Jamaica Labour Party government, Hugh Shearer, and then by a representative of the People's National Party opposition, Michael Manley.[24] Conscious of the importance of this settlement in the Jamaican popular imaginary, these politicians could not pass up such an occasion to announce their "familiarity" with the question of return, which had, nonetheless, been sidelined since independence.

This group, which left in 1969, joined the first group of "pioneers" that had arrived the year before. The new arrivants had made the trip to Ethiopia under the aegis of the EWF, regardless of the fact that, to do this, they had had to oppose international officers, raise funds by themselves and transform the Ethiopian organization from the bottom up in order to reach their objectives. When Cecil Gordon, then the president of Local 19, returned from the first mission to Africa in 1961, he had boasted about his ability to organize departures to the continent even without the approval of the government – a boast on which he was never able to make good.[25] Eight years later, in 1969, the Rastafari had won and become the first Jamaican members of the EWF to repatriate to Shashemene, thanks in particular to Wolfe, who had managed to establish Local 43 and to encourage its members to take practical measures.

Shashemene Land Grant Development and Re-settlement Committee

Solomon Wolfe was very influential, and, in view of encouraging new departures, he returned to Jamaica in 1972, three years after his own departure and the settlement of the first returnees on whom we will focus later. In Shashemene, he had founded the Shashemene Land Grant Development and Re-settlement Committee

(SLGDRC), of which Carmen Clarke was the secretary. This administration was meant to serve as a base for raising funds to develop the land on which they had settled. On his return to Kingston, Wolfe created, on 16 September 1972, a branch of the SLGDRC, which was administrated as a working committee of the EWF, and brought together members of Locals 25 and 43.[26] Made up of nine officers and seven members, the authority of this new committee was to prevail in all future communication between the EWF and the returnees in Shashemene. A petition and two letters dated 14 October 1972 and addressed to the imperial government explained the expectations and requests of the SLGDRC.[27] They opened with "Greetings to our Lord and Saviour, His Imperial Majesty, Emperor Haile Selassie", or with "Our Father His Imperial Majesty Emperor Haille [*sic*] Selassie I", and specified, by way of introduction, the privileged role of Solomon Wolfe in these relations with the government. The letters required work and administrative facilities to be placed at Wolfe's disposal in Ethiopia: an office, a car with an English-speaking chauffeur, a secretary, a lawyer and an architect "to carry out the speedy development on the land" and some ready money. The petition requested a temporary dwelling in Addis Ababa, with precise details regarding size and amenities, and a loan of one hundred million Ethiopian dollars (or *berrs*) "to begin the development", not to mention the opening of negotiations between the emperor and the Jamaican government. This idea was to get the government to agree to buy the belongings of the members before their departure. Brother Redwood was the president of Local 25 and of the committee elected on 14 January to forward this petition to Ethiopia.[28] It was decided the following week that he had full powers to represent the EWF in Jamaica and the world.[29] Was this a type of internal coup d'état? This might have been the case since, during the meeting of 28 January 1973, these decisions were presented to Wolfe as the consequence of "his long absence [when] he left us at a cross road where we were faced with great difficulties [*sic*] and frustration", Wolfe left the meeting before the end.[30] At a subsequent meeting, the "intolerable" absence of the officers elected in September 1972 forced the committee to elect new ones, and the departure of Redwood for Ethiopia was deferred.[31]

Other documents dated 8 April 1973 followed the letters and petitions addressed to the emperor. The distribution of the budget that they hoped to obtain from the Ethiopian government is as follows: a quarter of the budget for transportation to Ethiopia; a quarter for the construction of houses with at least seven rooms, a shopping centre, a swimming pool, a reception hall accommodating twenty thousand persons, a theatre, a private clinic, a school, a sports ground, an Orthodox Church, an office, a telephone connection, a gas station, a used water treatment facility; a quarter for the development and the maintenance of mechanized agriculture; the last quarter for miscellaneous expenditure and as a reserve.[32] These requests, projected on a loan which was not yet granted, may seem, at first sight, extravagant or disproportionate. They certainly did not take into account the general condition of the city and region of Shashemene. They nonetheless formulated the representation that the Jamaican members had of a "model city", dreamed up as the complete opposite of the conditions in which they lived. This vision of a "complete" city in which the same importance is given to transportation, housing, entertainment, agriculture and pocket money is revealing as concerns both their idea of the attributes of development and the gulf that yawned between the Jamaican committee and the attainment of such a level of development.

In the itinerary in Ethiopia imagined by the delegates of the committee, this distance is subtly reformulated in the various requests that they presented:[33] adequate clothing; social, economic and financial assistance; protection; logistical support for transportation and settlement; and international passports – in fact, everything they lacked in Jamaica and would need in Ethiopia. This social ambition, this hunger for resources was sustained by the confidence they had in the powers of the emperor, referred to at the end of the document as "Our God and King". The tribulations of the committee illustrate how difficult it was for a grassroots initiative to become a solid institution and to present to governments a viable plan of settlement in Ethiopia. In the words of Jah Bones: "Governments have got to come in here but only when Rastas are thoroughly organised and are ready to force Presidents and Prime Ministers, worlds councils and churches to respect Rasta by listening and responding positively to a just demand" (Jah Bones 1985, 36). In 1972 and 1973, the Rastafari sometimes had unrealistic requests, as seen in the case of the SLGDRC, and they were far from obtaining the desired attention in ministries and governments. Consequently, the dynamic of departure played out among individuals.

Harold Reid

After some hesitation, Harold Reid recalls that he was born in 1927, in Kingston. His parents attended the Baptist Church. He remembered the benches on which he fell asleep during the long sermons. He grew up in the ghettos of Kingston: "Life in Jamaica terrible ting [thing] dat, you know. I wasn't a rude boy, I was a humble man, but the ghetto where I in, we grow up into rude boys, some terrible rude boys I grow among, see dem time, we nah deal with school business, we a deal with rudeness."[34] He did not stay long in school, not enough to learn to read and write. He had to get up too early and run to get there; it was too far, and the road that led there offered too many distractions as well as older people who helped him, sometimes, to forget the hunger in his stomach. Reid remembers how brawls used to be settled with stab wounds from knives or broken bottles, before the day of firearms – those of young gunmen manipulated by politicians or those of the police. Reflecting on urban violence, he keeps repeating: "Dat cause me reach Africa you know, dem something cause me reach Africa."[35] Violence was omnipresent in the large and numerous ghettos of Kingston. Sometimes, spaces of peace were to be found in the yards of the Rastafari. Reid lived in various places, but he circulated a great deal within the city, among these yards and the older Rastafari who occupied them, like Bra Watto in Trench Town, Bra P in Key Fire, Bra Phillip in Waterhouse, where Bra Sala (Solomon Wolfe) also lived (Jah Bones 1985, 24–29). Harold Reid knew Wolfe's "church":

> "Wolfe is a man who have a church, a temple like, keep a likkle [little] service like, and you a go outside and listen to what him a say. Man deh [there] a smoke herb, bigger man than me, and hear dem a likkle reasoning. So is deh so now me get my likkle wisdom, through likkle reasoning, so I get groundation of Africa, cause de man who sit dung [sit down] dere a talk two, three, four a whol' heap [many] of man did dere fe [to] done a talk you know."
>
> "Dem sitting down were Rastaman?"
>
> "Yes! . . . They were Garveyites, bedwardites and binghi deh deh too, federation. . . . All the people were speaking of Africa and then we decide we a come Africa."
>
> "Some talk about Liberia?"
>
> "Liberia, Sierra Leone, Ghana man used to talk about, but Ethiopia, speak about Ethiopia more *hayläñña* than Ghana and de rest of de country dem. Ethiopia me say to you."[36]

In this interview, Reid used the Amharic term, *hayläñña*, derived from *haylä*, as in the name Haile Selassie, meaning strong, powerful. He thus underlined that, in Rastafari evocations of Africa, Ethiopia had a special place, elevating it above all other African nations. The meetings he mentions are characteristic of the long sessions of Rastafari "reasoning", in which the older brothers officiated, occupying the space through their words and teachings. Those of the generation before Harold Reid had been disciples of Alexander Bedward or Marcus Garvey, two religious and nationalist figures who were still popular in the 1950s. The terms *binghi* or *nyabinghi* designated dreadlocked Rastafari attached to the ritual of the drums. They were at the time in full expansion, the foundation of the great cultural changes of the movement at the time: dreadlocks, Italk and the ganja protocol (Homiak 1985). The members of the federation who, like Reid, took part in this lifestyle, the binghi livity, were also in charge of a constitution and of the gift of land in Ethiopia. Harold Reid, a young man at the time, fasted once a week with his Rastafari brothers and began to grow dreadlocks, putting his trust in "the power of the uncombed wool or hair and that the people had a dread or fear of the locks" (Jah Bones 1985, 31). He was also a member of EWF Local 25.

While the atmosphere in which the Waterhouse Rastafari lived is narrated to a great extent by Jah Bones (1985, 22–37), Reid underlines how hard it was not to become a rude boy. The rude boy was a prototype of the Jamaican urban culture: he represented the young man from the country arriving in Kingston, or born in town, without resources, bred into inhospitable ghettos and forced to become a delinquent. Sometimes elder Rastafari, like Solomon Wolfe, gave work to the youth to prevent them from stealing and falling into the hands of the police. Conflicts between Rastafari and the police were commonplace between the great repressions of Coronation Market in 1959 and those of Coral Gardens in 1963. It is precisely in this period that migration became a way out of this world of poverty, unemployment and violence, especially since migrants sometimes returned to their old neighbourhoods, impressing their neighbours with imported clothes and wealth. Harold Reid illustrates this tension between migration and repatriation mentioned above. In fact, leaving the country to reap apples or potatoes in the United States or to try out the benefits of the dole in England formed part of the perspectives of this social landscape. Reid learned masonry to fend for himself and had even put aside money to pay for the trip to England, but really "It nah make nah sense I man nah like col' . . . no sun no shine deh a [there in] England. No sun no shine deh."[37] Thanks to an imagination nurtured by numerous sessions spent among the Rastafari, he had something else in mind: Africa. Sitting on the street corner, he shared this thought with Elie, one of his friends who had come back from the United States. The migrant, who was passing through, replied: "What you a talk about Reidy, about Africa? You mad man, come America man." To this, Reid retorted:

> "Me I like know Africa believe me how de breeze a blow like," me a say to him, "me like know Africa you know, me hear about Ethiopia me like know about dem place deh, cause me nah go dem place deh yet. . . . Man deal wid [with] America, I man deal wid Africa." "Alright," him say, "me see you interested in Africa but me see man out deh a die, man nah have nothing to eat, so why you a go a place like dat?" Me say "well bwoy [boy] me radder [rather] go see wha' a gwaan."[38]

Reid resisted the temptation of migration and remained focused on repatriation. For several years, Africa had been *the* topic of discussions, and, like Carmen Clarke, he underlined the paradox: "When we ready fe [to] come, nobody ready fe come yet . . . de amount of people who a suppose to reach nah [didn't] reach yet."[39] One event forced him to prepare in a concrete manner. He had been present at the departure of the previous group in 1969, and Solomon Wolfe had returned to Kingston in 1972 with news of land, which had then been divided up among the twelve persons present in Shashemene. "[Wolfe] say him get the land now, me say to him, 'land dere for me too?' him a say 'a no problem. If you look 'pon it that way deh, if you nah get no land, me give you land, you nah haffi [don't have to] buy nah land, me give you land'. 'Me nah haffi buy no land?' him say 'no'."[40]

Given the prospect of direct, facilitated access to land, Reid's decision was made, although perhaps, with the passing of the years, he resented Wolfe a little for not having informed him of the real financial and food situation in Ethiopia. Anyway, he got organized, applied for a passport, sold his business and his yard, as he had no intention of returning to Jamaica. Alongside Wolfe, who had left behind the SLGDRC in great turmoil; "Mother" Isolene Swearine Thompson, from the Church of God; Ewart Tulloch, a young student; and Mr Baker, he went through the maze of the American and English immigration services to find out the conditions of obtaining a visa. Without informing his parents, but only his brother and his sister, Harold Reid embarked with this small group for Ethiopia, with his son and daughter. After a long journey which passed through Rome, where they encountered problems of overweight baggage, and they finally arrived in Ethiopia on 8 March 1973.

Thanks to the activism of its officers, Local 43, based in Unity Lane, was recognized by both the EWF in New York and the imperial government in Ethiopia. It had facilitated the departure of a first group in 1969, closely following that of the "pioneers" in 1968, and despite the failure of the SLGDRC, Solomon Wolfe had succeeded in taking another group with him in 1973. But a complex and important event was about to bring to a halt the plans of Local 43: the Ethiopian revolution of September 1974, under which the Ethiopian empire was going to collapse. We will return later to the local consequences, in Shashemene, of this political and social upheaval; suffice it to say for the moment that most – but not all – of the members of these first three groups returned to Jamaica between 1975 and 1976. Associated with the emperor because they were Rastafari and with the dominant class because they had land, they feared for their life and made the return voyage, this time to Kingston. This other return might have spelled the failure of repatriation to Ethiopia and, more generally, of the Rastafari claims to the right of African descendants to return to Africa.

Figure 5.6. Harold Reid left Jamaica in 1973. He is seen here a few years later in front of his house in Shashemene with his son Mike and his daughter Colleen, who had travelled with him. Shashemene, Ethiopia, January 1981. Photograph: Derek Bishton © DR.

The Ethiopian Revolution and the Rastafari

The only article addressing the impact of the Ethiopian revolution on the Rastafari movement was written by Barry Chevannes in 1975 in a socialist newspaper. Based on the work of Engels and on his thesis developed in *The Peasant War in Germany* (1926), Chevannes's article admitted that all religious wars, and all heresies, were manifestations of class struggle. Consequently, in addition to a future theological interpretation of the fall of the emperor, he predicted two alternatives for the Rastafari movement: an inevitable absorption in the proletarian movement or an increased religiosity no longer seeking redemption through the struggle – economic and racial – against oppressors, but via individual and spiritual rebirth (Chevannes 1975). For Horace Campbell, the revolution elucidated one of the fundamental contradictions of the Rastafari movement, which he summarized thus: "Rastas cannot be against Babylon in the West and support reaction in Africa" (Campbell 1994, 229). Using a Marxist and political economy approach, Campbell stressed that one of the resounding paradoxes of the Rastafari was their refutation of any association with the West, with "Babylon", while identifying with what was considered, at the time, to be an autocratic and retrograde Ethiopian regime opposed to popular aspirations to reform and social change. His wish was that the regime change in Ethiopia would force the Rastafari to erase their ideas and ideologies and to face up to African political realities. This was without considering that the social and economic conditions which had governed the formation of the Rastafari movement had not, in 1975, changed to the point of enabling a reformulation of the root reasons for belonging to the movement. On the contrary, with the increasing violence of the Jamaican society and the emerging prestige of reggae contributing to the popularization of their identity, the Rastafari in Jamaica still embodied an appealing cultural and spiritual alternative.

In Jamaica, the fall of the Ethiopian empire was important at at least two levels – political and religious. For about ten years, Jamaican Black Power activists, gathered around the periodical *Abeng*, had been proposing a Marxist critique of Jamaican society and opposing its capitalist development (Nettleford 2001, 125–28). The Black Power activists were former Garveyites or people influenced by Garvey and Rastafari: young people from the middle class or from the black farming or urban communities, residing in modest neighbourhoods; others from the more established middle class, who had become the voice of the movement and who were sometimes filled with the guilt characteristic of persons of mixed race; young intellectuals, black beneficiaries of the social change following the great 1938 uprisings. The relations between Rastafari and the proponents of Black Power were complex, sometimes revealing clear distinctions between militants, sometimes showing a juxtaposition of ideals and practices. The Black Power activists at the university were often involved in social studies. Their relations with the Rastafari provided a bond with the poorest classes which they probably would not have had otherwise, one that reopened a cultural and militant dimension which had existed before, and in whose continuity they positioned themselves, although the Rastafari had formerly gone much further in their claims (Nettleford 2001, 151).

One still comes across many people in Jamaica whose trajectory passed from radical Marxism to the militant spirituality of Rastafari, or vice versa – a phenomenon which deserves attention. The fact is that the tools of class struggle and those of eschatological battle were not the same. The Black Power critique of the social structure of Jamaica formulated itself in more economic, industrial and political terms. Walter Rodney's (1942–80) stay in Jamaica is revealing in this respect (Lewis 1998a). A Guyanese with a doctorate in African history and an activist, he had studied in England, had taught in Tanzania and had accepted a position in the department of history on the Mona campus of the University of the West Indies in 1967. He had a radical vision of the role of intellectuals: they should never forget the people and should put their knowledge at the service of the black revolution (Alpers 1982). His meeting with Jamaican Rastafari was important; it contributed to the opening of a dialogue between the various social classes. Recalling his interactions with Rastafari, Rodney (1996, 67) wrote:

> And above all, I would like to indicate my own gratification for that experience which I shared with them [the Rastas]. Because I learnt. I got knowledge from them, real knowledge. You have to speak to Jamaican Rasta, and you have to listen to him, listen very carefully and then you will hear him tell you about the Word. And when you listen to him, and you can go back and read *Muntu*, an academic text, and read about *Nomo*, and African concept for Word, and you say, Goodness the Rastas know this, they knew this before Janheinz Jahn.[41] You have to listen to them and you hear them talk about Cosmic Power and it rings a bell. I say, but I have read this somewhere, this is Africa.

Rodney was impressed by the knowledge of the Rastafari, born outside universities, in the streets and ghettos of the city; he was impressed by their ability to produce a culture of this kind through their words and arts, while surviving in such abject living conditions. Rodney was deported and banished from Jamaica for having participated in the congress of black writers held in Toronto in October 1968, and his forced departure gave rise to great riots in Kingston. The intensity of the exchanges between Marxist intellectuals and Rastafari indicated the extent of the contestation which was brewing in Jamaica, but the Ethiopian revolution fissured these alliances. Rodney spoke in respectful terms about Haile Selassie and, more generally, about the ancient heritage of Ethiopia (Rodney 1996, 40–46), but at the onset of the revolution, for many Marxist militants, the fall of the old empire marked another step forward towards the abolition of feudal structures and the liberation of black peoples, an opinion at variance with that of the Rastafari, for whom Haile Selassie I represented not only political but also religious values.

The fall of the empire, the disappearance and, perhaps, the death of the emperor were of extreme significance for Rastafari: these events posed the question of the sustainability of the movement, of the adaptation of their social and ritual practices, and of the legitimacy of their claims. Few testimonies of the times have remained, but it is probable that there were multiple reactions, going from a break with the Rastafari movement to a total negation of the events which had occurred. An elder Rastafari woman, who was an activist from the 1950s, narrates in these terms her memory of 1975 and her reaction to the news of the death of the emperor:

> Listen now – When dey [they] come and tell we [us] dreadful lie, we know is lie for His Majesty cannot dead [*sic*]. He is life ever living, so when dey come wid dis [with this] propaganda and dis false prophet we burn dem out! And make dem know Haile Selassie can't dead, is Him give life and if him dead everyting [*sic*] dead. Haile Selassie is true and living life. . . . [*Sings*:] "Don't try to tell me Jah is dead he wake I up dis morning, don't try to tell me Jah is dead him live within my heart." We know Jah live in our heart so him can't dead. We laugh after dem, the great Bob Marley come in and sing dis great song, *Jah live*. . . . [*sings*].[42]

She denied the reality of this news coming out of Ethiopia and qualified the news as lies relayed by the Jamaican press. We must imagine the confusion which seized the Rastafari, the popular pressure that surrounded them at the time, how they were mocked, how their beliefs were ridiculed by others. The argument of this Rastafari woman adds up to this: Haile Selassie I was the Living God on earth and could therefore never die, the existence of the Rastafari themselves being the most concrete proof of this. The refusal of bodily mortality, especially that of the divine black body, forced Rastafari to come up with arguments and to develop, as Chevannes had foreseen, theological interpretations centred on the fact that Jah could not die because he was regarded as living by Rastafari. She then referred to Bob Marley's "Jah Live", sung in September 1975, a retort by the artist at the height of his glory. By quoting the words of the psalms, Bob Marley challenged the assertions of "fools" who said that Jah had died and forced the "children" to see the rising glory of Jah:

> Fool say in their heart
> Rasta your god is dead
> But I and I know, Jah Jah
> Dread it shall be dreader dread
> . . . .
> Let Jah arise
> Now that the enemy are scattered.

This song helped to restore the confidence of the Rastafari and to point out that *they* were not about to die. This was also the state of mind of the new generation of Rastafari which was preparing to leave for Ethiopia:

> Well as far as I was concerned all of that didn't touch me none at all. Because I was so strong faith and deep root in Ethiopia, the King of Kings, although it was affecting other people, cause people start cut off dem dread and leave the faith. Me was a yout'

just vibrant in the faith so den [then] I come into Ethiopia. And the organization start to send us. At the same time you had some people leave from Ethiopia to come back to Jamaica as well. Because a lot of things was going on in Ethiopia and people were not going to stay to see what happen after, so people was coming out .[43]

This Rastafari recognized that many people, upset by the news, had cut off their dreadlocks, thus abandoning the external sign of their faith, but he attributed his certainty to his own youth and faith. Although certain Rastafari were returning from Ethiopia to Jamaica, he was one of those who still made a point of leaving. The organization to which he refers, the one which sent him to Ethiopia, functioned with two names – EWF Local 15 and the Twelve Tribes of Israel; we will return to this in a moment. The leader of this organization, called Prophet Gad, had warned his members that important political changes were on the way, thus preventing them from being caught completely unawares, as was the case of many others: "We know the King would step down, our Prophet told us long before that the Emperor is going to step down, so we were prepared for it, it didn't came as a shock. We receive it not quite pleasing, but we understand the situation, the forces against him."[44]

This form of "preparation" limited their exposure to the shock experienced by most Rastafari after the emperor was deposed, and the foresight of the leader of this organization tempered the anxiety of those around him. For these Rastafari, leaving for Ethiopia regardless of a revolution in full swing was, contrary to Horace Campbell's opinion, a radical way of facing up to African realities without giving up their identity and ideology. Most members of EWF Local 43 returned to Kingston between 1975 and 1976, but Solomon Wolfe made the journey to Ethiopia again a few years later in 1981, in the company of another officer of the local, Berthal J. Moody. Born in 1936 in Kingston, the latter became the chaplain of the local in 1960 and its second vice-president in 1963. He had made the trip to New York in 1964 for the EWF annual convention, but, at the time of the departures of the 1969 and 1973 groups, he had remained in Kingston to take care of the affairs of the local. One of the decisions he had had to make in the absence of Wolfe was to accept or refuse to cooperate with another EWF local, Local 15, based in Trench Town, which counted many members and was very organized. At the head of Local 15 was the leader who was just mentioned: Prophet Gad. This is how Moody explains his choice:

When Gad come fe [to] hand over the people and the money to EWF, I man refused. . . . No organization respecting the leadership can suddenly hand over to another organization without some kind of agreement as to what it is all about, consolidation or merging of two bodies under what condition. . . . Not a case when you hand over your money and your people and say do this [and] hand over to you. So what happen to you? What happen to your administration? Not so.[45]

This defensive position illustrates the importance the officers of EWF Local

43 accorded to its administration. They had overcome many difficulties of an organizational nature: short-circuiting the established channels of the EWF controlled by non-Rastafari, transformation of the EWF to prioritize repatriation, obtaining passports and visas, organizing departures by air, establishing the local in Ethiopia and working to keep members of the Jamaican local mobilized. The other local, Local 15, thus represented, in one way or another, a threat to Local 43, and the impossible cooperation between these two locals was going to have a great impact on the settlement in Shashemene and the development of the Rastafari movement. Let us focus for a moment on Local 15, which went on to be known internationally as the Twelve Tribes of Israel, in order to underline its specificities and the reasons why it was perceived as a threat.

From Local 15 of the Ethiopian World Federation . . .

The Twelve Tribes of Israel remains one of the least-known Rastafari organizations, regardless of the fact that, in terms of membership, it is still the most prominent on the international scene. During the 1970s and 1980s, it was occasionally mentioned, in passing, in the literature without new sources or interpretations. The updated edition of Leonard Barrett's book offers a few pages on the Twelve Tribes of Israel, but in the face of the refusal of the members to speak to him, his insights are supported essentially by remarks made by persons outside the organization (1997, 225–34). In 1988, Frank Jan van Dijk (1988) published an article dealing specifically with the Twelve Tribes of Israel. Van Dijk presented the characteristics of their doctrines, seen as relatively Christian; their internal functioning, which followed a strict protocol; and their social composition, which included members of the middle class. He also noted that the Twelve Tribes formed the broadest and best-organized of group of Rastafari in Jamaica. He remained evasive on the history of the formation of this organization and on its relation to repatriation to Ethiopia. Yet this history is important for the clarification of the complex relations between the EWF and the Twelve Tribes of Israel.

Local 15 did not obtain its charter from the EWF general headquarters in New York but from a local based in Chicago, which had been directed since 1947 by an African American, Reverend Winston G. Evans. Evans had met the emperor at the time of his official visit to the United States in 1954 and had gone to Ethiopia in 1955 for the Silver Jubilee celebrating the twenty-five years of reign of Haile Selassie I. That year, Evans had become the "Minister for the religious section of the EWF".[46] At the time of another visit of the emperor to the United States, in 1967, he had taken the initiative of asking for land on which black migrants could settle. His request was approved, and land was assigned to him in the wonderful region of Bale Goba, to the east of Shashemene. This individual initiative illustrated the fragility of the organization in the United States. In fact, Evans recognized his detachment from the New York offices by underlining: "we are independent of that local [of New York] and working as an independent organization. . . . We believe in togetherness but we don't believe in any one holding us back."[47] While using the name of the EWF, he gave himself a degree of independence vis-à-vis that organization founded in 1937. The emperor and Evans, pictured shaking hands in *African Opinion*, brought the Jamaican Rastafari to contact him.[48]

Figure 5.7. Winston G. Evans of EWF Chicago visiting EWF Local 15, 7 Davis Lane, Trench Town, Kingston, 1970. Archives E.L. Smith, Shashemene © DR.

Thus, at the request of a few Rastafari and through the intermediary of Evans and his Chicago local, two EWF locals were established in Jamaica in 1968: Local 15 in Kingston, headed by Gad, and Local 16 in St Thomas, in the east of the island. Later that year, Reverend Evans left for Ethiopia with his treasurer, Mr Dewey Weaver, in order to discover the land in Bale. They failed to say whether their enthusiasm was dampened by the time needed to arrive at their destination, by the lack of roads and the isolation of the region, but that was undoubtedly the case. They had planned to establish on this site "community building, raising live stock, agriculture and other undertakings, by returnees in collaboration with the brothers there and with the help of both governments, the Ethiopian and the United States".[49] It was an ambitious programme, and when Reverend Evans went to Jamaica at the beginning of 1970, he was received with great enthusiasm by the members of Local 15, although he must have appeared somewhat out of place among its members, there in the ghetto, dressed as he was in a suit and a bowler hat.

Thanks to Evans, settlement in Ethiopia seemed to be possible, and Local 15 developed its base by recruiting new members. At the time, Joseph Owens was conducting his research on the Rastafari movement in Kingston, and he noted:

> The group which is currently most insistent upon pursuing repatriation and is most actively taking steps towards it is Local 15 of the Ethiopian World Federation. Members of that local have almost completely eschewed the notion of waiting passively for their deliverance [and are] currently trying to raise money to send small groups to Ethiopia. . . . Of key importance to them is membership in the Federation, and much of their exhortation is aimed at proselytising. . . . Local 15 leaders are convinced that once people realise the potential of the organisation, they will join in vast numbers, save their money, and soon return home to Ethiopia. (Owens 1995, 241–42).

Local 15 was thus, in terms of mobilization for the return to Ethiopia, one of the most active and dynamic places. It is interesting to note that their proselytizing was closely related to the claim to return but also to membership in EWF as the organization that would make return possible. When passing through Kingston, Evans had promised to send scores of members to Ethiopia, but facing the absence of concrete progress, the leader of Local 15, Gad, decided to visit the EWF head office in Chicago. Accompanied by another Rastafari, he left for Chicago but returned home extremely disturbed. Not only were the members of Evans's local old, but Evans, moreover, avoided the two Jamaicans, in order to sidestep the mention of financial issues which would quite likely have resulted in a confrontation. The Jamaicans returned disappointed to Kingston, where they qualified the EWF as a "joke" and a "fraud" and recognized that the charter establishing their local was probably illegitimate.[50] The investigation continued. Gad and other officers of his local visited Ethiopia, where they remained for a month. They went to Bale, where they noted that the donated land was neglected. They later contacted the returnees residing in Shashemene and the Ethiopian government.[51] On their return, they presented a detailed report to the members of the local, to whom they also presented a symbolic handful of soil collected in Ethiopia.[52] *Seeing* this land was like getting tangible "proof" of its availability, not in Bale, which was too remote, but in Shashemene, where several Jamaicans had already settled. At the time, Local 15 counted 118 highly organized members and was ready to send a first group to Ethiopia.

The impression that Reverend Evans had misled them, because he made fraudulent use of the EWF label, and the refusal of Local 43 – the only local with active bonds with Shashemene – to merge with the many members of Local 15 brought the latter to give up their intentions of collaboration with the EWF. They were thus forced to rely on their own organizational, economic and doctrinary principles. These were the very principles that Local 43 saw as a threat. Since its formation in 1968, Local 15 had developed a particular form of internal organization, called the Twelve Tribes of Israel. It had affiliated with the EWF in the certainty that the latter was the legitimate organization through which repatriation to Ethiopia would occur. Due to the dysfunction of the EWF, the Twelve Tribes decided to eschew this legitimacy and to seek their own means of accomplishing return. One Twelve Tribes member explained it this way:

> Even with federation [EWF] we were functioning Twelve Tribes of Israel. Two organizations, we set up Twelve Tribes, like a church. Federation was the state part of it. We function both Twelve Tribes of Israel and federation. It was easy to rest federation and own the function as Twelve Tribes of Israel, free from attacks and things government could try. . . . Chapter 15 wasn't legal some say, so Gad say let's function Twelve Tribes. There is the federation thing but we ready fe deal wid something positive, and it seems like a skeleton, just like a ghost. There is no administrative body as such of the federation. Federation didn't take the people home. . . . If federation say people sent

back to Africa, is Gad who did that through dues and buying tickets – none of dem did this. . . . If federation was to investigate, federation would go to prison. Where did the money go? Like Marcus Garvey. Gad warn that Garvey mistake is a land mark. Something else but not federation. Federation died.[53]

The distinction between the two organizations was made in terms of function: on the one hand, a *statical*, state-like function, represented by the EWF, and, on the other, a *churchical*, ecclesiastic function, filled by the Twelve Tribes. Whereas the EWF was an ecumenical organization to which Rastafari had difficult access, the Twelve Tribes formulated a unitary doctrine, which all its members accepted and which excluded those who did not share it. Activities included pooling resources through a weekly contribution by members. While under the aegis of the EWF, the funds collected weekly by members were sent to Reverend Evans and the Chicago local. Upon the rejection of the EWF, Twelve Tribes members were able to disperse the funds they collected. That was the meaning of the reference to Marcus Garvey, who had been accused of fraud in 1923, brought to justice and imprisoned in Atlanta until his deportation from the United States. The financial racket whose outcome was so disastrous for Garvey was interpreted as a precedent of that of the EWF, and it was in the interest of the Twelve Tribes to benefit from the resources they generated.

. . . to the Twelve Tribes of Israel

Reference has already been made to Gad and his role is continuously underlined by the members of his organization. His name was Dr Vernon Carrington (1935–2005), but he was also called Gad, Prophet Gad or Gadman. He did not wear dreadlocks and had previously belonged to another EWF local.[54] In 1968, he founded the Twelve Tribes of Israel and became, at the same time, the president of EWF Local 15. In his own terms, Gad "got converted" in 1961, the year of the first mission to Africa. It took him three and a half years to read the Bible "a chapter a day from Genesis to Revelation", followed by a second reading; seven years in all to "to vision" the Twelve Tribes of Israel.[55] The twelve tribes theme referred to the identification with the children of Israel, archetypes of divine election and of the promise of return, shared by the Rastafari, but it also reflected a surprising influence, that of Charles Fillmore (1854–1948) and the Unity School of Christianity. Fillmore's theology belonged to a vast American metaphysical movement at the base of neo-liberal Christian fundamentalism. It was founded on the unity and universality of God, the regeneration of man by Christ, the power of thought and the spiritual interpretation of the Scriptures.[56] Fillmore's *Metaphysical Bible Dictionary* (1931) thus offered a metaphysical interpretation of the Bible. This book was one of the readings recommended by Gad to the members of the Twelve Tribes of Israel.[57] Prosperity and healing were interpreted as divine attributes procured by faith in Christ, and they characterized fundamentalist Christian congregations which experienced a decisive expansion after the 1960s. In what has sometimes been identified as a Rosicrucian influence, Fillmore identified twelve seats of power within the human body, corresponding to twelve faculties, like faith, strength, judgement and so on, and to the twelve disciples of Christ. Gad's stroke of genius consisted in juxtaposing these twelve seats of power with the twelve months of the lunar year, which begins in April, associating them with the names of the tribes of Israel, and ascribing a colour to each. This allowed the members of the organization, according to their birth date, to identify with a given tribe and, consequently, a given colour, a faculty, a part of the body, and a disciple of Christ. Hence, a man or a woman born in April was of the tribe Reuben, had the colour of silver, the faculty of strength, the part of the body was the eyes, and the corresponding disciple of Christ was Andrew. Table 5.1 summarizes these correspondences.[58]

Table 5.1

Month	Tribe	Colour	Faculty	Body	Disciple
April	Reuben	Silver	Strength	Eyes	Andrew
May	Simeon	Gold	Faith	Ears	Simon-Peter
June	Levi	Purple	Love	Nose/ breathing	John
July	Judah	Brown	Generation	Mouth/ heart	Judas
August	Issachar	Yellow	Zeal	Hands	Simon the Zealot
September	Zebulon	Pink	Order	Belly	James the son of Alpheus
October	Dan	Blue	Judgment	Back	James the son of Zebedee
November	Gad	Red	Power	Private parts	Philip
December	Asher	Grey	Understanding	Thigh	Thomas
January	Naphtali	Green	Elimination	Knees	Thaddeus
February	Joseph	White	Imagination	Calf	Bartholomew
March	Benjamin	Black	Will	Foot	Matthew

Figure 5.8. The first executive body of the Twelve Tribes of Israel, 7 Davis Lane, Trench Town, Kingston, April 1972. Archives E.L. Smith, Shashemene © DR.

With a few modifications and the addition of the corresponding elements of the calendar, this chart was based on that developed by Charles Fillmore (Judah 1967, 248–49) and provided the Twelve Tribes of Israel with a concrete framework in which to develop their doctrine. The appropriation of these external references brought a certain "solidity" to Rastafari doctrine as it was expressed in the streets of Kingston. Gad's primary goal was to fill the executive bench of his organization by recruiting members representing each tribe. There were two series of executive members: *first* and *second*, each bringing together the twelve tribes. These forty-eight seats were supplemented by Dinah, representing "the only lady child that Jacob had", and who was dressed, as a result, in multicoloured clothing.[59] During meetings, the executive members wore long robes in their respective colours and sat in a circle, with Dinah in the centre. Six tribes faced the six others, thus establishing symbolic modes of relations among themselves.[60]

This photograph dated April 1972 shows the first executive body of the Twelve Tribes of Israel, dressed in colours and forming with their hands the symbol of the Star of David, modelled on the official photographs of the emperor, and representing a sign of identification common to all Rastafari. They are wearing tams, knitted headgear, in the Ethiopian colours characteristic of their organization. Sister Dinah and Prophet Gad are at the centre; behind them are an Ethiopian flag and a panel in the colours of the rainbow. Several books are present in the picture, probably Bibles which were read in the preferred Scofield version.[61] Two frames (one square and the other heart-shaped) contain photographs of the executives and of the emperor, a map of Africa and other characteristic Twelve Tribes documents. This photograph was taken at the first Twelve Tribes headquarters on Davis Lane, Trench Town. The zinc of the dwellings, the wobbly fence and the bare earth of the yard attest to the humble origin of the organization.

Yet, despite such origins similar to that of other Rastafari, the Twelve Tribes, by reason of their dynamism, posed a threat to the officers of Local 43. Their extremely active proselytizing, always carried out in a group, whether in Kingston or in the country, their reformulation of Rastafari doctrine and social identity, and the expansion of their social base often disturbed Rastafari attached to other organizations or practices. What Berthal J. Moody refused was not so much cooperation with another EWF local but rather the incorporation into his EWF local of this group of a hundred Rastafari affiliated with the Twelve Tribes. The charisma of their leader, Gad, the discipline of the members and their proselytizing around the issue of repatriation transformed them into a rising force. The Twelve Tribes saw the American EWF administration as fraudulent and ineffective and considered its Jamaican branches to be weak and disorganized. By rejecting the EWF, Twelve Tribes were able to centralize their own resources and finally send some members to Ethiopia. This unworkable cooperation had two consequences: the choice of the primacy of the name Twelve Tribes of Israel by Local 15 occurred in 1973, but it was applied retroactively from the foundation of Local 15 in 1968. The recognized date of the foundation of the Twelve Tribes is therefore 1968. Second, the separation of the two bodies, the EWF and the Twelve Tribes, led to consequences that are still visible today in the settlement in Shashemene, especially in terms of legitimacy, power and sociability and, more largely, regarding the international diffusion of the movement. But before touching on that subject, it would be helpful to focus for a moment on the trajectories of the Twelve Tribes members who left for Ethiopia, in order to clarify the specific nature of the organization.

Eric L. Smith

In the photograph of the Twelve Tribes of Israel in Kingston, the fourth person from the right is Eric L. Smith. Born in 1949, he grew up in the neighbourhood of Trench Town in Kingston. His parents were Christians. Because of their poverty, he was forced to drop out of school around age ten to learn to fend for himself. As mechanics was not his forte, he chose woodwork. His mother and her sister moved house regularly, but Smith was often in Trench Town, and around age twelve or thirteen, he was already in contact with Rastafari. Thanks to them, he had heard about the teachings of Marcus Garvey and the 1961 and 1963 Back-to-Africa missions. At age nineteen, he met Gad in this neighbourhood and became one of the first members of the organization, which was

Figure 5.9. Eric Smith, Gerald Brissett and Millward Brown in Addis Ababa, 1972. Archives E.L. Smith, Shashemene © DR.

functioning at the time as EWF Local 15. He explains as follows his reason for becoming a member of the EWF:

> The whole thing is back to Africa, repatriation to Africa that was the cry of the Rastaman, that was my aim and desire to return back to Africa. So I start federation as a mean to return back to Africa, cause at the time, most Rasta couldn't really afford a ticket to come to Ethiopia, including myself. Now the federation work co-operatively, a ticket could be purchased for any member that was chosen to come that's even how I get a chance to reach here.[62]

Smith had met Reverend Winston G. Evans during the latter's visit to Kingston. Given the reverend's promise to send Jamaican members to Ethiopia in the near future, the EWF represented a concrete prospect of financing transportation, which was beyond the means of the Rastafari. Smith became an executive member of the organization, and was given the name of Asher 1st, but he relinquished his seat on the first bench to someone else. When Gad and Naphtali returned from their visit to Ethiopia, Smith was quickly called: was he ready to leave for Africa? He answered yes, accepted his plane ticket and had very little time to prepare for departure. He left behind a woman and a three-month-old baby, who was not to survive. He left on 28 September 1972 for Ethiopia, where he arrived after a two-day journey and a transit through London. Smith was the first of a series of persons sent by the organization. Millward Brown (Dan) was to follow him three months later.

In 1973, another executive member arrived in Ethiopia in order to prepare a report for the organization. He was accompanied by Brother Green (Simeon), but the latter "couldn't cope with the conditions, so he went back to Jamaica".[63] Despite this return to Jamaica, it seems that Green remained a member of the organization, but he was the first of a long list of persons who, once in Ethiopia, were astounded by the difficult conditions of settlement and who returned shamefacedly to their point of departure. The next person, Brother Leard (Benjamin), arrived the same year but promptly fell ill and died in hospital in Addis Ababa. Nevertheless, he had had the time to pass on an important piece of information to the first members who had settled in Ethiopia: relinquishing the name and structure of the EWF was a must; the organization was henceforth to be known as the Twelve Tribes of Israel.

> "When that news reached you, did that change anything in the relation with the people here?"
>
> "Well to be truthful, to the old federation members, the Twelve Tribes was kind of strange, they were indoctrinated in the federation thing, and the Twelve Tribes thing is dealing with Jesus Christ as the returned Messiah, so that created differences between we and those old federation. But it wasn't too obvious then to really create a division their belief is their belief and they do not accept Jesus Christ and we say Rastafari is Jesus Christ revealed in the personality of His Imperial Majesty. We are orthodox, this is orthodox teachings, but we understood the difference and we don't make that become a problem, so we just go through still with them as Rastaman."[64]

The tense relations between the EWF and the Twelve Tribes of Israel might have had consequences at the local level. Smith expressed the distinction in religious terms: over and beyond the existence of different administrations, there was a difference regarding the interpretation of the nature of Haile Selassie I. At the time, for the majority of Rastafari, Jesus Christ was seen as the prerogative of the Christian churches of missionary origin, whose proselytizing concerned a "white Christ". The Rastafari of the Twelve Tribes appropriated the Christian discourse and constructed their unitary doctrine around the recognition of the second coming of Christ, manifested in the "personality" of the emperor. This is why the first phrase of the official greeting, known to all their members, begins: "Greetings in the Divine Name of our Lord and Saviour Jesus Christ who has revealed himself in the personality of His Imperial Majesty Haile Selassie I." This patently "Christian" leaning is one of the elements that ensured the success of the Twelve Tribes in Jamaica, a largely Christian nation. Such a leaning was especially acceptable in the light of the fact that many of the speeches of Haile Selassie I referred to the Bible, Christ and the Christian Church of Ethiopia. Thus, a young Rastaman, who was in the habit of "licking out against Jesus Christ", went to Prophet Gad to ask for explanations concerning the nature of the link between Christ and Haile Selassie I. Gad's answer was: "Look here that is why we always say greetings in the name of our Lord and Saviour Jesus Christ because His Majesty a reveal himself that way, all a revealed himself through His Majesty cause he is the only person in our time having all these titles fit, from the Bible that God use to remind us of the coming of God."[65]

It took three months of reflection for the young Rastafari to understand and accept Gad's explanation, which was at variance with the young man's position up to that point. In substance, Gad's reasoning was that it was not as much Haile Selassie I who was divine but rather Christ himself, who had appeared in this dispensation through the personality of the emperor, based on the titles of the latter. This interpretation had more to do with the spiritual, messianic character represented by the emperor than with the physical, human nature of his presence. Such an interpretation might have appeared contrary to the interpretation offered by other Rastafari, for whom the divine nature of the emperor rendered indissociable – and immortal – his spirit and body. Furthermore, the adjective "orthodox", invariably used by the Twelve Tribes to qualify their faith, functioned as a legitimating attribute and suggested, if not competition, at least an alternative to the Ethiopian Orthodox Church, which had opened its first branch in Kingston in 1970 (Archbishop Yesehaq 1997, 204). These distinctions on the nature of Haile Selassie I – Christ returned or Living God – had great impact in Jamaica, where the Twelve Tribes offered an alternative in a previously dense array of Rastafari affiliations. In Ethiopia, the small size of the community did not initially exacerbate the theological differences. However, after the departure of the majority of arrivants, following the Ethiopian revolution, and while other Twelve Tribes members were arriving, the community balance was transformed.

Figure 5.10. Ethiopian Orthodox Church, Maxfield Avenue, Kingston, 2002, Photograph: G. Bonacci © DR.

Desmond Martin

Theophilus Edward, also called Brother Zion (Gad), was the next to arrive in Ethiopia, in 1974. Born in 1933, he was a little older than the other members already present. He was soon followed by Donald Leach (Reuben), joined by his wife, then by Desmond Martin (Judah), who arrived in November 1975. The fifth of seven children, Martin was born in Kingston into a middle-class family in 1952. His Pentecostal family gave him a Christian education, and he was a regular attendant at church and prayer meetings. In 1966, he received a scholarship to finish his schooling.

Martin was not in Kingston when Haile Selassie I made his official visit, but he watched on television the crowd that hurried to welcome the King of Kings. He recalls: "I was terrified; this is the man who Rastafarians say he is God." One of his brothers, Everton, was Simeon 1st, an executive member of the Twelve Tribes, who invited him to a meeting of the organization in 1970.

> I went to a meeting, and the first meeting I went to I was so impressed, just by seeing the brothers, how they organize. . . . They were functioning at the moment EWF charter 15. However the first meeting I went I joined the organization, I set down my name to be a member, and there was an application form . . . asking the reason why

Figure 5.11. Function to celebrate the high school graduation of two future pioneers, the first and the fourth from the left. Desmond Martin, James Francis, Likkle Roy Earl Lowe, Maurice Lee, Everett Peart, Kingston, 1969. Archives D. Martin, Shashemene © DR.

> you want to join the organization and I wrote because it was to send people to Africa. I joined the organization in order to reach Africa.[66]

The discipline of the Twelve Tribes had a profound impact on Martin. The order, the cleanliness, the uniforms, the clearly established authority and the references to Christ drew him to this Rastafari life, by which he was already fascinated. Martin had finished his studies by then and was working as accountant in an office. He was representative of this Jamaican middle-class generation which launched out in the Rastafari movement through the Twelve Tribes and transformed it. The success of the Twelve Tribes was due to their policy of inclusive membership, irrespective of class, race or gender – a crucial difference from other Rastafari groups and organizations, restricted for the most part to the poorest classes, black persons and men, at least as far as public functions were concerned. The Twelve Tribes were able to attract members from different milieux, to give a place to women and to accept even white persons. This inclusive outlook was reinforced by the conception that all humans were descendants of the three sons of Noah, Ham/black people, Shem/brown people and Japheth/white people, thought to have repopulated the earth after the flood. Among them could be found and reunited the dispersed tribes of Israel. As noted by a Jamaican commentator: "A quiet, unobstructive revolution is taking place among the Rastafarians. This revolution is having far-reaching implications for traditional Rastafari theology and ideology. Respectable, well-educated middle-class sons and daughters are drifting into Rastafarianism, leaving behind a trail of horrified and embarrassed parents and friends as well as frightened Christians."[67]

Up to that point, the Rastafari movement had been a phenomenon primarily limited to the poorest and blackest classes of Jamaica, which had innovated on the basis of older practices of resistance and popular contestation, by formulating social criticism in a political and religious language, a system of beliefs and a lifestyle based on the image of Haile Selassie I. The movement had been severely repressed in Jamaica, but the Rastafari progressively influenced the culture and the dominant sectors of society. Subsequent to the visit of Haile Selassie I, through various exchanges with intellectuals and Black Power activists and owing to the growing influence of reggae, Jamaican society began to reappropriate Rastafari culture, and the entry of the middle class into the movement helped to accelerate this process.

Another member of the Twelve Tribes, Anthony Nevers (Issachar), born in 1955, also came from this middle class, for which respectability was a crucial value. He explained that, in school, he was one of the first to grow dreadlocks, to refuse to wear the mandatory belt and epaulettes of his school uniform and to oppose conventional authority and conformity. The Rastafari identity was well adapted to this state of mind. These young men were "uptown boys" but were irresistibly attracted by "downtown" life: they "wanted to know what was happening in the ghetto".[68] They found ghetto culture to be much more exciting than that in which they had been brought up. They were educated, sometimes light-skinned, and navigated between very different worlds – on the one hand, their astounded families, and, on the other, elder Rastafari, from whom they learned to smoke chalice, the water pipe used to burn ganja. They were sometimes sent packing or were scorned by these Rastafari, who reproached them with their privileged background, their education and their attachment to Christianity. As Nevers put it: "All the elders looked down upon us as youths, like we don't have the right to say nothing. But we go to Africa and not them. . . . We came to revolutionarize [*sic*] the Rasta movement."[69]

"Revolutionizing" the movement transited via the accomplishment of a tenacious Rastafari claim – to go back to Africa – which some managed to do, thanks to their involvement in the Twelve Tribes. With the inclusive approach promoted by the Twelve Tribes, the Rastafari movement changed, little by little. Rather than losing its defenders in downtown Kingston, the movement became more and more socially and theologically complex. Researchers were not welcome at Twelve Tribes meetings unless they became members. Their relations with the University of the West Indies were not as close as those formerly encouraged by elders like Mortimo Planno, who had contributed to the notoriety and recognition of the movement and its claims. The reservations of intellectuals and Black Power activists regarding dialogue with the Jamaican middle class, associated with capitalist forces and the bourgeoisie – from which they themselves sometimes originated – probably contributed to the frequent perception of the Twelve Tribes as an "inauthentic" branch of the Rastafari movement. Indeed, the Twelve Tribes did not place the claim to blackness at the top of its ideological agenda, notwithstanding the departure of many of its members for Ethiopia. Martin wanted to be a "soldier", although his appearance was closer to that of an office employee, and he took the road to Ethiopia at the end of 1975. His wife and his two children, aged two and three, went to join him. The arrival was particularly difficult for her, a fact Martin attributed to her middle-class background: "She was disappointed. She said 'this land is too heavy for me' because when she came, how her family brought her up it was more sophisticated. I can understand it."[70] She returned, transiting through Kenya, then through Jerusalem, and settled in the United States. Two years later, her children, who had remained in Shashemene with their father, joined her.

The Year 1976

The year 1976 was one of the densest, in terms of Twelve Tribes members' returns to Ethiopia. Seven persons arrived between January and November, including two women. One of them, Joan Douglas, was born in 1952 into a Catholic family. She had fourteen brothers and sisters, but only she and one of her brothers were Rastafari. After her schooling, she left to work in a factory, and, in 1972, she became a member of the Twelve Tribes of Israel (Naphtali). As she explained, her affiliation with the organization is indissociable from her desire to return to Ethiopia: "When I joined the Twelve Tribes, that's when I became conscious of coming to Ethiopia. After we have meetings we use to sing theme songs, always sing this one especially 'we want to go back to Ethiopia', it was one thing being built up in us, wanting to come to Ethiopia. When you become a member, every focus is Ethiopia."[71]

By maintaining images of Ethiopia through meetings and songs, by basing its proselytizing on the need for repatriation, the organization played a significant role in the perpetuation of the desire to return to Ethiopia even after the Ethiopian revolution. Thus, Douglas, who was married before her departure, joined, in April 1976, her husband, who had preceded her to Ethiopia by about seven months. She was quickly followed by Norval Marshall. Born in 1949 in St Catherine, he grew up in Kingston in a family with a comfortable living but felt alienated, at a very early age, from the religious education which he had received and from the hypocrisy that reigned in his Church of God congregation (Bonacci 2011). After a "vision" of Haile Selassie I in uniform, he formed a habit of fasting two times a week with his friends. He was only about fifteen years old and was approached by one of his schoolmates, who came to his home one afternoon and said to him:

> "You know that Selassie I is God?" and [I] say "Yeah tell me more about that." And him start explaining to me "Well Selassie is the King of Africa. There was a man call Leonard Howell he started about when the King is crowned in Ethiopia, Black people should look for redemption." And this guy my school mate was telling me all of this. But the most thing he tried is what I can tell you is Haile Selassie is the Almighty God. Well because he was showing me certain Bible scriptures as well and I was convinced is that, I went home from this place and told my mum Haile Selassie is God, I don't want no more pork feet and I don't want to do this and I don't want to do that and eventually I was thrown out of my mum's place because of that. My mum told me I must go and live with these people that is Haile Selassie followers.[72]

The combination of all these elements – fasting, vision, the oral transmission of concept-keys related to Leonard Howell, African redemption, the coronation of the emperor and the literal reading of the Bible – was an explosive mixture for a young man searching for identity. In the middle of his teenage life, through identification with a king and an African God in the person of Haile Selassie I, Marshall took a decisive step, broke with his family and became a Rastafari. He lived downtown with his friends, then went up to the hills for three years to undergo a kind of natural initiation into Rastafari livity instead of finishing his schooling. His dreadlocks began to grow; he ate ital food and stopped wearing "Babylon" clothing. He had previously met Prophet Gad and assimilated his teachings, especially concerning the nature of Christ. Coming down from the hills, finally, he visited his mother and became a member of the Twelve Tribes (Dan). When his turn came, the organization paid for his plane ticket, leaving him with two things to do. First, application for a new passport, as his old one had just expired. An executive member with relations in the government handed him a new one – this was one of the advantages of membership in an organization with contacts in the middle class, including the political and social elite. Then, he organized a dance (party) with reggae on the agenda.

The Twelve Tribes were reputedly "the house of reggae". More than any other Rastafari group, they contributed to the explosion of reggae, which they called "the music of the king" (Hepner 1998, 144). Twelve Tribes reggae parties still bring back vivid memories in Kingston, and they accounted, to a great extent, for the success of Twelve Tribes. During the 1970s, a Twelve Tribes party was the place to be. Enthusiastic crowds would gather, made up of members, well-known personalities, reggae artists (many of whom belonged to the organization), other Rastafari, from uptown and downtown, well-dressed hooligans, middle-class girls and even international guests from Twelve Tribes offshoots (which will be addressed later). This variegated crowd formed queues hundreds of metres long, at the entrance. These events had themes and colours corresponding to the month in which they were held. The year 1976 was marked by the famous khaki dance that is still remembered today, at which everyone had to wear khaki. These events started with prayers, the reading of the Bible and the presentation of the artists, often local talents and members of the organization (Hepner 1998, 144). Before his departure, Marshall organized a dance, as was the practice of most future returnees, in order to raise funds for an easier settlement in Ethiopia: "This was my first and only dance until today in my life, I never kept another dance. There was a send-off dance, and I came with a lot of money, maybe I came with I can't remember exactly now, but I sure I came with like five thousand Jamaican dollars at that time, or more, which could get me a nice *č'eqa* [mud] house even, like that or maybe bigger."[73] The send-off parties for members also served another purpose: to make public show of the fact that the Twelve Tribes were really sending people to Ethiopia and fulfilling repatriation goals. For Marshall, everything was ready. He left in August 1976 with his seven-month-old son, as, unlike the other members who had preceded him, he did not want to leave the baby behind.

The year 1976 drew to a beautiful end for the Twelve Tribes: in December, thirteen members of the organization made the trip to Ethiopia together. For a first departure of this importance, the *Daily Gleaner* published a photograph of those who accompanied the travellers to the airport, "hundreds of happy and peaceful 'brethren' and 'sistren' who wore banners (knitted tams) of red, gold and green which are the colours of the Ethiopian flag".[74] Six executive members and Sister Dinah accompanied them, in order to make a report to the general headquarters. Six members of the delegation had the intention of settling in Ethiopia. Only three of them remained. One did not want to leave his wife in Jamaica, and the others were probably discouraged by the military atmosphere reigning in Addis Ababa and by the tense social situation in Shashemene. Patrick Campbell (Zebulon), Vincent Wisdom (Naphtali) and Anthony Nevers (Issachar) remained. The last, already mentioned, had worked in the cement factory in Spanish Town, but had left his job about a year earlier. Anthony Nevers reported that they too had organized a dance, but that, in their case, the money had disappeared and that he was left, literally, with twenty-five cents in his pocket at the time of departure. They were all determined to leave, but the situation was particularly difficult: "It pressure we, put we [sucks his teeth] – I never talked about that – that was a test in I and I faith. Jah know. Real testing."[75] Refusing to leave for lack of money implied insufficient trust in the divine plan of gathering the Twelve Tribes of Israel in Shashemene – it was a test of faith. The three bredrens promised each other to keep the faith, and they left. Nevers was only twenty years old at the time; he left a pregnant woman and a child behind, in what he called a "sacrifice".

Many Twelve Tribes members left families, women and children behind. Only four, perhaps thanks to their position in the organization, were joined by their wives. The latter were members, but one of them left after four months. Only one unmarried woman arrived. Only one man came with his young child, while the others left theirs in Jamaica – a fact which sets them apart from the groups of Jamaican arrivants who had preceded them to Ethiopia. The 1968 "pioneer" group comprised four adults and four children. The 1969 group comprised an unmarried woman and a child. In the group of 1973, an adult arrived with his two children. The difference with Twelve Tribes members was that they functioned within an organized framework, received a plane ticket and then had to leave in an order determined by their date of membership in the organization. Norval Marshall puts it this way:

> Being a member of the organization, we were called up in a meeting and what the Prophet [Gad] ask us is if we are ready to go to Ethiopia. And we say yes. Are you ready to leave your wife and kids? Cause I had a woman and a baby boy. Are you ready to leave your mum and everything you have? Me say yes. . . . It wasn't her [his wife's] time, not her turn to come. People had their turn in according to when you joined the organization. So they were sending me and after that I was promised that my wife would come and I wanted my son to travel with me, I wasn't leaving him. So I brought him. We came here.[76]

Marshall is an exception among the Twelve Tribes members who arrived in Ethiopia, as he himself financed the ticket for his son. The call to leave everything behind in order to join the collective project of gathering the Twelve Tribes in Shashemene is reminiscent of Christ who asked his disciples to give up their activities and families to follow him, to let "the dead bury their dead" (Matthew 8:22). Some members who were recently married did not have the heart to give up their wife, but others did so. Anthony Nevers, who left behind a pregnant woman and a child, recalls the difficulty and the stake of this act:

> We know we some stone heart [laughs]. Some people say we was stone heart people, that we never give a damn, but it wasn't like that, a true you don't know, we missed beloved ones, yeah, but a sacrifice we know we have to make, it was so fortunate – or say unfortunate? – that it had to be me as Issachar that would have to step forward for holding that seat. I was just twenty years old. One of the youngest yout' who a came through ina dem time. Even years after years you realize the bold step of that time.[77]

The intermingling of sorrow and determination are palpable in these words. The allegiance to the organization, the certainty of partaking in a larger project, the possibility of accomplishing the dream, and the responsibility of representing one of the tribes in Shashemene took precedence over personal and familial situations. It was, therefore, a sacrifice and, as such, reflected both the prophetic and the patriarchal leaning of the Rastafari movement. Although the Twelve Tribes had opened up to the participation of women in the internal and public functions of the organization, male initiatives prevailed, exacerbated by the pioneering nature of the settlement in Shashemene. These personal and family ruptures induced by the departures later influenced family practices in Shashemene, leading to a kind of "added value" to Jamaican women, compared to their Ethiopian counterparts, who belonged to a different language and culture – an issue that will be addressed later. Members were sent based on their order of membership. The discipline of the organization led to fissures in family relations, but a few members found ways of working around this.

Freedom of choice was left to the members of the Twelve Tribes who had joined in view of going back to Africa: "So when your number call, they call you up and ask if you ready or don't ready, you say yes or you say no."[78] After the great departures of the 1976 and the return to Jamaica of the majority of EWF members who had previously settled in Shashemene, certain members refused to leave when their turn arrived, leading to tensions within the group. Winston Simons, born in 1945, was from the tribe of Benjamin. Three persons from his tribe refused to leave, prior to his turn. He was only the fourth on the list, but, in 1981, he was the one who went to Ethiopia. His wife quickly followed, and his older brother was already in Shashemene, having made the trip in 1977.

As the news of the new military regime in Ethiopia came to Jamaica, the letters written by the transatlantic migrants were read and commented on in Kingston. They reported on the increasingly difficult financial and social situation in Shashemene and advised a deceleration in the sending of members, since their safety could not be guaranteed and the land concession had been severely reduced subsequent to the land reforms of 1975. In 1981, Simons and his wife were among the last Jamaicans to arrive directly from Kingston. They arrived a few months after the settlement of Berthal J. Moody, the chaplain of EWF

Local 43 who had been reticent about accepting Twelve Tribes members in his local, but who eventually had made the trip with Solomon Wolfe. The return to Ethiopia had scarcely begun to be take form, with more regular arrivals, when the Ethiopian revolution and the living conditions in Shashemene weakened the determination of "Ethiopian volunteers" to return.

THE FIRST GROUP OF "PIONEERS" TO LEAVE JAMAICA for Ethiopia, in 1968, was followed by forty-four persons, between 1969 and 1991, all of whom were members of an organization. None had prior experience of migration, and the departure for Africa was sometimes chosen as an alternative to migration to English-speaking metropolises. The first group bonded around family ties, but those who followed were either members of the EWF or, for the majority, members of the Twelve Tribes. The first had legitimacy concerning the administration of the land, but few Jamaican members were able to depart. By investing effort, the officers of EWF Local 43 finally succeeded in appropriating this pan-Ethiopian organization, which had initially rejected them. They reformulated its objectives in order to enable and legitimate their return to Africa.

The Twelve Tribes of Israel were created in reaction to the fragility of the EWF and had numerical and financial clout. They placed Shashemene at the core of their proselytizing. They participated in the evolution of the Rastafari movement, owing, in particular, to a fundamentalist reading of the Bible, the acceptance of Christ, the identification with the twelve tribes of Israel, an inclusive racial policy, an organic link with reggae, and the acceptance of middle-class members. Elements previously regarded as characteristics of the Rastafari movement, notably the exclusiveness in the claim to blackness, the wearing of dreadlocks, the nyabinghi ritual and membership of the most underprivileged classes, underwent transformation.

The history of the arrivals in Ethiopia throws light on that of EWF Local 43 and that of a new organization, the Twelve Tribes of Israel, whose members made the return to Shashemene. These two organizations structured the mobility of return as they were formed and divided around the issue of the land in Shashemene. Notwithstanding the Ethiopian revolution leading to a temporary discontinuation of return, the centrality of the settlement in Shashemene to the development and activities of these groups determined their status as heirs to the nationalist and pan-African claims, in which return was a right worth defending. In the wake of Jamaican migrations and of the international diffusion of reggae music, the Rastafari movement was about to grow beyond the confines of Jamaica and to undergo other deep mutations. The revitalization of the EWF in England and the establishment of eighteen international branches of the Twelve Tribes of Israel sustained the contemporary imaginary of return in view of settlement in Shashemene, where the complexity and diversity of the international Rastafari movement were finally reflected.

CHAPTER 6

THE INTERNATIONALIZATION AND DIVERSITY OF THE ARRIVALS IN SHASHEMENE

THE RATE OF ARRIVALS IN ETHIOPIA SLOWED FROM the end of 1970s onwards. The Rastafari communities in Jamaica and elsewhere received letters from the returnees in Shashemene, relating the difficulties of life on the ground and advising against new settlements. The memory of the fall of the empire was still fresh, and the great famine of 1984 and the restrictions imposed by the government of Mengistu Haile Mariam did little to brighten the prospects of settlement in Shashemene. The road to return seemed definitively blocked. Without the opening up of Ethiopian politics, without the reactualization of the country's pan-African policies, the Rastafari community in Shashemene, which at the time counted some fifty adults and numerous children, might have remained as it was, continuing its fragile development. By combining life stories collected in Shashemene with primary sources such as Rastafari printed material, this chapter will show that the dynamics of return were reinvigorated by the development and internationalization of the Rastafari movement. Between 1992 and 2003, around ninety-five persons settled in Shashemene on the land granted to "the black people of the world". Acceleration was noted at the approach of the year 2000: fifty-one returns were recorded between 2000 and 2003, but only time will tell if these returns are permanent.

As we shall observe, several elements characterized these arrivals. In the beginning, those who came were Caribbean migrants who had transited via the northern cities of the United States, a few Americans, then Jamaicans who arrived directly from Kingston through the EWF and the Twelve Tribes of Israel. The arrivals of the 1990s were marked by the role that these organizations played in the practices of return to Shashemene and the revival of nyabinghi practices, as well as the arrivals of individuals with no formal affiliation. The multiplication of the points of departure of the actors, their mobility prior to arrival and the diversification of their social origins bore witness to the transformations at work in the "Ethiopian nation of the world". The Rastafari who arrived in

Shashemene during the 1990s showed that the legacies of Ethiopianism and nationalism were still alive. They also reflected the internationalization of the Rastafari movement, which travelled abroad in the wake of Jamaican migrations. The movement was also carried into the world on the wings of reggae music, which became its voice.

The Dynamics of the Internationalization of the Rastafari Movement

The Jamaican Migrations

The internationalization of the Rastafari movement occurred quickly, following various itineraries which sometimes converged, worked together, then separated again – namely, Jamaican migrations and the worldwide success of reggae music. Harry Goulbourne has insisted: "Caribbean Africans have arguably been the most mobile members of the African diaspora within the Atlantic world" (Goulbourne 2002, 8). We have already seen how Caribbeans, and Jamaicans in particular, circulated in the direction of West Africa, Central America, the United States and the United Kingdom. During the second half of the twentieth century, Jamaican migrations continued in the direction of the English-speaking urban centres, regardless of the various legislations that were passed in the United States and the United Kingdom.

The passing of the Immigration and Nationality Act in 1965 in the United States opened the door to mass migration, by annulling the small quota that had been allotted to Jamaica since 1952. This opportunity was quickly reflected in statistics (Foner 1987, 198; Kasinitz 1992, 32). Conversely, in the United Kingdom, the passing of the Commonwealth Immigrant Act in 1962 put an official end to the former tradition of freedom of movement and settlement in the metropolis for the citizens of the colonies and the Commonwealth. The conditions of entry into British territory became even more stringent in 1968, when the conservative far right came to power. These legislations resulted in a reduction of primary immigration, whereas the Caribbean population was still undergoing natural increase (Lassalle 1997, 22, 35–37). Entire regions and neighbourhoods became identified with these Caribbean migrants: Brooklyn, Bronx and Queens in New York, as well as Brixton in London, West Midlands, Birmingham and Manchester in the United Kingdom. The migrants who debarked in the English-speaking urban centres in the 1960s came from the educated urban elite desirous of protecting its wealth against economic fluctuations. Among them were an increasing number of women and children of the middle class seeking broader opportunities, as well as many poor people in search of a higher standard of living and responding to the need for manpower (Foner 1987, 199–200; Kasinitz 1992,

27–28; Lassalle 1997, 22). These two destinations for migration, the United States and the United Kingdom, were extremely different in terms of social structure, economic opportunities and population, but, in both cases, a change occurred that Nancy Foner accurately explains regarding the United States: "Perhaps the most jarring change was that being black took on a new, and more painful meaning. As part of the larger black population in a racially divided America, blackness became more of a stigma than it had been in Jamaica" (Foner 1987, 202).

This is not to say that being black in Jamaica was easy, for black skin was undervalued in that country. For most Jamaicans, whiteness represented power and wealth, whereas blackness represented poverty and a lower social status. But, after independence, colour no longer formed the same obstacle to social mobility. One of Foner's informants asserted that in Jamaica class prejudice was more important than colour prejudice. Accordingly, another informant was able to report, "I wasn't aware of my color till I got here, honestly" (Foner 1987, 203). He knew, of course, that he was black, was aware of American racism, which he had probably already experienced during a first visit. But it was one thing to hear about colour prejudice and another thing to experience it on a day-to-day basis. At the crossroads of the nineteenth and twentieth centuries, the migratory process laid the ground for the emergence of a black consciousness. There has been a wealth of research in the United States on the complex relations between Jamaicans and African Americans, on the one hand, and between Jamaicans and other English-speaking, Spanish-speaking Caribbeans and Haitians, on the other. Consequently, there is no need to develop this question here. These relations affected the representations that the Caribbean or Jamaican communities had of themselves and also impacted their social and economic positioning (Hintzen 2004). As migrants to the United States or the United Kingdom, Jamaicans formed large contingents of workers who brought with them their language, culture and music.

Among them were Rastafari, who spearheaded the spread of the movement. In the beginning, they were invariably associated, in public terms, with criminal practices, violence, dealing in drugs and weapons, and murder. It is true that Jamaica, via its mass migrations, had also "exported" its gangs. Laurie Gunst's book (1995) brilliantly relates the criminal internationalization of Jamaicans, who confronted American gangs over the control of territories and trafficking. While they sometimes sported Rastafari attributes like dreadlocks, they were not Rastafari, for all that, but the Rastafari, for their part, suffered from this association with Jamaican criminals and, more generally, with black criminality in Jamaica and elsewhere. As of the 1970s, the New York police conducted vast operations against the emerging Rastafari movement and suggested that violence was inherent in the beliefs of Rastafari (Hepner 1998, 126–31). Crimes were arbitrarily laid at their door, and, during the 1980s, the American media was flooded with violent and sinister images of Rastafari. In the United Kingdom, between

1971 and 1973, the police and the media launched a programme describing black youth as aggressive criminals. In the report "Shades of Grey", concerning the relations between the police and Caribbeans in Handsworth, a Birmingham neighbourhood, police brutality was justified through the construction of a "criminalised dreadlock subculture" (Campbell 1994, 191–92). The image of a "Rasta menace" was diffused in the British media and legitimated by the thesis of Ernest Cashmore (1979), in the absence of any questioning of the racist British police practices of the 1970s. However, this negative construction of Rastafari managed to quell neither the movement nor its music: reggae.

Reggae

Roots reggae, which contains the message of Rastafari, appealed to a vast international public and was one of the primary means of diffusion of the Rastafari movement in the world (van Dijk 1998; Savishinsky 1994a; Bonacci 2003). Reggae derives from African rhythms (burru and kumina) and the impact of American pop music on Jamaica (rhythm and blues, soul, jazz). In the Jamaican melting pot, these beats were transformed into gospel, mento, ska (1960–66) and rocksteady (1966–68). Born in 1968, reggae itself was, during the 1970s and 1980s, closely associated with the Rastafari movement (Reckord 1977; Bilby and Leid 1986; Blum 2004). Rastafari and reggae are not reducible to one another, but it is thanks to reggae that Rastafari produced their most resounding contribution to Jamaican popular culture. While certain important artistes like Prince Buster or Jimmy Cliff did not identify with Rastafari, the Rastafari nonetheless gave to the ghetto and to the prophets a voice which was universally acclaimed. The artistes who embraced Rastafari faith worked with the instruments and the sound engineering of their time. But they also disturbed and recreated contemporary sounds, notably by improving the art of remix and inventing dub, while conserving the use of nyabinghi drums. Numerous groups and individuals marked the beginnings of roots reggae, including the Ethiopians, the Abyssinians, Burning Spear, Alton Ellis, Dennis Brown, and so on, but few benefited from the investments of the British record industry. Among these chosen few, Bob Marley remains a central figure. In the words of Roger Steffens (1998, 253), reggae archivist and biographer of Bob Marley: "Marley is the most famous Rastaman who ever lived."

The biographical details of Bob Marley are generally well known (Davis 1991; Blum 2004). Born in 1945, of mixed race, embodying the contradictions of the colour line, he arrived in the ghettos of Kingston when he was still a child, then left to work in the United States in 1966, missing the visit of Haile Selassie I to Jamaica. On his return to Kingston, Marley got to know the Rastafari and their practices: reasoning, nyabinghi rhythms, the egalitarian language of Italk, and ital livity. After many recordings of gospel, soul, ska and rocksteady, Marley's first Rastafari recording, in 1968, was "Selassie Is the Chapel". The words were entrusted to him by the charismatic Mortimo Planno, evoked earlier in this book.[1] After several commercial failures of the trio founded in 1963 with Winston "Peter Tosh" McIntosh and Bunny "Wailer" Livingston, at the end of 1972, Marley finally found funding, an art director and a distributer in London. The first two albums of the trio diffused in Europe, *Catch a Fire* (1973) and *Burnin'* (1973) were quite militant and met with little success despite the carefully crafted lyrics and music. The first solo album, *Natty Dread* (1974), in which the I Three chorus line comprising Rita Marley, Judy Mowatt and Marcia Griffiths replaced Tosh and Bunny, sold no better. The Jamaican attained international media acclaim only after Eric Clapton's 1974 interpretation of Marley's composition "I Shot the Sheriff". Facing journalists, Bob Marley never hesitated to defend his music, his opinions, his Rastafari interpretations regarding the nature of Haile Selassie I, the incarnation of God in man, and the diabolic character of the Vatican and of Babylon.

With the album *Rastaman Vibration* (1976), Marley finally achieved major success and the sufferer influenced Jamaica: he had gained notoriety and financial success while remaining militant. He spoke out against illiteracy as the instrument of capitalism in "Slave Driver", protested against the influence of churches in "Get Up, Stand Up" and chanted about the return to Africa, to the accompaniment of nyabinghi drums, in "Rastaman Chant". His subsequent albums, including *Exodus* (1977), *Survival* (1979) and *Uprising* (1980), riding the waves of great international tours, made of him the triumphant icon of the

Figure 6.1. Desmond Martin, Alan "Skill" Cole, Bob Marley holding Yosef "Baba" Leach, Maurice Lee, Brother Malachi, Sister Yvonne Leach, Ronald Simmons, Shashemene, 1978. Photograph: Yohannes Bisrat. Archives M. Bekele, Shashemene © DR.

Figure 6.2. From top to bottom and from left to right: Desmond Martin, Donald Leach, Bob Marley, Kassaye Araya, Youth Simeon, Maurice Lee, Eric Smith, Ruel McLaughlin, Yohannes "Johnnie" Bisrat, Ronald Simmons, Lip, Alan "Skill" Cole, Llewellyn "Zulu" Campbell, Vincent Wisdom, in Wondo Genet, Ethiopia, 1978. Archives M. Lee, Shashemene © DR.

downtrodden people of the world. Marley also expressed a sharp critical view of Jamaican neocolonial politics. He survived a murder attempt in 1976 and was on stage two days later. After sixteen months of exile, in the hope of calming urban violence, in 1978, he united on stage in Kingston the political rivals Edward Seaga (Jamaica Labour Party) and Michael Manley (People's National Party) during the One Love Peace Concert. A few months later, in New York, he accepted, "on behalf of 500 million Africans", the United Nations Peace Medal honouring his commitment to peace and solidarity (Steffens 1998, 260).

References to Africa run through Marley's albums and life: the claim of an African identity, solidarity with the liberation struggles of the continent ("Africa Unite"), the quotation of Haile Selassie I's 1963 speech to the United Nations ("War") and the claim of the right to return to Africa interpreted literally (*Exodus*). In 1999, *Time* magazine qualified the album *Exodus* as "the most important pop recording of the twentieth century" (Gilroy 2005, 227). Bob Marley made only one visit to Shashemene, in 1978, where he met with his brothers from the Twelve Tribes of Israel, an organization of which he was a member (Joseph).[2] Some of his songs, like "Zimbabwe", were written there.[3]

In 1980, Marley made two trips to the African continent. He played at two free concerts in Gabon, at the invitation of the daughters of President Omar Bongo Ondima, who had been in power since 1967. Afterwards, he received an official invitation to the celebrations of the independence of Zimbabwe, where he did two

Figure 6.3. From top to bottom and from left to right: Kassaye Araya, Eric Smith, Maurice Lee, Bob Marley, Donald Leach, Lip, Alan "Skill" Cole, Vincent Wisdom, Llewellyn "Zulu" Campbell, in Wondo Genet, 1978. Archives M. Lee, Shashemene © DR.

concerts, one for the officials and another, the following day, with free admission, for all those who were unable to attend the day before (Campbell 1994, 144–47). This was a great honour for Marley; here he was at last, officially welcomed on African soil. For the local youth, he represented a unique model of success embodied in the voice of a rebel. Robert Mugabe, then prime minister, went as far as inviting him to take up residence in Zimbabwe (Steffens 1998, 262). In 1981, "Get Up, Stand Up", recorded with the Wailers, was adopted by Amnesty International as the theme song of their worldwide campaign in defence of the Universal Declaration of Human Rights (Gilroy 2005, 229).

Marley's exceptional career drew international attention to Jamaica, reggae and the Rastafari message. It attracted to Jamaica many visitors in search of culture, faith and symbolic grounding. Reggae music was a crucial component in the diffusion of the symbolism associated with the Rastafari movement: the colours green, gold and red; dreadlocks; the use of the ganja; and the figure of Haile Selassie I. It allowed the diffusion of the ideology of rebellion, survival and liberation embodied in Rastafari. Although reggae lyrics are not always understood, due to the specificity of Jamaican language and context, this music was the first channel of diffusion of the Rastafari movement in Africa (Savishinsky 1994b), but also in more remote places like Australia, New Zealand, and the small Pacific islands of Fiji, Tonga and Samoa. Research on the international diffusion of the movement remains scanty. The presence of the Rastafari movement has been studied more in the continental or insular Caribbean – Guyana, Dominique, Antigua, Trinidad, St Kitts, St Vincent and so on – than in continental Europe, where only the Netherlands and Italy have drawn the attention of researchers (Bonacci 2001–2, 2003), whereas the communities in France, Portugal, Spain, Germany and Finland, which are not the least important, are still ignored. The dissemination of Rastafari ideas and practices gave rise to a heterogeneous counterculture, but lack of data prevents the arrival at overall conclusions (van Dijk 1998, 194). These "new" Rastafari began by adhering to the social, political and cultural ideas associated with the movement rather than to the religious message per se. However, as has been demonstrated in the case of Italy, communities of a religious character developed in the framework of more secular forms, often owing to international contacts and encounters with Rastafari elders.

The specific cultural context in which the Rastafari movement was founded might have prevented its diffusion and its international readjustment. Shaped by black internationalism and popular Jamaican religious traditions such as Revivalism, the Rastafari movement had remained, to a certain extent, typically Jamaican. In Caribbean contexts similar to Jamaica, or in places marked by an important Jamaican presence, like the United Kingdom, Rastafari ideas and practices were easily adaptable. But in very different cultural contexts, some of these were liable to pose problems of incorporation and were even liable to appear senseless. Rastafari celebrations in Italy attempting to stage the nyabinghi ritual offer an example: in this foreign space, the ritual was recreated and reinvented, stripped of its Jamaican singularity (with no circular space, fire or ritual representation of Africa) (Bonacci 2003, 88). The tensions at work between a local culture and an international diffusion underlined the limits of the reappropriation of a black identity, its adaptations and the global potential of the movement.

Reggae and Return

Generally speaking, reggae themes cover a wide spectrum: local current affairs, social and political critique, love and friendship, call to revolt, black pride, diaspora and pan-African consciousness, Rastafari beliefs, and so on. But there exists, besides, a lesser-known corpus, directly related to the return to Africa. Bruno Blum, a specialist of Jamaican music, was thus able to select 125 titles making explicit references to the return to Africa, the promised land, Zion and Ethiopia. Without claim to exhaustiveness, this selection covers the years 1958 to 1983 and forms a rich musical corpus called "repatriation reggae", the details of which are provided at the end of this book.

The theme of the return to Africa existed in Jamaican popular music before the advent of reggae. It is possible to cite in this regard: the song "Ethiopia" by the Jamaican Calypsonians, interpreted by Lord Lebby, which was one of the first mentos, recorded in 1958; "Exodus", played in 1962 by the Skatalites, then one of the major groups on the island; "Carry Go Bring Come" by Justin Hines and the Dominoes, in 1963, and "I've Got to Go Back Home" by Bob Andy, in 1967. These were hits describing the miserable living conditions in the ghettos and explaining the reason behind the desire to go back "home". Nine recordings by Bob Marley and the Wailers appear in this selection, including three versions of "Exodus". Three songs and an instrumental dated 1959 are covered by Count Ossie and his percussion band, which later became known as the Mystic Revelation of Rastafari.

Count Ossie was killed in a car accident in 1976, but not before establishing an arts centre in his West Kingston neighbourhood, at the foot of Wareika Hills. This centre epitomizes the ties that bind Rastafari to their neighbourhood community. Count Ossie and his band were among the first to publicly promote the Rastafari music called nyabinghi. Using the fundeh, the repeater and bass drums, they often widened their orchestra to include the flute, wind instruments, trombone, trumpets and saxophone, guitars and double bass, and played an important role in the transmission of the classics of the Rastafari "sacred" repertoire (nyabinghi), as opposed to the "profane" reggae corpus.[4] The titles of these pieces are evocative – "Leaving This Land", "Going Home to Zion Land" – and representative of a much broader nyabinghi corpus.

Up until 1965, almost all the songs in our selection were sung to a very characteristic, fast ska rhythm, perceptible in a song like "Dreamland" (1964) by the Wailers. As time went on, the rocksteady rhythm evolved, ultimately producing, in 1968, the famous "one drop" reggae beat. It is interesting to note that, despite a few recordings made at uncertain dates and regardless of the partiality of this selection, there are years when the theme of return reached a considerable peak, for example, in 1970, 1976, 1977 and 1978. The years following the Ethiopian revolution and the political upheavals it generated were characterized by numerous reggae songs evoking return. This phenomenon is due in part to Bob Marley's success at this time, as it encouraged many reggae artistes to appropriate Rastafari themes. But it is, above all, the constancy of these themes which is underlined in table 6.1, indicating on the top line the year of recording and on the bottom line the number of relevant songs in our corpus between 1968 and 1983.

The songs in this selection, in fact, develop a repertoire of classic themes – the continuous evocation of slavery and captivity, contrasted with the liberating representation of Africa and Ethiopia, evident in several titles and in almost all lyrics. The theme of the departure of the train to the promised land, probably dating from the nineteenth century, already present in the classic American gospel song "This Train", was regularly revisited: "Freedom Train" by Laurel Aitken (1964), "Train to Glory" by the Ethiopians (1968), "Rasta Train" by Lee Perry and Jimmy (1974), "Train to Rhodesia" by Big Youth (1975) and "Zion Train"

Table 6.1.

1968	**1969**	**1970**	**1971**	**1972**	**1973**	**1974**	**1975**
4	5	11	4	2	8	4	7
1976	**1977**	**1978**	**1979**	**1980**	**1981**	**1982**	**1983**
17	18	9	8	3	1	4	1

by Bob Marley and the Wailers (1980). References to the traditional trope of the boat, in this instance that of Marcus Garvey, are visible in songs like "Black Starliner Must Come" by Culture (1977), "Black Starliner" by Reggae Regular (1978), or evoked, as in "Selassie Ship" by Niney and Errol (ca. 1979). Biblical themes are omnipresent – references to Jerusalem (Carlton and the Shoes, 1969), to Jordan (Sugar Minott, 1979) and, of course, to Zion: "Forward on to Zion" by the vocal trio the Abyssinians (1976), "Holy Mount Zion" by the Heptones (1976), "In Zion" by Ras Michael and the Sons of Negus (ca. 1976), which were reinterpreted with a nyabinghi rhythm. The theme of land is also strong. It is evoked in terms of a land of joy, a promised land, the Holy Land, the land of the judgement, the land of Ethiopia or the land of dream, traversing, as such, many texts. Far from representing a defeatist vision, the lyrics of several songs invest in action. Some examples are: "let me lead you / and take you to the Promised Land", sung by Gregory Isaacs (1972) and "I'm going / going back to Africa / 'cause I'm black", intoned by Alton Ellis. Other songs are explicitly titled, like "Repatriation" by Dennis Brown (1978) or Burning Spear's (1983) powerful and heart-rending cover.

Africa – Ethiopia – is represented as the "free land", and return as a desire, a will and a right. Many other reggae songs could probably be added to this corpus. They have all contributed to perpetuate and maintain the classic symbolism identifying return as an act of liberation, emancipation and redemption. Indissociable from the Rastafari movement, reggae has allowed the circulation of Rastafari identity far beyond the spaces of Jamaican migratory dynamics. This identity, reinterpreted, reappropriated and reformulated, has served to shape the contemporary Rastafari movement, of which the diverse elements arrived in Shashemene.

The EWF in the United Kingdom

In the interest of concisness, the history of the Rastafari movement in England cannot be developed here. Such a task has, moreover, been tackled elsewhere (Cashmore 1979; Campbell 1994; van Dijk 1998; Adams 2002). It will suffice to underline some of the salient points of the history of the EWF, before introducing the members of this organization who went to Ethiopia from the United Kingdom. Few and far between, Rastafari were nevertheless present in the United Kingdom as of the 1950s and had sporadic contacts with Jamaica and Ethiopia (Adams 2002, 35–43). At the time, they had little impact on the black communities, although several of them left for Ethiopia, on foot, as in the case of Noel Dyer, or by plane, in that of Desmond Christie. Another group of four is said to have left by car in 1962, via France, Spain and Morocco, from where they reportedly went to Ethiopia, but I was unable to unearth any other traces of this expedition.

At the end of the 1960s, in addition to the overwhelming entry of reggae on the British pop scene, another element contributed to the fecundity of the ground on which Rastafari developed. Black Power groups, like the Racial Adjustment Action Society headed by Michael X (de Freitas), and the Universal Colored People's Association, set about articulating the interests and claims of the black communities in the country (van Dijk 1998, 179; Naipaul 1980, 1–91). They emerged from the dynamics impelled by Stokely Carmichael's visit in 1967, but were short lived. As underlined by Horace Campbell: "A direct co-relation has been made in the United Kingdom between the decline of Black Power Movement and the rise of Rastafari" (Campbell 1994, 179). In 1969, two Jamaican Rastafari, Ascento Foxe and Keith Berry, founded the Universal Black People's Improvement Organization, whose members were not all Rastafari but included Garveyites and intellectuals. Like Marcus Garvey's organization, their hymn was the Universal Ethiopian Anthem, written by Rabbi Arnold Josiah Ford in 1920. Despite the fact that it assembled mostly Jamaicans, the organization was instrumental to the development of a social and political consciousness among black British youth.[5] At a time when serious clashes between black youth and the police were on the rise, the Universal Black People's Improvement Organization became the People's Democratic Movement. With more distinctly political objectives, the People's Democratic Movement published a monthly newsletter called the *Rastafarian Cry*. In 1972, a delegation from the movement left for Jamaica, while departures of Jamaican EWF members to Ethiopia were still regular. On the return of the delegates, the People's Democratic Movement became Local 33 of the EWF with a charter delivered by the New York headquarters (Adams 2002, 59). Local 111 of the EWF was later opened in Birmingham. As indicated by one leader of the People's Democratic Movement and, later, of Local 33: "by the early part of 1973 a new generation of hard-core Rastafarian youth had emerged within the Federation" (Adams 2002, 65). This new generation is the one that turned up in Ethiopia.

Another delegation went in 1973 to New York and to Jamaica, this time in the name of Local 33, to re-establish contacts with the Ethiopian Orthodox Church and Rastafari elders. Thanks to their efforts, a branch of the Ethiopian Orthodox Church was finally established in London in 1974. Notwithstanding doctrinal disagreements within the church in subsequent years, these relations between the Ethiopian faith and the EWF allowed the development of a strong Rastafari cultural identity. Following the first great Rastafari conference held in London in January 1975, a demonstration and a petition, sent the same year, expressed their enduring affection and support to Haile Selassie I. Confrontations with the authorities became a matter of public knowledge, and in 1977 the report "Shades of Grey", amalgamating dreadlocks with a criminal culture, was published. The constant repression of the black communities, the economic crisis which suffocated the British industry, and the arrival of the government of Margaret

Thatcher prepared the ground for a radical growth of black mobilization and of the Rastafari movement. Great riots shook England in 1980 and 1981, and open confrontations between blacks and the police erupted in the streets of Brixton and Southall in London. Escalating to national dimensions, this violence also affected Liverpool, Manchester, Birmingham, Leeds, Southampton, and so on. Angry black youth were sometimes joined by white youth, equally tired of unemployment and disgusted with the politicians in power (Campbell 1994, 205). A new generation of radical, black and determined Rastafari came out of these riots of 1980 and April 1981, rendered in the poetry and music of Linton Kwesi Johnson (2002).

Tagesse King

Born in 1956 of a Sierra Leonean father and an English mother, Tagesse King exemplified the expansion of the base of the Rastafari movement in England, which evolved from a Jamaican phenomenon into a pan-African affair, assembling various nationalities. Raised in a Catholic family, he did brilliantly in his studies in construction engineering and began to work in England. Of mixed blood, but passionate about the issue of racial purity, which he deemed necessary because "you're either or either", he became black, and, referring to the biblical verses about the leopard unable to change its spots, he became Ethiopian. Seeing God through the lenses of Ethiopia, he became a Rastafari. Permeated by reggae and brought to consciousness by American Black Power, he attended the Ethiopian Church and engaged in discussion with Rastafari elders. He was a frequent visitor to St Agnes Place in London, a large building occupied by Rastafari who went under the name of "Rasta International". In 1981, they organized the second grand Rastafari conference, during which positions seemed to diverge between prioritizing repatriation and prioritizing organization and centralization (Adams 2002, 122). Tagesse King made a stand for establishing repatriation as *the* priority. These years, as he reported, were a turning point:

> We progressed to Rasta International and then to federation as Research and Repatriation Committee. At that time the head of the federation was dormant . . . so we couldn't apply for a charter. We did call ourself Research and Repatriation Committee. Meaning to say that we assist in revitalizing the federation and research repatriation at the same time. It was very much as a yout' man involved in those works in England, and coming through the big riots that took place in early eighties, Brixton, Liverpool riot, riot all over England, and we went to Parliament as young Rasses and represent the Rasses from Brixton.[6]

The revitalization of the EWF was therefore driven by a strong interest in the questions of return – black nationalism was back on the top of the agenda. In the British Rastafari landscape, marked by the opening of branches of well-known organizations such as the Twelve Tribes of Israel and of others, lesser known, allegiance to the EWF provided a militant answer to social difficulties:

> Looking at the social ladder, black is at the bottom and in order to rise, they have to organize themselves, that's a black problem, so we must have a black government for the black nation that has been missing since slavery. Our understanding and teaching is that the constitution of the federation is the government for the nation. His Majesty gave it to the black people of the world in order to unite and come home. . . . He grant a constitution for Ethiopians outside of Ethiopia Africa, Ethiopians all over the world, Ethiopians meaning black.[7]

Over and above working to change the existing living conditions in England, Tagesse King and the Rastafari engaged in the Research and Repatriation Committee revitalized the organization in the United States and Jamaica, where it had lost steam. This revitalization was intrinsically related to the status of the EWF, the pan-Ethiopian historical organization to which the administration of the land in Shashemene was entrusted. While return was not mentioned, as such, in the constitution of the EWF, mention of Ethiopia as the "divine heritage" of the black people of the world activated identification. This constitution, designed to serve as a factor of social cohesion for groups of at least twenty-five persons and to organize the international support for Ethiopia, was also used as a metaphor of black government. The aim was to be the "federating organization" asserting the legitimacy of return and of the settlement in Shashemene.

Two documents of importance to the movement were published in 1982 in the United Kingdom: a report by the Catholic Commission for Racial Justice (1982) questioned the appropriate attitude to adopt regarding Rastafari, and another by the Ethnic Minorities Committee, a part of the London administration (Minority Rights Group 1982). Their conclusions were positive: Rastafari was recognized as a legitimate religion, its members were to be respected by the authorities, the Catholic churches should lend them their buildings, and their social projects could be financed by the government. These important advances in Rastafari status in England and the resulting social improvements did not prevent Tagesse King from making his first visit to Ethiopia in 1982, in the company of another brother. They stayed for two months. The Wollo region was already experiencing the pangs of famine. On their return to London, they launched a fundraising musical campaign, Jamming for Ethiopia, before the launching of Bob Geldof's Band Aid in the United States. These Rastafari in England took care of the daughter of a Jamaican who settled in Ethiopia in 1973: Colleen Reid suffered from a heart condition requiring surgery in England. Tagesse King placed Ethiopia and Shashemene at the centre of the London activities of the EWF, and the survival of the Rastafari community on the continent, on the land formerly granted to the EWF, served as a driving force and as a factor of cohesion. To show that Rastafari could settle in Ethiopia despite the military regime, Tagesse King went there in 1988 with his family, whereas others, perhaps wary of the Ethiopian situation, left for Ghana.[8] At first, he settled in Shashemene, with frequent stays in Addis Ababa, where it was easier for him to continue his work. The engagement of the Rastafari in England continued, and many followed suit and settled in Shashemene.

The EWF Officers in Shashemene

In Shashemene, it took months of patience before I was able to sit down with the officers of the EWF who represented this new generation of what Norman Adams has referred to as "hard-core" Rastafari. They were reticent about confiding in a European woman whom they hardly knew. Presided over by Brother B.J. Moody, who had arrived in 1981, and who was, for his part, a member of the "older generation", the accounts were woven together.[9] The three other officers who finally agreed to the interview had been long-standing members of the EWF in England, and they were thoroughly immersed in racial consciousness. All three arrived in the 1990s, following rather distinct trajectories.

The first, the eighth child of Jamaican parents, was born in 1965 in England. His days in school were few, and he got involved in the movement as a young man. Circulating between various Rastafari groups, he was comfortable with the objectives of the EWF and became a member in 1982. He left for Ethiopia in 1990 and remained there for two months, thus realizing what he said was an enduring dream. In 1992, at age twenty-seven, he decided "to leave the west" and settled in Shashemene, leaving a woman and three children behind. He has since made several round trips and hopes to take his parents to Ethiopia.

The second was born in 1960, in England, to parents from St Kitts and Montserrat who had migrated to England. He returned to Montserrat when he was only a few years old and grew up there hearing about James Piper, who was a member of his family and the first person to arrive on the land in Shashemene. This Rastafari finally returned to England in 1988. In 1989, he settled in Birmingham, where he became a member of Local 111 of the EWF. He was certain about wanting to leave for Africa but hesitated somewhat to go to Ghana. His encounter, during a celebration, with Tagesse King and Desmond "Kabinda" Trotter, who was already living in Ethiopia, helped him make up his mind. As he was poor, the EWF financed half the cost of his plane ticket in 1992, but he was forced to return to England the following year for health reasons. He set out again in 1994, and, this time, the EWF covered the entire cost of his journey. He was thus able to accomplish his mission, which was to finish the construction of the EWF headquarters in Shashemene.

It is also following a contact with Tagesse King that the third EWF officer I interviewed became a member of the EWF. A little older than the two others, born in Jamaica in 1954, he migrated at age eleven with his family to the

United Kingdom, where, like many other Caribbeans, he suffered from racism. Although a habitué of Jamaican and Rastafari circles, he was never affiliated, estimating that this was in contradiction with his commitment as a Rastafari. He nevertheless attended the Ethiopian Orthodox Church. A mechanical engineer by training, his illegal activities sent him to prison on several occasions. He travelled widely and resided in Jamaica and Ghana. On his return to England around 1987, he attended a presentation by Tagesse King and decided to become a member of the EWF. Caught up in family problems, he lived for a time at St Agnes Place, and, encouraged by EWF brothers and sisters, he finally left for Ethiopia in 1998.

The narratives of the EWF officers in Shashemene underscore the influence of Tagesse King. His commitment and regular trips to England enabled him to keep the members of the British EWF mobilized. It sometimes appeared easier to concretize the prospects of return to Ghana. Jerry J.K. Rawlings, the president of Ghana since the 1996 elections, visited Jamaica that same year and offered land to the EWF to allow its members to settle. Proximity in terms of language, the greater political stability of the country and the pan-African policy of the government attracted many Rastafari to Accra and to the western coast of Africa. Nevertheless, the ideologies and practices of the Rastafari movement sustained the reference to and the identification with Ethiopia. To this extent, the constitution of the EWF and the land offer made by the emperor almost fifty years earlier continued to play a role in the Rastafari movement. The officers I interviewed all experienced the urban centres from their point of view as blacks and were often members of a modest and marginal class. Yet their proselytizing in favour of the EWF was not homogeneous. This came to light when, asked what was the exact number of EWF members in the Shashemene Rastafari community, one officer answered: "As far as I am concerned everybody is member."[10] He was defending the primacy of this historical organization, although only fifteen of its members had settled in Shashemene. This relativizes, if not the symbolic power of the EWF, at least its real local authority, especially since the constitution requires a minimum of twenty-five people for the creation of a branch. In England, the Rastafari movement, which at the outset was closely linked to Jamaica through its organizations and actors, opened up to persons of non-Jamaican origin. Some of these came from other Caribbean islands and were sometimes of Jamaican parentage, but all had a background as migrants or children of migrants. The great mobility of those who were not so poor facilitated their cosmopolitan experiences.

The trajectories of these three officers, who grew up to the beat of migrations, reggae, Black Power and Rastafari, not to mention a permanent grappling with the British government, exemplify the long-standing, deep-seated diasporic and transnational character of the Caribbean. The persistence of the Ethiopian imaginary was represented by the fortune of the EWF: founded in New York, popular and fragile in Kingston and revitalized in London. Because the returns to Ethiopia transited through the EWF, the organization allowed, in the face of the Ethiopian revolution and famines, a new production of the nationalist and pan-African claims of the "Ethiopian nation of the world".

The Eighteen Branches of the Twelve Tribes of Israel

The Twelve Tribes of Israel in Jamaica started sending their members to Ethiopia with a degree of success by 1972. Following a slowing of their initiatives due to the social and political situation in Ethiopia, the Twelve Tribes began to widen their international base.[11] The organization was already well known to Rastafari, thanks to its close ties to the reggae scene. In England, the Twelve Tribes was also called the Reggae House of Rastafari (van Dijk 1998, 181). Its expansion was remarkable, considering that, beyond reggae, which did not necessarily proselytize in favour of the organization,[12] no communication media was used; it was purely a matter of personal and family contacts. Below is a table showing the sites of implantation of the eighteen branches of the Twelve Tribes of Israel. The opening dates of fifteen of these sites were verified based on several sources. However, there remains a degree of uncertainty concerning the opening dates of three branches, which the various Twelve Tribes officers consulted could not dispel (table 6.2).

The various local situations could not all be verified, but the openings of these branches followed a similar protocol. A person on the spot, with the endorsement of Prophet Gad, was given the authorization to open the branch: an American in New York, a Trinidadian in Trinidad, a Kenyan in Kenya, and so on. The embryonic organization took the name Brotherhood of Rastafari while waiting for the forty-eight executive members (twenty-four men and women from each tribe) and Sister Dinah to come together as "full benches".

Table 6.2.

New York, USA	1976	Manchester, UK	1976
Port of Spain, Trinidad	1977	London, UK	1979
St George, Grenada	1981	Bridgetown, Barbados	1985
Montreal, Canada	1985	Los Angeles, USA	1985
Scarborough, Tobago	1985	Georgetown, Guyana	1986
Nairobi, Kenya	1986	Accra, Ghana	1986
Weiden, Germany	1995	Brisbane, Australia	1995
Paramaribo, Suriname	2006	Auckland, New Zealand	–
Stockholm, Sweden	–	Cayman	–

This took a certain amount of time. For example, the Kenyan branch kept the name Brotherhood of Rastafari for more than fifteen years as the forty-nine persons whose "approval" was needed were not present.[13] This first criterion was probably a way of protecting the organization as a whole from the difficulties liable to result from incomplete or floundering branches. Given the inclusive racial policy of the Twelve Tribes, its members sometimes came from different cultures, but most were middle-class or salaried individuals, at least in the case of large cities (Hepner 1998, 142–43). Consequently, in New York, the organization was situated in neighbourhoods with a Caribbean majority, and most members were Jamaicans. Jamaicans were far less numerous in Los Angeles, which counted migrants from various other locations. The multiethnic character of Los Angeles was therefore reflected in the Twelve Tribes membership there, which included Jamaicans and other Caribbeans as well as African Americans, Indians or Euro-Americans. White people, who were allowed to become members, flowed into the organization, especially in England, attracted by the culture, the music and the Rastafari symbolism. They contributed to the marking of a sharp distinction between the Twelve Tribes and the EWF.

The branches attempted, sometimes with proud success, to become owners of the local in which their Sunday meetings and weekday social activities were held. The resemblance between the various headquarters is striking. Assimilated to embassies, they flew flags of Ethiopia and of the host country and featured photographs of the two heads of state. Two frames were hung, one presenting the photographs of the executive members. On another wall, painted in Rastafari colours (green, gold and red), several of these words: Loyalty, Joy, Life, Peace, Wealth, Health, Charity, Faith, Hope, Goodness, Happiness, Love, God.[14] A map of Africa, painted on the wall or on paper, was also present as well as portraits of Gad (the founder), of Haile Selassie I, his son, Asfa Wossen (1908–97), and grandson, Zere Yacob (1953–). The focus on the emperor's descendants became a characteristic of the Twelve Tribes subsequent to the Ethiopian revolution. For them, Israel and the mythical line of King David were thus perpetuated, while for many Rastafari Haile Selassie I was "King Alpha and Omega", the first and last of the kings (Hepner 1998, 180). What is more, Asfa Wossen and Zere Yacob became involved with Rastafari communities.

In the draft of a constitutional monarchy drawn up by the new Ethiopian military regime before the formation of the *derg*, the successor designated by the emperor, his son Asfa Wossen, was to rule as emperor of Ethiopia, under the name Amha Selassie (Bereket Habte Selassie 1980, 179–91). At the time, Asfa Wossen was in convalescence in England. During the 1980s, members of the growing Ethiopian expatriate community rallied around him to defend the monarchy and, in 1991, founded the monarchist party Mo'a Anbessa, literally the "Conquering Lion". Ascento Foxe, the Jamaican Rastafari who founded the Universal Black People's Improvement Organization, then Local 33 of the

EWF in England, approached the royal family in exile in 1983, and Asfa Wossen offered him his support.[15] Adopting a royalist, imperialist and anti-communist line, Foxe left the EWF and created the Imperial Ethiopian World Federation, thus increasing the fragility of the historical organization. This incident marked the first direct intervention of the royal family in the organizational affairs of Rastafari (Hepner 1998, 173–221). As crown prince, Zere Yacob became the "king" in the eyes of the Twelve Tribes on the death of his father, Asfa Wossen, in 1997. He was close to members of the organization. Members of the English branches had welcomed and surrounded him in his illness, and strong bonds were thus woven between them. In 1992, Zere Yacob was the guest of honour at a Twelve Tribes function in New York, called the HIM Amaha Selassie I Ball, and in 1996, with an entourage from the royal family, he visited several of the organization's headquarters, including those in Kingston and New York.[16] Zere Yacob currently makes public appearances in the company of Rastafari, especially in Ethiopia, to which he has been able to return.

Subcommittees were organized within each branch of the Twelve Tribes of Israel, with officers in charge of security, finance, communication, music, arts and so on. Moreover, the development of new branches followed a precise "programme of events", as underlined by an English member established in Addis Ababa: "Gadman told us the purpose is to publish the word and gather the people. . . . Very simple you'll do things, when you finish one stage, you'll get more instructions. So we had executives, members, meetings, executive's dances, members' dances, colour parties, all stage of dances and celebrations and we had programme with international function, khaki, leather and suit."[17]

After the establishment of executive members, ordinary members and weekly meetings, these functions set the pace for the development of the branches. Their international dimension was underlined by clothing themes such as khaki, leather and suits. The use of one colour theme, added to the symbolism of the uniform, contributed significantly to the feeling of togetherness, of being part of the same family. Years later, one could still hear emotional accounts about the atmosphere of these events in which reggae was omnipresent, where everyone presented herself or himself as a member of a tribe. These festive activities offered an attractive public image of the organization and contributed substantially to its popularity. In 1983, active members in England numbered more than a fifteen hundred – that is, more than the revitalized locals of the EWF – and at least two thousand counted thereafter.[18]

The proselytizing of each branch of the Twelve Tribes, a very centralized and organized body, gave precedence to the theme of return to Africa, and to Shashemene in particular. "Ethiopia is the key of the Twelve Tribes", insisted the founder of the New York branch; it was the objective targeted by the collective and financial efforts, despite the fact that, for many years, arrivals in Ethiopia were few and far between.[19] After Brother Karl (Zebulon), who was sent to Ethiopia by the New York branch in 1979, the two next arrivants, in 1981, were Handell Paris (Reuben) from New York and Brother David (Issachar) from England. Unable to obtain immigration status in Ethiopia, they were deported by the *derg* to Tanzania, where Handell Paris died. Hence, contacts were completely interrupted. Following the example of the founding branch in Kingston, the other branches tried to send their executive members for a visit to Shashemene as soon as they could, and the mandated officers gave a detailed report to members on their return. This mobility was rapid in the case of New York but was liable to call for several years' preparation when originating elsewhere. In the 1980s, six branches were thus able to send their executive members. This was proof of their proper functioning and a milestone in their development. In Shashemene, the private photographs of certain residents continue to testify to the importance of these visits. New Zealand, Trinidad, England, the United States, Germany, and Canada – the whole world went to Shashemene, wearing faces of all colours, originating in all of the twelve tribes. Among certain residents of Shashemene, childhood photographs or photographs of relatives are rare, and the pictures in their possession usually represent this mingling of the Twelve Tribes, experienced as an extended international family.

The temporary moral and financial support provided by these visitors was important for the branches that sent them, as their proselytizing in favour of Shashemene was thereby reinforced. But it was even more so for the residents in Ethiopia. Larry Curtis, the founder of the New York branch, making a direct reference to the role played by the organization in the lives of the returnees to Shashemene, declared: "We kept them alive."[20] Members of the international branches sometimes visited Ethiopia out of pocket when their group was too slow in doing things "in order" and in sending executive members to visit. One executive member, born in England in 1959 of Jamaican parents, made the journey in 1988 with the intention of settling. This tendency developed especially in the 1990s, a period during which many members financed their own departure and settlement, bearing witness to the fact that the members of the Twelve Tribes had easier personal access to cash than was the case when the organization operated in Jamaica alone. Furthermore, when the Jamaican members migrated to English-speaking urban centres, where they were usually able to improve their standard of living, they joined the local branches and gave life to the international network formed by the Twelve Tribes. Albert Allen (Issachar) is exemplary in this respect.

Albert Allen

The Allens were a well-established family in Black River, St Elizabeth. A grocery shop and a pharmacy bore their name; one uncle had served as minister of education; and Allen's parents were members of parliament. Albert Allen, born in 1956, was a brilliant pupil. His last years of schooling took place in Kingston, where his parents rented a room for him so that he could continue his studies in chemistry, physics and mathematics. For a year, he taught technical education. At the occasion of football games organized by a professor, he met members of the Twelve Tribes of Israel and "started to develop interest in the Twelve Tribes religion".[21] He had to go back to his parents' home in St Elizabeth, where he taught for five years. But the back-and-forth journeys to Kingston to attend the meetings of the organization, of which he had become member in 1977, proved expensive. He decided to find a position in the capital and taught mathematics in a school in Trench Town. His dreadlocks, which had began to grow, disturbed the Ministry of Education, but, thanks to his good work, he was allowed to keep his job; in the final analysis, a brilliant teacher with dreadlocks was not a bad model for students. Recalling the influences which helped to shape him, Allen has this to say: "We were Africa conscious but I think we were dealing with blackness at the time, I don't know if you hear about Dr Rodney and Stokely Carmichael, they visited Jamaica, especially the university and they were talking a lot about blackness so I think the whole Caribbean was influenced by these people at the time."[22]

Walter Rodney was banished from Jamaica in 1968, but his influence continued via the militant Black Power groups operating in the university and in the capital. Contrary to other militants, Allen did not lose interest in religion. His parents were believers who attended a Presbyterian Church affiliated to the Church of England, and, in his younger years, he had won a prize for church attendance fifty-one Sundays in the year. This Christian education was not in conflict with the teachings of the Twelve Tribes:

> The real thing about Twelve Tribes is that we grew up in the church, we were very conscious about Jesus Christ being the Saviour of the world as the Bible teaching and the Old Testament part of the Bible so when we link up with Twelve Tribes and they accept the Bible in its entirety, both the Old and the New Testament, we could identify with that organization, it was like semi-Christian.[23]

This proximity between the Twelve Tribes and Christian teachings and doctrines differentiated them from the other Rastafari and attracted Allen. He, too, nurtured the hope of leaving for Shashemene, as so many others had done. Facing the slow-down induced by the situation in Ethiopia, he decided to migrate to England in 1987 and stayed there for four years. He took the opportunity to specialize in civil engineering, then left for the United States in 1991. He settled in New York but travelled extensively. Not wanting to get stuck in the United States, and heeding the encouragement of other resident members of the Twelve Tribes, he finally left for Ethiopia in 1997. He financed his own trip because "one of the things we learned in the earlies, is whosoever who can afford their fare should pay it so that you take off pressure from the organization, so we paid our own fare and went to Germany, cause there's a House in Germany, we stayed for six weeks and come from Germany into Ethiopia. We arrived with two hundred fifty dollars with the intention to start a school."[24] He arrived with more money than his predecessors, had twenty-five years earlier. He was also older than the early returnees, with more experience and with recognized skills as a teacher. Like them, however, he left behind a woman and six children, who were not yet ready to make the move. The international branches of the organization served as milestones and way stations for Jamaican members engaged in the process of return. Allen circulated within the organization's network in England, the United States and Germany. Others, like Winston Laurence (Gad), also a Jamaican member since 1975, followed a similar itinerary. He left first for Germany, where he remained for a month, then for Ghana in 1993, where he stayed five years, at a time when the local branch was in development. Due to malaria and medical problems, Laurence decided to leave the African coast and went instead to Ethiopia in 1998.[25]

During the 1990s, identification with Ethiopia continued and was activated, sometimes in different ways, by organizations like the EWF and the Twelve Tribes. The Ethiopian government headed by Meles Zenawi, in power since 1991, was not prepared to recognize the legacy of Haile Selassie I – that is, the historical symbol of a free Ethiopia that had never been colonized – but return continued to afford the Rastafari "the redemption of [their] body from slavery".[26] The incarnation represented by Haile Selassie I was sometimes "diluted" on the fringes of the movement, where the reggae culture and dreadlocks were transmitted devoid of the religious and nationalist corpus. As soon as Ethiopia reopened, in 1991, the Rastafari mobilized, reminding the country of the symbolic importance of its own history. The Rastafari returnees to Ethiopia were of one mind concerning the importance of persevering in celebrating the emperor. To that end, some resorted to the calendar: 1992, marking the centenary of the birth of Haile Selassie I, was called the "Year of the Creator".

The Centenary of Emperor Haile Selassie I

The festivities organized in 1992 in Ethiopia surrounding the centenary of the birth of the emperor must be interpreted in the framework of the dynamics of the internationalization of the movement, previously marked, on several occasions, by international encounters. The main actors behind these encounters were Rastafari elders who, in Jamaica, embodied the ritual and memorial foundation of the Rastafari movement. Jake Homiak (1994, 52) counted between seventy-five and a hundred elders, belonging to several generations, on whom this ritual continuity reposed. They were assembled under the name Theocratic Order of Nyabinghi, an association of "free men" rather than a structured organization, in charge of the nyabinghi ritual, held several times a year in the hills of

Jamaica (in particular on 23 July, the birthday of the emperor; 2 November, his coronation; and 21 April, the anniversary of his visit to Jamaica). In response to an international request to meet with the elders and learn from them, given the development of the movement beyond Jamaica, and owing to contacts with researchers of Rastafari, in particular Carole Yawney and Jake Homiak, Rastafari elders went to speak at various conferences and made several "trods" (journeys) in the 1980s. These events occurred in places where the authority of the Order of Nyabinghi was officially recognized regarding questions of livity and spirituality: in Toronto in 1980; in Kingston in 1982; in the Eastern Caribbean in 1983; in Toronto, again, in 1984; in London in 1986; in New York, Washington, DC, and California in 1988; and finally, in New York, Baltimore and Washington, DC, in 1989–1990. On each of these occasions, Jamaican elders made the journey, thus taking advantage of the opportunity to represent Rastafari "tradition" abroad, to establish lineages of authority, to develop contacts with other communities and to institute a certain cultural orthodoxy within the movement. These conferences resulted in a "rebirth of the nyabinghi traditions" in Jamaica and the world (Homiak 1994, 72). The Rastafari press, like *Rastafari Speaks*, published in Trinidad, or *Jahug*, published in London, provided information on these encounters in the form of testimonies, photographs and reports.

These Rastafari international conferences formed important watersheds in the development of the movement and were both the consequence and the agents of its globalization. Moreover, the place of women in the organization of these encounters and the choice of the themes explored illustrated an awakening: it was high time to reconsider and to recognize the place, role and responsibilities of women in the movement (Yawney 1999). These events have been studied elsewhere; it will suffice here to underline their importance in the dynamics which drove the trod to Ethiopia, in honour of the centenary of the emperor's birth. For the first time, one of these international events was held in Ethiopia, underscoring the fact that the Rastafari movement had not abandoned its enthusiasm for Ethiopia or its faith in the divine character of Haile Selassie I. This renewed focus on the nature of the emperor and concern about the fate of Ethiopia characterized the Rastafari of the 1990s. The next section examines the process of the trod to Ethiopia through the itinerary of Ras Mweya Masimba, who was one of its driving forces.

Ras Mweya Masimba

The trajectory of Ras Mweya is characteristic of that of the Rastafari of his generation, who grew up in different places when the Rastafari movement was developing international roots. Born in England in 1964, following six half-brothers and -sisters, he remained there until age seven, when his mother decided to return to Jamaica. During his school days, he lived in the Liguanea neighbourhood in Kingston, and he retains a vivid memory of the Rastafari he saw downtown and of the first times he heard about Haile Selassie I. Although his older brother, Carl Bradshaw, had played a role in Perry Henzel's famous film, *The Harder They Come* (1972), starring Jimmy Cliff, he had been warned about the Rastafari, as was the case in many Jamaican families: "We were told of the black heart man, living in the gully, and going there you see Rastaman in the gully, identifies as black heart man."[27] In 1980, due to family difficulties and facing the escalating urban violence in which the elections were being prepared, his mother decided to return to England. At age sixteen, this was a decisive change for Ras Mweya, who confided: "Rastafari came to me when I left Jamaica."[28] He explained in confident terms his search for identity once he arrived in England, so as not to become "like them", like the English, adding: "And what I am holding to is my African identity or Jamaican identity."[29] This identity took the form of a refusal to give up the Jamaican dialect, learning about African history and slavery, the adoption of an African name, the growing of dreadlocks and the prioritizing of black social circles. In the beginning, for him, Rastafari mainly involved a culture comprising publications, reggae and the return to Africa. Ras Mweya became familiar with the members of the Twelve Tribes, but also frequented other organizations and sat down with several Rastafari elders for the purpose of reasoning and learning. While the cultural aspect of Rastafari initially struck him as the most important, the young Ras was fully aware that an important phase of the search for identity was related to the comprehension and acceptance of the divinity of the emperor:

> The divinity of His Majesty for me was the bridge to cross, that's what one Rastaman showed me, you're not a Rasta until you don't know from your perspective not from what a next man show you. From by now what I had gathered of His Majesty was the manifestation of Christ in flesh, of God in man. From that time to this time, it never stopped growing, every rastaman you talk you get a next friend to the knowledge of HIM being divine, you hear a next story that firms up all what you already known, you see a next revelation, some works, some words who a confirm HIM is God, everyday, every time. That's how I would know who a rastaman is, as to the sentiments he shared for His Majesty, that's what I judge him on, how much he love His Majesty, it equate to the love I have for His Majesty, and the things pertaining to His Majesty.[30]

Ras Mweya's testimony illustrates how, in the face of the cultural "dilution" of Rastafari due to the internationalization of the movement, a young generation centred its beliefs and practices on the concept of the divinity of man and on the divine character of Haile Selassie I. He encountered the most adequate expression of this in the traditions of nyabinghi and the association of "free men". Indeed, participating in nyabinghi required no formal membership, and Ras Mweya was wary of institutions susceptible of trying to control him. He thus abandoned the hope of finding a position as a wage earner, got even more involved in the local community and started working in Rastafari art through painting, drawing and video. In 1989, he left for Zimbabwe but soon returned to London. It was then that he had an encounter which turned out to be decisive in the organization of the events of the centenary.

A committee of seven persons, including several Rastafari sistren, played a significant role: Sister Benjie, a Jamaican from the Order of Nyabinghi; Sister Liveth Ivory, who had organized the international encounter "Rastafari Focus" in 1986; and Sister Wellete Medhin of the EWF. At least two years were spent in coordination, discussions, on-the-ground missions to Ethiopia, intermittent personalities clashes, as well as a shared determination. In April 1992, the announcement became public: a month of celebrations was to be held in Ethiopia in July, and the Rastafari were invited to take part in it. The international response was immediate, the more so as the committee was successful in sponsoring the tickets of several Jamaican elders: Empress Baby I, Bongo Rocky, Ma Ashanti, Ras Ivi, Sister Faye. They all belonged to the Order of Nyabinghi and represented two generations of Rastafari. Bongo Solomon coordinated between the committees based in London and Jamaica, and participated in the celebrations in Ethiopia.[31] The official delegation comprised fifty persons, and many Rastafari joined it. In Ethiopia, the members of the trod visited the palaces of the emperor, the buildings of the Organization of African Unity, performed in a function at the national theatre and played the nyabinghi drums on several occasions in Addis Ababa. On the emperor's birthday, 23 July, they converged in Shashemene. The Rastafari ritual space, the tabernacle, had been built for the occasion. Video recordings as well as several publications, including a report in *Jahug*, bore witness to the event.[32]

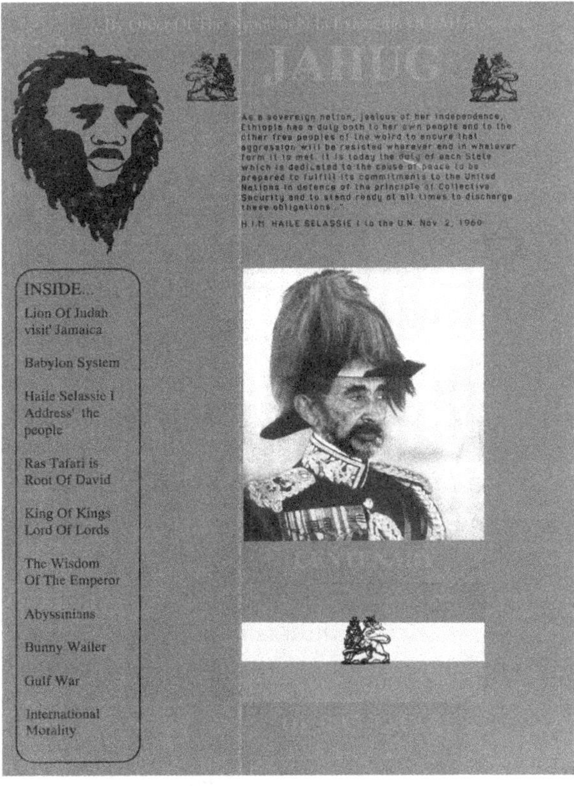

Figure 6.4. An issue of the Rastafari magazine *Jahug* devoted to the centenary of the emperor, 1995. © DR.

The symbolic and political impact of this event did not go unnoticed in Ethiopia. The country was fully engaged in the process of redefinition following the change of regime in 1991, whereupon an important international delegation of Rastafari arrived to celebrate the emperor. The two regimes succeeding the empire had been constructed in opposition to the image of Haile Selassie I's power, and the new regime could hardly be described as fans of the monarchy. Haile Selassie I was still, in the eyes of many Ethiopians, the icon of tyrannical absolutism and political backwardness, and an obstacle to social change. However, the Rastafari encountered no major impediment on the part of the government, and the celebrations proceeded without tension. For the international Rastafari movement, the centenary of the emperor's birth in Ethiopia was a landmark signalling redeployment; following a decade of decline, its interest in Ethiopia was reignited. While divisions did not fail to emerge, owing especially to efforts here and there to appropriate the positive results of the trod, the delegations to the centenary event gave precedence to the pragmatic questions related to the return to Ethiopia, and many people readied themselves for this repatriation. Confirming the revival of nyabinghi practices, a few elders finally went to Shashemene in 1999: Bongo Rocky, Empress Baby I (who had participated in the centenary event), Bongo Ruppa and Bongo Ezekiel. Whereas they had all been involved in the Rastafari movement as of the 1950s, their late arrival brought to Shashemene a historical reference mark within the movement – a matter in which active organizations like the EWF and the Twelve Tribes had preceded them, as far as repatriation was concerned. The elders had arrived shortly after Ras Mweya, who returned in November 1995 with the project – to be addressed further – of establishing a permanent tabernacle in Shashemene. Its establishment marked the successful conclusion of a long personal quest and represented the result of the commitment of the Rastafari community, enabling him, eventually, to make the statement: "That's who I am, one of these Ethiopians who came home."[33]

Ethiopia Africa Black International Congress

Beginning in the 1950s, Prince Emmanuel made a point, in his letters to the colonial government, of demanding the return of the sufferers to Africa. In 1958, he attained national notoriety by convening, in Kingston, the first great congress of Rastafari, in which thousands of persons participated and during which, over twenty-one days, the drums had resounded in the ears of a scandalized public (see chapter 4). In 1966, he was one of the Rastafari invited to the official receptions in honour of the emperor. It is not my intention here to delve into the details of Prince Emmanuel's foundation of the Ethiopia Africa Black International Congress in the hills of Bull Bay, to the east of Kingston, or to discuss his full correspondence, comprising hundreds of letters addressed to Haile Selassie I, the British government and international institutions like the United Nations and the Organization of African Unity. Prince Emmanuel's congregation is known as "Bobo Ashanti" and is marked by a strong distinction of ecclesiastical character. The Bull Bay camp, to the east of Kingston, comprises a tabernacle, dwellings, visitors' quarters, and quarters in which women are secluded twenty-one days per month, during and after their menstrual period. Among the Rastafari, the Bobo congregation retains the closest ties to Jamaican

Figure 6.5. Entrance to the Ethiopia Africa Black International Congress camp, Bull Bay, Jamaica, 2002. Photograph: G. Bonacci © DR.

revivalist practices (Chevannes 1994, 171–88). The death of Prince Emmanuel in 1994 probably encouraged change within the congregation. It took on a global dimensions and Bobos from the United States and elsewhere began to make regular visits to the camp, for stays lasting from a few days to several weeks.[34] What is more, an entire young generation of dancehall artists (Sizzla, Capleton, Determine, Luciano, for example), the contemporary Jamaican popular music artistes, identify with the Bobos and adopt their distinctive markers, the tight turban covering their dreadlocks, radical vegetarianism and a black supremacist ideology opposing racial mixing. Large-scale return to Africa, seen as the inalienable right of black people the world over, had always figured in Bobo claims. In a letter to Queen Elizabeth II in 1966, Prince Emmanuel once again asked that Liberia be opened up to the descendants of slaves, and he readily resorted to older images, like that of Garvey's fleet: "I would like you to get our transportation, such as the Black Starliner seven miles to go up the Nile."[35] Besides, the attributes of the black nation – Ethiopian nationality; the green, gold and red flag; and the Universal Ethiopian Anthem, written by Arnold Josiah Ford – were continuously foregrounded, forming an integral part of the camp's landscape.

The first Bobo delegation arrived in Ethiopia in 1992. Wesley Phang, better known as Priest Paul, was a member. Born in 1959, he was an "Ethiopian" in Kingston, who dropped out of school at around fourteen to experience "a more practical way of life".[36] After becoming a Rastafari in the 1970s, he spent eleven years in the hills of Bull Bay and became a priest of the congregation. While the celebrations of the centenary were in full swing in 1992, a delegation of Bobos was invited, apparently by the Jamaican embassy in Addis Ababa, to meet with Ethiopian officials and to look into the possibilities of establishing a congregation in the country. Ethiopian Airlines sent two tickets to Prince

Emmanuel, but the charismatic leader was unable to make the trip due to age, and these tickets went to others, including Priest Paul. Thirteen people formed this delegation, but all except Priest Paul were forced to leave the country after a clash with Ethiopian authorities.

He was joined in January 2001 by Prophet Kenny. Born in the Bahamas, Kenny was a former professional golfer who had not succeeded in making a mark and who encountered a tragic end in Ethiopia, as he was shot and killed in the Bobo camp in April 2002. Priest Paul was joined by his son, who had lived in Ghana, where the Bobo congregation was growing. A limited number of Bobos arrived and settled officially, but a few others arrived over the years, especially women. One of them was a Haitian who had lived in New York. During her three stays in Jamaica, she had lived in the Bull Bay camp but came away with a memory of constraint, due in particular to the practice of reclusion. She arrived in 1998 with a Trinidadian companion who had migrated to New York.[37] Another of these women was born in England. She had lived for two and a half years in the Bull Bay camp before moving to Trinidad, then to London, to raise funds. She arrived in Ethiopia at the beginning of 2001, joining her husband.[38] Bobo presence in Shashemene, now visible thanks to a large camp decorated in the Ethiopian colours, is significant, for, despite their small number, they represent a historical organization of Rastafari, one whose symbols, liturgies and practices have strongly impacted the development of the movement in Jamaica.

The English-Speaking and French-Speaking Caribbean

In the wake of the Rastafari movement, individuals, families and groups prepared for their return out of the Caribbean. At the time of this research, few representatives from Trinidad, Bermuda, Barbados, or Dominica were present in Shashemene. Given the history of the movement, which is young and active in these regions, many will probably take the road to Ethiopia. All over the Caribbean, the development of Rastafari communities occurred in the context of a continuous grappling with the insular governments. Rastafari doctrines, their disapproved appearance and their revolutionary commitment, which was occasionally armed and violent, emerged against a background of political and cultural confrontation (Tafari 2001). For example, in the island of Grenada, Rastafari joined forces with Maurice Bishop to overthrow Eric Gairy's despotic regime (Campbell 1994, 162–66; Tafari 2001, 331–32). In Antigua, Barbados and Guyana, the few existing reports focus, above all, on the forms of repression to which Rastafari have been subjected – imprisonment, death in police custody – according scant attention to the life stories of the actors. In the Cayman Islands and the Virgin Islands, Rastafari were forbidden entry as late as the 1990s (van Dijk 1998, 193). Rastafari organizations – Nyabinghi, EWF and Twelve Tribes – were established in the Caribbean, but other local structures were also created, and the Rastafari returnees to Ethiopia carried them there. The examples of Trinidad and Tobago, Dominica and the French-speaking Caribbean are enlightening in this respect.

The most important contingent, after that of Jamaica and the English-speaking urban centres, is that of Trinidad. At least nineteen persons from Trinidad and Tobago settled in Ethiopia between 1992 and 2000. The Rastafari movement in Trinidad had been active since the middle of the 1970s, with nearly a thousand five hundred practising members at the end of that decade (van Dijk 1998, 191). The close contacts between Trinidad and Jamaica, the principal English-speaking islands of the Caribbean, the visit of the emperor in 1966 and the early establishment of the Ethiopian Orthodox Church contributed to the diffusion of the movement. Besides the EWF and the Twelve Tribes, whose establishment was particularly important, several other organizations were formed there, like the Ras Tafari Brethren Organization, responsible for the publication of the internationally distributed newspaper, *Rastafari Speaks* (van Dijk 1998, 191). According to Horace Campbell (1994, 171), Trinidad "was one of the few areas outside Jamaica where young blacks still revere Haile Selassie". Campbell took into account neither the United States nor England, but there was a bond between the strength of the Rastafari movement in Trinidad and the fact that Trinidadians formed one of the important contingents of arrivants in Shashemene. Some arrived as members of the Twelve Tribes. Malcolm Philip, born in 1952, had been a member since the 1980s. He was fourteen years old when Haile Selassie I visited Trinidad. He left shortly after for the United States. He lived in New York and Miami and spent five years in prison before returning home for two years. In 1998, he left for Kenya before arriving, finally, in Ethiopia.[39] Many Trinidadians in Shashemene, but not all, were members of the Twelve Tribes; others followed the nyabinghi traditions. The Trinidadians repatriated alone or as a family, and most had lived cosmopolitan experiences in England, in the United States or Canada.

Only one Dominican lives in Shashemene. He is an active militant for the return to Africa and is well-known in francophone circles. At the beginning of the 1970s, when Dominica was still a British colony, relatively heterogeneous groups of Rastafari emerged but were quickly perceived as "subversive and dangerous elements" (van Dijk 1998, 186). Upon the death of an American tourist during the carnival of 1974, two dreadlocks were convicted with the murder based on ambiguous declarations. The first was relased but the second, Desmond "Kabinda" Trotter, was condemned to the death penalty. His sentence was changed to life imprisonment following a vigorous international mobilization. A few months later, the government introduced the Prohibited and Unlawful Societies and Association Act, specially targeting persons with dreadlocks. Section 9 of what was dubbed the Dread Act was a "permission to kill" the dreads, who fled to the hills. About twenty of them were pursued and killed by the police. In the confusion that followed the independence of Dominica in 1978, Desmond "Kabinda" Trotter managed to escape but soon gave himself up. He was ultimately released by the new – and disputed – head of state, Patrick John, when the latter revealed that Trotter had been wrongfully accused. The repression to which the Rastafari were subjected continued into the 1980s. Desmond Trotter and the Inity of Rastafarian Idren group spoke out on several occasions against this religious denigration and constant harassment. Desmond Trotter finally migrated to England in 1987 and arrived in Ethiopia a few years later, probably in 1994.

A few francophone Caribbeans also went to Shashemene. During the 1990s, French-speaking visitors from Martinique and Guadeloupe passed through Ethiopia. Some were present at the time of celebrations of the centenary of the emperor's birth and others went individually to the "Holy Land". At the end of the decade, a few persons prolonged their stay and rented a room in Shashemene. The first arrivants with the intention of staying were a couple who debarked in 2002. They were young, born in 1976 and 1980, hailing from Martinique, Schoelcher and Fort de France, respectively, and accompanied by a small child. They have been followed by others, including the founders of the Zion Train Lodge in Shashemene, but the impact and visibility of francophone Rastafari remains extremely limited to date. The Rastafari movement is little known in the French-speaking Caribbean. Yet Rastafari existed there as of the end of the 1970s. Guadeloupe's proximity to Dominica and Martinique's proximity to St Lucia facilitated exchanges and encounters among Rastafari (van Dijk 1998, 188). Guadeloupian groups, like the Jah family, settled in Benin in April 1997. Generally speaking, their negligible presence in Shashemene seems to be due to several factors at the root of the formation of the francophone Rastafari movement: (1) distance from the English-speaking movement, owing to language; (2) scarcity of formal organizations despite efforts to open EWF locals in the islands or in France; (3) weak delegations at international Rastafari events; (4) the particularities of the French historical, social and political context. The passion for Ethiopia is, nevertheless, quite present in the francophone milieu, as witnessed by the success of the Ethiopian Orthodox Church, which has baptized many Rastafari in Martinique.

Jamaicans have always been in the majority among the repatriated population in Shashemene, but Rastafari from all over the Caribbean followed them during the 1990s. Trinidadians formed the largest contingent, with about twenty persons, but a few representatives of the other islands – Bermuda, Barbados, the Bahamas, St Vincent, Dominica and Martinique – have also settled. The Rastafari movement in the Caribbean took shape during the 1970s in different local contexts, to which it adapted. There are, for example, "Indian" Rastafari in Trinidad, home to a large East Indian population, descendants of the Indian indentured workers engaged by the British after the abolition of slavery. Possibly owing to the revolutionary political significance of the movement in that island, no Grenadians went to Ethiopia. Discrimination and prejudice were similar in the anglophone contexts, whereas the francophone situation was different, marked by a patently more fragmented Rastafari movement. The Caribbean arrivants in Ethiopia reflected the regional influence of the Jamaican Rastafari movement, but without dissimulating the tensions related to the legitimacy and "authenticity" which is still frequently attributed to Jamaican Rastafari, who were pioneers of the movement.

Of Some White Repatriates to Ethiopia

These various trajectories between the Caribbean, the United States, England and Ethiopia formed a transnational fabric inherited from Ethiopianism, pan-Africanism and black nationalism – revived, reformulated and transformed in new and changing contexts through the Rastafari movement. Persons from the Caribbean became Rastafari, with or without previous migrant experience, regardless of whether they were born in the country, in town or in an English-speaking urban centre; affiliated with an organization or not, they formed waves of returns to Shashemene. There, they came face to face with their black imaginary, in a country with a black majority, often in conditions worse than those they had left behind. The body of the myth, whether divine or human, which Haile Selassie I represented and which they themselves incarnated, was black and "Ethiopian", but this did not prevent white people from identifying with Rastafari and from going to Shashemene. Given the territorial and nationalist symbolism of Shashemene, their arrivals are astonishing. They were very few in numbers but embodied the appropriation of this black, "Ethiopian" imaginary within European societies. They could have remained in Europe, participating in the development of their own communities which, to date, are heterogeneous, fragmented and dispersed. But they, too, chose to take part in the "fulfilment of prophecy" and made the move that brought them to Ethiopia. The questions raised by the presence of white persons in Shashemene are of several orders. How can white people be Rastafari? How can white people claim "to repatriate" to Africa? How can they settle on land that Haile Selassie I gave specifically to the "black people of the world"?

The process which leads young white persons to become Rastafari has been studied in England (Jones 1988) and Italy (Bonacci 2001–2, 2003), but such studies are still rare. The influence of reggae has been crucial. Among the multitude of fans of this music in continental Europe, few persons chose the path of comprehension and reappropriation of the Rastafari symbolism and faith. Context has played a significant role in this process. Whereas in England the proximity and interactions between black and white youth raised, essentially, questions about the cultural influence of Jamaica, interracial co-education and the adoption of militant countercultures, these interactions were rarer in continental Europe, owing to the scarcity of Jamaicans there. The Rastafari of continental Europe thus had, overall, fewer occasions to think about their involvement, as they were less often confronted with black discourses and practices. Through travel to England, they were able to make contacts within the Rastafari social environment, initially around music production, the purchase of Rastafari literature and, sometimes, close ties with other Rastafari. But those who decided to settle on the African continent as returnees all explained their commitment in religious terms, as a testimony of their faith. Though highly informed on black history and imaginary, and though never denying the right of the black people to return there, their only means of justifying their presence in Ethiopia, when all is said and done, was through a literal interpretation of the divine plan, calling them to live in Africa within Rastafari communities. It is thus as Rastafari that they justified their return.

Their arrival was more or less facilitated by their proximity with Rastafari organizations. The inclusive racial policy of the Twelve Tribes largely facilitated the interaction or membership of young whites, although, once in Shashemene, they were liable to run into black members of the Twelve Tribes who had reservations about the presence of whites. The EWF, especially since its revitalization in England, had espoused a sharper viewpoint. One of its officers in Shashemene expressed it in these terms: "We're not racist, we're race conscious."[40] There is sometimes a very thin line between racism and race-consciousness, and it was easily observable on the ground. The young EWF generation interacted at times with white people at the individual level, but their milieu and friends were black and their activities exclusively geared towards the improvement of the condition of black people. The Bobos were notorious for their attachment to the defence of black supremacy and their refusal of intermingling, although one of their members in Ethiopia had a love affair with a young woman who was both Bobo and white and lived elsewhere. Within the Order of Nyabinghi, whiteness was symbolically negative, but certain white Rastafari, due to long years of fellowship with practitioners of nyabinghi, were accepted by the congregation. Nonetheless, there were occasionally strong tensions, as we will see in a moment. Whereas, in England, the black Rastafari involved in nyabinghi were keen on racial distinction, others progressively changed their opinion once they were in Ethiopia, thanks in particular to the encounter with white Rastafari, a rare occurrence in Western cities.[41] The Twelve Tribes could explain the presence of white persons with the aid of their doctrines on the twelve tribes issuing from the three sons of Noah, Ham, Shem and Japheth, representing the three "colours" and great characters of humanity. However, most of the other Rastafari could be only surprised by the presence of white persons in Shashemene. One of them, who was a member of the Twelve Tribes, confided: "You have to understand, we never thought we would see people like you [white] here."[42]

This reaction was all the more acute given the nature of Shashemene itself. Even the most exclusive Rastafari did not refuse the possibility of white Rastafari settling in Ethiopia, and they often cited the example of Haile Selassie I, who had had European advisers, and of Sylvia Pankhurst, who was buried in the Church of the Trinity in Addis Ababa – but *not* in Shashemene, seeing that the grant was made specifically to black people by the emperor and was a place where the survivors of slavery should be the only ones with the right to settle. The presence of white persons living in Shashemene was, symbolically, a form of delegitimation of the black claim and of the right to return and, as such, was liable to disrupt the efforts at realization. There were various takes on this phenomenon, varying from one individual to another, depending on doctrinal persuasion, specific social practices and group influence. An Austrian Rastafari who had settled in Shashemene in 1997 thus reported that she had amicable relations with most members of the EWF and with the Order of Nyabinghi, but that, due to group pressure, unfavourable opinions on her presence were expressed. Let us return for a moment to the itinerary of this woman.

Sister Isheba Tafari

Sister Isheba, born in 1971, is very discreet concerning her first steps in the Rastafari faith, thus colluding with the widespread idea that Rastafari is an "innate conception" and is not acquired through a process of conversion. Her life story certainly did not begin with the growing of her dreadlocks or with her first contact with the name of the emperor, but her account flows in a manner suggesting that this identity had always been a part of her. She makes discreet reference to a family tragedy, a sister who was a drug addict, who had traced for herself a fatal trajectory, whereas the path that she, Isheba, had traced, thanks to Rastafari, had allowed her to stay alive: "My mum realize say that if you question and you find Jah is the only way you can survive, so she could see the two roads, even though my way must have been strange for her."[43] And Isheba questioned many things: the sense of authority, the nature of Jah, the borderline separating the oppressors and the oppressed. She was very isolated in Austria; the first Rastafari she met were a couple from Jamaica who had lived in the United States and England and had finally opened a reggae record shop in Vienna. In 1993, they left to settle in Tanzania, and she joined them for the summer. She registered in a course in African studies at the university and began to learn Kiswahili but left, the following year, on another journey that was something of a pilgrimage. She went from Israel to Ethiopia, following the path of the Ark of the Covenant, as described by Graham Hancock's book *The Sign and the Seal* (1997). Four months later, she arrived in Shashemene for the first time. Notwithstanding her growing attachment to Ethiopia, she decided to go back to Vienna to finish her studies in a state of solitude: "I really needed some contacts with ones and ones, I started going to England and buying cultural books, Rasta, Africa, I was juggling a bit in Austria, videos as well, that's how I got to know Ras Mweya 'cause I order some videos."[44]

She put together a small catalogue in Austria and kept in contact with the Rastafari brothers and sisters in England, some of whom had left to settle in Ghana. She was then a strict vegetarian, was interested in alternative medicines and fasted regularly. With a master's thesis in preparation on the question of repatriation to East Africa, and aiming to study the practical aspects of settlement in Africa, she set out again in 1997 for Tanzania, where, thanks to earlier contacts, her arrival was facilitated. She left from there for Ethiopia via Kenya. Once in Shashemene, she found accommodation in the home of a Rastafari in Malka Oda, the village on the other side of the river bordering the lands on which the community was established:

> "I was supposed to go back to Tanzania to continue my research. Ras Mweya was encouraging me as well, 'no, you can make it here'. Is most spiritually, I just know say Jah him say, I can't say well wait for me until I finish my master and so on and so me stay. My mum was supposed to come and spend some time together in Tanzania just for holiday. Me call and say bring as much stuff as you can because I am not coming back."
>
> "What? And school?"
>
> "I know, it's all nice and important but Jah tell me fe stay here. I am not going nowhere."[45]

Having made this radical decision, Sister Isheba was the second European to settle permanently in Shashemene. The first, who arrived in 1991, came from Manchester and was a member of the Twelve Tribes of Israel. This implies that she was already a part of a wide Jamaican and international network. This facilitated her arrival, but did not prevent her from suffering a very violent attack, leading to the loss of the use of one finger. The circumstances behind the violation of her home at night by a man armed with a machete remain unelucidated, but the origin or colour of this English woman who spoke like a Jamaican might have had some bearing on the aggression. Sister Isheba remained in Malka Oda. Highly conscious and sensitive regarding the nature of the land in Shashemene, she was not disturbed about living on the other side of the river. The ritual at the nyabinghi tabernacle was just beginning, and this is where she invested her energy, whereas few other Rastafari attended. Rastafari from England visiting Shashemene, who had heard about her, questioned the legitimacy of her presence during the nyabinghi ritual:

> That night and one start attacking I verbally and question my presence in the tabernacle and on the land altogether, question I as a Rasta sistren, all levels. I respect all dem ones cause many of them is my elders and went through a lot of things, I know. But the thing was like is a group phenomena and ones and ones, everybody was meant to

> speak on my case. . . . One after the other, especially ones I don't expect, say like "Let she go she is a problem."[46]

Sister Isheba made the distinction between the persons she did not know, who came from England bent on confrontation, and her friends and brothers living in Shashemene. The experience was painful, as she considered herself as belonging to "I and I community praising Rastafari" and knew that most of the residents in Shashemene had no problem with her presence. The separatist drive came from the outside and was, in her case, decisive. It serves to illustrate the racial tension traversing the Rastafari movement, which was inevitably exacerbated in Shashemene. The social policy of racial exclusion or inclusion continued to be a line of separation among Rastafari. It was particularly acute in Shashemene and in the English-speaking urban centres where cultures and races are more sharply highlighted than elsewhere. Arguments in favour of or against including white people in the Rastafari movement abounded. In the words of the Austrian Rastafari:

> Their question of race is one of the question that is gonna make break I and I as people, it is because the spiritual thing we function has to be based on truth, whenever you get into racial talk, is pure contradiction you gonna get yourself no matter which way you want to turn it. . . . Me I am convinced is everyone here is supposed to be here according to plan of Jah no matter what you may see, whether you like it or not, he who is here is supposed to be here, you can't tell nobody who fe [to] be here and who not fe be here. Not a people choice or decision because Jah decide that one. That's why the race thing become irrelevant in that sort of way, because Jah decide.[47]

By insisting that repatriation to Shashemene represents a divine calling, this Rastafari woman displaced the debate from a racial and social question to the level of spiritual interpretation. One reference to the emperor often quoted by "inclusive" Rastafari underlines the fact that he did not speak in terms of whites or blacks but rather in terms of Europeans and Africans. The idea here is that Haile Selassie I did not advocate racial identification, notwithstanding his position and that of Ethiopia in the black imaginary and the political battlefield, both of which durably incarnated a symbol of sovereignty and independence. After the departure of the quarrelsome delegation, calm returned to Shashemene, although the question of the presence of white people on the land given to the "black people of the world" remains unsettled. A few other Europeans have arrived, like a mixed Finnish and Swedish couple who came in 2000 with their two children. Based initially in Addis Ababa, the family gradually settled in Shashemene.[48] The father was familiar with the nyabinghi circle, as he had made long stays in Jamaica and, to a certain extent, a white couple was less "threatening" than a mixed couple. The number of white visitors have increased. Since the end of the 1980s, white members of the Twelve

Tribes have arrived regularly from the United States, England and New Zealand. Others have preferred to settle in Addis Ababa, due in particular to questions of employment. Germans, Italians and French, these sometimes improbable Rastafari have also the made voyage in a quest for identity which, at times, had them become "living contradictions" (Jones 1988, 177).

THE COMMON DENOMINATOR OF ALL THESE INTERNATIONAL RASTAFARI remains the process of identification with Haile Selassie I, Ethiopia and the Rastafari movement, which has assumed different forms and itineraries depending on contexts, encounters, opportunities or financial means. The Rastafari movement offers an answer to the identity quest of people who are sometimes very different. This answer takes the form of the appropriation of various spiritual, interpretative and material practices. It often involves a name change, sometimes including the administrative process of changing personal documents such as birth certificates. This deep-seated identification, this Ethiopian imaginary, continues to be fuelled, more than thirty years after the deposition of the emperor, by concrete practices of return. It is around these practices that the following are formed: the Rastafari movement, organizations, networks and sites of symbolic power, interest groups, and chains of solidarity linking the spaces traversed by these returnees. The racial question is often posed with acuity, but other, subtler distinctions are surfacing within the Shashemene community, especially with respect to country of origin or practices. A Trinidadian does not always want to be mistaken for a Jamaican; a Jamaican from England is not always able to live like a Jamaican from yard; a strict vegetarian cannot not eat at the Twelve Tribes; someone who observes the Sabbath is not available for a community activity taking place on Saturdays, and so on. The diversity of these attitudes reflect the diversity inherent in the Rastafari movement, which does not detract from its black, nationalist and pan-African legacies. The Rastafari of Shashemene represent the "Ethiopian nation of the world" which has "returned home", to "its own land". In the final analysis, what is to be found there is almost a Rastafari "nation" – one which took shape despite the diversity, the sometimes contradictory doctrines and the presence of highly contrasted actors, on the basis of two points of unanimous accord: the centrality of the figure of the emperor and the imperious need to go back to Africa.

CONCLUSION TO PART 2

THE CLAIMING OF THE RIGHT TO RETURN TO Africa first emerged, in Jamaica, as a reaction to the social and economic conditions in which the majority of the black population lived. It served as a radical critique of the Jamaican society through the very act of offering another national identity (the black nation, Israelites) along with a racial identity (Ethiopian). Various segments of the population followed this dynamics, including the Rastafari, for whom return was the "fulfilment of the prophecy". Haile Selassie's invitation influenced the racial identification with Ethiopia by adding to the symbolism a territory represented by the land in Shashemene. During the 1950s, return to Africa became an issue of public debate in Jamaica. At times, it took the shape of an alternative migratory opening for the Jamaican workers. The independence of Jamaica in 1962 eclipsed the discussions of return, while the Rastafari movement gained visibility. Four years later, Haile Selassie's official visit to Jamaica, providing a living symbol of the independence and divinity of the black body, encouraged some Rastafari to move beyond passive waiting and to organize their return.

The desire to return to Ethiopia guided the efforts mustered by the Rastafari, in view of collective organization. Not without difficulty, some were able to transform the EWF "from the bottom up" in a bid to legitimate their return to Shashemene. Others founded the Twelve Tribes of Israel and placed the fate of Shashemene at the heart of their proselytizing. Mobilizing reggae artistes and young people from the middle class, this organization helped to transform the Rastafari movement. Far from the long-expected mass movement and despite the Ethiopian revolution which closed up the country, these groups played a major role in perpetuating the black imagination of Ethiopia.

Their international expansion, sustained by the migrations of Jamaicans and by the worldwide diffusion of reggae, marked the new spaces invested by the contemporary "Ethiopian belt". Various representatives of this diversity found themselves in Ethiopia, thereby exemplifying, in this other history of the Rastafari movement, the persistence of the desire for return and of its realization. It is possible to be an "Ethiopian" in Kingston, London or New York, but how does one continue to be an Ethiopian upon arrival in Shashemene? The discourses on authenticity produced by these "true Ethiopians" were sorely tried in Ethiopia, where the heirs of the Ethiopianist legacy and of the gift of land in Shashemene were transformed into foreign pioneers. The last section of this work will consider the endless contradictions of the diasporic subject who finds herself or himself back "home".

Part 3

THE "TRUE" ETHIOPIANS IN SHASHEMENE

"I am here not by law but by grace."
– *Brother Teach, Shashemene*

"I don't know much about the land, I live 'pon the land sister, I don't even know how much a hectare is."
– *Ras Mweya Masimba, Addis Ababa*

"If we don't build new Jerusalem, is not gonna fall from heaven. Is we haffi build it."
– *Sis Isheba Tafari, Shashemene*

BEFORE THEIR ARRIVAL IN ETHIOPIA, THE "ETHIOPIANS OF THE WORLD" expected to integrate their nation, a land flowing with milk and honey, the *elsewhere* that would procure freedom and safety. To date, history has been silent concerning the consequences of these arrivals, the shocks of discovery and the adventures of settlement. Yet the challenges they encountered were not unsubstantial: what would transpire when Utopia finally found its *topos*? How would the contradictions, inherent in the diaspora, be redefined? How would Ethiopians interpret the image of Ethiopia produced by the returnees? Was it possible to be Ethiopian in a new land without becoming a foreigner at home? An understanding of the history of the return to Ethiopia cannot be restricted to an evaluation in terms of success or failure. What this history offers, instead, is the possibility of a complex, multilayered analysis.

Two approaches have been chosen to guide this account: land relations and social relations. The centrality of the homeland, of land, of national territory, is common to the black nationalist imaginary and to Ethiopian societies and authorities. Approaching the issue of return via the land rapidly emerged as an inevitable pathway into the dynamics and modalities of the encounter between Caribbean Rastafari and Ethiopia. The focus on social relations is its corollary: on the land, we can read the economic, social and familial impacts of return. These traces are, as we will see, simultaneously embedded in the local and diaspora contexts. Moving from one level to another, on several occasions, I will reveal the entanglement of identities and belonging as well as their interactions with the national context. The contradictory situations in which the returnees to Ethiopia evolved will thereby emerge. The comparison between their living conditions and those of the Ethiopians is made difficult by the lack of social history on Shashemene and its environs. Nevertheless, I will show that the experiences of the Caribbeans testify to the major transformations of the Ethiopian state in 1974 and 1991. Their experience also illustrates the place of foreigners in the Ethiopian society and clarifies the concomitant processes of urbanization and integration in Ethiopia. Beyond territory, the Caribbean settlement in Shashemene has also become the symbolic centre of a certain black, emigration-oriented, nationalist and Ethiopian consciousness in which the power struggles among Rastafari organizations have been reformulated. The land in Shashemene allowed the encounter between reality and the imaginary. There, the Rastafari movement has survived, not without difficulties, giving form, at last, to a "Rastafari nation" within that of Ethiopia.

CHAPTER 7

IN THE HEART OF THE ETHIOPIAN EMPIRE

BASED ON THE CAREFUL INTERSECTION OF ORAL, PRINTED and Ethiopian archival sources, this chapter offers a reconstruction and a historical cartography of the beginning of the settlement in Shashemene. The questions related to the status, the surface area and the location of the land granted "to the black people of the world" seemed particularly interesting. This chapter discusses the power stakes linked to the arrival of the Jamaicans in a space in which few other Caribbeans and Americans had previously settled. It focuses on the changes in the configuration of the settlement in the period immediately preceding the Ethiopian revolution, which shook the social and political landscape of the country.

Entry into the Territory

Leaving Addis Ababa by its southernmost gates, the road progressively silences the effervescence, on the outskirts of the capital, of myriad merchants and carriers, buses, trucks, mules and walkers. It stretches between the fields of *t'ef* and the human density that mark the landscape. At Mojo, the road turns fully to the south and cuts into the furrow of the grand valley of the Rift which splits the continent, creating an anciently populated environment. Beyond the river Awash, there is a chain of lakes, which blossom into grandeur further south, in Kenya, Uganda, Tanzania and Malawi. Here, each can be embraced in a single glance: Lakes Koka, Ziway, Langano, Abyiata, Shala, Awasa and Chamo, surrounded by vegetation or inhospitable rocks. Some are stained blood red by iron ore; others are so dark that legend has it they are bottomless. Some abound in fish, while others attract tourists and townspeople. Abandoning the heights of the capital, the road descends endlessly, still almost two thousand metres above sea level. It crosses cultivated fields, semi-arid zones and herds of hundreds of heads of cattle, while churches, Muslim tombs and dusty villages succeed one another. The temperature mounts gradually as we enter what is conventionally called the "Ethiopian south", an appellation which covers, awkwardly, more

Figure 7.1. Map of Ethiopia

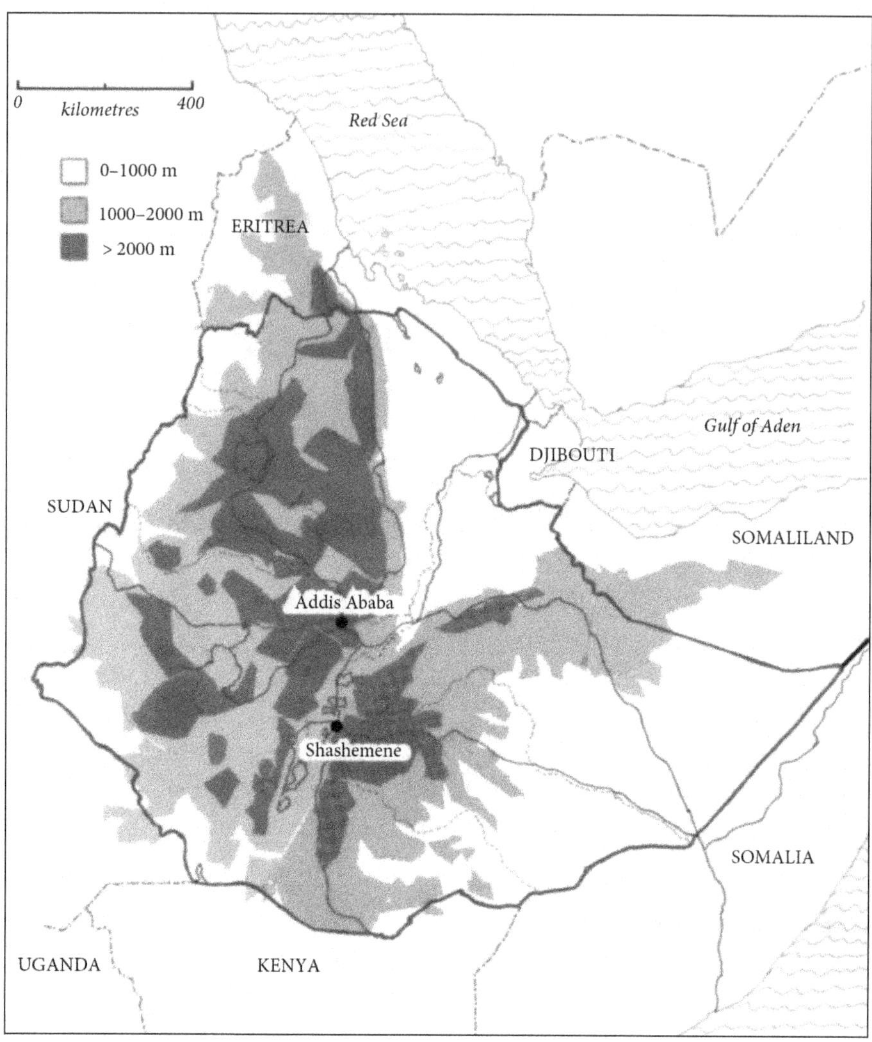

than a third of the national territory, covered by heterogeneous landscapes, populations, languages and cultures.

The Land in the South of the Ethiopian Empire

The Ethiopian south has often been perceived as a periphery of the modern Ethiopian state, a state whose centre is supposedly represented by the political and administrative institutions emanating from the region of Choa, in the high plateaux. The southerly expansion of the hegemony of Choa, begun in the early nineteenth century, was pursued decisively by Menelik II, who became King of Kings in 1889, after having fought for Yohannes IV (1872–89). The domination of Choa over this Oromo land resulted from the great battles of the second half of the nineteenth century, which redefined the relation between the centre of power and its new peripheries and founded the modern Ethiopian

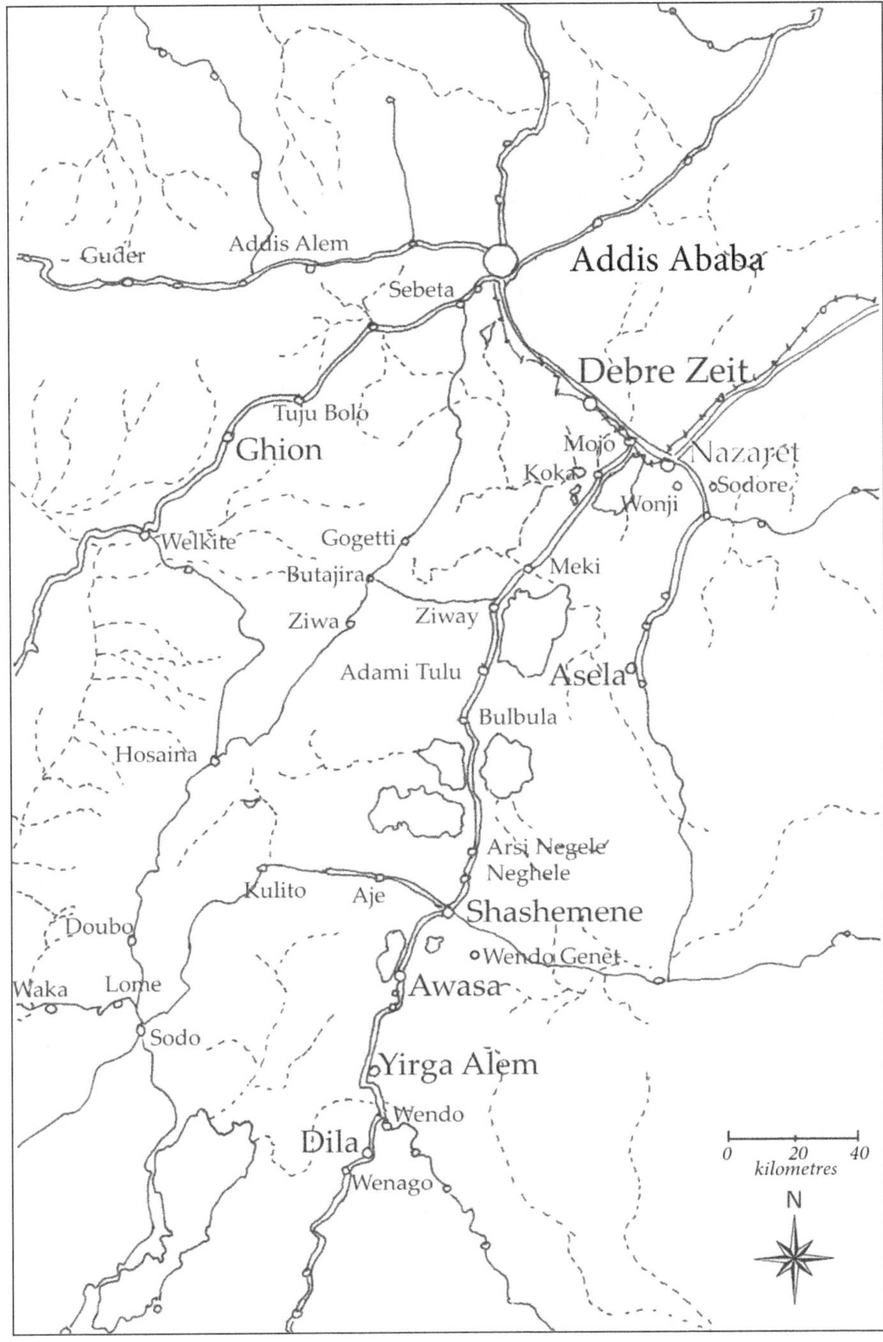

Figure 7.2. Map of the Southern Road

state (Darkwah 1975; Donham 2002a, 23). Following Ethiopia's momentous entry on the international scene, due to the victory of Adwa (1896), the forceful annexation of the lands in the south provided the sovereign with a reinforced territorial base, allowing him to control the extended trade route traversing these territories (Bahru Zewde 2000, 60). Designating a centre and borders is not a matter of simple, stationary and immutable dichotomy. To the contrary, in the peripheries, a variety of local situations fell into place. Fluctuating relations were reformulated around numerous stakes of power and representation of authority, but especially around the control of agricultural land and modes of production. Donald Donham (2002a, 37–44) defines three types of economic relations and policies linking the centre and the peripheries of the south and illustrating the diversity of the subjected regions:

1. Regions that were formerly independent kingdoms, in which the local leaders became dependent on the centre. As of the beginning of the twentieth century, most of these enclaves lost their specific structures and moved slowly towards the second mode of relation.
2. Regions in which the system of *gäbbar* was established: governors from the north were named and the local populations subjected. *Gult* land was given to governors, soldiers and local leaders who became *balabbat* or intermediaries of the administration. The *gult* land implied that the local population, previously living in weakly stratified societies, became peasants obliged to pay a tribute, that is, a *gäbbar*. The tribute covered a share of their agricultural production as well as forced labour and gifts. This system, imported from the north and suddenly imposed on the regions of the south, was assorted with a profound sense of cultural superiority on the part of the northerners. The region surrounding Shashemene falls into this category.
3. Regions on the far outskirts are low-altitude land, inhabited by hunters or farmers. In these borderland regions, *balabbat* were named and the exaction of tribute initially took the shape of the capture of cattle and humans, taken as slaves. This system was progressively normalized through the collection of taxes.

Generally, the history of the land politics of the centre and the north of the country is complex but relatively well known. Historians carried out their work based on various sources: the royal chronicles, the lives of saints and, at times, documents related to property (Crummey 2000). The land history of the Ethiopian south did not benefit from similar documented analyses. It is nonetheless possible to shed some light on the origin of the land in Shashemene on which the transatlantic migrants settled. In these peripheral spaces, a great deal of the land was seen as unoccupied and referred to as *yä-negus märét*, the land of the King, with no regard for the local populations who lived there (Berhanou Abebe 1971, 1–7). In the case of the recently acquired provinces, and especially the regions which interest us, the idea that the land was unexploited or unoccupied meant that there was a better use to which it could be put by the king. According to Donham, the ideology behind this formulation was similar to that of European colonists, especially in South Africa and Kenya (Donham 2002a, 41). John Cohen and Dov Weintraub (1975, 46–47) distinguish, for their part, four types of government land holdings:

1. Palace land, whose agricultural produce and cattle were reserved for the government and the court;
2. *Gebretel* land, reappropriated by the government when the owner was unable to pay taxes;
3. *Madäriya* land, granted in usufruct by the government in lieu of wages. The recipient acquitted all taxes due, except land tax. He had the right to lease the land and to retain the agricultural produce. Nevertheless, this land was the property of the state, and its usufruct could neither be sold nor inherited;
4. *Mängest* land, which formed the majority of government land. It was either left vacant or leased as pastureland. This land comprised most of the land grants or attributions made by the emperor.

Around Shashemene, a substantial amount of government land was thus distributed to several types of people, thereby further reducing the land available to the local populations. The *näft' äñña* – name derived from the word *näft'*, meaning rifle – were soldiers from the provinces of the north who had fought in the armies of Menelik. Many remained on the lands of the south. The church as well as many royal family members and government officials were also beneficiaries of these redistributions (Benti Getahun 1988, 9). The attribution of these "vacant" concessions had more to do with political concerns than with developmental objectives. Indeed, the recipients were often civil servants, police officers and soldiers rather than peasants. These gifts of land rewarded loyalty and services rendered by the recipients and were not accompanied by mandatory conditions of development (Cohen and Weintraub 1975, 59).

Subsequent to the liberation of Ethiopia, with the support of the English armed forces in 1941, between three and five million hectares were allocated, thus accelerating the privatization of the land, particularly in the south (Cohen and Weintraub 1975, 60; Bahru Zewde 2000, 191). Cohen and Weintraub (1975, 60–61) have identified three main decrees legislating land distribution via the Ministry of the Interior. The decree of the 16 *hamlé* 1934 *a.m.* (23 July 1942)[1] offered to veterans, patriots and refugees of the Italian occupation the possibility of converting up to forty hectares of their *madäriya* land into *gäbbar* and allowed those who had no land to acquire forty hectares of *gäbbar* land. The proclamation of the 16 *hamlé* 1936 *a.m.* (23 July 1944) offered forty hectares of vacant government land to each soldier, civil servant and serviceman. Lastly, the proclamation of 23 *t'eq'emt* 1945 *a.m.* (2 November 1952) offered twenty hectares of *gäbbar* land to each landless or unemployed Ethiopian citizen. The recipients, however, were seldom peasants. Moreover, special gifts, in the form of *gäbbar* and *madäryia* land, were lavishly granted by the emperor, through the Ministry of the Pen. These usually went to the powerful partisans of the crown and the *protégés* of the emperor. Out of a total of three million hectares, these land grants represented a little more than six hundred thousand hectares (Cohen and Weintraub 1975, 60).

The land in the south of the Ethiopian empire was therefore a conquered territory, gradually taken over by governors and military men, forming the local branches of an extremely centralized power. Through being progressively dominated by the centre, the peripheries of the south yielded, not always without rebellion, to a process of acculturation called "abyssinization" (Donham 2002a, 10–13). The appropriation and redistribution of the land and its corollary, the alienation of the local population, formed a kind of "scramble" for the lands of the south, or, in other words, an imposed and uneven division of a space with multiple resources, executed for political and economic reasons. It was therefore not particularly surprising that the land earmarked for the "black people of the world", to thank them for their moral and financial support during the war against the Italians, was situated in this southern region. For the black communities of the United States and the Caribbean, this gesture was a clear sign of pan-African consciousness; they perceived it as a policy of assistance, one which inscribed the Ethiopian south in their collective imaginary and influenced several generations of nationalist and emigrationist militants. From the Ethiopian perspective, this gesture was a commonplace political act; the localization of the land grants followed a dynamics of occupation in vogue since the end of the nineteenth century. The recipients were, of course, a peculiar population, but they were recognized as allies in the struggle for the defence of Ethiopian independence and as partisans of the crown, who could, like the other patriots and veterans, be rewarded for their unconditional support.

The Town of Shashemene

Situated 250 kilometres from the capital, Shashemene offers a moment of respite to the traveller on the road of the south. Bordered by the heights of the Rift, the city climbs to almost nineteen hundred metres and is characterized by its position at the centre of numerous intersections. Shashemene was a time-honoured crossroads of commercial exchange in the region. It was at the junction of medieval trade, leading to the creation of important markets, whether permanent or temporary, which received produce and merchants from all over the region (Benti Getahun 1988, 24). Routes leaving Shashemene lead to the mountainous eastern regions of Bale, to Sidamo in the southeast, Kembata in the west, Gamu Gofa in the southwest, and, in the extreme south, to Walayita, the Konso region and the town of Moyale, situated on the border with Kenya, a little more than five hundred kilometres away. The name Shashemene recalls the town's historical fortune as a place of passage and circulation: *Shash* is said to be the name of a woman from the beginning of the century, who offered food, the local beer, *t'älla*, and accommodation to merchants and passers-by. *Mene* is an Oromo word meaning "house". The "house of Shash" reportedly gave its name to the urban development.[2] Two opposing opinions address the

Figures 7.3a–b. Entrance of Shashemene, 2002. Photograph: G. Bonacci © DR.

origin of the town of Shashemene: Gunilla Bjerén thinks that it was a garrison town, like many others in the south (Bjerén 1985, 86), whereas Benti Getahun stresses that Shashemene was an important junction, prior to the settlement of soldiers, and was not, fundamentally, a garrison town.

At the intersection of trade routes and an outpost of the armies of Menelik II, Shashemene became a strategic space. At the end of the nineteenth century, the region around Shashemene was integrated into the large Arussi province, within the sub-province (*Awrajja*) of Kembata. The city was then almost at the intersection of the Arussi, Bale and Sidamo provinces (Benti Getahun 1988, 1). The old customs of land tenure definitively deteriorated due to the nominations, among the local leaders, of *balabbat* to whom land was entrusted in return for tax and administrative and military services. *The balabbat* were joined around 1915 by *näft'äñña*, and later by *shialäqa*, mobile, landless servicemen, many of whom were attracted by the numerous land grants available, along with authority over the local population. Their settlement was sometimes bloody in the event of resistance by the local population (Joireman 2000, 89), but their presence transformed Shashemene into the administrative and commercial hub of the region, where a large market, later known as Alelu, was established (Benti Getahun 1988, 28). Coinciding with the arrival of the *näft'äñña*, several groups of merchants settled in Shashemene. Their names continue to designate certain neighbourhoods of the city. The C'orré, Oromo traders, as well as others from Jimma, or the Guragués from Soddo, in the Walaiyta region, helped, through trade, to make Shashemene a centre of distribution of produce brought from all over the south or from Addis Ababa (Benti Getahun 1988, 27, 32–36).

Shashemene was occupied by the Italians during their Ethiopian campaign. After liberation, in 1941, the city remained in the same Arussi province but was placed in the Chilalo *awrajja*, and its municipality was founded in *hedar* 1936 *a.m.* (November–December 1943) (Benti Getahun 1988, 98). Perpetuating a policy of centralization targeting the control of the lands of the south, many land grants were accorded following the war. Concessions to foreign investors, missionaries, royal family members or government officials were meant to secure the loyalty of influential persons or, sometimes, served as a means of displacing opponents.

The case of the Hamassiens illustrates this post-bellum wave of land appropriation and redistribution. Originating in the region of Hamassien, in Eritrea, and enlisted in the Italian armies, they deserted massively and joined forces with the Ethiopian patriots. In recompense, land was granted to them in 1944 near Neghele, to the north of Shashemene. Eight hundred soldiers from Hamassien received approximately forty hectares per person. Moreover, between 1948 and 1949, the village of Malka Oda, bordering on the river situated near the entry of the town of Shashemene, was also given to these migrants from the north. Certain veterans sold their land, but many others settled there. The village covered an area of approximately one hundred and twenty hectares and comprised some two hundred houses.[3] More will be said later concerning the importance of Malka Oda for the Caribbeans who settled in Shashemene. This village populated by persons from Hamassien was in fact closer to them than the town of Shashemene itself, and the colonists from the North were, as it were, their immediate neighbours.

These continuous settlements contributed to the development of the town, and Shashemene quickly emerged as a major space of migration within the country. Yet the city offered few employment opportunities. Whereas Ethiopian industrialization began in the early 1950s and the first five-year development plan was completed in 1962, industrial activity was almost totally nonexistent in and around Shashemene (Eshetu Chole 1995). But the economy burgeoned in the 1960s, marked by the constant increase in services offered and a sustained economic expansion due to the development of commercial farms (Benti Getahun

Figure 7.4. The entrance to Shashemene during the dry season, 2003. Photograph: G. Bonacci © DR.

1988, 181). Thanks to this development, Shashemene was integrated into the province of Choa in 1960 and became a district capital, a *wäräda* of the Hayqoch and Buta Jira *awrajja*, whose capital was eventually established further north, in Ziway (Benti Getahun 1988, 1–2). During the 1980s, following the creation of smaller administrative units, the *wäräda* of Shashemene was divided into seventy-eight peasant associations, while the town was subdivided into ten districts, or *qäbälé* (CSA 1996, 33, 139). The ten *qäbälé* varied exceedingly in size. The smallest included the most populous districts of the city, made up ofthe central spaces of the bus station and main trade venue. These small districts were surrounded by the largest districts, made up of less populated and more residential areas, or quasi-rural zones. Shashemene is now the capital of the most populated and densest *wäräda* of the East Shäwa Zone. The East Shäwa Zone is one of the twelve zones of the regional state of Oromiya, created by the constitution of 1995. It borders another regional state called Southern Nations, Nationalities and People (Master Plan 2000, 4–5, 24).

The population of the city increased rapidly: the first population census dates back to 1962 and registered 5,048 inhabitants. In three years, the population doubled to 10,000 inhabitants (Master Plan 1967, 16). In 1984, 32,376 inhabitants were listed in the town (Benti Getahun 1988, 2). In 1994, the figure advanced was 45,208 inhabitants (Master Plan 2000, 69), and in 2003, coffee-house gossip raised that number to more than 100,000 inhabitants. Various migrant populations, from the north or the south, were to be found in Shashemene: Amharas as well as Tigreans, Oromos, Guragués, Walayitas, Kembatas, Sidamas, Soddos, Dorzes and so on. These populations formed an ethnic mosaic distributed among the districts and the social levels. At times adding themselves to the ethnic diversity, at times intermingling, they were distinguished by their religion,

Figure 7.5.
The centre of Shashemene, 2007. Photograph: G. Bonacci © DR.

cultural attitudes and economic activities (Bjerén 1985, 137–236; Benti Getahun 1988, 133–66; Mesfin Getahun 2001). In the absence of industrial activity, transport, trade and prostitution became, in a way, the pillars of the development of Shashemene, where the informal economy has always dominated. Despite the economic niches offered to the new arrivants, today's Shashemene is a typical, overpopulated town of the Ethiopian south, in which infrastructure fails to keep pace with a rapidly increasing demography, and where social mobility is almost non-existent, while new migrants are constantly settling, forming a large population of unemployed persons, "squatters" and hooligans (Benti Getahun 1988, 157–58). Shashemene's reputation is not spotless. In the city and beyond, many Ethiopians and foreigners have heard about its social instability and constant insecurity – or have experienced it.

Despite its strategic location at the crossroads of migrations, Shashemene is a town that has received scant academic attention, one whose social dynamics are still largely ignored. The rare works of reference on Shashemene were written in the 1980s. They offered, on the one hand, data and analysis capturing its role in urban migrations (Bjerén 1985) and, on the other, a history of its foundation and development until 1974. The second remains unpublished (Benti Getahun 1988). The presence, on its periphery, of a group of foreigners from the Americas is never mentioned. This silence is puzzling: were the transatlantic migrants so disregarded during the 1980s that their identification was considered irrelevant, even in the form of a simple footnote? Or were they so few in number as to go unnoticed by censuses and the careful examination of historians[4]?

Other important sources on Shashemene, the master plans, were reports on the progress and objectives of urban development. The first, financed by the Ministry of the Interior, harks back to 1967 and was conducted by Italian consultants who, strangely enough, compared the region of Shashemene with the plain of Pô as it was between the fifth and the third centuries BC (Master Plan 1967, 58–59). The second, and last, master plan dates back to 2000 and was carried out by the National Urban Planning Institute in Addis Ababa. In the section dealing with "history, culture and tourism" in Shashemene, essentially a summary of the works of Gunilla Bjerén and Benti Getahun, a single reference is made to the Jamaican families:

> The most interesting thing that makes Shashemenie [*sic*] unique is the presence of the Jamaican community in it. In the late 1960s, Emperor H/Selassie brought 10 families of Jamaican community to Ethiopia and allotted them 1.5 *gashas* [60 hectares] of land on the outskirts of Shashemenie. Though some members of this community left Ethiopia in the 1970s, after the nationalisation of their land by the *Derg* regime, still the remaining members intermingled with the natives of the region and, as a result, their number have been rising. According to Desmond, currently there are 40 families with 120 members of whom 80 are born in Ethiopia.
>
> The Jamaican community which are also known as the "*Ras* Taferians" ("Rasta") have their own unique culture which is associated with the late Emperor H/Selassie (the former *Ras* Taferi). Though the culture is widely apparent all across the world, it is interesting to see this community in Shashemene giving a new impetus to the historical ties that have existed between Ethiopia and African Americans" (Master Plan 2000, 52).

In the absence of a classified architectural or historical legacy in Shashemene, the Jamaican community emerged as a cultural asset and an important tourist attraction on the southern road. The numerical and historical importance of the

Figure 7.6. On the road which goes towards the town, a *gari* drawn by a horse, with the colours of Ethiopia. Photograph: G. Bonacci © DR.

Jamaican presence was stressed by the name, *Jamaica säfär, säfär* being used to designate a neighbourhood in which at least twelve foreign nationalities cohabited. The historical narrative was somewhat fanciful, the dates and the area of the land originally granted erroneous, but the bond between this community and a specific culture associated with the emperor remained relevant. Moreover, the inscription of this community into the broader history of the relations between Ethiopia and African Americans revealed an understanding of the dynamics that gave rise to this settlement. The adviser mentioned by the experts in charge of elaborating the master plan was a Jamaican who arrived in 1975. At the end of the final report, thirty-two photographs illustrated Shashemene: main roads, markets, transport and school children. Illegal constructions also appeared, as well as the Jamaican neighbourhood, its place of worship and homes. After fifty years of presence on the periphery of Shashemene and as many years of absence in the reference books on the city, the returnees appeared for the first time in an administrative document. In the project of an arts centre and museum recommended by the master plan, to preserve the "mosaic of cultures" that Shashemene represented, a small place was finally projected for them.

The Land Granted to the "Black People of the World"

The land granted to the "black people of the world", according to the terms of the constitution of the EWF, was part of a larger territory that became the property of the imperial government. This was a land marked by ancient stories of conquest and alienation of the local populations, Oromos for the most part. Were they the personal property of the emperor or, rather, that of his daughter, Princess Tenagne Worq, who was decidedly interested in the transatlantic migrants who settled there? The land archives of the princess, comprising several hundreds of files filled with official documents, lists of personnel and legal documents, which are often serious but sometimes frivolous, are silent on this subject and offer no clue concerning the status and original occupation of the land near Shashemene.[5] One of the first newcomers, Gladstone Robinson, claims that when the land was granted as a sign of gratitude, it had a *madäriya* status.[6] This implied that the recipients acquitted all taxes except land tax. They were allowed to lease out the land and to retain the agricultural produce. Nevertheless, the land belonged to the government, and the usufruct could be neither sold nor transmitted. The private character of *madäriya* land did not facilitate the settlement of the other migrants who were expected. A major change of status occurred in 1955, at the time of a proclamation, which bestowed "permanent and complete property" on those who had been gratified with *madäriya* land at the conclusion of the war (Mahteme Selassie, 1957, 301). This transformation into permanent property recalled the *rest* status existing in the lands in the centre and north of the country. In general terms, *rest* land

Figure 7.7. The Shashemene land grant. Photograph: G. Bonacci © DR.

conferred to peasants the inalienable right to cultivate the land and especially to transmit it to their children (Crummey 2000, 9). Thus, the lands granted by Haile Selassie I to the black peoples of the Americas remained in their hands and could benefit their families.

Uncertainty about the area of the land grant was largely maintained by the numerous references in the Jamaican press at the time, often repeated in the literature on the Rastafari movement. The land in Shashemene given to the "black people of the world" was thus variously reported to cover two hundred acres, five hundred acres, approximately thirty hectares, sixty hectares, five hundred hectares or treated with an embarrassed silence by authors relatively unfamiliar with the question of Ethiopian land tenure.[7] It is now possible to state with certainty that the granted land covered an area of five *gashas* (two hundred hectares or a thousand acres).[8]

At the beginning of the century, the authorities set out to determine the area of the agrarian unit. The objective was not really to constitute a registration of urban and rural land holdings, but rather to facilitate the taxation of occupants. The *gasha* served both as a unit of agrarian measurement in the subdivision of domains and as a unit of taxation in the division of fiscal dues (Berhanou Abebe 1971, 96). The *gasha* was originally a shield made of hippopotamus hide, carried by soldiers, who subsequently gave this name to the land granted them by the state (Gebre Wold Ingida Worq 1962, 303; Crummey 2000, 172). The *gashas* were measured with the aid of thin straps of leather called *qälad*, measuring 133 cubits (66.75 metres), but the area varied with the fertility of the land or the degree of exploitation and human settlement. Thus, there were at least three or four ways of determining the *gasha*, varying from an area of seven to twelve *qälads* in width by twenty *qälads* in length (Gebre Wold Ingida Worq 1962, 303; Berhanou Abebe 1971, 99). This unit lacked precision and was not the same all over the country, but in the places that interest us, the *gasha* delimited a category of relatively fertile land and was nine *qälads* wide by twelve *qälads* long, that is, 509.25 metres by 781 metres. In other words, a *gasha* was about forty hectares. A field of five *gashas* was not particularly large; big landowners and foreign concessionaires sometimes possessed land covering dozens of *gashas*.[9] At the time of the numerous post-bellum distributions, most recipients were granted between half a *gasha* and one *gasha* per person. Five *gashas* were therefore likely to be distributed to five persons.

The manager of Princess Tenagne Worq's land, *Fitawrari* Guebre Heywot Wolde Hawariat, a rather elderly gentleman, vaguely recalled that five people came to him expressing their wish to cultivate the land. He did not remember how these people came to contact him, but he recalled having written to the governor of Shashemene to ask that five *gashas* be granted to them. The *Fitawrari* had been informed that many others would come, but seemed nevertheless disappointed by the agricultural performance of these five persons whose names escaped his memory.[10] Herein lies, perhaps, one of the paradoxes linked to this land grant. Admittedly, many people were expected, but apparently only five persons showed up, so the targeted land was allotted to them. If this land, granted before 1955, fell under the *madäriya* category, it was meant for a specific recipient: were these individuals the recipients in question? Or was the recipient in fact the EWF? This administrative uncertainty will be discussed later; the focus, for the moment, is on a recapitulation of the approach used to map this land.

Today's memory constructs a territory of variable dimensions. The narrative is sometimes vague, but often grandiose, accompanied by the body language of arms spread wide and hands extended: "it goes from Malka Oda River to Bale Goba road", "from far back over there, to far far down over there", "from river to river, and mountain to mountain". Memory sometimes rediscovers the shapes and contours of the traces left on the ground. *Ato* Aduna, an architect who knows the neighbourhood well and who works with the municipality, marks a blue paper with a black lead pencil. The paper is a 1998 map made by the Ethiopian Mapping Authority.[11] He points with a ruler to a landmark, situated in a corner, just below the road. *Ato* Tesfa Giorgis grew up in the village of Hamassien, in Malka Oda, then left to study electronics in Russia in 1964. His eyes slip away from the map and his fingers point:

> From the main road, the land goes on both sides and borders the river. The other side of the river belong to veterans. Up to Bac'aré, where there is the *werka* [sycamore] it belonged to them. Italians set up an old airport for military purposes, there were some cactus, up to that it belonged to them. Up to the high school it belonged not to Piper but to *Ababa* Asamani. After the high school, there is a house called *Villa bella*, after that where there is the hotel construction it didn't belong to them. Landmarks

> were big trees, and you know you never touch that tree.[12]

Figure 7.8. The Malka Oda River. Photograph: G. Bonacci, © DR.

One owner of neighbouring land was called *Ababa* Asamani. He had granted a part of his field, on a twenty-year lease, to the Sudan Interior Mission in 1958. After sixteen years, the mission was transferred to Kuyra, a few kilometres to the north, and the Territorial Army took over the lease (Benti Getahun 1988, 83, 96n139). A military camp is still there. But to return to the issue of mapping, in the company of a small team, and guided by the map in our possession, I tried to find the trees and found the traces, departing from the hollow of Malka Oda River, which forms a fine natural border. The land slopes sharply down to huge rocks over which the river flows; birds take refuge in the trees which wave their branches over the water. The land spreads out, bordered by the river. It slopes gently to the southeast and the northwest. On the northern side is a road, extending to the site of the old runway, covered with short grass. Cactus gives way to *wärka*, a line of tall sycamores near which the land stops, before climbing up to the road. It continues southeast, then curves to another tree, following which the domain resumes, until it reaches the river. The numerous trees, serving as landmarks, show the signs of a territory inhabited by the Oromos. *Malka*, in Oromo, means a green space at the edge of the water, of a river or lake, and also designates a sacred space. *Oda* are the venerated trees near which arguments, judgements and parliaments are presided over by the elders.[13]

A resident once said: "Let me tell you a secret: I walked the boundaries and it took me three days and a half."[14] But one is obliged to conclude that he went out to discover the region, as opposed to walking around the boundaries of the concession. A perimeter of six kilometres might take several hours to cross, especially when one is stumbling along by a riverside, skirting dwellings, following paths and meeting neighbours.

Fifty years ago, the boundaries of this concession traversed a few fields, passing by long-horned cattle and cutting through tall grass. It waxed green after the rains, turned golden the rest of the year, and was sometimes scorched by the dry season. Old photographs show an open space with nothing to arrest the glance save these tall trees and, in the distance, the elevations of the Rift.

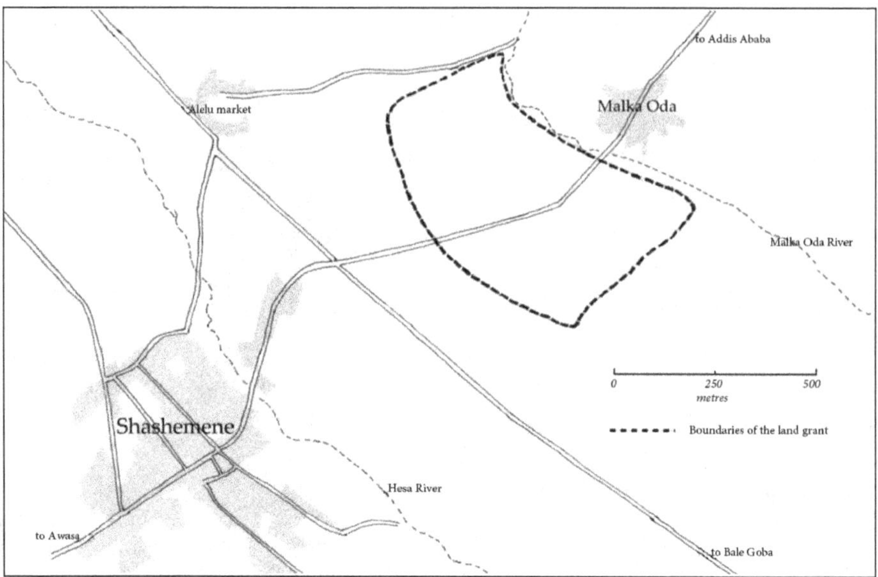

Figure 7.9. A map of the land grant, ca. 1950.

But the forest nearby was dense, and a few round houses huddled together, sometimes at its edge. Besides Gogeti and Hesa, intermittent streams crossing Shashemene, the Malka Oda River was the main source of water for the local population – it provided water for drinking, cooking, washing, cleaning, watering of cattle and irrigation of the fields. The land formed an intermediary space close to the river, bordering the town, traversed by the rocky road on which, a few months each year, mud replaced dust. In the direction of Shashemene, this road leaves, to the right, the neighbourhood called Alelu and the large regional weekly market by the same name. It leaves, on the left, the neighbourhood called Awasho, then the path to Bale. Two kilometres ahead, it traverses the small bridge spanning the river Hesa and enters the town. The *garis* – small unstable horse-drawn carriages – trucks and people follow a paved road. Finished in 2002, the new road coming from Addis Ababa circles the town before continuing to Awasa, transforming the former trail into a highway attracting business and new directional signage.

In fifty years, this territory has changed substantially. This rural region became one of the dynamic peripheries of the city. In the two kilometres which separate this periphery from the town, the fields have disappeared, leaving only residential buildings, two hotels, two gas stations, restaurants, a mechanic, a bakery, a few shops, two schools, high fences maintaining the privacy of family lives and, especially, many more people. Residents, passers-by, visitors, travellers, idlers, blue-collar workers, women bent double, and men with bicycles traverse it continually. The landscape has undergone profound transformation, although it is sometimes enough to leave the road, enter the hearts of neighbourhoods and then leave them behind to find yourself in the fields and the vast open spaces subjected to the endless pressure of population.

At the beginning of the 1950s, the first representatives of the black peoples of the world, who had never been landowners in their lives and who had lived in overpopulated and segregated urban neighbourhoods, came into fertile land holdings and exerted an unquestionable power over the local peasant populations. Settling on the periphery of Shashemene, at the time, was an extraordinary achievement, an unimaginable social mobility, unattainable in the United States or the Caribbean. Contrary to an American dream of thirty-year post-war boom, which, though in full swing, remained inaccessible, the Ethiopian dream, for its part, was a tangible reality beneath their feet.

The Settlement of the Pipers

Born in Montserrat, Helen and James Piper were American citizens who arrived in Addis Ababa in 1948. They were Garveyites and black Jews, and figured among the countless technicians, teachers and African American professionals committed to playing a part in the reconstruction and development of Ethiopia after the end of the war in 1941. James taught at the Gundrandt Technical School in Addis Ababa, and Helen worked at the airport. They frequented the fast-growing African American community and had close ties with David Talbot due to their shared Caribbean origin and militant commitment. A photograph showing the three of them was diffused time and again in the pan-African press.[15] A Guyanese journalist who arrived in Ethiopia in 1943, David Talbot was also president of the Addis Ababa local of the EWF, of which James and Helen Piper were, respectively, the secretary and the treasurer.[16] In November 1952, the Pipers returned to the United States to give an account of their Ethiopian experience and to promote the settlement in Shashemene. At a meeting in a Chicago local of the EWF, "their description of the wonderful life and opportunities in Ethiopia aroused great enthusiasm".[17] They were back in Ethiopia by 1953 and settled on the outskirts of Shashemene. The social break represented by this choice of residence should not be underestimated: the other African Americans had remained, in the majority, in urban areas, in Addis Ababa and Harar. At the beginning of the 1950s, Shashemene was at quite a distance from Addis Ababa, a daylong trip on a bad road. While several elements support the belief that they arrived in Shashemene before the proclamation of 1955, which transformed the temporary use of the *madäriya* land into a permanent and inalienable property, sources remain uncertain regarding the date of their arrival. One EWF officer cites 1952;[18] for the inhabitants of Malka Oda, it was in 1953 or 1954 (1946–47 *a.m.*),[19] while the journalist Yacob Wolde Mariam claims that it was in 1956.[20] They did not go to Shashemene alone. It is said that they had assembled between five – a hesitant recollection of *Fitawrari* Guebre Heywot Wolde Hawariat – and twenty persons, as noted in an internal correspondence between the Ministry of the Interior and Agriculture and the Ministry of Foreign Affairs.[21] No trace remains of the names, origins and trajectories of the other families who were reportedly present in Shashemene in the 1950s. The Jamaican press mentioned another Caribbean family, but on their departure, the Pipers "took over the whole concession", and only they have survived in local memories.[22]

Imprints on the Land and the Society

James Piper became the administrator of a land holding of two hundred hectares,[23] but that did not prevent him from returning regularly to Addis Ababa to visit David Talbot. The latter was a familiar face in the imperial ministries and administration. This facilitated their meetings with *Ras* Mesfin Sileshi in the Ministry of the Pen, for discussions concerning the development of the land and the legal problems that had already arisen with a neighbour on an adjoining property, *Balambaras* Negasso. As they had settled *madäriya* land that had been redistributed to them, the place where the Pipers arrived was not vacant but was part of a domain on which the *Fitawrari* Jula formerly lived. In his absence, the lands had been placed in the keeping of Bekele Debabé and *Abba* Shukko, and of the Oromo farmers who lived there: *Abbas* Balu, Gamechu, Fotto and Kerbo. Before the arrival of the Pipers, this space was partially occupied by a mechanized government cereal farm.[24] The Pipers continued this exploitation of the land, to which they added fruit trees and groundnuts. Moreover, James developed an irrigation system that facilitated the agricultural and domestic use of water from the Malka Oda River. They installed a *wäfc'o bet*, a mechanized mill, and they had a car. These were signs of wealth that clearly revealed their superior economic power in the local landscape of Ethiopian peasants.[25]

The first house the Pipers built is still standing today – it is small, solid, with walls made of long, horizontal planks and two small windows, a slightly tilted roof and two wooden doors. While this two-room rectangular house was in construction, they lived in a "pretty government house with a thatched roof".[26] Their house was naturally situated on the Awasho side, slightly elevated above the road. In its "cozy" interior hung a photograph of Melaku E. Beyen, the founder of the EWF. A neat fence, all around their *gebbi*, enclosed their house and the garden, in which they planted flowers. Located a bit further was a structure sheltering the mill. Beside it, they built another small, two-room house, in which they taught school in the evening – the alphabet, English and mathematics – to the children of the vicinity, the smaller children in one room, and the older ones in the other. Constructed entirely of wood, these buildings were reminiscent of the houses in the Caribbean and signalled James Piper's reproduction of a familiar architectural style. At the beginning of the 1960s, on the other side of the road, the Pipers built a school, a bigger one, named the Melaku E. Beyen School after the founder of the EWF. It had a zinc roof,

Figure 7.10. The Melaku E. Beyen School, Shashemene, ca. 1965. Archives G. Robinson, Shashemene © DR.

walls of wood and an annex at the back.[27] To the right of the main door, a panel announced, in Amharic and English, the "Children's Institute". This is the school on the map of Shashemene presented by Gunilla Bjerén (1985, 89), the first school to be built between the town and the Adventist college of Kuyra, founded at the end of the 1950s. At the local level, the Melaku E. Beyen School offered an invaluable educational alternative, as the other schools were several kilometres away. It accommodated up to sixty pupils at a time.

Two Ethiopian teachers assisted the Pipers, but a considerable amount of the teaching was done in English, which was seen as prestigious. Despite the lawsuits in progress over joint property borderlines, their neighbour *Balambaras* Negasso was unable to resist the temptation of sending his children to their school so that they could learn to speak English.[28] A small infirmary called the "Ethiopia Clinic" was built next to the school. Although it was not round, it resembled the surrounding houses, as it was made of cob, called *č'eqa*. Cob is

Figure 7.11. Ethiopia Clinic, Shashemene, ca. 1965. Archives G. Robinson, Shashemene © DR.

a mixture of manure, soil and straw applied to a structure of vertical branches in which stones are wedged. Once the walls were dry, cement was sometimes projected onto them, then smoothed over, giving rise to a solid, long-lasting structure. It is probable that Ethiopians were employed in its construction, as it is quite unlikely that the Pipers themselves adopted this method.

The Pipers left a significant mark on the area, in terms of agriculture and construction. They represented an administrative authority, as they were responsible for the administration of their land concession, and a social authority, since the peasants who worked for them were not on the same footing. An elderly peasant who spent his entire life in the environs of Shashemene thus reports that, even when the *balabbat* changed, their situation as peasants, on the other hand, remained the same, one of dependence, inherent to the *gäbbar* status:

> "You see, the land belonged to a *balabbat* and when it was given to Piper we started paying taxes to the Piper."
>
> "So to the farmers, Piper was like a *balabbat*?"
>
> "Yes, he was like a *balabbat*."
>
> "Did Piper cultivate all the five *gashas*?"
>
> "When Piper first come all the land was uncultivated forest and grassland except a few patches that we farm. And so when Piper came, he started selling the grass for the people and the people on the land gave tribute to Piper. . . . For the grass every year one pays a young ox, and the produce of the farm he gives the half to Piper."[29]

Abba Medina used, inappropriately, the term *balabbat* to define the social status of the Pipers. In actual fact, in the Ethiopian south, the *balabbat* were usually named among the chiefs of the local population to serve as the administrative intermediaries of the state. This amalgamation with the situation of the Pipers nonetheless reveals that they charged the peasants fees in much the same way as the *balabbat*, who had the right to collect tribute (Donham 2002a, 39). The Pipers received their tribute in kind. Besides, two practices characteristic of this relation of domination linked them to the peasants. First, that of grazing: the Ethiopians grazed their herd on the Pipers' domain in return for a yearly tribute in heads of cattle. The Pipers thus raised a herd, kept by the peasants, but the milk and other dairy products were reserved for the use of the owners. Second, the practice of tenant farming: one half of the crops harvested by the Ethiopians was turned over to them.[30] The peasants retain a bitter memory of this period during which they were subjected to the *balabbat* and other property owners. It is summed up in an Amharic expression used repeatedly by *Abba* Médina during our conversation in Oromo: *ayqerbunim*, "they were not close to us". While the spatial proximity was obvious, the social distance was not less patent.

This said, those employed by the Pipers, especially for domestic tasks, spoke peaceably about their relations with them. Berhanou Teffera came from Wollayta when he was a young man, and he worked for them as a *zäbäñña* or watchman for a long time. He was a salaried worker in the employ of the Pipers, who paid him a relatively good wage, hence his positive appreciation: "the people had respect for her . . . and he was a good man, no problem with anybody and people loved him".[31] One sign of this appreciation was the presence of two little girls entrusted to them by a Muslim Oromo neighbour. The children helped with domestic tasks. They were fed and sheltered, and they absorbed the culture of their hosts. One currently works with Ethiopian Airlines in Addis Ababa, and the other, Berba Tulu, a mother of ten, lives in Kuyra, some five kilometres from Shashemene. The latter retains an enchanted memory of the Pipers. She was their interpreter, spoke for them in Amharic and accompanied them on their trips to Addis Ababa. She reported that they taught her how to stay healthy and to work conscientiously, a principle she claims to have transmitted to her children. She is proud and grateful to the Pipers that her children have all done well in school and, later, in tertiary institutions.[32]

The Pipers seemed to have enjoyed good relations with their neighbours from Hamassien who had settled in Malka Oda, on the other side of the river. The young people from Malka Oda often came to spend the weekend with them and crossed the ultimate cultural boundary by sharing their meals. As *Ato* Tesfa Giorgis reports: "we drink the same river water", a picturesque way of expressing the perceived "social equality" between the beneficiaries of royal liberality on southern lands. The Pipers, too, had their own story to tell – but all that remains are the bits and pieces preserved by memory. The residents of Malka Oda remember having heard "lady" Helen Piper say that the Pipers had participated in demonstrations in the defence of Ethiopia during the war. Others thought that Helen Piper was formerly the emperor's cook or that the Pipers had convinced the emperor that they were Ethiopian patriots, hence their invitation to settle on this land.[33]

On a legal document dated 1952 *a.m.* (1960), endorsing the purchase of a *rest* property comprising five *gashas* by *Ras* Andergachäw Masaï, the husband of Princess Tenagne Worq, an important mention is made of the Pipers. The boundaries of the acquired property were indicated by reference to all the neighbouring property owners. Whereas the other neighbours were identified by name, the neighbours in the east, the Pipers, were identified as *sedätäñña färänj.* The term *färänj* was commonly used to designate foreigners and probably comes from an old word referring to the French, who had spread all over the East during the crusades. It is often taken for granted that *färänj* specifically designates white foreigners. The Pipers were not white, but some of their practices were probably interpreted as white. They spoke English, drove a car, sometimes wore a suit and a tie or a skirt and a hat, cooked standing up and ate their meals at a table set with cutlery. It possible that, for such reasons, the Ethiopians saw them as white although they were black. The term *sedätäñña* as used here functions as an agent and designates them as refugees or migrants. The action implied by *sedät* contains, moreover, the concept of exile, of a departure from home. The root of this word is *säddädä*, subsuming the idea of expulsion, banishment, and putting down roots in the land (Kane 1990, 576–77; Leslau 1976, 58). The expression *sedätäñña färänj*[34] is apparently unusual, like the Pipers, who were no ordinary foreigners. These words identified them as foreigners but not only that. They were also recognized as migrants and refugees in Ethiopia, where they had planted new roots.

The settlement of the Pipers on the land in Shashemene was characterized by their exploitation of the land and the construction of several houses but also by contrasted social relations. A certain solidarity was possible between the Pipers and the Hamassiens, who were both foreigners to the region and recipients of post-bellum land grants. The employees of the Pipers, who served them on a daily basis, seem to have had only good memories. However, for the peasants, Oromos for the most part, the Pipers were merely the new faces of an inevitable class of rich and powerful people who constrained their work, their production and their lives. The complexity of the impact the Pipers had on the land and the local society is scarcely visible in the letters they sent abroad, as this correspondence required the construction of an ideal situation.

The Imprint on the Diaspora

The pan-African press served as a channel of dissemination for the Pipers' letters and photographs, which were published regularly. In one of these letters, this is how the Pipers described the territory on which they had settled:

> Our colony is not in the forest; it is situated on both sides of the main highway leading into Kenya. It is in the suburb of the City of Shashamane. There are thousands of homes, nice ones all around us. There is a Bank in Shashamane also, and a Post Office where we get our mails. Our home is just a few feet from the road. It is the most lovely spot on earth.[35]

An idealized image of Shashemene was spread to the West: "a large area of flat, fertile land",[36] something like a modern garden of Eden, lying close to the city and its amenities. The Pipers reassured the readers of the pan-African press by specifying that they did not live in the forest, a space likely to evoke stereotyped images of Africa, but they failed to mention that Addis Ababa was a good day's journey away, that Shashemene was more than two kilometres away and that the beautiful houses surrounding them were made of cob. The photographs showed Helen in her garden and James leaning with proprietorial ease against a wooden fence overhung with a sign bearing the inscription "Land Grant Ethiopian World Federation Colony. Malcoda Shashamane. James Piper administrator."[37]

On several occasions, they defined their settlement as a "colony", a term

Figure 7.12. Helen Piper in front of her house, Shashemene, *African Opinion* 7, nos. 1–2 (June–July 1965): 6 © DR.

of varying connotations depending on the language and the period (Green et al. 2008). The term as they used it must be placed in the context of the black emigrationist heritage, which saw the "colonization of Africa by Negroes as solution of race problem".[38] Inherent in the term *colony*, the power struggle between the colonizer and the colonized on the continent, once displaced, represented the struggle between blacks and whites. The black colonies in Africa represented, in principle, a space of freedom, a refuge for populations subjected to the racial politics of the western states in which they lived. In the words of the Pipers: "[Ethiopia] is a place where none can lynch you, stop you from voting, segregate, burn, despise or hate you on the basis of colour."[39] However, the escape from segregation did not automatically generate a position of equality or neutrality, once in the colony. The Pipers came into a superior social status in Shashemene, where they were, at the same time, the managers of a domain with peasants at their service, and teachers and role models for their neighbours. The diffusion of this ideal image targeted the interest and investments of the pan-Africanists, who felt drawn to settlement on the continent. Indeed, the Pipers had many plans and hoped for the fast development of their colony. The pan-African press thus diffused an ambitious five-year plan:

Figure 7.13. James Piper in front of his place, Shashemene, *African Opinion* 7, nos. 1–2 (June–July 1965): 7 © DR.

1. Repatriation (settlement)
2. Industries
3. Farming equipment
4. Building of a large community house

5. Water supply construction
6. Building of roads
7. Enlargement of Dr Melaku E. Beyen School
9 [*sic*]. Transportation
10. Building of Religious Temple of Worship.[40]

This plan reveals the priorities established by the Pipers. At the top of the list were physical settlements in Shashemene, the life force for all future development. Although there was an African American community in Addis Ababa, the Pipers remained alone in Shashemene until the middle of the 1960s, waiting for the other "pioneers", who were in no hurry to make the trip down south. Their solitude struck the journalist Yacob Wolde Mariam, at the time of his visit in 1962: "One thing that I found rather striking with the Pipers was how they could bear the isolation in which they found themselves. Here were a couple who knew of life and civilization living remote from everything beautiful the world could offer. I wondered how many of us Ethiopians would make similar sacrifices to offer our own people in distant places something to improve their lot."[41]

For this journalist, leaving America for Shashemene, leaving behind the modernity of the West for a social position that was certainly enviable but far from the capital, in an isolated rural locality, was a sacrifice few Ethiopians would readily make. What is more, few African Americans were prepared to make this sacrifice. The Pipers invited others to take up the challenge of coming and settling alongside them, and these calls to people were indissociable from an appeal for the funds needed for settlement: "We have arranged a five-year program to develop the land and we are asking you to donate what you can. Even to help buy a brick. We hope you will decide and just come to Ethiopia for the rest of your days."[42]

Despite their many achievements, there was a severe lack of funds, and the couple tried to obtain the financial support that, apparently, was not forthcoming from the EWF. The points presented in the expansion plan all concerned infrastructure, whether of a local nature, like a community house, the expansion of the school, the construction of a temple; or of a more general character, such as industries, irrigation, roads, transport and farming equipment. The lack of infrastructure, underlined in this plan, explained the perceived need to make amends for the shortcomings of the Ethiopian state, unable to implement the development of its provinces. The fragility of the pan-African networks interested in this type of settlement was also underscored, since little or no funds arrived in Shashemene. To no avail, the Pipers emphasized the facilities available to future arrivants, including the possibility of obtaining an individual parcel of land: "each family is allowed a home site, including a garden and space for a garage free, except $11 fee with your application for certificate, deed and postage".[43] They also stated that Ethiopian banks could provide loans to help with settlement.[44]

William Hillman sent funds to have a house prepared for him. A Baptist pastor from Georgia, he first heard about Shashemene during a Malcolm X conference which took place in Pennsylvania in the early 1960s (Bishton 1986, 29). After a year of preparation, in 1965, Hillman, his wife and their daughter arrived in Shashemene. James Piper had chosen for him a site to the left of the Melaku E. Beyen School, and Hillman seemed delighted: "This is the most beautiful country in the world. We found our home well built by the Administrator, Mr James Piper. He and his wife, Mrs Helen Piper, had planted beautiful flowers around our home and also a garden and now we are enjoying the undescribable [*sic*] freedom."[45]

Given the publicity surrounding the settlement of the Hillmans, how did the Pipers explain the absence of newcomers? How did they interpret the gulf between the hopes of massive settlement by Afro-descendants searching for freedom and justice, and the feeble response to their appeals? Disregarding the rising influence of the newly independent African nations on pan-Africanists, they put the blame on "the race", stigmatizing what they regarded as the "fundamental" defects of black people: a lack of commitment and organization, the loss of important referants, their preference for a life in a society dominated by white people over separation and freedom in the motherland, Africa. They wrote: "If this 'land grant' was given to another race, one month after there would not be an inch of this land left."[46] This was not the case in Shashemene, at least not until the middle of the 1960s. But other people eventually arrived, in a trickle, one by one or in small family units, thus posing a crucial problem for the Pipers. Their accusation of "the race" was restaged in Shashemene. How could their dominion over the territory be reconciled with the settlement of new arrivals?

New Arrivants and Initial Tensions

Between 1964 and 1974, at least thirty-six people arrived in Shashemene. The requests for access to the land increased accordingly, putting pressure on the aged administrator. The relations between the first occupiers and the new arrivants were neither simple nor serene. On the contrary, numerous conflicts resulted from their encounter on the land in Shashemene. The Pipers rejected several people preventing them from settling; some, like Gladstone Robinson, found it impossible to live near them; and others, like Clarence Johnson, were driven out. Reverend Hillman and Desmond Christie, a Jamaican, were exceptions, and they settled in the vicinity of the Pipers. Several persons sought refuge in the town, in rented rooms, like Delval and his wife, Doughty, who were African Americans and themselves black Jews; Lynch and Tuwills, a black Muslim with his two wives and two daughters; and Dawson, another African American.[47] Although James Piper was the administrator of the land concession, it would appear that welcoming and taking charge of new arrivants was not his main concern. To the contrary, an Ethiopian neighbour recalls the strategies the Pipers used to chase people away:

> [Piper] will put [newcomer] in his home and feeds him, but he will not allow him to go out and he will also charge him a lot of money for the lodging and food, for example fifty *berr* for an egg and a hundred *berr* for a chicken, and when the man finishes all his money Piper chases the man away. . . . Nobody could share the land with him. Many people came and went back because of similar problems.[48]

The Pipers charged outrageous prices, a tactic that did not fail to rid them of undesirable arrivants, who fled once their pockets were empty. Why did the Pipers behave in such a manner? If the land grant concerned all members of the EWF, as announced internationally, how can we interpret this resistance on the part of the Pipers? After spending fifteen years alone in Shashemene, did they suffer from the final evolution of the situation? Were they unable to relinquish the solitude, which might have become a precious asset in their eyes? Why were certain newcomers accepted and not others? The criteria of origin was not, apparently, of crucial importance: like the Pipers, most of the new arrivants came from urban centres in the United States. Two came from the Caribbean, but had lived in England. The religious criteria did not seem weightier: the Pipers' neighbour, William Hillman, was a Baptist, while the other black Jews had had to seek lodgings in the town.

What is certain, though, is that they were not familiar with the practices of the Rastafari and reacted strongly to these migrants who "had deified" Haile Selassie I, especially Gladstone Robinson, who was, for his part, an American. Robinson recalls: "[Piper] didn't like Rastas, he knew I was federation, he couldn't deny me, but when he found out that I was a Rasta, I had to go."[49] Indeed, most of these newcomers were members of the EWF, and each had the right to a lot of the land and to a piece of the Ethiopian dream offered to the members of the organization. In fact, the Pipers' decision to facilitate the settlement of an arrivant or not was based on personal criteria: affinity, appreciation, level of funding.

Gladstone Robinson and the Quest for Power

The Pipers encountered a fierce opponent in the person of Gladstone Robinson, who arrived in 1964, while they were still the only occupants of the land. Robinson was young, educated, American, a member of the EWF, with close contacts among the black Jews but asserting a Rastafari identity, and he was the first to dispute the authority of the Pipers. He was accommodated for a year in the first school the Pipers had built next to their house, and which later served as lodgings for several persons. Living close to the Pipers, he had an ideal vantage point from which to observe in detail the reception of new arrivants and the tensions that accumulated. Thanks to his profession as a pharmacist, he managed to obtain a licence for the Melaku E. Beyen School from the Ministry of Education. Nevertheless, two reasons forced him to leave Shashemene: the deterioration of his relations with the Pipers and a job proposal from the Saint Gabriel Pharmacy in Addis Ababa, where he worked for two years.[50] G. Robinson was acutely critical of the efforts made to develop the two hundred hectares. To the five-year plan diffused in the press, Robinson added handwritten notes on the state of progress visible on his arrival:

1. Repatriation (settlements)	*Tiny*
2. Industries	*Nothing*
3. Farming equipment	*1 tractor, some cattle*
4. Building of a large community house	*Nothing*
5. Water supply construction	*Tiny*
6. Building of roads	*Tiny*
7. Enlargement of Dr Melaku E. Beyen School	*Partial*
9 [*sic*]. Transportation	*Nothing*
10. Building of Religious Temple of Worship	*Nothing*[51]

Probably tired of the manner in which the Pipers opposed new settlements and impatient to see real progress, G. Robinson got ready for confrontation. With the support of Princess Tenagne Worq, with whom he had lengthily discussed the obstacles in the way of development, he vied to be appointed as the administrator of the land and the legitimate representative of the EWF, persuaded that he would be able to solve the problem of tense relations among the migrants. On 15 January 1967, the officers of the EWF in New York finally accorded the responsibility he had requested, instating him as "the sole true and lawful attorney of the Ethiopian World Federation Inc. with the title of Administrator, hereby revoking any and all other powers of attorney heretofore issued by it, for it and in its name".[52] As defined by the EWF, the function of administrator proved to be almost boundless. All interests and all business regarding the land, the buildings and their occupants were the responsibility of the administrator, who was mandated to manage, evict, collect lease money or funds. The officers of the EWF insisted on a regular correspondence in the hopes of reconnecting with Ethiopia. The irregular communication between the New York headquarters and the Pipers accounted for their ignorance concerning the land that had been granted more than fifteen years earlier: "Please give us an idea of what we are supposed to own. . . . You know that we have in the past suffered from the blight of silence on the part of our representatives in Ethiopia."[53] Furthermore, George E. Bryan, then the international president of the EWF,[54] signed and addressed an official letter to the Ministry of the Pen, informing the imperial government of the change of administrator.[55] Given the correspondence between the ministries in charge of the land and of public administration, the governor of Hayqoch and Buta Jira, and the *wäräda* of

Shashemene, this change seemed perfectly accepted.[56] Through their consulate in the United States, the Ethiopian authorities checked on the legality of the EWF, which was confirmed.[57] The governor of the region wrote to inform the authorities of the *wäräda,* in view of a peaceful handover: "Mr Piper should give [power] to Mr Gladstone [Robinson] and show him all the borders of the land grant and hand it over to Gladstone. If there are tenants or farmers on the land, they are directly obliged to be ordered by newly appointed chairman."[58]

The Pipers never accepted this legal assumption of office by Robinson. Besides, for more than ten years, they had built relations with their neighbours and the Ethiopian peasants. It is possible that the Pipers incited them to give Robinson a hard time. Despite his new title as administrator, Robinson resided far from Shashemene, first in Addis Ababa, where he worked at the Saint Gabriel Pharmacy, then in Asmara, where he spent two years. In 1969, he returned to Shashemene and finally succeeded in obtaining a lot of land from the Pipers, next to Reverend Hillman's house. The steps taken by Robinson, though justified by the fact that the Pipers discouraged the settlement of new arrivants, did not allow him to exercise his authority as administrator of the land in Shashemene. In the United States, internal divisions weakened the EWF, and individuals sometimes made use of its name while refusing to follow the rulings of the New York headquarters. The example of Reverend Winston G. Evans, based in Chicago, who made fraudulent use of the name of the organization, was of this order.[59] This fragility also resulted from the general decline in EWF membership, owing to the relocalization of the pan-African interests in the direction of the newly independent nations. Thus, Robinson could rely only on theoretical support from the United States, as the US EWF had no fresh American members and no real budget. Such a "support" was hardly helpful when the new administrator came face to face with new arrivants, from Jamaica this time, with members of the EWF among them, who seemed willing to accept neither the authority of the Pipers nor his own.

The Jamaican Arrivants

The Jamaicans displeased the Pipers in every conceivable manner: they came from the ghettos of Kingston; they had not been "polished" by years of residence in the United States their language was sometimes difficult to understand and, worst of all, they were Rastafari. Yet, symbolically and culturally, black Jews and Rastafari partake of the same "Ethiopian heritage" and have the same overlooked relation with freemasonry. They honour Marcus Garvey, held in common as a prophet, and sing the same "Universal Ethiopian Anthem", composed by Rabbi Arnold Josiah Ford. But the Pipers and the Jamaicans represented two different generations of "Ethiopians", formed in different contexts. After Noel Dyer, who arrived on foot in 1965, Desmond Christie arrived from England in

1967. He settled in the Pipers' shack while constructing a brick house. Probably unable to get accustomed to cob, the Pipers began to make bricks, and, at the beginning of the 1970s, several constructions were in progress. Christie's house was a large structure, built in three parts, with a zinc roof and an awning above two of the doors.[60] The Pipers evicted Clarence Johnson, another Jamaican Rastafari, because he had married an Oromo woman and had become much too "popular". Johnson went to live on the property of David Talbot, who had five *gashas* in Ambo, north of Addis Ababa. A talented craftsman, he was employed by a technical training school in the capital.[61]

Figure 7.14. Inez Baugh in the window of her boardhouse with two of her children. Photograph: D. Bishton © DR.

When the group of "pioneers" arrived in 1968, the Baughs initially rented a room in town while waiting for the Pipers to give them a site near their house. There, they constructed a small wooden structure, meant to be temporary, comprising two rooms with a kitchen at the back. Inez and Clifton Baugh lived in one room with their children, and Vivian Thompson, with whom they had travelled, occupied the other. Baugh's brother, for his part, built himself a house on the other side of the road, at a small distance, in the direction of the town.[62]

The following year, the members of the Kingston EWF arrived: Solomon Wolfe (president of Local 43), Gerald Brissett, Zeptha Malcolm and Carmen Clarke (the only woman). They swelled the small Jamaican contingent and were not prepared to endure the rule of the Pipers. They arrived from Kingston where, for dozens of years, the Rastafari had appropriated the claim of return, formerly brandished by the Sierra Leoneans, the veterans of the colonial wars and the UNIA. They had removed themselves from the deadlock with the Jamaican government and the repression to which they were once subjected. They saw themselves as rightful members of the EWF, thanks to their control of Local 43, and were particularly concerned by the promise of the land. Above all, their Rastafari faith added a particular feeling of legitimacy to their presence: their king and their God had prepared a land for them, hence the aura of holiness that surrounded Shashemene. Robinson defined himself as a Rastafari; they had already seen him on the occasion of his visit to Jamaica in 1964, but, even then, the difference in social class had not escaped them. Wearing a suit and a tie, being of mixed race, a graduate and a pharmacist, Gladstone Robinson represented a different social class from that of the Jamaican sufferers, who had grown up in the vicinity of Rastafari from the ghetto. The four EWF members settled in turn in the Pipers' first school, Carmen Clarke in a room by herself, and the men in the other. But they were unable to accept the tension on the land and the struggles between the Pipers and G. Robinson over the administration of the EWF. They took several steps in view of a more equitable distribution of the land and the power associated with it.

The Division into Lots in July 1970

The merging of two dynamics helped to improve the situation on the land in Shashemene: the arrival of Jamaican politicians on the Ethiopian scene and the mobilization of the Jamaican Rastafari in Shashemene. The Jamaican prime minister, Hugh Shearer (Jamaica Labour Party), made a stopover in Ethiopia in September 1969, in the course of an African tour, which took him to Kenya, Zambia, Uganda and Liberia. The object of this visit was to develop contacts with the imperial government, to discuss the possibility of opening a Jamaican embassy in Ethiopia and to ensure that Jamaicans could settle there, even if this required the search for a place to accommodate them, with the aid of the emperor. In fact, the prime minister sought to understand "why the Rastafarian sect . . . is apparently slow to seize what they regarded, literally, as a heaven-sent opportunity to migrate".[63] Shearer visited the settlement in Shashemene and reported that the complaints concerned the access to and enjoyment of the land as well as conflicts with the administrator, James Piper.[64] A form of agreement with Haile Selassie I was concluded: "[Shearer] said the Emperor agreed that the two governments should work out plans to move the Rastafarians to new land and to settle them in satisfactorily before any move is made to expand the colony."[65]

The two governments agreed on a cooperation which would allow a new departure by moving Rastafari to another land concession, while linking their settlement there to the reception of other arrivants. This approach was regarded as the best way of responding to the situation of conflict in Shashemene, but the location to which the settlement was to be displaced was left unspecified. Shearer attempted to reprimand the returnees by pointing out the importance, as Jamaicans abroad, of being good citizens who helped the local community. He issued a warning: even if boundless land were offered, Jamaicans would not have the right to "flock here". On the contrary, they should be ready to adapt "into the ways and means, the life and standards, the laws, rules and regulations of the society".[66] This turn of phrase revealed a fear which haunted the

Figure 7.15. Jamaican politicians visit Shashemene, Clifton Baugh on the left, Douglas Manley and his brother, Michael Manley, leader of the opposition People's National Party. Standing, with a beret, Gladstone Robinson, Shashemene, 1969. Archives G. Robinson © DR.

Jamaican government: the eventuality of facing an uncontrollable movement of poor, black masses. Shearer was soon followed by Michael Manley, the leader of the Jamaican opposition (the People's National Party), on a semi-official visit. Manley visited Shashemene and met with the representatives of a few diplomatic missions, the secretary general of the Organization of African Unity and trade union representatives.[67]

As the two parties vied for political influence in Jamaica, playing on popular cultural references, their almost simultaneous visit to Ethiopia emphasized the interest they accorded, at last, to the settlement of the Rastafari in Ethiopia, given the political stake that they represented in Jamaica. Their presence also announced a paradox: whereas Rastafari defined themselves as the true Ethiopians, once settled in Ethiopia, they were immediately identified as Jamaicans, and thus dependent on their government and the negotiations it had initiated.

In January 1970, Aston Foreman, the Jamaican high commissioner in London, also visited Ethiopia to pursue discussions with the imperial government concerning the conditions of resettlement of the Jamaicans living on the territory. While no specific decisions were relayed by the press, Aston Foreman nevertheless met the Ethiopian ministers of foreign affairs, of the interior and of agriculture.[68] On 1 November 1970, he became the first ambassador to represent Jamaica in an African nation, Ethiopia, while Jamaica awaited accreditation from other countries on the continent. The opening of a Jamaican embassy in

Ethiopia was a concrete step by the government of that island state in view of initiating relations with the Organization of African Unity, in the framework of a general broadening of its diplomatic relations. The presence of Rastafari in Ethiopia played a driving role in the development of these diplomatic relations. When Aston Foreman presented his letters of accreditation to the emperor on 23 December 1970,[69] a capital change had already occurred on the land in Shashemene: it had been divided up between twelve persons.

For the Rastafari who arrived in Shashemene, there was no question of moving anywhere else. They did not want to be regarded as a "sect", to quote Hugh Shearer, an odd cult at the beck and call of the Jamaican political imperatives. They wanted to be seen as worthy "Ethiopian" heirs who had defended the sovereignty of Ethiopia, who were members of the EWF, created in 1937, at the order of Haile Selassie I. Consequently, for them, their desire to settle in Shashemene was legitimate. Together with Solomon Wolfe, the president of EWF Local 43, the settlers from Kingston made various requests to the emperor in an attempt to avoid the measures already taken by the Pipers. Assembled under the name "Pioneers Settlers Corps", their numbers did not meet the legal requirements for the constitution of an EWF local, so they wrote a letter and a petition to the emperor and signed them as "the Rastafarian brethren in Shashemene".[70] These were handed over to the emperor during his visit to the community in Shashemene, probably in the early part of 1970. This visit is remembered in graphic and emotional terms. A few members of the community had already seen him in 1966 in Kingston, but this was their first meeting, face to face, with the King of the Kings. Baugh's son remembers the story, one he must have heard hundreds of times, of the dialogue between Haile Selassie I and the Rastafari:

> Haile Selassie I asked Mister Piper: "Where are the people?" And then my mum was closer to the car, she said, "We are the people, Your Majesty.' He looked up and said, "Are you from Jamaica?" "Yes, Your Imperial Majesty, we are from Jamaica, and we came home to stay." He said, "You want to stay here in Ethiopia?", she said, "Yes Your Imperial Majesty, we want to stay." And then he looked around at Mister Piper and said three times "Why not? Let them stay, let them stay, let them stay," that's what [was] His Majesty word to Mister Piper. That's when they heard that, they felt secure that they really were accepted in their home, that's when they settled. That was a strong motivation.[71]

To feel that the emperor approved their request and to hear him order James Piper to let them settle must have been a great relief and a great source of pride for the Jamaicans. Before taking leave, the emperor shook hands with them, a memory which still strikes them as incredible. Carmen Clarke was holding Baugh's daughter in her arms; she recalls her emotion: "The hand was soft, I've never seen in me life, I never feel hands like those, and believe you me, . . . I was transformed that day inside so, if I come back to Ethiopia and go on with corrupted life then I know what my hand will be because after having that experience, that day, I know who I am dealing with, you know what I mean."[72] What Clarke meant was that to touch the hand of the Living God, Haile Selassie I, as she had done, was to be blessed, through direct physical contact with the man who incarnated the myth and who had embodied Rastafari claims and identity. In fact, it is on this occasion that the letter and the petition were given to him: "The letter was asking him to enable us to get the land, to get land sekklement [settlement], land sekklement, that's what was in the letter."[73] A direct result of this meeting, the division of the land into lots was going to change the destiny of the settlement and of its residents.

Figure 7.16. Haile Selassie I dressed in a suit, as when he met the pioneers in Shashemene, ca. 1960 © DR.

Following the agreement of the imperial government and under the supervision of *S'ähafé Tezaz* Teferi Worq, a minister in the court, two people came to measure and divide the land, *Ato* Aneyo Mulate and *Ato* Belachew Goshame. On 7 *hamlé* 1962 *a.m.* (14 July 1970), twelve people received ten hectares each, that is, three *gashas* out of the five granted to the EWF. James Piper refused to attend, complaining that they had destroyed his farm. The governor of the *awrajja*, *Däjazmač* Shousa Boahe, authorized him to make his harvest before moving back to the two *gashas* granted to him.[74] Up until the day of division, two persons were absent: Gladstone Robinson was in Addis Ababa, but informed in time, he arrived the second day to sign the documents; Noel Dyer, who worked in Sidamo, was able, in absentia, to receive his share. The twelve people involved were thus the two Americans, Gladstone Robinson and William Hillman, and the ten Jamaicans: Gerald Brissett, Solomon Wolfe, Desmond Christie, Noel Dyer, Zeptha Malcolm, Uriah Brown, Carmen Clarke, Clifton Baugh, Vincent Beckford and Landford Baugh. Three of them were not members of the EWF, the Baughs and Noel Dyer. Vivian Thompson, fed up with the tensions with the Pipers, refused the land. Stones were used to mark the boundaries; an official document was signed by the governor of the *awrajja*, *Däjazmač* Shousa Boahe, and a copy presented to each grantee. The parties concerned carefully preserved this document bearing the written proof that five *gashas* had, in fact, been given to the EWF and had been divided among them. Nevertheless, Robinson pointed out the potential distance between the

Figure 7.17. Gerald Brissett with his original document of division of the land between twelve persons dated 14 July 1970, Kingston, 2002. Photograph: G. Bonacci © DR.

papers and the land: "The thing is that they never gave us maps, they should have given us maps . . . but at that time we don't know the land, the runnings, we just accept everything and we never know what a priceless gift we were given."[75] Robinson spoke in these terms thirty years later, when he had finally come to understand the symbolic and monetary importance of the land. As we will see, many upheavals modified the status of the land and changed the life of the residents. The lack of cartographic evidence made it extremely difficult to document and justify subsequent claims. It is nevertheless possible to propose a map of this division, by combining the recollections of the older residents of Shashemene, who were present at the time of the division.

The members of EWF Local 43 played a decisive role in this division, from which they derived great prestige. Gerald Brissett reported with a big smile: "Melaku [Beyen] did everything and so established a charter [of EWF] in New York and a likkle [little] local come now [Local 43], and get the land through the same establishment. Nobody else would have done it. Only we."[76] The pride of the Jamaican Rastafari, members of Local 43, was understandable. They, the poor and often illiterate black people from Kingston's ghettos, the Rastafari, had demonstrated they could organize themselves. Often accused of aggravated utopia, they showed they had the will to fulfil their back-to-Africa claim. By integrating with the EWF, they had succeeded in settling in Shashemene. What our interlocutor omitted to say, however, is that this division of the land among twelve individuals definitively

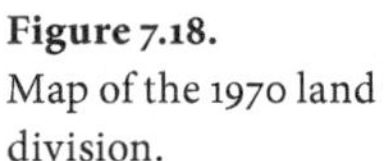

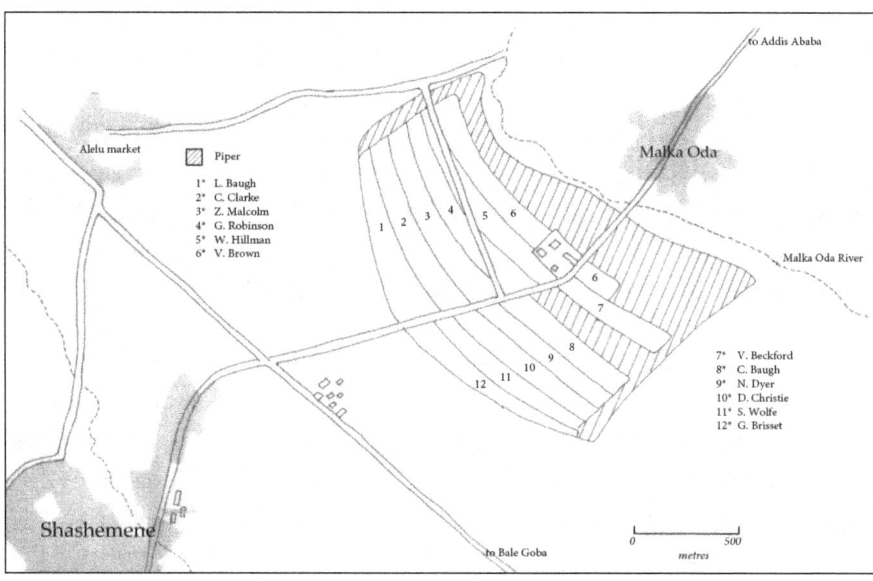

Figure 7.18. Map of the 1970 land division.

annulled the hopes of collective ownership and sharing implicit in the terms of operation of the EWF. But these individual attributions did not prevent the residents from helping one another and working together when necessary.

The Occupation of the Land

Once the land was divided, a feeling of power traversed the small community that had benefited from the largesse of Haile Selassie I. To have the right to the land, to see the boundaries of this property concretely outlined, was the fulfilment of a long-standing dream. David Baugh was not yet born at the time, but he remembers the account of his parents:

> [The land was] from the road back to the sycamore tree behind. The land we had it takes you at least fifteen minutes to walk from end to the other end. . . . It was like a whole empire. Seeing that happened it really stirred up the hearts of the people around, they were amazed, they didn't expect people to possess that amount of land. It really caused a lot of uprising among the people. Even Mister Piper was crazy over the happenings. Because the land is no more under his control, everybody got its own piece so the original people that were there got their land.[77]

"A whole empire" – these are touching words when pronounced by individuals who, formerly, were merely the subjects of an empire, the vast British Empire. As colonial subjects and landless subalterns, they found themselves in charge of an empire of their own in Ethiopia, comprising hectares of fertile lands, by the side of a river, crossed by a road. They were far from the marginalization experienced in the urban ghettos from which they came, but this access to the land, directly facilitated by Haile Selassie I, aroused great jealousies, especially

Figure 7.19. One of Carmen Clarke's harvests, Shashemene, ca. 1970–73. Archives C. Clarke, Shashemene © DR.

in the Pipers who, while they had not lost everything, had suffered a serious affront to their power and authority. The Ethiopian peasants were also jealous of these newcomers who immediately received more wealth than they had ever had throughout their life of labour.

Previously, the lands had been only partially cultivated by the Pipers. It was therefore necessary to cut down trees and to push back the forest in order to prepare the lands for more intensive agriculture. While the lands were being prepared, a few arrivants set about planting their gardens, meant to provide for their personal subsistence. The Jamaicans had the power because they had the land: "We had the land, the land was the big thing."[78] Many peasants in the vicinity did not have land, thus tenant farming on larger surfaces remained the common mode of working the land. The seeds were provided by the Ethiopians, the cost of the manure bought from the government was divided, but the physical labour was provided by the Ethiopians alone. Day labourers were sometimes engaged. The Jamaicans, who considered their "fixed" wages to be extremely low, immediately offered to double it, bringing it to one *berr*. Harvests were divided into two and shared between the Ethiopian farmer and the Jamaican owner, allowing the latter to begin construction. Thanks to his contacts in England, Desmond Christie had succeeded in gathering sufficient funds to buy a tractor.[79] He drove it with Gerald Brissett, and the two were thereby able to collect payment from other properties and to cultivate their own without the help of the Ethiopians. Mechanized farming was initiated. Government offices rented to the property owners machines such as a grader, a reaping-machine and a pulverizer. Moreover, following the elections which brought Michael Manley (People's National Party) to power in Jamaica in February 1972, the multiple requests of the community were heard and funding was offered in support.[80] This allowed the cultivation of a greater quantity of soya, peas, beans and corn, resulting in a decisive contribution to Ethiopian agricultural production.[81] In the words of David Baugh: "They started farming, it was going on and good. We had vegetables, carrots, everything. Life start looking up."[82] The living conditions improved, but those able to find paid employment did not hesitate. Hillman and Beckford were employed by the Imperial Road Authority, established in 1951. Its regional branch was situated in the centre of the granted land since 1952 and dealt with the development of road infrastructure (Benti Getahun 1988, 46). Noel Dyer, who was a painter and a mason, travelled the region, working for various local societies and non-governmental organizations. Besides his work with the tractor, Brissett worked for a while in a bakery opened in downtown Shashemene by a Jamaican from England, Alston Sinclair.[83]

The Pipers had several houses. William Hillman's had been finished for a long time, Desmond Christie's was already in construction, and there were also a few shacks hastily built by the Jamaicans. Strung out along the road, with a few a bit further inland, they spoke eloquently to the challenges of space

Figure 7.20. Ten years of Jamaican independence celebrated in Shashemene, 1972. In front of St Michael Church, from left to right: Israel Brown, Malvease Hillman, Carmen Clarke, Desmond Christie, Uriah Brown, Mr Symes for the Jamaican embassy, Eva Christie, *Abba* Meshesha, Gerald Brissett, Reverend William Hillman, ?, Landford Baugh, Clifton Baugh and in front of him his daughter Jasmine or his niece Anne Marie, Zeptha Malcolm, Vincent Beckford, an Ethiopian driver from the embassy. Archives, C. Clarke, Shashemene © DR.

facing the community, despite uncertainty regarding the exact site of some of the houses (including those of A. Sinclair and Z. Malcolm). In fact, in the centre, there were the Pipers and their four houses, with Christie's building beside them. On the other side of the road was the house of Hillman, to which the reverend had added a small cob church by the roadside. Beside that, slightly off-centre, was the house of Robinson, to which he had added an annex. As a wage earner, he had been able to invest on his lot of land: "I put so much money in that compound, the water system, new buildings, I have a little house that is empty now, and the big house my bedroom is there and another room too."[84] Between the Piper's land and the river, Brown and Beckford alone used cob for their houses facing the buildings of Imperial Road Authority. Dyer settled a good distance from the centre, probably because of his misunderstanding with the Pipers. Between the Pipers and Dyer, the Baughs built their small wooden house. Further to the west, the Jamaican members of the EWF settled next to one another; the houses of Gerald Brissett, Carmen Clarke and Solomon Wolfe faced each other on either side of the road. The houses were built little by little, and new arrivants were placed there, usually while waiting for access to their own lot or for the money to build. A sign of the confidence which reigned among the Jamaican arrivants in 1968 and 1969 was the personal arrangements that allowed them to settle in as best as they could. Carmen Clarke remembers:

> So when he [Gerald Brissett] made up his house there [on his land], he asked me seen that he wanted to do, that was on the main road we have, back, which is a back road now, this is were the road is, he says he want to build up a business place 'cause that was a frontage. So we agreed, he got that house spot from me and he gave me back the amount of land over by his side to do my farming over too, the same amount of the land that he took for his house spot, he gave me back so I farm over there too.[85]

A lot along the road was a better commercial space than a site further back, in the middle of the fields, but no land was "lost", as the roadside location was exchanged for arable land. While memory remains the primary means of reconstructing these settlements, the oral and friendly nature of these arrangements is sometimes a challenge to clear recollection.

Once survival was ensured thanks to the construction of houses, the produce from the gardens and the first harvests, development became the main concern of the residents. They had understood that Shashemene was destined to become one of the important cities of the country, and they wanted to take part in its growth. To develop their lands, they needed money, and, for this reason, they formed the SLGDRC, of which Carmen Clarke was the secretary. We saw in a previous part how, during a visit to Jamaica in 1972, Solomon Wolfe had unsuccessfully attempted to establish the SLGDRC there.[86] The unrealistic – though comprehensible – ambitions of the committee had been set out in a letter and a petition addressed to Haile Selassie I, which probably never arrived at its destination. The Jamaican administration of this committee did not grow, but

Figure 7.21. The pioneers. From left to right: Gerald Brissett, Gladstone Robinson, Uriah Brown, Desmond Christie, Eric Smith, Reverend William Hillman, Millward Brown, Noel Dyer, Shashemene, ca. 1973–1974. *Archives C. Clarke, Shashemene* © DR.

Solomon Wolfe had returned to Ethiopia in 1973 with another group of persons. They joined the first members of Local 15 of the EWF, who had arrived before their organization became known as the Twelve Tribes of Israel. "Repatriating" to Ethiopia less than one year before the revolution, which would sweep away the empire in its wake, how did they manage to settle in Shashemene?

A Brief Calm before the Storm

At least ten people, including two children, arrived from Kingston between 1972 and 1973, but, contrary to their expectations, they found themselves in an uncomfortable position in Shashemene. They were without resources for the most part, and, as no support mechanism had been put in place, they had no easy access to land. They discussed this with the residents, on whose advice they addressed a letter and a petition to Haile Selassie I, signed by six persons, all members of the EWF. One of them, Eric Smith, was the first member of Local 15 to arrive to Ethiopia. In Addis Ababa, he ran out in front of the emperor's car to give these letters to him. General Assefa took the letters and invited the petitioners to the palace. The minister of the court who had ordered the 1970 division, *S'ähafé Tezaz* Teferi Worq, received them and directed them towards the Ministry of Land Reform.[87] On 17 June 1974 (10 *säné* 1966 *a.m.)*, the ministry asked the land administration in Choa to grant five hectares of land to each of the six petitioners, to be subtracted from the two *gashas* remaining in the possession of the Pipers. The letter insisted on the fact that the land was to be registered in the name of the EWF and that the taxes were to be received in accordance with the law, also from the EWF.[88]

On 8 July 1974 (1 *hamlé* 1966 *a.m.*), six parcels of five hectares each were allotted. They were rectangular in shape and the boundaries were marked by stones.[89] But, this time, the petitioners were made to finance the travel expenses of the government employees sent to record the new lots. The recipients were Ewart Tulloch, who was studying in Addis Ababa; Harold Reid and his two children; Clarence Johnson, who had returned from his stay at David Talbot's in Ambo and who was still working in Addis Ababa; a woman, Mother Swearine Thompson, who was not a Rastafari but a member of the Church of God; and Eric Smith and Millward Brown, the first members of Local 15 of the EWF.

On the Awasho side, three lots were staked out along the road to the river and one on the Alelu side followed the river, whereas the two others were situated to the rear of the buildings of Imperial Road Authority.[90] In conditions that remain unclear, another Jamaican newly arrived from England, Alston Sinclair, settled on ten hectares, probably negotiated directly with the Pipers.[91] After the 1970 division, the two *gashas* that had remained in James and Helen Piper's possession covered eighty hectares. They had lost thirty hectares in the last official attribution and had relinquished ten more for practical reasons.

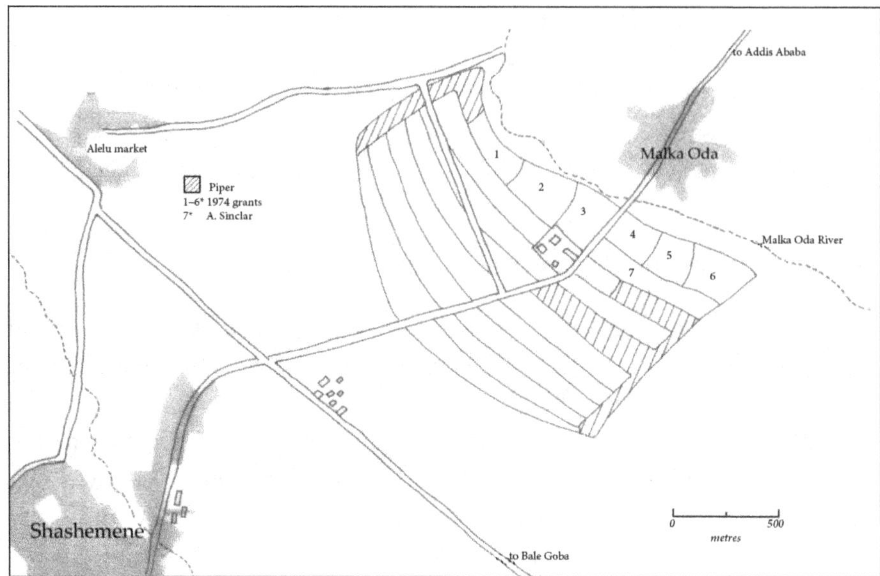

Figure 7.22.
Map of the 1974 land attribution.

About twenty years after their arrival, the Pipers had seen Jamaicans arrive, their power decrease and their land divided. On the eve of the revolution, they had only forty hectares left, a fifth of the original area.

To the petition of 1974, Millward Brown and Eric Smith added a request: they asked the emperor for a job. They did not see this as inconsistent with a request for land. A job would take care of immediate necessities, and there was urgent need for cash. They were both quickly employed at the school of arts and craft in Addis Ababa. The construction of a house required funds, and Smith regretted that they did not receive more direct aid from Local 15, which became, in 1973, the Twelve Tribes of Israel. As he recalls:

> It was a sudden calling so I didn't come [prepared financially]. It was said the mansions were prepared for us; we have to start a new life over in Ethiopia. . . . Although they were a few Rastaman, you were still alone, understand? You had to fight your way to make a start. I didn't get a chance to build on my portion. Being young at that time, I had more expected from the organization, 'cause I didn't consider that land as my personal although we received it individually.[92]

He blamed the financial problems encountered in Ethiopia on a lack of preparation. His words hint at the tension between the collective project, which had allowed his departure, and the individual dynamics that took over upon arrival. The lack of money was not, in fact, the only obstacle to construction and settlement. The arrivants also came up against the resistance of the Oromo peasants. The six lots of five hectares each were occupied by the Ethiopians who cultivated them, probably as tenant farmers of the Pipers. None of them wanted to run the risk of losing the harvest by giving up a piece of land, so they remained on the spot. In support of the Ethiopians, the *wäräda* told the recipients to wait six months before settling, until after the harvest. But the year 1974 was marked by numerous events: agitation, popular uprisings and strikes, all tending towards a transformation of the society. The Oromo peasants did not hesitate for long; they soon launched a new cycle of farming, preventing the disinherited Jamaicans from settling on the six lots of land.[93] The empire fell on 12 September 1974, and the aftermath of the Ethiopian revolution transformed the life of the community, the status of the peasants and the exploitation of agricultural land. These events led to an appreciable decline in arrivals and in the development of the land in Shashemene offered to the "black people of the world".

IT WAS IN THE SOUTH OF THE COUNTRY that land was earmarked for allocation to the partisans of the Ethiopian crown originating in the black world. Characteristic of the expansionist policy of the Ethiopian government, the localization of this gift placed the returnees, *de facto*, in an unequal social relationship with their neighbours. The latter regarded them as *färänj* or *balabbat*. Their itineraries, which took them from the status of marginalized communities in the United States and Jamaica to that of landowners in Ethiopia, represented an indisputable upward social mobility. For this reason, the power over the land was difficult to share. The severe tensions that developed between the transatlantic migrants led, due to the steps taken by the Jamaican members of Local 43 of the EWF, to a division of the land among twelve persons in 1970. This division, encouraged by the need for the individualization of the land ownership, may be seen as the failure of a collective project. The new arrivants set themselves to work, farming and building houses. Impecunious for the most part, they benefited more from the agreement between the Ethiopian and the Jamaican governments than from financial mobilization in the diaspora. Some were forced to seek salaried employment from the Ethiopian government. While their situation interested the emperor, who visited them on several occasions, the local relations were distended and difficult, notwithstanding spatial proximity. The arrival of the first Jamaicans in Shashemene marked the beginning of the reappropriation of the land by the Rastafari. Members of the EWF and of the Twelve Tribes of Israel, they continued to arrive despite the upheavals announced by the Ethiopian revolution of 1974.

CHAPTER 8

REVOLUTION AND REFORMS IN SHASHEMENE

HOW DID THE SMALL REPATRIATED COMMUNITY EXPERIENCE THE Ethiopian revolution? How did the Rastafari adapt to an Ethiopia without Haile Selassie I? With the change of regime, political contingencies impacted the process of settlement of the Caribbean migrants, transforming their land and their social space, constraining some to departure and the others to survival. Thanks to interviews, which fill the archival void on this period, this chapter will consider the ways in which their land, status, social position, faith and identity were completely reconfigured and diminished. While the Rastafari movement was spreading far beyond the confines of Jamaica, influencing youths of all colours and diffusing a pan-African message, the presence of the small group in Ethiopia became extremely problematic, leading to a period of great paradoxes and contradictions.

The Ethiopian Revolution

A great deal has been written about the Ethiopian revolution, giving rise to an impressive historiographical production. Several works examine the social structure of Ethiopia on the eve of the revolution, offering in-depth analyses of the social inequalities and the economic issues which marked the beginning of the 1970s (Markakis 1975; Cohen and Weintraub 1975). The curtain of the year 1974 rose on the horrific images of the famine in the Wollo region. These images, which travelled the world, currently remain hard to bear and to assume. That year also began with the image of a country devastated by the economic crisis due to the closure of the Suez Canal, the rise in the price of oil and the inflation of consumer goods and food. By mid-February, taxi drivers and teachers went on strike, while students took to the streets. The latter formed a radical intelligentsia, many of whom had studied abroad and had espoused Marxism. Their call for a reduction of taxes on gasoline, for better wages and for profound political reforms influenced large sectors of the society, including workers, civil servants, merchants, Muslims and even a part of the Ethiopian clergy. Soldiers quickly joined their ranks. The first mutinies broke out in spring 1974 and led to the creation of the *derg*, the coordination committee of the armed forces (Markakis 1979). The first programme of the *derg*, in July 1974, was flagged by a slogan, *Itiop'ya teqdem*, Ethiopia first. It did not announce the revolution but launched, in thirteen points, a "movement" aimed at bringing about "sustainable change" (Lefort 1981, 97). In an attempt to respond to the call for reforms, the emperor revoked several ministers, and Mikael Imru, of aristocratic background, replaced the recently designated prime minister, Endelkachew Makonnen. The propaganda campaign against Haile Selassie I was in full swing when, on 12 September 1974, he was overthrown by the army and imprisoned alongside the members of his family. Led by General Aman Andom, the *derg* changed its name, became the Provisional Military Administrative Council and took over the reins of the state.[1] Although a constitutional monarchy was initially considered by the military in their dialogue with the ministers of the imperial government, upon the overthrow of the emperor, radical and conservative factions clashed within the council. The radical faction, in which Major Mengistu Haile Mariam had already emerged as a spearhead, carried the day. On 22 November, General Aman Andom was assassinated, and fifty-nine officials, generals, officers, aristocrats and royal family members were condemned and executed (Marcus 1994, 181–201). Up to that point, the military takeover had occurred without bloodshed, but the massacre of November 1974 shocked the country and the world. What had been, in the words of the historian Harold Marcus, "a standard African revolutionary process, replacing one elite with another" (Marcus 1994, 190), finally established in Ethiopia a "garrison socialism" (Markakis 1979). The military elite had surpassed the claims of the street. A socialist ideology was promoted and a centralized bureaucratic administration imposed, giving rise to a "garrison state", supported by other socialist states and by the Soviet Union.

At the end of the 1970s appeared the first books and papers analysing the upheavals which had provoked the fall of the empire and the introduction of a military regime (Ottaway 1978; Markakis 1979). In the 1980s, the studies by Fred Halliday and Maxine Molyneux (1981) and by René Lefort (1981) applied to the Ethiopian revolution a Marxist analysis of the revolutionary processes. Christopher Clapham criticized this approach by stressing the importance of taking the Ethiopian historical context into account. Since a revolution never completely erases the past, his aim was to study the transformations of the Ethiopian state through the prism of its continuities (Clapham 1988). Other approaches of the Ethiopian revolution also emerged, focusing on social change based on circumscribed objects. For example, the relations between the Ethiopian Orthodox Church and the state were studied (Haile Mariam Larebo 1986; Bonacci 2000), and John Cohen and Peter Koehn published a work of reference on the transformations of the provincial and municipal administration in Ethiopia (1980). Comparative approaches, like Edmond Keller's (1987), helped to reposition Ethiopian events within the broader problematics of African Marxist regimes.

The decade of the 1990s, opening with the fall of the *derg* in 1991, made room for a more distanced perspective, and a few general works quickly became indispensable, like Harold Marcus's *History of Ethiopia* (1994), which includes the revolutionary period, or more targeted works, such as Kiflu Tadesse's remarkable books (1993, 1998) retracing the fortunes of a generation engulfed in the political and social mutation of Ethiopia. Ethnography opened a decisive pathway into the historiography of the revolution, thanks to Donald Donham and his *Marxist Modern: An Ethnographic History of the Ethiopian Revolution* (1999). Combining concepts derived from various disciplines surfaced as a fruitful strategy, as demonstrated by the collective work published by James, Donham, Kurimoto and Triulzi, *Remapping Ethiopia: Socialism and After* (2002). Using the notions of space and cartography, the typology between the centre and peripheries proposed in *Southern Marches of the Ethiopian Empire* (Donham and James 2002) was re-actualized to analyse its considerably intensified instrumentalization by revolutionary Ethiopia, through the military government's project of "encadrement" – that is, through its control of the national space. The great land reform of 1975 was a watershed moment of the transformation of the rural and urban administrative space in Ethiopia. In view of a better understanding of the social and political stakes involved, I will focus briefly on its local consequences in Shashemene.

A Great Upheaval on the Land

Following the massacre of November 1974, the *derg* stood in need of popular success in order to rally civilian support and to mobilize manpower and materials. Mengistu Haile Mariam and the most radical members of the Provisional Military Administrative Council's left wing conceived of a radical land reform that meant buying the favour of the populations of the Ethiopian south, in particular the Oromos, whose lands had been expropriated under the reigns of Menelik II and Haile Selassie I. Through proclamation number 31 of 4 March 1975, all of the rural land in Ethiopia was nationalized and became the collective property of Ethiopians. The Soviet Union advised against this reform, while the Yugoslav and Chinese embassies recommended moderation, to prevent interference with production and conflicts among the peasants (Ottaway 1978, 67). It was nonetheless applied and, "fulfilling the revolution's leading motto, Land to the tiller, would destroy the patron and client and sharecropping political economy prevailing in southern Ethiopia since the 1920s and stop the development of capitalistic agriculture " (Marcus 1994, 191). The impact of the land reform on the rural populations did not assume the same form in the north and the south of the country. In the north, the reform affected the daily life of the peasants, whereas, in the south, the impetus provided by the land reform led, according to certain observers, to an agrarian revolution. Until 1976, violent confrontations between peasants, farm owners and local elites were frequent in Keffa, Sidamo and Arsi (Kiflu Tadesse 1998, 1–9).

In the wake of the reform, peasant associations were created throughout the country. They were simultaneously new organizations of the masses and organs of the government. Each peasant association was declared responsible for eight hundred hectares of land, and the farmers who farmed them came together in general assemblies and elected their representatives. They had authority over matters relating to security and economic life and were responsible for the equitable redistribution of the rural land under their jurisdiction (Marcus 1994, 192). Hence, in September 1977, 24,700 peasant associations existed, assembling almost seven million persons (Cohen and Koehn 1980, 286). Proclamation number 31 established the peasant associations without defining the bounds of their authority or the nature of their relationship to the provincial administration. These issues were clarified later. The enthusiasm with which the Ethiopians integrated the peasant associations was remarkable. It owed much to the fact that this was their first access to the exercise of local power, and a first in the social history of Ethiopia itself (Cohen and Koehn 1980, 280–81).

In Shashemene, in the vicinity of the land granted "to the black people of the world", the Oromo farmers did not wait for the great land reform to radically redefine their relations with the Caribbeans who held sway over five *gashas*. In several areas of the south, the echoes of the events of summer 1974 in Addis Ababa sufficed to provoke the eviction of owners and the destruction of tractors and machines (Lefort 1981, 154). The former relations between the Oromo peasants and the Caribbeans were often limited to questions concerning tenant farming and the payment of daily wages. As it was, they were marked by spatial proximity and a vast social gap, and the local situation rapidly deteriorated. Clifton Baugh reported that, shortly after the overthrow of the emperor, on 12 September 1974, he heard the sound of horns blowing to announce an assembly. Standing on his doorstep, he saw that "they were tons of people, thousands on horse with stone and spears and stick and they took control of the land".[2] The Caribbeans felt threatened by this invasion of their land. For the Oromos, the overthrow of the emperor meant the end of all outside prerogative on the land, of which they were constantly deprived since the reign of Menelik. To a certain extent, the land nationalization of March 1975 validated the spontaneous move of the Ethiopians to reappropriate the land. Without waiting for the land to be officially redistributed by the peasant associations, the farmers took possession of the areas they cultivated and of the product of their work. According to an official of one of these peasant associations in the vicinity of Shashemene: "The day the proclamation 'Land to the tiller' was promulgated, the farmers took all the land they worked on, only they paid the taxes imposed on it and all the produce they took to themselves."[3]

The great land reform was a blow to the small American and Caribbean community that had settled in Shashemene. The reversal of the social situation was a bitter pill to swallow for the foreign residents, stripped of the land to which they had been invited. They were severely traumatized by the overthrow of the emperor and saw their dreams crumbling at their feet. Their confrontation with the peasants was open and direct and has left a bitter memory: "Sometimes I [used to] cook and I give them [the Ethiopians] and believe you me they was like a *jebb* [hyena], after the coup they look at me and say '*anshi, bäfit, märét, yät allä märét ahun? Yät allä?*' I used to tell them before 'this is my land' and after they say 'where is my land?' They are ungrateful people these black people dem, very much ungrateful!"[4]

The fact that they had given food to the peasants, the sign of a dominant position, had little weight in the new balance of power. The Rastafari defended their land as best as they could, but they lost most of it and their harvests as well. Their property shrank to the buildings and the land that they were able to border and protect. The tractor and their harvests – quite moderate that year, since the peas had been attacked by worms – were nationalized along with the rest, thus hampering, as Harold Marcus has underlined, the mechanized agriculture which had developed. The land at the disposal of members of the EWF dwindled dramatically, all the more so as lots had been sold or yielded shortly before the proclamation. James Piper had sold part of his land to a high-ranking official, and Alston Sinclair, hard-pressed for cash, had sold part of his concession to Ethiopians.[5] Many houses were also nationalized. This was the case of all the property held by the Pipers, with the exception of their house, which was later occupied by Ethiopians, and of the first school, in which other arrivants were accommodated. The Melaku E. Beyen School became national property, as well as the structures surrounding it, including the private clinic, the house and the small church of William Hillman. A certain sum was offered to Hillman in compensation, of which he gave part to Eric Smith so that the latter would give up his house for him, causing the Twelve Tribes of Israel to lose a parcel of land.[6]

The reconfigurations induced by the 1975 reform did lead to social and land changes, and also affected relations with the administration. The Ministry of the Pen no longer existed. The administration of the Hayqoch and Buta Jira *awrajja*, to which the small community formerly had recourse, was no longer there; it was replaced by the Ministry of Foreign Affairs of the provisional military government, the *derg*, which forwarded decisions concerning the settlement of the land directly to the Jamaican embassy, worried about the status of its nationals. A letter dated April 1975 indicated the decision of the *derg* to "grant use right over farm lands not exceeding ten hectares to every

Figure 8.1. William Hillman was born in Georgia, in the United States, and heard of the donation of land in Ethiopia at a meeting organized by Malcolm X. In 1981, he had already spent fifteen years in Ethiopia, the last fourteen of which were spent working for the Road Authority. His wife is Ethiopian, and, as a Baptist pastor, he was in charge of a small church until the authorities forced him to close it after the revolution. The church is now used as a school. Shashemene, Ethiopia, January 1981. Photograph: Derek Bishton © DR.

Jamaican family who has previously been allotted land in Shashemene".[7] Ten hectares was the area officially allocated to each peasant family (Marcus 1994, 192). This was therefore a relatively lenient dispatch, since, in spite of two early departures, eighteen families were still present: twelve of whom had benefited from the 1970 division and six of whom had received land in 1974, but had been unable to settle on it. In theory, the latter were to receive the double of the 1970 allocation, which rose from five to ten hectares. Usufruct of parcels of over ten hectares thus comprised a total area of 180 hectares, almost five *gashas*, the area of the first grant, prior to reduction. The only proviso on the gesture of the new government was the decision that "no land will be made available to new settlers until the Provisional Military Government is satisfied that the present project has been fully and effectively developed".[8] This decree was of crucial importance. It implied that all future installation would depend on the way in which the land was occupied, managed and developed. But the new Ethiopian government went back on its decision. In a letter dated 3 October 1975, the Ministry of Foreign Affairs acknowledged receipt of a verbal note dated 22 May from the Jamaican embassy, regarding complaints lodged by Jamaicans.[9] These complaints were due to the escalation of tension between the settlers' community and the peasants. The government had decided to maintain the right of use of the land to the persons who had settled there, but the peasants, farmers,

Figure 8.2. The "Jamaican neighbourhood" in 1976. Archives C. Clarke, Shashemene © DR.

employees and neighbours had decided otherwise. The compromise decided by the ministry was to limit to one *gasha*, or forty hectares, the land allocated to all the participants, locals and migrants, in this quarrel. Forty hectares meant 2.2 hectares per person – that is, an area equivalent to the allocation ultimately received by the Ethiopians following the rural land reform.[10] But this attribution took neither departures nor arrivals into account.

Departures and Arrivals

After some twenty years spent on the land, the Pipers left for the United States. They invited Berba Tulu, whom they had raised, to follow them, but as she was pregnant with her second child, she preferred to stay with her family.[11] The exact date of the Pipers' departure remains uncertain: Berhanou Teffera recalls that they left before the proclamation of the land reform,[12] which seems coherent with their last land transaction; but, for *Abba* Médina: "When the declaration 'Land to the tiller' came out, all *balabbat* had to leave their possessions and Piper too said the land belongs to the people, the farmers. He said he would leave and that he doesn't want the land and he left."[13] Shortly before or after March 1975, the Pipers left. They were the first to make the trip back to the Americas, but almost all those who had settled on the land eventually left, because "they were afraid cause people were being killed even by local people, uprising, stoning, a lot of people was afraid for their life".[14]

Physically threatened, disorientated by the profound social changes taking place before their very eyes, many left Ethiopia, entrusting their houses to whomever they could. Before departing for Kenya, Desmond Christie left one of his houses to Donald Leach, who had arrived in 1975, and his brick house later became the headquarters of the EWF Local.[15] Carmen Clarke, who had health problems, returned to Jamaica for an operation. She entrusted her house to Ivan Coore, who had settled a few years earlier in Ethiopia. He later passed it on to R. Simons, a member of the Twelve Tribes, who arrived in 1977. Following Gerald Brissett's departure to Jamaica, his house was occupied by Norval Marshall, who arrived in 1976. William Boyd arrived only in 1973, but had had the time to build a small cob house by the roadside, close to Clarke's house.[16] When Boyd left, Tyrone took over the house in which he had lived. The newcomers could expect no additional grants and were therefore not entitled to the 2.2 hectares allocated by the *derg* in October 1975. Only those who did not abandon Shashemene were able to conserve the few parcels that had escaped reallocation.

Without the perseverance of those who remained and the presence of those who arrived, the totality of the land would have been lost and only a few houses, made of cob or bricks, would have remained, and these would have been occupied in short order by the Ethiopians. Tagesse King, an officer of the EWF, has underlined the importance of this tiny flock:

> Those that remained are the real pioneers cause if they wouldn't remain, the land grant would have been .... It would have been the end of the Rasta movement so to speak, it would have been written off as another cult, like the hippies. But the fact that we had land granted, a gift, saying thank you for the help of our parents through the federation again, had given Ethiopia, it couldn't be written off as a myth.[17]

The few remaining parcels of land, covering an area of eleven hectares, situated on both sides of the road, thus symbolized the reality of the land grant. They continued to represent Haile Selassie's pan-African commitment. Above all, as emphasized by Tagesse King, this salvaged land formed the tangible

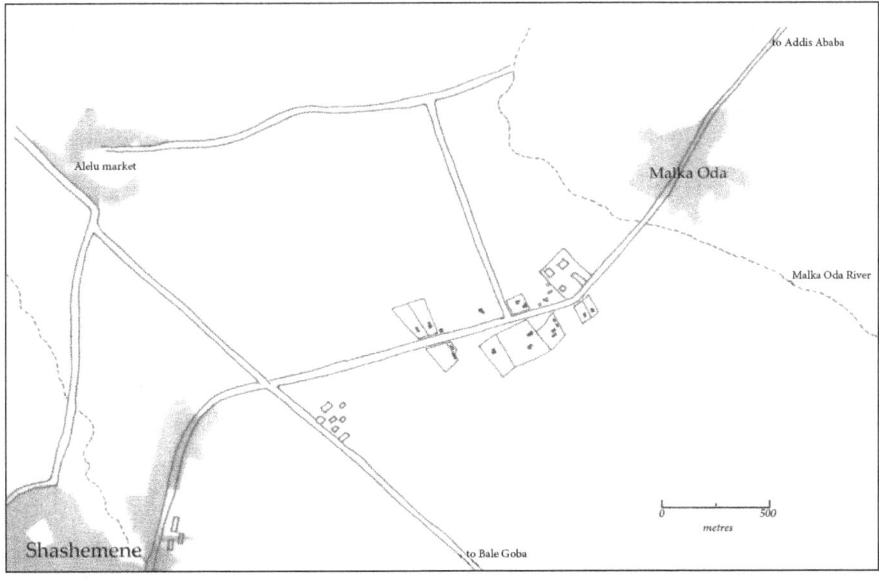

Figure 8.3. Map of the 1975 parcels after land reform.

heritage legitimating, "abroad", the Ethiopian identity, the right to return and, consequently, the Rastafari movement. It allowed the survival of the Rastafari movement subsequent to the revolution and transformed those who remained into pioneers.

In their political response to the affection of the returnees for Haile Selassie I, the new authorities ratified the loss of the two hundred hectares granted twenty-five years earlier, without the least consideration for the underlying pan-African motivations of the returnees' devotion. Whittled down to almost nothing, the land in Shashemene continued to territorialize the race, the nation and the identity so dear to the hearts of the Rastafari of Jamaica and the rest of the world.

A Young Generation Comes to Settle

Although the Ethiopian revolution had shaken the Rastafari movement, members of the Twelve Tribes of Israel arrived regularly from Kingston between 1972 and the early 1980s. They represented a younger generation, the majority of them being about twenty years old. They were all members of the Twelve Tribes, originating in the former EWF Local 15, the dissident branch that had contributed significantly to the renewal of the Rastafari movement in Jamaica and in its places of international diffusion. Disappointed by the EWF, which was unable to channel and support their determination to settle in Ethiopia, they arrived bearing the legitimacy derived from their membership in the Twelve Tribes of Israel, the first organization to finance the journeys of its members. The arrival was nonetheless daunting for some, for those who discovered in Ethiopia a world for which they were ill prepared. The first Twelve Tribes member arrived in 1972. His financial resources were soon depleted, and he was forced to find a job in Addis Ababa. He remembers: "I was here, I fought to survive and I had many problems, not as I expected it, because I thought that Shashemene would be a better place, even materially, all the gold of Solomon and Sheba."[18]

The gold of the palaces of King Solomon and the Queen of Sheba, a promised land flowing with milk and honey, was in part what Ethiopia evoked. Shashemene, upon the donation of land by the emperor, had raised expectations in those who had militated long enough to be entitled to their share – but the reality was quite different. Another Jamaican was completely disorientated when he arrived in 1976. He spent three days in a hotel in Addis Ababa before he found the bus station and got into the bus for Shashemene:

> When the bus filled up I told to myself "oh my God, this is a nightmare", I mean people having flies and nose snot and all kind of stuff on them which normally no people would go about that way. But people was like that. When the bus start driving, no one would allow the bus to be open, the windows – it would be the stink, it give you want to vomit, at least those things happened to me. I tried to shield up my yout'

and open the window but although I couldn't open it even though I pull it open and people say "ooohhh!!" All kind of things. I couldn't understand and had to close it. We got to Shashemene.[19]

The arrival was hard; this Jamaican understood neither the language nor the differences in clothing, attitude and sociability. One of the first shocks he experienced was caused by what he took for dirtiness and a lack of hygiene. Several of the returnees interviewed stressed that even if, as children, they went to beg in the streets of Kingston to find food, they had always paid great attention to the cleanliness of their appearance. Their clothes had holes, but they were ironed; if they had shoes, they were polished and made to look as new as possible. Besides, it was a challenge for our traveller – as for any traveller new to Ethiopia – to understand why the bus windows had to be shut tight: evil spirits had a way of coming in with the draught, so to open the window of a moving bus was to look for trouble! The disconnect between his expectations and the on-the-ground reality was violent:

> "I couldn't take what was here 'cause my expectation wasn't fulfilled at all! What I expect how Shashemene and Ethiopia generally stay? Weren't like that – a lot of flies."
>
> "What were you expecting?"
>
> "Well let me try see if I can find the words . . . because I was coming from a modern world I was actually expecting Ethiopia to have proper toilets, and proper sanitary convenience and people being hygienic and all of that. The place not being so bushy. My expectation was a bigger one, like maybe it should be more developed then and people would be more clean in their appearance but it weren't so."[20]

He wanted more hygiene and more development, less bush and more urbanization; the young Jamaican soon realized that there was no milk and honey flowing in the land of Shashemene. He settled there, nonetheless, and gradually became accustomed to this new world. Like the other Twelve Tribes members, he had arrived at a watershed moment, when most of the former residents had left the land after its nationalization and their expropriation. Only three EWF members (Reid, Hillman, Beckford), three other non-affiliated Jamaicans (Dyer, the Baughs), and an administrator who was prevented from exercising his authority (Robinson) remained on the spot. Immediately before the great land reforms, Robinson had attempted to sue James Piper, whom he accused of usurpation of authority, fraud and embezzlement. His letter addressed to the Provisional Military Administrative Council and signed by the most recent arrivants was probably left unanswered, and legal action became useless following the reforms and the departure of the Pipers.[21] Robinson was later forced to leave Ethiopia as, in spite of his pharmaceutical and medical activities in the country, in close collaboration with the Ministry of Health and the Russian and Cuban doctors, he was seen as a potential enemy due to his American nationality. The Cold War was in full swing in Shashemene. The new arrivants replaced the old, and the new influx of arrivants occupied the existing buildings. Purchase, resale, loan and sharing were some of the modes of occupation practised by the newcomers. These sometimes resulted in conflict, especially following the unexpected return of the first owners in the 1980s.

Thus, the EWF was falling apart in Ethiopia, and the arrival of Twelve Tribes members, formerly members of EWF Local 15, did not facilitate the survival of the historical, pan-Ethiopian organization. But these arrivals nevertheless allowed the returnees "to keep the land", to occupy the lots that had escaped the reforms and ultimately to preserve a few parcels out of the two hundred hectares that had been granted by the previous regime. The tense relations between the Pipers and the new arrivants had adversely affected the administration of the land. It was reconfigured by the departure of the EWF members and the arrival of the members of the Twelve Tribes of Israel. The fortune of Uriah Brown's house illustrates the power stakes linked to the change in occupants of the buildings: Brown had settled there with his Ethiopian wife but decided to leave the country and return to Jamaica, subsequent to the reforms. He sold his house and the lot of land surrounding it to the new arrivants and left behind his wife, who joined her family in another region. Uriah Brown's house became the headquarters of the Twelve Tribes on the land. It was a two-room brick house, with a kitchen and an awning at the back. A few trees were already there, and the land was occupied by a small vegetable garden and surrounded by a barbed-wire fence. It quickly became a community house, accommodating young newcomers who lived, cooked and slept together. At the end of the 1970s, five houses were under the control of the Twelve Tribes: the headquarters, the house of M. Lee (Piper), that of D. Leach (Desmond Christie), that of R. Simons (Carmen Clarke) and that occupied by N. Marshall (Gerald Brissett/Solomon Wolfe), where a workshop was set up. This new configuration, in which the

Figure 8.4. Inez Baugh and her two sons, Dawit and Andrew, Shashemene, Ethiopia, 1981. Photograph: D. Bishton © DR.

members of the Twelve Tribes used their numerical force to occupy all the existing houses and to emerge as the legitimate occupants and administrators of the remaining land, crystallized the division between the two organizations and has left a currently visible impact, locally and internationally.

New Social Configurations

The Rastafari were naturally associated with the emperor, since he had invited them to come and settle in Ethiopia and was an integral part of their ideology, practices and worldview. This connection unleashed a downpour of insults: "We were being attacked as lovers of His Majesty, imperialists, feudalists, we were insulted. It wasn't nice."[22] As the last local embodiments of a defeated society, the Rastafari were not the targets of direct attacks, but rather the victims of popular revenge and, as such, were insulted and attacked in the streets of the city: "You have to be really strong fe really stay. You kind of feel fear at times, knowing we are people who are praying to His Majesty."[23] They were forced to grin and bear it in order to remain in Shashemene. For the new local government, the peasant associations and their urban equivalent, neighbourhood cooperative associations called *qäbälé*, the Rastafari represented the residues of the former regime and were not respectable: "[One day], the *qäbälé* came, took all photographs [of the emperor] and burn them. They went through all of our houses, which at the time was nothing, they took all the photos on the wall, the table, wherever and burn them. We replaced them the next day with what we have. That didn't stop us from loving His Majesty, defending the faith."[24]

Horace Campbell (1994, 229) stressed that putting up photographs of the emperor, which was an act of protest and resistance in colonial Jamaica, became a reactionary act in Ethiopia. Such was, to his mind, the contradictory position of the Rastafari in revolutionary Ethiopia: "Rastas cannot be against Babylon in the West and support reaction in Africa." But to what extent did the Rastafari of Shashemene, by defending the emperor, support the old Ethiopian social hierarchy and the agricultural modes of production that exploited the farmers? There is no doubt whatsoever that leaving the ghettos for land on the continent, in Ethiopia, represented an extraordinary upward mobility, but, after the revolution, they were forced to find the means of integrating into the lowest Ethiopian social rung while facing the mistrust of the Ethiopians. As foreigners engulfed in social conflicts, what were the Rastafari of Jamaica defending by remaining faithful to the image of the emperor, to the body of the myth, if not their own identity? Locally, they ran into violent conflicts with their neighbours, with the peasants and the local government desirous of restoring popular power over the land of the south. Yet, with the officers, soldiers and high officials of the *derg*, the situation was different, and relations of confidence were established: "People in high power loved to speak to us at that time, because there was no one they could talk to. When they see us they see strength. They admire the strength – we were at the time, the Red Terror time. Lot of them was touched by that. Lot of them will treat us good, call us, feed us; they could see our plight at that time."[25]

The returnees who remained in Ethiopia earned the admiration of some Ethiopians. They stood in contrast with the many Ethiopians who were fleeing the country and forming the first large migratory wave from Ethiopia (Abye Tasse 2004, 141–69). Thanks to their marginal but constant presence, the Rastafari gained the confidence of certain officers, who spoke to them about the political situation, the great changes in progress and the difficulties they were experiencing. These strange relations illustrated the position of the stranger, evoked by Georg Simmel (1971, 145): "[The stranger] often receives the most surprising revelations and confidences, at times reminiscent of a confessional, about matters which are kept carefully hidden from everybody with whom one is close." Despite the community's identification with the royal family, the residents never engaged in the local or national political action – nor were they in a position to do so. Disqualified from membership in political parties and excluded from internal power struggles, they were seen merely as foreigners.

While the military government was being undermined by the radical intelligentsia, by civilian parties like the Ethiopian People's Revolutionary Party, by the war in Eritrea and by the invasion of Ogaden by Somalia, Mengistu Haile Mariam launched his internal coup d'état and took full control of power. Many members of the *derg* and General Tafari Bente, who had succeeded Aman Andom as head of state, were prepared to negotiate with the Eritreans and the civil opposition, but, accused of conspiracy by Mengistu, they were reluctantly condemned by the other members of the *derg* and executed. Thus, on 12 February 1977, the *derg* proclaimed Mengistu as the head of state and president of the *derg* (Marcus 1994, 195–96). Mengistu launched a campaign of repression, sadly remembered as the "Red Terror", with the intention of breaking all forms of civilian opposition. The country was engulfed in war and trauma, thousands of Ethiopians were killed or forced into exile and the conflict with Eritrea entered a deadlock. All presumed opponents to the new regime were systematically eliminated, and the small community in Shashemene probably owed its safety only to its foreign status. The Jamaicans sometimes hid young Ethiopians, sent from Addis Ababa by parents fearing their conscription by the army, thus revealing, by the same token, the confidence placed in the Rastafari and their marginal position in the political arena. A few years prior to the fall of the *derg* in 1991, Mengistu Haile Mariam visited Shashemene, leaving an amused recollection in the local community:

> Mengistu love we still, he came pass here and greet we. The farmers who wait 'pon him with corn and banana he never looked on them, yet a we him wave to. . . . Him

> never stop he just drive through. He never stop by the rastaman them. [laughter]. Me sure he was afraid but he greet we and the people who stand up! Never really brutalize we no way, we have to give him credit for that, when the policy was real bloody.[26]

The Rastafari had gathered along the road with their Ethiopian flags when they heard that Mengistu was to pass through the region. But how could Mengistu love them? He must have recognized their determination and seen it as a reflection of his conquering nationalist ideology; he probably held them up as a counterexample to the Ethiopians who sought to flee; or maybe he felt admiration for these foreigners who, despite their lack of means, had decided to tie their destiny to that of Ethiopia, even under a revolutionary regime.

The image of an entire society opposing migrants faithful in their affection for the emperor thus appears more complex and nuanced than one might have thought. The contrasting reactions of the peasants, the local government and the officers of the *derg* allotted a contradictory position to the Rastafari, who were, at the same time, accepted in their midst, protected by the government, but also kept at a distance, limited to their role as foreigners present in the social landscape without being an organic part of the community which hosted them. These new social configurations for the Rastafari, torn between insults and confidence, rejection and absorption, played out on the land in Shashemene, where the Jamaicans developed survival strategies in a context in which no economic initiative was possible.

Paralysis and Land Insecurity

A reproach often levelled against the members of the Twelve Tribes of Israel in Shashemene claimed that they had done little to develop the land under the *derg*. The land had been preserved, but was barely cultivated and was left undeveloped. This reproach sometimes addressed a specific point of their doctrine, according to which, Jerusalem was the final objective of the movement, not Ethiopia. Ethiopia was said to represent the place of assembly of the 144,000 elect, originating in the twelve tribes of Israel, who would then move on to Jerusalem. This numerical reference to the book of Revelation (8:1–4) is a recurrent theme of millenarian movements (Desroche 1969, 27) and fitted in logically with the identification with the twelve tribes of Israel promoted by the Jamaican organization. This insistence on Jerusalem was probably a reformulation of the doctrines of the Twelve Tribes following the blockade of the situation in Shashemene during the 1970s and 1980s, in a bid to facilitate the continuation of the organization's propaganda. In an interview in 1997, Prophet Gad, the founder of the Twelve Tribes, emphasized that Jerusalem was absolutely a part of Africa:

> "The Twelve Tribes of Israel currently has the largest settlement on Shashemene."
>
> "Is Ethiopia the final home and what about the rest of Africa?"

"Just Shashemene is not the final home. The whole of Africa [is], because one King shall rule over them. And also, the whole of Africa, especially Jerusalem. . . . Yes Jerusalem is Africa. Jerusalem is a part of Africa, is only certain things happen, and it break away. But there is no argument that Jerusalem is not a part of Africa, we are sure!"[27]

By arguing that Jerusalem was in Africa, Prophet Gad resorted to a line of argument common to many black congregations, especially the black Jews and their more contemporary heirs, like Ben Ammi's African Hebrew Israelites. The latter, following the failure of their return to Liberia in 1967, settled in Dimona in Israel (Markowitz 2006). For certain members of the Twelve Tribes, the idea that Ethiopia was not Zion might have been no more than a means of rationalizing the trauma related to their arrival in Shashemene. For others, although future entry into Jerusalem represented a tenet of their doctrine and a promise, it was not an obstacle to their involvement in Ethiopia:

> As Twelve Tribes we know our names are already written over the gates [of Jerusalem] and when fullness come, we'll be going in. Really Ethiopia is a resting place for a time, where Twelve Tribes is supposed to be gathered with our king which is David and Jerusalem is for the future. . . . Ethiopia is my home, the end of my journey for now. I wouldn't go to Jerusalem now. . . . My professional career, raising my kids, that's what I'll do here. I want to buy land, build a house, establish something as solid as possible.[28]

But this Twelve Tribes member was speaking in 2003 in Addis Ababa and his situation was quite different from that of the others who lived in Shashemene during the *derg*. The criticism of Twelve Tribes members concerning their lack of development of the land during the 1980s probably erred through a lack of consideration of the material conditions in which the young residents lived. The community had no specific opportunities, whether economic or social – quite the contrary – and nobody settled in Shashemene between 1977 and 1981. Narratives are often silent regarding this period. Evoking those years was still painful, and not everyone was willing to do so: "Being foreigner and under communist regime, it was really terrible. You're not allowed to build, to trade, no business, no nothing. . . . We were afraid, some of us, afraid, and anyone would be still. You couldn't blame people to be afraid in a communist government."[29] For them, everything was prohibited. The political upheavals, and their status as foreigners, imposed a total lack of initiative. Contrary to those who had preceded them, they were of urban origin, with no solid rural or agricultural experience. Most had come without a penny to their name, and the coercive economic and social situation established by the *derg* offered no opportunity for material development.

Regardless of the nationalization of the land and the loss of the two hundred hectares ratified by the government, several elements suggest that land was allocated and reclaimed several times between 1975 and 1986. Their location has,

Figure 8.5. Threshing *tef* in front of Inez Baugh's house. Shashemene, Ethiopia, January 1981. Photograph: D. Bishton © DR.

for the most part, been lost to memory and has left no visible trace on the land, but at least two such lots have been identified. The first is the current location of Eric Smith's house. The latter had sold his piece of land to William Hillman and had found himself landless and homeless. Based on the recent Ethiopian custom making it possible to request an allocation of land from the local government, he tried his luck but addressed his request directly to the senior officer, the *astädädar*. Following a letter addressed to the peasant association of Alelu, in charge of the land north of the road leading to Shashemene, a parcel of 2.2 hectares was finally granted to him in 1981.[30] As he had no resources, he settled there in a very modest manner.

In response to petitions written by the other Jamaicans, the local government also granted the second space, which was a collective allocation. Located on the southern, Awasho side of the road, it started at the sycamore tree marking the centre of the original land grant, went up to a yellow house, then reached the Bale road, where a workshop was built. It was intended for seven persons, at about two hectares per person.[31] As the prerogatives of the *balabbat* had become a thing of the past, tenant farming was no longer practised – the land had to be farmed by those who occupied it. Paradoxically, this grant turned out to be too large for the handful of Jamaicans to manage, as they lacked the farming experience needed to exploit it fully. They were thus obliged to pay five or six *berrs* a day to the Ethiopians who ploughed and guided the oxen. But the lack of money to pay for labour, the lack of tools and expertise hampered development, and the fifteen hectares of land were left fallow. On the pretext that the land was neglected and underexploited, the authorities confiscated it four years after its allocation. The Jamaicans were obliged to fall back on the small spaces surrounding their few houses, where they practised subsistence farming – potatoes, cabbage, corn and peas, the "*Shashemene wät'* ", on which they lived for many years: "Sometimes we nah even want to see it, you never want to see a cabbage because years of that [*laughter*]!"[32] The land insecurity in which the young arrivants lived highlights the extent to which the access to ground became a major challenge following the great reforms. Adding layers of complexity to current interpretations that perceive the loss of the original land grant as a failure and as the end of the pan-African settlement, these new allocations illustrate the ways in which the community worked its way through the maze of the Ethiopian administration while continuing to survive in a situation of great instability. As noted by Norval Marshall, who arrived in 1976, "Since we came here, since the early times we had always been issuing land and taking away land from us."[33] These endless negotiations with the Ethiopian authorities increased the instability and insecurity of their lives, by adding to the general climate of fear and impediment.

This phenomenon is also reflected in the complete cessation of construction, as a result of the restrictions imposed by the government on the access to raw materials (sand, cement, wood) and by the eternal lack of funds. Moreover, the unwillingness of the municipality to support construction initiatives was a permanent hindrance. To give an example, once he had moved to the lot of land purchased from Eric Smith, Reverend William Hillman began to build a small shop, a *suq*, but municipal civil servants came, confiscated his tools and stopped the construction.[34] Following his letter of complaint, the municipality wrote to Addis Ababa concerning the trouble they were having with the Jamaicans: "Jamaicans used to live as peasants and without permission they are building

Figure 8.6. Noel Dyer in Shashemene, Ethiopia, January 1981. Photograph: D. Bishton © DR.

little unpleasant houses and fences. We never know them so we don't allow them to build and fence. We want to clarify their case."[35] Yet Hillman had lived there for over fifteen years and had worked for a long time as a mechanic at the Road Authority, so it is unlikely that he was unknown to the local administration. Addis Ababa sent the following response: "This case is new for us, we have to investigate more, until then, let them finish their construction, but nothing new."[36] The relative leniency of Addis Ababa contrasted with the attitude of the local authorities. This did not prevent a ten-year paralysis of the small community; adults and newborn babies were crammed together in the few houses they had managed to keep. Carmen Clarke's remarks concerning the struggles, at the end of the 1960s, for access to land, in spite of the Pipers, can also be applied to the 1980s: "You see Jamaican black people? Anywhere they go and want to stay, no care how the fire is hot, they stay!"[37]

Life in Shashemene during the *Derg*

Without development of agriculture or resources, the Jamaicans had no choice but to get acquainted with their Ethiopian neighbours, who were sometimes resentful, and to learn to survive in a hostile rural environment. They experienced integration at the lowest rung of the Ethiopian social ladder, and their standard of living, which was already low in Jamaica, declined even further in Ethiopia. The first stage of their social integration was the learning of Amharic, the common language in this multiethnic town. With no knowledge of the language, the Rastafari were easily ripped off by traders: "It was difficult at first when I came here, didn't know what they were saying, they robbed us so much, they did us so bad when we came here."[38] They were unable to discuss prices or to strike a good bargain. They thus developed various ways of learning the language. Some walked around the market paying careful attention and wrote down all that they heard. Afterwards, they tried to find out the meaning of the words and gradually plucked up the courage to make a few sentences. Others attended the classes taught by students sent out in the programme of the *zämäč'a*, the large development campaign "through cooperation". These young civil servants helped to implement the land reform, to set up peasant associations and also contributed to the elimination of illiteracy among the rural populations. This educated population was often more radical than the government (Kiflu Tadesse 1993, 214–16; Marcus 1994, 192). These lessons were taught in town, and, although they were sometimes close to political indoctrination, they allowed the Jamaicans to learn the language. Of course, it was with women that they first practised their new linguistic skills: "The word *eshi* [okay] it get us in a lot of troubles [*laughter*]. If you go into the bar and a girl come and talk and you don't know what she saying and you say *eshi* and when you pay the bill is big! *Eshi* is the first word we learn."[39]

It took them several months to acquire the rudiments of Amharic, and the majority learned neither to read nor write it. Some of the Jamaicans were not literate in English; some could neither read nor write the Latin script; and only a few were able to switch effortlessly from the Jamaican dialect to standard English. The efforts they made in order to be understood by a population that spoke no English at all were no small matter. Several managed only a basic mastery of the language. The discovery of Amharic went hand in hand with that of the city. Every evening, the young men walked the two kilometres to town, without, apparently, being forced to observe the curfew. The local people made no effort to conceal their surprise when the Jamaicans ran into them: "When we came here is as if we came from space, into the town, everyone surround us and look at us."[40] They felt no less free, for all that, and are still amused by such recollections of their youth. Shashemene by night offered few distractions except for the bars, brothels and *bunna bet* – the Ethiopian "coffee houses" – where a few musicians sometimes played, and the girls were easy: "Bars, *bunna bet* in the ghettos, we see how people live. First thing we do is go in the ghetto and see how people live. We learn a lot of things in the ghetto. The economy of the people, how they economize."[41]

The knowledge of the economic life of Shashemene, which began through commercial exchange, was refined in these places of consumption. Having scant resources, the Jamaicans quickly found ways of having a drink on the soldiers, who were all over the city, and of misleading the young women into thinking that lottery tickets were cashable cheques. Once in a while, the Ethiopian youth taught them a thing or two – how to get away without paying, how to swindle or trick people: "A lot of troubles, we used to fight in the town. . . . We didn't afraid in those days. We come from Jamaica, we nah afraid of nobody, everywhere we go we fight! [*laughter*]."[42] Such nights often ended in brawls, in which quarrels were settled with blows, "between men", even with the soldiers, almost in the same way as they were back in Jamaica. The reputation of the Jamaican rude boys had not reached Shashemene, but the members of the Twelve Tribes present helped to establish it, by repeating old practices imported from Kingston.

As getting by on subsistence farming alone was nigh impossible, street smarts and innovation became crucial. Though they lacked tools, they had many skills – they were painters, masons, carpenters, shoemakers and upholsterers – and attracted customers from all over the region, and sometimes from Addis Ababa. In the house occupied by N. Marshall, a small workshop with a few workstations was set up. They turned out articles that were carefully crafted and painted: decorated wooden combs (Afro picks) with teeth made of bicycle spokes, coffee tables, padlocked boxes for securing telephones, as well as cupboards, beds and tables. They bought wood from *Ato* Hailu, who lived on the Alelu side of the road, but also from as far as Jigessa or Neghele. In reaction to the market success of these articles in wood, the Ethiopian competition quickly organized

Figure 8.7. The men are wearing their Sunday best – the kickers, made in France, a gift sent by sympathizers, are highly appreciated. Shashemene, Ethiopia, January 1981. Photograph: D. Bishton © DR.

itself: other workshops making manufactured combs, coffee tables and the like were set up, causing prices to fall. For example, the Jamaicans made between ten and fifteen *berrs* for their combs, but the Ethiopians put theirs on the market for three *berrs*, thus destroying the trade for those who had initiated it. The few women present started to sew panties, an initiative which caught on very well. Like the other articles, they were sold in town, on the street, on the move, or in offices, or on the market days, like everyone else did; "That's how we survive, selling things, trading, small trading, knitting, sawing, carpentry and so on."[43] They were sometimes forced to sell the few clothes they possessed and their cutlery and personal belongings, in order to eat. Some sold cigarettes to the other members, when they managed to get a pack, or even a little *aräqé*, a potent local brew.

A few found temporary wage-earning jobs: Millward Brown was employed by the United Nations Economic Commission for Africa, which had its offices in the capital; Hillman and Beckford worked for the Road Authority; and a few others worked on and off on construction sites for the Catholic Mission in Shashemene or for German or Norwegian non-governmental organizations which had contracts with the state. They sometimes spent months away from the land, in Bale or Sidamo, overseeing construction sites. Working with foreign organizations was their only viable option, since the wages paid by the Ethiopians were very small. The rest of the time, other survival strategies were needed. They shot birds for food and got food from the Oromos who lived in the surrounding countryside. As they were not registered by the *qäbälé*, they

Figure 8.8. A festive moment in Shashemene: Mamouche's third birthday (*he is seated at the table, left*) offers the opportunity for the two Jamaican women (*left*) to invite their Ethiopian neighbours to a party. Shashemene, Ethiopia, January 1981. Photograph: D. Bishton. © DR.

were not entitled to the rations handed out by the government. Nevertheless, they circulated among the various *qäbälés* where, depending on their relations with the persons in charge, they received food products or were turned down. Surplus rations fuelled the black market, and the Jamaicans used this channel to obtain food items like sugar that were always scarce and unavailable through legal means.

Their practice of sports facilitated the local integration of the Rastafari in Shashemene during the *derg* years. Prior to the revolution, G. Robinson had already nourished the ambitious project of founding a Haile Selassie I stadium and had tried his hand at training basketball teams. As an American, basketball was the game he knew the best. Most of the Jamaicans present were sportsmen and trained regularly with their Ethiopian neighbours. At the end of the 1970s, the long visit of Alan "Skill" Cole, the great Jamaican footballer, engaged in the Rastafari movement and a member of the Twelve Tribes, contributed to the enhancement of the community's reputation through sports, especially given his participation in the Ethiopian national team.[44] In Shashemene, an Ethiopian-Jamaican team was founded, and it won the *wäräda* cup: "We had a very good relationship with the people who live around us, especially we involved in sports, most of us are very young and Ethiopians like sport, so because of that they embrace us."[45] Moreover, Desmond Martin was an excellent track athlete. The government organized a national athletics competition. Play-offs started at the level of the *wäräda*, then of the *awrajja*, in which Martin won the 100- and 200-metres races, qualifying for the finals in the grand stadium in Addis Ababa in March 1981. Clocking 10.03 seconds in the 100 metres, he broke the national record and received the honours reserved for winners – the press, television and medals. Omitting to expand on the conditions of the participation of a foreigner in a national competition, all he had to say was: "The people rebelled when I went on the first race, but they organized so that I could be accepted as a person living here and a black man and the record was broken and I was emulated by the people. . . . That is the greater achievement that I made in Ethiopia."[46] This victory, for which the ministers of the *derg* congratulated him, gave him a certain celebrity in Shashemene. Representing the community before the local government in the 1980s, he was recognized and respected for this sporting achievement.

Figure 8.9. A Desmond Martin win; first on the podium in Ziway, 1981. Archives D. Martin, Shashemene © DR.

The life of the small community organized itself, regardless of the difficulties, hunger and poverty, which it shared with its Ethiopian neighbours. They created occasions to party, sometimes in honour of a visitor, a birthday, or a birth. Alongside memories, dog-eared photographs bear witness to this period. While doing their best in a constrained economic situation, certain Jamaicans, fed up with being penniless, feeling more isolated than ever and discouraged by the poor circulation of news between Ethiopia and Jamaica, made various attempts to return to Jamaica. Nevertheless, the community held on and survived. For Martin: "We were lonely but we survive, 'cause the Bible teaches us that whatever situation we found ourselves in, environment, we contented, because you can't do better, and you have to work for betterment, better standards of living, that's what we are working on in Ethiopia, to uplift the standards of living for ourselves and the people, Ethiopian people."[47]

They were nonetheless in a bind, and development was a long way off. The standard of living remained quite low, despite occasional aid from the Jamaican embassy. Since its opening in 1970, it had offered mainly administrative support, taking care of questions relating to documents and passports. Given the extremely limited commercial exchange between Ethiopia and Jamaica, the problems and the future of resident Jamaicans were the chief concern of the embassy. Mr Symes succeeded Mr Foreman for four years, followed by Mr Pearce and, finally, by Mr Sing in 1987.[48] It was to the embassy that the Jamaicans turned to plead the acceptance of their application for the extension of their residence permits. They went there to especially rally support for the additional allocation of land, in view of accomplishing their long-standing dream of a better standard of living. Paradoxically, the Jamaicans present in Ethiopia during the *derg* saw themselves as the "true Ethiopians" and had literally taken on this identity by settling in Ethiopia. Upon their arrival, they were completely excluded from the local political and economic scene and were forced to rely on their embassy for administrative matters. As foreigners, they were regarded as Jamaican citizens, dependent on their national representation. The *derg* years also saw a change in their designation. In the past, when many black persons in Ethiopia were Americans, the Jamaicans were commonly called *t'equr americawi*, literally black Americans. They worked to change this appellation:

> Average Ethiopians will address you as *t'equr americawi*, Black American, we never liked this, we consider to change this concept, perception, so we say Jamaicans, 'cause we try to break across the enlightenment of His Imperial Majesty. In Jamaica he said Ethiopians and Jamaicans are blood brothers. It wasn't that easy, and after a while we get them to do that. Here in Shashemene community [we are] known as Jamaicans, we emphasize that we are one people.[49]

The declarations of the emperor at the time of his visit to Jamaica in 1966 had left a deep imprint on the minds of the Jamaican people. The monarch, in his speech at the national stadium in Kingston, had mentioned the blood ties between Ethiopians and Jamaicans, which the Rastafari had asserted long before. Unable to fully affirm their Ethiopian identity under the regime of the *derg*, they fell back on their status as Jamaicans, which offered, in the terms of

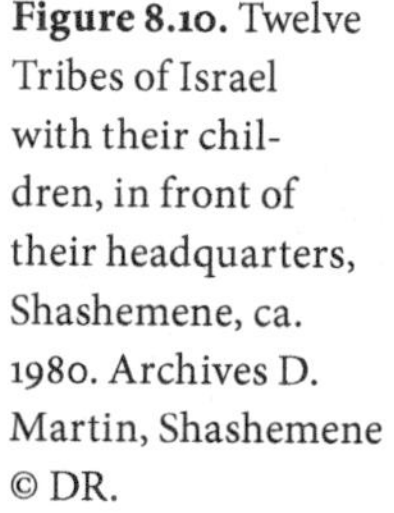

Figure 8.10. Twelve Tribes of Israel with their children, in front of their headquarters, Shashemene, ca. 1980. Archives D. Martin, Shashemene © DR.

Haile Selassie I, a common filiation. The word Jamaican was thereafter adjoined to the neighbourhood in which the returnees lived.

The Final Land Grant

Despite a tense and difficult economic situation, the members of the Twelve Tribes continued to put pressure on the Jamaican embassy and the government for the granting of arable lands to enhance their subsistence. There are perhaps several reasons behind the breakthrough in the land situation: the Jamaicans were very insistent; their families were growing, and the limited number of houses led to promiscuity; their Ethiopian neighbours had come to know them. By 1983, the Ministry of Agriculture in Addis Ababa had carried out investigations into the surface area of the land occupied by the Jamaicans. The report, approved by the mayor of Shashemene, indicated that twenty-seven families occupied 5.23 hectares on the Alelu side and 7.43 hectares on the Awasho side, hence a total of 12.66 hectares, all enclosed.[50] Forty hectares had been officially allocated in October 1975, following the land reform. But 60 per cent of the land formerly occupied by the Jamaicans had been "lost" between 1975 and 1983. This was due as much to the departure of residents as to their inability to occupy and exploit it. Following this report, but in no hurry, the Ministry of Agriculture decided to distribute parcels of land to the Jamaicans. The Alelu and Awasho peasant associations, in charge of this matter, implemented the decision in 1986, and the residents received it with relief. Ambac'o Dagné, the president of the Awasho Peasant Association from 1979 to 1989, relates how the two peasant associations in charge of the land at the town entrance shared what they possibly regarded as

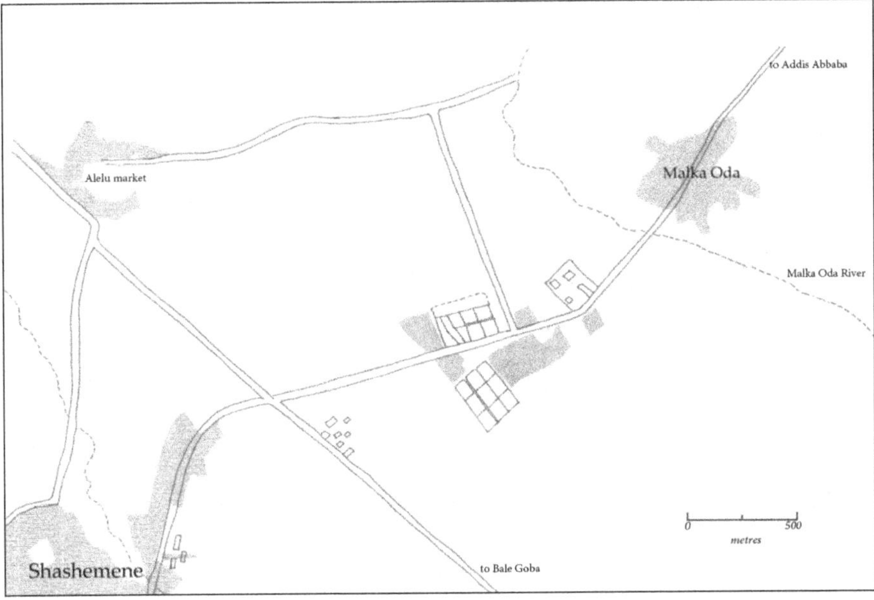

Figure 8.11. Map of the 1986 attribution of eighteen parcels.

a burden by accommodating the same number of persons: "What we did then was, below the highway at Alelu Peasant Association we put nine Jamaicans to be holders of the land and beyond the highway at Awasho Peasant Association we put another nine, that is in two groups."[51] One recipient, offering another perspective on this distribution, explained that two persons were in charge of the distribution to specifically named individuals in these two spaces: "They gave [the land] to one of the bredren on this side and the bredren divide that land among all the bredren that was on this side. And they give that land over there to one bredren and that bredren divide all the land to the people on that side."[52]

The fact that they were put in charge of the distribution of these spaces was a sign that certain individuals in the community enjoyed a degree of power, but arrangements remained possible. For example, Llewellyn Campbell gave up his parcel to a woman who got no land, and went to settle on the parcel allocated to Anthony Nevers. Winston Simons gave his to Nevers in exchange for another small lot in Nevers' control, located behind the few occupied houses at the centre of the land. Simons had arrived only in 1981, but he was ready to build. His lot of land was closer to the existing houses, whereas the eighteen parcels distributed had been specifically reserved for farming. On the Alelu side, an Ethiopian construction firm was set up directly behind the newly allocated lots of land, thus amputating part of the new acquisition. This space was left vacant for several years, but the Jamaicans were unable to reclaim it, and it was ultimately taken over by an agricultural educational college in 2002.[53]

This official division was an ultimate compromise with the tenacious Jamaicans and represents the last land grant authorized by the local government. It was unaccompanied by any official document: "None of us have proper papers regarding land titles," said Norval Marshall.[54] This continual lack of documents legitimating their presence on the land reinforced the residents' feeling of insecurity and instability. These attributions were, nevertheless, decided at a crucial moment, when acute tensions had resulted from the arrival, in 1981, of two representatives of EWF Local 43; Solomon Wolfe had returned to Jamaica after the revolution, and so had Berthal J. Moody, the former chaplain of the local. On their return to Shashemene, they attempted to recover the building that Wolfe and Brissett had constructed. It had become a workshop producing combs, coffee tables and other articles made of wood, which had allowed the Twelve Tribes members to survive during the hardest years of the *derg*. Marshall had been living there since 1977; the house was registered by the *qäbälé* in his name; and it was out of the question, for him, to leave the place. Moody refused the room offered to him and lodged a complaint with the *qäbälé*, requesting the recognition of his rights and those of Wolfe. They were recognized, probably because, in 1970, when the land was divided, Wolfe had been attached to a specific lot. In addition, a cob house had been built on the land and was apparently registered by the local authorities. Marshall went to prison three times because of his refusal to return the house to the EWF officers. He was allowed to appeal twice, but, following his third imprisonment, the representatives of the *qäbälé* came with weapons and soldiers to remove his goods and expel him. Moody, who had been living at Harold Reid's house since his arrival, recovered the house, and Marshall found lodgings on the other side of the road, in the small workshop belonging to Simons.[55] The allocation of individual lots of land in 1986 thus came as a relief; each and every one was able to find his own space and land to feed the growing families. This internal war surprised the local authorities, oblivious of the distinctions that were playing out between the members of the EWF and the Twelve Tribes. As Moody put it: "They wondered why we are acting like enemies."[56] With the return of the EWF to Shashemene, the power relations surrounding the legitimate administration of the land were reconfigured, leading to numerous conflicts, which later crystallized, in 1992, during the election of an official representative of the community.

Visitors to Shashemene

At the end of the 1980s, the appearance of the first post-revolution visitors brought a breath of fresh air to the residents of the Jamaican neighbourhood in Shashemene. The visitors came with news of the West, the inside stories of the various houses as well as a significant material support. In fact, until then, financial aid, coming mainly from America and England, was particularly difficult to send to Shashemene via the banks, due in particular to the mistrust of the authorities regarding interaction with these "capitalist" countries.[57] Prophet Gad's visit in 1986 helped to change the relations among Twelve Tribes members. Two major decisions were made. The first was to develop the headquarters, located in Uriah Brown's old house that had become a community dwelling. With an external financial contribution, the building was renovated, painted and improved by the addition of two new rooms, a kitchen and an office. In a little under four years, the headquarters had an entirely new appearance and became the first "finished" house on the land. The second decision was "to nationalize" the international funds, in order to avoid partiality in the support of members with more external contacts than others.[58] Using a rhetoric that had become fashionable in Ethiopia more than ten years earlier, this second decision was meant to facilitate the creation of "central funds" and a more equitable distribution, in the interest of the community as a whole. This measure was also intended to protect aid recipients from sponsors liable to claim, at a later date, any type of ownership of the goods they had helped to finance. In addition to these improvements, a more regular flow of visitors began to arrive. Following a period of six or seven years with no visit whatsoever, it was good once again to have visitors in the community, although their trip to Shashemene was made difficult by the need to obtain a travel licence beforehand. Upon their arrival in Addis Ababa, the visitors applied and paid for this licence. But their application was not always successful; they were sometimes forced to waste their time and money in the capital and to leave the country without seeing Shashemene. "We had to bring some of them by night from Addis, so they could get just a glimpse of Shash. We had to hide them. It was really terrible at that time. We had to hide them because there was a immigration officer here, who might see a new face and back to Addis they might trick and imprison him."[59]

Figure 8.12. Handell Paris in Shashemene, 1981. Photograph: D. Bishton © DR.

Due to the need for clandestinity when travellers failed to obtain the licence required for circulation inside the country, certain visits ended in trouble. Handell Paris, a member sent by the New York branch of the Twelve Tribes, was accused by the Ethiopian authorities of being a Central Intelligence Agency spy and sent to prison. His Rastafari identity, which, to his mind, legitimated his visit, was completely denied, "And the worse thing you can do is deny a Rasta faith, being a Rasta, a Rasta image."[60] He contracted malaria in prison and was eventually released and deported. Refusing to be sent to the United States, he went to Tanzania where he soon died of illness.[61]

Starting in the mid-1980s, many Twelve Tribes branches opened in the wake of the international diffusion of the organization. Focus on the return to Shashemene was central to their propaganda and contributed to the arrival of new residents in Shashemene. The new branches were all allowed to send their executive members to visit Shashemene and submit a report on the state and the development of the place on their return home. In the preceding years, a message asking for the cessation of visits and new settlers, given the danger and precariousness of the local situation, had been widely diffused, leading to the slow-down of arrivants and visitors. Now, executive members were arriving in groups. The most outstanding among the first wave of group visits was probably that of twelve sisters from the Jamaican executive, who spent a month in Shashemene in 1986. Thereafter, members from Trinidad, the Bahamas, Canada, the United States, New Zealand, London, Manchester and Germany provided an irregular influx of visitors. Their stay allowed residents to obtain goods, funds, clothing, music – commodities that enhanced their daily lives. By the same token, the creation and development of commercial links between the residents and the outside world were facilitated: "We start getting visitors, people start to trade outside, like for example I was knitting craft and I was selling a lot of craft into the West, hats, belts, plaited things, hammocks and start making money from there."[62] This relative opportunity was a result of the residents' personal relations. For example, with the help of an Italian friend, Anthony Nevers was able to buy a mill and install it in 1989 on his plot of land on the Awasho side. He had seen the Ethiopian women travelling several kilometres to grind of thirty kilos of cereal. So, the demand was there, and his mill turned out to be useful, even lucrative.[63]

Out of England, the EWF, revitalized by radical young Rastafari, had attempted to reconnect with the elders who were still in residence on the land. One among them, Tagesse King, had already made an initial, two-month visit in 1982. He returned to England with the news that famine was becoming endemic in certain parts of the country and organized a humanitarian campaign, "Jamming for Ethiopia". His settlement in Ethiopia in 1988, with his three children was used to show that it was still possible to settle, despite the restrictions imposed by the government.[64] It also contributed to a tightening of the links between Ethiopia and the Rastafari community in England. In 1985, the "Colleen Reid" appeal was launched on behalf of the daughter of Harold Reid, who had arrived in 1973. Colleen suffered from a malformation of the heart, and a huge mobilization in England garnered the funds for her operation in that country. The operation was successful, and she returned to Ethiopia with her father in January 1986. During a second operation in England in 1991, Colleen died at the age of twenty-five.[65] Notwithstanding this failure, the effort spearheaded by the EWF represented the first signs of the renewal of its relations with Ethiopia, which were to develop after 1991, following the change of regime.

The first visitors to the community in Shashemene, at the end of the 1980s, had a real and positive, albeit limited, impact. Most were from Jamaica, with a few from England; their organizations, the EWF and the Twelve Tribes, attracted an increasing number of persons, from diverse origins and with various trajectories. Reinscribing the diasporic space in the economic and social life of Shashemene, these mobilities were the beginning of a more complete movement, which took shape after 1992. Before considering the decisive openings brought about by the regime change in 1991 and the celebration of the centenary of Haile Selassie I in 1992, it is important to focus for a moment on an aspect already mentioned at several points in this discussion – namely, the issue of the families of the residents and, more particularly, that of the women.

On a Few Women

A few women too came from Jamaica to live in Shashemene. They arrived as part of a couple, like Helen Piper, Inez Baugh and Joan Douglas, or alone, like Carmen Clarke. They were few in number for at least two reasons. First, because of the patriarchal character of the Rastafari movement, in which the women had no ritual responsibility and where their social position was often regarded as one of subjection to a man or to a male assembly. Then, there is the masculine character of the settlement on a new land, exacerbated by the symbolism linking virile strength to the work of pioneers. Mobility in the direction of Ethiopia was, consequently, mainly a masculine affair, and men left alone, often leaving their women, wives, children and newborn babies behind. This male mobility had two consequences on the form of the settler families in Shashemene: a kind of "added value" was attached to female returnees with a shared culture, language and practices, alongside numerous relations with Ethiopian women, with whom families were founded. These relations assumed various forms. Certain men arrived as part of a couple but sowed many wild oats among the Ethiopian women. Others had only one Ethiopian woman or several, sometimes bequeathing a legacy of difficult relations among children born to the same father but to different Ethiopian mothers. Complex bonds were sometimes woven between various returnee families. Here are a few examples, without claim of exhaustiveness. The first illustrates the "added value" of repatriated women; the second considers the will of certain Ethiopian women to appropriate the Jamaican culture by becoming Rastafari; and the third approaches the place of those who became mothers while working for Jamaicans.

The "Added Value" of Repatriated Women

The expression *added value* is not derogatory and is used, instead, to convey the idea that a common cultural background was seen as a "plus" in the male/female relationship. This attitude is illustrated by the ties of kinship woven between two repatriated women, which governed the relationship between three families living in Shashemene (see figure 8.13).

In the family chart shown in figure 8.13, all the men were Jamaicans (Δ), and so was one woman (O1). Their date of arrival in the country is noted in brackets. Woman number 2 (O2) was a black Briton who arrived in Ethiopia with her parents who had travelled to the region. The third was Ethiopian (O3), probably also migrant in Shashemene. O1 and Δ2 had two children. The first was born in Jamaica and arrived in Ethiopia with his father. The second was born in Ethiopia. After giving birth to the second child, O1 moved in with another Jamaican (Δ1), and they had nine children, five of whom died. O2 had three children with Δ3 in Shashemene; the second child died. After her third child was born, O2 went to live with Δ2 and they had nine children. Finding himself single, Δ3 got involved with an Ethiopian woman (O3), and they had five children. Three families were thus inextricably linked by blood relations. It may be noted that many children died shortly after their birth, probably due to local sanitation and medical conditions. Without entering into the details of some conflicts arising from such separations and recompositions of family units, it should be stressed that certain offspring suffered from this configuration, having grown up without their mother or without the care they may have needed. Some have

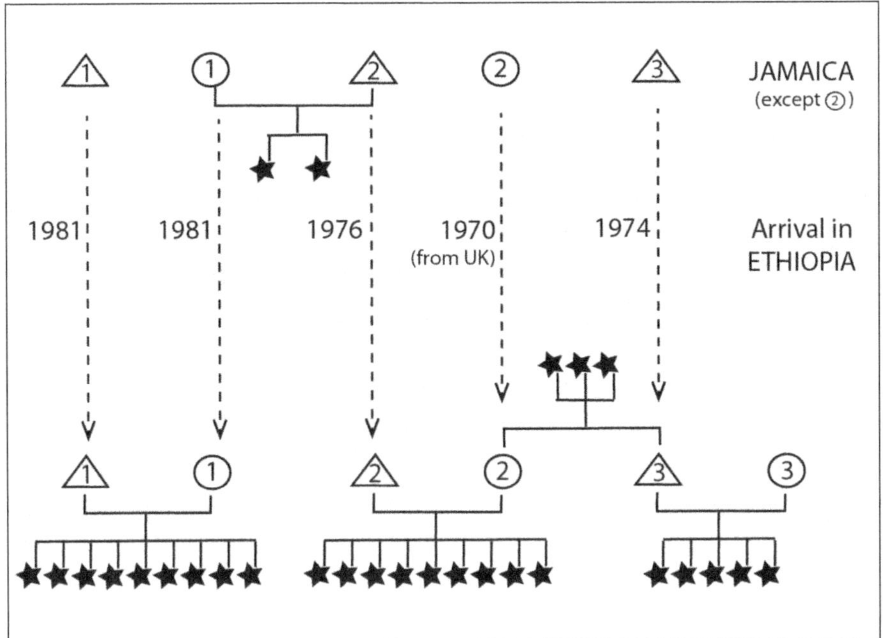

Figure 8.13.
Family chart

become parents themselves in recent years. However, the tensions of the first generation, due to the separation and recomposition of family units, had only partial repercussions on the second generation. Hence Δ1 sees the children of his first wife fathered by Δ2 as his own. The third child of O2 and Δ3 regards the children of O2 and Δ2 as his brothers and sisters. The bonds between the children are generally close, except perhaps in the case of the children of O3 and Δ3, who are half Ethiopian. Besides, one of the latter has become notorious for the numerous acts of theft and vandalism committed in the community.

These ties of cross-kinship around two repatriated women, a Jamaican and a black Briton, illustrate the "added value" associated with them. They were the object of intense competition among the men but tried to live as best as they could. Jamaican women were rare and precious in Shashemene. They were fewer than the men, and even those who settled as part of a couple were obliged to deal with loneliness. Thus, in one of the large Jamaican families in Shashemene, one child was visibly the offspring of another father, also Jamaican, but this seemed to have no decisive repercussion on how he was considered within his family unit. Could the complexity of these relations of cross-kinship, seemingly due to the dominantly masculine nature of the immigration to Shashemene, also reflect, at a broader level, the mode of operation of the organization, the Twelve Tribes of Israel, to which these people belonged? Further research is needed to respond to this question. Nevertheless, the proximity induced among members by the centrifugal force of collective organization and the focus on family via the numerous activities that brought them together suggests that the family issue is central to the development and sustainability of the organization.

Ethiopian Rastafari Women

The predictable and numerous encounters and interactions between Ethiopian women and Rastasfari form another consequence of this male-dominant immigration. As highlighted above, the first Ethiopian women they encountered were the women of easy virtue who worked in the *bunna bets* in town. As far as families are concerned, two categories emerged: Ethiopian women who became Rastafari and, in the majority, Ethiopian women who went to work for Jamaicans and became mothers. Several Ethiopian women were involved in the life of the small repatriated community during the years of the *derg*. Three of these women significantly impacted the community: in addition to mothering children sired by Jamaicans fathers, they also appropriated the Rastafari identity.

One of these women was born in Asmara in 1953, in an Amhara family, and was educated in an Italian private school. Her family was forced to leave Eritrea for Addis Ababa in the early 1970s. While passing through Shashemene, she met the Jamaicans and started a relationship with a member of the community whose Jamaican wife had returned home with their children owing to the hardships of rural life in Ethiopia. The young Ethiopian woman, for her part, remained in Shashemene, where she found work and started a family with this Jamaican. They had four children. She underscored her curiosity with respect to the Jamaicans, her desire "to become like them", "to take on their culture", and defined herself as a Rastafari: "Before I had never thought of the emperor, I liked him as my emperor but I never said that he was God. They [the Jamaicans] taught us many things, about him and about the Bible. I discovered the emperor as a God."[66]

As an Ethiopian woman, becoming a Rastafari during the 1980s was a choice resulting in marginalization among her compatriots, leading to the taking on of another cultural identity. While stressing that her parents did not oppose her choice of lifestyle, she admitted that it was always difficult to talk about the emperor with her compatriots: "I can talk to everybody, but not everybody understands me when I talk about the emperor. There are many Ethiopians who hate him. If you say something good about him, they don't want to listen you; few will have anything positive to say."[67]

The Ethiopian women who became Rastafari on account of their interaction with the Jamaicans in Shashemene found themselves on the margins of the two populations: they were marginalized by the Ethiopians because they shared with the Jamaicans a divine representation of Emperor Haile Selassie I; and by the Jamaicans because they were Ethiopians, when all was said and done. Indeed, despite their intimate relations with Jamaicans, the Ethiopian women in the community were the first victims of their cultural autarky. Yet these three young Ethiopian Rastafari women tried to facilitate the community's learning of the lifestyle in Shashemene, of the Ethiopian society and, beyond, of the local modes of social relations. But they brought to light the reserve and the misgivings of the Jamaicans and admitted that, after twenty years of living with them, they were still "not integrated" among the Jamaicans:

> They do not like foreigners, and even now are still not open to foreigners; whether Black or White, a foreigner remains a foreigner. . . . They think that only Jamaicans can be Rastas, but is just impossible! . . . They do not like others to get close to them and they don't want anybody else to believe in their God. They are jealous of their God and even today they do not care for foreigners.[68]

Hence the following paradoxical situation: how could foreigners, in this case the Jamaicans living in Ethiopia, express feelings of xenophobia? Our interviewee explained that she could understand certain reservations of the Jamaicans with respect to opening up to Ethiopians. First, they had suffered a great deal due to their minority position in the local society, and, above all, they had often been mistreated in the years following the revolution. They had been tricked and beaten, had suffered robbery on numerous occasions, sometimes aggravated by violence, resulting in a feeling of mistrust and resentment. The most current forms of violence in Shashemene will be considered later, but they impacted the reciprocal representations of one's neighbours. Second, they were reticent concerning the conversion of others to Rastafari. It is surprising to observe that the women who had shared the lives of these Jamaicans for such a long time were never regarded as bonafide members of the Twelve Tribes of Israel. This limited their access to the community house in Shashemene as well as their role in community affairs. A member of the Twelve Tribes explained why Ethiopians could not become members:

> We never had the full bench, twelve bredren, twelve sistren and Dinah. . . . We have only finance meeting. Twelve Tribes are not open in Ethiopia yet. We'll do that properly when we have people and problem solved. We can fill the bench, our children can sit on the bench. If the House is ready to form here, people would come from the west, and have executive in Shashemene. We've had no Twelve Tribes functioning properly in Ethiopia. . . . We couldn't bring Ethiopians members yet because we're not there yet.[69]

During the 1970s and 1980s, members of the Twelve Tribes of Israel formed the overwhelming majority of returnees, and Shashemene was at the centre of the propaganda of the organization. However, contrary to other places, there was no official inauguration of a Twelve Tribes branch. In the absence of such an inauguration subject to the attainment of the required number of executive members, Shashemene was unable to deliver cards of membership and to take advantage of the development of activities common to all the other branches. Consequently, Ethiopians could only become members by leaving the country and joining branches in line with all the institutional requirements. Of the three Ethiopian women who became Rastafari, only one became a member. The

Ethiopian Rastafari woman I interviewed saw no reason to leave the country: to be on the inside was enough, as far as she was concerned, and she was not motivated to become a member at all costs, even if that meant exclusion from certain community affairs. It is hard to determine to what extent this observance of institutional rules served to exclude Ethiopian Rastafari during the *derg*, but it partook of the cultural protectionism implemented by the Jamaicans in Shashemene. The treatment reserved for Ethiopian Rastafari portended what other Rastafari, the large majority, might expect. Most of the Ethiopian women involved with the community of returnees never identified with Rastafari and claimed no relation to this Caribbean culture. The following distinction was made by the Ethiopian women I interviewed: "Many girls nowadays don't want to resemble them, we wanted to become like them. All these girls that you see don't even want even to hear about the emperor."[70]

The *Serratäñña*

Let us return for a moment to the itineraries of the "many girls" – that is, the other women – the majority of those who became wives and mothers while working among the Jamaicans. Several circumstances were observed. Certain women grew up in the neighbourhood or came from nearby towns, while others arrived from further afield and displayed a more fragmented migratory or family history. Without going into the fine points of matrimonial practices in Ethiopia and the collective representations of intercultural marriages, a few remarks made by an Ethiopian father living in the neighbourhood provides introductory insights into these questions. I asked whether, in his opinion, their marriage with Ethiopian women might contribute to the integration of the Jamaicans. His answer was:

> I suppose so. If indeed the people lawfully do such thing, it will be good. But we see some strange things, which are contrary to the culture of the society. . . . For example when my daughter wanted to marry [a Jamaican], I wasn't happy she was first impregnated and I cannot disown her. But if one does it ceremoniously, first sending a *shimagele* [an old person] to ask the parents for the bride's hand, we wouldn't refuse so long as they love each other. But when [a woman] is hired in one's house as a servant and someday they make them pregnant, culturally it is an insult to the family, and if the girl don't really love or the man don't really love, it may be a big problem, a girl wouldn't go out publicly for the shame of it.[71]

This response pinpointed several factors: first, his contempt for extramarital relations – which, by the way, are not specific to Jamaicans – as illustrated by the case of his own daughter. His idea of culture, respectful of the proper procedures of requesting the hand of a bride through a third party, an elder, was damaged by the relational practices of the younger generation. He seemed, nonetheless, quite open, stressing the importance of feelings and a lack of prejudice towards marriage with Jamaicans, as long as proper protocol is observed and provided the children are born after the wedding. He made a very clear distinction between women like his daughter and the *serratäñña*, the women who, employed by the Jamaicans as domestic helpers, became pregnant, whether they liked it or not. A situation like this, in which love was thought to be absent, was seen as resulting in the dishonour of the community and of the woman. The reality of this shame is difficult to evaluate, but many women found themselves in this kind of situation. They started out as domestic helpers employed by Jamaicans, became pregnant and ended up in a social dilemma. One of these women, Amina, agreed to share her story.

Amina was born in the Wollo countryside. While she was still a child, upon the death of her mother, she was taken in charge by the government of Haile Selassie I and sent to an orphanage. She was later transferred to a "young workers" training centre, where she learned handicraft and agriculture. The course included a month's training in beekeeping, in Wondo Genet, about fifteen kilometres away from Shashemene. On her way back to the Wollo region, she was caught in an exchange of fire between the army and the Ethiopian Popular Revolutionary Democratic Front and was shot in the leg. At nearly fifteen years old, she was sent back to the orphanage and, after another year there, returned to Wondo Genet. Like many others before her, she eventually landed in Shashemene, in 1983, at age seventeen. Following a friend, she went to the Jamaican neighbourhood to look for work. Without knocking, she entered the first house she came across; they called her a *balegue*, a "good-for-nothing", and refused to give her a job. At the second attempt, she was engaged as a *serratäñña*, or general helper in charge of all the domestic chores. The Jamaicans were known to offer slightly better wages than the Ethiopians. Her friend Alemitu tells Amina's story in these terms:

> The [Jamaican] said that he would pay her twenty *berrs*. I asked her: 'Amina, do you want to go to his place? He will pay you twenty *berrs*. At this time the Jamaicans paid twenty *berrs* a month. . . . With the *habäshas*, it was five or ten *berrs* a month. She went to work [for the Jamaican]. At that time, the house was not like that. There was gold, all that. There was no telephone anywhere else in the houses of the Jamaicans, the only telephone was at his place.[72]

At the beginning of the 1980s, the Jamaicans seemed much richer than they really were, to these two women. With the arrival of the first visitors to Shashemene, the Jamaicans were able to start selling their goods abroad, thus fetching a better price than in the local market. Their international relations created a sizeable economic gap between them and most Ethiopians. Amina moved into the small cob house with this Jamaican, who was a carpenter and an upholsterer. He was making a living and had customers who came from far for his services. Amina explains how her situation began to change:

In the beginning it was like that [twenty *berrs* per month], but finally he stopped paying me any wages. The twenty *berrs*, I felt that . . . when he told me *bäqa*, that's it, I was pregnant. I was pregnant, I gave birth but while I was living, here, I was going to the *Yekatit* [local] school. In 1977 [1984] when I was going to enter grade 7, I had my daughter.[73]

Stuck as she was in an unequal relationship, as a servant, then as a companion, to top it all, she was now pregnant. She tried to abort, but it did not work. After the birth of her daughter, the Jamaican's previous woman, an Ethiopian from Walayita, who had had a child with him, returned for a while and then left again. Then there was a decline in the economic situation of the Jamaican. After the visit in 1986 of Prophet Gad, who had founded the Twelve Tribes of Israel, the Rastafari started to collectively organize the successive construction of their houses. I will focus later on the development of construction in the early 1990s, but in the case of this Jamaican, collective work was apparently the end of his independent activity and resulted in a deterioration of the living conditions of the Jamaican man and the Ethiopian woman. With a growing family, counting six children, and a house still to be built, poverty and alcohol added to a breakdown of their relationship.

The Ethiopian women who had working relationships with Jamaicans and became mothers had various ideas about the Rastafari faith and identity. Overall, they cast a critical glance on the Rastafari faith. Those who had recently arrived in the community spoke little English and sometimes found the reasoning about the nature of the emperor difficult to grasp. They were equally amazed at the distinctions the Rastafari made among themselves based on phenotype or insular or cultural origin. Beyond the question of economics, the reputation of Rastafari was not always the best in the public opinion. Moreover, some of their practices, like the wearing of dreadlocks, added to prejudice. Alemitu, whose parents had separated when she was seven, arrived in Shashemene with her father. After school, she sold *qolo* in the street. A friend inveigled her into visiting the Jamaican neighbourhood when she was still a teenager and she remembers her first reaction to the sight of a Rastaman's hair:

"It was *dread* [frightening]! His hair down to there! I screamed: 'a monster'; I ran back to town [*laughter*]."

"Were you afraid?"

"Very! Why? We had never seen hair like that! When we were small, there wasn't anything like that, we didn't see any, we didn't know. . . . When you see somebody strange, you think of a monster. There were stories, that monsters ate people. When I saw the guy with his hair down, I was afraid of him and ran away, telling my girlfriend to come, that it was a monster!"[74]

This young girl's first reaction to dreadlocks was a typical one, at the beginning of the movement, in Jamaica and Ethiopia alike. The surprise and alarm facing the long locks of the Rastafari were frequent, despite the fact that Ethiopians, especially priests or monks, sometimes wear locks. Dismissed from her home, Alemitu eventually found a Jamaican who helped her to continue her schooling. She went to live at his place and had a child. She and Amina spent nearly twenty years in the community and were well informed on the practices and habits of the Rastafari. They were familiar with the doctrines of the Twelve Tribes, the calendar that amalgamated the birth month, the belonging to a specific tribe and the character of the members; but they both defined themselves as orthodox Christian women and attended church regularly. Belief in the divine nature of the emperor was a threshold they did not cross. Alemitu was the first to talk about this:

> "You know, Haile Selassie was a man. We knew him. We have to follow what is in the Bible. At one time, he was the sovereign of Ethiopia. In the Bible, it is written that you must respect the sovereign, so I love him and respect him. But as for me, it is to God that I listen. That's it."
>
> "And you, Amina, what do you think of the Rastafari faith?"
>
> "What do they say? They say that *Ababa Janhoy* [Haile Selassie] is God. But, there are also Rastas who says that he is like a prophet, that he is not God. They say that and Jah Rastafari Selassie I is their way of saying '*temesgen amlaké, egziabehér*' [thanks to the king, to God]. For us, he used to be the sovereign of our country, *Ababa Janhoy*. When he got old, he was like our father. I do not think that he is God. But God gave something to him. He said things which came to pass, that, I believe. He is like a prophet. He was a man, like other men. But he believed in the Bible, like a good orthodox. Like every orthodox, he loved the church. . . . But we do not think that *Ababa Janhoy* is God."[75]

By insisting on the human nature of the emperor, they refuted his having a divine nature and interpreted his role with the aid of a mixture of biblical and political references. In a general way, they were attached to the idea of royalty in Ethiopia, being under the impression that the subsequent regimes, which they identified as Marxism, then democracy, had served to deteriorate their living conditions. However, their opinion was firm: Haile Selassie was only a man, and he was, moreover, an orthodox Christian – a position that comforted their faith. Amina showed her understanding of the diverse conceptions of the emperor circulating within the Rastafari movement, where some affirmed that he was God, others that he was a prophet, and others still that he was a mortal being. The variety of interpretations they produced was not to the advantage of the Rastafari and did not facilitate the spread of the movement's ideologies in the direction of the Ethiopians. Moreover, the close connection of several non-Rastafari women with the Rastafari community sometimes led to tensions over the upbringing of children or the local modes of sociability. More generally, the reciprocal impressions that "the other" was wrong sometimes resulted in a lack of understanding or in mutual contempt.

The relations among the Caribbean and Ethiopian women, whether Rastafari or not, were sometimes interdependent, given the common economic and social pressures to which they were all subjected, but the Caribbeans often had an economic edge thanks to their external contacts and sponsors. Their relations were conflict-ridden when reposing on social or cultural prejudice, or in the event that one group or the other felt threatened or undermined. For a Jamaican wife and mother, any Ethiopian woman represented a potential risk of adultery by her husband. And for an Ethiopian wife and mother, being excluded by the Jamaicans was experienced as a sign of contempt, a refusal of intercultural integration, which was nonetheless indispensable, given the situation of proximity. Whereas the Ethiopian women interviewed recognized that most Jamaicans were "proud to be Ethiopian" and loved "the Ethiopian flag", their tone of voice sometimes betrayed a certain bitterness:

> "And although they have settled among us, Ethiopians, they do not like us."
>
> "The Jamaicans don't like Ethiopians?"
>
> "No. The Ethiopians? The Ethiopian women? They do not like them, the Jamaicans. Why? Well, I . . . I don't know why. We receive them in peace. We are willing to live peacefully with them, but they . . . ."[76]

The feminine landscape of Shashemene was diverse and complex with these various permutations: Caribbean women who arrived alone or as part of a couple, Ethiopian women who become Rastafari, and *serratäñña* who became mothers. I have underlined the main characteristics, without disregarding their constant evolution, influenced by new and more regular arrivals of Caribbeans and Ethiopians. This question will be considered later from the perspective of the offspring of these families and the ways in which their feelings of belonging sometimes supersede the contradictions inherent in the encounter of experiences and identities involving, on the one hand, Caribbean foreigners who saw themselves as Ethiopian returnees, and, on the other, Ethiopians who felt marginalized in their own community.

THE ETHIOPIAN REVOLUTION AND THE FALL OF THE empire almost resulted in the death of the Rastafari movement and the end of the Caribbean settlement in Shashemene. But it probably required more than these events to completely demolish the dream. Nevertheless, their impact was direct and brutal: the returnees lost almost all of the land that had been granted by Haile Selassie I. They found themselves in open conflict with their Ethiopian neighbours, who now had a power that was felt and exercised via the peasant associations. The returnees were forced to learn the ropes of survival in a hostile environment. Many left, and new arrivals decreased to a trickle. Those who remained experienced a downturn in their situation but maintained, through their presence, the clearly potent symbolism of the land. Paradoxically, their status as foreigners protected them from the war that was raging in the country, but it also hindered actions of development, construction and ownership. They integrated with Ethiopian society at the lowest level, lost even the standard of living that was formerly theirs in Jamaica and experienced the same poverty and fear as the Ethiopians. But to a certain extent, they refused integration: protected their identity, closed themselves to the outside, and remained wary in their relations, especially with women. The end of the 1980s introduced a breath of fresh air: a final land grant, a few visitors, and the beginnings of trade with the outside, which helped to set them apart from the Ethiopians. The changes induced by the fall of the *derg* in 1991 will be examined in chapter 9.

CHAPTER 9

SHASHEMENE AT THE AGE OF "DEVELOPMENT"

THE 1990S IN SHASHEMENE WERE MARKED BY A regular increase of arrivals and their impact on the general development of the neighbourhood. Based on interviews conducted with the Rastafari and the Ethiopians and on the archives of the municipality and of the region of Shashemene, this chapter will attempt a more precise definition of the Jamaican neighbourhood. A change of scale will allow us to observe the development of distinctions among the various component spaces. The community was confronted with the challenges of the Ethiopian context, characterized by the need for resources and growing insecurity. Whereas a certain resurgence of returns may be observed during this period, tensions surrounding the legitimacy of the administration of the land hardened among the different organizations on the spot. But this did not prevent the residents, Ethiopians and Rastafari alike, from living together and establishing unprecedented relations among themselves.

The Change of Regime in Ethiopia

The change of regime in 1991 put an end to the People's Democratic Republic of Ethiopia. It had been founded in 1987, based on a new constitution drawn up by the militaries of the *derg*. In 1974, the *derg* had replaced the fourteen imperial provinces (*t'äqlay gezat*) with fourteen administrative regions (*keflä agär*), and the 1987 constitution added five autonomous regions, Ogaden, Dire Dawa, Tigray, Asab and Eritrea, itself subdivided into three administrative regions (Fontrier 1999, 28). But at the end of the 1980s, the Soviet Union's support to Ethiopia was on the decline, while clashes continued to break out inside the country. The opposition to the *derg*, notably represented by the Eritrean People's Liberation Front, the Tigrean People's Liberation Front, the Ethiopian People's Revolutionary Party and the Oromo Liberation Front, began to conduct coordinated actions. The foundation of a common organization, the Ethiopian Popular Revolutionary Democratic Front, dominated by the Tigrean People's Liberation Front, was intended to allow, despite divergent political ideologies, a coalition against their common enemy (Henze 2000, 312–14, 320–23). This was a done deal in May 1991, when the Eritrean People's Liberation Front occupied Asmara, and troops from the Ethiopian Popular Revolutionary Democratic Front entered Addis Ababa. Mengistu Haile Mariam fled to Zimbabwe, where he was welcomed by President Robert Mugabe. A temporary government was put in place in Addis Ababa, and national conferences were organized, in view of initiating dialogue among the different factions of the victorious opposition.

Without going into the details of the vicissitudes of the new temporary government established by Meles Zenawi, chief of the Ethiopian Popular Revolutionary Democratic Front, it will suffice to recall that the front embarked upon the reconstruction of the country with the aim of founding a federal republic and chose ethnic federalism as the basis of its administration (Henze 2000, 334–38). The independence of Eritrea was proclaimed in 1993, and the constitution of the Federal Democratic Republic of Ethiopia was promulgated in August 1995. A new national cartography was deployed, comprising the creation of nine federal states: Afar; Amhara; Beneshangul Gumuz; Gambella; Oromiya; Somali; Southern Nations, Nationalities and People; Tigray; and Addis Ababa, which enjoyed a special status. Nazaret became the capital of the regional state of Oromiya, comprising twelve zones. Shashemene became the county seat of the most populated *wäräda*, situated at the far south of one of these twelve zones (the East Shäwa Zone).

Several works have studied the question of the "nations" and "nationalities" of Ethiopia, from ideological origins to political establishment (Barnes and Osmond 2005; Turton 2006). With the institutionalization of the ethnic groups and nationalities, the federal model prevented the breaking up of the country without thereby eliding various tensions and contradictions born of the search for a political compromise between unity and diversity (Turton 2006, 11–12). The reinterpretation of the genesis of the Ethiopian state was one of these contradictions, featuring the opposition between an ethno-nationalist perspective and a multiethnic one. With the rise of the ethnic nationalisms, the history of the country became a battlefield (Triulzi 2002, 276–88). Differing conceptions regarding origin and policy clashed, highlighting the difficulties inherent in holding together federal states guaranteed the right of secession by the constitution. "Indeed, the federal structure did not always succeed in producing a viable national imaginary for the Ethiopian populations" (Barnes and Osmond 2005, 17). In this context of the "ethnicization" of social relations and its corollary, the erosion of the national imaginary, the return to Ethiopia went through a certain renewal. The opening up of the borders of the country, the rising discourse on development, the readaptation of political ideologies to fit the capitalist economy were some of the factors that impelled the "Ethiopians of the world" to continue their arrival and settlement in Shashemene.

The Reconfiguration of Power Relations on the Land

With the change of regime and the progressive opening up of the country, more regular arrivals and new settlements occurred in Shashemene. Besides, the festivities organized in 1992 to celebrate the centenary of the birth of Haile Selassie revived diasporic interest in the Ethiopian cause and in the situation in Shashemene. The questions of power and legitimacy regarding the administration of the remainder of the land granted to the "black people of the world" became increasingly acute. Under the regime of the *derg*, the Twelve Tribes of Israel had ensured their domination thanks to their numerical superiority and their ongoing relations, through the intermediary of their representative, with the local Ethiopian authorities. The EWF, for its part, was split between an American administrator, named almost twenty-five years earlier by the headquarters in New York, who had returned to Ethiopia in 1990 after eight years of absence, and the officers of EWF Local 43 in Kingston, who had returned to Ethiopia in 1981 and had called for the division of the land in 1970. The tension between these two camps was extremely high. It crystallized around the symbolic attributes of EWF authority held by the American: a sign in front of his house which could be seen from the road, signalling the presence of the EWF, and the official seal of the organization. To make matters worse, a few EWF officers enjoying close ties with their Jamaican elders arrived from England.

The issue of the future settlement and development of Shashemene was on the agenda of an encounter between the contending forces on the spot. The encounter occurred following the centenary celebrations, which many people attended. Called the "All Houses Reasoning", this meeting was held in the EWF local in Shashemene and assembled at least forty people, visitors for the most part, including some well-known personalities of the Rastafari movement, as well as residents, present since the former regime or newcomers of recent years. All the "houses" of Rastafari were supposed to be represented, but EWF members formed the bulk of the assembly. Men and women sat on benches, or stood, with their backs against the wall or jammed together in the doorway, leaving a small central opening for the different speakers. Two cameras filmed the event, leaving a trace of this meeting, during which, for the first time, the future of the settlement was debated collectively, on site, in Shashemene. The videos were not commercialized and have become a part of the archives the community has created for its own memory-keeping. The analysis of one of these videos offers insight into the questions that were discussed and the points of disagreement.[1] The assembly took the form of a "reasoning". In this characteristic discursive space of Rastafari, during which the history of the movement is shared and transmitted, a satisfactory solution is generally sought after.

Inez Baugh gave a public reading of a few archives, the petition sent out in 1969 to call for a division of the land and the document that formalized this partition in 1970. These documents provided the historic reference marks that launched the discussion. One of the first questions debated was: who were the recipients of the land grant? Was it "all the black people of the world" or simply the members of the EWF? Various opinions were expressed, but the assembly came to the agreement that not all black peoples had supported Ethiopia during the crisis of the Italo-Ethiopian war and that it was, above all, the members of the EWF who had, through their moral and financial support, engaged in the defence of Ethiopia's sovereignty. An officer from England underlined the importance of the EWF constitution, which the emperor had endorsed. He also recalled that the revitalization of the EWF in England during the 1980s represented the last chance to centralize competing energies within the movement. The assembly agreed that the land had been granted to the EWF and that membership in this organization was open to all the black peoples of the world. But Inez Baugh took the floor. She had arrived in Ethiopia in 1968, had never been a member of the federation and had nonetheless remained on the land since then, experiencing three political regimes: "We came as pioneers, not members of federation. . . . Look how long we've been here, and I've been suffering, suffering so much and we're not members of the federation but we hang on to the land. . . . Why don't we stop talk and talk foolishness, why don't we get together?"[2] Her husband, seated in the centre, bowed his head, apparently discommoded by this speech. Inez Baugh defended a non-exclusive vision of settlement and pointed out that, in spite of the legitimacy of EWF Local 43, the first settlers to arrive from Jamaica were not members of the EWF and that the administration founded there at the beginning of the 1970s was called the "Pioneers Settlers Corps". This term was challenged by Noel Dyer, who insisted on the fact that he had never seen himself as a pioneer, that he had come back to Ethiopia to recover his legacy as a deported black man: "Me nah pioneer, dis ya me heritage, Iman came back to my heritage."[3] His contribution was highly appreciated by the assembly. The next to take the floor was a woman, a representative of the Twelve Tribes of Israel. She recalled the origins of the Twelve Tribes, the disappointment of Prophet Gad over the administration of the EWF and the need for a stable financial base, in view of the repatriation of members to Africa. She insisted on the fact that it was not the federation that had given them land and that the Twelve Tribes now had more than sixty children born in Shashemene. She also recollected that during Gad's last visit in 1986, he, the leader, had been ready to give up the name "Twelve Tribes of Israel" for another susceptible of fostering greater unity, thus allowing the Rastafari to work together under an "umbrella" organization.

The questions of unity and centralization have been recurrent since the beginning of the movement and are constantly evoked in its discourses and discussions. To centralize meant organizing a joint administration and sharing the powers of decision making and management. A proposal of this type, put forward by the Twelve Tribes, posed no threat to them, given their numerical weight. But for the federation, on the other hand, centralization has often been perceived as a risk and as a betrayal of the objectives of their constitution. The assembly seemed to approve the idea of a common organization that would not prevent the houses from treating their internal business separately. Furthermore, all speakers, Twelve Tribes and EWF members alike, constantly emphasized the pre-eminence of the Order of Nyabinghi. The Order of Nyabinghi was highlighted as the root, the wellspring of the Rastafari movement, whose power resides in the elders and in their musical and ritual traditions. Livity, the moral and behavioural code of Rastafari conduct, was mentioned on several occasions; it was the point of dissension separating those who claimed the ital, vegetarian, nyabinghi practices – who do not smoke tobacco, do not drink alcohol – and those with other Rastafari practices, Twelve Tribes members in particular, who have the reputation of greater laxity and impose no doctrines concerning food. Such distinctions contribute to the creation of symbolic barriers between the groups.

One of the young actors from the Order of Nyabinghi in Shashemene took the floor to stress the complementarity of the different houses and practices and to propose the creation of a neutral space favourable to collective work. One of his remarks, expressing reservations about the way in which EWF members "sacralize" and rigidify their constitution, jolted the assembly, but his insistence on discipline went undebated. There was a large consensus around the need to develop local facilities and infrastructure. One speaker insisted that all those who had helped in development were not EWF members, but were nevertheless important. Another Rastaman summed it up this way: "Me a member of federation, but me nah deal wid dem. De issue is not who and who is member, but who a go develop [the land]."[4] Yet, moving beyond boundaries to develop the neighbourhood was not a sacrifice everyone was willing to accept. Accordingly, the EWF officer from England seemed quite unwilling, for his part, to set aside the supremacy and legitimacy of the EWF. Plan in hand, he presented a project of industrial development, insisting that the business spirit was to be promoted within the community and that the creation of a legal entity in Ethiopia was a prerequisite.

No decision concerning the formation of a common organization came out of this gathering of representatives from the different organizations present in Shashemene, the EWF, the Twelve Tribes of Israel and the Order of Nyabinghi. However, the promotion of development and the legalization of facilities via development projects emerged as priorities endorsed by all attendees. Faithfulness to the Rastafari tradition was incessantly reiterated and connected Shashemene, following a biblical terminology, with the "Kingdom of Rastafari". Similarly, shouts of "Jah Rastafari! Haile Selassie I!" punctuated the allocutions. The shared racial and spiritual consciousness was quite strong, but the weight given to the discrepancies surrounding livity and membership in different organizations hindered a collective and united synergy.

These internal rifts were publicly staged when the Ethiopian authorities requested the election of a community representative in late 1992. They surfaced in the letters addressed to the municipal authorities by the EWF representative, Berthal J. Moody, on the one hand, and by Reverend William Hillman, a Twelve Tribes supporter, on the other. The latter was a member of the EWF, but the *derg* years, spent among the Twelve Tribes members, had probably served to strengthen their bonds. It would appear that Moody was initially designated as the representative of the community, but some immediately contested his legitimacy. According to Hillman, twenty-nine people refused to recognize him as their representative.[5] Moody complained to the municipality that the members of the other group had refused to cooperate and stated his intention to call on the authorities in Addis Ababa.[6] The mayor, Negaw Gebreal, later asked that the representative be elected from among the eighteen families to whom parcels of land had been allocated at the end of the 1980s and who were well known to the administration. All were members of the Twelve Tribes of Israel.[7]

The opposing actions of the returnees, their inability to come to an agreement and to choose a representative undermined their standing in the local society. The Ethiopian authorities eventually realized that a historical rift opposed the EWF, whose history they had begun to understand, and the Twelve Tribes, most of whose members were familiar, and whom the municipal archives designated as "the Jamaican community". The municipal authorities had called for only one representative, but a double-phased dialogue was ultimately established with representatives from each group. This compromise hindered settlement and hampered the execution of development projects. The other stumbling block was the local Ethiopian administration, the returnees' primary interlocutor, and an unavoidable link in the establishment of a development project. Let us go back for a moment to the transformations that took place in what was already often referred to as the *Jamaica säfär*, the "Jamaican neighbourhood". They illustrate the complex modes of communication between the local administration and the returnees as well as the dynamics of urbanization around the town of Shashemene.

The Transformations of the "Jamaican Neighbourhood"

Revised after 1991, the bureaucratic network became even more complex after the federalization of the country, and the process of application for construction permits became exceedingly laborious. Infrastructure developed at a snail's pace in the neighbourhood, whereas arrivals and settlements were in full swing during the 1990s, with a considerable acceleration near the end of the decade. The municipal archives overflow with applications for building permits addressed by the community. These were of several orders: home construction, the rehabilitation of existing constructions, or the construction of a wooden or brick fence.[8] To be valid, these applications had to be accompanied by a master plan, providing information on the site, the area of the lot and the construction project. But as the town maps used by the authorities were totally outdated – the latest having been made in 1967 – they failed to show most of the existent land parcels. On the whole, the procedures of construction permit followed no clearly defined or transparent mechanism and were, in some cases, inconsistent or even contradictory. Moreover, the official borderlines of the town divided the neighbourhood in two, placing certain parcels under the authority of the municipality and others under the authority of the peasant associations, in charge of the management of increasingly inhabited residential and urban land. In the urban development plan of 2000, the remainder of rural land before the river was to be incorporated into the town, and its status was supposed to change from land administered by the peasant associations to holdings managed by a *qäbälé*. We must study this issue on another scale in order to understand the stakes involved in settlement on the land in Shashemene.

Within the "Jamaican neighbourhood", several spaces may be distinguished:

a. A rural space undergoing transformation: the eighteen parcels allotted in the 1980s, which spilled over the boundaries of the town, under the control of the municipality;
b. The lots that escaped the 1975 reforms, situated beyond the limits of the town, which were transformed due to interpersonal arrangements;

Figure 9.1. Four Spaces maps.

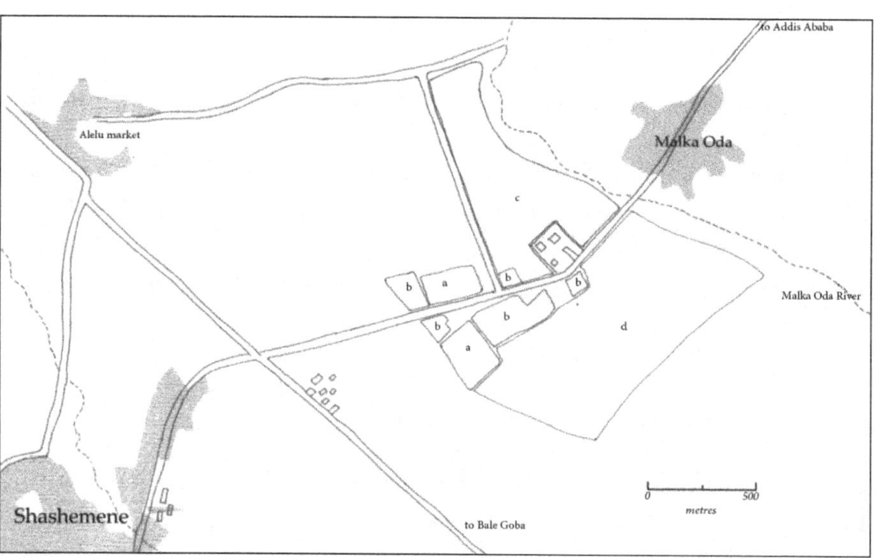

c. Alelu, the "*addis säfär*", the new neighbourhood, situated beyond the limits of the town until the Master Plan of 2000, where more than one hundred new lots were marked off in the space of a few years;
d. Awasho, beyond the limits of the town until the Master Plan of 2000, occupied since the mid-1980s by Oromo people, who came from the neighbouring countryside.

A change of scale, moving beyond the neighbourhood for a closer look at its component spaces, highlights the different types of housing developments, which in turn illustrate the complexity of the dynamics of settlement after 1991.

A Rural Space Undergoing Transformation

The Alelu and Awasho peasant associations allotted eighteen parcels to the Jamaican members of the Twelve Tribes in 1986. These parcels, cut squarely in two, were situated on either side of the road, just before the entrance to the town of Shashemene. As they were defined as rural land at the time, it was not possible to build there, and the lack of funds during the *derg* years precluded construction anyway. During the 1990s, the administration of these eighteen parcels changed hands and status; from the peasant associations to the municipality, from farming land to urban land. Until that period, given the former rural status, the residents paid no taxes to the town and were consequently not registered there. When the residents decided to begin construction and submitted their plans to the municipal authorities, their applications were rejected based on the lack of "certificates" of legal residence.[9] To solve this problem resulting from the change of status of the lots on which they lived, in 1994, the residents asked a Shashemene architect to draw up a map showing their sites, in view of integration into the municipality's urban development plans.[10] This land registration map was in fact the first cartography of the settlement on the land. The original document is in the keeping of the municipality of Shashemene, with a copy in the possession of the Twelve Tribes representative.[11] It indicates the form and confines of the lots and the names of those living there, but it is not really a property title.

A second difficulty arose: once these parcels had been consigned by a land surveyor and could be officially registered by the municipal authorities, it was discovered that they were larger than the other residential lots granted by the town, measuring five hundred square metres at the time,[12] whereas theirs measured between thirteen hundred and twenty-one hundred square metres.[13] A paradoxical situation emerged: the town recognized the residential character of these spaces but could not apply the usual procedures, especially regarding taxation, since the lots exceeded the authorized dimensions and were therefore illegal as urban residential spaces. As a solution, the town proposed the

Figure 9.2. Registration of the eighteen parcels, Shashemene, 1994. Archives D. Martin, Shashemene © DR.

application of a lease tax to all residential lots exceeding five hundred square metres, thus allowing another rate of taxation. From an annual tax of about five hundred *berrs* for an urban lot of the usual size, the annual land tax on each of the eighteen lots jumped to three thousand *berrs*, which was too much for the residents to afford.[14] In short, the eighteen lots had to change status from rural to urban land for construction to be allowed, but obtaining property titles for the new residential status was beyond the means of the residents, given the size of their concessions. The solution arrived at may be summarized as follows:

> [The municipality] advised us not to worry about the paper in our hand because it is money, so do what you want to do, build. They don't want the permission to build, so that's how we build, even with no money still, but customarily you should have documentation in order to build, being untouchable. There is a problem amongst us, a query, they shouldn't take tax on us, on the land grant.[15]

Authorized to build without an official permit, but nevertheless uncomfortable with the absence of bonafide property titles, this interviewee underlined the existence of a "litigation", constituting another sore point. The returnees felt that they should be exempted from land tax as they had been invited to settle on the land by the former regime. This claim could not be countenanced by the municipality, which was already hard put to integrate these oversized residential lots into the urban plan. There was therefore no question of taking on the recognition of the right of the "Ethiopians of the world" to come and settle in Shashemene. Despite this litigious factor, whose solution was in the hands of the Ethiopian government, not in those of the municipality of Shashemene, constructions took off: a few houses were constructed collectively, following a system of work rotation, meant to offer to each, according to the order of arrival, a house financed by the Twelve Tribes and built by resident members.[16] While awaiting their turn, some residents managed to find the means of building on their own. Some of the buildings at the time were made of bricks, but most were made of cob with an overlay of cement, covered with a zinc roof. Some "ate up" the funds made available to them and continued to live in unfinished houses made entirely of cob or wood. Others had access to more direct outside assistance and were thus able to build large houses in strong, durable materials. The situation was nonetheless precarious: the local authorities, willing to "close their eyes", delivered no property titles but allowed construction to proceed, leaving intact the risk of a sudden application of the law, or a change of administrative personnel and the consequent cessation, without notice, of the numerous constructions in progress.

The case of one resident illustrates this insecurity: he arrived in 1976 but settled on one of these lots only in 1992; up until then, he had lived in a two-room hut made of wood and zinc, with his wife and nine children. Without outside financial help, he had managed, in 1999, to lay the foundations of a house in durable materials on the same lot. Four years later, when the house was nearly finished, it was destroyed, and the employees of the municipality confiscated the materials, thereby provoking the anger and incomprehension of the residents:

> Land grant was given to us and we are recognized here by the government that we are settlers from Jamaica and we do everything official through community, and we have a chairman of the community body, a executive body and they look after all official business. This particular house including all the houses that we built on the land is processed through the government, Nazaret and Addis Ababa and the Shashemene *meker bet*. Now all these things are being processed. Especially since they destroyed my house, the process step up.[17]

The destruction without notice of this house provoked the outcry of residents demanding respect for their constructions. They addressed their protest to every level of the administrative hierarchy – the municipality, the regional government (Nazaret) and the federal government (Addis Ababa) – in an attempt to gain the recognition, once again, of their right to live and to build on the allocated land. The expansion of the town, sanctioned by the Master Plan of 2000, transformed this neighbouring space into a stake for a municipality faced with the challenge of exercising its authority over formerly rural parcels of land and probably disturbed by the general expansion of constructions in the neighbourhood, as will be seen later. The modus vivendi that had prevailed for several years between the residents and the municipality revealed its limitations, and the precariousness of the situation provoked numerous correspondences and discussions at various levels.

The municipality found itself between the devil and the deep blue sea – a predicament that was probably not unrelated to the ill will of its administrators, indisposed to facilitate the settlement of the Jamaicans. On the one hand, they were bombarded by the applications of the Jamaican residents, and, on the other, they repeated the argument that the absence of official certification prevented the approval of their permit application: "It was not found possible to give them proper certificate because they don't have any basic information."[18] Yet the municipality was perfectly aware that the Ministry of Foreign Affairs had "very strongly reminded us that their rights should be kept and their piece of land shall not be taken or touched".[19] Besides, given the fact that the residents had been in Shashemene for twenty-five years and had the requisite construction plans, the regional government of Oromiya impressed on the regional Urban Development Office that "this land is owned by them, they should get letter of ownership and you should certify them they can construct".[20] The protection provided by people in high places expressed a more general policy of respect for the residents. But it was no substitute for direct and concrete orders to the municipality and provided no explanation for the destruction of the house in question. The lack of legitimacy thwarted the development undertaken by the residents on these eighteen lots of land, and the problems encountered illustrated, moreover, the struggle between the local, regional and central authorities and, more generally, the circuitous channels of communication and the internal complexities of the Ethiopian administration.

The Land That Escaped the Reforms

Despite the great land reform of March 1975, which nationalized all the land in the country, the Jamaican inhabitants managed to retain a few parcels of the original grant. Most of these were situated outside the town limits, and their dimensions allowed further settlement possibilities for the arrivants who came after 1991. This room for manoeuvring was nevertheless limited, as these spaces were enclosed and surrounded by numerous dwellings and pressured by a greater population density. Settlement on these parcels of land depended mainly on personal or organizational contacts with previous settlers. Several scenarios emerged: conflicts, for instance, when Rastafari returning after many years of absence found that the place had changed and that they were unable to reintegrate their former concessions; then, there was the case of the amicable interpersonal arrangements which facilitated insertion. These examples highlight the fragmentation that threatened these parcels, which were among the largest.

The case of Carmen Clarke illustrates one type of conflict that arose when a returnee reintegrated into Shashemene after years of absence. A member of the EWF, Carmen Clarke had arrived in Ethiopia in 1969, at the age of thirty-five, and was allocated ten hectares following the 1970 division of the land. After the revolution, she left for Jamaica. She took up residence in Trench Town, where political violence was still in full swing, making such a neighbourhood increasingly dangerous. She resumed her studies, became a nurse and took up responsibilities within the Ethiopian Orthodox Church, which had opened in Kingston in 1970 (Abuna Yesehaq 1997, 203–17). According to her report, she was sure that one day she would return to Ethiopia. Following her mother's death in 1994, she left everything behind, once again – husband, job, house – and, at sixty-one, returned to Shashemene.[21] She was unable to recover her ten hectares of land, which had been nationalized, and her small cob house, left in the keeping of another. In fact, this person had passed it on to a member of the Twelve Tribes who had arrived in 1977 and had lodged two other persons there during the *derg*. Clarke had given notice of her return and of her intention to recover her house, but as soon as he received this news, the occupant went to the *qäbälé*, registered the house in his name and paid the annual tax, amounting to 350 *berrs*. Clarke appealed his action as soon as she returned, but had no document to prove her entitlement to the property and she had, moreover, entered the country on a tourist visa, whereas the occupant, for his part, had a valid residence permit. For the local authorities, the situation was clear: Clarke's appeal was rejected and, following twenty years of absence, she was unable to reclaim her house.[22] She lived in the home of one of the EWF officers for nine months, after which a small lot was finally placed at her disposal, a little further away, on the Alelu side. Disappointed and bitter, she opened an orphanage there, under the patronage of the Orthodox Church.

Gladstone Robinson's itinerary offers another example; he came back from the United States in 1990, after eight years of absence and several short visits. He had left his land and house in the keeping of his Ethiopian wife and in-laws. But he was unable to recover them upon his return. In fact, they maintained that these goods had been gifted to them and that it was out of the question for them to leave. Robinson and his in-laws got into a number of lawsuits, with several appeals. Things took a dramatic turn with the use of false documents, the corruption of witnesses and the intervention of the army. Fearing that they would lose everything, the in-laws started selling the zinc roofing, after which they subdivided the land and sold pieces to Rastafari or to Ethiopians. Robinson hastily purchased them, at an exorbitant price. After ten years of legal proceedings and threats on all sides, Robinson was still unsuccessful in reclaiming his house, located on the lot of land.[23] Throughout this crisis, he lived almost in front of his former home, with his new family, in a little house by the roadside, on what remained of the lot that had been given to Vincent Beckford, in 1970.

In other cases, a certain number of arrangements were made and did not lead to conflicts of such proportions. On the contrary, they corresponded to existent needs for space, on the one hand, and for funds, on the other hand. One example is the use of the parcel of land adjoining Beckford's. Belonging to Inez Baugh, it was one of the largest to have escaped nationalization. On the occasion of the centenary celebrations for Haile Selassie I, in 1992, a temporary tabernacle was constructed there, facing the Baugh home. The tabernacle is a sacred space in which Rastafari venerate Haile Selassie I, and it falls under the ritual authority of the Order of Nyabinghi. The tabernacle is circular in shape, covered by a roof made of branches and zinc, but open on the sides. Surrounding a central pillar, on a table usually covered with a white cloth, are placed Bibles, pictures of the emperor, Ethiopian flags and a few offerings. The space of the tabernacle is intimately related to the Jamaican religious context, since its organization and ritual objects bespeak the cultural proximity existing between the ritual practices of the Rastafari and those of Revivalism, studied notably by Barry Chevannes (1994, 21–22). Following the centenary festivities of summer 1992, the organizing committee of the centenary was put in charge of the construction of a permanent tabernacle in Shashemene. Pursuing the international campaign that had contributed to the centenary's success, the committee sold certificates of contribution to the construction of the tabernacle in Shashemene, to the tune of five pounds sterling each. In 1995, with the income from several hundreds of certificates sold to the Rastafari international community, the foundations of the tabernacle were laid in Shashemene, next to Baugh's house. A lot of land was subtracted from the Baugh property, rented for the sum of a thousand dollars a year. The money was sent from England.[24] Two persons were put in charge of the first works and lodged on site to protect the materials. One was Bongo Solomon, who had already built a tabernacle in Jamaica as well as the previous, temporary one in Shashemene in 1992: "When me come Shashemene, I bring light to Shashemene by building the tabernacle. . . . Me serious, me come build foundation in name of Selassie I cause none of this was in Africa before, plus it is the only one in Africa, one in South Africa now, where people go and praise the black God. Everywhere else is the White Christ. It has its purpose and Shashemene get bright."[25]

The foundation of the tabernacle was an important stage in the settlement of the Rastafari in Shashemene. As our interlocutor underlined, there was a tabernacle in South Africa, of recent construction, but the one in Shashemene was the first, thus symbolizing the realization of the physical and spiritual return of the Rastafari to Africa, following the promise of the black God. The localization of the tabernacle on the Baughs' large concession showed how a community space came into being thanks to consensual fundraising efforts launched in collaboration between the returnees residing on the spot and the Rastafari arriving in search of land. This initiative was also an indirect means of "protecting" the Baughs' land. As the couple were elderly and unable to exploit it completely, they were exposed to the threat of a change of mind by the local administration, susceptible of reappropriating these unoccupied spaces by the roadside. Indeed, with the general growth of Shashemene, the value of roadside lots had escalated. Other parcels that escaped nationalization, like Beckford's, accommodated newcomer initiatives: one Rastafari rented a space on Beckford's land, where he opened Rasta Alem, "Rasta World", comprising a large shipping container, in which he worked and lived for several years, and which housed a macramé shop and a library, visible from the road to passers-by and visitors.[26] These facilities on the parcels of land that had slipped through the net of the reforms signalled a fragmentation of the land in the neighbourhood, partaking of the broader dynamics of population density and increasing pressure on the land, to which numerous persons sought access.

The Opening of Alelu

Alelu formed a gentle slope alongside the Road Authority buildings, bordered, on one side, by the river and, on the other, by a large footpath. The population density was one of the lowest in the neighbourhood up until the middle of the 1990s, and the Ethiopians, through the peasant associations, controlled these large parcels of land strictly reserved for agriculture.[27] Yet, strategies of negotiations between the peasants and the Rastafari were put in place in order to facilitate the settlement of the growing numbers of newcomers. However, it is only in 2000 that a letter from the *wäräda* of Shashemene was sent to the Alelu administration to notify concern over the land transactions practised in the neighbourhood: "Around the community of Jamaicans, illegally, lands are sold and bought. Therefore if the matter continues, in future, peasants will not have anymore farming land. It will also be against the Master Plan. Therefore from today onward the case has to be followed."[28]

The preoccupation of the *wäräda* was double: the future of the peasants, who would soon be unable to cultivate due to a lack of space, and the uncontrolled development of the town of Shashemene. Yet, settlement had been progressing for years and had managed to sidestep the law. Marking the gap between the law and the local practices, an Ethiopian neighbour had this to say about these common practices of informal deviation:

> "During the *derg*'s regime, people couldn't buy land but now they can buy?"
>
> "Well, in a round about way. Not directly. We can buy only on contract. For example you want to buy a piece of land from me who am an owner, you pay me the money and I give you a signed receipt. But to make it legal, in the public office you'll sign on a contractual basis for twenty years or thirty years contract. Before there was such things as *gult*, *madäriya*. After the *derg* came all this is no more. After the declaration of 'Land to the tiller' land is given only on contract for lengths of time. But secretly after I've sold you my land and received the money I give you a receipt. But before the law I'd say it was given to you as a gift from me. This way it's possible to have a piece of land in your name. . . . Before it was not like now . . . and this is not for the Jamaicans alone, it is for everybody, it is within the city it become expensive, out of the city it is cheaper."[29]

Figure 9.3. Cactus fences in Alelu, 2003. Photograph: G. Bonacci © DR.

This testimony reveals the extent to which, for the Ethiopians, the arrivals of these Rastafari turned out to be more lucrative than attempts to preserve agricultural land. Above all, these transactions help to explain the influx – defying statistics – of Ethiopians to the neighbourhood. The latter, thanks to their nationality and to their understanding of the runnings of the local administration, had easier access to land than the foreigners who, for their part, had no rights. It is best not to underestimate the stakes behind the settlement of Ethiopians in the Jamaican neighbourhood, where quick money could be made on land speculation. Priest Paul, from the Bobo Ashanti congregation, arrived in 1992, and he lived for two years in a rented house. He was instrumental to the opening of the Alelu neighbourhood. He narrates his search for land:

> Since land was available, as land was granted to people of the West, I seek a little plot for ourself. So I come down and seek for land 'cause I want to sekkle [settle] Iself to live the land which Jah inspired us to live as Rastaman. Coming here, you haffi [have to] understand that the land was occupied by the farmers. Seeking me get fe meet with a farmer, a man that work in Ministry of Agriculture, so to get land. Not just for myself, but for Rastaman in general.[30]

He discreetly refrained from specifying the position of the civil servant in question. In fact, negotiations were about to begin with the farmers who worked, occupied and managed the land: "The land was given to the people, [and] because the people wasn't here the land was occupied by the natives. You couldn't blame them fe that, cause if you have land you haffi occupy the land."[31]

Negotiations began between this mediator and the peasants who occupied the land. They came to the agreement that money should be paid to the Ethiopians who would then free up the land and "donate" it. Due to administrative regulations, even "granted" or "donated" land could not be left empty but had to contain a construction of one type or another. Accordingly, a small house was constructed quickly on such sites, shortly before or right after the land changed hands. The peasants were then "compensated" for whatever was built on the land, be it a building or crops, at the time of the handover:

> To my understanding of what is happening here still, the land, you can't buy land, land belong to Almighty God. But now is compensate you a compensate for a thing, whether for a building – yeah or a crop on the land or something, you a recompense. Speaking of buying land, here we nah buy land here, we recompense for the one who dwelt on the land and kept the land for a period of time.[32]

The financial transaction was thus configured as an exchange between the "legitimate" owners, the returnees, and the "occupants", who thereby became the custodians of the land. At least eighty out of the one hundred and fifty parcels or so that formed, in 2002, the *addis säfär* – that is, the new Alelu neighbourhood – were made available to the Rastafari by this same mediator, who took care of the negotiations with the peasants.[33] Once obtained, the land was rapidly enclosed with fences of cactus, barbed wire, planks, or bricks, for the more fortunate. But even after this, many parcels remained vacant, as the new owners were in Addis Ababa or abroad. Cob houses were for a long time the only constructions, but many big cement houses were also built, most of them over a period of several years, thus providing work for Ethiopians and Jamaicans with construction skills. This architecture stands in contrast to the more current Ethiopian style, mainly in cob. The Ethiopian houses are no longer round, in the style of the yesteryear *täkul*, but are now either square-

Figure 9.4. Haile Selassie and Empress Menen painted on the zinc fences of Alelu, 2007. Photograph: G. Bonacci © DR.

shaped or rectangular, and their size is measured in the number of zinc sheets required for the roof. The new houses, which usually take time to complete, have private gardens with flowers, fruits, vegetables and legumes, terraces, spacious interiors, windows protected by burglar bars, walls often colourfully decorated with representative paintings, and, of course, external toilets made of durable materials.

Let us make a visit to one of the recently settled *gebbis*. A young couple, a Caribbean man from England, and an Ethiopian woman of mixed blood, adopted and raised in Germany, set up house between the Road Authority building and the river. After a first visit to Ethiopia in 1998, they repatriated in 1999. They stayed for a while in Addis Ababa and acquired land in Shashemene in 2000. They chose a site that they liked, which was still free, with trees already planted and a beautiful view. They had no immediate neighbours at the time and occupied three lots of farm land, each measuring a little over eight hundred square metres, for a total area of twenty-five hundred square metres. There was a set price at the time, about 4,600 *berrs* per parcel, but they were obliged to pay a grand sum of 13,200 *berrs* (1,320 euros). Of this amount, 2,300 *berrs* went to the peasant occupant, and 2,300 *berrs* to the *qäbälé*. A document was signed by the purchaser, the mediator and two Ethiopians, one of whom applied his seal. This document stipulated that the land had been donated with an eight-zinc-sheet cob building, which did not, in fact, exist. Within a week, the space was enclosed, and the young couple built a cob house, in which they lived for two years. Another peasant complained that this land had been leased to him, that he was unaware of the sale, and claimed that he wanted to harvest his crops. Ethiopian soldiers came several times to ask the couple for money, threatening to stop the brick construction that was underway. The couple was eventually obliged to give them money for a peaceful life. A Rastafari with experience in technical drawing made a construction plan for the sum of 700 *berrs*. With the financial help of their family in England, they began to build a slightly elevated heptagonal house, using regular bricks, with a water tank in the basement and large, painted, wrought-iron windows. Although internal toilets were included in the plan, the installation of external latrines allowed better water management. Two bedrooms and a large living room with an American-style kitchen were simply furnished, and two doors let in the breeze.

When the house another resident was constructing on one of the eighteen parcels of newly granted land was destroyed in 2003, alongside those of other people in a similar residential situation, this young couple went to the municipality to apply for the registration of their installations. Accordingly, several parcels were surveyed that same week, and a retroactive land tax was applied. One resident reported the sense of security derived from the application of this tax: "I hear since you have that land tax, you are legal in the municipality, the land is yours, you are recognized legally as you pay, the land is yours. And then once you have that, you can have plan for your house." Nevertheless, the process of legalization of these new installations remained unclear, and this was only the beginning, as the Rastafari had occupied more than eighty parcels in Alelu. This was the location of the large Ethiopia Africa Black International Congress camp and several of its members, the Bobo Ashantis, lived in the ajacent neighbourhood, together with members of the Twelve Tribes, of the EWF and of the Order of Nyabinghi. Access to land in Alelu was not determined by membership in a specific organization, and many Rastafari, individually or as a family, found land there. Alelu is where the first collective house was constructed, financed by four individuals, three of whom had previously resided in Malka Oda, on the other side of the river. One lot of land had been identified and selected, and a huge one-storey house was built there. One of the persons who worked on this project explains the symbolic importance of this house built by four people: "I think that's the purpose of coming home to me, it's about not taking selfish European values, as Rasses [Rastafari] we should be able to live and work together. . . . It's a expression of unity, Rastafari unity, that's its purpose, Rasta coming home we have to be united, but if we can't live together, what's the point of it all? We must have some works that express togetherness."

Unrelated to any type of official membership in an organization, the energy spent in creating this common space bore witness to the desire for unity expressed by the Rastafari who came together in Shashemene. This shared effort integrated the general dynamics of the partition of rural space that went into the creation of this "new neighbourhood". The rise in the number of returnees during the 1990s had contributed to an increased pressure on the land. Consequently, in Alelu, where land soon became available, there was a high concentration of fresh arrivants and new houses. On the other side of the road, in Awasho, similar strategies of land occupation existed, but this was a different environment, in a neighbourhood that was already fairly occupied by a majority of Oromo people.

Integration in Awasho

Awasho had found itself, since 1985, at the centre of a "villagization" programme. Villagization was a vast campaign of population displacement launched by the *derg*. Its objective was to regulate and control the rural population by concentrating the peasants who lived scattered all over the region into villages. Following this residential centralization, the peasants continued to work the same farmlands as before, although these were sometimes at a distance from their homes (Clapham 2002, 19; Taddesse Berisso 2002, 117). Close to 40 per cent of the rural population was concerned. One of these new villages was situated at the centre of the land that was initially granted, a little way back from the road. The division into blocks, a characteristic of the villagization process, occupied four blocks by eight, each subdivided into eight narrow parcels, leaving no

Figure 9.5. Map of Alelu and Awasho in 2002.

space for a home garden. Most of these dwellings were *täkuls*, round structures made of cob with a thatch roof.[34] The farmlands were set further inland, and space for new installations along the roadside were extremely limited. A few Awasho Peasant Association officials appropriated parcels of land between the road and the homes of the Jamaicans. Following the pattern of the new village in Awasho, another village was established on the other side of the river, next to the old Malka Oda settlement. This new settlement was, however, much smaller, occupying five blocks by six, each comprising sixteen parcels. The establishment of the villagization project at the centre of the first land grant, in Awasho, signalled the *derg*'s intention to curtail all future requests for land.

This is not the place to launch an in-depth study of the impact of villagization on the environs of Shashemene. A few remarks will suffice. Taddesse Berisso has underlined the economic decline induced by the villagization campaign. This was due to the increased distance of access to farmlands and the difficulties of keeping livestock close to home, owing to a lack of space. The promiscuity resulting from the creation of these new villages led to tensions between families and individuals. It destroyed the privacy of families as well as local social practices (Taddesse Berisso 2002, 131–32). More than 250 parcels were drawn up and built in Awasho, bringing together, en masse, the bulk of the population present in the neighbourhood at the end of the 1980s. This led to a significant demographic growth, and the population density surpassed that of Alelu, situated on the other side of the road. Awasho remained unenclosed for a long time, but fences began to spring up near the end of the 1990s. These were rarely made of durable materials, consisting rather of pickets made of wood or branches. Many homes have hens, goats and cows instead of a kitchen or a decorative garden. Here, returnee settlement occurred in a more populous residential and demographic context than that of Alelu and transited through mediators distinct from those on the other side of the road.

For example: A young Martinican couple arrived in Addis Ababa in late November 2002 and got to Shashemene a few days later. They began by finding lodgings in the community and later met an Ethiopian who introduced them to a peasant who was willing to sell a parcel at some distance from the Awasho road, within an overwhelmingly Oromo population. The parcel of land measured fourteen hundred square metres and was first quoted at 18,000 *berrs* (1,800 euros), but was finally sold, after bargaining, for 12,000 *berrs*. The Ethiopian mediator explained that they had to build quickly to prevent the authorities from catching on – although the latter were in connivance. The former owner built a small cob house with cement plaster for 7,000 *berrs*, though rumour had it that the real price was 4,000 *berrs*. Another 2,000 *berrs* were demanded for the construction of a high bamboo fence. These payments were all honoured in monthly instalments. A document signed before four witnesses attested that the land had been "given". But the mediator explained that he needed cash and received a certain sum. On top of that, 2,500 *berrs* were paid to the *qäbälé* for the registration of the transaction, but no document was signed. Later, they were told that, to have their property registered, they needed to obtain a residence permit. The young couple sent a third party with 250 *berrs* to apply for the permit but, here again, the local identification card regularizing their presence was refused. It took 300 *berrs* to finally obtain the document, against the normal local price of about 35 *berrs* for Ethiopians. The young returnees spent 21,000 *berrs* for their lot of land and their tiny house and fence and another 2,800 *berrs* on various local administrative fees, hence a total of almost 24,000 *berrs* – a huge amount of money in Shashemene – the equivalent of a mere 2,400 euros at the time.

This case speaks to the significant economic gap between the Ethiopians and the new arrivants. The foreigners had no idea of the local cost of living, and the

Figure 9.6. Awasho after the rainy season, 2003. Photograph: G. Bonacci © DR.

Ethiopians took advantage of the situation and fleeced them as much as possible. This economic gap marked the entire range of relations woven in Shashemene and also differentiated the 1970 returnees from those of the 1990s. The newcomers often arrived from United States or England and, generally speaking, had more cash and were thus able to invest more quickly in large, solid houses. Furthermore, there was a sharp rise in inflation. While Awasho was, for a long time, less expensive than Alelu, prices soon rose there as well, and the cost of a parcel of land tripled within two or three years. Roadside lots escalated to as much as 125,000 *berrs* for an empty, non-cultivated lot and 80,000 *berrs* for a commercial site. Before this inflation, some preferred to settle in Malka Oda, in rented houses which they refurbished to fit their needs. Others found lodgings in town, sometimes as a transitional phase, while awaiting the funds needed to begin construction. The pressure resulting from newcomer practices had a double impact: they were inevitably informal, related to the overall conditions of the reception of returnees to Ethiopia; and this informality helped to create an unequal and corrupt social climate.

Changing scale, by shifting our focus from the Jamaican neighbourhood to its constitutive spaces, allows us to highlight the disparity in residential development characterizing the complex settlement dynamics after 1991. These were marked by the diversity of actors within the Rastafari community and among their Ethiopian interlocutors. Members of Rastafari organizations, both families and individuals, increasingly applied for and negotiated land access and residence permits. The municipality, the peasant associations and the Ethiopian occupants controlled the land. Consequently, to obtain access, the Rastafari officially applied to the administrative services. On the whole, more or less formal solutions were found. But these left numerous issues unresolved. Where was the documentary proof that the Caribbeans had a right to the land granted by

Haile Selassie I? How could a government policy acknowledging their presence be implemented by the town authorities? How would the day-to-day search for solutions and the current negotiations play out in the wider perspective of the town's development? The Caribbean presence in Shashemene raises a number of unusual questions in the Ethiopian society regarding the place and the rights of foreign actors. Yet, the difficulties foreigners encounter are not necessarily different from those faced by the Ethiopians themselves, who are also confronted with the complications of the administrative system. At any rate, the settlement of the Caribbean Rastafari in Shashemene helped to transform the space that rapidly became known as the *Jamaica säfär*, the Jamaican neighbourhood. They paved the way for future development: residential development was a prerequisite for the overall development of the neighbourhood and for the establishment of social or commercial projects on a larger scale. The urban development plans, designed in 2000, will contribute, when executed, to the transformation of the neighbourhood. The space managed by the town will then extend to the river, embracing the Rastafari installations and reclaiming the power placed in the hands of the peasants' associations of Alelu and Awasho.[35] New roads, new services and new land-tenure statuses will once again curtail returnee settlement and installations, in the absence of specific policies designed to clarify the ambiguous land tenure situation which currently exists.

Local Impact and Social Life

The land tenure relations encounter those of social life. Life in the Shashemene of the 1990s might be approached from several angles, notably that of ethnographic analyses addressing the dense strata of social dynamics connecting the returnees with the Ethiopian social context and the diaspora networks. A few aspects of these dynamics will be underlined below.

Relations

Arrival in Shashemene was never easy, and, in the first weeks, the new arrivants were easy targets. They were generous, had few reference marks and were unaware of the jealousy they were likely to arouse. They all passed through the phase they later called "the test of fire". This expression resonates with the Bible story of Shadrach, Meshach and Abednego, whom King Nebuchadnezzar threw into the fiery furnace when they refused to disown their God. Preserved by their faith, they escaped death by fire (Daniel 3). The Rastafari arriving in Shashemene associated the furnace with their experience when subjected to robbery, injury, suffering and loneliness due to their choice of existence. Returnees felt that they had passed through the fire upon making the decision to remain in Shashemene, in spite of everything, for the accomplishment of their Rastafari faith and of the divine plan of return. Among the numerous biblical images reactivated in Shashemene, that of the test by fire was often evoked, offering a spiritual interpretation of the difficulties encountered and the determination needed to remain. These difficulties were sometimes induced by the other Rastafari present, from whom the new arrivants expected greater support.[36] Indeed, certain insular distinctions reared their heads in Shashemene, where a Trinidadian, for example, was possibly welcomed with less warmth by the Jamaicans, compared to one of their compatriots. The French-speaking Rastafari, who were usually uncomfortable with English and even less so with the Jamaican dialect, seemed isolated within the community. But the difficulties encountered also had to do with the relations with the Ethiopians. William Shack characterized thus the relation that the Ethiopians established with the foreigners in their midst: "Tolerance and indifference, and the absence of overt forms of hostility, for the most part characterize the attitudes of Ethiopians towards strangers, whatever the strangers' racial or ethnic origins or religious leanings" (Shack 1979, 44).

Taking a closer look at the overall Ethiopian situation, Shack underlined the fact that "religious strangers" were probably those that posed the greatest problems for the Ethiopian authorities. He was thinking about Christian missionaries. But to a certain extent the Rastafari were also "religious strangers". They did not threaten the politico-religious structure of the monarchy as Christian missionaries did, but were perhaps a threat to the anti-monarchist ideologies of the post-imperial regimes. Furthermore, the Rastafari, in their effort to integrate with the poor peasant stratum of the Ethiopian society, came up against greater hostility on the part of the Ethiopians than many other foreigners in the country did.

In Shashemene, the hostility of the Ethiopians surfaced in the form of insults, for example, linking social status and phenotype, notably through use of the term *baria*. *Baria* means slave and *barnet* is the condition of slavery and servitude. For the Caribbean Rastafari who saw themselves as free men and women who had returned "home", to be called *baria* was a serious insult. A few Ethiopians who took the risk of pronouncing this slur were severely battered and ended up in hospital. Slavery and the slave trade had been endemic in Ethiopia but were abolished at the beginning of the 1920s (Rouaud 1998). Current usage of the term *baria* covers a variety of meanings, beginning with a low social status. Calling the Caribbean Rastafari *baria* might have referred to their ancestors' deportation from Africa and to their origin as the descendants of enslaved Africans and would have implied a certain knowledge of the history of black people in the Americas. But the transatlantic slave trade has little resonance in the Ethiopian national memory, compared to coastal countries such as Ghana or Benin. Instead, the term in Amharic has a rather southern resonance. It was linked to a geographical space, the Ethiopian south, whence slaves were extracted and over which imperial control weighed heavily. This political domination often went hand in hand with cultural prejudices. As used today, the term *baria* still seems loaded with prejudices of this kind, expressed in terms of civilization or skin tone.

One illustration of colour prejudice cropped up in a conversation I had with an Ethiopian woman, a teacher at the Ethiopian school in the Jamaican neighbourhood. She explained that she did not like Jamaicans because they were black (*t'equr*).[37] She herself would have been black in Europe, for example, but the disconnect between her self-representation and her prejudice regarding the colour of certain Jamaicans was obvious. Conceptions linked to skin colour in Ethiopia have not yet been studied, but the association between a social status (*baria*), and a skin colour (*t'equr* or black), a legacy of Ethiopian history, is sometimes reconfigured in the register of the insult slung at Caribbean settlers in Shashemene, thus revealing the mutual ignorance marking the relations between the two populations. This situation bears witness to a shared ignorance of each other's history, drives, customs and practices. Nonetheless, social and economic dynamics emerged in Shashemene and were expressed through ties binding Rastafari and Ethiopians to one another.

Securities

A distinction must be made between the Rastafari who had resided durably in Shashemene and the new arrivants. The first were usually – but not always – better integrated. A few participated in an *edder* or mutual aid society, to which people contributed in order to receive financial support during illness or for funerals (Tubiana 1995). Others were invited to Ethiopian weddings or other family celebrations held in the town as representatives of the community. More rarely, some participated in the numerous religious festivals of the Ethiopian Orthodox Church and joined the press at the church doors, alongside the Ethiopians. Nevertheless, a slight disconnect persisted: the Rastafari spoke a different language, had a different culture, higher levels of income as well as connections to the outside world. These differences were exacerbated by the presence of the new arrivants. They were obliged to seek, without delay, means of generating income. The community resorted to a variety of economic strategies and often relied on its connections to foreign markets. At the end of the 1980s, external trade circuits had developed. The Rastafari sought foreign outlets for the sale of materials bought in Ethiopia (textiles, jewellery) or local handicraft productions (crochet, knitting, clothing). A few workshops had opened, and produced articles in wood or metal, while others specialized in handicraft articles (macramé, clothing). Following in the footsteps of a Rastafari from St Vincent who pioneered the production of organized handicraft among the Ethiopians, one Rastafari woman narrates how she set up a clothing workshop, in which training and work were remunerated:

I just brought my sawing machine and start from there, very basic, some ideas of design, working on a few blockets, piled on top of rough board, that's how me started, and the meditation of training Ethiopian daughters at practical skills they can use. That project went to different phases and learning experiences, but a number of daughters passed through. InI got my inspiration on how to set up this works from Ras Hailu directly in that sort of way. I have nuff [a lot of] respect for the works he does, Banana Art, and I met him from an early time, observe how he was functioning, training Ethiopians, paying them at the same time like an underjob training and they continue to work like they have a job and he train them and I like that idea. Seeing how the economic situation of a lot of Ethiopians is and difficulty paying for education, especially in Shashemene, I directly did a similar thing, encourage some daughters to come, buy some more machines and learn with InI, some went through good, and some through distance, nuff experience, teaching, language. What InI do is we produce our own design and sell them.[38]

At the outset, she was forced to leave the country once a year to sell her goods, but she ultimately turned, little by little, towards the local market, adapting to the demands of visitors and residents, by sewing school uniforms, for example. Thanks to her contacts in Tanzania, another market opened up. After spending several years organizing this collective production and travelling to sell it, it dawned on her that the pan-African market was the way forward, as it allowed the Rastafari communities in Africa to offer mutual financial support by facilitating the circulation of local productions. Valuable initiatives of this kind helped to consolidate the commercial activities of the returnee community and those of the local economy alike.

In addition to the typical Ethiopian economic and social life of their environment, the Rastafari also developed certain forms of solidarity among themselves. Everyone was confronted – despite the difference in background – with poverty and hardship, and the forms of solidarity, developed on a day-to-day basis, often overlooked cleavages in ritual practices, lifestyles and earnings. People gave clothes and food to the neediest in their midst, and, from time to time, a helping hand opened spontaneously. Sporting tournaments were also organized, as well as excursions to Wondo Genet, the hot springs situated about fifteen kilometres from Shashemene. Skills were corporatized for work projects, events and concerts. Musical groups were formed, such as the Twelve Tribes of Israel Band, conducted by Sydney Salmon, a Jamaican who had arrived from the United States. The group included musicians who were not all members of the organization. Their songs, comprising a mixture of English and Amharic, brought the Rastafari universe closer to the Ethiopians and was an immediate hit in the country. This success inspired Ethiopian artists to make reggae music as well.[39] The EWF and Twelve Tribes community houses usually opened their doors to the public on Friday and Saturday evenings for domino games, movies or music, thus providing leisure time at the end of a busy week.

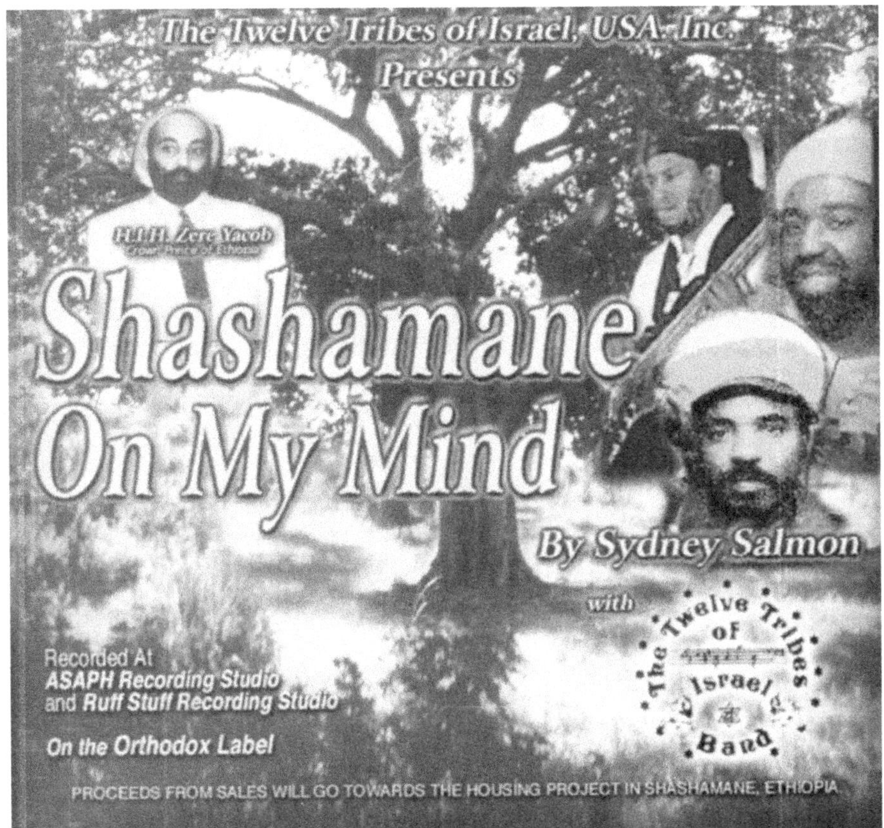

Figure 9.7. The jacket of a Sydney Salmon record, *Shashamane on My Mind*, 2000. © DR.

High points of the year included the holidays and the ritual celebrations of the Rastafari calendar – 23 July (the birth of Haile Selassie I) and 2 November (his coronation) – offering the occasion for huge assemblies attracting numerous visitors from Addis Ababa and abroad. At the crack of dawn, nyabinghi drums would sound in the tabernacle, where the service continued until midday, when big dishes of ital food were shared.

In the evening, a reggae concert would be organized by the Twelve Tribes. Local groups like the Twelve Tribes of Israel Band performed, as well as other artistes from the community or visiting artistes. Due to the gradual improvement of their infrastructure, the Twelve Tribes were able to put up a stage and accommodate hundreds of people. Besides, with municipal authorization, a great parade was usually organized for the July celebration. Several trucks loaded with participants, drums and flags woul leave the neighbourhood, followed by numerous passers-by. In town, amused Ethiopians watched the parading Rastafari, proudly bearing aloft the Ethiopian colours. These celebrations bonded the community together due to the returnees' partaking in the production of a shared identity. The social life of the Rastafari, with its activities, projects and celebrations, enhanced their visibility and obliged the Ethiopians to identify and recognize them as Rastafari.

Figure 9.8. Rastafari beating nyabinghi drums in front of the tabernacle in Shashemene, 2003. Photograph: G. Bonacci © DR.

Insecurities

Other, less festive events also contributed to the unity of the Rastafari community. Violent attacks were the main problem causing social insecurity in Shashemene. They were sometimes perpetrated by members of the community – that is, Rastafari returnees – who, at one point, turned against their neighbours in a violent manner. During the *derg*, two persons, Eric Smith and Inez Baugh, suffered cruel attacks by fellow Jamaicans. A redoubtable weapon, the machete, was used against them, resulting in the loss of the use of a hand and an arm. One attacker was jailed and later deported, while the other was ostracized by the community. These serious acts of abuse troubled many in the neighbourhood and added to the social insecurity already rampant in the everyday life of Shashemene.

A comprehensive inventory of the cases of theft, with or without aggression, would fill a book. The Caribbeans appealed time and again to the authorities for support in remedying the security problem in the neighbourhood.[40] The persons with whom I spoke all agreed that incidents of robbery had escalated during the 1990s. Several causative factors might be advanced: the demobilization of the soldiers of the *derg* and the exponential circulation of weapons, the constant inflation of consumer goods, in-migration and the evolution of the state system, added to a haphazard application of the law. The increase in robbery and violence was not restricted to the Jamaican neighbourhood, but its residents were choice targets. They lived in a less densely populated area than the rest of the town of Shashemene and often possessed more interesting goods than the Ethiopians, thus provoking jealousy and daily episodes of robbery. Racket created in the street, threats addressed to the new arrivants and the burglary of homes revealed a high level of social insecurity, often affecting the overall relations between Rastafari and Ethiopians.

A Jamaican who arrived in 1981 lost the entire contents of his small cob house on nine occasions. These incidents were sometimes aggravated with assault, and the thieves beat his wife, who was present at the scene of the crime. This Jamaican, embittered by such frequent violent experiences, finds it difficult to befriend Ethiopians. And many others share this experience. A Jamaican who arrived in 1976, and who was repeatedly robbed, revealed that she had been tempted to leave Ethiopia on two occasions because of this. In recent years, armed robbery has been on the rise, and several Caribbeans attempting to defend their belongings have been threatened at gunpoint and seriously wounded by machetes and knives. When the victims of such aggression caught or injured a thief, they found themselves obliged to pay for his transportation, hospitalization and care. For an arrested thief to remain in the town jail, the victims were forced to bring food for him to eat. The insecurity generated by robbery impacted everyday life; houses could never be left without someone inside. In a context where residents were isolated, lived alone, or at some distance from their neighbours, this generated a climate of anxiety.

Without going into the details of returnee mortality, it may be noted that the rate was high, corresponding to the situation of the wider Ethiopian population.[41] Infantile and maternal mortality, death due to poisoning, short- and long-term illnesses (tuberculosis, cancer, HIV) left a deep impact on the community, underlining issues related to hygiene, medical coverage and the preservation of life. But death was sometimes violent. A few cases of murder or attempted murder affected the members and the history of the community. There was, first, that of Zeptha Malcolm at the end of the 1980s. He had arrived in 1969 and was found dead one morning, on the ground, in the main street. The motive of the crime and the identity of the perpetrators – were they Ethiopians? Jamaicans? – was never officially discovered, and suspicion and accusations led to great tension. A Rastafari woman from England was attacked in 1992, a year after her arrival, on her doorstep, at dusk. The man, armed with a machete, probably did not expect her to defend herself. But she did, saving her life but losing, in the process, a finger and some nerves. Here again, the motive was left unelucidated. Was it because she was white? Because she had been able to afford a house? Because she was new? The attacker fled and was never brought to justice. In April 2002, a Rastafari from the Bahamas was killed by being shot in the back at point-blank range by an Ethiopian. In this macabre series, this last murder brought the community together to protest the arbitrariness of the act. The information was circulated all over the world by the Rastafari communities, and the residents in Shashemene reacted by informing the Ethiopian authorities and calling on them to arrest the criminal, a former soldier employed as a security guard.[42]

The mobilization of the Rastafari around these problems of violence and mortality is interesting, since death had always been a taboo subject within the Jamaican Rastafari communities. Extolling eternal life, the victory of the body and incarnation over mortality, the Rastafari feared the "contamination of death" and never participated in funeral ceremonies, including those of their loved ones (Chevannes 1998b, 36–37). This taboo was challenged in Shashemene, where the death of children and adults in their families obliged the Rastafari to confront the mortality of the body. Some members of the community knew how to prepare a body for burial and took charge of several discreet funeral ceremonies. Even more significantly, faced with the existence of specific cemeteries for each religious faith, the Rastafari, who lacked resources, applied to the authorities for a lot of land to be used as a cemetery.[43] This was an unprecedented initiative in the history of the movement, an adjustment born of the local reality in which the Rastafari evolved. Whereas living in Shashemene contributed to the accomplishment of the Rastafari faith, the reality of death also forced the settlers to take their responsibilities in the various phases of social life.

In its density, complexity, and multiple facets, the impact of local social life on the Jamaican neighbourhood underscored the specificity of Rastafari life in Shashemene. They encountered the same problems as other foreigners in Ethiopia: indifference, distance, sometimes hostility. These, added to the specific land issues, increased insecurity. But contrary to all other foreigners residing in Ethiopia, they were the only ones to attempt such a level of social integration, in a space fully engaged in the process of urbanization, alongside Oromo peasants with whom they shared the same access to weak Ethiopian infrastructure. Generating an income and creating a Rastafari and Ethiopian social life were the challenges they had to tackle. The need for development was so urgent that the Rastafari organizations – the EWF and the Twelve Tribes of Israel – reformulated their discourses around this question, by decisively linking repatriation and development.

Repatriation for Development

The Rastafari of Shashemene were taxed with a lack of initiative. This was a characteristic of the *derg* years, during which they were unable to act, build, or grow. With the liberalization of the economic exchanges and the slow development of infrastructure and services, the Rastafari apprehended the importance of the development discourse. Adaptation to the changing economic dynamics of the 1990s induced a discursive shift: repatriation to Shashemene was no longer simply a matter of "fulfilling the prophecy"; its objectives also concerned the development of the country. This credo of residents and visitors was expressed in "Africa awaits its Creator".[44] There were two interpretations of what this meant. First, a spiritual interpretation, linking the future of Ethiopia and Africa to the adoption of the Rastafari faith, implying that when Africa recognizes its creator – Haile Selassie I – many of its problems will disappear. The second is a "classic" pan-African interpretation, assigning to the African diaspora a role and a decisive responsibility in the evolution of the continent. These interpretations served to re-actualize and renew the African Renaissance discourses that Edward W. Blyden, Alexander Crummell and Martin R. Delany had championed in their day. The "civilizing" framework of the pan-Africanists and black emigrationists of the nineteenth century was re-actualized by the Rastafari arriving in Ethiopia. They demonstrated the resilience of their pan-African commitment to the development of the country, despite the regime change of 1974. Consequently, the Rastafari organizations in Shashemene adapted themselves to the new situation and reformulated their development objectives.

They were handicapped by their inability to designate one individual to represent them before the local administration. Hence, two organizations continued to represent the interests of the returnee community: the EWF and the Twelve Tribes of Israel. In an internal report written in 1991, the EWF offered a clear reformulation of its objectives by insisting that "the development of Shashemene is the principal aim of the EWF at this present moment in time. We ardently believe that Shashemene cannot be built by mere rhetoric – neither can it be developed by wishful thinking alone."[45] At the time of the writing of this report, the EWF was working on three specific projects, funded by lotteries or events organized in England: the renovation of the headquarters in Shashemene, the purchase of a machine to make building blocks for construction and the development of a water storage system in the neighbourhood, to palliate the insufficiency of the town's distribution of drinking water.[46] Ten years later, in 2002, the EWF obtained from the Ethiopian Ministry of Justice the status of an international non-governmental organization, and a consultative status was accorded them by the United Nations.[47] The project accompanying these applications concerned the establishment of a "model city" in Shashemene. The term "model city" resonates with the symbolism of the ideal city, the heavenly Jerusalem coming down to earth, present in the biblical corpus and circulating in the "Ethiopian belt". Beginning with the "Zion Cities" developed by the "Ethiopian" religious communities, evoked in part 1, the image of the ideal city was remodelled to fit the requirements of its promoters and those of state-of-the-art technology. One EWF officer explained the "vision" behind their development projects as follows:

> We want to establish a self-sustainable model city and we are using our status at UN to promote this. A model city that will not need to rely on nothing outside of it, that will harness the natural resources of modern age. We will have our solar sub-station distributing solar energy to each and every dwelling, to the industrial estate, recreational area, residential area, we will have gas tank giving distribution to every household and every business, we will take harness of the wind and have wind pumps. This is the kind of model city we want to establish in Shashemene, as a model not only

to Ethiopia but to the rest of the continent, as what can be achieved in unity between Blacks returning from the West and our brothers and sisters here.[48]

Including the use of solar energy, wind energy, gas storage, the exploitation of natural resources and their distribution in the neighbourhood, the vision promoted by the EWF was appealing, given its will to afford access to the latest technology in clean and renewable energy production. By presenting an objective of this order, which will probably require years of research, funding and execution, the EWF was, in fact, proposing an alternative vision of development. The latter was meant to be equitable, clean and effective, corresponding to the general values of respect for the environment advocated by the Rastafari, who value nature and are wary of consumer society.

One of the first stages of this ambitious project was the creation of a "vocational centre" in Shashemene. This project, presented in 2000 to an Ethiopian government agency, the National Disaster Prevention and Preparedness Commission, in Addis Ababa, had several objectives. Targeting the youth, who are often idle and unemployed, its agenda included various types of technical training (metalwork, electricity, carpentry, construction, sewing), promoted the development of organic farming, of research in herbal medicine, and also offered various services (sports, access to computers) to the residents in the community.[49] While corresponding to local needs, this development project not only made sense in terms of infrastructure but was also formulated to allow, in the long-term, the development of relations between the returnees and Ethiopians. Advancing these pan-African relations was thus seen as a central stake in the future development of the community, although the relations among Rastafari organizations were neither simple nor easy. Indeed, parallel to the efforts formulated by the EWF, the Twelve Tribes of Israel also reformulated their objectives and participated in the foundation of a new organization.

In December 2001, the Jamaican Rastafarian Development Community was recognized by the government and accorded the status of a local – that is, Ethiopian – non-governmental organization.[50] The aim of the Jamaican Rastafarian Development Community was to provide an umbrella organization, bringing together the different Rastafari organizations in Shashemene. The EWF had refused to take part, to avoid the risk of losing its historic prerogatives over the administration of the land in Shashemene. Members of the Order of Nyabinghi and the Ethiopia Africa Black International Congresses, in addition to members of the Twelve Tribes of Israel, joined the main initiators, who occupied several positions of responsibility within this new organization. Other positions were occupied by Rastafari originating in other organizations, but the predominance of Twelve Tribes was such that the Jamaican Rastafarian Development Community was sometimes assimilated with the Twelve Tribes and was thus sometimes seen as an old association with a new name. Whereas the reluctance of certain residents (notably, EWF members) was understandable, the new organization soon became an important interlocutor with the local administration. It relayed appeals and applications, complaints and information between the municipality and the residents. The presence of the word "Jamaican" in the organization's name was sometimes criticized. Although the returnee community had become quite international by the end of the 1990s, the general community and the neighbourhood were still often identified as Jamaican, owing to the origin of the majority. Nevertheless, many Rastafari arrivants found it difficult to accept this insular identity. Despite lengthy discussions, the word "Jamaican" was finally adopted, regardless of its unsatisfactory representation of the community's diversity.

The field of action of the Jamaican Rastafarian Development Community was reflected in its structure: a general council – which collected the proposals submitted by a committee representing the different "houses" of Rastafari – and three bodies, in charge of their execution: (1) a project director and his operational team; (2) an accountant and an external auditor; (3) the subcommittees for agriculture, education, health, sports and culture, entertainment, trade and industry, construction, and the media and communication.[51] At Jamaican Rastafarian Development Community general council meetings, the persons in charge of the different committees present the results of their activities, ask questions and table the problems encountered, for discussion by the council. The community also created another project, similar to that of the EWF "vocational centres", called the "Shashemene Community Education, Skill Training and Recreation Centres", never mind the risk of disconcerting the Ethiopian authorities by this duplication of projects with similar objectives. More importantly, the neighbourhood school was taken in charge by the Jamaican Rastafarian Development Community, and its development quickly emerged as one of the first challenges successfully tackled by the community.

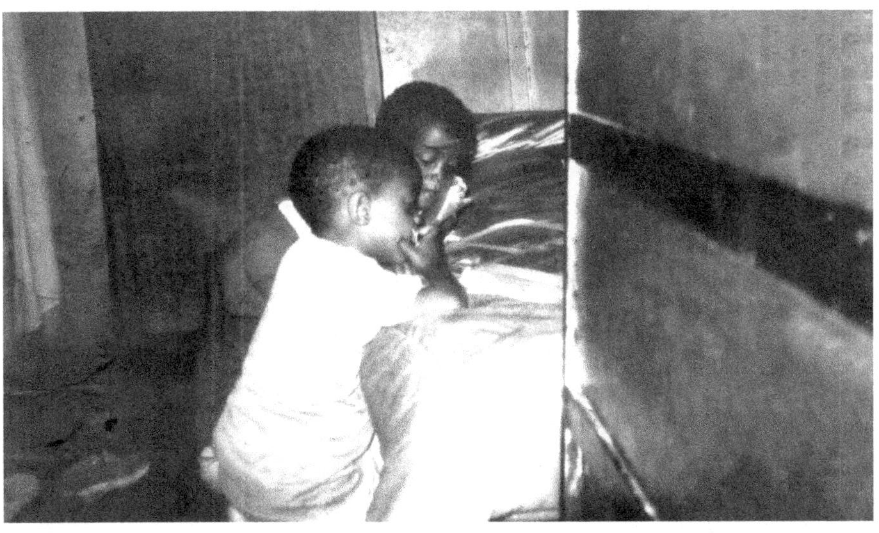

Figure 9.9. One of the first schools in the community, late 1980. Personal archives, D. Martin, Shashemene © DR.

The second school established by the returnees, during the *derg* years, was housed in a small room with a sheet metal roof, within the Twelve Tribes of Israel community. It had functioned for several years thanks to a Jamaican teacher, Karl Hamilton (Zebulon), who had arrived from the United States in 1979. Starting again from scratch, following the nationalization of the first school, established by Pipers, this tiny school supplemented the instruction the children received at the Ethiopian school. Above all, it allowed the young generation born in Ethiopia to make friends, socialize and spend time together.

The school was soon overwhelmed by demands, and was moved, in 1999, to another site, formerly occupied by a dairy industry. This new school opened with close to thirty-five pupils, a number which hiked to one hundred and seventy in 2003, comprising mainly Ethiopian children with no family connections to the Caribbean. The school's principal pointed out that he had been forced to turn down many pupils,[52] due to a lack of space and infrastructure. Eleven teachers and two volunteers, a mix of Ethiopians and Caribbeans, were in charge of teaching, giving courses in English and Amharic. After several years of operation without government recognition, the Ministry of Education accorded a permit in May 2003, allowing the adoption of the official curriculum from kindergarten to eighth grade. Registration fees were the same as those of the Ethiopian government schools: for kindergarten, five *berrs* for registration plus one *berr* a day and, for primary school, an annual fee of fifty *berrs* a year. Furthermore, every year, the organization sponsored about fifteen school children from more distant Oromo villages. As Shashemene had about fourteen schools, with an average of seventy-five pupils per class and only three schools covering the last four years of education, the Jamaican Rastafarian Development Community School played an important role.[53] The permit from the Ministry of Education enhanced sponsorship opportunities and the development of the school took off to a good start.

The development actions were the fruit of a double dynamic, originating in both the local society and the diaspora. The local development actors produced a project relating the history of the school and detailing its needs (classrooms, canteen, computers, gate, and so on). Many Rastafari living in Shashemene were engaged in the everyday life of the school as teachers or administrators. They organized countless activities, concerts or family days in order to raise funds. Over the years, mobilization kicked off in the diaspora, thanks to foundations created in the United States. They took charge of fundraising, sales, events and shows for the benefit of the school. Some conducted more small-scale actions at the individual level, as a contribution to the school's development. This double dynamic is characteristic of the development action undertaken in Shashemene in recent years. It reposes primarily on the feeling of solidarity and identification with the community in Shashemene, which traverses diaspora spaces and Rastafari networks. A proper history of the mobilization of the diaspora in favour of Shashemene would require multi-site investigations extending beyond the objectives of this book.

It is possible, nevertheless, to highlight the importance of the extroversion of the development economy in Shashemene. The investments in and the funding of development objectives formulated by the residents came from the outside. They integrated the activities of the two main organizations in Shashemene, the EWF and the Jamaican Rastafarian Development Community, both of which placed a premium, in their discourse and practice, on the need for development in Shashemene. These organizations also attracted the individuals, groups, and foreign investors who visited the community. They invested, to alleviate the insufficiencies of the Ethiopian infrastructure, financing, for example, the electricity and water connections, whose execution had proved to be an overwhelming challenge for the municipality.[54] Plans for a hotel, a restaurant, shops and a hospital were made, all dependent on drawn-out discussions with the Ethiopian authorities.[55] Generally speaking, it is too early to assess the success or failure of these projects and the processes of economic dependence they might incur. Mobilization, enthusiasm and determination are the heart and soul of most of these actions, impeded by the tensions reigning among the representatives of the Rastafari community, the overall economic conditions in the town and in the country and, once again, by the twists and turns of the Ethiopian administration.

Nationality and Belonging

At this point, approaching the end of our discussion, we return to the questions of nation, national imaginary and nationality. Representatives of the black peoples of the world have come a long way, from the imagined black nation and the dream of its realization, projected onto the territory of Shashemene, to the actual returns that have helped to keep the dream alive. Alongside land, social relations and development, acquiring or failing to acquire Ethiopian nationality is a concrete issue impacting heavily on the life of the returnees in Ethiopia. These final concerns will now be examined in an attempt to discuss the community formed in Shashemene. I will recall the conditions laid down for obtaining Ethiopian nationality and propose a few perspectives concerning the dialectical processes renewed by the children of returnees in Ethiopia.

The Rastafari Nation

In a master's thesis on the Rastafari community in Shashemene, submitted at the University of Addis Ababa in 1997, an Ethiopian student, Ababu Minda (1997, 6–8), offered an interesting approach by analysing the Rastafari in Ethiopia as an ethnic group, following the classic definitions of Max Weber and Fredrik Barth.

Figure 9.10. D. Leach of the Twelve Tribes of Israel, with Danakil, Shashemene, Ethiopia, January 1981. Photograph: D. Bishton © DR.

The identity markers studied were mainly rituals, symbolism and language. Presenting an Ethiopian perspective on the subject, he stated in the conclusion of his work that "Rastafarians are in the process of forming an ethnic group. Although we are convinced they are an ethnic group when we see them from the native's point of view, it takes some time for an objective observer to see them in the same light" (115).

Considering the Rastafari in Ethiopia as an "ethnic group" has more to do with the process of identity transformation in Ethiopia through which the ethnicization of social relations became the cornerstone of the country's federal politics (Barnes and Osmond 2005; Turton 2006) than with the forms and social conceptions developed by the Rastafari themselves. The Rastafari, of course, present "ethnic differences", some of which are identified by Ababu Minda (dreadlocks, ital food, Italk, the use of ganja, musical and family culture, and so on). Yet speaking of a Rastafari "ethnic group" in Ethiopia precludes the analysis of the relations between Rastafari and Ethiopians as well as that of the multiple differentiations among Rastafari. Indeed, many families are mixed, Caribbean and Ethiopian, and the family legacies passed on are neither strictly Caribbean nor completely Rastafari. Besides, the social interactions between Rastafari and Ethiopians are constant, manifold and diverse. The Shashemene community bonds during the ritual celebrations of the Rastafari calendar, although everyone does not participate in the same rituals. The tabernacle and the Twelve Tribes' concerts fail to assemble all of the Rastafari living in Shashemene. Many adopt Italk characteristics, but all residents do not share the same mother tongue, in a situation marked by various forms of English as well as French and diverse Caribbean creoles. The biological criteria assigned to ethnic groups is formulated in the discourses on the need for racial purity that cropped up time and again in the history of the movement, but black people, people of mixed blood and a few white people live or have lived in Shashemene. Even a question as crucial as the interpretations of the emperor's nature, as human and divine, is not a matter of consensus among the returnees.

But community consensus coheres around the national symbolism of the Ethiopian colours – red, gold and green. This shared national symbolism represents the black imagination of Ethiopia, the identification with Ethiopians and with the land of Shashemene, as well as the various cultural practices of the Rastafari. Consequently, this is not an ethnic imaginary but rather that of the black nation, simultaneously associated with Ethiopia and with Rastafari. The local population recognizes this double identity when they call out to Rastafari: "When they [the Ethiopians] see us they say Rasta! Selassie I! We accept that, we think it is a title, an honour, every time they see us, Selassie I! Rasta! Jamaican! We don't get that title nowhere in the world, that honour. We can put on His Majesty button and red, green and gold and they might even be timid to wear a red, green and gold hat, so I think we is courage and inspiration to them."[56]

Representing both Rastafari and a certain Ethiopian national pride, the Rastafari in Ethiopia form a Rastafari nation within the Ethiopian nation – and the two are intimately connected. Identification with Rastafari had to be discreet during the *derg* years, and it resurfaced during the 1990s. The new Rastafari arrivants were not afraid to claim this name: they explained it, taught it, shared it, asked to be called and recognized by it. Little by little, a process of transformation occurred in which previous appellations (such as "Jamaican") gave way to the "new name" (that is, Rastafari). A Rastafari from Shashemene offered this explanation: "Rasta is the only outside body they [the Ethiopians] accept as their own. That's who they identify as Jamaicans. When the realization will come eventually, it will be the acceptance of Rastafarians."[57]

The complexity of this nation within the nation is crystallized in the first part of this remark: Rastafari is the only foreign body recognized as Ethiopian. By impelling the Ethiopians to recognize their own political past and to make allowances for the symbolic body of Haile Selassie I, which the Rastafari represent, they amuse, provoke or disturb the Ethiopians, as well as making them proud. Rastafari identity spurs identification with the Ethiopian nation and with the sovereigns of Ethiopia, bringing both into the limelight in Ethiopia. Hence, the identification that has been in circulation in the black world since the eighteenth century has survived its territorialization in Shashemene. What is more, it has resisted the challenges of the social reality of Ethiopia. However, this does not imply the absorption of the Rastafari into the mainstream of the Ethiopian nation. The government finds itself in a quandary: how to recognize Rastafari without validating their interpretation of the body of Haile Selassie I, or legitimating disturbing social practices like the use of ganja? A Rastafari in Shashemene commented on this state of indecision, characteristic of the Ethiopian authorities: "I think they're still not sure what the hell is we about, dem kinda watching we, they don't really overs [overstand] the seriousness of InI spiritual aspiration and trod. Hard for them as well. . . . I'm just watching, they have a problem, cause as much as they like or dislike we, we love Ethiopia so much they can't help like we! [*laughter*]."[58]

Can Ethiopia reject the only people in the world to construct a positive, victorious, mythical image of their country? Will it be able to recognize those who affirm that the last emperor of Ethiopia is of divine nature? Rastafari often say that love opens all doors, yet this Rastafari nation, imagined and staged in Shashemene, which endlessly asserts its love for the country despite the harsh realities of settlement, continues to occupy an extremely precarious position in Ethiopia. Nations are constructed on the basis of the imaginary, but to what extent? The prerogatives of the nation – nationality, laws, rights, vote and civil involvement – do not apply to the returnees and are systematically refused. Let us pause for a moment to consider the question of nationality, a right that is often claimed in the black world, and one that remains out of reach in Ethiopia.

Ethiopian Nationality

The first article of the law of 1930 on nationality, promulgated on the occasion of the emperor's coronation, indicated that Ethiopian nationality could be obtained by having one Ethiopian parent, and under certain conditions, such as marriage and good legal standing. The articles on naturalization were vague. They mentioned the case of the nationality of an Ethiopian woman married to a foreigner but were silent regarding the naturalization of foreigners married to Ethiopians.[59] Yet, under the previous regime, a few returnees – notably, Helen and James Piper as well as Vincent Beckford – received Ethiopian nationality. The *derg* years killed all desire for naturalization on the part of the returnees, who were clearly placed, at the time, under the responsibility of the Jamaican embassy. In its census of the Shashemene community in 2003, the ministry in charge of immigration attempted to analyse the legal status of the returnees. Out of the one hundred and twenty adults registered, none had Ethiopian nationality. Seventy-six reportedly entered the country with a tourist visa (63.4 per cent), thirteen with a business visa (10.8 per cent), and thirty-one declared possession of a residence permit (25.8 per cent). Among the last, only nineteen or twenty paid the yearly residence tax validating their permit.[60] The eighty-nine persons who arrived with a visa, with a validity period varying between a few months and two years, depending on their nationality, had been on the territory for years with expired visas. Given the frequency of robbery, many personal documents had either been stolen or lost, with no possibility of renewal. The lack of papers would be highly problematic, since a security check, a fine or jailing would likely result in expulsion. In the face of the – sometimes arbitrary – application of the law, certain returnees have had to call on the help of the embassy representing their country.

Eight months after the completion of this official census of the community, the new proclamation number 378/2003 on Ethiopian nationality replaced the law of 1930. Owing to the war with Eritrea, the complex question of binational Ethiopians and Eritreans had to be legislated in order to decrease the risk incurred by their presence on Ethiopian soil (Barnes 2006, 29–37). As for the acquisition of Ethiopian nationality by foreigners, this was made possible by part 2, paragraph 5 of the new law, ruling that

> a foreigner who applies to acquire Ethiopian nationality by law shall:
> 1. Have attained the age of majority and be legally capable under the Ethiopian law;
> 2. Have established his domicile in Ethiopia and have lived in Ethiopia for a total of at least four years preceding the submission of his application;
> 3. Be able to communicate in any one of the languages of the nations/nationalities of the Country;
> 4. Have sufficient and lawful source of income to maintain himself and his family;
> 5. Be a person of good character;
> 6. Have no record of criminal conviction;
> 7. Be able to show that he has been released from his previous nationality or the possibility of obtaining such a release upon the acquisition of Ethiopian nationality or that he is a stateless person; and
> 8. Be required to take the oath of allegiance stated under Article 12 of this Proclamation.[61]

Most returnees have a strong desire to acquire Ethiopian nationality. But without a foreign passport, with no documentation and no legal status, it is extremely difficult to even begin this process. Normally, fulfilling these criteria should enable returnees to apply for naturalization. A few hundred have attained the age of legal majority and have lived in Ethiopia for more than four years. Most speak Amharic, sometimes with difficulty, but the other criteria are a bit more delicate. A good reputation seems highly subjective, in particular when the possession or the use of cannabis is seen as an offence, thus barring the eligibility of certain would-be candidates. Besides, the prohibition of a double nationality is perceived by the returnees as a sacrifice, since, for the purposes of international mobility, an American passport, for example, is more useful than an Ethiopian one. The following paragraph of this proclamation facilitates the acquisition of the nationality for foreigners married to an Ethiopian citizen, but most of the unions in Shashemene are not sanctioned by an official marriage contract. This proclamation, primarily concerned with the Eritrean situation, probably opens up an avenue of greater flexibility for the repatriated Rastafari. But, while they await clear signs of change, the question of obtaining Ethiopian nationality continues to mobilize them.

In a collective letter, signed by the Rastafari of Shashemene in 2001, addressed to the general secretary of the Organization of African Unity, requesting the assistance of the pan-African institution at several levels, the first item raised was that of their legal status: "The majority of us who left the West to return to Ethiopia, came expecting to be accepted as Africans, with the rights to African citizenship. We therefore desire to have full legal status, and to be recognized as citizens of Ethiopia, with all the privileges and rights to live, work and travel freely as Ethiopians."[62] The bottom line of the issue of obtaining Ethiopian nationality has to do with whether or not Afro-descendants have the right to an African nationality. Several hundred people are directly concerned by this question, and it is not in the interest of Ethiopia to host a large resident population whose status is unclear, invalid or maladjusted. Granting Ethiopian nationality to all Caribbeans residing in the country would sign the acceptance and absorption of the Rastafari nation into the Ethiopian nation and would create an urgently needed jurisprudence for all future applications. But, in this context, the sovereign gesture of according or retrieving an individual's nationality is no longer simply a national question; it is also a pan-African one. This internal problem confronting Ethiopia also exists on a larger scale. It is best approached as a broader policy issue concerning the relations that African countries entertain with the African diasporas. This pan-African responsibility, which Ethiopia is unable to tackle by reason of the overwhelming impact it would have at the national level, leaves a constantly increasing repatriated population in limbo. It is obviously beyond the scope of this book to predict the solution of these major problems linked to the relation between the returnee population and the Ethiopian state regarding the right to nationality. Further studies, of a juridical nature especially, should throw light on the contradictory dynamics underscored by this situation. These contradictory dynamics are particularly acute in the

Figure 9.11. Flag floating in Entotto, above Addis Ababa, 2003. Photograph: G. Bonacci © DR.

case of the increasing number of children born in Ethiopia, within the returnee community. The main cause of the returnees' reluctance regarding a change of nationality concerns their children. As foreigners, the children have no rights, although they have lived only in Ethiopia. But as Ethiopians, they would not only be obliged to do military service, a practice that seems unacceptable to the Rastafari, but would, moreover, run the risk of being drafted for one of the multiple wars regularly erupting in the country. Let us take a closer look at the situation of these returnees' offspring.

The Ethiopian and Foreign Offspring

The law of 1930 indicated that anyone born of an Ethiopian parent was Ethiopian. It nonetheless stipulated that a child legally recognized by its father adopts the father's nationality. If born out of wedlock, such a child, born to an Ethiopian mother and a foreigner, was deprived of its mother's Ethiopian nationality. The legal terms are somewhat obscure for non-specialists, but it would appear that the father's nationality prevails, and that it is only by default that Ethiopian nationality may be granted to a child born to parents of mixed nationality. Only the child born to a Caribbean father who is a naturalized Ethiopian, or one not recognized by its Caribbean father, has the right to Ethiopian nationality. In their first interpretation of the 2003 census, the Ethiopian authorities found seventy-three children from mixed families, with a Caribbean father and an Ethiopian mother. Thirty-four children originated in families with two foreign parents. These numbers must be taken with a grain of salt, since they are only partially representative and serve, instead, to highlight a tendency: the Jamaican neighbourhood has twice as many Ethiopian-Caribbean children as Caribbean children. There are no accessible statistics retracing the evolution of the birth rate within the returnee community. But, whereas the average fertility rate of Ethiopian women in Shashemene was approximately 3.3 children per woman in 1994 (Master Plan 2000, 73), Ethiopian-Caribbean and Caribbean families were usually larger. Another distinction must be made: of the thirty-four children born to two Caribbean parents, how many were born in Ethiopia? Until the middle of the 1990s, this was probably the case of the majority, whereas, subsequently, with the increase in arrivals, especially of whole families, this number might have been slightly on the decline. The children of returnees in Shashemene are registered by the *qäbälé*, who issue a local identification card making no mention of the holder's nationality but only of his or her place of residence. In fact, as these cards always mention the father's nationality, the young people born in Ethiopia continue to be identified as foreigners. At their majority, they are forced to begin the administrative process needed to legalize their status, a process often complicated by their fathers' illegal status.

The children of the returnees have all learned Amharic in school at a very young age and sometimes speak Oromo as well. Interesting linguistic research could be done on the children of returnees, most of whom are not only multilingual (Amharic, Oromo, English, Jamaican patois) but also speak to each other in a subtle mixture of these languages, so as not to be understood by their parents and relations. Ababu Minda (1997, 102) noticed that the children of an Ethiopian-Caribbean family spoke Amharic but not the Jamaican dialect, while the fact was that the children did not speak the Jamaican patois with him since he did not understand it. It is not easy to evaluate how being raised in a Caribbean or an Ethiopian-Caribbean family influence the development and education of the children. Most of them grew up in Shashemene with Ethiopians. They went to the same schools, shared the same trips and sporting activities, experienced the same changing rural environment and endured similar sanitary conditions. They all have friendly and intimate relations with Ethiopians, with whom they spent their childhood and adolescence. Those with an Ethiopian mother are certainly closer to the local cultures than those with two foreign parents. In mixed families with a distant or absent Caribbean father, familiarity with the father's culture is, no doubt, further compromised.

Vincent Beckford's family offers a good illustration of this type of situation.[63] He left Jamaica in 1968 with the first group of "pioneers" and acquired Ethiopian nationality in a manner that remains unclear. He had permanent employment in the regional road works office, formerly called the Imperial Road Authority, situated in front of his house. He had ten children with an Ethiopian woman, all with Ethiopian nationality, before his death in about 1993 (1986 *a.m.*). His first three children were girls; the first two did not finish school and spoke no English at all. They married Ethiopian men and had many children. One daughter, Aster, receives her guests in the Ethiopian manner. On a low seat, she sells *t'älla*, the local beer, and *aräqé*, a clear alcohol, to neighbours and peasants from the neighbourhood. Nothing in her appearance or manner alludes to her Caribbean origin. She understands neither English nor the Jamaican patois, and Jamaica means nothing to her. Beckford's third daughter, Yeshimabet, after a first marriage and two children, remarried in 1998 to Gladstone Robinson, the American, many years her senior, who had repatriated to Shashemene in 1964, and had three more children with him. Yeshimabet, who had dropped out earlier, resumed her schooling and set about learning English. Beckford's two following children are boys. Owing to this, they finished school and speak English. One opened a small food store on the main street in 2003. The last five children, two boys and three girls, all finished school, and the oldest of this set lives with his eldest brother, while the others live with their mother. Beckford's last daughter was born the year of her father's death. Beckford's ten children are therefore representative of a situation in which children raised by an Ethiopian mother became Ethiopian, heirs of their mother's cultural legacy and that of their environment, not that of their Jamaican father, originating in a country which seems of little interest to them. Two of them have moved closer to the paternal legacy in their adult life: the third daughter, by marrying an elderly American Rastafari, learning English and growing dreadlocks and the first son, by deciding to work in the neighbourhood, where he will probably be influenced by Caribbean culture.

In the same group as Vincent Beckford, a Jamaican couple made the journey with their daughter and their niece. The story of their family legacy is quite different. After settling in Ethiopia, the couple had two sons. Their daughter died, following a caesarean at the Kuyra hospital; the second son died from an infection due to a head injury when he was small; and their niece later married a Jamaican who had repatriated from the United States. The surviving son, born just before the revolution, tells how his immediate environment was steeped in Rastafari culture, contrary to that of Beckford's children:

> Our house was like a congregation, a HQ [headquarters], everybody comes, smoke herb, the Rasta movement, the Rasta reasoning, and you hear about Rastafari, we sit down, we were kids, we play around but we still hear the history, of how the Black man came, that's why I can talk about it, I grew up in it, day and night, His Majesty and how he came to be and how he came to Jamaica, right until now. I grew up in it. We were properly taught, there was nothing hidden from us pertaining to the faith, from families, friends, we hear, we listen, they call us and say sit down and listen to the history of the Black man. We were aware of where we are from.[64]

Given this legacy, which is typical in families with two Caribbean parents, going to school in the *derg* years was particularly challenging. Added to the fact of their identification by fellow pupils as Jamaicans, as people who were different, those who had dreadlocks had their hair pulled by the other children, and all were teased about their origin. But the hardest thing to bear was the obvious contradiction between what was taught in school, including the obligatory political education, and the education, permeated with Rastafari culture, received at home:

> We used to take political education at school, the things we used to learn about His Majesty, sometimes I used to even fight hard to write it into my book from the teaching I'm getting at home. And when I come to school, the teachings I am getting, it really created a big contradiction, cause they telling you all the bad that His Majesty [has] done. . . . But I still come back home and take that, and have that teaching, it never really . . . it affects you but it never reaches as far as getting you crazy. Still come home and ask questions, look, they told us about His Majesty at school today and they say bla bla, no [my parents] say, that's the propaganda they're trying to teach. It's just the government who is trying to degrade His Majesty but it is not true.[65]

The lessons taught in school clashed with those received at home, especially concerning the emperor's personality. This was exacerbated under the political climate of the *derg* and has been resolved over time, following the stages of individual personality development and the identity construction of a people. This type of difficulty lessened in the 1990s, without totally disappearing. The number of returnee children has increased; the political climate has evolved; and the Rastafari environment is no longer restricted to home and domestic spaces, thanks to the arrival of new families and the greater visibility this entails. Most children have gone, at least for a time, to the community school mentioned above. Directed by a few Rastafari, alongside Ethiopian teachers, this school helps to provide the children with role models. It offers a home-like environment in which neither politics nor religion is evoked.

Many questions remain concerning the complex situation of a Jamaican child, of Rastafari parentage, in Ethiopia. More research is needed to understand their itineraries. A few insights may however be derived from the two depictions that follow. In their adult lives, these two have varied relations with the community in Shashemene, but, while they were growing up, they both chose another religion. One, born in 1978 in Shashemene, notes:

> My father used to tell me Haile Selassie is God and I used to do all this and say Haile Selassie is God, not understanding, [but] because my father tell me Haile Selassie is God, he is the only spirit, I used to say it cause I was a little boy then, I didn't have my own understanding to read the Bible and see the truth. But after some time I read the Bible myself and I know Haile Selassie is not God.[66]

Brought up by his Ethiopian stepmother, he was soon exposed to contradictory messages about the nature of the emperor, and, when he finally made his choice, he became a "penté", a member of a Pentecostal church, but retained a certain respect for King Haile Selassie I. This unleashed his father's indignation and the sarcasm of his Caribbean friends. His sense of ease in the Ethiopian environment is evidenced by his adoption of some common Ethiopian gestures like holding hands with another man. He felt rejected by the community, which suspected him of being a homosexual – an experience he considers worse than rejection on account of his new faith. His discretion on all this could not conceal his pain, and, at the first opportunity, he left Shashemene for Addis Ababa, to work as a cook in a Rastafari family.

The other returnee offspring pointed out that he had, in fact, grown up between the two faiths, Rastafari and Orthodox Christianity, because, like him, his Rastafari parent had been baptized. While recognizing the influence of the Rastafari environment on his development and identity, he defined himself at age thirty as an Orthodox Christian and did not defend the emperor's divinity:

> I don't really defend him [Haile Selassie] on that kind of way [divine], but I would say yeah some things about him, some mystical things about him, some kingly character and he does a lot of work, he teaches, inspires our fore-parents. Everybody has its own

way of seeing things and this is the way I see it. Great King. That's something I really got into me after being growing up, before I was in the same thing, I used to defend him, because of what I learned. When I grow up now and start reading, realizing, seeing.[67]

As the son of one of the first Jamaican families, he has often been rebuked for not being a Rastafari, for not wearing dreadlocks, especially by the visitors, who expected him to be a worthy representative of the community. Although he did not choose to follow his parents' religion, he was, nevertheless, concerned with Shashemene. As a mechanic in Addis Ababa, he worked with the Rastafari of Shashemene to preserve the land of his elderly parents and to implement the technical training aspects of the community's development project.

It is not easy for a child raised in Ethiopia to identify with the Rastafari faith, since everything in the surroundings claims that this is a mistake, and intercultural gateways remain rare. These are only two examples out of some two hundred returnee children living in the community, and, in a context where many things have changed significantly, there are multiple modes of reappropriating parental cultural identity. Research is needed to understand how certain individuals play with the criteria of distinction and differentiation. Due to ambient prejudices, the wearing of dreadlocks in Ethiopia complicates many social interactions while facilitating identification with the Rastafari. Remaining in Caribbean or Rastafari social networks probably offers, at first, greater economic opportunities, not to mention international contacts with a demand for middlemen. Although the young generation in Shashemene has various ways of reappropriating their parents' Rastafari faith while growing up, they nevertheless define themselves as Ethiopians. Offering yet another stage in the dialectics of identity and identification, they use an expression that probably belongs to their parents – "we are Ethiopians" – but they use it for other reasons and in a different way:

"How would you define yourself?"

"Ethiopian. My father is a Jamaican, my mum is a British. . . . I know I am Jamaican and I am proud of that, not to be even a Jamaican but to be black, I am a black African, not Jamaican, I would prefer that. . . . Mostly I would like to be Ethiopian because I born here, I know a lot of things about Ethiopia, I have lots of friends, I learned here, I know many things, the *bahel* [customs]. I prefer to say I am an Ethiopian, but I am still a Jamaican and I am happy for that."[68]

This testimony reveals the entanglement of identities this young man experiences. He spontaneously defined himself as an Ethiopian then revised his statement for greater nuance. He felt Ethiopian but was Jamaican despite himself, and defining himself as black or African seemed preferable to the insular or foreign identity. Is identification with blackness or Africanness a spontaneous phenomenon among the youth of Addis Ababa? It is hard to say. But his Jamaican

Figure 9.12. The land of Shashemene, 2003. Photograph: G. Bonacci © DR.

father and black British mother owned this identity. Parents and children share the Ethiopian identity, imagined, for the first, and, let us say, lived for the latter. What is the importance of being born in Ethiopia, even when one is deprived of Ethiopian nationality associated with this identity?

> My roots are here. Why I say that is I feel even though we passed through so many hardship, I feel now more grounded, I feel living in Ethiopia wouldn't be an headache for me, but I would still like to be more mobile, travel. . . . But my roots are here. *Etebté ezzih yätäq'äbbäräw*, meaning your navel string is buried here, meaning originally, no matter what happens, your roots are here.[69]

Jamaicans and many others have crossed the world in search of their roots, but their children born in Ethiopia have theirs right there, beneath their feet. Are the second more legitimate than the first? This is really not the question. The real question concerns the process through which the first, the imagined roots, allowed the second, the roots anchored in the land, to become a reality. The confidence with which these young people define themselves as Ethiopians does not prevent them from wanting to travel to the other place, the *elsewhere* of their parents' origin, or to the big wide world that the returnees left behind, and which crops up in their conversations. Some of these children born in Ethiopia have lived for a time in England or the United States, thanks to family networks that bear the cost of their education. It might seem ironic that those who left Babylon at the price of great sacrifice must watch their children leave for it. However, regardless of their itineraries, these offspring are bound to Ethiopia by their "navel strings", their childhood and their memory. And this bond, made up of the first life experiences, is impossible to forget. In the same way that it is probably impossible to forget the green hills of Jamaica, or the ghettos of Kingston, Brooklyn or Brixton – even in the heart of Zion itself.

DURING THE 1990S, AND ESPECIALLY NEARING THE APPROACH of the following decade, an increasing number of Rastafari arrivals contributed greatly to the transformation of the Jamaican neighbourhood. This appears evident, although more distance is needed to evaluate whether these later arrivants will remain. Settlement in Shashemene is marked by insecurity, in terms of land availability and in social relationships, and is also characterized by the creation of new relations among Rastafari, and between Rastafari and Ethiopians. The returnees' profiles show insular or metropolitan origins, affiliations to various organizations, different languages and contrasted practices of livity. Such distinctions preclude their definition as an ethnic group, although they may appear to be such to Ethiopians influenced by the ethnicization of social relations since the 1990s. The bond cementing these profiles is that of the imaginary of the nation. The Ethiopian people, with whom the Rastafari identify, cohere beneath a symbolic, national Ethiopian flag. Whereas the imaginary may suffice, for a time, for formation of a nation, access to nationality would represent a giant step forward in the direction of change. The naturalization of the Afro-descendants who have settled in Ethiopia would be a gesture of pan-African responsibility that post-imperial Ethiopia is yet to make. This would signify a politics of welcome on the part of the country, a recognition of the Rastafari religion, documented legalization of residential facilities and an agreement concerning the status of the land that the Rastafari occupy and see as their own. Nearly all of the Rastafari in Shashemene are illegal, meaning that "the law" does not recognize their status, while they claim that their legitimacy reposes on "grace". New policies are necessary, especially in the face of the growing number of returnee children. Caught between the law and their identity, the children are at once Ethiopians and foreigners. Their entangled identities, situated between here and elsewhere, reality and symbolism, surfaces as one of the fruits of this return to Ethiopia, an extension of the dialectics that guided their parents' steps. These children are "true Ethiopians", since they were born in Ethiopia. They are sometimes heirs to conflicting legacies but remain pioneers; the first to raise crucial questions pertaining to the future of pan-African relations and to the identity that Ethiopia is designing for itself.

CONCLUSION TO PART 3

MY RESEARCH ON THE FATE OF THE "ETHIOPIANS OF THE WORLD" was guided by a focus on the land tenure and the social relations they experienced upon their arrival in Ethiopia. The land, donated at the turn of the 1950s, was located in Shashemene, in the Ethiopian south, whose history is marked by the conquest and alienation of the land. The authority of the first arrivants, the Pipers, was contested by those who followed them and who also claimed rights to the land. Unequal relations with their Ethiopian neighbours were established from the beginning. The fragmentation of the land grant in 1970 and 1974 signalled the will of the imperial government to accommodate these transatlantic migrants who enjoyed a special relation with the emperor and the palace administration.

The Jamaican Rastafari took possession of this land grant, but, following the Ethiopian revolution and the swathe of nationalizations in 1975, they lost most of their possessions and were forced to integrate with Ethiopian society at the lowest rung of the social ladder. Their insecurity in terms of land was maintained by the tug-of-war with the new local administrations, until a few parcels were finally allocated to them once again. Individual legitimacy, protected by their status as foreigners and their connections with the Jamaican embassy, was nevertheless severely compromised. Learning how to survive rural life, poverty and political marginalization while protecting their culture was a determinant factor in most of the returnees' social relations, especially with women.

With the change of regime in 1991 and the celebration of the birth centenary Haile Selassie I in 1992, the living conditions of the returnees began to improve. But the struggles for power and legitimacy between the EWF and the Twelve Tribes of Israel continued over the little land that remained, and complicated their dealings with the government. Besides, exemplifying the tensions generated by the creation of a federal republic, the central government and the local government had contrasting attitudes with regard to the Rastafari. The first considered that their rights should be respected, while the second attempted to force them into a tight corner in order to establish their own authority. Despite the prevailing absence of legal clarity, the Jamaican neighbourhood underwent rapid transformation, due to strategies of amicable arrangement between Ethiopians and Rastafari. The increasing economic distinction between the Ethiopians and the new Rastafari arrivants aggravated the general climate of social insecurity. Sometimes insulted as "slaves" by Ethiopians, the Rastafari were also admired for their love of Ethiopia.

The identification with Ethiopia that had been in circulation in the black world since the eighteenth century survived its territorialization in Shashemene, for, regardless of the difficulties encountered and the two post-imperial political regimes endured, the "Ethiopians of the world" kept coming. The Ethiopians did not always easily accept their presence. Under the former regime, they were treated with a certain attention; under the *derg*, their faith had to be hidden but their nationalism was admired; under the last regime, they have been endangered by the lack of specific policies. The Rastafari went against the grain when, in the era of ethnic identification, they attempted to perpetuate a certain image of the Ethiopian nation, one that was royal, Amhara, centralized, and a thing of the past. They continue to press for what they consider to be a right: the access of Afro-descendants to land in Africa and the nationality of an African state. Representing a unique example of returns to Africa, Shashemene also became the symbolic hub of the Rastafari movement, a place of gathering for organizations, visitors, pilgrims and returnees realizing the dream of return. We do well to ask ourselves whether, paradoxically, the Rastafari movement, which allows certain individuals to return owing to a powerfully impelling imaginary, does not, by the same token, also prevent the crossing of the pan-African bridge of recognition by the Ethiopian government, repelled by Haile Selassie's role. The place of Haile Selassie I in the Rastafari movement is felt more acutely in Ethiopia than anywhere else. In that country it becomes a central issue because of its national, memorial and political stakes. On the battlefield of history and of national identity, Rastafari and Ethiopians have told their – often conflicting – interpretations.

CONCLUSION

"I hope you have at least a piece of the history. You never get a history straight. Things like this give you more motivation, that people are interested to hear what you have to say, at least life's worth living."

– *David Baugh, Addis Ababa*

Africa, unite!
'Cause we're moving right out of Babylon
And we're going to our Father's land
How good and how pleasant it would be before God and man
To see the unification of all Africans
As it's been said already, let it be done
We are the children of the Rastaman
Africa, unite!
'Cause the children wanna come home.

– *Bob Marley, "Africa Unite" (1979)*

ALMOST EIGHT HUNDRED PERSONS – MEN, WOMEN AND children, with an overwhelming majority from the Caribbean – currently live on the outskirts of Shashemene, a town of the Ethiopian south counting at least a hundred thousand inhabitants. They are few in number, and the "Jamaican neighbourhood" where they live is populous, noisy and sometimes dangerous. The great expanses of fertile land on which cattle once grazed has given way to houses, hedges, and business places. At the entrance to the town, a traveller going from Addis Ababa to Shashemene sees portraits of the emperor painted on walls and flags of red, gold and green floating in the wind. If he stops for a while, our traveller might eat ital food while listening to reggae music and, perhaps, discover bits and pieces of the history of his host who came thirty years ago, from Kingston or Trinidad, or a few years ago, from New York or Manchester. Hitting the road once more, he would soon enter the chaos of the town, with its trucks, dust and heteroclite traffic. Here, like elsewhere, he would encounter the miseries of the world in the guise of poverty, alcoholism, disease, injustice and violent death. Has Shashemene – which, thanks to the land granted by Haile Selassie I, has become a "Zion City", where the "Ethiopians of the world" can come together – fallen short on its promises? Whatever the case may be, Shashemene continues, like a powerful magnet, to attract "Jah people" prepared for the sacrifice needed to participate in the edification of the dream: to build on that land a new town, a new world and another life.

The history of this Caribbean settlement is not really a matter of success or failure but rather one of the complex ties that bind a territory to identities. Between Shashemene and the black worlds, a specific social history took shape, one marked by the circulation of myths, the reappropriation of songs and the transformation of congregations. The – often involuntary – impact of Ethiopia on these worlds runs deep. It was reinforced by the pan-African policies of the Ethiopian sovereigns and the invitation to settle in Shashemene in order to contribute to the development of the country. The land grant allowed two ideologies to coalesce; on the one hand, that of the return to Africa, meant to erase the alterations caused by slavery and to restore the black nation; on the other, Ethiopianism, a symbolic reservoir of racial, royal, and even divine identity. Caribbeans, who were already in the vanguard of the nationalist and pan-African struggle, answered the call of the land. There were a number of Rastafari in their midst.

The study of the waves of settlement on these two hundred hectares makes room for the emergence of another history of the Rastafari movement. The desire for return implied a critique of the insular Jamaican society and a denunciation of the social violence of its living conditions. The choice of return suggested that working towards transforming these conditions was not the solution. What was required, instead, was leaving them behind by going "back home". The Rastafari, by centralizing nationalist and religious symbols in the black body of Haile Selassie I, transformed the desire for return into a social alternative. Various segments of the Jamaican population were mobilized in view of this objective – namely, the realization of the biblical prophecies, which they believed they were elected to fulfil.

The return to Africa out of Jamaica was not accomplished through government policies. In the likeness of British colonial administration, the independent Jamaican state denied any responsibility regarding the return to Africa of the descendants of the enslaved. By the same token, return did not occur through divine intervention, despite the hopes of some Jamaicans who, even today, are still waiting for the boats sent by the hand of Jah to carry them home. As most of the attempts to return have fallen through, many Rastafari have rationalized the Back-to-Africa project through a new way of thinking introducing the option of spiritual or cultural return without leaving Jamaica. It is on this basis that Barry Chevannes (1998b, 30) indicated that "no" physical return occurred after 1960.

Of course, no mass return occurred, but some, nevertheless, took place, thanks to the convergence of several factors: individual determination, including that of Noel Dyer, whose return on foot from England was a telling example; the mobilization of families; the formation of small groups; and, especially, the collective engagement of two organizations, the EWF and the Twelve Tribes of Israel. The social history of these two organizations, reconstructed herein through the combination of oral and written sources, offers insight into the popular practices of organization within the Rastafari movement. The EWF and the Twelve Tribes of Israel structured the movement, while contributing to its transformation. They sent officers and members to Shashemene, first from Jamaica, then from the Caribbean and the English-speaking urban centres. Shashemene thus became a mirror reflecting the international diffusion of the Rastafari movement and, consequently, the most recent transformations of the "Ethiopian belt", a term designating the spaces in which the identification with the Ethiopian nation was reformulated.

The history of the returns to Shashemene also makes way for a solid inscription of continental Africa in the back-to-Africa discourses, which are often limited to the spaces of the Americas and the diaspora. Putting Ethiopia at the centre of the modalities of return has allowed another glance at the local and national contexts. The various waves of arrival in Shashemene and the social hardships encountered, depending on the period, highlight the mutations in Ethiopia's pan-African policies, which moved from a programme of invitation and reception to the marginalization of returnees. The administration of these two hundred hectares passed from the jurisdiction of the imperial palace to the assembly of the peasant associations and finally to the *qäbäle*, thereby illustrating the revenge of the peripheries on the centre. It was their turn to exercise their newfound power, to defend their interests and to protect their land from external claims. The parcelling out of the land grant in Shashemene and the densification of the population went hand in hand with the dynamics of urbanization, which extended the town limits and the quirks of the municipality. The arrival of the Caribbeans in Shashemene helped to attract Ethiopians, who came in search of work or land speculation.

The returnees arrived bearing the characteristic contradictions of black identity and the diasporic experience, the "double consciousness" evoked by W.E.B. Du Bois (1996, 5). Many years after their arrival in Ethiopia, they still describe themselves as both heirs and pioneers. Far from resolving the identity dialectics, return has served to exacerbate and reformulate them. Caught between the double need for integration into the world of their Ethiopian neighbours and that of preserving their own culture, which was brutalized in the context of the revolution, the returnees leave an ambiguous trace in the Ethiopian landscape. Sometimes attracting and sometimes repulsing Ethiopian men and women, they have in turn been supported or rejected by them. While the love the returnees have for Ethiopia often forces the admiration of the Ethiopians, the returnees also pose a symbolic threat to the Ethiopian national identity, currently in search of new points of reference.

According to Tsegaye Guebre Medhin, an artistic and intellectual personality of the twentieth century, the returnees are at once "sons who have come home" and "profane strangers" (see appendix 3). Many contradictory representations of these transatlantic migrants have emerged, dependent on the places from which the Ethiopians observed them and on the staging of national power. At the local level, in Shashemene, the Rastafari were associated with the emperor, whom the Oromos saw as a coercive central power. In a region still marked by a history of alienation of the land and by economic and social domination, the symbols of imperial power were inevitably despised. At the national level, a group like the Rastafari, which identifies with an imperial, Amhara, and centralized Ethiopian nation is also in contradiction with a national imaginary in the process of construction, one based, since 1991, on ethnic distinction and the autonomy of the federal regions. Paradoxically, the Rastafari identity and the power of their imaginary allowed them to leave everything behind in order to settle in Shashemene, but this same identity also hinders their acceptance by and their "absorption" into the Ethiopian nation.

Ethiopia's pan-African identity was reaffirmed in February 2005 in Addis Ababa, through events staged by the Rita Marley Foundation to celebrate the sixtieth birthday of Bob Marley, the "most famous Rastaman who ever lived" (Steffens 1998, 253). These events went by the name "Africa Unite", the title of a Bob Marley song, a pan-African hymn linking the return of Afro-descendants to the unity of the continent. The events were widely diffused in the country and abroad. The Ethiopians saw their ministers welcoming Rita Marley with all the honours of protocol and attending the concerts in which the Marley children, like their father thirty years earlier, brandished the portrait of Haile Selassie I and the red, gold and green flag emblazoned with the Lion of Judah, the symbol of imperial Ethiopia. But this event was merely a staging of pan-African unity rather than a concrete step forward in the direction of solidarity between Africans and Afro-descendants. Indeed, no specific measures have since been taken in favour of the repatriated population, which remains deprived of land, rights and nationality.

If applied, the pan-African ideology, which posits the unity of nature and destiny of all black people, would imply, despite their divergences, the sharing of power and fraternal sentiments between the Oromos in Shashemene, the Tigreans in power and the Rastafari. However, their identies conflict, crystallizing around the memory of Haile Selassie I, and seem to prevent the emergence of such a pan-African fraternity. Is it possible, when all is said and done, to be at the same time a pan-Africanist – that is, one who adopts a world vision that asserts universal solidarity between Africans and Afro-descendants – and specifically a Rastafari, an Oromo or a Tigrean? In other words, do the racial and nationalist identities that allowed the emergence of pan-Africanism also form the main stumbling block to its practical application?

A response to the question might reside in the trajectories of those who went from one identity to the other: the increasingly numerous children of returnees, as well as the Ethiopians who became Rastafari. Some of the latter were born in the United States or England to parents who had fled the revolution, the power of the *derg*, or the regime change of 1991. In their life abroad, Rastafari became for them, as for others, an identity resource, and some of these young Ethiopians returned to Ethiopia to live this Rastafari identity. In Ethiopia, Rastafari represents an identity and cultural alternative for young Ethiopians in search of an opening. In urban areas, especially Addis Ababa, dreadlocks are the hallmark of the young Ethiopians who play reggae. This hairstyle facilitates their contacts with visitors and tourists familiar with the global reggae culture. Will these Ethiopians who have become Rastafari encounter new difficulties with their families or with society? Will they manage to bridge the tensions generated by identity conflict?

These questions form one aspect of the relations between Africa and its diasporas, both old and new. The African Union, in its official replacement of the Organization of African Unity, took these relations into account through the creation of a sixth region of Africa: the diaspora. This African Union "Diaspora Initiative" formally encourages African member states and leaders to react positively to initiatives aimed at promoting relations and cooperation between the diasporas and Africa.[1] It reflects the transformations that have occurred in the conceptualization of pan-Africanism. Initially formulated out of the diaspora on a racial basis, it became a continental question in the era of African independence. Recent African Union interest in the diasporas is probably guided by economic imperatives acknowledging the potential of the most recent African diasporas. Nevertheless, far removed from the sociopolitical models of Liberia and Sierra Leone, the oldest diasporas, originating in the Atlantic slave trade, are present and active in Africa, from Senegal to Benin, from Ghana to Tanzania, from Ethiopia to South Africa. Their settlements, investments, contributions and claims are yet to benefit from methodical investigations.

The history of the return to Shashemene has demonstrated that a practice of history linking Africa to its diasporas allows, thanks to the interweaving of documentation from these different spaces, the formation of new objectives which clarify the social processes at work in both the diasporas and Africa. The history of this return is also a call for comparative studies involving other returns – to Africa, of course, but also other instances of return, such as the return to Israel, in which Ethiopian Jews participated. Let us go back for a moment to the end of the book of Isaiah:

> I will gather all nations and tongues; and they shall come, and see my glory. And I will set a sign among them and I will send those that escape of them unto the nations; . . . to the isles afar off, that have not heard my fame, neither have seen my glory; and they shall declare my glory among the Gentiles, and they shall bring all your brethren for an offering unto the Lord out of all nations, upon horses, and in chariots and in litters, and upon mules and upon swift beasts, to my holy mountain, Jerusalem, saith the Lord. . . . For as the new heavens and the earth, which I will make, shall remain before me, saith the Lord, so shall your race and your name remain. (Isaiah 66:18–22)

These words of the persecuted prophet Isaiah evoke the organic unity between a people, a land and God. They refer to situations in which the language of the Bible, the link to origins, the quest for "home" and the national imaginary are intimately intertwined. They offer a summary of the archetypes that mark the human imagination, over and beyond local or cultural particularities. A comparative perspective should shed new light on the various histories and contradictions – those that perpetually uprooted peoples, the world over, carry around with them, as part and parcel of their double heritage as heirs and pioneers.

Figure C.1. An issue of the Rastafari magazine *Jahug*, devoted to the return to Africa, 1995. © DR.

APPENDIX 1

VERSIONS OF THE ETHIOPIAN PRAYER

"The Shepherd's Prayer" by Athlyi

This is the original version, published within The Holy Piby *(Rogers 1924, 11).*

O God of Ethiopia, thy divine majesty; thy spirit come in our hearts to dwell in the path of righteousness lead us, help us to forgive that we may be forgiven, teach us love and loyalty on earth as to heaven, endow us with wisdom and understanding to do thy will, thy blessing to use that the hungry be fed, the naked clothed, the sick nourished, the aged protected and the infant cared for. Deliver us from the hands of our enemies that we prove fruitful, then in the last day when life is o'er, our bodies in the clay, or in the depths of the sea, or in the belly of a beast, O give our souls a place in thy kingdom forever and forever. Amen.

"The Ethiopian Prayer"

This version was provided by G.E. Simpson (1955, 140), the author of the first publications on the Rastafari. It was used in the 1950s in Rastafari communities in Kingston. Although it remains almost identical to the original, there is nonetheless the addition, in the first line, of a verse designating the Ethiopianist corpus, Psalm 68:31, as well as the transformation of "Amen" to "Selah", a common occurrence in the psalms of the King James Version of the Bible.

Princes have come out Egypt; Ethiopia now stretches forth her hands unto God. O Thou God of Ethiopia, Thy divine majesty, Thy spirit come into our hearts to dwell in the paths of righteousness. Lead us, help us to forgive that we may be forgiven. Teach us love, loyalty on earth as to Heaven, endow us with Thy wisdom and understanding to do Thy will. Thy blessing to use that the hungry be fed, the naked clothed, the sick nourished, the aged protected and the infant cared for. Deliver us from the hands of our enemies that we prove fruitful for the last days. When our enemies are passed and decayed in the depths of the sea, in the depths of the earth or in the belly of a beast, Oh give us all a place in Thy kingdom for ever and ever. Selah.

The "Nyahbinghi Creed"

Preceded by a few Psalms (1, 121, 122, 133, 24), this version of the Ethiopian Prayer forms the creed of the Order of Nyabinghi (Ancient Order of the Nyahbinghi Guidelines, n.d., 8). The practice of Italk is obvious here; in addition to the pronoun I and I, many terms are transformed, for example: divine is changed to ivine, Ethiopia to Ithiopia, Creation to Iration and understanding to overstanding, thus operating a symbolic reversal of the value attributed to words. Also worthy of note is the addition, at the end of the text, of titles and qualities attributed to Haile Selassie I.

Princes and Princesses must trod out of Egypt,
Ithiopians now stretch forth their hands to JAH
O' I JAH of Ithiopia, I n I Ivine Majesty
Thy irits trod into I to dwell in the paths of Righteousness lead I n I
Help I n I to forgive that I n I must be forgiven
Teach I n I love, loyalty on earth as it is in Zion
Endow I n I with wise mind, knowledge and overstanding to do thy will
Thy blessings to I n I O' JAH
Let the hungry be fed, the naked clothed; the sick nourished; the aged protected, and the infants cared for
Deliver I n I from the hands of our enemies
That I n I must prove fruitful in these perilous days
When our enemies are passed and decay, in the depths of the sea, the depths of the earth or in the belly of a beast
O' give I n I a place in thy iverliving kingdom
Through the power of the Kings of Kings, Lord of Lords,
Conquering Lion of the Tribe of Judah
Ilect of himself and light of this world, I n I ivine Majesty Emperor Haile Selassie I, JAH Rastafari first incient king of iration JAH art the Alpha and the Omega the beginning without end the first and foriver, the protectorate of all human faith and the ruler of the ineverse, so I n I hail to our JAH and King Emperor Haile Selassie I JAH Rastafari!!!!
Almighty I JAH Rastafari great and thunderable I JAH Rastafari!!

"A Little Prayer"

This is a version of the "Ethiopian Prayer", which was sung, or rather chanted, by Mortimo Planno. This charismatic Rastafari began the chant by a loose usage of the ritual formula of the Ethiopian Orthodox Church: Bäsem ab, bäwäld, bämänfäs qeddus, and ehadu amlak, amen, meaning "In the name of the Father, of the Son, and of the Holy Spirit, One God, amen". The last refrain, which is an addition, is often used by Rastafari to conclude their songs and prayers. This version was recorded on 8 June 1968, in the studio of the Jamaican radio, JBC, in Kingston, as the flip side of a Bob Marley and the Wailers record, "Selassie Is the Chapel", produced by Mortimo Planno. This extremely rare recording was recently re-edited by Bruno Blum in the Bob Marley and the Wailers' DVD compilation Rebel *(JAD/55/EMI France 2002).*

Bless Be ab, Ufu, Manfat Adu, Adu, Amlak, Aman
Princes has come out of Egypt
Ethiopians now stretch forth their hands unto God
Oh God of Ethiopia
Our Divine Majesty
Thy spirit hath cometh into our heart
To dwell in the path of righteousness leads us
Help us to forgive
That we must be forgiven
Teach us love, loyalty on earth as it is in Zion
Endow us with thy wisdom
Knowledge and understanding to do thy will
Thy blessing to you
That the hungry be fed
The naked be clothed
The sick nourished
The aged protected
And the infants cared for
Deliver us from the hands of our enemies
That we may prove fruitful
In these last days
When our enemies are passed and decayed
In the depths of the sea
In the depths of the earth
Or in the bowels of a beast
Oh give us all
A place in thy kingdom
For ever

Selah

Let the words of our mouth
And the meditations of our heart
Be acceptable in thy sight
Oh Jah
Thou art the strength and our redeemer
That liveth and reigneth
In the hearts of man
For ever
Selah

APPENDIX 2

VERSIONS OF THE "UNIVERSAL ETHIOPIAN ANTHEM"

THE ORIGINAL VERSION, BY BENJAMIN EBENEZER BURRELL (1892–1959) and Arnold Josiah Ford (1877–1935), was called the "hymn of the black race" during the First Convention of the Black Peoples of the World organized by Marcus Garvey in New York in 1920. (See also Bonacci 2014.)

I
Ethiopia thou land of our fathers
Thou land where the gods loved to be,
As storm cloud at night suddenly gathers
Our armies come rushing to thee.
We must in fight be victorious
When swords are thrust outward to gleam;
For us will the vict'ry be glorious
When led by the red, black and green

Chorus
Advance, advance to victory,
Let Africa be free
Advance to meet the foe
With the might
Of the red, the black and the green

II
Ethiopia, the tyrant's falling
Who smote thee upon thy knees,
And thy children are lustily calling
From over the distant seas;
Jehovah the great one, has heard us,

Has noted our sighs and our tears,
With His spirit of Love He has stirred us
To be the One through the coming years.

Chorus

III
Oh Jehovah the God of the ages,
Grant unto our sons that lead
The wisdom Thou gave to Thy sages,
When Israel was sore in need.
Thy voice thro' the dim past has spoken,
Ethiopia shall stretch forth her hand,
By Thee shall all fetters be broken,
And Heav'n bless our dear fatherland

Chorus

The following version, used in the 1950s and 1960s in Rastafari communities in Kingston, Jamaica, was contributed by Douglas Mack (1999, 73).

Eternal Thou God of the Ages
Grant unto thy sons that lead
Thy wisdom Thou gave to the sages
When Israel was sore in need.
Thy voice through the dim past has spoken.
Ethiopia shall stretch forth her hands
By thee shall all barriers be broken
And heaven help our Dear Father's Land.

Chorus
Advance, Advance to victory
Let Africa be Free
To Advance to meet the Foes
To Advance to meet the Foes
With Righteousness leading
We haste to the call
Humanity's pleading
One God for us all.

Ethiopia the Land of our Fathers
The Land where all God's love to be,
As swift bees to hive suddenly gather
Thy children come rushing to thee

With the red-gold-and green
Floating o'er us
And our Emperor to shield us from wrong
With our God and our Future before us
We hail Thee with shouts and with song.

Chorus

Ethiopia the Tyrants are fallen
Who smote thee upon thy knees
And thy children are lustily calling
From over the distant seas.
Jahovah the Great One has heard us
He has heard our cries and our tears,
With the Spirit of Love he has taught us
To be one through the coming years.

Chorus

The next version transcribes almost phonetically the usages of *dread talk*. Thus the expression *I and I* is therein transcribed as *Ihi yahnh Ihi*. The term "Jehovah", which appears in the original version, and which became "Jahovah" in that of 1950, is replaced here by the characteristic contraction, "Jah" or by "Jah Rastafari". This version appears in a Rastafari publication by Faristzaddi (1991, 3). The signature "Order of Nyabinghi" graces it with a ritual legitimacy.

Ithiopia the land of our Fathers
The land where Ihi Jah loves to be
As the swift bee to hive sudden gathers
Thy children are gathered to thee
With Ihi Red, Gold and green flowing over Ihi
With Ihi Emperor to shield Ihi yahnh Ihi from wrong
With Ihi Jah and Ihi future before Ihi yahnh Ihi
Ihi yahnh Ihi hail and shout Ihi chant;

Chorus
Jah Jah is Ihi Negus Negus Ihi
Who keeps Ithiopia free
To advance in truth and rights, truth and rights
To advance in love and light, love and light
With righteousness pleading
Ihi yahnh Ihi haile to Ihi yahnh Ihi Jah and King
Ihimahnhihtih pleading
One Jah for Ihi yahnh Ihi.

Ihiternhnahlh Ihi Jah of all ages
Grant unto Ihi a son that leads
Thy wise minds thou hast given the ages
When Israel was sore in need
Thy voice through the dim past has spoken
Ithiopia now stretch forward her hands
And by Jah shall all barriers be broken
And Zion bless our dear Motherland

Ithiopia the tyrants are fallen
Who smote thee upon thy knees
Thy children are lovingly chanting
From over the distant seas
Jah Rastafari the Great One has heard Ihi yahnh Ihi
Jah has noted Ihi sighs and Ihi tears
With the Ihirihthzhs of Love Jah hath filled Ihi yahnh Ihi
To be one through all the trodding years.

Chorus

H.I.M. Haile Selassie Ihi Order of the Nihyahbihnghi Anthem

APPENDIX 3

TSEGAYE GUEBRE MEDHIN, "HOME COMING SON"

TSEGAYE GUEBRE MEDHIN (1937–2006) IS AN ETHIOPIAN POET, playwright and translator. He studied in Chicago, London and Paris. He served as the director of the Ethiopian National Theatre and created the Department of Theatre at the University of Addis Ababa. He was named permanent secretary in the Ministry of Culture by the *derg,* which later imprisoned him for his positions on legal rights and freedom of speech. His works have often been censored in Ethiopia, but he remains a great artist and cultural figure of the twentieth century. He is the composer of the "Hymn of the African Union". The following poem, "Home Coming Son" is a beautiful testimony to his pan-African commitment; it is a song of welcome to those who return. It was published in the *Reporter* (Addis Ababa), 4 December 2002.

Look where you walk unholy stranger
This is the land of the eighth harmony
In the rainbow: Black
It is the dark side of the moon
Brought to light
This is the canvas of God's masterstroke.

Out, of your foreign outfit unholy stranger
Feel part of the great work of art
Walk in peace, walk alone, walk tall
Walk free, walk naked
Let the feelers of your motherland
Caress you bare feet
Let her breath kiss your naked body.

But watch where you walk forgotten stranger
This is the very depth of your roots: Black
Where the tom-toms of your fathers vibrate
In the fearful silence of the valleys
Shook, in the colossus bodies of the mountains
Hummed in the deep chest of the jungles,
Walk proud.

Watch, listen to the calls of the ancestral spirits prodigal son
To the call of the long awaited soil
They welcome you home, home. In the songs of birds
The wind whispers the golden names of your tribal warriors
The fresh breeze blown onto your nostrils
Floats their bones turned to dust.
Walk tall. The spirits welcome
Their lost-son returned.

Watch, and out of your foreign outfit brother
Walk in laughter, walk in rhythm, walk tall
Feel part of the work of art
Walk free, walk naked.
Let the roots of your motherland caress your body
Let the naked skin absorb the home-sun and shine ebony.

GLOSSARY

INTERVIEWS WERE CONDUCTED IN ENGLISH, JAMAICAN PATOIS, AMHARIC, Oromo translated into Amharic and, on one occasion, in Italian. The archives consulted were mostly in English, Amharic and Oromo, with a few in French and Italian. I wish to extend special thanks to Wahib Adamu, who accompanied me during most of the interviews in Amharic, and with whom I was able to check that I had a correct grasp of what the interviewees had to say. He also supported my consultation of the archives in Amharic in the town of Shashemene. Groum Hailu also helped with this on one occasion. Ayele Olana's translations from Oromo to Amharic allowed me to spread out my investigations around Shashemene. Fetha Negest and Katia Girma were responsible for the translation of interviews recorded in Amharic into English and French, respectively.

Amharic

All terms transliterated from Amharic are given in the singular, even when used in the plural. In order to facilitate reading for non-users of these languages, a simplified spelling has been adopted for the most current proper nouns such as the names of cities, places and regions. For example:

Täfäri	Tafari
Shashämäne	Shashemene
Haylä Sellassé	Haile Selassie
Addis-Abäba	Addis Ababa
Täwodros	Tewodros
Shäwa	Choa
Menilek	Menelik
Wällo	Wollo
Mäkonnen	Makonnen
Tänaññä Wärq	Tenagne Worq
Mängestu Haylä Mariam	Mengistu Haile Mariam

Ababa Janhoy	አባባ፡ጃንሆይ	our father, majesty; popular name given to Haile Selassie
Abba/Abun	አባ / አቡን	our father; title given to bishops
aräqé	ዐረቄ	brandy
arash	አራሽ	cultivator
astädädar	አስተደዳር	director
ato	አቶ	mister
awrajja	አውራጃ	district, sub-province
azaž	አዛዥ	commander, chief
bahel	ባህል	custom, tradition
balabbat	ባላባት	of good family, landowner
balambaras	ባላምባራስ	commander of troop
balegué	ባለጌ	good-for-nothing
bäq'a	በቃ	that is enough
baria	ባሪያ	slave
barnet	ባርነት	slavery
berr	ብር	Ethiopian currency
bitwäddäd	ቢትወደድ	honorary title
blatténguéta	ብላቴንጌታ	honorary title, confidant of the king
bunna	ቡና	coffee
č'eqa	ጭቃ	mud, cob
däjazmač	ደጃዝማች	general
därg	ድርግ	committee
edder	እድር	society of mutual aid
Egziabehér	እግዚአብሔር	God
enjära	እንጀራ	wafer made of t'ef
eshi	እሺ	term of approval, ok, alright
fära	ፈራ	to fear, to be afraid
färänj	ፈረንጅ	foreigner, white foreigner
fitawrari	ፊታውራሪ	avant-garde general
gäbbar	ገባር	serf, land taxpayer
gari	ጋሪ	horse-drawn buggy
gasha	ጋሻ	unit of land measurement
gebbi	ግቢ	palace, residence, enclosed property

geber	ግብር	tax, taxation, duty
gebretel	ገብርትል	land reclaimed for non-payment of taxes
gult	ጉልት	concession of the tax revenue from a territory to a dignitary
habäsha	ሐበሻ/ አበሻ	Ethiopian
jeb	ጅብ	hyena
käntiba	ከንቲባ	the mayor of Addis Ababa or Gondar
keflä agar	ክፍለ ፡ ሀገር	provinces under the derg
lejj	ልጅ	son, title attributed to aristocrats
madäriya	ማደሪያ	temporary tenure
mängest	መንግሥት	government
märét	መሬት	land
meker bét	ምክር፡ቤት (ም/ቤ)	municipality
näft'äñña	ነፍጠኛ	who has a rifle, soldier
negus	ንጉሥ	king
negusä nägäst	ንጉሠ ፡ ነገሥት	King of Kings
qäbälé	ቀበሌ	smallest unit of urban administration
qälad	ቀላድ	unit of land survey
qés	ቄስ	priest
qolo	ቆሎ	roasted grain
ras	ራስ	title of governor, head
rest	ርስት	land domain
säfär	ሠፈር	neighbourhood
s'ähafé tezaz	ጸሐፌ ፡ ትእዛዝ	Minister of the Pen
seddät	ስደት	exile, departure from home
seddätäñña	ስደተኛ	refugee, immigrant, migrant
selt'an	ሥልጣን	authority
serratäñña	ሠራተኛ	worker, domestic help
shemagelé	ሽማግሌ	elder, elderly person
shialäqa	ሺአለቃ	commander of a thousand men
suq	ሱቅ	shop
tabot	ታቦት	replicas of the Ark of the Covenant

täkul	ተኩል	round house made of cob
t'älla	ጠላ	local homemade beer
t'äqlay gezat	ጠቅላይ ፡ ግዛት	province under the former regime
t'ef	ጥፍ	the cereal used to make enjära
t'equr	ጥቁር	the colour black
wäfč'o bét	ወፍጮ ፡ ቤት	mill
wäräda (gezat)	ወረዳ (ግዛት)	province, district, subdivision of an *awrajja*
wärka	ወርካ	sycamore
wät'	ወጥ	flat
zäbäñña	ዘበኛ	guard
zämäč'a	ዘመቻ	campaign (for development)

Figure G.1.
Consonants

ሀ/ሐ/ኀ	ha	ኸ	hä
ለ	lä	ወ	wä
ረ	rä	ዘ	zä
መ	mä	ዠ	žä
ሰ/ሠ	sä	የ	yä
ሸ	shä	ደ	dä
ቀ	qä	ጀ	jä
በ	bä	ገ	gä
ተ	tä	ጠ	t'ä
ቸ	čä	ጨ	č'ä
ነ	nä	ጸ/ፀ	s'ä
ኘ	ñä	ጰ	p'ä
አ/ዐ	a	ፈ	fä
ከ	kä	ፐ	pä

Figure G.2.
Vowels

ለ	lä
ሉ	lu
ሊ	li
ላ	la
ሌ	lé
ል	le/l
ሎ	lo

Jamaican Patois and Dread Talk

The language spoken by Jamaicans, called dialect, patois, or Jamaican English, is not officially standardized, although the dictionary by Cassidy and Page is a work of reference (1980). Long undervalued, it is nevertheless increasingly used in the Jamaican public space, in newspapers, on the radio and in literary, theatrical and, of course, musical creations. The term *dread talk* indicates the transformations Rastafari have brought to this language. More than a mere linguistic stance, it is a subversive cultural practice, studied notably by Velma Pollard (2000). I have opted for the simplest and most readable transcription of the Jamaican patois and dread talk.

brother/bredren/Idren bra brother, a Rastafari male

babymother/babyfather the mother of a child, the father of a child

chalice designates the water pipe used in the ritual smoking of ganja

dance party; in this case, a night event of the Twelve Tribes of Israel

deh there, adverb of place

dreadlocks the hair of the Rastafari, natural, uncombed locks, which, literally, "frighten" (dread); symbolically likened to the lion's mane

ganja, Cannabis sativa weed; it is seen as a sacrament by the Rastafari, and may also be used in teas or cooking

grounation/groundation a combination of "ground" and "nation"; a ritual of the Rastafari, also the process by which one becomes a Rastafari

gully one of the open irrigation canals which crisscross Kingston

gunmen armed men, gangsters

HIM acronym of "His Imperial Majesty", the title given to Haile Selassie; homonym of the pronoun "him"

I substituted for the pronoun "me"; homonym of the ordinal I (first) which follows the name of Haile Selassie

I and I/InI us, signifying the respect of subjectivities

ital literally vital, natural; characterizes Rastafari food and, more generally, their livity

Italk/dread talk the language of the Rastafari, source of many innovations, notably the intensive use of the pronoun "I" (creation becomes Iration, unity becomes Inity, and so on), and the inversion of the meaning of certain words. See *overstand* below.

Jah God, contraction of Jehovah; a common exclamation, often followed by "Rastafari"

likkle little, small

livity Rastafari lifestyle, including food, behavioural and ritual practices

nyabinghi/binghi/nyahbinghi Rastafari ritual lasting from one to seven days; name of the section of the Rastafari movement, the Order of Nyabinghi, which perpetuates the ritual; name of the rhythm played on drums (bass, fundeh, repeater); the name of a corpus of songs. Term designating a cult of Central Africa, which arrived in Jamaica in 1935 through a fascist propaganda article on the secret army of Haile Selassie. Means, symbolically, "Death to white and black oppressors."

nuff much

overstand to understand, inversion of "understand", since one is not "below" (under) but rather above (over) when one understands. Numerous symbolic inversions of this type exist. Thus the "university", University of the West Indies (UWI), which was former called UC (University College), corresponding to the homonym "You see", becomes "ublind" for the Rastafari, since universities are thought to prevent people from seeing and from differentiating good and evil (or truth and lie)

pickney child

reasoning mode of Rastafari discussion and sociability; oral spaces in which Rastafari history and identity are transmitted

rude boy bad boy, prototype of the country boy who comes to town and becomes a criminal

sekkelement settlement

sister/sistren sister, a Rastafari female

sufferer poor people in dire straits; from the 1930s onwards, denotes poor black Jamaicans; a term popularized by reggae music

tam knitted bonnet in the red, gold and green Ethiopian colours

trod to journey, to travel; metaphor referring to the spiritual itinerary of the Rastafari

wid with

yard unit of urban residence and, for Jamaicans abroad, a metaphor of their country, Jamaica

NOTES

Introduction

1. Whereas one sometimes finds, in particular in the press, the terms "Rastafarism" and "Rastafarianism", I observe in this book the scientific usage established some twenty years ago in the English-speaking literature, after discussing it with colleagues at the University of the West Indies. Hence the preference for the term "Rastafari" to indicate the Rastafari movement, practitioners and identity. Rastafari names are sometimes preceded by the term "Ras", recalling the title *Ras* Tafari and applying only to men. They are also sometimes preceded by "Bro or "Bra", meaning "Brother", or by "Sis" or "Sister". Among themselves, Rastafari often use these appellations.
2. Many thanks to *Ato* Girma Balcha, then in charge of immigration and nationality affairs, for having accepted to share with me the details of this census as well as his initial analyses.
3. See Frédéric Tonolli, *Les derniers Rastas* (RFO, 1998).

Chapter 1

1. The maroons are the Africans and the Afro-descendants who escaped from the plantations to form autonomous communities in the hinterland. See Price (1996).
2. This term is borrowed from Roger Bastide, who used it to designate the black cultures and civilizations of the United States, Central and South America and the Caribbean. See Bastide (1996).
3. Pan-African Conference, London, 1900; First Congress, Paris, 1919; Second Congress, London, 1921; Third Congress, London and Lisbon 1923; Fourth Congress, New York, 1927; Fifth Congress, Manchester, 1945; All-African Peoples Conference, Accra, 1958.
4. Firmin wrote his remarkable treatise *Égalité des races humaines: Anthropologie positive* (1885), aimed at countering Gobineau's racist theories. We will return to the trajectory of Benito Sylvain, particularly interesting since he travelled several times to Ethiopia and also attended the 1900 Pan-African Conference in London.
5. Figures mentioned by Ousmane Power-Greene during his conference at Yale University, 22 April 2006. His presentation, "The Means of Alleviating the Suffering: Pan-Africanism, Black Nationalism and the African American Led Haitian Emigration Movement of the 1820s", quoted documents provided, inter alia, by Charles Dixon (2000).

6. Paul Cuffe to Peter Williams Jr. (1816) and to James Forten (1817), and James Forten to Paul Cuffe (1817), in Moses (1996, 42–52).
7. Cited in Moses (1996, 171).
8. See Hill (1983–1990), 11 vols.
9. See Garvey (1986, 44).
10. David Walker (1829), in his famous *Appeal in Four Articles*, had already evoked the "God of the Ethiopians" who was about to save black people from an abject oppression. In the next chapter, I will return to the question of Ethiopianism.
11. The *Universal Negro Catechism* is published in Hill (1989, 4:160–61).
12. See the correspondence between M. Garvey and E. Cox, in Hill (1989, 4:160–61, 168). E. Cox wrote *Let My People Go* and dedicated it thus to Marcus Garvey: "To a black Negro making herculean effort to do for the Negro what the greatest of white Americans sought to do for the Negro and encouraged the Negro to do for himself – To Marcus Garvey, a martyr for the independence and integrity of the Negro race." Cited in Garvey (1923, 414).
13. The photographs of the period showing parades, exhibitions, and receptions provide an extremely rich source depicting the dramatization of the black nation. A few of these photographs may be seen in Garvey (1923). See as well Raiford (2013).

Chapter 2

1. J. Booth published a short book entitled *Africa for the Africans* (Baltimore, 1897). The use of this slogan probably came to him from a three-month visit to the American Negro Baptists in 1895. Forming a personal criticism of the African situation, this book evokes the initiatives of return to Africa but also launches a vigorous protest against the partition of the continent by Europeans. He was not the author of the slogan, contrary to certain claims – as we have seen, Martin Delany had already used it in 1852. See Shepperson and Price (1963, 109–12 and 504).
2. These texts by G. Schuyler, originally published in the form of serials, were republished by Hill (1994).
3. Reference may be made to Blyden's *The Negro in Ancient History* (1869, 3–6), clearly illustrating the historical use the author makes of the Bible.
4. It is not possible in this framework to cover the details of Afrocentrism which offered a central place to Egypt without restricting it to Egyptocentrism. See, for example, W. Moses (1998), who adopted a historical perspective in his brilliant study of Afrocentrism.
5. They are assembled in file 1B/5/79/41 Hamatic Church, National Archives, Spanish Town, Jamaica.
6. *The Holy Piby* has recently been re-edited (2000). In the Jamaican archives, the same texts comprising the *Piby* appear, but in a slightly different order, and with one booklet less. For greater clarity, reference is made here to the 2000 edition. The preface by Miguel Lorne (Rogers 2000, 7–14), a lawyer and editor who is also a well-known and respected Jamaican Rastafari, provides some interesting information.
7. It is also in Newark that Noble Drew Ali (1886–1929) settled with his family in the 1880s. He founded the Moorish Science Temple, which quickly took root in a dozen

American cities, with nearly three thousand members and numerous well-wishers. The movement of the Moorish Science Temple, largely inspired by the mystic freemasons, was one of the first to identify with Islam. See Nance (2002).

8. The police reports indicate on several occasions that the concerns with the AACC were of an entirely religious nature, having nothing to do with politics, which was, in all likelihood, one of the worries of the colonial authorities. See the reports dated 19 February 1926 and 1 September 1927, respectively, in 1B/5/79/41 Hamatic Church, National Archives, Spanish Town, Jamaica.
9. "The Living and Trading Scheme", one double-sided page, in 1B/5/79/41 Hamatic Church, National Archives, Spanish Town, Jamaica.
10. Police report, 16 February 1926, in 1B/5/79/41 Hamatic Church, National Archives, Spanish Town, Jamaica.
11. See in appendix 1 (this volume) the different versions of the Ethiopian prayer (1924, 1950, 1968, ca. 2000).
12. The inspector was unable to determine the validity of this affirmation concerning the foundation of the AACC in South Africa. It seems to be confirmed by Miguel Lorne (in Rogers 2000, 8). See police report, 16 February 1926, in 1B/5/79/41 Hamatic Church, National Archives, Spanish Town, Jamaica.
13. Police report, 19 February 1926 and 27 February 1926, in 1B/5/79/41 Hamatic Church, National Archives, Spanish Town, Jamaica.
14. Police report, 16 February 1926, in 1B/5/79/41 Hamatic Church, National Archives, Spanish Town, Jamaica.
15. Police report, 27 February 1926 and 1 September 1927, in 1B/5/79/41 Hamatic Church, National Archives, Spanish Town, Jamaica. This detail on broom-making is interesting: there still currently exists a Rastafari congregation, the Ethiopia Africa Black International Congress, to be discussed later, whose members are renowned for the making and selling of brooms.
16. Police report, 1 September 1927, in 1B/5/79/41 Hamatic Church, National Archives, Spanish Town, Jamaica.
17. Handwritten letter by Goodridge, dated 31 August 1927, in 1B/5/79/41 Hamatic Church, National Archives, Spanish Town, Jamaica.
18. *The Hamatic Church Hymn Book of AAC Gaathly under the auspices of the House of Athlyi. Kimberley, South Africa, Universal Headquarters* (Kingston: H.F. Hogg Printer, 1925), in 1B/5/79/41 Hamatic Church, National Archives, Spanish Town, Jamaica.
19. Preface by Miguel Lorne in Rogers (2000, 8).
20. Their emergence was influenced by John Alexander Dowie, who founded, in 1896, a "theocratic" and apocalyptic church, the Christian Catholic Apostolic Church in Zion, and a "Zion city" near Chicago. His main teachings were the "miraculous cure", the "Trinitarian baptism", and the conviction that the second coming of the Lord was imminent. Missionaries of this church baptized Africans by 1904, thus creating a first generation of leaders at the origin of many Zionist churches in South Africa. See Sundkler (1961, 48–49).
21. Here are some examples: Shembe's Nazareth Church at Ekuphakameni on Mount Nhlangakazi (Durban, 1912); Simon Kimbangu's Zion City at Nkamba, in Lower

Congo (its ministry started in 1921); Mutendi's Zion City on Mount Moriah in North Rhodesia (1923); Engmasi Lekhanyane's Church Zionist and the Morija Zion City in North Transvaal (1920s); Eduard Lion's Zion City in Basutoland (1917); the Musamo Christo Disco Music Church and Zion at Mozano in the Gold Coast (1923); Mtisi's Zion City at Umtali (1918).

22. This hymn is reminiscent of Lee Scratch Perry's roots reggae (1977): "Open the gate let's repatriate I say / Open the gate before it's too late I pray", in which gates symbolize both an entrance and the return to Zion.
23. R. Pemberton (1998, 600–601) quotes a calypso from 1936, by an unknown songwriter. The first couplet begins:

    Mussolini's only playing de fool
    We know Ethiopia will bring him cool
    It's the very country that gave them licks
    It was in the year 1896
    You know they altered them and they were so sore!
    And look at hell, they going back for more
    But this time what they'll have to do
    Is to hold Mussolini and alter him too

24. Besides, in 1898, a group of one hundred black delegates from West Africa and from the Western metropoles are reported to have gone as far as Ethiopia to ask Menelik for moral and financial support. While the financial support was not possible, the delegation nevertheless returned home strengthened by this visit. I received this information from Kifle Sellassie Beseat (Paris, 29 June 2006), but there is no corroborating source available at the moment. Future research might elucidate this remarkable initiative.
25. This is the case of all the public events reported by the pan-African press and of all the speeches, edited and published in English, made by the emperor. See for example, Haile Selassie (1967, 190, 203, 206 and so on). Once, to distinguish among Americans, the emperor used the term "black Americans" (Haile Selassie 1994, 27).

Chapter 3

1. See Hill (1983, 2:575–76). Different versions of the Universal Ethiopian Hymn are to be found in appendix 2.
2. For references to the Universal Ethiopian Hymn sung by these American activists, see *New Times and Ethiopia News* (hereafter *NT&EN*), 18 October 1952 and 15 November 1952. These groups will be discussed below.
3. *The Universal Ethiopian Hymnal*, 16 pages, compiled by Arnold J. Ford, published by *Beth B'nai Abraham*, no date, probably 1922. In SC Scores Ford, Schomburg Center for Research in Black Culture, New York Public Library. Two songs were republished in Ethiopia: "Africa" and "Ethiopia's children" in "Arnold J. Ford's 'Universal Ethiopian Hymnal': A Note", *Ethiopia Observer*, 1973.
4. Rabbi Arnold Ford to Rabbi Matthew, June 5 1931. In Wentworth A. Matthew MS, Schomburg Center for Research in Black Culture, New York Public Library.

5. Ibid.
6. Ibid. Formatted in the original.
7. His racial theories were blamed in the 1960s for justifying segregation; he stepped down from the position of president of the American Association of Physical Anthropology.
8. Telegramme from the UNIA branch in Kingston to the consul of Italy in London, 19 August 1935, in 1B/5/77/290 1941 Abyssinian/Italian dispute. Protests against action of Italy, National Archives, Spanish Town.
9. Resolution adopted 5 October 1935 at a public assembly in Kingston, in 1B/5/77/290 1941 Abyssinian/Italian dispute. Protests against action of Italy, National Archives, Spanish Town, Jamaica.
10. Petition "of loyal Jamaicans of colour" addressed to the secretary of state for the colonies in London, 8 October 1935, in 1B/5/77/290 1941 Abyssinia/Italian dispute. Protests against action of Italy.
11. Letter from the Spanish Town branch of the UNIA and African Community League of the World addressed to the secretary of state for the colonies in London, 9 October 1935, in 1B/5/77/290 1941 Abyssinian/Italian dispute. Protests against action of Italy.
12. Letter from the secretary of state for the colonies in London April 1936, in 1B/5/77/290 1941 Abyssinian/Italian dispute. Protests against action of Italy.
13. See *Black Man* 1, no. 7 (June 1935): 16–17.
14. See *Black Man* 1, no. 8 (July 1935): 17.
15. For example, "The Abyssinian rape", reproduced from *New Statesman and Nation*, in *Black Man* 1, no. 9 (August–Septepmber 1935), 16–17, and "Ethiopia Has Never Been Conquered", reproduced from the *New York Sun*, in *Black Man* 1, no. 10 (October 1935): 14–15.
16. See *Black Man* 1, no. 11 (December 1935): 10.
17. "Italy's Conquest?", *Black Man* 2, no. 2 (July–August 1936): 4.
18. Ibid., 6.
19. For example, in *Black Man* 2, no. 6 (March–April 1937): 1–2, 8–9.
20. Una Brown to the editor, *Black Man* 2, no. 3 (September–October 1936): 15. The author of this letter could be Una Marson (1905–65), a young, brilliant Jamaican poet and feminist employed by the Abyssinian Legation in London in 1936. Her autobiography, which was never published, was entitled "The Autobiography of a Brown Girl". She may have taken the pen name Una Brown to sign this letter. See Jarrett-Macauley (1998, 80–85, 98–105).
21. G.H. Blackett, M.E. Gardner and Melaku's wife, Dorothy H. Beyen, were appointed as presidents until the first annual meeting of the organization. Aida Bastian and Eudora Paris, who had resided in Ethiopia at the beginning of the 1930s also signed the certificate of incorporation of the EWF (Certificate of Incorporation, New York, 28 July 1937, private archives, Gladstone Robinson, Shashemene).
22. EWF Inc., Constitution and By-laws, article 1, section 2 (a), 1937.
23. For example, Joel Rogers and Colonel John Robinson were members of EWF. See their photographs in EWF (2003).
24. EWF Inc., Constitution and By-laws, articles 2 and 4, 1937. These groups were called

chapters or charters, terms with a religious or legal connotation, but also locals, followed by the number that identified them.

25. C.L.R. James and A. Phillip Randolph, two well-known pan-Africanists, figured among the numerous speakers. Many associations were also represented (churches, trade unions, the UNIA, the Young Men's Christian Organization, the Royal Order of Ethiopian Hebrews, and so on). See Harris (1994, 136–39).
26. *NT&EN*, 26 March 1955, 1.
27. Letter on the Eritrea question by Mr Mattavous, EWF international chaplain, published on the first page, *NT&EN*, 5 July 1952, 1 and 3.
28. See, for example, *NT&EN*, 6 September 1952, 3, and 18 October 1952, 3.
29. Letter from the EWF to the Council of Foreign Affairs Ministers of the United Nations on the Question of Eritrea in 1948, *NT&EN*, 28 February 1948, 3.
30. Sylvia Pankhurst (1882–1960), an Englishwoman, the leader of the anti-fascist movement in the 1920s, edited *NT&EN* (1936–56) and the *Ethiopia Observer* (1956–60) in Addis Ababa. She died there and was buried in the cathedral of the Trinity. Her mother, Emmeline Pankhurst (1858–1928), was a well-known feminist figure, speaker and organizer, who served several terms in prison and inspired constitutional change on women's rights. See Hill (1989, 6:197).
31. This was a common concern of the speakers of the fifth Pan-African Congress, held in Manchester in 1945. The second session on October 17 was entirely devoted to the question of Ethiopia. See *History of the Pan-African Congress* (1947, 44–45).
32. T.R. Makonnen co-organized the fifth Pan-African Congress held in Manchester in 1945 and took the floor in the name of Ethiopia to denounce the imperialist stronghold of the British subsequent to the treaty signed between the two countries in 1941 and renewed in 1944. See *History of the Pan-African Congress* (1947, 44).
33. Interview with Gladstone Robinson, Shashemene, 28 April 2003.
34. D. Talbot, *Musical Bride*, 1962. The story of this young woman could be that of the daughter of *Käntiba* Gebru Desta, the mayor of Gondar, who was well-known to the Afro-Americans. Issue 21 of the musical collection *Ethiopiques* presented the music of *Emahoy* Tsegaye-Maryam Gebrou, and the booklet that narrates her story, edited by Francis Falceto, is strangely reminiscent of the destiny of David Talbot's heroine.
35. An article in *Ebony* 6, no. 7 (May 1951): 79–83, offers interesting portraits, and *African Opinion* (hereafter *AO*) is full of information on these professionals in Ethiopia. See, for example, the issues of August 1949, 1, 3, 3; January 1950, 1, 4, 3, and so on.
36. *AO* 7, nos. 1–2 (1965): 6.
37. *NT&EN*, 15 November 1952, 4.
38. *AO* 6, nos. 11–12 (1965): 4.
39. Interview with Berba Tulu, Kuyra, 13 May 2003. Although the term *tabot* was probably not used by the Pipers, it is not surprising on the part of an Ethiopian woman.
40. Interview with G. Robinson, Shashemene, 19 March 2003.
41. Interview with Tesfa Giorgis, Shashemene, 29 April 2003.
42. Letter from Emperor Haile Selassie I to the members of EWF in New York, 30 September 1947. Private archives, G. Robinson, Shashemene. The impact of the official correspondence between the emperor and the members of the federation was

very strong and speedily affected the sales of the *Voice of Ethiopia* and the growth of membership. See the example given by Harris (1994, 138) regarding the message from the emperor received at the end of the first international congress in 1939 and the cable from his daughter Princess Tsehay to the women of EWF.

43. *Ebony* 6, no. 7 (May 1951): 80.
44. *NT&EN*, 15 November 1952, 4.
45. In 1962, five thousand residents were counted in a census of Shashemene. They were certainly less numerous in previous years. See Master Plan, Shashemene (1967, 16).
46. Letter from EWF, New York, to the Emperor of Ethiopia, May 1950. Private archives, G. Robinson, Shashemene.
47. Collective interview with the officers of EWF, Headquarters, Shashemene, 30 September 2003.
48. Interview with T. King, Addis Ababa, 10 August 2003.
49. See *Majority Report* (1961, 5).
50. Interview with G. Robinson, Shashemene, 19 March 2003.
51. Letter from G.A. Bryan, executive secretary, EWF New York, to Miss Iris Davis, Local 31 in Kingston, 8 July 1950. In 1B/5/77/367 [1933] Repatriation to Africa III, National Archives, Spanish Town, Jamaica.
52. *NT&EN*, 3 March 1956, 3, and *AO* 6, nos. 3–4 (1964): 8–9.
53. *AO* 1, no. 4 (1950): 11.
54. *AO* 1, no. 4 (1950): 12.
55. *AO* 9, nos. 3–4 (1969): 7.
56. *NT&EN*, 6 September 1952, 3, and *NT&EN*, 15 November 1952, 4.
57. *NT&EN*, 6 September 1952, 3.
58. Interview with G. Robinson, Shashemene, 19 March 2003.
59. Ibid.
60. Ibid.
61. Diary of the trip to Jamaica, 1964. Private archives, G. Robinson, Shashemene.
62. The organizations represented were the Rastafarian Movement Church Triumphant; EWF Locals 7, 15, 19, 25, 37, 43; Ras Sam Brown's Rastafari Movement; Apostles of the Negus in East Kingston and Montego Bay; the Rastafarian Movement in Trench Town; and the Ethiopian Orthodox Church. They are listed in Robinson's diary, in private archives, G. Robinson, Shashemene. See also the *Star*, 24 June 1964, on this encounter.
63. *NT&EN*, 19 June 1954, 2.
64. Many artistes made music about the independence of Ghana: for example, Lord Kitchener, with his calypso song "Birth of Ghana" (Trinidad, 1957), and John Coltrane, who recorded his album *Africa/Brass* in 1961, subsequent to several pieces like *Tanganyika Strut* and *Gold Coast* in 1958.
65. Era Bell Thompson, "Are Black Americans Welcome in Africa?", *Ebony* 24, no. 3 (January 1969): 44–50.
66. *AO* 5, nos. 1–2 (1959).
67. Thompson, "Are Black Americans Welcome?", 50.
68. *Ebony* 24, no. 10 (August 1969): 90–94.

Chapter 4

1. Afro-descendants form an estimated 76 per cent to 91 per cent of the Jamaican population, placing Jamaica among the "blackest" islands of the Caribbean, alongside Haiti, Guadeloupe, St Lucia, St Vincent, Antigua and Grenada (quoted by Chivallon 2004, 66–67).
2. G. McKenzie to Sir Edward Denham, governor of Jamaica, 20 May 1935, and G. McKenzie to B.H. Easter, colonial secretary, 28 May 1935, in 1B/5/77/394 [1933] Repatriation to Africa I (1933–42), National Archives, Spanish Town, Jamaica.
3. G. McKenzie to Sir Alexander Ransford Slater, governor of Jamaica, 12 March 1933, in 1B/5/77/394 [1933] Repatriation to Africa I.
4. G. McKenzie to Sir Alexander Ransford Slater, governor of Jamaica, 1 May 1933, in 1B/5/77/394 [1933] Repatriation to Africa I.
5. G. McKenzie to Sir A.S. Jelf, colonial secretary, 9 April 1933, in 1B/5/77/394 [1933] Repatriation to Africa I.
6. G. McKenzie to Sir Alexander Ransford Slater, governor of Jamaica, 12 March 1933, in 1B/5/77/394 [1933] Repatriation to Africa I.
7. G. McKenzie to Sir Alexander Ransford Slater, governor of Jamaica, 20 March 1933, in 1B/5/77/394 [1933] Repatriation to Africa I.
8. G. McKenzie to Sir Alexander Ransford Slater, governor of Jamaica, 1 May 1933, and G. McKenzie to the colonial secretary, 29 May 1933, in 1B/5/77/394 [1933] Repatriation to Africa I.
9. Minutes 13, 25 April 1933, in 1B/5/77/394 [1933] Repatriation to Africa I.
10. Minutes 14, 25 April 1933, in 1B/5/77/394 [1933] Repatriation to Africa I.
11. Minutes 14, 26 April 1933, as formatted in the original, 1B/5/77/394 [1933] Repatriation to Africa I.
12. Minutes 14, 26 April 1933, in 1B/5/77/394 [1933] Repatriation to Africa I.
13. G. McKenzie to the colonial secretary, 29 April 1933, in 1B/5/77/394 [1933] Repatriation to Africa I.
14. G. McKenzie to Sir Edward Denham, governor of Jamaica, 20 May 1935, and G. McKenzie to B.H. Easter, colonial secretary, 28 May 1935, in 1B/5/77/394 [1933] Repatriation to Africa I.
15. G. McKenzie and twelve other signatories to the secretary of state in London, 18 June 1935, first typewritten letter in 1B/5/77/394 [1933] Repatriation to Africa I.
16. Tract "To the Ethiopians" in 1B/5/77/394 [1933] Repatriation to Africa I.
17. J.A. Atkinson and twelve other signatories to the secretary of state in London, 23 June 1939, in 1B/5/77/394 [1933] Repatriation to Africa I.
18. Copeland Robinson to the colonial secretary, 24 October 1938, in 1B/5/77/394 [1933] Repatriation to Africa I.
19. Nilton Gordon to A.G. Grantham, colonial secretary, 30 August 1939, in 1B/5/77/394 [1933] Repatriation to Africa I.
20. F. Pitters, "Garvey Movement Takes Momentum", *AO* 1, no. 3 (1949): 13.
21. Florence Pitters, UNIA, to Sir Arthur Richards, governor of Jamaica, 24 September 1941, in 1B/5/77/394 [1933] Repatriation to Africa I.
22. Florence Pitters, UNIA, to Sir Arthur Richards, governor of Jamaica, 13 October 1941, in 1B/5/77/394 [1933] Repatriation to Africa I.

23. Florence Pitters, UNIA, to Sir Arthur Richards, governor of Jamaica, 14 January 1942, and Repatriation Bill of Jamaica and the West Indies, in 1B/5/77/390 [1933] Repatriation to Africa II (1942–46), National Archives, Spanish Town, Jamaica.
24. Although published only in 1947, the book of T. Bilbo and, in particular, its chapter 15 entitled "The Negro Repatriation Movement" (200–220) resorted to arguments developed earlier and echoed by the Repatriation Bill of the UNIA in Jamaica.
25. Repatriation Bill of Jamaica and the West Indies, chapter 8 and conclusion, in 1B/5/77/390 [1933] Repatriation to Africa II.
26. Florence Pitters to Sir Cosmo Parkinson, secretary of state for the colonies, 20 October 1942, in 1B/5/77/390 [1933] Repatriation to Africa II. In 1944, these figures go up to eighty-five thousand; see Florence Pitters to Sir Franck Stockdale, chairman of Caribbean Conference, Barbados, 22 March 1944, in 1B/5/77/390 [1933] Repatriation to Africa II.
27. Florence Pitters to Sir John Huggins, governor of Jamaica, 14 October 1943 (no indication of receipt), and Florence Pitters to Sir Franck Stockdale, Chairman of Caribbean Conference, Barbados, 22 March 1944, in 1B/5/77/390 [1933] Repatriation to Africa II.
28. Florence Pitters to the governor and the executive council, 4 August 1948, and joint petition with the Afro–West Indian Welfare League, 5 July 1948, in 1B/5/77/367 [1933] Repatriation to Africa III (1946–1951), National Archives, Spanish Town, Jamaica.
29. Samuel Hall to the accounting officer, 14 June 1948, in 1B/5/77/367 [1933] Repatriation to Africa III. S. Hall's handwritten letter shows his difficulty with the language, as many words are written almost phonetically.
30. Colonial secretary to Florence Pitters, 20 May 1950, in 1B/5/77/367 [1933] Repatriation to Africa III.
31. During various conversations in Accra, Ghana, in July 2004, I had confirmation that Jamaican Garveyites arrived there in 1948 and in subsequent years.
32. G. McKenzie to Sir Alexander Ransford Slater, governor of Jamaica, 12 March 1933, in 1B/5/77/394 [1933] Repatriation to Africa I.
33. *AO* 1, no. 3 (August 1949): 13.
34. See p. 8 of *The Universal Ethiopian Hymnal* (18 pages), compiled by Arnold J. Ford, published by Beth B'nai Abraham, no date, probably 1927. In Ford, Arnold, SC Scores, Schomburg Center for Research in Black Culture, Public New York Library.
35. See hymn number 15 of *The Hamatic Church Hymn Book*, published in 1925 in Kingston, in 1B/5/79/41 Hamatic Church, National Archives, Spanish Town, Jamaica.
36. Jean Besson (2002, 265) published a photograph, taken in the William Knibb Memorial Baptist Church in Trelawny, of a plaque commemorating emancipation and signalling, through Psalm 68:31, the bond between Baptists and Ethiopianism.
37. *Daily Gleane*r (hereafter *DG*), 6 June 1927.
38. *DG*, 6 June 1927, quoted by Ras Miguel Lorne in the foreword to the 1996 edition of *The Royal Parchment Scroll of Black Supremacy.*
39. My analysis is based on the copy published in Accra.
40. The first translation into English was that of E.A. Wallis Budge in 1932. It was made more accessible by Miguel F. Brooks in 1995 and almost denatured by Gerald Hausman in 1997.

41. See 1 Kings (10:1–13 and 2) and Chronicles (9:1–12). Ullendorf (1997, 132–39) mentions other Talmudic and Koranic occurrences.
42. The Ethiopian Salvation Society founded by Howell in 1939 made it possible to gather the funds which were used for the establishment of the Pinnacle. The constitution of Ethiopian Salvation Society seems to be inspired by that of EWF and had a similar objective of creating a network of solidarity and popular mutual aid. My thanks to Louis Moyston for having entrusted me with a copy of the constitution of Ethiopian Salvation Society.
43. C. Jones to the colonial secretary, 28 April 1948, in 1B/5/77/390 [1933] Repatriation to Africa II.
44. Dawson African to Sir John Huggins, governor of Jamaica, 21 May 1945, in 1B/5/77/390 [1933] Repatriation to Africa II.
45. R.E. Bennett and M.L. Henderson to Sir John Huggins, governor of Jamaica, 15 December 1943, in 1B/5/77/390 [1933] Repatriation to Africa II.
46. B.L. Wilson to the colonial secretary, 1 September 1944, 15 September 1944, 20 October 1944 and 5 January 1945, in 1B/5/77/390 [1933] Repatriation to Africa II.
47. C. Jones to the colonial secretary, 5 June 1943, in 1B/5/77/390 [1933] Repatriation to Africa II.
48. C. Jones to the colonial secretary, 28 April 1943, in 1B/5/77/390 [1933] Repatriation to Africa II.
49. Letter of Mrs Annie Harvey to the secretary of state, George Hall, 31 March 1946, in 1B/5/77/390 [1933] Repatriation to Africa II. See also Hill (2001, 27).
50. Note of the commissioner of police to the colonial secretary, 3 July 1946, in 1B/5/77/390 [1933] Repatriation to Africa II.
51. Egbert Smith to the colonial secretary, 14 May 1943, in 1B/5/77/390 [1933] Repatriation to Africa II.
52. R.E. Bennett and M.L. Henderson to Sir John Huggins, governor of Jamaica, 15 December 1943, in 1B/5/77/390 [1933] Repatriation to Africa II.
53. R.E. Bennett and M.L. Henderson to Sir John Huggins, governor of Jamaica, 10 December 1943, in 1B/5/77/390 [1933] Repatriation to Africa II.
54. B.L. Wilson to the colonial secretary, 15 September 1944, in 1B/5/77/390 [1933] Repatriation to Africa II.
55. B.L. Wilson to the colonial secretary, 5 January 1945, in 1B/5/77/390 [1933] Repatriation to Africa II.
56. B.L. Wilson to the colonial secretary, 20 October 1944, in 1B/5/77/390 [1933] Repatriation to Africa II.
57. Letter from EWF Local 17 to Sir Arthur Richards, governor of Jamaica, 11 December 1939, in 1B/5/77/145 [1939], National Archives, Spanish Town, Jamaica.
58. Letter from EWF Local 17 to Sir Arthur Richards, governor of Jamaica; received 13 February 1940; and the police report, Minutes 3, in 1B/5/77/145 [1939].
59. George Bryan, EWF New York, to Miss Iris Davis, EWF Local 31, Kingston, 8 July 1950, in 1B/5/77-367 [1933] Repatriation to Africa III.
60. Richard A. Brown, EWF Local 31, to Sir John Huggins, governor of Jamaica, 6 September 1950, in 1B/5/77-367 [1933] Repatriation to Africa III.

61. The colonial secretary to Richard A. Brown, EWF Local 31, 12 September 1950, in 1B/5/77-367 [1933] Repatriation to Africa III.
62. Richard A. Brown, EWF Local 31, to the colonial secretary, 20 September 1950, in 1B/5/77-367 [1933] Repatriation to Africa III.
63. Richard A. Brown EWF Local 31, to the colonial secretary, 21 October 1950, in 1B/5/77-367 [1933] Repatriation to Africa III. Like *DG*, 11 November 1950.
64. *NT&EN*, 24 February 1951, 3.
65. Minutes, no. 197, 13 November 1950, in 1B/5/77-367 [1933] Repatriation to Africa III. See also Lawson's declaration to the press in *DG*, 13 November 1950.
66. As indicated in *DG*, 27 September 1950.
67. Letter from Joseph Myers to the governor, 22 August 1950, and Minutes 148, 21 July 1950, in 1B/5/77-367 [1933] Repatriation to Africa III.
68. Letter from Claudius Barnes, Afro–West Indian League, to the colonial secretary, 27 September 1950, in 1B/5/77-367 [1933] Repatriation to Africa III.
69. *DG*, 22 October 1955, 3.
70. *NT&EN*, 6 September 1952, 3.
71. *DG*, 30 September 1955.
72. This visit by Richardson and the public announcement of the gift of land explains why, in historiography, the date of the gift is always noted as 1955, whereas, as we have seen in the preceding part, it occurred before this date. See also "Local Organization Gets Land Concessions in Ethiopia", *DG*, 31 July 1950, 1.
73. Executive committee, EWF New York, to the executive committee, EWF Local 31, Kingston, 24 September 1955, in Smith et al. (1960, 39–40).
74. See the photographs in *NT&EN*, 11 June 1955, 1.
75. *NT&EN*, 3 March 1956, 3.
76. "Tribute to the Patriarchs", *Rastafari Speaks* 1 (Spring 2002): 11.
77. Besides the videos which circulate among Rastafari and which are not easily accessible, see the documentary by John Dollar, *The Emperor's Birthday* (1992), and that of Frédéric Tonolli, *Les derniers Rasta*s (1998).
78. For example, Ras Bongo Watto in Shashemene in 1996. See *Papa Dyer and Bongo Watto*, I-Vision Productions, 1996.
79. "Tribute to the Patriarchs", 11.
80. Prince Emmanuel Charles Edwards, to Sir John Huggins, governor of Jamaica and to the colonial secretary, five letters dated 7 July 1948 and 24 January 1950, two dated 13 September 1950 and 21 September 1950, in 1B/5/77-367 [1933] Repatriation to Africa III.
81. Prince Emmanuel Charles Edwards to the colonial secretary, 13 September 1950, in 1B/5/77-367 [1933] Repatriation to Africa III.
82. Prince Emmanuel Charles Edwards to the colonial secretary, 21 September 1950 in 1B/5/77-367 [1933] Repatriation to Africa III.
83. *Jamaica Times* (8 March 1958, 1) indicated the presence of three thousand people. Prince Emmanuel thereafter founded, in Bull Bay, to the east of Kingston, the Ethiopia Africa Black International Congress, a self-sufficient church community named Bobo Ashanti, to which I will return later.

84. Enquiry carried out in December 1958, following the "Report on Rastafari Cult", attached to the Special Branch Report for January 1957, dated 13 January 1959, p. 3 in CO 1031/2767, Public Record Office, London.
85. An original of this blue card may be found in CO 1031/2768, Public Record Office, London.
86. *DG*, 6 October 1959.
87. Interview with H. Reid, Shashemene, 3 April 2003.
88. *AO* 4, nos. 11–12 (1959): 6–7.
89. *AO* 5, nos. 3–4 (1959): 9.
90. *AO* 5, nos. 1–2 (1959): editor's note, 7.
91. See *Majority Report* (1961, 1).
92. *DG*, 16 September 1960.
93. Ibid.
94. *DG*, 8 September 1960.
95. The delegates also met other Caribbeans residing in Ethiopia, like Julia Green from Anotto Bay, Jamaica, and David A. Talbot from Guiana.
96. Interview by van Dijk with Roy Augier, Kingston, 20 March 1990, in van Dijk (1993, 157).
97. Ras Sam Brown was a candidate to these elections with a programme in twenty-one points. It was a first in the movement. He gained few votes and his political involvement was sometimes disparaged. See Barnett (2000, 34–42).
98. Van Dijk (1993, 164) qualified as "anti-nationalists" the forces represented by the Rastafari. I think however that "alter-nationalist" would be more adequate, as it was not national allegiance per se that the Rastafari refused but, specifically, subordination to the Jamaican nation.
99. *DG*, 7 March 1965, quoted by van Dijk (1993, 169), and on Robinson's visit to Jamaica, see part 1, chapter 3 of this book.
100. See *Janhoy bäcaribiyan dässétoč*. Ministry of Information and Tourism, Addis Ababa: 1958 a.m. (1966). Haile Selassie I had initially been invited by Eric Williams, then head of the Government of Trinidad and Tobago, although various Rastafari who had taken part in the 1961 and 1963 missions sometimes attribute the invitation to themselves.
101. Confidential report by J.D. Murray, the British high commissioner to Jamaica, to the secretary of state for the Commonwealth, 14 June 1966, p. 2 in DO 200/170, Public Record Office, London.
102. Up until today, many Ethiopians believe that the divinity of the emperor was revealed to Rastafari *thanks to* this rain. The vernacular transmission of this event reversed the course of the events: whereas the plane landed *just after* the rain, Ethiopians take it that the arrival of Haile Selassie I *caused* the rain, which would have been a divine action, a "miracle" event, from the standpoint of a country which, contrary to Jamaica, suffers regularly from drought.
103. Confidential report by J.D. Murray, the British high commissioner to Jamaica, to the secretary of state for the Commonwealth, 14 June 1966, p. 3 in DO 200/170, Public Record Office, London.
104. Photographs in *Janhoy bäcaribiyan dässétoč*. Ministry of Information and Tourism,

Addis Ababa: 1958 a.m. (1966). See also the documentary *The Lion of Judah Visits Jamaica*, Vin Kelly (1966).

105. Confidential report by J.D. Murray, the British high commissioner to Jamaica, to the secretary of state for the Commonwealth, 14 June 1966, p. 4 in DO 200/170, Public Record Office, London.
106. These two watchwords, still in wide circulation in Jamaica today, are often quoted by Rastafari who chose not to go to Africa. It is in reference to these words that the Rastafari organization founded in 1995 was named the Rastafari Centralisation Organisation. See their publication *The Edifier: The Bearer of Light* (Kingston, 2001).
107. Confidential report by J.D. Murray, the British high commissioner to Jamaica, to the secretary of state for the Commonwealth, 14 June 1966, p. 4 in DO 200/170, Public Record Office, London.

Chapter 5

1. Interview with D. Baugh, Addis Ababa, 4 October 2003.
2. Interview with I. Baugh, Shashemene, 9 November 2001.
3. Interview with D. Baugh, Addis Ababa, 4 October 2003.
4. Ibid.
5. Ibid.
6. *DG*, 8 February 1968.
7. Letter to the editor by Mortimo Planno, *AO* 8, nos. 7–8 (1968): 11. Original formatting.
8. Interview with B.J. Moody, EWF officer, Shashemene, 1 April 2003.
9. Ibid.
10. Ibid.
11. Interview with officers of EWF Local 43, Waterhouse, Kingston, 23 March 2002.
12. My thanks to Brother Reid, who gave me this text, and to Jake Homiak, who helped me to complete its referencing. Despite my long sojourns in Shashemene, I never managed to meet Solomon Wolfe, who was always on international trips.
13. Interview with B.J. Moody, Shashemene, 1 April 2003.
14. *Jah*, probably a contracted form of Jehovah, is a synonym of God – that is, Haile Selassie I for the Rastafari.
15. *DG*, 29 December 1966, 3, article reproduced in *AO* 8, nos. 1–2 (1967): 7.
16. Interview with C. Clarke, Shashemene, 11 November 2001.
17. Ibid.
18. Ibid.
19. *NT&EN*, 3 July 1954, 3.
20. *NT&EN*, 11 September 1954, 3. This well-known hymn is part of the *nyabinghi* corpus; it is sung and was sung by others before them.
21. Interview with C. Clarke, Shashemene, 21 January 2003.
22. Ibid.
23. *DG*, 6 September 1969.
24. See, for example, *DG*, 28 and 30 September 1969, for Hugh Shearer, and *DG*, 12 October 1969, for Michael Manley. The visit of Jamaican politicians to Ethiopia will be addressed later.
25. *DG*, 30 April 1962.

26. SLGDRC, creation of the committee, 16 September 1972, in archives of the Ethiopian Orthodox Church (hereafter EOC archives), Kingston, Jamaica.
27. SLGDRC, letters and petitions dated 14 October 1972, in EOC archives, Kingston.
28. SLGDRC, nomination dated 14 January 1973, in EOC archives, Kingston.
29. SLGDRC, communiqué dated 21 January 1973, in EOC archives, Kingston.
30. SLGDRC, minutes, 28 January 1973, in EOC archives, Kingston.
31. SLGDRC, minutes, 18 March 1973, in EOC archives, Kingston.
32. SLGDRC, plan, 8 April 1973, in EOC archives, Kingston.
33. SLGDRC, "Land Grant Development. Delegates. Working Itinerary in Ethiopia", 8 April 1973, in EOC archives, Kingston.
34. Interview with H. Reid, Shashemene, 2 April 2003.
35. Ibid.
36. Ibid.
37. Ibid.
38. Ibid.
39. Ibid.
40. Ibid.
41. Janheinz Jahn's *Muntu: The New African Culture* was published in English in 1961 and was popular in academic and intellectual circles of the time. This reference was used to revalidate African and neo-African cultures (Lewis 1998, 121).
42. Interview with Empress Baby I, Shashemene, 16 September 2003.
43. Interview with N. Marshall, Shashemene, 27 September 2003.
44. Interview with L. Campbell, Shashemene, 9 September 2003.
45. Interview with B.J. Moody, Shashemene, 1 April 2003.
46. Programme celebrating the fortieth anniversary of the EWF, Chicago, in EOC archives, Kingston.
47. Reverend W.E. Evans, EWF Chicago, to G. Ascott, Kingston, 14 October 1967, in EOC archives, Kingston.
48. *AO* 8, nos. 3–4 (1967): 5, and interview with R. Morrison, Kingston, 22 March 2002.
49. *AO* 8, nos. 11–12 (1969): 9.
50. Interview with R. Morrison, Kingston, 22 March 2002, and E. Smith, Shashemene, 3 May 2003.
51. Interview with R. Morrison, Kingston, 22 March 2002, and E. Smith, Shashemene, 3 May 2003.
52. Interview with D. Martin, Shashemene, 28 January 2003.
53. Interview with A. Nevers, Shashemene, 5 September 2003.
54. Interview with R. Morrison, Kingston, 22 March 2002.
55. Prophet Gad interviewed by Andrea Williams for "Running African", 13 July 1997, Irie FM, Kingston, Jamaica.
56. On the congregation of Charles Fillmore, see, for example, Larson (1985, 322–57). Some of the theological concepts developed by Fillmore were similar to those of Emanuel Swedenborg (1688–1772), a scientist, philosopher and Swedish theologian, whose mystical experiences, exegeses, and vision of a spiritual and authentic Christianity translated in the establishment of the New Church. Thanks to Jean-François Mayer of the University of Freiburg for the many references he lent me on the subject.

57. The other readings recommended by Gad were *Philosophy and Opinions* of Marcus Garvey, *Selected Speeches* of Haile Selassie I, a work of an interpretative nature on the place of the West in the biblical prophecy of Herbert Armstrong, as well as the daily newspaper. See "What Gadman Has Taught Us", compiled by the New York branch of the Twelve Tribes of Israel (ca. 2005), entrusted to me by its founder, Larry Curtis. New York, 16 April 2006.
58. Correspondances are based on close reading of Fillmore (1930, 1931). Thanks to Timothy Green of the Los Angeles branch of the Twelve Tribes of Israel (21 June 2005) and Larry Curtis of the New York branch (30 January 2015) who revised this chart. The names of the Apostles in the chart were not part of the teachings of Prophet Gad, but they appear in Fillmore's work and are reported herein. Fillmore (1931, 214) explains the chart could be "expanded or changed to suit a broader understanding", and changes can be observed in different sources.
59. Interview with D. Martin, Shashemene, 28 January 2003.
60. Hence, Reuben faced Dan, Simeon Gad, Levi Asher, Judah Naphtali, Issachar Joseph and Zebulon Benjamin.
61. The American Cyrus Ingerson Scofield (1843–1921) published the first version of the Scofield Reference Bible, based on the text of King James Version (1611) in 1909, revised in 1917. Numerous comments frame the text and develop an intertextual frame of reference. Characterized as a pre-millenarian Bible, with many eschatological speculations, Scofield promoted dispensationalism, the belief that, between creation and the final judgement, there existed seven dispensations of relations between God and man, which offered a temporal symbolic framework to the biblical message. Scofield had a large impact on the fundamentalist Christian milieu.
62. Interview with E.L. Smith, Shashemene, 3 May 2003.
63. Ibid.
64. Ibid.
65. Interview with N. Marshall, Shashemene, 27 September 2003.
66. Interview with D. Martin, Shashemene, 28 January 2003.
67. Ian Boyne, "Rasta and the Middle Class", *Sunday Sun*, 22 March, 29 March, 5 April 1980, cited by van Dijk (1988, 1).
68. Interview with A. Nevers, Shashemene, 5 September 2003. The juxtaposition of spatial and social distinctions is quite visible in Kingston. These are articulated around different points, Parade, Crossroads, Halfway Tree, New Kingston, Papine, and so on. "Downtown", the old city centre near the waterfront, refers to popular, poor and violent neighbourhoods, sometimes with zinc houses. The former Back-o-Wall, Trench Town, and Tivoli Gardens are situated there. Other, more decentred ghetto zones are to be found elsewhere, like Waterhouse or Wareika Hills. "Uptown" refers to the more well-to-do residential, commercial or institutional neighbourhoods. The middle class lives uptown, not downtown.
69. Interviews with A. Nevers, Shashemene, 7 March 2003 and 5 September 2003.
70. Interview with D. Martin, Shashemene, 28 January 2003.
71. Interview with J. Douglas, Shashemene, 29 September 2003.
72. Interview with N. Marshall, Shashemene, 27 September 2003.
73. Ibid.

74. *DG*, 10 December 1976.
75. Interview with A. Nevers, Shashemene, 28 September 2003.
76. Interview with N. Marshall, Shashemene, 27 September 2003.
77. Interview with A. Nevers, Shashemene, 28 September 2003.
78. Interview with L. Campbell, Shashemene, 9 September 2003.

Chapter 6

1. Mortimo Planno financed this record, of which only six copies were made (Steffens 1998, 257). It has since been released by Bruno Blum (JAD/EMI, 1997).
2. A few months before his death, in November 1980, Bob Marley was baptized in in the Ethiopian Orthodox Church in New York. He received the name Berhane Selassie, meaning Light of the Trinity.
3. Several Rastafari who were present in Shashemene during Bob Marley's visit relate their participation in the elaboration of Bob Marley's song "Zimbabwe".
4. Samuel Clayton, a member of the second Jamaican Back-to-Africa Mission, 1963–65, was a part of this musical ensemble. Mystic Revelation of Rastafari remains quite active socially and performs regularly at school concerts, in order to sensitize children regarding black music and identity in Jamaica. On the occasion of Samuel Clayton's birthday in 2002, celebrated in the Wareika cultural centre, a back-to-Africa project was again reformulated. Notes and interview with Samuel Clayton, Kingston, 27 March 2002.
5. Situated on Portobello Road in the west of London, the organization promoted the learning of African history, the transmission of the Rastafari conception of Haile Selassie I, and political action through mobilization against apartheid in South Africa (Adams 2002, 46–53).
6. Interview with T. King, Addis Ababa, 10 August 2003.
7. Ibid.
8. Ibid. See also Adams (2002, 110).
9. Interview with EWF officers, Shashemene, 30 September 2003.
10. Ibid.
11. In the absence of references, the information collected on the Twelve Tribes is the fruit of observation and informal discussions carried on over several years with numerous members. In the course of this research, I was able to visit Twelve Tribes of Israel Headquarters in Kingston, Shashemene, New York, Los Angeles and Accra.
12. Singers were, however, quite explicit at times, like Tappa Zukie, who sang "A Chapter a Day" (1977), advocating the daily reading of the Bible as practised by the Twelve Tribes of Israel.
13. Interview with G. Cohen, Addis Ababa, 4 October 2003.
14. "What Gadman Has Taught Us", document compiled by The Twelve Tribes in New York ca. 2005, entrusted to me by Larry Curtis.
15. The archives of the Ethiopian Orthodox Church on Maxfield Avenue, in Kingston, contain several documents and letters exchanged between Ascento Foxe and Asfa Wossen as well as declarations on the occasion of the creation of the EWF.
16. *Dr Vernon Carrington*, publication on the occasion of Prophet Gad's funeral (2005, 8).

17. Interview with G. Cohen, Addis Ababa, 4 October 2003.
18. Ibid.
19. Interview with L. Curtis, New York, 16 April 2006.
20. Ibid.
21. Interview with A. Allen, Shashemene, 9 September 2003.
22. Ibid.
23. Ibid.
24. Ibid.
25. Interview with W. Laurence, Shashemene, 24 September 2003.
26. Interview with A. Allen, Shashemene, 9 September 2003.
27. Interview with Ras Mweya Masimba, Addis Ababa, 18 August 2003.
28. Ibid.
29. Ibid.
30. Ibid.
31. Interview with Bongo Solomon, Shashemene, 22 September 2003.
32. Ras Mweya Masimba filmed this event in its entirety. The film was edited and distributed by I-Vision Productions. See also John Dollar's documentary film, *The Emperor's Birthday* (1992) and *Jahug* 4 (1995): 8–11 and 32–34.
33. Interview with Ras Mweya Masimba, Addis Ababa, 18 August 2003.
34. I met with some of them during my stay in the Bull Bay Bobo camp in March 2002.
35. Prince Emmanuel to the Queen of England, 3 March 1966, in EABIC, *Black Supremacy* (n.d., 64–66).
36. Interview with Priest Paul, Shashemene, 28 September 2003.
37. Interviews in Shashemene with Marie Cummings, 22 April 2001, and her companion, Kristos, 8 November 2001. They have since left Ethiopia, due to increasingly difficult material conditions and the death of their second child, a daughter.
38. Interview with Sis Inanda, Shashemene, 24 April 2001.
39. Interview with Malcolm Philip, Shashemene, 24 March 2003.
40. Interview with EWF officers, Shashemene, 30 September 2003.
41. Interview with Ras Mweya Masimba, Addis Ababa, 18 August 2003.
42. Informal interview with W. Simons, Shashemene, 2003.
43. Interview with Isheba Tafari, Shashemene, 19 September 2003.
44. Ibid.
45. Ibid.
46. Ibid.
47. Ibid.
48. Interview with Ras Ibi, Shashemene, 4 September 2003.

Chapter 7

1. Ethiopia uses the Julian rather than the Gregorian calendar. The year begins in September and is divided into thirteen months. Twelve months have thirty days each, and one month has five or six days, depending on the year. The years are calculated based on a starting point situated seven years before the Gregorian calendar. All Ethiopian dates are provided with the Gregorian equivalent. They are followed by

the abbreviation *a.m.* (*amätä mehrät*) meaning "year of mercy" in Ge'ez, the ancient language of Ethiopia.

2. This is the way in which most of the residents questioned narrate the origin of the town. See the Master Plan (2000, 44). Benti Getahun also reports a story, according to which the name "Shash" was that of one of the officers of King Lebnä Dengel (1508–40), who purportedly settled on this spot (Benti Getahun 1988, 40n71).
3. Interview with Tesfa Giorgis, Shashemene, 29 April 2003. Benti Getahun's account of the settlement of the Hamassiens is based on oral sources (1988, 8).
4. Thus the only map of Shashemene presented by Gunilla Bjerén (1985, 89), dated 1973, indicates, right before the Malka Oda River, a few traces of construction and the mention of a clinic and a school. They were constructed, as we will see, by the first Caribbeans who settled on this land, but Bjerén never mentioned them.
5. *Tänaññä Wärq/bét rest*, Welde Meskel Memorial Archives Research Centre, Addis Ababa.
6. EWF document, "The Shashemene Story", private archives, G. Robinson, and G. Robinson, interview, Shashemene, 19 March 2003.
7. See, for example, *DG*, 13 February 1960 and 7 March 1960, and Campbell (1994, 221), Fikru Negash Guebrekidan (2005, 179), as well as Master Plan (2000, 52).
8. Document dated 29 January 1975, private archives, G. Robinson; interviews in Shashemene with Ambac'o Dagné, 3 February 2003, and Berhanou Teffera, 21 April 2003.
9. For example *Ras* Andergachaw Mesaï or the Italian concessioners at Wondo Genet; see files 90 5/90 and 10/3310 in *Tänaññä Wärq/bét rest*, Welde Meskel Centre, Addis Ababa.
10. Information collected over the telephone, Addis Ababa, 13 August 2003, with the help of Berhanou Abebe and *Ato* Mikias, professor at the Building College in Addis Ababa.
11. Shashemene, 1998, 1:5000, EMA. Older urban maps stop at the fringe of the town, and no registration or map of *ex-urbi* land has been found.
12. Interview with Tesfa Giorgis, Shashemene, 29 April 2003.
13. My thanks to Thomas Osmond and *Ato* Gemechu for their explanations of the meaning of Malka Oda.
14. Interview with G. Robinson, Shashemene, 5 November 2001.
15. *AO* 6, nos. 1–2 (1964): 6, and *AO* 6, nos. 7–8 (1964): 5.
16. Interview with G. Robinson, Shashemene, 28 April 2003.
17. See *NT&EN*, 15 November 1952, 4, and the photo of the Pipers on the runway, *AO* 6, nos. 11–12 (1965): 5.
18. Interview with T. King, Addis Ababa, 10 August 2003.
19. Interview with Tesfa Giorgis, Shashemene, 29 April 2003.
20. Yacob Wolde Mariam, *Menen* 6, no. 2 (1962): 22.
21. Minister of the interior and of agriculture to the minister of foreign affairs, 16 June 1982 *a.m.* (23 February 1990), in *Jamayca* DMJ 2/1–7, archives of the Ministry of Foreign Affairs, Addis Ababa.
22. Correspondence between the British ambassador in Addis Ababa and the editors of the Jamaican *Daily Gleaner*, published by the *DG*, 13 February 1960.

23. Although it certainly occurred later, T. King states that this nomination took place in 1952. Interview in Addis Ababa, 10 August 2003. See also *AO* 7, nos. 1–2 (1965): 6.
24. Interview with Berhanou Teffera, Shashemene, 21 April 2003. See also Master Plan (1967, 13) on the use of the soil, and *NT&EN*, 28 November 1953, 4, on the experimental cultivation of alfalfa in Shashemene.
25. Interview in Shashemene with Tesfa Giorgis, 29 April 2003, and Berhanou Teffera, 21 April 2003.
26. Interview with Berhanou Teffera, Shashemene, 21 April 2003.
27. This part is not visible when the building is photographed from the front (private archives, G. Robinson). However, in a side-view picture taken for the *Daily Gleaner*, this annex is quite visible. Nevertheless, the caption to the photograph in this newspaper reads: "meeting place for the children of the colonists" and is attributed to the Ethiopian government, although the building shown is clearly the Melaku E. Beyen School (*DG*, 7 November 1971).
28. Interview with Berba Tulu, Kuyra, 13 May 2003.
29. Interview with *Abba* Medina, Shashemene, 22 April 2003.
30. Several forms of tenant renting were practised in Ethiopia. The most common forms were: the *siso arash* in which the peasants provided the seeds and the cattle and reverted a tenth of their produce (*asrat*); the *irbo arash*, in which, in addition to the *asrat*, a quarter of what they produced was given to the *balabbat*; the *ekul arash*, in which the *balabbat* provided the seeds and the cattle, the peasants paid the *asrat* and the remainder of the produce was spilt equally between the two parties. See Cohen and Weintraub (1975, 53).
31. Interview with Berhanou Teffera, Shashemene, 21 April 2003.
32. Interview with Berba Tulu, Kuyra, 13 May 2003.
33. In May 2003, *Ato* Tesfa Giorgis took me to Malka Oda for a funeral so that I could meet certain residents. Sitting under a great tent, the conversation on the Pipers unearthed an interesting variety of recollections.
34. File 90 5/90, *yärest mäshashač'a wäyem mawerärsha wäyem yäsät'ota marägagäč'a säséda*, 14 *genbot* 1952 (22 May 1960), page 2, in *Tänaññä Wärq/bét rest*, Minsitry of Home Affairs, Addis Ababa. Many thanks to Shimelis Bonsa, with whom I studied this document, and to Katia Girma, who helped me think about the meaning of these terms.
35. *AO* 7, nos. 1–2 (1965): 7.
36. *AO* 9, nos. 3–4 (1969): 6.
37. *AO* 7, nos. 1–2 (1965): 6, 7.
38. Marcus Garvey, "Plan for the Colonization of Liberia", in Garvey (1923, 380–85).
39. *AO* 7, nos. 1–2 (1965): 6.
40. *AO* 6, nos. 7–8 (1964): 5.
41. Yacob Wolde Mariam, *Menen* 6, no. 2 (1962): 23.
42. *AO* 6, nos. 7–8 (1964): 5.
43. *AO* 7, nos. 1–2 (1965): 7. A few years later, this forfeit was increased to fifteen dollars. See *AO* 9, nos. 3–4 (1969): 6.
44. *AO* 7, nos. 1–2 (1965): 7.
45. *AO* 7, nos. 9–10 (1966): 5.

46. *AO* 6, nos. 11–12 (1965): 5.
47. Interview with G. Robinson, Shashemene, 19 March 2003.
48. Interview with *Abba* Médina, Shashemene, 22 April 2003.
49. Interview with G. Robinson, Shashemene, 19 March 2003.
50. Ibid.
51. See the photocopied page from *AO* 6, nos. 7–8 (1964): 5, with annotations. Private archives, G. Robinson, Shashemene.
52. "Power of Attorney", registered 4 February 1967 in New York. Private archives, G. Robinson, Shashemene.
53. Letter from G. Bryan, EWF, New York, to G. Robinson, 2 February 1967. Private archives, G. Robinson, Shashemene.
54. George E. Bryan had served as the EWF international secretary from 1952 (*NT&EN*, 6 September 1952, 3, and 15 November 52, 4), before becoming the executive secretary from 1955 to 1958 (*NT&EN*, 26 March 1955, 1 and 4; *AO* 4, nos. 5–6 [1958]: 3).
55. Letter from G. Bryan, EWF, New York, to *Ato* Yohannes Kidane Mariam, vice-minister, 2 February 1967. Private archives, G. Robinson, Shashemene.
56. See, for example, Ministry of the Interior and Administration to R*as* Mesfin Sileshi, 25 *miyazia* 1959 *a.m.* (3 May 1967), and the governor of Hayqoch et Buta Jira A*wrajja* to the *wäräda* of Shashemene, 10 *genbot* 1959 *a.m.* (18 May 1967), in the archives of the *wäräda* of Shashemene, S-8.
57. See the certificate delivered by Ethiopian consulate to the United States, 8 *hamlé* 1959 *a.m.* (15 July 1967), in the archives of the *wäräda* of Shashemene, S-8.
58. The governor of Hayqoch and Buta Jira A*wrajja* to the *wäräda* of Shashemene, 10 *genbot* 1959 *a.m.* (18 May 1967), in the archives of the *wäräda* of Shashemene, S-8.
59. See this volume, part 2, chapter 5, "From Local 15 of the EWF . . .".
60. See photographs, *DG*, 7 November 1971.
61. Interview with G. Robinson, Shashemene, 19 March 2003.
62. Interview with D. Baugh, Addis Ababa, 4 October 2003.
63. *DG*, 28 September 1969, 1.
64. *DG*, 17 October 1969, 1.
65. *DG*, 30 September 1969, 1.
66. *DG*, 17 October 1969, 1 and 5.
67. *DG*, 12 October 1969, 1.
68. *DG*, 23 January 1970, 22.
69. *DG*, 9 January 1971, 2.
70. Reading of the petition by Mama Baugh, *All Houses Reasoning*, video, I-Vision Production (1992).
71. Interview with D. Baugh, Addis Ababa, 4 October 2003.
72. Interview with C. Clarke, Shashemene, 21 January 2003.
73. Ibid.
74. Official document on the division of the land into twelve lots, 7 *hamlé* 1962 *a.m.* (14 July 1970), in Amharic, and translated on the spot into English by Desmond Christie. I received a copy from Gladstone Robinson in Shashemene (4 November 2001), and was able to consult the original in Kingston, in Gerald Brissett's hands (23 March 2002).

75. Interview with G. Robinson, Shashemene, 19 March 2003.
76. Interview with the officers of EWF Local 43, Kingston, 23 March 2002.
77. Interview with D. Baugh, Addis Ababa, 4 October 2003.
78. Interview with C. Clarke, Shashemene, 21 January 2003.
79. Adams (2002, 41). Berba Tulu (Kuyra, 13 May 2003) remembers that this tractor was called Israel. It features on a photograph in the *DG*, 7 November 1971.
80. Interview with C. Clarke, Shashemene, 21 January 2003. It would appear that this funding, between twelve thousand and eighteen thousand Jamaican dollars, at the time, according to informants, was managed by Ivan Coore (the son of the Jamaican minister of finance), who was a Twelve Tribes member then residing in Ethiopia.
81. Interview with C. Clarke, Shashemene, 21 January 2003. On the modernization of agricultural production in Ethiopia before 1974, with the aid of the United States, see Dessalegn Rahmato (1995, 166–78).
82. Interview with D. Baugh, Addis Ababa, 4 October 2003.
83. Interview with the officers of EWF Local 43, Kingston, 23 March 2002.
84. Interview with G. Robinson, Shashemene, 19 March 2003.
85. Interview with C. Clarke, Shashemene, 21 January 2003.
86. See this volume, part 2, chapter 5, "Shashemene Land Grant Development and Re-settlement Committee".
87. Interview with E. Smith, Shashemene, 3 May 2003.
88. Ministry of Land Reform in the province of Choa (*t'äklay gezat*), 10 *säné* 1966 *a.m.* (17 June 1974), in the archives of the municipality of Shashemene, *Yädassé qut'er gä* 8.
89. The *wäräda* of Shashemene to the province of Choa (*t'äklay gezat*), 8 *hamlé* 1966 *a.m.* (15 July 1974), in the archives of the municipality of Shashemene, *Yädassé qut'er gä* 8.
90. Interview with E. Smith, Shashemene, 3 May 2003.
91. Interview with G. Robinson, Shashemene, 21 March 2003.
92. Interview with E. Smith, Shashemene, 3 May 2003.
93. E. Smith to the Provisional Military Administrative Council, Addis Ababa, 20/5/1967 *a.m.* (28 January 1975). Private archives, E. Smith, Shashemene.

Chapter 8

1. Whereas the term *derg* referred to the Provisional Military Administrative Council which directed Ethiopia until September 1984, popular usage of the term designated the government until the fall of the regime in 1991. The term *derg* is used herein in the popular sense. See also Donham (2002b, 3n1).
2. Interview with D. Baugh, Addis Ababa, 4 October 2003.
3. Interview with Ambac'o Dagné, Shashemene, 3 February 2003.
4. Interview with C. Clarke, Shashemene, 21 January 2003.
5. Interviews with C. Clarke, 21 January 2003, and G. Robinson, 21 March 2003, in Shashemene.
6. Interview with E. Smith, Shashemene, 3 May 2003.
7. Letter from the Ministry of Foreign Affairs of the Provisional Military Government

to the Embassy of Jamaica, stamped 21 April 1975. Private archives, A. Nevers, Shashemene.

8. Ibid.
9. Letter from the Ministry of Foreign Affairs of the Provisional Military Government to the Embassy of Jamaica, dated 3 October 1975. Private archives, A. Nevers.
10. Ibid.
11. Interview with Berba Tulu, Kuyra, 13 May 2003. It seems that James Piper was murdered in New York in 1981. See Bishton (1986, 40).
12. Interview with Berhanou Teffera, Shashemene, 21 April 2003.
13. Interview with *Abba* Médina, Shashemene, 22 April 2003.
14. Interview with T. King, Addis Ababa, 10 August 2003.
15. Interview with the officers of the EWF, Shashemene, 30 September 2003.
16. Interview with W. Boyd, Kingston, 3 March 2002.
17. Interview with T. King, Addis Ababa, 10 August 2003.
18. Interview with E. Smith, Shashemene, 3 May 2003.
19. Interview with N. Marshall, Shashemene, 27 September 2003.
20. Ibid.
21. Letter from the EWF, signed by G. Robinson, to the Provisional Military Administrative Council, 4 February 1975. Private archives, G. Robinson.
22. Interview with A. Nevers, Shashemene, 28 September 2003.
23. Interview with E. Smith, Shashemene, 3 May 2003.
24. Interview with A. Nevers, Shashemene, 28 September 2003.
25. Ibid.
26. Ibid.
27. Prophet Gad interviewed by Andrea Williams for "Running African", 13 July 1997, Irie FM, Kingston, Jamaica.
28. Interview with G. Cohen, Addis Ababa, 4 October 2003.
29. Interview with A. Nevers, Shashemene, 28 September 2003.
30. Interview with E. Smith, Shashemene, 3 May 2003.
31. Interview with A. Nevers, Shashemene, 28 September 2003.
32. Ibid.
33. Interview with N. Marshall, Shashemene, 27 September 2003.
34. W. Hillman to the municipality of Shashemene, 4 *t'er* 1973 (12 January 1981). Municipal Archives, *Yädassé qut'er gä* 8.
35. Letter from the municipality to the Ministry of Urban Development and Housing, Office of the Choa Province in Addis Ababa, 6 *t'er* 1973 (14 January 1981). Municipal Archives, *Yädassé qut'er gä 8*.
36. Ministry of Urban Development and Housing, Office of the Choa Province in Addis Ababa, to the municipality of Shashemene, 18 *t'er* 1973 (January 1981). Municipal Archives, *Yädassé qut'er gä 8*.
37. Interview with C. Clarke, Shashemene, 21 January 2003.
38. Interview with J. Douglas, Shashemene, 29 September 2003.
39. Interview with V. Wisdom, Shashemene, 30 January 2003.
40. Ibid.
41. Ibid.

42. Ibid.
43. Interview with D. Martin, Shashemene, 28 January 2003.
44. Interview with G. Robinson, Shashemene, 19 March 2003.
45. Interview with D. Martin, Shashemene, 29 January 2003.
46. Ibid.
47. Ibid.
48. Interview with Guebre Egziabeher Guebru, Jamaican consul in Ethiopian, Addis Ababa, 15 August 2003. Officially for financial reasons, the embassy was closed in 1992, and, in 1994, a consulate was opened. It does not have the same means and is unable, for example, to renew passports. The consul is Ethiopian and had entered the embassy as the ambassador's secretary in 1972.
49. Interview with B.J. Moody, Shashemene, 2 May 2003.
50. Report from the municipality of Shashemene to the Ministry of Agriculture in Addis Ababa, 10 April 1983, Municipal Archives, *Yädassé qut'er gä* 8.
51. Interview with Ambac'o Dagné, Shashemene, 3 February 2003.
52. Interview with N. Marshall, Shashemene, 27 September 2003.
53. Ibid.
54. Ibid.
55. Interviews with B.J. Moody, 2 May 2003, and N. Marshall, Shashemene, 27 September 2003.
56. Interview with B.J. Moody, Shashemene, 2 May 2003.
57. Interview with A. Nevers, Shashemene, 28 September 2003.
58. Interview with N. Marshall, Shashemene, 27 September 2003.
59. Interview with A. Nevers, Shashemene, 28 September 2003.
60. Ibid.
61. Interview with Larry Curtis, New York, 16 April 2006.
62. Interview with N. Marshall, Shashemene, 27 September 2003.
63. Interview with A. Nevers, Shashemene, 28 September 2003.
64. Interview with T. King, Addis Ababa, 10 August 2003.
65. EWF, *Official Black Paper* (1991, 9).
66. Interview with Mebrat Bekele, Shashemene, 6 September 2003. This interviewee went to an Italian school and speaks the language fluently. The interview was conducted in a strange mixture of Italian and Jamaican dialect, peppered with a few interjections and phrases in Amharic.
67. Ibid.
68. Ibid.
69. Interview with G. Cohen, Addis Ababa, 4 October 2003.
70. Interview with Mebrat Bekele, Shashemene, 6 September 2003.
71. Interview with Ambac'o Dagné, Shashemene, 3 February 2003.
72. Interview with Amina and Alemitu, Shashemene, 5 September 2003.
73. Ibid.
74. Ibid.
75. Ibid.
76. Ibid.

Chapter 9

1. *All Houses Reasoning*, video (I-Vision Productions, 1992).
2. Inez Baugh, in *All Houses Reasoning*.
3. Noel Dyer, in *All Houses Reasoning*.
4. *All Houses Reasoning*.
5. W. Hillman to Negaw Gebreal, mayor of Shashemene, 30 November 1992. Municipal Archives, Shashemene, *Yädassé qut'er gä* 8.
6. B.J. Moody to Negaw Gebreal, mayor of Shashemene, 7 December 1992. Municipal Archives, Shashemene, *Yädassé qut'er gä* 8.
7. Negaw Gebreal, mayor of Shashemene, to W. Hillman, 8 December 1992. Municipal Archives, Shashemene, *Yädassé qut'er gä* 8.
8. Most of these may be found in the *Yädassé qut'er gä* 8 file, Municipal Archives in Shashemene.
9. Interview with J. Douglas, Shashemene, 29 September 2003. The Municipal Archives (*Yädassé qut'er gä* 8) show only two property titles, one dated 4 *yekatit* 1986 *a.m.* (11 February 1994), for a house in *qäbälé* 01, and a second, without date, for a house in *qäbälé* 010.
10. Interview with D. Martin, Shashemene, 29 January 2003.
11. Land survey produced by the Technical and Land Administration Department of the municipality, dated 21 March 1994, Municipal Archives, *Yädassé qut'er gä* 8, and private archives, D. Martin.
12. See the handwritten notes on a letter from the *qäbälé* 010 to the municipality, dated 3 May 1995. Besides, in the 2000 Master Plan, this area was reduced to a maximum of 200 square metres in town, see Master Plan (2000, 126).
13. This data is derived from the various land surveys appearing in the Municipal Archives (*Yädassé qut'er gä* 8). They comprise a dozen surveys, often rudimentary drawings, and the large size of the lots (5,000 square metres) is due to the fact that several of these parcels had escaped the 1975 reforms and were thus larger than subsequent allocations.
14. Interview with D. Martin, Shashemene, 29 January 2003.
15. Ibid.
16. Interview with A. Nevers, Shashemene, 28 September 2003.
17. Interview with N. Marshall, Shashemene, 27 September 2003.
18. Municipality of Shashemene to the Urban Development Office of the *East Shäwa Zone*, 22/3/1994 *a.m.* (1 December 2001), Municipal Archives, *Yädassé qut'er gä* 8.
19. Municipality of Shashemene to the Urban Development Office of the *East Shäwa Zone*, 22/3/1994 *a.m.* (1 December 2001), Municipal Archives, *Yädassé qut'er gä* 8.
20. The Government of Oromiya to the Urban Development Office of the *East Shäwa Zone*, 11 November 1994 *a.m.* (17 August 2002), Municipal Archives, *Yädassé qut'er gä* 8.
21. Interviews with C. Clarke, Shashemene, 12 and 13 November 2001.
22. Interview with Amina and Alemitu, Shashemene, 5 September 2003.
23. Interview with G. Robinson, Shashemene, 19 March 2003.
24. Interview with Empress Baby I, Shashemene, 16 September 2003.
25. Interview with Bongo Solomon, Shashemene, 22 September 2003.

26. Interview with Ras M. Masimba, Addis Ababa, 18 August 2003. See also *Rastafari Repatriate to Shashemene*, video (I-Vision Productions, 2000).
27. The EMA Maps 1:5000 published in 1998 were drawn up on the basis of an aerial photograph taken in 1994. On it, Alelu looks totally empty, with no construction in sight.
28. The *wäräda* of Shashemene to Alelu Peasant Association, 22 December 1993 *a.m.* (29 July 2001), in the archives of the *wäräda*, S-8.
29. For reasons of discretion, I have refrained from citing the names of most of the persons who provided information on issues relating to land tenure and construction.
30. Interview with Priest Paul, Shashemene, 28 September 2003.
31. Ibid.
32. Ibid.
33. Ibid.
34. This remained the most common type of dwelling in Shashemene in 2000 (Master Plan 2000, 125). Square-shaped houses with zinc roofs are a recent phenomenon, and are built when funds become available.
35. See the NUPI maps, Shashemene Development Plan, 1: 2,000 (2000).
36. This is the opinion of a young American Rastafari who went to Ethiopia with his wife and son in 1999. See *Rastafari Repatriate to Shashemene* (I-Vision Productions, Shashemene, 2000).
37. Field notes taken at the Yekatit School in Shashemene, 24 April 2003.
38. Interview with I. Tafari, Shashemene, 19 September 2003.
39. The most famous among them, Teddy Afro and Jonnie Ragga, made songs that were aired over and over again for months all over the country. Some of their songs evoke Bob Marley and Haile Selassie, while certain videos show scenes of Rastafari life in Shashemene.
40. For example, D. Martin to the *wäräda* police, 2 May 1995 and 16 July 1996 in the archives of the *wäräda*, S-8.
41. In 2000 in Shashemene, the infant mortality rate of children under one: 109/1,000; under five: 158/1,000. Life expectancy at birth: fifty-two years. In Master Plan (2000, 71).
42. Jamaican Rastafarian Development Community to the *wäräda* of Shashemene, 1 May 2002, in the archives of the *wäräda*, S-8.
43. Jamaican Rastafarian Development Community to the *wäräda* of Shashemene, 23 May 2002, in the archives of the *wäräda*, S-8.
44. Several interlocutors mentioned this phrase. See, for example, *Rastafari Repatriate to Shashemene.*
45. EWF, *Official Black Paper* (1991, 14–15).
46. Ibid.
47. *Ethiopian Herald*, 19 June 2002, and *Addis Tribune*, 21 June 2002, in Ethiopian World Federation, *Vision Statement*, Addis Ababa, 2003.
48. Interview with T. King, Addis Ababa, 10 August 2003.
49. The EWF to the Disaster Prevention and Preparedness Commission, Addis Ababa, Project Proposal: Establishment of a Vocational Training Centre in Shashemene, May 2000, in EWF, *General Overview* (ca. 2005, 4–11).

50. Jamaican Rastafarian Development Community to the *wäräda* of Shashemene, 19 January 2002, in the archives of the *wäräda*, S-8.
51. Field notes, presentation of the structure of the Jamaican Rastafarian Development Community, community meeting, Shashemene, 30 March 2003.
52. Interview with A. Allen, Shashemene, 9 September 2003.
53. Figures calculated based on information provided in the Master Plan (2000, 79).
54. The Jamaican Rastafari Community, D. Martin to the administration of the *wäräda*, report concerning water pipes in Jamaican community, water-pipe development made in the peasant association, 6 January 1999. In the archives of the *wäräda*, S-8.
55. Two big development projects, a hotel and a restaurant, promoted by a Trinidadian couple living in the United States, and a hospital project promoted by the Nurses of Israel, an American association close to the Twelve Tribes, were in gestation for years. The construction of the first was completed at the time of my field enquiry whereas the second was impeded by the presence of Ethiopian squatters on the land granted by the government. See, respectively, the correspondence of L. Chapman with the municipality, Municipal Archives, *Yädassé qut'er gä* 8, and that of the Nurses of Israel with different government agencies, in the archives of the *wäräda*, S-8.
56. Interview with A. Allen, Shashemene, 9 September 2003.
57. Interview with Ras M. Masimba, Addis Ababa, 18 August 2003.
58. Interview with I. Tafari, Shashemene, 19 September 2003.
59. The proclamation of the 1930 law on nationality was published in *Berhannena Selam* 6, no. 30 (24 July 1930), and amended in *Berhannena Selam* 9, no. 41 (5 October 1933).
60. Many thanks to *Ato* Girma Balcha, formerly in charge of Immigration and Nationality Affairs, for having accepted to share his analyses of the census conducted under his jurisdiction.
61. *Negarit Gazeta*, Proclamation no. 378/2003 on Ethiopian Nationality, 23 December 2003, part 2, point 5.
62. The Rastafari Community to the general secretary of the Organization of African Unity, 27 June 2001, published in *Rastafari Speaks* 1 (Spring 2002): 8 (reissue 1).
63. My sincere thanks to Ayele Olana, the late husband of Aster, Vincent Beckford's second daughter, for welcoming me into his family and for patiently relating the itineraries of Beckford's ten children. Family interview with Ayele Olana, Shashemene, 27 September 2003.
64. Interview with D. Baugh, Addis Ababa, 4 October 2003.
65. Ibid.
66. Interview with T. Theophilos, Addis Ababa, 29 August 2003.
67. Interview with D. Baugh, Addis Ababa, 4 October 2003.
68. Interview with T. Theophilos, Addis Ababa, 29 August 2003.
69. Interview with D. Baugh, Addis Ababa, 4 October 2003.

Conclusion

1. Decision of the third extraordinary session of the executive council on the execution of the diaspora initiative in the framework of the African Union, DOC. Ext/EX/CL/5, 21–24 May 2003, Sun City, South Africa.

DISCOGRAPHY

The following 125 titles selected by Bruno Blum, specialist in Jamaican music, are on the theme "Repatriation Reggae".

1. "Ethiopia", The Jamaican Calypsonians (alias Lord Lebby)
   Produced by Stanley Ivan Chin, 1958
2. "So Long (The Negus Call You)",* Count Ossie and the Wareikas
   Produced by Harry Mudie, 1959
3. "Leaving This Land",* Count Ossie and the Wareikas
   Produced by Harry Mudie, 1959
4. "African Shuffle",* Count Ossie and the Wareikas
   Produced by Harry Mudie, 1959
5. "Going Home to Zion Land",* Count Ossie and the Wareikas
   Produced by Harry Mudie, 1959
6. "African Blood",* Raymond Harper and the Prince Buster All Stars
   Produced by Clement "Coxsone" Dodd, 1961
7. "Exodus", The Skatalites
   Produced by Harry Mudie, 1962
   Cover version of Ernest Gold's theme, interpreted by Eddie Harris for the soundtrack of the film *Exodus* by Otto Preminger.
8. "Carry Go Bring Come", Justin Hines and the Dominoes
   Produced by Arthur "Duke" Reid, 1963
9. "Dreamland", The Wailers, featuring Neville "Bunny" Livingston
   Produced by Clement Dodd, 1964
   Adapted from "My Dream Island" by El Tempos (Vee Jay, 1961)
10. "Bongo Man",* Bongoman Byfield
    Produced by Vincent "King" Edwards, 1964
    Parody of "Wonderful World" by Sam Cooke
11. "Freedom Train",* Laurel Aitken
    Produced by Laurel Aitken, 1964

12. "Addis Ababa", The Skatalites
Produced by Harry Mudie, 1965

13. "Rude Boy" (a.k.a. "Walk the Proud Land"), The Wailers
Produced by Clement "Coxsone" Dodd, 1965
Contains an abstract of "I've Got to Keep on Moving" by Curtis Mayfield

14. "Mount Zion", Desmond Dekker and the Four Aces
Produced by Leslie Kong, 1965

15. "Ethiopia",* The Hiltonaires
Produced by Edward Seaga and Ronnie Nasralla, 1965

16. "The Train Is Coming", Ken Boothe
Produced by Clement "Coxsone" Dodd, 1966

17. "Africa", The Gaylads
Produced by Clement "Coxsone" Dodd, 1967

18. "Pretty Africa", Desmond Dekker and the Aces
Produced by Leslie Kong, 1967

19. "I've Got to Go Back Home", Bob Andy
Produced by Clement "Coxsone" Dodd, 1967

20. "Train to Glory", The Ethiopians
Produced by Edward Seaga and Ronnie Nasralla, 1968

21. "Walk the Proud Land",* The Gaylads
Produced by Clement "Coxsone" Dodd, 1968

22. "Bongo Jah",* The Immortals
Produced by Joe Gibbs, 1968

23. "Happy Land",* Carlton and the Shoes
Produced by Clement "Coxsone" Dodd, 1968

24. "Forward Jerusalem",* Carlton and the Shoes
Produced by Clement "Coxsone" Dodd, 1969

25. "Satta Massa Gana", The Abyssinians
Produced by the Abyssinians, 1969

26. "Thunderstorm", Bongo Herman
Produced by the Abyssinians, 1969

27. "A Place Called Africa", Junior Byles
Produced by Lee Perry, 1969

28. "Ethiopians Live It Out/Live It Out", Burning Spear
Produced by Clement "Coxsone" Dodd, 1969

29. "Selah", The Ethiopians
Produced by J.J. Johnson, 1970

30. "Imperial I", Prince Jazzbo and Burning Spear
Produced by Clement "Coxsone" Dodd, 1970

31. "Land Call 'Africa' ",* Alton Ellis, ca. 1970
Adapted from "The House of the Rising Sun" by Alan Price

32. "Holy Mount Zion",* Zion Star (feat. Count Ossie)
Produced by Clement "Coxsone" Dodd, 1970

33. "Dreamland" (alternate), The Wailers (with Neville "Bunny" Livingston)
Produced by Lee "Scratch" Perry, 1970
Adapted from "My Dream Island" by El Tempos (Vee Jay, 1961)

34. "Way Back Home", U Roy
Produced by Arthur "Duke" Reid, 1970

35. "Rocking to Ethiopia",* Dennis Alcapone (with the Ethiopians)
Produced by J.J. Johnson, 1970

36. "Open the Gate", The Ethiopians
Produced by Clement Dodd, 1970

37. "Sunny Side of the Sea", Slim Smith
Produced by Edward "Bunny" Lee, 1970

38. "A Place Called Africa", Dr Alimantado and the Upsetters
Produced by Lee "Scratch" Perry, 1970

39. "Way Back Home", U Roy
Produced by Arthur "Duke" Reid, 1970

40. "Freedom Train",* The Gladiators
Produced by Lloyd "The Matador" Daley, 1971

41. "Freedom Train", The Gladiators
Produced by Lloyd Daley, 1971

42. "Alpha and Omega",* Dennis Alcapone
Produced by Lee "Scratch" Perry, 1971

43. "African People", Funky Brown, 1971

44. "Behold the Land", Culture
Produced by Clement "Coxsone" Dodd, 1972

45. "Promised Land", Gregory Isaacs
Produced by Sidney Crooks, 1972

46. "Far Beyond", Leroy "Horsemouth" Wallace and the New Establishment
Produced by Clement "Coxsone" Dodd, 1973

47. "Africa We Are Going Home", Time Unlimited
Produced by Lee Perry, 1973

48. "Africa Dub (Africa We Are Going Home)", The Upsetters
Produced by Lee "Scratch" Perry, 1973

49. "Walk the Proud Land" (a.k.a. "Rude Boy"), Bob Marley and the Wailers
Produced by Chris Blackwell, 1973

50. "Deliver Us to Africa", Alton Ellis, 1973

51. "Salvation Train", Scotty
Produced by Lloyd Charmers, 1973

52. "East of the River Nile", Augustus Pablo
Produced by Herman Chin-Loy, 1973

53. "Rasta Man Chant", Bob Marley and the Wailers
Produced by Chris Blackwell and the Wailers, 1973

54. "A Change Me Mind"* (a.k.a. "Ethiopia"), Count Lasher
Produced by Clement "Coxsone" Dodd, 1974

55. "Ethiopian (Version)",* Count Lasher
Produced by Clement "Coxsone" Dodd, 1974

56. "Rasta Train", Lee and Jimmy (with Lee "Scratch" Perry)
Produced by Lee "Scratch" Perry, 1974

57. "School Train", The Black Brothers (with the New Establishment)
Produced by Clement "Coxsone" Dodd, ca. 1974

58. "Train to Rhodesia", Big Youth
Produced by Tony Robinson, 1975

59. "Dub Ethiopia", Augustus Pablo
Produced by Lee "Scratch" Perry, ca. 1975

60. "A Place in Africa" (a.k.a. "Addis Ababa"), Delroy Wilson
Produced by Keith Hudson, ca. 1975
Adapted from "The House of the Rising Sun" by Alan Price

61. "Open the Iron Gate" (parts 1 and 2), Max Romeo
Produced by Max Romeo, 1975

62. "Zion Land", Ras Michael and the Sons of Negus
Produced by Tommy Cowan, 1975

63. "Repatriation", Horace Andy
Produced by Winston "Niney" Holness, ca. 1975

64. "Rainbow Country", Bob Marley and the Wailers
Produced by Lee "Scratch" Perry, 1975

65. "Africa We Want to Go",* The Maytones
Produced by Alvin Ranglin, 1976

66. "Holy Mount Zion", The Heptones with Nago Morris
Produced by Winston "Niney" Holness, 1976

67 "Forward on to Zion", The Abyssinians
Produced by Bernard Collins, 1976

68. "Ethiopian Land", Peter and Paul Lewis
Produced by Lee "Scratch" Perry, 1976

69. "African Talk", I Roy
Produced by Edward Sullivan "Bunny" Lee, 1976

70. “Africa”, Mighty Diamonds
Produced by Pat “Jah Lloyd” Francis, 1976

71. “MPLA”,* Tappa Zukie
Produced by David “Tappa Zukie” Sinclair, 1976

72. “MPLA (Version)”,* Tappa Zukie
Produced by David “Tappa Zukie” Sinclair, 1976

73. “In Zion”, Ras Michael and the Sons of Negus
Produced by Ras Michael and Tommy Cowan, ca. 1976
Adapted from “On Broadway” by Cynthia Weil, Barry Mann, Jerry Leiber and Mike Stoller, interpretation by the Drifters

74. “Forward onto Zion”, The Abyssinians
Produced by the Abyssinians, 1976

75. “Dream Land”, Bunny Wailer
Produced by Neville “Bunny Wailer” Livingston, 1976

76. “This Train”, Bunny Wailer
Produced by Neville “Bunny Wailer” Livingston, 1976

77. “The Exile Song”, Skiddy and Detroit
Produced by Keith Hudson, ca. 1976
Adapted from “The House of the Rising Sun” by Alan Price

78. “Babylon Queendom”, Peter Tosh
Produced by Peter Tosh, 1976

79. “Yi Mas Gan”, The Abyssinians
Produced by Clive Hunt, ca. 1976

80. “Yi Mas Gan (Dub)”, The Abyssinians
Produced by Clive Hunt, ca. 1976

81. “Mandela”, Tommy Mc Cook
Produced by the Abyssinians 1976

82. “Exodus”, Bob Marley and the Wailers
Produced by Bob Marley and the Wailers, 1977

83. “Exodus (Version)”, Bob Marley and the Wailers
Produced by Bob Marley and the Wailers, 1977

84. “Exodus (Advertisement)”, Bob Marley and the Wailers
Produced by Bob Marley and the Wailers, 1977

85. “Open Up the Gate”, The Congos
Produced by Lee “Scratch” Perry, 1977

86. “Rasta Train”,* Raphael Green and Dr Alimantado
Produced by Lee “Scratch” Perry, 1977

87. “Get Ready to Ride the Lion to Zion”, Culture
Produced by Joel “Joe Gibbs” Gibson, 1977

88. "Judgement on the Land", Vivian Jackson and the Prophets
Produced by Vivian "Yabby You" Jackson, 1977

89. "Repatriation Rock (Judgement on the Land)", King Tubby's
Produced by Vivian "Yabby You" Jackson, 1977

90. "A Chapter a Day",[*] Tappa Zukie
Produced by David "Tappa Zukie" Sinclair, 1977

91. "Roots Train", Junior Murvin and Dillinger
Produced by Lee "Scratch" Perry, 1977

92. "I Know a Place", Bob Marley and the Wailers
Produced by Lee "Scratch" Perry, 1977

93. "My Father's Home Land (Extended)", Sylford Walker
Produced by Glenmore "Glen" Brown, 1977

94. "Kunta Kinte",[*] Ray I
Produced by Derrick Harriott, 1977

95. "Mount Zion Version", Yabby You and Michael Prophet (feat. King Tubby)
Produced by Vivian "Yabby You" Jackson, ca. 1977

96. "Black Starliner Must Come", Culture
Produced by Joel "Joe Gibbs" Gibson, 1977

97. "Open the Gate", Watty Burnett
Produced by Lee "Scratch" Perry, 1977

98. "Repatriation Time", Dillinger
Produced by Lester "Dillinger" Bullock, Webster Shrowder and Larry Sevitt, 1977

99. "Holy Mount Zion", Gladstone Anderson
Produced by Mike Brooks and Pat "Jah Lloyd" Francis, ca. 1977

100. "Repatriation", Dennis Brown
Produced by Joel "Joe Gibbs" Gibson, 1978

101. "Behold the Land",[*] Culture
Produced by Sonia E. Pottinger, 1978

102. "Leaving to Zion", Black Uhuru
Produced by Sly Dunbar and Robbie Shakespeare, 1978

103. "Black Starliner",[*] Reggae Regular
Produced by Lloyd "TCB" Patten, 1978

104. "Steppin' Out of Babylon",[*] Marcia Griffiths
Produced by Sonia E. Pottinger, 1978

105. "Africa Here I Come", Freddie McGregor
Produced by Clement "Coxsone" Dodd, 1978

106. "Ethiopia", Aisha Morrison 1978
Produced by Lee "Scratch" Perry, 1978

107. "My Home Land (Extended)", Dave Robinson
Produced by Dudley "Manzie" Swaby, ca. 1978

108. "Holy Mount Zion", Culture
Produced by Sonia E. Pottinger, 1978

109. "Addis Ababa", Willie Williams
Produced by Clement "Coxsone" Dodd, 1979

110. "Free Africa", The Twinkle Brothers
Produced by Norman Grant, 1979

111. "River Jordan", Sugar Minott
Produced by Lincoln "Sugar" Minott, 1979

112. "Long Way", Junior Delgado
Produced by Winston "Niney" Holness, ca. 1979

113. "Selassie Ship", Niney and Errol
Produced by Winston "Niney" Holness, ca. 1979

114. "Africa Unite", Bob Marley and the Wailers
Produced by Bob Marley and the Wailers and Alex Sadkin, 1979

115. "Repatriation", U Brown
Produced by Huford "U Brown" Brown, 1979

116. "The Land We Belong", Culture
Produced by Sonia E. Pottinger, 1979

117. "People of the World",* Sugar Minott
Produced by Winston "Niney" Holness and Joseph Hookim, 1980

118. "Train to Zion" (Discomix) with Linval Thompson, U Brown
Produced by Huford "U Brown" Brown and Tony Welch, ca. 1980

119. "Zion Train", Bob Marley and the Wailers
Produced by Bob Marley and the Wailers, 1980

120. "Forward to Africa", Culture
Produced by Joseph Hill, ca. 1981

121. "Land of Love", The Heptones
Produced by Winston "Niney" Holness, ca. 1982

122. "Ethiopian National Anthem", The Ethiopians
Produced by Winston "Niney" Holness, ca. 1982

123. "His Future In Africa? Plots on His Life", Peter Tosh
Produced by Roger Steffens, ca. 1982

124. "Holy Mount Zion", Wayne Jarrett
Produced by Lloyd "Wackies" Barnes and Clive Hunt, 1982

125. "Repatriation", Burning Spear
Produced by Burning Spear and the Burning Band, 1983

Note: *Titles digitalized from original LPs.

REFERENCES

Note: Following the usage in Ethiopian historiography, Ethiopian authors are listed by their first names.

Primary Sources

Archives and Manuscript Collections

Jamaica

National Archives, Spanish Town

1B/5/77/394 [1933] Repatriation to Africa I (1933–1942)
1B/5/77/390 [1933] Repatriation to Africa II (1942–1946)
1B/5/77/367 [1933] Repatriation to Africa III (1946–1951)
1B/5/77/145 [1939] Application for permission to form EWF Inc. and kindred societies (1939–1940)
1B/5/79/41 Hamatic Church
1B/5/79/430 Existence of dangers arising from race hatred (1930)
1B/5/79/87 Spread of anti-white propaganda (1926)
1B/5/79/174 Bolchevist activities among Negroes (1930)
1B/5/77/232 1935 Ethiopian-Italian war, joining of West Indians to fight for Ethiopia
1B/5/77/52 1941 Assistance to Abyssinia
1B/5/77/290 1941 Abyssinian/Italian dispute. Protests against action of Italy (1935–1938)

Ethiopian Orthodox Church, Kingston

Files Ethiopian World Federation
Files Imperial Ethiopian World Federation
Files Shashemene Land Grant Development and Re-settlement Committee (SLGDRC)

United Kingdom

Public Record Office, London

Foreign Office

FO 371/125389 Immigration to Ethiopia
FO 371/138036 Attempt by Haile Selassie to bring together the emerging nations of Africa and the European powers still interested in Africa

FO 371/108283 Emperor of Ethiopia's visit to United Kingdom 1954
FO 371/27528 Egyptian 1941 Ethiopia File no. 25, pp. 2317 to end
FO 371/27527 Egyptian 1941 Ethiopia File no. 25, to pp. 2289
FO 371/19176
FO 371/19124 Political Egyptian Ethiopia Files 1, pp. 3622–721.
FO 371/3500 Abyssinia Files 70539–178490

Colonial Office

CO 96/552 Negro immigration from USA
CO 96/554 Negro immigration from USA
CO 318/432/2 Marcus Garvey and connected associations
CO 1031/2545 West Indian clubs and associations in the United Kingdom
CO 1034/2545 Study of the migration movement between Jamaica and the United Kingdom
CO 1031/2768 The activities of Mr C.V. Henry and his "Back to Africa" movement in Jamaica, 1957–1959
CO 1031/3998 The activities of Mr C.V. Henry and his "Back to Africa" movement in Jamaica, 1960–1962.
CO 1031/2767 Activities of the Rastafarians in Jamaica

Dominions

DO 200/170 Political implications of Emperor Haile Selassie Visit to the West Indies 1964–66

War Office

WO 336/32 Internal Security – Rastafarians, April–May 1960
WO 336/33 Secret Rastafarians Log Sheet, 16 June–28 December 1960
WO 336/34 Rastafarians sitreps and reports to War Office, 22 April 1960–?
WO 336/35 Rastafarians – OP orders, OP instructions and confirmatory notes. April–July 1960.

United States of America

Arthur Schomburg Center for Research in Black Culture, New York

Ford, Arnold, SC Scores Ford
Wentworth A. Matthew Collection SCM 97-9

Private Archives, Long Beach

Randal Hepner, anthropologist

Ethiopia

Ministry of Foreign Affairs, Addis Ababa

Files *Jamayca* DMJ 2/1–7, 7 volumes

Welde Meskel Memorial Archives Research Centre, Addis Ababa

Tänaññä Wärq/bét rest, Land Archives of Princess Tenagne Worq

Immigration and Nationality Affairs, Addis Ababa

Individual files of Jamaicans in Ethiopia selected by the archivist

National Urban Planning Institute, Addis Ababa

Shashamane 1971, 1: 2,500
Shashamane 1976, 1: 50,000, ETH4 (DOS 450)
Shashamane 1984, 1: 2,500
Shashamane 1998, 1: 2,000, sheets 5, 10
Shashamane 1998, 1: 5,000, sheet 2
Shashamane 1998, 1: 5,000, Development plan, sheets 4, 8, 9,
Existing land use
Proposed land use

Ethiopian Mapping Authority, Addis Ababa

Shashemene 2002 1: 2000, air photographs of Oromiya region
ETH 01 R13 ST 43
ETH 01 R13 ST 44
ETH 01 R13 ST 45

Shashemene Municipality (*meker bét*), Shashemene

Yädassé qut'er gä 8. Bäshashemene kätäma ymigägnu yäjamaicanoč täwäladoč mänoriya bét
Ga-54 *Arsä Af Esraél* (Nurses of Israel) *Gaafi heeyaama ijjaarisa dhabatta*

Shashemene Region (*wäräda*), Shashemene

S-8 1994 AM *Saba-Jamayiika*
Shashemene wäräda 2200 *A*-2135
Shashemene Hayqočnna Buta Jira 211-2113
Arussi 2067

Private Archives of Shashemene Settlers, Shashemene

Mebrat Bekele
Carmen Clarke
Desmond Martin
Anthony Nevers
Gladstone Robinson
Eric L. Smith
Vincent Wisdom

Government Documents

CSA (Central Statistical Authority). 1996. *1994 Population and Housing Census of Ethiopia. Oromiya Region, Addis Ababa,* Vol. 1: Statistical Report. Addis Ababa: CSA.

Janhoy bäcaribiyan dässétoč (Haile Selassie in the islands of the Caribbean). 1966 [1958 *a.m.*]. Ministry of Information and Tourism, Addis Ababa.

Ministry of Immigrations and Nationality Affairs. 2003. "Census of the Rastafari Community in Shashemene". Unpublished data. February.

Master Plan. 1967. Shashamane. Consorzio italiano di studi urbanistici. Imperial Ethiopian Government, Ministry of Interior, Municipality Department: Addis Ababa.

Master Plan. 2000. Shashemene. National Urban Planning Institute: Addis Ababa.

Newspapers

Exhaustive Reading

African Opinion [*AO*], New York (1949–76)

Blackman/Black Man, Kingston and London (1933–39)

Daily Gleaner [*DG*], Kingston (1927–2000)

New Times and Ethiopia News [*NT&EN*], London (1948–56)

Voice of Ethiopia, New York (1937–39)

Selective Reading

Ebony, Chicago

Berhannena Selam, Addis Ababa

The Crisis, New York

Ethiopia Observer, Addis Ababa

Jamaica Times, Kingston

Menen, Addis Ababa

Negarit Gazeta, Addis Ababa

Negro World, New York

Plain Talk, New York

Public Opinion, Kingston

Rastafari Speaks, Trinidad

Star, Kingston

Sunday Star, Kingston

Interviews by the Author

Marie Cummings, Shashemene, Ethiopia, 22 April 2001

Sis Inanda, Shashemene, 24 April 2001

Kristos, Shashemene, Ethiopia, 8 November 2001

Inez Baugh, Shashemene, Ethiopia, 9 November 2001; 22 January 2003

Mortimo Planno, Kingston, Jamaica, 7 February 2002

William Boyd, Kingston, Jamaica, 3 March 2002

Roy Morrison, Kingston, Jamaica, 22 March 2002
Officers of EWF Local 43, Kingston, Jamaica, 23 March 2002
Samuel Clayton, Kingston, Jamaica, 27 March 2002
Carmen Clarke, Shashemene, Ethiopia, 11, 12 and 13 November 2001; 21 January 2003
Desmond Martin, Shashemene, Ethiopia, 28, 29 January 2003; 2 February 2003
Vincent Wisdom, Shashemene, Ethiopia, 30 January 2003
Ambac'o Dagné, Shashemene, Ethiopia, 3 February 2003
Abba Haji, Shashemene, Ethiopia, 5 February 2003
Berthal J. Moody, Shashemene, Ethiopia, 8 February 2003; 1 April 2003; 2 May 2003
Anthony Nevers, Shashemene, Ethiopia, 7 March 2003; 5 September 2003; 28 September 2003
Bac'oré Andargé, Shashemene, Ethiopia, 16 March 2003
Groum Hailu, Shashemene, Ethiopia, 18 March 2003
Gladstone Robinson, Shashemene, Ethiopia, 4, 5 November 2001; 19, 21 March 2003; 28 April 2003
Malcolm Philip, Shashemene, Ethiopia, 24 March 2003
Harold Reid, Shashemene, Ethiopia, 31 March 2003; 2, 3 April 2003
Kim Shaw, Addis Ababa, Ethiopia, 13 April 2003
Berhanou Teffera, Shashemene, Ethiopia, 21 April 2003
Abba Médina, Shashemene, Ethiopia, 22 April 2003
Abraham Anota, Shashemene, Ethiopia, 24 April 2003
Tesfa Giorgis, Shashemene, Ethiopia, 29 April 2003
Eric L. Smith, Shashemene, Ethiopia, 3 May 2003
Berba Tulu, Kuyra, Ethiopia, 13 May 2003
Dej. Zwede Guebre Sellassié, Addis Ababa, Ethiopia, 17 July 2003
Yacob Wolde Mariam, Addis Ababa, Ethiopia, 1 August 2003
Tagesse King, Addis Ababa, Ethiopia, 10 August 2003
Guebre Egziabeher Guebru, Addis Ababa, Ethiopia, 15 August 2003
Ras Mweya Masimba, Addis Ababa, Ethiopia, 18 August 2003
Teferi Theophilos, Addis Ababa, Ethiopia, 29 August 2003
Ras Ibi, Shashemene, Ethiopia, 4 September 2003
Alemitu and Amina, Shashemene, Ethiopia, 5 September 2003
Mebrat Bekele, Shashemene, Ethiopia, 6 September 2003
Qés Bariyé, Shashemene, Ethiopia, 7 September 2003
Albert Allen, Shashemene, Ethiopia, 9 September 2003
Llewellyn Campbell, Shashemene, Ethiopia, 9 September 2003
Empress Baby I, Shashemene, Ethiopia, 16 September 2003
Isheba Tafari, Shashemene, Ethiopia, 19 September 2003
Bongo Solomon, Shashemene, Ethiopia, 22 September 2003
Sis. Wellete and Bro. Paul, Shashemene, Ethiopia, 22 September 2003
Winston Laurence, Shashemene, Ethiopia, 24 September 2003
Ras Kawintseb Mehert Sellassié, Shashemene, Ethiopia, 25 September 2003
Ayele Olana, Shashemene, Ethiopia, 27 September 2003
Norval Marshall, Shashemene, Ethiopia, 27 September 2003
Priest Paul, Shashemene, Ethiopia, 28 September 2003
Joan Douglas, Shashemene, Ethiopia, 29 September 2003

Officers of EWF, Shashemene, Ethiopia, 30 September 2003
David Baugh, Addis Ababa, Ethiopia, 4 October 2003
Gideon Cohen, Addis Ababa, Ethiopia, 4 October 2003
Yeweneshet Beshimared, Addis Ababa, Ethiopia, 5 October 2003
Abere Jembere, Addis Ababa, Ethiopia, 7 October 2003
Sophie Heckett, Addis Ababa, Ethiopia, 7 October 2003
Larry Curtis, New York, United States, 16 April 2006

Audio-Visual Sources

Video archives constituted by Ras Mweya Masimba, I-Vision Productions, Shashemene, 1992–1996:
Full interview between Papa Baugh and Mama Baugh by Sister Faye Tammani
Sistren's reasoning in the tabernacle, July 1996
Seal of the July 1996 gathering with Bongo Watto and meeting with Papa Dyer
Papa Dyer and Bongo Watto, July 1996
Bongo Watto talks of Prince Emmanuel
Bongo Watto in Wondo Genet
All Houses reasoning during 1992 Centenary in EWF Headquarters
The Lion of Judah Visits Jamaica, Vin Kelly, 1966.
The Emperor's Birthday, John Dollar, 1992.
Prophet Gad interviewed by Andrea Williams for *Running African*, 13 July 1997, Irie FM, Kingston, Jamaica.
Les derniers Rastas, Frédéric Tonolli. RFO, 1998.
Au nom de Jah, Luc de Saint Sernin. RFO, 1998.
Rastafari Repatriate to Shashemene. I-Vision Productions, Shashemene, 2000.

Published and Unpublished Primary Sources

Adams, Norman (Jah Blue). 2002. *A Historical Report: The Rastafari Movement in England*. London: GWA Works.

"Arnold J. Ford's Universal Ethiopian Hymnal: A Note". 1973. *Ethiopia Observer* 15, no. 4: 246–47.

Bilbo, Theodore G. 1947. *Take Your Choice: Separation or Mongrelization*. Poplarville, MS: Dream House.

Blyden, Edward W. 1856. "A Voice from Bleeding Africa". In *Black Spokesman: Selected Published Writings of Edward Wilmot Blyden*, edited by H.R. Lynch, 7–10. Reprint, 1971. London: Frank Cass.

———. 1862. "The Call of Providence to the Descendants of Africa in America". In *Black Spokesman: Selected Published Writings of Edward Wilmot Blyden*, edited by H.R. Lynch, 25–33. Reprint, 1971. London: Frank Cass.

———. 1869. "The Negro in Ancient History". *Methodist Quarterly Review*, reprinted in *The People of Africa: A Series of Papers on Their Character, Condition, and Future Prospects by E.W. Blyden (and others)*, edited by H.M. Schieffelin, 1–34. New York: A.D.F. Randolph, 1871.

———. 1880. "Ethiopia Stretching Out Her Hands unto God; or, Africa's Service to World".

Conference to the American Colonization Society. In E.W. Blyden, *Christianity, Islam and the Negro Race*, 113–29. Reprint, 1994. Baltimore: Black Classic Press.

Catholic Commission for Racial Justice. 2002. *Rastafarians in Jamaica and Britain*. Notes and Reports, no. 10 (January).

Coon, Carleton S. 1935. *Measuring Ethiopia and Flight into Arabia*. Boston: Little, Brown.

Cuffe, Paul. 1816. "Letter to Peter Williams Jr". In *Classical Black Nationalism. From the American Revolution to Marcus Garvey*, edited by W. Moses, 48–49. Reprint, 1996. New York: New York University Press.

———. 1817. "Letter to James Forten" and "Letter from James Forten to Paul Cuffe". In *Classical Black Nationalism. From the American Revolution to Marcus Garvey*, edited by W. Moses, 49–51. Reprint, 1996. New York: New York University Press.

Crummell, Alexander. 1861. "The Progress of Civilization along the West Coast of Africa". In *Classical Black Nationalism. From the American Revolution to Marcus Garvey*, edited by W. Moses, 169–87. Reprint, 1996. New York: New York University Press.

Delany, Martin R. 1852. *The Condition, Elevation, Emigration and Destiny of the Colored people of the United States*. Baltimore: Black Classic Press, 1993.

———. 1861. "Official Report of the Niger Valley Exploring Party". In *Classical Black Nationalism. From the American Revolution to Marcus Garvey*, edited by W. Moses, 145–68. Reprint, 1996. New York: New York University Press.

Dr Vernon Carrington. 2005. Booklet published for the funeral of Prophet Gad.

Du Bois, W.E.B. 1946. *The World and Africa: An Enquiry into the Part Which Africa Has Played in World History*. Reprint, 1972. New York: International.

EABIC (Ethiopia Africa Black International Congress). N.d. *Black Supremacy in Righteousness of Salvation*. Kingston: EABIC.

EWF (Ethiopian World Federation). 1937. *Constitution and By-laws*. New York: Headquarters.

———. 1991. *Official Black Paper, Shashemene Land Grant (1975–1991)*. Report authorized by the EWF Inc., Birmingham.

———. 2003. *Vision Statement*. 50-page pamphlet containing various documents. Addis Ababa: EWF.

———. 2005. *General Overview*. New York: EWF Headquarters.

Faristzaddi, Millard. 1987. *Itations of Jamaica and I Rastafari: The First Itation*. Miami: Judah Anbessa.

———. 1991. *Itations of Jamaica and I Rastafari: The Second Itation*. Miami: Judah Anbessa.

———. 1997. *Itations of Jamaica and I Rastafari: The Third Itation*. Miami: Judah Anbessa.

Fillmore, Charles. 1930. *The Twelve Powers of Man*. Unity Village, MO: Unity. Reprint, 1995.

———. 1931. *Metaphysical Bible Dictionary*. Mineola, NY: Dover. Reprint, 2

Fleming, G. James, and Christian E. Burckel. 1950. *Who's Who in Colored America*. New York: C.E. Burckel and Associates.

Garvey, Marcus. 1923. *The Philosophy and Opinions of Marcus Garvey: Or, Africa for the Africans*. Reprint, 1986. Dover, MA: Majority.

Haile Selassie I. 1966. "Discourse of Haile Selassie I in Jamaica, 21 April 1966". Reprint, 1986. *Reggae and African Beat* 5, nos. 5–6.

———. 1967. *The Third Testament: The Ilect Verses of Emperor Haile Sellassie I*. [Selected speeches]. Reprint, 1997. Kingston: Headstart.

———. 1976. *My Life and Ethiopia's Progress: The Autobiography of Emperor Haile Sellassie I*. Vol. 1. Translated by E. Ullendorf. Reprint, 1999. Chicago: Research Associates School Times Publications.

———. 1994. *My Life and Ethiopia's Progress: The Autobiography of Emperor Haile Sellassie I*. Vol. 2. Translated by E. Ullendorf. Reprint, 1999. Chicago: Research Associates School Times Publications.

Hill, Robert, ed. 1983. *The Marcus Garvey and Universal Negro Improvement Association Papers*. Vol. 1: *1826–August 1919*. Berkeley: University of California Press.

———. 1983. *The Marcus Garvey and Universal Negro Improvement Association Papers*. Vol. 2: *27 August 1919–31 August 1920*. Berkeley: University of California Press.

———. 1984. *The Marcus Garvey and Universal Negro Improvement Association Papers*. Vol. 3: *3 September 1920–August 1921*. Berkeley: University of California Press.

———. 1985. *The Marcus Garvey and Universal Negro Improvement Association Papers*. Vol. 4: *1 September 1921–2 September 1922*. Berkeley: University of California Press.

———. 1986. *The Marcus Garvey and Universal Negro Improvement Association Papers*. Vol. 5: *September 1922–August 1924*. Berkeley: University of California Press.

———. 1989. *The Marcus Garvey and Universal Negro Improvement Association Papers*. Vol. 6: *September 1924–December 1927*.Berkeley: University of California Press.

———. 1990. *The Marcus Garvey and Universal Negro Improvement Association Papers*. Vol. 7: *November 1927–August 1940*. Berkeley: University of California Press.

———. 1994. *George S. Schuyler: Ethiopian Stories*. Boston: Northeastern University Press.

History of the Pan-African Congress. 1963 [1947]. London: Susan Tully.

Howell, Leonard Percival [G.G. Maragh]. 1935. *The Promised Key*. Accra: The African Morning Post.

———. 1939. *Rules of the Ethiopian Salvation Society, Friendly and Benevolent Society*. Kingston, Jamaica.

Jah Bones. 1985. *One Love Rastafari: History, Doctrine and Livity*. London: Voice of Rasta.

Jahug. 1991–2000. 7 volumes. London.

Mack, Douglas. 1999. *From Babylon to Rastafari: Origin and History of the Rastafarian Movement*. Chicago: Research Associates School Times Publications.

Majority Report of Mission to Africa. 1961. Kingston: Government Printer.

Mérab, Docteur. 1912. *Médecins et Médecine en Ethiopie*. Paris: Vigot Frères Editeurs.

———. 1922. *Impressions d'Ethiopie (L'Abyssinie sous Ménélik II)*. Vol. 2: *La Capitale et ses environs; la cour et le peuple; une page d'histoire contemporaine (1908–1914)*. Paris: Éditions Ernest Leroux.

Minority Report of Mission to Africa. 1961. Kingston: Government Printer.

Minority Rights Group. 1982. *The Rastafarians*, Report no. 64, written by E. Cashmore.

National Geographic. 1931. 59, no. 6 (June).

Malaku E. Bayen. 1939. *The March of Black Men: Ethiopia Leads – An Authentic Account of the Determined Fight of the Ethiopian People for Their Independence*. New York: Voice of Ethiopia Press.

Order of the Nyahbinghi. N.d. *Ancient Order of the Nyahbinghi Guidelines*, 18 pp.

Pettersburgh, Reverend Fitz Balintine. 1926. *Royal Parchment Scroll of Black Supremacy*. Reprint, 1996. Kingston: Headstart.

Rastafari Centralisation Organisation. 2001.*The Edifier: The Bearer of Light*. Kingston.

Rastafarian Advisory Service. 1988. *Focus on Rastafari: A Report*. London.
Robbins, Jerrold. 1933. "The Americans in Ethiopia". *American Mercury* 29, no. 113: 63–69.
Rogers, Joel A. 1936. *The Real Facts about Ethiopia*. Reprint, 1982. Baltimore: Black Classic.
Rogers, Sheperd Robert Athlyi. 1924. *The Holy Piby*. [Distributed by the House of Athlyi (Woodbridge, NJ), published by the Athlican Strong Arm Company. 37 pp.]
———. 2000. *The Holy Piby: The Blackman's Bible*. Chicago and Kingston: Research Associates School Times Publications/ Headstart.
Sylvain, Benito. 1901. *Du sort des indigènes dans les colonies d'exploitation*. Paris: L. Boyer.
———. 1906. *L'Étoile africaine*, no. 1.
Talbot, David. 1952. *Contemporary Ethiopia*. New York: Philosophical Library.
———. 1962. *The Musical Bride*. New York: Vantage.
———, ed. 1966. *Ethiopia: Liberation Silver Jubilee, 1941–1966*. Addis Ababa: Ministry of Information.
"Technical Mission to Africa (Nigeria, Ghana, Ethiopia). Summary Report (January–March, 1962)". Reprinted 2010 in *Rastafari: The Reports*, edited by R. Augier and V. Salter, 77–107. Kingston: Caribbean Quarterly.
Walker, David. 1829. *Walker's Appeal in Four Articles*. Reprint, 1969. New York: Arno/ New York Times.
"What Gadman Has Taught Us". 2005. Document compiled by the Twelve Tribes of Israel, New York.
Williams, Prince Elijah. 2005. *Book of Memory: A Rastafari Testimony*. St Louis, MO: N.p.
Yacob Wolde Mariam. 1962. "Journey to Awassa". *Menen* 6, no. 2: 18–24.
Young, Alexander. 1829. "The Ethiopian Manifesto". In *Classical Black Nationalism. From the American Revolution to Marcus Garvey*, edited by W. Moses, 60–67. Reprint, 1996. New York: New York University Press.
Zervos, Adrien. 1936. *L'Empire d'Éthiopie: Le miroir de l'Éthiopie moderne. 1906–1935*. Alexandra: Imprimerie de l'école professionnelle des Frères Alexandrie.

Secondary Sources

Ababu Minda. 1997. "Rastafarians in the Promised Land: A Study of Identity, its Maintenance and Change". MA diss., Addis Ababa University.
Abera Awano. 2003. "A Brief History of the Rastafarian Settlement in Shashamane". BA diss., Addis Ababa University.
Abye Tasse. 2004. *Parcours d'Éthiopiens en France et aux Etats-Unis: De nouvelles formes de migrations*. Paris: L'Harmattan.
Adeleke, Tunde. 1998. *UnAfrican Americans: Nineteenth-Century Black Nationalists and the Civilizing Mission*. Lexington: University Press of Kentucky.
Adi, Hakim. 2000. "Pan-Africanism and West African Nationalism in Britain". *African Studies Review* 43, no. 1: 69–82.
Ahmad, Abdussamad H., and Richard Pankhurst, eds. 1998. *Adwa: Victory Centenary Conference, 26 February–2 March 1996*. Addis Ababa: Addis Ababa University Press, Institute of Ethiopian Studies.
Akpan, M.B. 1973. "Liberia and the Universal Negro Improvement Association: the Background to the Abortion of Garvey's Scheme for African Colonization". *Journal of African History* 14, no. 1: 105–27.

de Albuquerque, Klaus. 1977. "Millenarian Movements and the Politics of Liberation: The Rastafarians of Jamaica". PhD diss., Virginia Polytechnic Institute and State University.

Alpers, Edward A. 1982. "The Weapon of History in the Struggle for African Liberation: the work of Walter Rodney". In *Walter Rodney: Revolutionary and Scholar – A Tribute*, edited by E.A. Alpers and P.-M. Fontaine. 59–75. Los Angeles: Center for Afro-American Studies and African Studies Center.

Anderson, Benedict. 1991. *Imagined Communities: Reflections on the Origin and Spread of Nationalism*. London: Verso.

———. 2002. *L'imaginaire national: Réflexions sur l'origine et l'essor du nationalisme*. Paris: La Découverte.

Anderson, Jervis. 1982. *This Was Harlem: A Cultural Portrait, 1900–1950*. New York: Farrar Straus Giroux.

Anglès, Eric, Chris Hensley and Denis-Constant Martin, eds. 1994. *Les tambours de Jah et les sirènes de Babylone: Rastafarisme et reggae dans la société jamaïcaine*. Les Cahiers du CERI 9. Paris: FNSP, CERI.

Anteby-Yemini, Lisa, William Berthomière and Gabriel Sheffer. 2005. *Les diasporas: 2000 ans d'histoire*. Rennes: Presses universitaires de Rennes.

Archbishop Yesehaq. 1997. *The Ethiopian Tewahedo Church: An Integrally African Church*. Nashville: James C. Winston.

Asante, S.K.B. 1977. *Pan-African Protest: West Africa and the Italo-Ethiopian Crisis, 1934–1941*. London: Longman.

Bahru Zewde. 2000 [1991]. *A History of Modern Ethiopia, 1855–1974*. London: James Currey.

———. 2002. *Pioneers of Change: The Reformist Intellectuals of the Early Twentieth Century*. London: James Currey.

Barnes, Cedric, and Thomas Osmond. 2005. "L'après-État-nation en Éthiopie. Changement de forme plus que d'habitudes ?" *Politique Africaine*, special issue, "Éthiopie: le fédéralisme en question", 99: 7–21.

Barnes, Kenneth C. 2004. *Journey of Hope: The Back-to-Africa Movement in Arkansas in the Late 1800s*. Chapel Hill: University of North Carolina Press.

Barnett, Michael. 2000. "The Political Objectives of Rastafari: A Case Study of the Life and Influence of Ras Sam Brown on the Rastafari Movement". *Caribbean Quarterly* (Rastafari Monograph): 34–42.

Barrett, Leonard E. 1997 [1976]. *The Rastafarians*. Boston: Beacon.

Bastide, Roger. 1996 [1967]. *Les Amériques noires*. Paris: L'Harmattan.

Becken, H.J. 1978. "Ekuphakameni Revisited". *Journal of Religion in Africa* 9, no. 3: 161–72.

Benti Getahun. 1988. "A History of Shashamanne from Its Foundation to 1974". MA diss., Addis Ababa University.

Bereket Habte Selassie. 1980. *Conflict and Intervention in the Horn of Africa*. New York: Monthly Review.

Berhanou Abebe. 1971. *Évolution de la propriété foncière au Choa (Éthiopie), du règne de Ménélik à la Constitution de 1931*. Paris: Librairie orientaliste Paul Geuthner.

———. 1998. *Histoire de l'Éthiopie d'Axoum à la révolution*. Paris: CFEE, Maisonneuve and Larose.

Berhanou Abebe, and Eloi Ficquet. 2003. *Dictionnaire Français–Amharique*. Addis Ababa: Shama Books.

Berthomière, William, and Christine Chivallon, eds. 2006. *Les diasporas dans le monde contemporain*. Paris: Karthala.

Besson, Jean. 2002. *Martha Brae's Two Histories: European Expansion and Caribbean Culture-Building in Jamaica*. Chapel Hill: University of North Carolina Press.

Bilby, Kenneth, and Elliott Leib. 1986. "Kumina, the Howellite Church and the Emergence of Rastafarian Traditional Music in Jamaica". *Jamaica Journal* 19: 22–28.

Bishton, Derek. 1986. *Black Heart Man: A Journey into Rasta*. London: Chatto and Windus.

Bjerén, Gunilla. 1985. *Migration to Shashemene: Ethnicity, Gender and Occupation in Urban Ethiopia*. Uppsala, Sweden: Scandinavian Institute of African Studies.

Blum, Bruno. 2004. *Bob Marley: Le reggae et les Rastas*. Paris: Éditions Hors Collection.

Blyden, Nemata A. 2000. *West Indians in West Africa, 1808–1880: The African Diaspora in Reverse*. Rochester, NY: University of Rochester Press.

Bonacci, Giulia. 2000. *The Ethiopian Orthodox Church and the State, 1974–1991: Analysis of an Ambiguous Religious Policy*. London: Centre of Ethiopian Studies.

———. 2001–2. "Discours et pratiques du mouvement rastafari en Italie: Continuités et discontinuités de la transmission religieuse". *Psychopathologie Africaine* 31, no. 1: 45–67.

———. 2003. "De la diffusion musicale à la transmission religieuse: Reggae et rastafari en Italie". In *Musiques populaires: Usages sociaux et sentiments d'appartenance*, edited by G. Bonacci and S. Fila-Bakabadio, 73–89. Paris: CEAf, EHESS.

———. 2011. "An Interview in Zion: The Life-history of a Jamaican Rastafarian in Shashemene, Ethiopia". *Callaloo* 34, no. 3: 744–58.

———. 2013. "L'irrésistible ascension du *ras* Tafari dans les imaginaires noirs". *Annales d'Ethiopie* 28: 157–76.

———. 2014. "L'Hymne éthiopien universel (1918): Un héritage national et musical de l'Atlantique noir à l'Ethiopie contemporaine". *Cahiers d'Etudes africaines* 56 (4), no. 216: 1055–82.

Braidwood, Stephen J. 1982. "Initiatives and Organisation of the Black Poor 1786–1787". *Slavery and Abolition* 3, no. 3: 209–42.

Brotz, Howard. 1964. *The Black Jews of Harlem: Negro Nationalism and the Dilemmas of Negro Leadership*. London: Macmillan.

Callahan, Allen D. 2006. *The Talking Book: African Americans and the Bible*. New Haven: Yale University Press.

Campbell, Horace. 1994. *Rasta and Resistance: From Marcus Garvey to Walter Rodney*. Trenton, NJ: Africa World Press.

Campbell, Mavis C., ed. 1993. *Back to Africa: George Ross and the Maroons, from Nova Scotia to Sierra Leone*. Trenton, NJ: Africa World Press.

Carmichael, Stokely, and Charles V. Hamilton 1967. *Black Power: The Politics of Liberation in America*. New York: Vintage.

Casely Hayford, J.E. 1969. *Ethiopia Unbound: Studies in Race Emancipation*. London: Frank Cass.

Cashmore, Ernest. 1979. *Rastaman: The Rastafarian Movement in England*. London: Allen and Unwin.

Cassidy, F.G., and R.B. Le Page. 1980 [1976]. *Dictionary of Jamaican English*. Cambridge: Cambridge University Press.

de Certeau, Michel. 1975. *L'écriture de l'histoire*. Paris: Gallimard.

Chaillot, Christine. 2002. *The Ethiopian Orthodox Tewahedo Church Tradition: A Brief Introduction to Its Life and Spirituality.* Paris: Inter-Orthodox Dialogue.

Chatwin, Bruce. 1980. *The Viceroy of Ouidah.* London: Jonathan Cape.

Chevannes, Barry 1975. "The Impact of the Ethiopian Revolution on the Rastafari Movement". *Socialism! Theoretical Organ of the Worker's Liberation League* 2, no. 3: 23–33.

———. 1976. "The Repairer of the Breach: Reverend Claudius Henry and Jamaican Society". In *Ethnicity in the Americas*, edited by F. Henry, 263–89. The Hague: Mouton

———. 1994. *Rastafari, Roots and Ideology.* Syracuse: Syracuse University Press.

———. 1998a. "Introducing the Native Religions of Jamaica". In *Rastafari and other African-Caribbean Worldviews*, edited by B. Chevannes, 1–19. The Hague: Institute of Social Studies.

———. 1998b. "New Approach to Rastafari". In *Rastafari and other African-Caribbean Worldviews*, edited by B. Chevannes, 20–42. The Hague: Institute of Social Studies.

———. 1998c. "The Origin of the Dreadlocks". In *Rastafari and other African-Caribbean Worldviews*, edited by B. Chevannes, 77–96. The Hague: Institute of Social Studies.

Chireau, Yvonne. 2000. "Black Culture and Black Zion: African-American Religious Encounters with Judaism, 1790–1930 – An Overview". In *Black Zion: African American Religious Encounters with Judaism*, edited by Y. Chireau and N. Deutsch, 15–32. New York: Oxford University Press.

Chisholm, Clinton. 1998. "The Rasta-Selassie-Ethiopian Connections". In *Chanting Down Babylon: The Rastafari Reader*, edited by N.S. Murrell, W.D. Spencer and A.A. McFarlane, 166–77. Kingston: Ian Randle.

Chivallon, Christine. 2004. *La diaspora noire des Amériques: Expériences et théories à partir de la Caraïbe.* Paris: CNRS Éditions.

Clapham, Christopher. 1988. *Transformation and Continuity in Revolutionary Ethiopia.* Cambridge: Cambridge University Press.

Clarke, Kamari M. 2004. *Mapping Yorùbá Networks: Power and Agency in the Making of Transnational Communities.* Durham: Duke University Press.

Cohen, John M., and Dov Weintraub. 1975. *Land and Peasants in Imperial Ethiopia: The Social Background to a Revolution.* Assen, The Netherlands: Van Gorcum.

Cohen, John M., and Peter H. Koehn. 1980. *Ethiopian Provincial and Municipal Government: Imperial Patterns and Postrevolutionary Changes.* Michigan: African Studies Center, Michigan State University.

Cohen, Robin. 1992. "The Diaspora of a Diaspora: The Case of the Caribbean". *Social Science Information* 31, no. 1: 159–69.

Constant, Denis. 1982. *Aux sources du reggae.* Roquevaire: Parenthèses.

Cottias, Myriam. 2007. *La question noire: Histoire d'une construction coloniale.* Paris: Bayard.

Cronon, Edmund David. 1969. *Black Moses: The Story of Marcus Garvey and the Universal Negro Improvement Association.* Madison: University of Wisconsin Press.

Crummey, Donald. 1969. "Tewodros as Reformer and Modernizer". *Journal of African History* 10, no. 3: 457–69.

———. 1998. "Imperial Legitimacy and the Creation of Neo-Solomonic Ideology in 19th Century Ethiopia". *Cahier d'Études africaines* 109, no. 28–1: 13–43.

———. 2000. *Land and Society in the Christian Kingdom of Ethiopia: From the Thirteenth to the Twentieth Century.* Urbana: University of Illinois Press.

Curtin, Philip D. 1969. *The Atlantic Slave Trade: A Census.* Madison: University of Wisconsin Press.

Daneel, M.L. 1987. *Quest for Belonging: Introduction to a Study of African Independent Churches.* Gweru: Mambo.

Daniel Getachew. 1984. "The Origin and Development of the Rastafarian Cult in Jamaica with a Reference to the Settlement in Shashemene". BA diss., Addis Ababa University.

Darkwah, Kofi R.H. 1975. *Shewa, Menelik and the Ethiopian Empire, 1813–1889.* London: Heinemann.

Davis, Stephen. 1991 [1983]. *Bob Marley.* Paris: Lieu Commun.

Daynes, Sarah. 2001. "Le mouvement Rastafari: Mémoire, musique et religion". PhD diss., EHESS, Paris.

Decraene, Philippe. 1970 [1959]. *Le Panafricanisme.* Paris: Presses Universitaires de France.

Del Boca, Angelo. 1969 [1966]. *The Ethiopian War, 1935–1941.* Chicago: Chicago University Press.

Desroche, Henri. 1969. *Dieux d'hommes: Dictionnaire des messianismes et millénarismes de l'Ère Chrétienne.* Paris: Mouton.

Dessalegn Rahmato. 1995. "Peasant Agriculture Under the Old Regime". In *An Economic History of Ethiopia*, vol. 1: *The Imperial Era 1941–74*, edited by Shiferaw Bekele, 143–93. Dakar: CODESRIA.

Dixon, Chris. 2000. *African America and Haiti: Emigration and Black Nationalism in the Nineteenth Century.* Westport, CT: Greenwood.

Donham, Donald L., and Wendy James, eds. 2002 [1986]. *The Southern Marches of Imperial Ethiopia.* London: James Currey.

Donham, Donald L. 1999. *Marxist Modern: An Ethnographic History of the Ethiopian Revolution.* Berkeley: University of California Press.

———. 2002a. "Old Abyssina and the New Ethiopian Empire: Themes in Social History". In *The Southern Marches of Imperial Ethiopia*, edited by D. Donham and W. James, 3–48. London: James Currey.

———. 2002b. Introduction. In *Remapping Ethiopia: Socialism and After*, edited by W. James, D. Donham, E. Kurimoto and A. Triulzi, 1–7. Oxford: James Currey.

Dorman, Jacob S. 2004. "The Black Israelites of Harlem and the Professors of Oriental and African Mystic Science in the 1920's". PhD diss., University of California at Los Angeles.

Drake, Saint Clair. 1966. "Negro Americans and the Africa Interest". In *The American Negro*, edited by J.P. Davis, 662–705. Englewood Cliffs, NJ: Prentice Hall.

———. 1991 [1970]. *The Redemption of Africa and Black Religion.* Chicago: Third World Press, Institute of the Black World.

———. 1993. "Diaspora Studies and Pan-Africanism". In *Global Dimensions of the African Diaspora*, edited by J. Harris, 451–514. Washington, DC: Howard University Press.

Du Bois, W.E.B. 1996 [1903]. *The Souls of Black Folk.* New York: Penguin.

Dufoix, Stéphane. 2003. *Les diasporas.* Paris: PUF.

———. 2011. *La Dispersion: Une histoire des usages du mot diaspora.* Paris: Editions Amsterdam.

Dunbar, Ernest. 1970 [1968]. *The Black Expatriates.* New York: Pocket.

Edwards, Brent H. 2003. *The Practice of Diaspora: Literature, Translation, and the Rise of Black Internationalism*. Cambridge, MA: Harvard University Press.

Eliade, Mircea. 1963. *Aspects du mythe*. Paris: Gallimard.

Elkins, W.F. 1977. *Street Preachers, Faith Healers and Herb Doctors in Jamaica, 1890–1925*. New York: Revisionist.

Ellison, Julian. 1977. "Afro-American Migration to Africa". *Africa* 72 (August): 76–77.

Esedebe, P. Olisanwuche. 1994. *Pan-Africanism: The Idea and Movement, 1776–1991*. Washington, DC: Howard University Press.

Eshetu Shole. 1995. "Running to Keep in the Same Place: Industrialization, 1941–74". In *An Economic History of Ethiopia*, vol. 1: *The Imperial Era 1941–74*, edited by Shiferaw Bekele, 194–231. Dakar: CODESRIA.

Fikru Negash Gebrekidan. 2005. *Bond without Blood: A History of Ethiopian and New World Black Relations, 1896–1991*. Trenton, NJ: Africa World Press.

Foner, Nancy. 1987. *New Immigrants in New York*. New York: Columbia University Press.

Fontrier, Marc. 1999. *La chute de la junte militaire éthiopienne (1987–1991)*. Paris: L'Harmattan.

Forsythe, Dennis. 1999. *Rastafari: For the Healing of the Nations*. New York: One Drop Books.

Franklin, John Hope and Alfred A. Moss. 2000 [1988]. *From Slavery to Freedom: A History of African Americans*. New York: Alfred A. Knopf.

Garretson, Peter P. 2012. *A Victorian Gentleman and Ethiopian Nationalist: The Life and Times of Hakim Wärqenäh, Dr Charles Martin*. Woodbridge, UK: James Currey.

Gebre Wold Ingida Worq. 1962. "Ethiopia: Traditional System of Land Tenure and Taxation". *Ethiopia Observer* 5, no. 4: 302–39.

Geiss, Imanuel. 1974 [1968]. *The Pan-African Movement: A History of Pan-Africanism in America, Europe and Africa*. New York: Africana.

Gellner, Ernest. 1983. *Nations and Nationalism*. Ithaca: Cornell University Press.

———. 1989 [1983]. *Nations et nationalisme*. Paris: Payot.

Gibson, Shirlie R. 1996. "African Repatriation: A Case Study of the Rastafarians and the Malcoda Land-Grant at Shashemane, Ethiopia from 1930 to Present". PhD diss., Howard University.

Gilroy, Paul. 1993. *The Black Atlantic: Modernity and Double Consciousness*. Cambridge: Harvard University Press.

———. 1995. "Could You Be Loved? Bob Marley, Anti-Politics and Universal Sufferation". *Critical Quarterly* 47, nos. 1–2: 226–45.

Glaude, Eddie S. 2000. *Exodus! Religion, Race, and Nation in Early Nineteenth-Century Black America*. Chicago: University of Chicago Press.

Glissant, Édouard. 1997. *Le discours antillais*. Paris: Gallimard.

Goldthree, Reena N. 2005. "'Precious African Links of a Mighty Chain': Amy Jacques Garvey and the Politics of Pan-Africanism". MA thesis, Duke University.

Goulbourne, Harry. 2002. *Caribbean Transnational Experience*. London: Pluto.

Green, Nancy L. 2002. *Repenser les migrations*. Paris: Presses Universitaires de France

Green, N.L., G. Bonacci, L. Hobson-Faure, E. Cuq-Monges, E. Rodrigues and Y. Scioldo-Zurcher. 2008. "Colonies d'ailleurs et colonies d'ici". *Hommes et Migrations*, no. 1276: 134–46.

Gunst, Laurie. 1995. *Born fi Dead: A Journey through the Jamaican Posse Underworld.* New York: Henry Holt.

Hahn, Steven. 2003. *A Nation Under Our Feet: Black Political Struggle in the Rural South from Slavery to the Great Migration.* Cambridge, MA: Harvard University Press.

Haile Mariam Larebo. 1986. "The Orthodox Church and the State in the Ethiopian Revolution 1974–84". *Revolution in Communist Lands,* 14, no. 2: 148–59.

Haley, Alex. 1976. *Roots: The Saga of an American Family.* Garden City, NY: Doubleday.

Hall, Stuart. 2001. "Negotiating Caribbean Identities". In *New Caribbean Thought: A Reader,* edited by B. Meeks and F. Lindahl, 24–39. Kingston: University of the West Indies Press.

Halliday, Fred, and Maxine Molyneux. 1981. *The Ethiopian Revolution.* London: NLB.

Ham, Debra Newman. 1993. "The Role of African American Women in the Founding of Liberia". In *Global Dimensions of the African Diaspora,* edited by J. Harris, 369–85. Washington, DC: Howard University Press.

Hancock, Graham. 1997 [1992]. *The Sign and the Seal.* London: Arrow.

Harris, Joseph E. 1987. *Repatriates and Refugees in a Colonial Society: The Case of Kenya.* Washington, DC: Howard University Press.

———. 1994. *African-American Reactions to War in Ethiopia, 1936–1941.* Baton Rouge: Louisiana State University Press.

Hastings, Adrian. 1994. *The Church in Africa, 1450–1950.* Oxford: Clarendon.

Hélénon, Véronique. 1997. "Les administrateurs coloniaux originaires de Guadeloupe, Martinique et Guyane dans les colonies françaises d'Afrique, 1880–1939". PhD diss., EHESS [L'Ecole des hautes études en sciences sociales].

Henze, Paul. 2000. *Layers of Time: A History of Ethiopia.* London: Hurst.

Hepner, Randal. 1998. "'Movement of Jah People': Race, Class and Religion among the Rastafari of Jamaica and New York City". PhD diss., New School for Social Research, New York.

Hill, Robert A. 1987. "Before Garvey: Chief Alfred Sam and the African Movement, 1912–1916". In *Pan-African Biography,* edited by R. Hill, 57–77. Los Angeles: African Studies Center, University of California, Los Angeles, and Crossroads Press/African Studies Association.

———. 2001. *Dread History: Leonard P. Howell and Millenarian Visions in the Early Rastafarian Religion.* Chicago: Research Associates School Times, Miguel Lorne.

———. 2008. "King Menelik's Nephew: Prince Thomas Mackarooroo, aka Prince Ludwig Menelek of Abyssinia". *Small Axe,* no. 26: 15–44.

———. 2013. "Our Man in Mona: A Conversation between Robert A. Hill and Annie Paul". *Active Voice,* http://anniepaul.net/our-man-in-mona-an-interview-by-robert-a-hill-with-annie-paul/.

Hintzen, Percy C. 2004. "Imagining Home: Race and the West Indian Diaspora in the San Francisco Bay". *Journal of Latin American Anthropology* 9, no. 2: 289–318.

Homiak, John. 1985. "The 'Ancient of Days' Seated Black: Eldership, Oral Tradition and Ritual in Rastafari Culture". PhD diss., Brandeis University.

———. 2001. "'Never Trade a Continent for an Island': Rastafari Diasporic Practice, Globalisation, and the African Renaissance". In *A United States of Africa?,* edited by E. Maloka, 186–233. Pretoria: Africa Institute of South Africa.

Jacobs, Sylvia M. 1981. *The African Nexus: Black American Perspectives on the European Partitioning of Africa, 1880–1920*. Westport, CT: Greenwood.

James, C.L.R. 1995 [1938]. *A History of Pan-African Revolt*. Chicago: C. Kerr.

James, Wendy, Donald L. Donham, Kurimoto Eisei and Alessandro Triulzi, eds. 2002. *Remapping Ethiopia: Socialism and After*. Oxford: James Currey.

James, Winston. 1998. *Holding Aloft the Banner of Ethiopia: Caribbean Radicalism in Early Twentieth-century America*. London: Verso.

———. 2004. "The Wings of Ethiopia: The Caribbean Diaspora and Pan-African Projects from John Brown Russwurm to George Padmore". In *African Diasporas in the New and Old Worlds: Consciousness and Imagination*, edited by G. Fabre and K. Benesch, 121–57. Amsterdam: Rodopi.

———. 2010. *The Struggles of John Brown Russwurm: The Life and Writings of a Pan-Africanist Pioneer, 1799–1851*. New York: New York University Press.

Jarrett-Macauley, Delia. 1998. *The Life of Una Marson. 1905–1965*. Manchester: Manchester University Press.

Jenkins, David. 1975. *Black Zion: The Return of Afro-Americans and West Indians to Africa*. London: Wildwood House.

Johnson, Linton Kwesi. 2002. *Mi Revalueshanary Fren: Selected Poems*. London: Penguin.

Joireman, Sandra F. 2000. *Property Rights and Political Development in Ethiopia and Eritrea*. Oxford: James Currey.

Jones, Simon. 1988. *Black Culture, White Youth: The Reggae Tradition from JA to UK*. London: Macmillan Education.

Judah, J. Stillson. 1967. *The History and Philosophy of the Metaphysical Movements in America*. Philadelphia: Westminster.

Kane, Thomas L. 1990. *Amharic-English Dictionary*. Wiesbaden: O. Harrassowitz.

Kasinitz, Philip. 1992. *Caribbean New York: Black Immigrants and the Politics of Race*. Ithaca: Cornell University Press.

Kebrä Nägäst (The Glory of the Kings). 1932. Translated by E.A. Wallis Budge in *The Queen of Sheba and Her Only Son Menyelek (I)*. London: Oxford University Press.

———. 1995. Translated by Miguel Brooks. Kingston: Kingston Publishers.

———. 1997. Edited by Gerald Haussman. New York: St Martin.

Keller, Edmond J., and Donald Rotchild, eds. 1987. *Afro-Marxist Regimes: Ideology and Public Policy*. Boulder: Lynne Rienner.

Kelley, Robin D.G. 2002. *Freedom Dreams: The Black Radical Imagination*. Boston: Beacon.

Kiflu Tadesse. 1993. *The Generation: The History of the Ethiopian People's Revolutionary Party*. Silver Spring, MD: Red Sea.

———. 1998. *The Generation Part II: Ethiopia, Transformation and Conflict – The History of the Ethiopian People's Revolutionary Party*. Lanham, MD: University Press of America.

King, Kenneth J. 1978 [1972]. "Some Notes on Arnold J. Ford and New World Black Attitudes to Ethiopia". In *Black Apostles: Afro-American Clergy Confront the Twentieth Century*, edited by R.K. Burkett and R. Newman, 49–55. Boston: G.K. Hall.

Ki-Zerbo, Joseph. 1972. *Histoire de l'Afrique Noire: D'Hier à demain*. Paris: Hatier.

Landes, Ruth. 1967. "Negro Jews in Harlem". *Jewish Journal of Sociology* 9: 175–89.

Landing, James E. 2002. *Black Judaism: Story of an American Movement*. Durham: Carolina Academic Press.

Langley, J. Ayodele. 1973. *Pan-Africanism and Nationalism in West Africa, 1900–1945: A Study in Ideology and Social Classes*. Oxford: Clarendon.

Lara, Oruno. 2000. *La naissance du Panafricanisme: Les racines caraïbes, américaines et africaines du mouvement au XIX° siècle*. Paris: Maisonneuve et Larose.

Larson, Martin A. 1985. *New Thought or a Modern Religious Approach: The Philosophy of Health, Happiness, and Prosperity*. New York: Philosophical Library.

Lassalle, Didier. 1997. *Les minorités ethniques en Grande-Bretagne: Aspects démographiques et sociologiques contemporains*. Paris: L'Harmattan.

Law, Robin, and Kristin Mann. 1999. "West Africa in the Atlantic Community: The Case of the Slave Coast". *William and Mary Quarterly* 56, no. 2: 307–34.

Lee, Hélène. 1999. *Le premier Rasta*. Paris: Flammarion.

Leenhardt, Maurice. 1976 [1902]. *Le mouvement éthiopien au Sud de l'Afrique de 1896 à 1899*. Paris: Académie des sciences d'Outre-mer.

Lefort, René. 1981. *Éthiopie: La révolution hérétique*. Paris: Maspéro.

Leslau, Wolf. 1976. *Concise Amharic Dictionary*. Berkeley: University of California Press.

Lewis, Rupert C. 1988. *Marcus Garvey: Anti-Colonial Champion*. Trenton, NJ: Africa World Press.

———. 1998a. *Walter Rodney's Intellectual and Political Thought*. Detroit: Wayne State University Press.

———. 1998b. "Marcus Garvey and the Early Rastafarians: Continuity and Discontinuity". In *Chanting Down Babylon: The Rastafari Reader*, edited by N.S. Murrell, W.D. Spencer and A.A. McFarlane, 145–58. Kingston: Ian Randle.

Lewis, William F. 1993. *Soul Rebels: The Rastafari*. Prospect Heights, IL: Waveland.

Lindsay, Lisa A. 1994. "'To Return to the Bosom of Their Fatherland': Brazilian Immigrants in Nineteenth-Century Lagos". *Slavery and Abolition* 15, no. 1: 22–71.

Lutanie, Boris. 2000 [1999]. *Introduction au mouvement Rastafari*. Paris: L'Esprit Frappeur.

M'Bokolo, Elikia. 1995a. *Afrique noire: Histoire et civilisations*. 2 vols. Paris: Hatier.

———. 1995b. "Des Amériques à l'Afrique: Les cheminements du panafricanisme". In *L'Afrique entre l'Europe et l'Amérique. Le rôle de l'Afrique dans la rencontre de deux mondes, 1492–1992*, edited by E. M'Bokolo, 145–56. Paris: UNESCO.

———. 2006a. "Le panafricanisme au XXIème siècle". *La Diaspora Africaine* (April). [From the first conference of Intellectuels d'Afrique et de la Diaspora, Union Africaine, Dakar, 2004.]

———. 2006b. "George Padmore, Kwame N'Krumah, Cyril L. James et l'idéologie de la lutte panafricaine". *La Diaspora Africaine* (April). [Council for the Development of Social Science Research in Africa thirtieth anniversary conference, "Intellectuels, nationalisme et l'idéal panafricain", 2003.]

MacGaffey, Wyatt. 1969. "*The Beloved City*: Commentary on a Kimbanguist Text". *Journal of Religion in Africa* 2: 129–47.

Mahteme Sellassie Wolde Maskal. 1957. "The Land System of Ethiopia". *Ethiopia Observer* 1, no. 9: 283–301.

Mais, Roger. 1974 [1954]. *Brother Man*. Oxford: Heinemann.

Marcus, Harold G. 1983. *Ethiopia, Great Britain, and the United States, 1941–1974*. Berkeley: University of California Press.

———. 1994. *A History of Ethiopia*. Berkeley: University of California Press.

Markakis, John. 1975 [1974]. *Ethiopia: Anatomy of a Traditional Polity.* Oxford: Clarendon.

———. 1979. "Garrison Socialism: The Case of Ethiopia". *MERIP Reports*, no. 79: 3–17.

Markowitz, Fran. 2006. "Finding the Past, Making the Future: The African Hebrew Israelite Community's Alternative to the Black Diaspora". In *Diasporic Africa: A Reader*, edited by M. Gomez, 123–46. New York: New York University Press.

Martin, Tony. 1985 [1983]. *The Pan-African Connection: From Slavery to Garvey and Beyond.* Dover, MA: Majority.

———. 1986 [1976]. *Race First: The Ideological and Organizational Struggles of Marcus Garvey and the Universal Negro Improvement Association*. Dover, MA: Majority.

Mathurin, Charles. 1976. *Henry Sylvester Williams and the Origins of the Pan-African Movement, 1869–1911*. Westport, CT: Greenwood.

Maunder, W.F. 1955. "The New Jamaican Emigration". *Social and Economic Studies* 4, no. 1: 38–63.

Meriwether, James H. 2002. *Proudly We Can Be Africans: Black Americans and Africa, 1935–1961*. Chapel Hill: University of North Carolina Press.

Merritt, Anthony Wayne. 2006. "Ethiopianism, Africanity and Repatriation: An Africentric Social History of Shashemene Repatriation Community, Ethiopia: 1955–2004". PhD diss., Union Institute and University.

Mesfin Getahun. 2001. "Shashemene". In *Living on the Edge: Marginalised Minorities of Craft Workers and Hunters in Southern Ethiopia*, edited by D. Freeman and A. Pankhurst, 269–85. Addis Ababa: Addis Ababa University.

Montilus, Guerin C. 1993. "Guinea versus Congo Lands: Aspects of the Collective Memory in Haiti". In *Global Dimensions of the African Diaspora*, edited by J. Harris, 159–65. Washington, DC: Howard University Press.

Moses, Wilson J. 1978. *The Golden Age of Black Nationalism, 1850–1925*. Hamden, CT: Archon.

———. 1990. *The Wings of Ethiopia: Studies in African-American Life and Letters*. Ames: Iowa State University.

———. 1996. *Classical Black Nationalism: From the American Revolution to Marcus Garvey.* New York: New York University Press.

———. 1998. *Afrotopia: The Roots of African American Popular History.* London: Cambridge University Press.

———. 2004. *Creative Conflict in African American Thought: F. Douglass, A. Crummell, B.T. Washington, W.E.B. Du Bois and M. Garvey.* London: Cambridge University Press.

Mutero Chirenje, J. 1987. *Ethiopianism and Afro-Americans in Southern Africa, 1883–1916.* Baton Rouge: Louisiana State University Press.

Murrell, Nathaniel S., William D. Spencer and Adrian A. McFarlane, eds. 1998. *Chanting Down Babylon: The Rastafari Reader.* Kingston: Ian Randle.

Naipaul, V.S. 1980 [1974]. *The Return of Eva Perón with the Killings in Trinidad.* New York: Alfred A. Knopf.

Nance, Susan. 2002. "Mystery of the Moorish Science Temple: Southern Blacks and American Alternative Spirituality in 1920s Chicago". *Religion and American Culture: A Journal of Interpretation* 12, no. 2: 123–66.

Negusse Ayele. 2003. *Ethiopia and the United States.* Los Angeles: Ocopy.com

Nettleford, Rex. 2001 [1970]. *Mirror Mirror: Identity, Race and Protest in Jamaica.* Kingston: LMH Publishing.

Nkrumah, Kwame. 1960 [1957]. *Ghana: Autobiographie de Kwame Nkrumah*. Paris: Présence Africaine.

———. 1979 [1957]. *Ghana: The Autobiography of Kwame Nkrumah*. New York: International.

Ottaway, Marina. 1978. *Ethiopia: Empire in Revolution*. New York: Africana.

Ottley, Roi. 1943. *"New World A-Coming": Inside Black America*. Boston: Houghton Mifflin.

Owens, Joseph. 1995 [1976]. *Dread: The Rastafarians of Jamaica*. Kingston: Sangster's.

Padmore, George. 1960 [1956]. *Panafricanisme ou Communisme? La prochaine lutte pour l'Afrique*. Paris: Présence Africaine.

———. 1971 [1956]. *Pan-Africanism or Communism*. Foreword by Richard Wright; introduction by Azinna Nwafor. New York: Doubleday.

Pankhurst, Richard. 1967. "Menilek and the Utilisation of Foreign Skills in Ethiopia". *Journal of Ethiopian Studies* 5, no. 1: 29–86.

———. 1972. "William H. Ellis – Guillaume Enriques Ellesio: The First Black American Ethiopianist?" *Ethiopia Observer* 15, no. 2: 89–121.

Patterson, Orlando. 1964. "Ras Tafari: The Cult of the Outcast". *New Society*, no. 111.

———. 1975 [1969]. *The Sociology of Slavery: An Analysis of the Origins, Development, and Structure of Negro Slave Society in Jamaica*. London: Associated University Press.

Pawliková-Vilhanová, Viera. 1998. "The African Personality or the Dilemma of the Other and the Self in the Philosophy of Edward W. Blyden, 1832–1912". *Asian and African Studies* 7, no. 2: 162–75.

Pemberton, Rita. 1998. "Ties Binding Trinidad and Tobago in the Caribbean to Ethiopia, 1896–1996". In *Adwa: Victory Centenary Conference, 26 February–2 March 1996*, edited by A.H. Ahmad and R. Pankhurst, 587–610. Addis Ababa: Addis Ababa University Press, Institute of Ethiopian Studies.

Perks, Robert, and Alistair Thomson, eds. 2004 [1998]. *The Oral History Reader*. London: Routledge.

Pétridès, S. Pierre. 1964. *Le livre d'or de la dynastie salomonienne d'Éthiopie*. Paris: Plon.

———. 1966. *Le Héros d'Adoua: Ras Makonnen, prince d'Éthiopie*. Paris: Plon.

Philpott, Stuart B. 1973. *West Indian Migration: The Montserrat Case*. London: Athlone.

Pollard, Velma. 2000 [1994]. *Dread Talk: The Language of Rastafari*. Kingston: Canoe.

Post, Ken. 1970. "The Bible as Ideology: Ethiopianism in Jamaica, 1930–1938". In *African Perspectives: Papers in the History, Politics and Economics of Africa Presented to Thomas Hodgkin*, edited by C. Allen, 185–207. Cambridge: Cambridge University Press.

———. 1978. *Arise Ye Starvelings: The Jamaican Labour Rebellion of 1938 and Its Aftermath*. The Hague: Martinus Nijhoff.

Price, Richard, ed. 1996. *Maroon Societies: Rebel Slave Communities in the Americas*. Baltimore: Johns Hopkins Press.

Prouty, Chris. 1986. *Empress Taytu and Menilek II: Ethiopia 1883–1910*. London: Ravens Educational and Development Services.

Raboteau, Albert. 2001. *Canaan Land: A Religious History of African Americans*. Oxford: Oxford University Press.

Raiford, Leigh. 2013. "Marcus Garvey in Stereograph". *Small Axe*, no. 40: 263–80.

Reckord, Verena. 1977. "Rastafarian Music: An Introductory Study". *Jamaica Journal* 11, nos. 1–2: 3–15.

Redkey, Edwin S. 1969. *Black Exodus: Black Nationalist and Back-to-Africa Movements, 1890–1910*. New Haven: Yale University Press.

———. 1974. "The Flowering of Black Nationalism: Henry McNeal Turner and Marcus Garvey". In *Marcus Garvey and the Vision of Africa*, edited by J.H. Clarke, 388–401. New York: Random House.

Renan, Ernest. 1996 [1882]. *Qu'est-ce qu'une Nation?* Paris: Imprimerie Nationale.

Revel, Jacques. 1989. "L'histoire au ras du sol". In *Le pouvoir au village: Histoire d'un exorciste dans le Piémont du XVII° siècle*, edited by G. Levi, i–xxxiii. Paris: Gallimard.

———. 1996. "Présentation". In *Jeux d'échelles: La micro-analyse à l'expérience*, edited by J. Revel, 7–14. Paris: Gallimard, Le Seuil.

Roberts, G.W., and D.O. Mills. 1958. *Study of External Migrations Affecting Jamaica, 1953–55*. Kingston: University College of the West Indies.

Rodney, Walter. 1996 [1969]. *The Grounding with My Brothers*. Chicago: Research Associates School Times.

Rogers, Claudia. 1970. "Toward a Typology of Group Organization and Group Activity within the Rastafarian Movement". Paper presented at a symposium. April.

Ross, Red. 1972. "Black Americans and Italo-Ethiopian Relief 1935–1936". *Ethiopia Observer* 15, no. 2: 122–31.

Rouaud, Alain. 1998. *Le Négus contre l'esclavage: Les édits abolitionnistes du ras Täfäri*. Paris: ARESAE.

Rubenson, Sven. 1965. "The Lion of the Tribe of Judah. Christian Symbol and/or Imperial Title". *Journal of Ethiopian Studies* 3, no. 2: 75–85.

Salewicz, Chris. 2000. *Rude Boy: Once upon a Time in Jamaica*. London: V. Gollancz.

Sanders, Edith R. 1969. "The Hamitic Hypothesis: Its Origins and Function in Time Perspective". *Journal of African History*, 10, no. 4: 521–32.

Savishinsky, Neil J. 1994a. "Transnational Popular Culture and the Global Spread of the Jamaican Rastafarian Movement". *New West Indian Guide* 68, nos. 3–4: 259–81.

———. 1994b. "Rastafari in the Promised Land: The Spread of a Jamaican Socioreligious Movement among the Youth of West Africa". *African Studies Review* 37, no. 3: 19–50.

———. 1998. "African Dimensions of the Jamaican Rastafari Movement". In *Chanting Down Babylon: The Rastafari Reader*, edited by N.S. Murrell, W.D. Spencer and A.A. McFarlane, 125–44. Kingston: Ian Randle.

Schmeisser, Iris. 2004. "'Ethiopia Shall Soon Stretch Forth Her Hands': Ethiopianism, Egyptomania and the Arts of the Harlem Renaissance". In *African Diasporas in the New and Old Worlds: Consciousness and Imagination*, edited by G. Fabre and K. Benesch, 263–86. Amsterdam: Rodopi.

Scott, William. 1971. "Going to the Promised Land: Afro-American Immigrants in Ethiopia 1930–1935". Paper presented at the Fourteenth Annual Meeting of the African Studies Association, Denver, 3–6 November.

———. 1972. "Malaku E. Bayen: Ethiopian Emissary to Black America, 1936–1941". *Ethiopia Observer* 15, no. 2: 132–38.

———. 1993. *Sons of Sheba's Race: African-Americans and the Italo-Ethiopian War, 1935–1941*. Bloomington: Indiana University Press.

———. 2004. "The Ethiopian Ethos in African American Thought". *International Journal of Ethiopian Studies* 1, no. 2: 40–57.

Shack, William A. 1974. "Ethiopia and Afro-Americans: Some Historical Notes, 1920–1970". *Phylon* 35, no. 2: 142–55.

Shack, William A., and Elliott P. Skinner, eds. 1979. *Strangers in African Societies*. Berkeley: University of California Press.

Shepperson, George. 1953. "Ethiopianism and African Nationalism". *Phylon* 1, no. 1: 9–18.

———. 1962. "Pan-Africanism and 'Pan-Africanism': Some Historical Notes". *Phylon* 23, no. 4: 346–58.

———. 1968. "Ethiopianism: Past and Present". In *Christianity in Tropical Africa*, edited by C.G.K. Baëta, 249–68. London: Oxford University Press.

———. 1993. "African Diaspora: Concept and Context". In *Global Dimensions of the African Diaspora*, edited by J. Harris, 41–49. Washington, DC: Howard University Press.

Shepperson, George, and Thomas Price. 1963 [1958]. *Independent African: John Chilembwe and the Origins, Setting and Significance of the Nyasaland Native Rising of 1915*. Blantyre, Malawi: Christian Literature Association in Malawi.

Shuler, Monica. 1980. *"Alas, Alas, Kongo": A Social History of Indentured African Immigration into Jamaica, 1841–1965*. Baltimore: Johns Hopkins University Press.

Sibley, Inez Knibb. 1965. *The Baptists of Jamaica*. Kingston: Jamaica Baptist Union.

Simmel, Georg. 1971 [1908]. "The Stranger". In *On Individuality and Social Forms: Selected Writings*, edited by Donald N. Levine, 143–49. Chicago: University of Chicago Press.

Simpson, George E. 1955. "Political Cultism in West Kingston". *Social and Economic Studies* 4, no. 2: 133–49.

Skinner, Elliott P. 1993. "The Dialectic between Diasporas and Homelands". In *Global Dimensions of the African Diaspora*, edited by J. Harris, 11–40. Washington, DC: Howard University Press.

Smith, M.G., Roy Augier and Rex Nettleford. 1960. *The Rastafarian Movement in Jamaica*. Kingston: Institute of Social and Economic Research, University of the West Indies.

Stein, Judith. 1986. *The World of Marcus Garvey: Race and Class in Modern Society*. Baton Rouge: Louisiana State University Press.

Steffens, Roger. 1998. "Bob Marley: Rasta Warrior". In *Chanting Down Babylon: The Rastafari Reader*, edited by N.S. Murrell, W.D. Spencer and A.A. McFarlane, 253–65. Kingston: Ian Randle.

Sundkler, Bengt G.M. 1961. *Bantu Prophets in South Africa*. London: Oxford University Press

———. 1976. *Zulu Zion, and Some Swazi Zionists*. London: Oxford University Press.

Sutherland, Bill, and Matt Meyer. 2000. *Guns and Gandhi in Africa. Pan-African Insight on Non-violence, Armed Struggle, and Liberation*. Trenton, NJ: Africa World Press.

Taddesse Berisso. 2002. "Modernist Dreams and Human Suffering: Villagization among the Guji Oromo". In *Remapping Ethiopia: Socialism and After*, edited by W. James et al., 116–32. Oxford: James Currey.

Tafari, Ikael. 2001. *Rastafari in Transition: The Politics of Cultural Confrontation in Africa and the Caribbean (1966–1988)*. Chicago: Research Associates School Times.

Teshale Tibebu. 1995. *The Making of Modern Ethiopia, 1896–1974*. Lawrenceville, NJ: Red Sea.

Tété-Adjalogo, Têtêvi Godwin. 1995. *Marcus Garvey: Père de l'unité africaine des peuples*. Paris: L'Harmattan.

Trevisan Semi, Emanuela. 2002. "The 'Falashisation' of the Blacks of Harlem: A Judaising

Movement in Twentieth-Century USA". In *Judaising Movements: Studies in the Margins of Judaism*, edited T. Parfitt and E. Trevisan Semi, 87–110. London: Routledge.

Triulzi, Alessandro. 2002. "Battling with the Past: New Frameworks for Ethiopian Historiography". In *Remapping Ethiopia: Socialism and After*, edited by W. James et al., 276–88. Oxford: James Currey.

Tubiana, Jospeh. 1995. "Regard sur les formes traditionnelles d'entraide en Éthiopie". In *Épargne et liens sociaux: Études comparées d'informalités financières*, edited by J.-M. Servet, 59–69. Paris: Cahiers Finance, éthique, confiance.

Tucker, Phillip T. 2012. *Father of the Tuskegee Airmen. John C. Robinson*. Washington, DC: Potomac Books.

Turton, David. 2006. Introduction. In *Ethnic Federalism: The Ethiopian Experience in Comparative Perspective*, edited by D. Turton, 1–31. Oxford: James Currey.

Ullendorff, Edward. 1997. *Ethiopia and the Bible*. London: Oxford University Press.

Uya, Okon Udet. 1993. "The Middle Passage and Personality Change Among Diaspora Africans". In *Global Dimensions of the African Diaspora*, edited by J. Harris, 83–97. Washington, DC: Howard University Press.

van Dijk, Frank Jan. 1988. "The Twelve Tribes of Israel: Rasta and the Middle-Class". *New West Indian Guide* 62, nos. 1–2: 1–26.

———. 1993. *Jahmaica: Rastafari and Wider Society, 1930–1990*. Utrecht: ISOR.

———. 1995. "Sociological Means: Colonial Reactions to the Radicalization of Rastafari in Jamaica, 1956–1959". *New West Indian Guide* 69, nos. 1–2: 67–101.

———. 1998. "Chanting Down Babylon Outernational: The Rise of Rastafari in Europe, the Caribbean, and the Pacific". In *Chanting Down Babylon: The Rastafari Reader*, edited by N.S. Murrell, W.D. Spencer and A.A. McFarlane, 178–98. Kingston: Ian Randle.

Venturini, Nadia. 1990. *Neri ed italiani ad Harlem: Gli anni Trenta e la guerra d'Etiopia*. Rome: Edizioni Lavoro.

Verger, Pierre. 1968. *Flux et reflux de la traite des nègres entre le Golfe de Bénin et Bahia de Todos os Santos du XVIIe au XIXe siècle*. Paris: Mouton.

Vergneault-Belmont, Françoise. 1998. *L'œil qui pense: Méthodes graphiques pour la recherche en sciences de l'homme*. Paris: L'Harmattan.

Vilakazi, Absolom, Bongani Mthethwa and Mthembeni Mapanza. 1986. *Shembe: The Revitalization of African Society*. Johannesburg: Skotaville.

Waquet, Jean-Claude, Odile Goerg and Rebecca Rogers, eds. 2000. *Les espaces de l'historien: Études d'historiographie*. Strasbourg: Presses Universitaires de Strasbourg.

Wariboko, Waibinte E. 2004. "I Really Cannot Make Africa My Home: West Indian Missionaries as 'Outsiders' in the Church Missionary Society Civilizing Mission to Southern Nigeria, 1898–1925". *Journal of African History* 45: 221–36.

Washington, Joseph R., ed. 1984. *Jews in Black Perspectives: A Dialogue*. London: Associated University Press.

Waters, Anita M. 1985. *Race, Class, and Political Symbols: Rastafari and Reggae in Jamaican Politics*. New Brunswick, NJ: Transaction.

Watkins-Owens, Irma. 1996. *Blood Relations: Caribbean Immigrants and the Harlem Community, 1900–1930*. Bloomington: Indiana University Press.

Weber, Max. 1963 [1959]. *Le savant et le politique*. Paris: Plon.

———. 1967 [1947]. *L'éthique protestante et l'esprit du capitalisme*. Paris: Plon.

Weisbord, Robert G. 1974. *Ebony Kinship: Africa, Africans, and the Afro-American.* Westport, CT: Greenwood.

Weisbord, Robert G., and Richard Kazarian, eds. 1985. *Israel in the Black American Perspective.* Westport, CT: Greenwood.

Wyse, Akintola J.G. 1993. "The Sierra Leone Krios: A Reappraisal from the Perspective of the African Diaspora". In *Global Dimensions of the African Diaspora*, edited by J. Harris, 339–68. Washington, DC: Howard University Press.

Yawney, Carole. 1978. "Lions in Babylon: The Rastafarians of Jamaica as a Visionary Movement". PhD diss., McGill University.

———. 1995. "Tell out King Rasta Doctrine Around the Whole World: Rastafari in Global Perspective". In *The Reordering of Culture: Latin America, the Caribbean and Canada in the Hood*, edited by A. Ruprecht and C. Taiano, 57–73. Ottawa, ON: Carleton University Press.

———. 1999. "Only Visitors Here: Representing Rastafari into the 21st Century". In *Religion, Diaspora and Cultural Identity*, edited by J.W. Pulis, 153–81. Amsterdam: Gordon and Breach.

———. 2001. "Exodus: Rastafari, Repatriation and the African Renaissance". In *A United States of Africa?*, edited by E. Maloka,133–85. Pretoria: Africa Institute of South Africa.

Yawney, Carole, and John P. Homiak. 2001. "Rastafari", "Rastafari in Global Context". In *Encyclopedia of African and African-American Religions*, edited by S.D. Glazier, 256–71. New York: Routledge.

Yelvington, Kevin. 1999. "The War in Ethiopia and Trinidad 1935–1936". In *The Colonial Caribbean in Transition: Essays on Postemancipation Social and Cultural History*, edited by B. Brereton and K. Yelvington, 189–225. Gainesville: University Press of Florida.

INDEX

Note: Ethiopians are listed by their first names. Ethiopian honorifics are indicated by italics.
Locators for endnotes are indicated thus: 410n2:7 (page number of note plus chapter number [if necessary] and note number).

Frequently used abbreviations: EWF (Ethiopian World Federation); UNIA (Universal Negro Improvement Association).